D1002033

WITHDRAWN LIBRARY

Macdonald at 200

Macdonald at 200

NEW REFLECTIONS AND LEGACIES

Edited by

Patrice Dutil & Roger Hall

DUNDURN
TORONTO

Copyright © Patrice Dutil and Roger Hall, 2014

All rights reserved. No part of this publication may be reproduced, stored in a retrieval system, or transmitted in any form or by any means, electronic, mechanical, photocopying, recording, or otherwise (except for brief passages for purposes of review) without the prior permission of Dundurn Press. Permission to photocopy should be requested from Access Copyright.

Editors: Patrice Dutil and Roger Hall
Copy-editor: Laura Harris
Design: Courtney Horner
Printer: Marquis
Cover design by Carmen Giraudy
Front cover images: Vintage Map of Canada: © I. Pilon/Shutterstock.com, Canada Topographic Map: © FrankRamspott/istockphoto.com, Rt. Hon. Sir John A. Macdonald: © William James Topley/Library and Archives Canada/PA-26999
Back cover image: Courtesy of Library and Archives Canada/PA-027002

Library and Archives Canada Cataloguing in Publication

Macdonald at 200 : new reflections and legacies / edited by Patrice Dutil and Roger Hall.

Includes bibliographical references and index.
Issued in print and electronic formats.
ISBN 978-1-4597-2459-4

1. Macdonald, John A. (John Alexander), 1815-1891. 2. Prime ministers--Canada--Biography. 3. Canada--Politics and government--1867-1896. I. Dutil, Patrice A., 1960-, editor II. Hall, Roger, 1945-, editor III. Title: Macdonald at two hundred.

FC521.M3M23 2014   971.05'1092   C2014-902134-8
                                               C2014-902135-6

1   2   3   4   5   18   17   16   15   14

 Conseil des Arts du Canada   Canada Council for the Arts  Canadä  ONTARIO ARTS COUNCIL CONSEIL DES ARTS DE L'ONTARIO an Ontario government agency un organisme du gouvernement de l'Ontario

We acknowledge the support of the **Canada Council for the Arts** and the **Ontario Arts Council** for our publishing program. We also acknowledge the financial support of the **Government of Canada** through the **Canada Book Fund** and **Livres Canada Books**, and the **Government of Ontario** through the **Ontario Book Publishing Tax Credit** and the **Ontario Media Development Corporation**.

Care has been taken to trace the ownership of copyright material used in this book. The author and the publisher welcome any information enabling them to rectify any references or credits in subsequent editions.
J. Kirk Howard, President

The publisher is not responsible for websites or their content unless they are owned by the publisher.

Printed and bound in Canada.

Visit us at
Dundurn.com
@dundurnpress
Facebook.com/dundurnpress
Pinterest.com/dundurnpress

Dundurn
3 Church Street, Suite 500
Toronto, Ontario, Canada
M5E 1M2

For Canadians observing the two-hundredth anniversary of John A. Macdonald's birth on January 11, 1815.

Descendants of this man and his times, for better and for worse.

Library and Archives Canada, C-003811.

John A. Macdonald, circa 1861–63 (age 46–48), photographed in Notman and Son Studios, Montreal.

Photo Archive, Museum of Civilization, C-021290.

John A. Macdonald, Prime Minister of Canada, 1867–73, 1878–91.

Contents

INTRODUCTION   13

Patrice Dutil and Roger Hall, "A Macdonald for Our Times"

PART 1 - MACDONALD AND SOCIETY   25

CHAPTER 1   27

Colin Grittner, "Macdonald
and Women's Enfranchisement"

CHAPTER 2   58

Donald B. Smith, "Macdonald's Relationship
with Aboriginal Peoples"

CHAPTER 3   94

David A. Wilson, "Macdonald and the Fenians"

CHAPTER 4   115

Timothy J. Stanley, "'The Aryan Character of the Future of
British North America': Macdonald, Chinese Exclusion, and
the Invention of Canadian White Supremacy"

CHAPTER 5   141

Michel Ducharme, "Macdonald and
the Concept of Liberty"

PART 2 - MACDONALD AND THE ECONOMY   171

CHAPTER 6   173

J.J. Ben Forster, "First Spikes: Railways in Macdonald's Early
Political Career"

CHAPTER 7   193

E.A. Heaman, "Macdonald and Fiscal *Realpolitik*"

CHAPTER 8   223

David W. Delainey and J.C. Herbert Emery, "The National
Policy's Impact on the West: A Reassessment"

PART 3 - MACDONALD AND GOVERNMENT   251

CHAPTER 9   253

Barbara J. Messamore, "Macdonald and the Governors
General: The Prime Minister's Use and Abuse of the Crown"

CHAPTER 10   282

Patrice Dutil, "Macdonald, His 'Ottawa Men,' and the
Consolidation of Prime Ministerial Power (1867–1873)"

CHAPTER 11   311

J.R. Miller, "Macdonald as Minister of Indian Affairs: The
Shaping of Canadian Indian Policy"

CHAPTER 12   341

Bill Waiser, "Macdonald's Appetite for Canadian Expansion:
Main Course or Leftovers?"

PART 4 - REMEMBERING MACDONALD   357

CHAPTER 13   259

Yves Y. Pelletier, "Politics, Posturing, and Process in Shaping
Macdonald's Public Memory (1891–1911)"

CHAPTER 14   379

Patrice Dutil and Sean Conway, "A Legacy Lost: Macdonald
in the Memory of His Successors"

CHAPTER 15   405

Ged Martin, "Understanding Macdonald:
Reviewing a Biographical Project"

AFTERWORD   437

Richard Gwyn, "Rediscovering Macdonald"

CONTRIBUTORS   451

ACKNOWLEDGEMENTS   455

INDEX   457

Introduction

A Macdonald for Our Times

PATRICE DUTIL AND ROGER HALL

There are no immutable laws in the writing of history, but there are customs, conventions, and traditions. One such persistent rule is that "each generation writes its own history." What is meant by that adage is that each generation, educated in a different way, shaped by a different past, has a unique perspective on what went before, a view largely informed by the circumstances of its particular present. This seems irrefutable — certainly it is unavoidable. Our conclusion is that it is time — high time — for a new take on John A. Macdonald. And what better occasion than the bicentennial of his birth in 2015?

Macdonald was born on or about January 11, 1815, in Glasgow, Scotland, the third child of Hugh Macdonald and Helen Shaw. At that time, Britons were savouring the fact that Napoleon had been exiled to Elba, and that wars with France were likely to end. The Treaty of Ghent, which brought peace between the United States and Britain, had just been signed on Christmas Eve. Little John was born when things were looking up.

Optimism is cruel, sometimes. For one thing, Napoleon returned to France and rallied his army, and was finally defeated decisively five months later at Waterloo. Victory over the French aside, Hugh Macdonald grew frustrated with the inevitable postwar economic downturn in Scotland

and, in 1820, moved his family to Kingston, Upper Canada to start afresh. Young John Macdonald attended school there, and proved an able student. He was apprenticed at age fifteen to become a lawyer with George Mackenzie, a cousin, was called to the bar in 1836 and started his own general law practice. Macdonald thrived in his work, and was already a prominent person in the town of Kingston by the time he turned thirty. He married Isabella Clark, a cousin from Scotland, in 1843. That same year, the siren calls of politics seduced him, and he never looked back. Supported by businessmen, Macdonald was elected an alderman in Kingston's city council. A year later, he was elected to the legislative assembly of Canada West as a Conservative. Four years later he was named Receiver General and for most of the next six decades would have a hand in shaping Canada's government.

Macdonald was singularly successful as a politician, a statesman, and as a man. His charm was known to both men and women; his reputation as a gentleman was uncontested on both sides of the Atlantic. His winning smile, his enduring optimism and willingness to overcome obstacles made him an easy colleague and companion. Macdonald was simply *likeable* and even people who cared little for his politics admitted their respect for his mind and industry. Yet he was not entirely a happy man for much of his life. His marriage to Isabella was blighted by her illness and depression. His resistance to alcohol was no match to its relief and by the time he had turned forty years old he was known to abuse the bottle with reckless abandon. Isabella died in 1857 and he remarried on the eve of Confederation. Agnes, his new bride, was the younger sister of his deputy minister, Hewitt Bernard. Macdonald had two surviving children, Hugh John (with Isabella) and Mary (with Agnes). Hugh John was a frustration for John A., and the two battled each other ceaselessly. Mary was born with hydrocephaly (which impaired her physical and intellectual growth), and while Macdonald loved her tenderly, he was denied the joy of seeing his daughter join the world as an independent woman.

Macdonald's personal battle with disappointments as much as his persistence in making things happen have endeared him to many Canadian commentators over the 120 years since his death. Their chief objectives have been to explain his accomplishments, and they were many. Confederation in 1867, of course, was the triumph of his career, but so too were his epic works in forging a country out of a continent within five years. He made terrible political errors in securing funding to build a transcontinental railroad and paid dearly for it in 1873. Nevertheless, he was re-elected five years later, and no one stopped calling him "prime minister" until he died in 1891.

• • •

THE AID OF A GLASS!

GORDON B.—"AH! YOU'RE RIGHT, SIR JOHN; LOOKING THROUGH *THIS* MEDIUM I DO SEE FACTORY CHIMNEYS IN EVERY TOWN AND VILLAGE IN THE COUNTRY."

Grip, 22 October, 1881.

This is not to romanticize Macdonald. The man worked hard to win, and had no pity for his adversaries. He was an ardent capitalist and made no apology for paying far more heed to those who had cash than to those who did not. He accepted the social order into which he was born, and did little to help the poor, the indigenous people, the imprisoned, the infirm, or the elderly. He went to war with the Métis twice, brutally crushing their revolts in the West. He was, like most people of his age, deeply suspicious of people who did not have the same skin colour as his own. He was a white Anglo-Saxon protestant and very proud of it. A British subject he was born, and a British subject he did die.

But he was not a snob. People remembered him as a kind man; he overcame the limits of his gender and pedigree and promoted the rights of women. He came to like French Canadians and was friendly with many men who hailed from Canada's First Nations. He respected people, but he knew his place.

Canadians have also been concerned about that place in history for a long time. A first generation of opinion was launched in 1883 when Joseph Edmund Collins, the Newfoundland-born, poetry-loving editor at the *Globe*, wrote a biography — a 635-page ardent defence of Macdonald (a surprising justification indeed, as Collins worked in the late George Brown's Liberal newspaper!). Collins's preface to *The Life and Times of the Right Honourable Sir John A. Macdonald: Premier of The Dominion of Canada* stated flatly that "we have no apology whatever to offer for the book. It must now fight its own way."[1] It did, and many of the stories first recounted by Collins are retold today.

Within months of Macdonald's death in 1891, three important books appeared in English in various parts of Canada, as did a short volume in French. Emerson Bristol Biggar published his *Anecdotal Life of Sir John Macdonald* in the summer of 1891 in Montreal and this singular work did not just entertain; it shaped what became the predominant understanding of Macdonald.[2] J. Pennington MacPherson, Macdonald's nephew, published a fat two-volume *Life of the Right Hon. Sir John A. Macdonald,* with the Earle Publishing House in Saint John, New Brunswick that fall. By Christmas that year, a third volume had appeared: Graeme Mercer Adam's update of Joseph Collins's book, now called *Canada's Patriot Statesman: The Life and Career of The Right Honourable Sir John A. Macdonald.* A twenty-page biography by John Francis Waters appeared in French translation, inaugurating a new series, *Les hommes du jour: Galerie de portraits cana-diens*[3] (alas, that short treatment was to be the last biographical treatment of Macdonald in French Canada as that *genre* never really took root in Quebec). Macdonald's long-time assistant Joseph Pope published *Memoirs of the Right Honourable Sir John Alexander Macdonald* shortly after in 1894, an 816-page volume filled with details.[4] He further produced the highlights of Macdonald's correspondence in 1921. These friends and admirers created nothing short of a chorus of posthumous praise.

Macdonald's star began to decline not long after the initial literary eruptions. It was now the turn of scholars to bring their scrutiny to Macdonald, but that generation was slow in producing. George Robert Parkin, headmaster of Upper Canada College and an ardent imperialist, felt the need to defend the memory of Sir John at a time when Wilfrid Laurier was marching to a fourth consecutive electoral victory, and so he published the substantial *Sir John A. Macdonald*.[5] Little was written on Macdonald for the next forty years. It would take two generations before another conservative scholar, Donald Creighton, frustrated by seemingly endless years of Liberal domination, dedicated himself to Macdonald and published his two-volume work (*John A. Macdonald: The Young Politician* in 1952 and *John A. Macdonald: The Old Chieftain* in 1955), both with Macmillan Canada, in Toronto.

History doesn't repeat but historians often repeat each other — at least until fresh evidence and more novel interpretations come to light. Donald Creighton saw the developing economy of the St. Lawrence-Great Lakes water chain as the key to understanding Canadian history, a view most completely expressed in his influential 1937 book *The Commercial Empire of the St. Lawrence*. Twenty years later, his sprawling biography placed Macdonald as one of the chief actors in this continuing drama. The first PM emerged as a colossus, a bulwark against the influence of the United States, and a strong advocate of the British connection — socially, culturally, politically, economically, and emotionally — and yet not a British Tory, but a man of action who bent conservative tendencies to fit his broad ambitions for the country. One could not succeed as the defender of a staid and static mercantilistic colony in a bustling new commercial world. Macdonald's distinct triumph was achieving a kind of political alchemy: he turned old ideas into new ones that looked convincingly similar.

The books were peppered, however, with intemperate descriptions of Macdonald's foes and skilful use of evidence to support Creighton's Laurentian thesis (while ignoring that which might be contrary). This partisan view of Macdonald and his times was challenged mildly — most noticeably through compilations of Macdonald's own writing, his papers and letters. As Canada celebrated its centennial, J.K. Johnson, a Carleton University historian, worked on bringing Macdonald's correspondence to light and edited *Affectionately Yours: The Letters of Sir John A. Macdonald and His Family*[6] as well as two large volumes of *The Letters of Sir John A. Macdonald* published by the Public Archives of Canada in 1968 and 1969 that covered the period of 1837 to 1861. Two other eminent scholars turned their hand at biography. Donald Swainson, at Queen's University, published *John A. Macdonald: The Man and the Politician*[7] and P.B. Waite, at Dalhousie University, published *Macdonald: His Life and World*.[8] These were enlightening works in their own way as they essayed explanations for Macdonald's longevity, but fell short on the colourful details that were features of the early works on Macdonald. Johnson and Waite collaborated on the masterful 1990 *Dictionary of Canadian Biography* piece on Macdonald (now easily accessible on the internet), which is a kind of capstone to the balanced synthetic histories that succeeded Creighton and characterized much of mid-twentieth century historical writing in this country.

A small number of scholars ventured articles on diverse aspects of Macdonald's actions and ideology, but they were few and far between. It seemed as though there was not much room for Macdonald in an age where professional history grew more aware of industrialization, capitalism, social developments, and Aboriginal affairs. At the same time, the interests of academic historians largely turned away from biography and particularly political biography. Social history — with myriad subcategories like women's, rural, and labour history — has largely dominated the field over the last half-century and micro studies have supplanted the fashion for grand, sweeping theories and accounts of national development. New methodologies and philosophies have further informed and modified professional study — not least being the emergence of quantitative history, or the application of postmodern theories that question the capacity to write history at all. In these studies, where Macdonald occasionally made cameo appearances, he and his governments appeared to be weak if not malicious.

The lack of interest among scholars seemed to spur a new generation of popular historians who turned to Macdonald as navigators once turned to the North Star. Writing in the late 1960s when Canada's identity as a country was being debated as never before, journalist Pierre Berton encapsulated his account of Macdonald's trials and tribulations by focusing on the construction of the Canadian Pacific Railway and entitled his work *The National Dream*.[9] The book (along with its sequel, *The Last Spike*, was made into a docudrama series in 1974 and its popularity set a viewership record for the CBC) cemented a renewed place for Macdonald in the popular imagination. Berton's work marked a new trend among popular accounts in that the theme attracted liberal writers, not the conservative friends that had chronicled his life at the turn of the twentieth century.

It took more than twenty years for yet a new generation of professional writers to find interest in Macdonald. Sandra Gwyn cast sidelong glances at Macdonald in her *Private Capital: Ambition and Love in the Age of Macdonald and Laurier*.[10] A few years later, Louise Reynolds published a study of Macdonald's second wife, *Agnes: The Biography of Lady Macdonald*[11] and Christopher Moore's *1867: How the Fathers Made a Deal*[12] devoted special attention to Macdonald as a negotiator and a political thinker. In the twenty-first century, it was again non-scholars who focused on Macdonald. Patricia Phenix's *Private Demons: The Tragic Personal Life of John A. Macdonald*[13] focused more on trying to understand his psychology while Richard Gwyn's *John A.: The Man Who Made Us: The Life and Times of John A. Macdonald: 1815–1867* and *Nation Maker: Sir John A. Macdonald: His Life, Our Times: 1867–1891*[14] adopted a classic recipe to explain Macdonald in terms of his context, but emphasized his more progressive traits: his understanding of women, the realities of politics, and Canada's indigenous population. It was, in sum, a new generation looking to Macdonald to make sense of contemporary Canada, in terms of its sensitivities to individual characteristics, aspirations, and origins. In Macdonald, these writers reflected and sometimes validated the country that had become the Canada of the twenty-first century.

Celebrations of anniversaries such as Macdonald's 1815 birth are themselves inventions, admittedly, and for convenience we divide the past into eras and epochs and give the passage of time some precision by introducing decades and centuries. Macdonald's lifetime stood astride one of the most energetic eras of the recent past — that of emerging democracies, rampant industrialization, and the consolidation of global European power. These monumental circumstances must always play a part in understanding him.

What follows in this collection, and what sets it apart, is the fruit of recent professional academic study. The collection is based on papers from a conference held in December 2010 at Ryerson University in Toronto, made possible by grants from the Social Sciences and Humanities Research Council and Ryerson University. For two days and through two dozen sessions, university historians, graduate students, archivists, and biographers examined and discussed the understanding of Macdonald during the past two centuries and his continuing relevance for today and tomorrow. These papers were immensely diverse and reflected both traditional historical approaches and more recent topics of interest and forms of analysis. The editors subsequently asked the participants if they would be willing to revise their papers for publication and the result is in your hands. Informed readers will recognize our contributors as experts in their respective fields. That the writers come from throughout the country and that they reflect so many diverse interests yet all have a fresh interpretations on Macdonald shows just how extensive a role Macdonald played in Canada's past, and how relevant an understanding of that role is to contemporary Canadians — inside and outside the academy. As a contrast to these new takes, we decided to select cartoons of the period, all of them (save for one) drawn by J.W. Bengough, the biting wit of late Victorian Canada whose *Grip*, the satirical weekly he established in 1873, mocked almost perfectly how Macdonald engaged with the issues of his day.

The papers are grouped into four broad areas and bring out various — and sometimes contradictory — interpretation. The first section, "Macdonald and Society," examines five aspects of how Macdonald reacted to what was happening in his times. Colin Grittner reveals Macdonald's perhaps surprising enthusiasm for women's suffrage. Timothy Stanley shows that Macdonald's prejudices and policies toward Chinese migrants — perhaps not unusual in his time — nevertheless set the stage for, and inflamed, popular white supremacy postures throughout Canada, with long-lasting effects. Donald Smith offers a penetrating analysis of

Macdonald's personal and political experiences with the First Nations — rooted in Upper Canada and in many ways unchanging over the decades — that shaped his complicated approach to the country's indigenous peoples. David Wilson, the biographer of D'Arcy McGee, explains how Macdonald took the Irish/Fenian threat very seriously indeed, casting them not as comic bumblers, as so many of his biographers like Creighton have, but rather as capable, determined opponents both within and without the country. There is no denying that Macdonald wanted the indigenous people to assimilate into the Canadian mainstream, or that he thought that Aboriginal peoples did not have a culture that was worth retaining. It was a blind spot that Macdonald shared with the majority, but its details divide historians: was Macdonald a racist? Did he discriminate on the basis of where certain segments of the population originated? There is room here for a lengthy debate. Finally, Michel Ducharme, an historian of ideas, places Macdonald in his eighteenth- and nineteenth-century context and shows how his idea of "liberty" was determined by the larger experiences of European and American revolutions that rocked his comparably safe Upper Canadian world. Macdonald, an intellectual in spite of himself, favoured autonomy in most things, but that hardly meant that he would fight in favour of vague ideas of "freedom."

The second part of the book examines Macdonald's handling of the economy. At the outset Ben Forster, in the aptly named "First Spikes," reminds us that Macdonald was easily convinced of the economic need for railways and was deeply involved in promoting them long before the Canadian Pacific Railway project came along. Elsbeth Heaman explains that, although Macdonald may have been flexible and pragmatic in much of his politics, when it came to fiscal matters, he had a fixed and essentially old-time Tory perspective of the way the world worked. Macdonald, the architect of Canada, worked to ensure that "poverty" was not something to be blamed on the federal government. David Delainey and Herb Emery radically reassess the National Policy in terms of western development. For them, this defining policy cannot be blamed for its legacy as it practically had no impact. It was and is an "inappropriate target of Western protest" and should be celebrated for saving the West for Canada, or as they put it, the policy was "a necessary geopolitical response given American nineteenth century expansionism."

The next section looks at Macdonald and the art of governing. Barbara Messamore shows how important, indeed central, to a government's success, was the nature of its relation to the Crown's representative — and how well Macdonald could play this game. In fact, no one exactly knew what the role of a prime minister was in the newly constituted Dominion and Patrice Dutil documents how in half-a-dozen years after taking the post Macdonald ensured his dominance in large part by ensuring that the public servants who worked in the East Block on Parliament Hill were fiercely loyal to him and his party. J.R. Miller sheds light on Macdonald as the minister responsible for native affairs — incidentally the longest-serving such minister in Canadian history — and examines how, for better or worse, he managed the shape and scope of western treaties, reserve policy, economic development on reserves, and a whole range of government programs that targeted First Nations' cultural identity, spiritual practices, and traditional governance. Bill Waiser demonstrates that Macdonald lived in an age dominated by emergent scientific thought and was not immune to its influence in both the stewardship and exploitation of the vast lands of the Canadian West and North.

The fourth and final section focuses on how Macdonald has been remembered. Yves Pelletier focuses on the two decades after his death and how the two principal political parties chose to employ his memory. That act of remembrance was shaped by partisan lines, with Tories arguing that Macdonald had forged a modern Canadian ideal while Liberals only perceived a man who was eager to protect mercantile interests and his ability to deploy patronage. Patrice Dutil and Sean Conway carry this analysis forward chronologically and show that Macdonald has all but been ignored by his political successors who seemed content to trot out his memory only when they were in trouble, or in need of a justification for their response to troubles.

Ged Martin, who recently authored a study of Macdonald's relationship with the denizens of Kingston, *Favourite Son? John A. Macdonald and the Voters of Kingston, 1841-1891*[15] as well as *John A. Macdonald: Canada's First Prime Minister*,[16] a short biography, takes a more individualistic measure of how the man can be remembered. Martin, who has written eloquently about Macdonald as a pre-confederation premier, as an alcoholic, and as a prime negotiator of relations between Canada and the British Empire, describes his long personal relationship with Macdonald as a subject. He examines the challenges that have come out of it, and the impact that the whole experience has had on his view of the role and nature of biography in historical writing. Richard Gwyn, the latest writer to contribute a major assessment of Macdonald's life and work, provides an Afterword. He makes the case that Macdonald's continuing significance is not simply in helping to build and shape a nineteenth-century country called Canada but that he was also in many respects a man far ahead of his time in terms of his attitudes toward democracy. For Gwyn, Macdonald's relevance to today's Canada is still central.

The picture of Macdonald that emerges from this volume is not inconstant with the traditional view that Macdonald has fair claim to be a principal builder of Canada. We would not go so far as to say that Canada could not exist without him; but we would argue that it would be a very different Canada than that in which we live and which he helped to shape at a critical juncture in its history. This book is the work of a new generation of scholars who have reflected on Macdonald's experience and revealed evidence of events and circumstances that resonate differently in contemporary Canada than the conventional interpretations of the man. These are the basis for what we have labelled the "new legacies" of our own Macdonald. In the pages that follow, Macdonald is presented as an "early adopter" of the idea that building infrastructure was the key strategy to strengthening Canada. Macdonald promoted the state as guarantor of private wealth, he shaped Canada's relations with the Empire with wisdom and not a little guile, he defined a particularly conservative ideology that favoured liberty, was a spymaster who fought terrorism. He worked as an economic protectionist that shielded Western development, and as a prime minister that centralized power, a man who left a heritage of hope for suffrage expansion but who promoted a hostile attitude toward Aboriginals and foreigners while hoping that both would be integrated into the mainstream quickly. In other words, Macdonald is as relevant to our time as he was representative of his. We struggle with many of the same prejudices, strengths, threats, and challenges he faced.

In short, this generation of historians sees in Macdonald, as he approaches his two-hundredth birthday, a man whose relevance to Canada is undiminished. To quote Joseph Edmond Collins, the first Macdonald biographer of

140 years ago, "we have no apology whatever to offer for the book. It must now fight its own way." We hope that these chapters will help contemporary Canadians distinguish between the monument and the man, and trust that future scholars will deepen the understanding of his legacy. What is certain is that other groups of historians, doubtless using new tools and perspectives, will in future sharpen the focus again and uncover yet other legacies reflecting their own times.

NOTES

1. Toronto: Rose Publishing, 1883, p. viii. See also Brook Taylor, "Collins, Joseph Edmund." In *Dictionary of Canadian Biography Online,* Vol. 12, University of Toronto/Université Laval, 2003, accessed September 16, 2013, *www. biographi.ca/en/bio/collins_joseph_edmund_12E.html*
2. Montreal: John Lovell & Son, 1891.
3. Published by La Compagnie de moulins à papier de Montreal, 1891.
4. The book was published by the Musson Book Company, Toronto, 1894.
5. Published in Toronto by Morang & Co, 1908.
6. Toronto: Macmillan, 1969.
7. Toronto: Oxford University Press, 1971.
8. Toronto: McGraw-Hill, 1975.
9. Toronto: McClelland & Stewart, 1970.
10. Toronto: McClelland & Stewart, 1984.
11. Ottawa: Carleton University Press, 1990.
12. Toronto: McClelland & Stewart, 1997.
13. Toronto: McClelland & Stewart, 2006.
14. Toronto: Random House, 2007 and 2011.
15. Kingston: Kingston Historical Society, 2010.
16. Toronto: Dundurn Press, 2013.

PART I

Macdonald and Society

Chapter 1

Macdonald and Women's Enfranchisement

Colin Grittner

Even at his bicentennial party, people still whisper about John A. Macdonald behind his back. Some want to hide the punch, seeing the Old Leader, above all else, as an inveterate drunk (despite a marvelously successful forty-seven-year political career).[1] Others want to hide the microphone. They are convinced that Macdonald was nothing more than a cagey manipulator — an unwavering opportunist who either possessed no political principles of his own, or adopted whatever principles he thought would ensure political success.

Fortunately for the man of the hour, historians are slowly dispelling these simplifications. Macdonald's most recent biographer, Richard Gwyn, for example, has taken dead aim against the last of these generalizations: that Sir John had no political ideas of his own. In both his two-part biography of Macdonald and his address to the "John A. Macdonald: Fresh Perspectives and New Legacies" conference, Gwyn has emphatically argued that Sir John possessed clearly developed political ideas *and* that he actively attempted to translate those ideas into reality.[2] As evidence, Gwyn has in part targeted the subject of this chapter: Macdonald's attempt to federally enfranchise women in 1885. Because of the unpopularity of women's suffrage within Macdonald's own Liberal-Conservative party, as well as amongst contemporary Canadian voters, Gwyn asserts that Macdonald's attempt to grant Canadian women the vote must have been ideologically motivated.[3] I could not agree more. The argument that follows, however, takes this conclusion a step or two further. Macdonald's relationship with women's suffrage does more than reveal the fact that he acted ideologically during his political career. I would argue that it also provides a window into Macdonald's take on political citizenship and, more interestingly, the political and cultural ideologies that may have fuelled this perspective. This window should be opened more fully to better understand our first prime minister.

Macdonald's flirtation with women's enfranchisement began formally in 1883. In that year he tabled his *Electoral Franchise Act*, a verbose piece of legislation he had written himself. Those within the House of Commons would not have been surprised. Since Confederation in 1867, Macdonald, as prime minister, had introduced six other franchise bills to Parliament. These unpassed bills all had the same goal: to implement a series of property and income qualifications that would apply uniformly across Canada during federal elections. Until that time, Canada did not have dedicated franchise legislation for federal elections. Instead, the Dominion government employed the various provincial franchises for that purpose. These laws ranged from the generally inclusive — that of Prince Edward Island — to the rather exclusive — those of New Brunswick and Quebec. Each contained its own peculiarities concerning property ownership, income, residency, and race.[4] These inconsistencies, however, did not extend to gender. No province at this time allowed women to vote. None would until 1916.[5] Consequently, only Canadian men had access to full citizenship within the young nation. Because the provincial franchises varied, a man who voted federally in one province may have faced disenfranchisement in the next. Like the six bills that preceded it, the *Electoral Franchise Act* sought to remedy this situation. Remarkably, it would do so through new federal property qualifications that essentially equalled the most restrictive property qualifications in the country: those of Quebec. The *Electoral Franchise Act* thus sought to *disenfranchise* poorer voters outside of Quebec who had previously managed to meet their provinces' less stringent restrictions. With the *Electoral Franchise Act*, however, Macdonald deviated from his earlier template in one key respect. For the first time, he sought to define the term "person."

The franchise bills of 1867, 1869, 1870, 1871, 1872, and 1873 all employed the term "person" freely. Yet, none of them indicated exactly to whom the term referred. The *Electoral Franchise Act* sought to correct such ambiguity. Not only did it offer a succinct definition of "person," it seemingly did so in the most radical way. According to section 2, "'Person' means a male person [who is] married or unmarried, including an Indian or a female person unmarried or a widow …"[6] By 1883, no country in the Western world, let alone the Dominion of Canada, had sought to define "person" in this manner. The next nation that attempted to do so in earnest, New Zealand, would not enact women's enfranchisement until a decade later in 1893. Canadians were stunned. The leader of Canada's Conservatives, by all appearances, had shunned British electoral tradition in order to spearhead a gendered upheaval of Canada's political order. Even though section 2 only allowed unmarried women who otherwise met the act's property qualifications to vote, the idea that *any* woman should vote represented a revolutionary departure from the male domination of official Canadian political participation.

After its first reading on April 12, 1883, the *Electoral Franchise Act* stagnated on the House of Commons' floor for a month and a half before

Grip, 24 October, 1885.

GETTING READY FOR THE KILLING.

Macdonald withdrew it.[7] Much the same thing took place in 1884.[8] The debate over the *Electoral Franchise Act* would finally occur in 1885. It lasted almost a dozen sleepless weeks as parliamentarians lobbed insults at one another to fill the time.[9] Through these protracted fits and bursts of franchise debate, Macdonald continuously defended his women's suffrage clause against the barbs of his parliamentary colleagues. In the end, he battled in vain. The clause died on the evening of April 28, 1885, largely at the hands of Macdonald's own party, mere months before the act became law.[10] Only a few members on either side of the aisle gave Macdonald's definition of "person" any support.[11] After its resounding defeat in the Commons, Macdonald never again attempted to enfranchise women at the federal level.

Within the current historiography, ambiguity and disagreement surround accounts of Macdonald's three years as Canada's most public champion of women's suffrage. Macdonald himself did not help historians very much in this regard. During the heated Commons debates concerning the *Electoral Franchise Act*, he commented very little upon his own bill. Neither did his fellow Liberal-Conservatives. The Old Leader had evidently instructed his party not to encourage or prolong the opposition's filibuster tactics.[12] Parliamentary sittings that lasted upwards of three days were long enough for the increasingly irritable members. The few times that Macdonald addressed Parliament, however, he spoke very plainly about his stance toward women's suffrage. For example, when Macdonald moved for the second reading of the *Electoral Franchise Act* on April 16, 1885, he remarked:

> There is one question, however, in this Bill in which, personally, I may be considered to be interested, and that is women's franchise. I have always and am now strongly in favor of that franchise. I believe that is coming as certainly as came the gradual enfranchisement of women from being the slaves of men until she attained her present position, almost the equal of man. I believe that time is coming, though perhaps we are not any more than the United States or England quite educated up to it, I believe the time will come, and I shall be very proud and glad to see it, when the final step towards giving women full enfranchisement is carried in Canada.[13]

When the women's suffrage clause finally found itself before the Committee of the Whole on April 27, 1885, Macdonald reiterated even more forcefully his comments of the previous fortnight. Regarding "female suffrage," he used his final remarks on section 2 of the bill to explain:

> I can only say that, personally, I am strongly convinced, and every year, for many years, I have become more strongly convinced, of the justice of giving women otherwise qualified the suffrage. I am strongly of that opinion, and have been for a good many years, and I had hoped that Canada would have the honor of first placing women in the position that she is certain eventually, after centuries of oppression, to obtain.[14]

During the same address he even went so far to assert that "I am ... in favor of giving ladies, married and unmarried, the franchise" (despite the fact that he did not include what he said he favoured within the legislation itself).[15] At face value, such language could not be plainer: Macdonald believed in the justice of women's enfranchisement. One might even call him a suffragist (at a time when suffragists represented only a small minority of the Canadian population).[16] Despite the apparent clarity of Macdonald's words, several scholars have remained unconvinced, distrustful of the prime minister's silver tongue and parliamentary wiles.

Drawing upon Macdonald's reputation for political opportunism, scholars such as Norman Ward, Diane Lamoureux, Jacinthe Michaud, and Carol Bacchi have maintained that Macdonald adopted the language of women's enfranchisement only to the extent that it could offer a partisan advantage. Ward, for instance, argues that Macdonald promoted women's suffrage solely to create a new group of voters "who were expected to vote Conservative".[17] Lamoureux and Michaud similarly see Macdonald as attempting to manipulate the inevitable implementation of women's enfranchisement for Conservative advantage.[18] These parallel assertions echo the patronizing words of one Liberal parliamentarian, who teased Macdonald as "desirous at all events of obtaining popularity amongst the ladies on the ground of promoting their enfranchisement."[19] And like Ward, Lamoureux, and Michaud, this member was unable "to discover yet that [Macdonald] is thoroughly sincere in his desire in this regard."[20] Carol Bacchi has even gone so far as to suggest that Macdonald already knew that women's enfranchisement would be a losing battle, and that he included it to distract the opposition's attention from other parts of the bill. In particular, Bacchi argues that Macdonald hoped to draw attention away from the bill's so-called revising barrister clause, which gave the prime minister the authority to select those individuals who had final say as to whom would receive a federal ballot.[21]

As evidence, the above authors have tended to rely upon Macdonald's actions rather than his words. They cite, for example, the fact that the prime minister flatly refused to whip his party into supporting his women's suffrage clause.[22] Macdonald clearly indicated that he would not "peril the bill on that point."[23] Indeed, he had even readied an alternative version of the bill from the outset in preparation for the clause's defeat.[24] Bacchi also points out that Macdonald managed in the end to have his revising barrister stipulation enacted without amendment.[25] If one believes that such actions do speak louder than words, then Macdonald's treatment of women's suffrage may have indeed reflected the actions of a sly politician who upheld pragmatism and opportunism as more important than any ideological position.

That being said, the evidence presented is not especially persuasive. Although an influential politician, Macdonald never could have conjured enough magic to convince the majority of his party to support a clause it so steadfastly rejected. Already knowing that the women's suffrage clause had little chance of survival, Macdonald, of course, would have had a replacement bill ready. A more sympathetic historian, Catherine Cleverdon, has recognized the difficult position in which Macdonald found himself. She asserts that while it "seems unfair to assume, as Macdonald's Liberal opponents did, that the women suffrage clause was political chicanery to win votes," it would be folly for him to "sacrifice either party unity or a bill he deemed very important in order to gratify personal preference for a noble but unpopular principle."[26] Yet, it is still hard to believe that "for many years, [he had] become more strongly convinced, of the justice of giving women otherwise qualified the suffrage." One merely has to examine Macdonald's track record regarding franchise legislation to find indications to the contrary. Oddly enough, none of the aforementioned scholars has cast her or his gaze much earlier than 1883 when analyzing Macdonald's relationship with women's suffrage.

Macdonald introduced six items of federal franchise legislation into the House of Commons between 1867 and 1873. Even by 1867, however, Macdonald was easily one of the most experienced politicians in Canada when it came to franchise law and debate. Between his first election to the Canadian Legislative Assembly in 1844 and his first election to the Dominion House of Commons in 1867, he witnessed five additional franchise bills — those of 1849, 1858, 1859, 1864, and 1866 — appear before the provincial legislature. As Attorney General for Canada West, he wrote and tabled the last four of these bills himself. With regard to each item of legislation, Macdonald seemed to treat the idea of women's enfranchisement in much the same way.

Macdonald was still a young politician in 1849 when he first sat in the opposition benches of the Canadian Legislative Assembly. During the 1849 session, the Reform majority introduced a bill before the legislature dealing with the women's franchise question. Instead of enfranchising women, however, the Baldwin-Lafontaine government wished to eliminate a technicality in Canadian law that permitted women to vote in the provincial elections of Canadas East and West. Because the *Constitutional Act* of 1791 allowed "persons" to vote, and not just men, some had inferred that women could receive the franchise as well.[27] As a member of the Conservative opposition, Macdonald had no real incentive to support any part of a Reform measure. The partisan nature of the legislation did not help matters either. According to historian John Garner, the Reformers desired to codify women's disenfranchisement in response to a sour experience during the 1844 provincial election. In West Halton, Canada West, a returning officer, citing the constitution, had accepted the votes of several women who endorsed the Conservative candidate. These few votes helped ensure a Conservative victory in Halton. As Garner neatly phrases it, "The Reformers were not to forget this incident."[28] After winning the 1848 provincial election, the Reformers hoped to prevent these irritating legal interpretations from costing them seats in the future.[29] To ensure that returning officers upheld the new law, the Baldwin-Lafontaine administration empowered the sitting government (or, in other words, itself) with the sole authority of selecting those returning officers.[30]

Unfortunately for historians, the legislative debates that exist for the *Election Act* of 1849 make no reference to the women's disenfranchisement clause. It is therefore difficult to tell how the House reacted to that particular section of the measure. The record does describe, however, the *Election Act's* third reading on April 25, 1849. Considering its egregiously partisan nature to Conservative eyes, one would have expected Macdonald to cast his vote against the legislation and thus support women's enfranchisement. Conservative Party leader Sir Allan MacNab certainly did so, and in grand style.[31] Yet, Macdonald did not follow his chief's lead. When the House divided, "Macdonald of KINGSTON" did not make a formal decision either way: his name was conspicuously absent from the final tally.[32] The debates regrettably do not indicate whether Macdonald was absent from the legislature that day or whether he chose to abstain from the division. Either way, it would seem that women's disenfranchisement was not a measure that necessitated an active interest. In the following few years, Macdonald rose rapidly through his party's ranks. Unable to miss or avoid key votes any longer, his subsequent actions provide greater evidence that he may not have always endorsed women's suffrage in and of itself.

Macdonald became Attorney General of Canada West in 1854. Four years after that, in 1858, he would write and table his first piece of franchise legislation, the *Act to define the Elective Franchise, to provide for the Registration of Voters, and other purposes therein mentioned.* Upon its first reading, Macdonald argued that its purpose was both to create an effective voter registration system and to establish new property qualifications for the franchise.[33] Until that time, the Canadian government had not established the necessary mechanisms to create and maintain voters' lists for the province (that is, lists of individuals who had proven they satisfied the qualifications placed upon the franchise). Instead, a potential voter merely had to swear a series of oaths at the hustings in order to cast his vote. These oaths represented the only means at returning officers' disposal to prevent voter fraud. Voter fraud, needless to say, was extensive.[34] Also by this time, the province had not altered its property qualification upon the franchise for sixty-seven years. It maintained the same forty-shilling freehold qualification found within the *Constitutional Act* of 1791, Canada's original constitution. Because of widespread property ownership, growing property values, rising inflation, difficulties in land assessment, and the introduction of decimal currency, the requirement to own at least forty shillings worth of real property had become essentially meaningless. As Macdonald himself put it, it "did not suit a young country such as this."[35]

Instead of a forty-shilling freehold, the *Act to define the Elective Franchise* established a minimum $200 property qualification upon the provincial vote.[36] Although this alteration seems severe at first glance, Macdonald argued that it would ensure a broad and inclusive franchise. Indeed, it would be so inclusive that supposedly "Laborers and young men alone would be excluded."[37] But this was not entirely true. The legislation also twice contained (within the very same section that outlined the property qualification) a caveat that enfranchisement should only be accessible to "Every male person entered on the then last Assessment Roll ..."[38] One finds no ambiguity in such language. If Macdonald passively promoted women's disenfranchisement in 1849, he actively advanced it in 1858. This stance against women's suffrage in 1858 would mark a trend in Macdonald's subsequent franchise legislation, a trend that would continue into his prime ministership.

In 1867, Macdonald became Canada's first prime minister. Between 1867 and 1873, he would almost annually table the immediate forerunner of the *Electoral Franchise Act*: the *Act respecting elections of members of the House of Commons*.[39] Although the bill underwent minor alterations over these years, no version reached the level of refinement displayed by the legislation of the 1880s. For example, the *Act respecting elections* never provided a clear distinction between the terms 'occupant' and 'resident' — an important distinction considering the terms were not synonymous and that one had to generally satisfy both categories to receive a vote.[40] Also, as mentioned earlier, it failed to define what it meant by the term "person" at the outset. Instead, one had to delve much further into the heart of the bill to discover exactly to whom it applied.

Peppered throughout the qualification clauses, of which one finds many, the bill indicates that a voter is a "male person" who owns the required amount of real property for the region of Canada in which he lives (four hundred dollars worth for city dwellers, and two hundred dollars worth for country dwellers).[41] To allay any gendered confusion, Macdonald also buried deep within the bill an abrupt clause that categorically stated, "No woman is or shall be entitled to vote at any election."[42] Thus, as late as 1873, Macdonald presented himself as disfavouring women's enfranchisement, limited or otherwise. True, he may have radically changed his opinion in the decade after 1873. The logic of the Canadian women's suffrage movement, first organized discreetly in 1876, and then openly in 1883, may have rapidly convinced Macdonald of its validity.[43] But first it would have had to break Macdonald of his quarter-century habit of resisting women's suffrage. Moreover, if he had, in fact, become a suffragist, why did his women's suffrage clause within the *Electoral Franchise Act* only seek to enfranchise unmarried women? Since the majority of adult women would have been married, one would expect a suffragist to offer married women the vote as well. A small group of writers have thus rejected the idea of 'Macdonald the suffragist' on these grounds in particular. Yet, this group has also largely dismissed the notion that limited women's enfranchisement reflected an outburst of pragmatic politicking. Instead, they see some other philosophy at work.

To discover this ideology, writers and scholars such as Sir Joseph Pope and Rod Preece have approached Macdonald's relationship to women's suffrage differently. Instead of highlighting what Macdonald said, or what sneaky manoeuvres he may have made, these authors have emphasized the wording of the women's enfranchisement clause itself and how it would have operated within the *Electoral Franchise Act* as a whole. One must remember that the bill sought to enfranchise only a select group of women: that is, unmarried property-owning women. Coupled with some of the most stringent property qualifications in the country, the act would have ensured that these unmarried property-owning women would have been fairly wealthy as well.

Throughout his political career, Macdonald had consistently stressed the importance of substantial property ownership as necessary for both receiving the franchise and for full citizenship. In 1858, he argued that "in this country, where we [are] all bent on acquiring and improving our properties, and defining the rights of property, that property ought to have a great influence on the qualification of electors."[44] At the Confederation Debates, he submitted that:

> [N]ot a single member of the Conference, as I stated before, not a single one of the representatives of the government or of the opposition of any one of the Lower Provinces was in favour of universal suffrage. Every one felt that in this respect the principle of the British Constitution should be carried out, and that classes and property should be represented.[45]

During the franchise debates in 1873, Macdonald again reiterated that "With regard to the franchise ... the Bill proposed to introduce a custom, not universal suffrage" but one based upon householding.[46] By 1883, Macdonald's belief in the importance of property ownership had not changed. What had changed was the number of Canadian women owning property.

Beginning in the mid-1870s, women's independent property ownership had seen marked growth due to the recently enacted Women's Property Laws. This was especially true for unmarried women. As Peter Baskerville relates, the protection offered by these laws to female property owners helped change land distribution patterns amongst the sexes. Knowing that bequeathed property would be legally guarded against potentially greedy or spendthrift future spouses, husbands and parents increasingly willed real property to their wives (to provide for their wives' future well-being) and their unmarried daughters (who were seen as particularly requiring financial support). With unmarried women's property ownership on the rise, it became increasingly evident by the early 1880s that a growing number of property owners as a group had no representation within Parliament.[47] Considering his esteem for property ownership, it is likely that this new situation led Macdonald to include the women's suffrage clause in his *Electoral Franchise Act*. Indeed, when the clause came before the Committee of the Whole, Macdonald immediately justified his stance by pointing out that, "By slow degrees women have become owners of their own property."[48]

For Macdonald, however, married women and unmarried women "do not stand on exactly the same footing."[49] Married women had their husbands to speak for them and their property on election day. Unmarried women had no such male representatives.[50] Although they "assume[d] most the responsibilities of men," and were "compelled to pay taxes on [their] property," these unmarried women had no one "to vote for laws, and the most important of which, in any country, are for the protection of property."[51] This situation became particularly apparent when an unmarried woman owned a substantial amount of real estate. Macdonald told an anecdote to make his point for his parliamentary colleagues:

> It seems very hard to argue that a lady who has a large property should not have a vote when her servants may have votes. A lady of large wealth and property said to me when I was

in England a short time ago: "I have no vote. My butler has a vote, my steward has a vote, my coachman has a vote and at least fifty of my servants have votes; but I have no vote." She thought it was rather an injustice to her that she had not a vote when so many who derived their means of living from her had votes, and were her superiors in that regard.[52]

Macdonald did not make the moral of his story complicated; when it came to the franchise, the propertied should trump the unpropertied, regardless of gender. Otherwise, gentility would be threatened and the structure of Canadian society would unravel. Some commentators have understood this moral keenly. Because of Macdonald's emphasis on property ownership, both Sir Joseph Pope and Rod Preece have argued that Macdonald's treatment of women's suffrage reflects a very specific set of ideas: those of an entrenched conservatism.[53]

Writing just after Macdonald's death in 1891, Sir Joseph Pope, Macdonald's private secretary, provided perhaps the earliest commentary on Macdonald's political life. Pope believed that a decidedly conservative outlook guided his former employer's political decisions. The *Electoral Franchise Act* was no exception. Like the member of Macdonald's own caucus who argued that the new franchise bill participated in the "grand conservative principle, that nobody should take part in the administration of public affairs unless he has something at stake in the land ... unless he has an interest at stake as a proprietor," Pope viewed the attempted enfranchisement of unmarried propertied women as part and parcel of the same conservative ideology.[54] According to Pope, this particular form of women's suffrage, if successful, would have introduced "a new and powerful conservative factor in politics, whose tendency [Macdonald] believed would be to strengthen the defences against the eruption of an unbridled democracy."[55] Pope unfortunately mentions little else about franchise politics before moving on to Macdonald's other exploits. Nor does he clarify his use of the term "conservative." Exactly ninety years after Pope published his *Memoirs*, political scientist Rod Preece sought to address these shortcomings. To that end, in "The Political Wisdom of Sir John A. Macdonald," Preece argues that Macdonald's political actions best reflected the conservative philosophy of English parliamentarian Edmund Burke.[56]

Scholars have traditionally viewed Burke as the father of modern conservatism.[57] Recorded at the end of the eighteenth century, Burke's political philosophy valued the concepts of prudence, order, and, above all, tradition. For Burke, the British constitution embodied the amassed sum of British experience. Because it provided directly for the freedoms, liberties, and advantages enjoyed by all Britons, Burke encouraged a strict adherence to the spirit of the constitution.[58] Highly skeptical of political change, Burke believed that any alteration to the constitution should take place only gradually, if at all. Preece argues that these same core values helped guide Macdonald during his own political career.[59] In discussing Macdonald's women's suffrage clause in the same breath as Burkean conservatism, though, Preece walks a very fine line. Burke in no way endorsed women's enfranchisement; in fact, he rejected any expansion of the franchise. Burke believed that "it would be more in the spirit of our constitution, and more agreeable to the pattern of our best laws, by lessening the number [of voters], to add to the weight and independency of our voters."[60] Macdonald's design, in Macdonald's own words, to enact an "extension of the franchise" through women's suffrage certainly flies in the face of Burkean ideology.[61]

Yet, Macdonald only desired to enfranchise propertied householding women. According to Preece, "Macdonald's view was predicated in part on the dying belief that it was families, not individuals, who held the franchise and that only one individual should represent each family."[62] Ever since England had adopted parliamentary institutions, it relied upon the notion that the ownership of freehold property conferred one's political independence. As both a constitutionalist and a staunch traditionalist, Burke refused to waver from this logic. He held that only the wealthy propertied classes should have a say in guiding the nation from the hustings.[63] Burke feared that a decision otherwise would empower the capricious, uneducated masses, and that they would ultimately disfigure England through "idleness and profligacy" and the "corruption of manners."[64] Because Macdonald's women's suffrage clause would have only enfranchised a select group of reasonably wealthy householding women, Preece could suggest that the clause at least *approached* the spirit of Burkean ideology.[65] Preece's article possesses one prominent shortcoming, however: it does not really address any other political outlook. Burkean conservatives did not hold a monopoly when it came to the valorization of real property. Property ownership and its protection were central to Victorian liberalism as well.

Nineteenth-century liberalism revolved around three central tenets: liberty, equality, and property. For the nineteenth-century liberal, this triptych was crucial to the creation and development of autonomous, self-sufficient individuals. These individuals in turn formed the foundational units for liberal society. Social institutions thus existed in the nineteenth-century liberal world to protect the individual's rights to liberty, equality, and property. While all esteemed, these three core values were not necessarily weighted equally. In his trendsetting essay, "The Liberal Order Framework in Canada," Ian McKay argues that nineteenth-century Canadian liberalism ordered liberty, equality, and property hierarchically, "with formal equality at the bottom and property at the top."[66] According to McKay, the preservation of property qualifications upon the franchise in nineteenth-century Canada reflected an attempt to limit the franchise to only those Canadians who met the required criteria for liberal individualism and, thus, liberal citizenship.[67] As leader of Canada's Liberal-Conservative Party, Macdonald seemingly marched at the forefront of this liberal movement to politically empower propertied individuals. At a time when most governments in the republican United States had already removed property qualifications from state franchises, he chose to defend Canada's property-based franchise to the bitter end.[68] In attempting to allow certain propertied Canadian women to vote federally alongside propertied Canadian men, it also appears that the prime minister upheld the liberal principle of equality as well. By doing so, Macdonald adhered quite closely to one of the English-speaking world's most noteworthy liberal thinkers: that is, John Stuart Mill.

Writing in 1861, British parliamentarian and philosopher John Stuart Mill recorded his thoughts regarding the franchise in his treatise entitled *Considerations on Representative Government*. As part of a new generation of liberal intellectuals, Mill believed in a considerably different set of voter qualifications than Burke, his parliamentary predecessor. For instance, Mill advocated women's enfranchisement, stating that he considered sexual difference "to be as entirely irrelevant to political rights, as difference in height, or in the colour of the hair."[69] He even went so far as to contend that "[i]f there be any difference, women require [the vote] more than men, since, being physically weaker, they are more dependent on the law and society for protection."[70]

Mill also argued that the franchise should be extended as widely as possible. Echoing American revolutionary rhetoric, he claimed that "if [an individual] is compelled to pay, if he may be compelled to fight, if he is required to implicitly obey, he should be legally entitled to be told what for; to have his consent asked, and his opinion counted at its worth, though not at more than its worth."[71] True to his words, Mill introduced a motion to the British House of Commons in 1867 "embodying the principle of female suffrage, which he said was a logical consequence of the constitutional maxim that taxation and representation should go hand in hand."[72] Despite these forward-looking claims and actions, Mill was no supporter of universal suffrage.

Like Macdonald, Mill steadfastly believed that clear limitations should be placed on who should have the *privilege* of voting. Although Mill did not necessarily see property as central to either the franchise or political citizenship more generally, he did believe that "he who cannot by his labour suffice for his own support, has no claim to the privilege of helping himself to the money of others."[73] Because his own liberal ideology upheld the individual as prime actor and the individual's independence as of prime importance, Mill recoiled from the notion that persons dependent upon and obligated to others should be allowed to speak publicly on equal terms. Within the British tradition, the property qualification itself was designed to ensure the independence and self-sufficiency of the electorate. Although Mill may not have agreed with Macdonald's insistence on a property qualification for the Dominion franchise, he may have fundamentally agreed with the spirit behind such a qualification. Furthermore, if one accepted dominant notions of patriarchy and male breadwinning, marriage could also be seen as another form of dependency: in this case, of a married woman upon her husband. From this perspective, Macdonald's endorsement of limited women's enfranchisement in 1883 does not appear as something necessarily Burkean or conservative at all. It instead appears as Millian or liberal, and illuminates Macdonald's motivations in a nineteenth-century liberal light. Such a conclusion, however, has the potential to create further theoretical problems.

When Burke and Mill published their works of political theory, they wrote with specific times and places in mind. Both Burke and Mill were Englishmen. It therefore comes as no surprise that they focused their treatises upon the English context. Burke wrote of England during the late-eighteenth century, when the spirit of revolution threatened to spill across the English

Channel. Mill hoped to guide England through the rapid technological and intellectual changes of the mid-nineteenth century. Canada, as a subject of interest, appeared rarely in their texts. Although Macdonald may have read the works of Burke and Mill, he rarely expounded upon political philosophy.[74] It is therefore difficult to know just how much of Edmund Burke or John Stuart Mill actually resided within him. Instead of making comparisons with men from other situations and circumstances, one could argue that an analysis of Macdonald's attitude toward women's enfranchisement should take into consideration Macdonald's own mid-Victorian Canadian environment. Nineteenth-century Canada unfortunately did not produce intellectuals as remarkable as Burke or Mill. Nevertheless, many of Macdonald's contemporaries maintained firm opinions as to the validity of women's enfranchisement and as to the structure of the franchise more generally.

During the second half of the nineteenth century, reformers' and liberals' opinions concerning the franchise in Canada appear much more prevalently than those of conservatives. Even amongst self-declared reformers and liberals, one finds little consensus as to who precisely should vote. For example, Edward Blake, leader of the federal Liberal Party throughout most of the 1880s, argued for an exceptionally inclusive franchise that mirrored the one promoted by Mill. Instead of property ownership, Blake believed that "the basis for [the Dominion] franchise should be citizenship, residence, and intelligence – that intelligence established by an easy test, which has been applied in several self-governing states and colonies, the easy test with reference to reading and writing."[75] Blake viewed property as too exclusive a foundation for the federal vote. With regard to women's suffrage, however, he was somewhat more ambiguous. In response to Macdonald's women's suffrage clause, he cited that "[i]f you once grant that it is for the good of the race that women should become political electors, you are driven to treat marriage not as a disability" by enfranchising both unmarried *and* married women.[76] Blake could not support Macdonald's women's suffrage clause not because it enfranchised women, but because it did not enfranchise enough women. One notices, however, that Blake himself did not recognize the desirability of full women's suffrage. Considering both his preference for electoral inclusivity and his general dislike of the *Electoral Franchise Act*, Blake perhaps did not wish to give Macdonald any quarter by admitting that he, at least in principle, favoured women's suffrage.[77]

Blake's reservation in this instance stands in contrast with the frankness of Wilfrid Laurier, the man who would take over the leadership of the federal Liberals from Blake. Laurier was already a party luminary when the Commons debated the *Electoral Franchise Act* in 1885. A self-declared "Liberal of the Liberals," Laurier's philosophy concerning the franchise looked decidedly non-liberal when compared with that of Blake.[78] As an advocate of provincial rights, he believed that the provinces should continue to govern the federal franchise (something he would enact as prime minister in 1898).[79] Moreover, as a Quebecer, he considered Quebec's provincial franchise — the most restrictive franchise in Canada at the time — suitable and sustainable legislation (for Quebec at least).[80] Concerning women's enfranchisement, Laurier's views also leaned toward restriction and exclusiveness. During the franchise debates he asserted that "in the Province of Quebec, so far as I know, there is not one single class in the community that would extend the right of the franchise to women, not even to that fair portion of them to whom it is intended to give it by this Bill."[81] Laurier included himself as a member of these classes. Although he may have felt "that the action of women must be most influential in politics as in everything else," he also believed that such "action is more effective if exercised in the circle of the home, by persuasion and advice, than if woman is brought to the poll to vote."[82] Laurier, like Blake, thus rejected Macdonald's women's suffrage, but he did so for a different reason. Instead of endorsing equality for both unmarried and married women, Laurier preferred to defend the principle of separate spheres and to fasten women's influence to the domestic realm.

Nineteenth-century Canadian liberals did not solely reside in the House of Commons, however. In 1871, Goldwin Smith, a former regius professor of modern history at Oxford University and a leading British liberal intellectual, took up permanent residence in Toronto. For the rest of his life, he worked as an editor and political commentator, promoting his liberal philosophy to all those willing to listen. Even before becoming a resident of the Dominion, Smith took particular interest in Canada and its political situation (more so than Mill ever did). Upon hearing of Canada's planned confederation, Smith wrote a short article for *Macmillan's Magazine* entitled "The Proposed Constitution for British North America." As part of his assessment, Smith particularly criticized the electoral franchise stipulation found within the draft *British North America Act*. According to Smith:

> [A]ssuredly it is not on the ground of special certainty or
> stability that, in a colony like Canada, political distinctions
> in favour of real property ought to be drawn: for there are
> few places, we apprehend, where the value of land and
> houses is more uncertain and variable.... But there seems
> to be a notion that because land itself is stable, property in
> it, though it may be the wildest of all possible speculations,
> is stable also: a mere illusion, as we need scarcely observe.[83]

Smith then went on to disparage those Canadians who defended the
property-based franchise — men like Macdonald, who himself had fashioned the *British North America Act's* franchise clause — by portraying them
as slaves to "the desire of imitating the British constitution."[84] Such a philosophy regarding the franchise stands up nicely beside those of Mill and
Blake. So does Smith's declaration that:

> He [Smith] has always been for enlarging the number of
> active citizens as much as possible, and widening the basis
> of government, in accordance with the maxim, which
> seems to him the sum of political philosophy, "That is the
> best form of government which doth most actuate and
> dispose all parts and members of the commonwealth to
> the common good."[85]

Unlike Mill and Blake, however, Smith categorically rebuked the idea
that women should vote alongside men.

Earlier in his life, Smith had actually endorsed women's enfranchisement.[86] During the 1860s he had even gone so far as to publicly support
Mill's call for "Female Household Suffrage."[87] By 1874, however, Smith had
changed his mind on the subject. In another article he wrote for *Macmillan's
Magazine* — this time reacting to a British government motion to "give the
suffrage only to unmarried women being householders" — he intimated that
"the [women's suffrage] movement was received with mistrust by some of the
best and most sensible women of his acquaintance, who feared that their
most valuable privileges, and the deepest sources of their happiness, were
being jeopardized to gratify the political aspirations of a few of their sex."[88]

Taking this revelation as his starting point, Smith argued that women's enfranchisement would yield calamitous results. Men and women within the same family "would be brought in direct and public collision."[89] Women would be unsexed.[90] In fact, Smith believed that "there can be little doubt that in all cases, if power were put into the hands of the women, free government, and with it liberty of opinion, would fall."[91] Like many of his contemporaries, Smith grounded his rhetoric in sweeping generalizations about "sentiment[s] inherent in the female temperament," the "female need of protection," and women's "preference for personal government, which finds its proper satisfaction in the family."[92] Needless to say, Smith would not have supported Macdonald's attempt to enfranchise unmarried property-owning women in 1883. In this regard, Macdonald appears as far more liberal than the liberal Smith.

Discovering late-nineteenth-century Canadian conservative voices concerning the franchise proves much more difficult. Current Canadian historiography does not necessarily help in this endeavour. For the longest time, one could point to Macdonald himself as a prime example of late-nineteenth-century Canadian conservatism. In one of the most widely read reflections on Canada's prime ministers, Michael Bliss portrays Macdonald's intense pro-British, anti-democratic tendencies as reflecting "the depth and consistency of [Macdonald's] conservatism."[93] Bliss goes so far as to assert that "by the end of his life [Macdonald] had become a somewhat rigid, reactionary Victorian."[94] The current historiography on liberalism in Canada, inspired by McKay's liberal order thesis, has profoundly complicated such portrayals.[95] As historians have applied this thesis to nineteenth-century Canada, they have come to re-evaluate the political philosophies of past individuals. Many Victorian Canadians, traditionally categorized as conservatives, are now depicted as ideologically liberal in their outlook. Macdonald, to a certain extent, has undergone the same treatment.[96] Pro-British and anti-democratic sentiments, after all, found support amongst self-declared liberals such as Wilfrid Laurier. As a result of this liberal emphasis within the historiography, late-nineteenth-century political conservatism has become somewhat nebulous in its definition.[97]

Within Macdonald's own nominally Conservative caucus, one does hear the voice of Thomas Linière Taschereau, of Beauce, Quebec. During an uncommonly long speech from the Government side of the House,

Taschereau offered his own "conservative" argument in favour of limited women's enfranchisement. From the backbenches he posed the following question to his fellow parliamentarians:

> If we take it as a conservative principle that the right of suffrage should be granted to whoever pays the taxes, and if a woman pays taxes, owns property and is interested in the good legislation [*sic*], and in the welfare and prosperity of the country, by virtue of what principle could we refuse to give her the right of voting?[98]

Although Taschereau may have made claims to conservative principles, Mill could have easily cited him for plagiarism. Even Taschereau's opponents commented upon the profoundly liberal attitude that tinged his supposedly conservative arguments.[99] If the Liberal-Conservative Party indeed shared Taschereau's definition of conservatism, then Macdonald's defence of limited women's suffrage would seem to speak to an exceedingly egalitarian form of liberalism in the Millian sense.

While such a conclusion may complement the recent historiography on liberalism in Canada, it does not persuade for at least three reasons.[100] First, Taschereau's argument concerning taxation and the franchise received no corroboration from either the *Electoral Franchise Act*, the Liberal-Conservative caucus, or Macdonald himself. Second, while it is true that Macdonald's attempt at limited women's suffrage would have created new voters, the women's suffrage clause participated in a larger act that, on paper at least, ultimately reduced the overall size of the electorate. Save that of Quebec, the provincial franchises replaced by the *Electoral Franchise Act* all contained far more lenient restrictions. Of course, it is impossible to tell whether the women's suffrage clause would have made up for the number of men disenfranchised by the higher property qualifications. That said, no nineteenth-century liberal thinker, whether in Canada or abroad, ever advocated *contracting* the overall electorate. One must turn to Edmund Burke to find such an opinion. In fact, Liberal members of Parliament specifically commented upon how non-liberal such a restriction of the franchise would be.[101]

Third, and perhaps most intriguing, limited women's enfranchisement was by no means an untried concept in Canada. Indeed, the *Constitutional*

Act of 1791 stipulated that all British subjects who met the forty-shilling freehold — including propertied women — could cast a vote. One finds evidence in early nineteenth-century Nova Scotia of propertied women voting provincially as well. By 1851, however, every British North America colony had amended its franchise to explicitly bar women from voting.[102] Although Macdonald may have commented unfavourably in 1858 upon the property qualification within the *Constitutional Act* of 1791, he offered no clear opinion as to the other parts of the legislation. With Women's Property Laws solidly in place throughout Canada by 1883, it now made more sense than ever to revisit the former constitutional practice of propertied women's suffrage. And if Macdonald wished to follow Burke's advice concerning tradition, then harkening back to the Canadas' first constitution made that much more sense. From this perspective, conservative ideology could have inspired Macdonald's endorsement of limited women's suffrage just as much as liberal theory.

To rescue us from this ideological cul-de-sac, I turn to the concept of constitutionalism. As a political philosophy, constitutionalism found its inception in seventeenth-century England. Championed by the supporters of England's Glorious Revolution, it centred upon the notion that individuals have certain natural or sacred rights to liberty, property, and security.[103] Within the constitutionalist framework, no one, not even the monarch, may arbitrarily incarcerate or injure another, or confiscate another's property. The constitution protects these sacred rights, and the mixed Parliament protects the constitution.[104] Michel Ducharme has convincingly revealed that both modern conservatism *and* modern liberalism, in both Great Britain and Canada, found their geneses within this constitutionalist tradition.[105] Such an interpretation further challenges what Janet Ajzenstat calls the "standard accounts of Confederation, [where] liberalism makes its appearance as one of a succession of political ideologies, preceded by conservatism and succeeded by socialism."[106] From the constitutionalist point of view, the link between conservatism and liberalism is not teleological at all. Instead, nineteenth-century conservatism and liberalism existed as part of an ideological web, branching from the constitutionalist tradition around the same time but with different trajectories. This common ancestry created a bond between the two, with conservatism and liberalism looking remarkably similar depending upon one's perspective. Nineteenth-century franchise debate in Canada provides a clear example of this overlap. Although conservatives and liberals may have disagreed over accessibility to the vote, property ownership and the property-based franchise played a vital role within both ideological frameworks.

Based upon this conceptual model, it seems that Macdonald's attempts to federally enfranchise property-owning women between 1883 and 1885 did not necessarily stem from a preformed set of liberal beliefs or a preformed set of conservative beliefs. Instead, his relationship with women's suffrage reflected an existence in both the conservative and liberal ideological worlds of his day, overlapping and entangling them both. Macdonald's advocacy of a property-qualified women's suffrage, in spite of his caucus's divergent views, placed him amongst the most forward-thinking liberals of the era. Indeed, even the cream of Canada's late-Victorian liberal intelligentsia — Blake, Laurier, Smith — refused to make that leap. If Mill had not suffered an untimely death during the previous decade, he may very well have offered Macdonald his support in this regard. That being said, Macdonald had also hoped to impose the most restrictive property qualification in Canada upon these unmarried women voters. In doing so, he looked decades back into the nation's colonial and constitutional past. The spirit of Burke would have smiled at the way Macdonald embraced the old constitution, even if Burke may not have agreed with extending the franchise to a new group of voters. By means of long-expired tradition, Macdonald thus attempted something socially and culturally liberal, in both the contemporary and the theoretical sense: to make independent propertied men and women equal citizens on election day. With the notions of enfranchisement and property ownership so inextricably linked in his mind, and the number of property-owning women in Canada growing annually, such a step made sense in Macdonald's tired eyes.

Because he rooted political citizenship so deeply in property ownership, nineteenth-century Canadian conservatives and liberals could both claim Macdonald as their own. After all, Macdonald was the original, and leading, Liberal-Conservative throughout his life. Since his death in 1891, scholars have made similar claims. Whereas twentieth-century historians have generally painted Macdonald as a conservative — if they viewed him as a man of ideas at all — twenty-first-century historians have often depicted him as a liberal. The constitutionalist heritage of Victorian conservatism and liberalism has allowed for both interpretations. Perhaps it is this philosophical intersection that has made it so difficult to classify Macdonald ideologically. He certainly had strong political ideas of his own. But these ideas did not necessarily fall neatly under the rigid labels of liberalism or conservatism. Macdonald's attempt to enfranchise unmarried property-owning women between 1883 and 1885 speaks directly to this theoretical liminality. In the end, though, very few Canadians shared Macdonald's vision of women's suffrage. Macdonald may have looked forward by looking backward. Or he may have looked backward by looking forward. But his vantage point was all his own.

• • •

The author wishes to thank Elsbeth Heaman and Michel Ducharme for their helpful comments on an earlier draft of this paper, and the other attendees of the "John A. Macdonald: Fresh Perspectives and New Legacies" conference for their keen remarks. The author would also like to acknowledge the Social Sciences and Humanities Research Council and the Peter Cundill Fellowship in History for their financial support of this research.

Notes

1. In his recent history of the 1891 Canadian federal election, Christopher Pennington also points out that Macdonald "is most commonly remembered for being an alcoholic" and that the "enduring public memory of Sir John A. Macdonald is that of a drunk." See Christopher Pennington, *The Destiny of Canada: Macdonald, Laurier, and the Election of 1891* (Toronto: Allen Lane, 2011), xv, 15. For more on Macdonald's drinking, see Ged Martin, "John A. Macdonald and the Bottle," *Journal of Canadian Studies* 40.3 (Fall 2006): 162–185.

2. Richard Gwyn, *John A.: The Man Who Made Us, Vol. 1* (Toronto: Random House: 2007), 294–297.

3. Ibid., "Macdonald @ 200," John A. Macdonald: Fresh Perspectives and New Legacies (conference), Ryerson University, Toronto, December 3, 2010. Also see Richard Gwyn, *Nation Maker: Sir John A Macdonald: His Life, Our Times, Vol. 2* (Toronto: Random House, 2011), 519–522.

4. For a good overview of these provincial franchise qualifications see Chief Electoral Officer of Canada, *A History of the Vote in Canada* (Ottawa: The Minister of Public Works and Government Services Canada, 1997), 46.

5. For more information on provincial women's enfranchisement in Canada see ibid., 61–68.

6. Sir John A. Macdonald Fonds [hereafter Macdonald Fonds], MG 26-A, "Political papers. Subject files" series, vol. 64, reel C1510, 25878, Library and Archives Canada [hereafter LAC]; House of Commons "Bill No. 103: An Act respecting the Electoral Franchise." See section 2. Although it is outside the scope of this chapter, one should note that the legislation also included "Indians" as persons. At this time, certain provinces (most notably British Columbia, but also Manitoba and Ontario) maintained racial restrictions that barred First Nations from voting. Considering the House of Commons debated the *Electoral Franchise Act* at the same time as the Northwest Resistance, and considering the racist invective the Resistance inspired amongst parliamentarians, it was a minor miracle that the final legislation upheld "Indians" as persons at all.

7. See Canada, *Official Debates of the House of Commons of Canada* [hereafter *Hansard*], vol. 13, April 12, 1883 (Ottawa: Maclean, Roger & Co., 1883), 593–596; Ibid., vol. 13, May 23, 1883, 1387.

8. Ibid., vol. 15, January 23, 1884, 31; April 16, 1884, 1627.

9. From the outset, the Opposition Liberal Party had realized that it had no hope of defeating the bill. It instead adopted filibuster tactics, hoping to delay the bill to such an extent that the government would end the session before the bill could pass. As a result, sessions of Parliament ran through the night and members of Parliament had to get whatever sleep they could on cots lining the corridors outside the House of Commons. I have discussed this debate elsewhere. See Colin J. Grittner, "'A Statesmanlike Measure with a Partisan Tail': The Development of the Nineteenth-Century Dominion Electoral Franchise," MA thesis (Carleton University, 2009), 91–140.

10. See ibid., volume 18, April 28, 1885, 1442.

11. In her overview of the franchise debates of 1885, Veronica Strong-Boag details in part the scant support that Macdonald received for his women's suffrage clause. Strong-Boag reveals that "The Prime Minister found the bulk of suffragists among the Liberal rank-and-file." The use of the word "bulk" in this instance is slightly misleading. Only eight Liberals supported the bill's women's suffrage clause. Even if one adds the four Conservatives who voted for the clause, a mere 5 percent of the House of Commons endorsed women's enfranchisement in 1885. See Veronica Strong-Boag, "'The Citizenship Debates': The 1885 *Franchise Act*," in *Contesting Canadian Citizenship*, eds. Robert Adamoski, Dorothy E. Chunn, and Robert Menzies (Peterborough: Broadview Press, 2002), 79–80.

12. Compared to the Liberal members' protracted speeches — for example, Liberal leader Edward Blake gave a speech on April 17, 1885, that lasted approximately four hours — the members of Macdonald's Party said very little during the debate. See *Hansard*, vol. 18, April 17, 1885, 1182–1195.

13. Ibid., April 17, 1885, 1134.
14. Ibid., April 27, 1885, 1388.
15. Ibid., 1389.
16. Strong-Boag argues that Macdonald's "declarations, while questioned, even ridiculed, by Edward Blake and the Opposition, placed Macdonald squarely within the pro-suffrage camp of the day." Strong-Boag does not go so far as to call Macdonald a suffragist though. See Strong-Boag, "Citizenship Debates," 77.
17. Norman Ward, *The Canadian House of Commons: Representation*, 2nd ed. (Toronto: University of Toronto Press, 1963), 217.
18. Diane Lamoureux and Jacinthe Michaud, "Les parlementaires et le suffrage féminin: un aperçu des débats," *Canadian Journal of Political Science* 21.2 (June 1988): 322–323.
19. See *Hansard*, vol. 18, April 27, 1885, 1441. The Liberal representative for North Brant, Ontario, James Somerville, made this somewhat off-colour remark.
20. Ibid.
21. Carol Lee Bacchi, *Liberation Deferred?: The Ideas of the English-Canadian Suffragists, 1877–1918* (Toronto: University of Toronto Press, 1983), 136.
22. See Ward, 218; Lamoureux and Michaud, "Les parlementaires et le suffrage féminin," 322.
23. *Hansard*, vol. 18, April 16, 1885, 1133.
24. Ibid.
25. Bacchi, 136.
26. Catherine Cleverdon, *The Woman Suffrage Movement in Canada*, 2nd ed. (Toronto: University of Toronto Press, 1974), 109.
27. According to section 20 of the *Constitutional Act*, 1791, members of the Legislative Assembly "shall be chosen by the majority of votes of such persons as shall severally be possessed" of either a freehold property with a yearly value of at least forty shillings, a house within a town with a yearly value of at least five pounds sterling, or a rental property with an annual rental value of ten pounds sterling. While Sections 22 and 23 prohibited minors under the age of twenty-one, non-British subjects, and those previously convicted of a felony from voting, the act did not contain any stipulations with regard to gender. Even by 1849, the United Province of Canada still adhered to this legislation. Consequently, Canadian women who met the above qualifications had technically possessed the right to vote at provincial elections in the two Canadas for over fifty years. Only unwritten Common Law could keep women from the hustings, and only where both Common Law was in force and returning officers chose to follow it over the letter of the constitution. Not all returning officers did so. See Great Britain, "An Act to repeal certain parts of an Act, passed in the fourteenth year of His Majesty's reign, intituled,

An Act for making more effectual provision for the Government of the Province of Quebec, in North America; and to make further provision for the government of said province," 31 Geo. 3, c. 31, sections 20–23.

28. John Garner, *The Franchise and Politics in British North America, 1755–1867* (Toronto: University of Toronto Press, 1969), 159.

29. Ibid.

30. Of all the members of the provincial assembly, former *patriote* leader Louis-Joseph Papineau spoke most fervently against government control of returning officer appointments. He argued (even after the clause had passed) that "by appointing officers who were dependent on the Ministry it would induce Returning-Officers to act in a partial manner in favor of the Party in power, from fear of losing their office. This would degrade representation, and increase in a most unjust manner the patronage and influence of the Administration." See Province of Canada, *Debates of the Legislative Assembly of United Canada*, vol. 8, part 2, March 13, 1849 (Montreal: Centre de recherche en histoire économique du Canada français, 1976), 1298. Besides Papineau, the Conservative members, including John A. Macdonald, also voted against the bill's registration clause. See ibid., March 6, 1849, 1163.

31. MacNab declared that he "would vote against the third reading of the Bill, as it created a new qualification for electors in Lower Canada, and also that it extended a franchise to Lower Canada, which was not accorded to Upper Canada." See ibid., vol. 8, part 3, April 25, 1849, 2043–2044.

32. Ibid.

33. Province of Canada, *Parliamentary Debates* [Scrapbook debates], reel 2, April 27, 1858 (Ottawa: Canadian Library Association, Newspaper microfilming project, 1954), 68.

34. Chief Electoral Officer of Canada, 2–3.

35. *Parliamentary Debates* [Scrapbook debates], reel 2, April 27, 1858, 67.

36. Province of Canada, "An Act to define the Elective Franchise, to provide for the Registration of Voters, and for other purposes therein mentioned," 22 Vic., c. 82, section 2, subsection 1.

37. *Parliamentary Debates* [Scrapbook debates], reel 2, May 11, 1858, 81.

38. Province of Canada, 22 Vic., c. 82, section 2, subsection 1.

39. The only year it was not tabled was 1868. For the final iteration of this bill, see Macdonald Fonds, MG 26-A, "Political papers. Subject files" series, vol. 73, reel C1513, 28688, LAC; House of Commons "Bill. An Act respecting Elections of Members to the House of Commons," 1873.

40. Ibid. See section 2. For comparison, see section 2 of the *Electoral Franchise Act* of 1885: Canada, "The Electoral Franchise Act," 48–49 Vic., c. 40, section 2.

41. "Bill. An Act respecting Elections of Members to the House of Commons, 1873." See sections 3–5, LAC.

42. Ibid. See section 12.

43. See Cleverdon, 20–21.

44. *Parliamentary Debates* [Scrapbook debates], reel 2, May 11, 1858, 81.

45. Province of Canada, *Parliamentary Debates on the Subject of the Confederation of the British North American Provinces*, 3rd Session, 8th Provincial Parliament of Canada (Quebec: Hunter, Rose & Co., 1865), 39.

46. *Parliamentary Debates* [Scrapbook Debates], reel 5, March 21, 1873, 32.

47. Peter Baskerville, *A Silent Revolution?: Gender and Wealth in English Canada 1860–1930* (Montreal and Kingston: McGill-Queen's University Press, 2008), 4–10. For a more regional study of Women's Property Laws, see Lori Chambers, *Married Women and Property Law in Victorian Ontario* (Toronto: The Osgoode Society, 1997).

48. *Hansard*, vol. 18, April 27, 1885, 1388.

49. Ibid., 1389.

50. Ibid.

51. Ibid.

52. Ibid.

53. Richard Gwyn has singled out political scientist Rod Preece as one of the very few scholars to treat Macdonald seriously as a man of ideas. See Gwyn, *John A.*, 295.

54. *Hansard*, vol. 18, April 17, 1885, 1175. Macdonald's secretary of state, Sir Joseph Chapleau, made this declaration. Its sentiment would have resonated with the majority of Macdonald's fellow Liberal-Conservatives.

55. Sir Joseph Pope, *Memoirs of the Right Honourable Sir John A. Macdonald*, volume II (Ottawa: J. Durie & Son, 1894), 247–248.

56. Rod Preece, "The Political Wisdom of Sir John A. Macdonald," *Canadian Journal of Political Science* 17.3 (September 1984): 464.

57. More recently, historian Michel Ducharme has updated Burke's image by defining him as a Whig constitutionalist whose work in part laid the foundation for modern conservatism. See Michel Ducharme, *Le concept de liberté au Canada a l'époque des Révolutions atlantiques 1776–1838* (Montreal and Kingston: McGill-Queen's University Press, 2010), 8; 31.

58. According to Burke, one cannot judge "whether the principles of the British (the Irish) Constitution be wise or not.." Instead, Britons "must assume that they are.." See Edmund Burke, "A Letter to Sir Hercules Langrishe, Bart., M.P., on the Subject of The Roman Catholics of Ireland and The Propriety of Admitting Them to the Elective Franchise, Consistently with the Principles of the Constitution, as Established at the Revolution" (1792), in *The Works of the Right Honourable Edmund Burke* (London: John C. Nimmo, 1899), 253.

59. Preece, "Political Wisdom," 486.

60. Burke, *Reflections on the Revolution in France*, ed. J.C.D. Clark (Stanford, CA: Stanford University Press, 2001), 370–371.

61. Again see *Hansard*, vol. 18, April 16, 1885, 1134.

62. Preece, "Political Wisdom," 475.

63. Burke, "A Letter to Sir Hercules Langrishe, Bart., M.P." (1792), 253.

64. Ibid., "The Present State of the Nation," in *The Works of the Right Honourable Edmund Burke*, 371.

65. Despite his argument, Preece admits that "Burke would have disapproved" of women's enfranchisement because it represented too drastic a change of British electoral politics. See Preece, "Political Wisdom," 475.

66. Ian McKay, "The Liberal Order Framework: A Prospectus for a Reconnaissance of Canadian History," *Canadian Historical Review* 81.4 (December 2000): 624.

67. Ibid., 625.

68. By 1855, only the states of Rhode Island and South Carolina maintained property qualifications upon their franchises. Rhode Islanders had to own $134 worth of real property to vote. South Carolina's property qualification was much less onerous: the state's constitution required citizens to possess a title to any piece of land, no matter the land's value. By the 1870s, some state governments began to revisit the institution of property qualifications upon their franchises. Very little of import came of these debates: no state re-established its former property qualifications. Certain states, such as Louisiana and Virginia, reincorporated property qualifications into their state laws, but only as an alternative to literacy qualifications already placed upon the franchise. See Alexander Keyssar, *The Right to Vote: The Contested History of Democracy in the United States* (New York: Basic Books, 2000), 363–367; 370.

69. John Stuart Mill, *Considerations on Representative Government* (Chicago: Gateway, 1962), 187.

70. Ibid.

71. Ibid., 169.

72. "Suffrage for Women," *Toronto Globe*, June 4, 1867, 1.

73. Mill, 174.

74. As authors such as Rod Preece and Richard Gwyn have argued, Macdonald rarely based his political speeches and discussions upon abstract ideas. See Preece, "Political Wisdom," 462; Gwyn, *John A.*, 294. Some have suggested that one could look to the voluntary associations to which Macdonald belonged to better determine Macdonald's own political ideology. For example, he participated in both the Orange Order (a Protestant political organization) and the British American League (an imperialist organization established in 1849 that sought to address Canada's economic turmoils in the face of Great Britain's withdrawal of imperial preference on trade and growing internal

demands for American annexation). One could argue that Macdonald's involvement with these groups offers evidence that he philosophically agreed with their mandates. Yet, as Ged Martin reminds us, Macdonald did not necessarily enlist with voluntary organizations out of ideological sympathy. Martin argues that Macdonald joined the Orange Order "in the early eighteen-forties, explicitly to advance his political career.." Macdonald may have done much the same thing with the British American League considering its first convention took place in Macdonald's own Kingston riding. Tellingly, Macdonald did not attend the League's second and final convention held in Toronto during the same year. See Ged Martin, *Favourite Son?: John A. Macdonald and the Voters of Kingston, 1841–1891* (Kingston, ON: Kingston Historical Society, 2010), 6. For more on the British American League, its mandate, and its participants, see Gerald A. Hallowell, "The Reaction of the Upper Canadian Tories to the Adversity of 1849: Annexation and the British American League," *Ontario History* 62.1 (March 1970): 41; 49–56. Also see British American League, *Minutes of the Proceedings of a Convention of Delegates of the British American League Held at Kingston (Canada West) on the 25th, and by Adjournment on the 26th, 27th, and 31st Days of July 1849* (Kingston: The Chronicle and News, 1849), 3–4; Ibid., *Minutes of the Proceedings of the Second Convention of Delegates of the British American League Held at Toronto, C.W. on Thursday, November 1, and by Adjournment on the 2nd, 3rd, 5th, 6th, and 7th of November, 1849* (Toronto: The Patriot, 1849), 3.

75. *Hansard*, vol. 18, April 17, 1885, 1187

76. Ibid., 1188.

77. Veronica Strong-Boag interprets Edward Blake's reticence differently. Because Blake never openly declared his support for women's enfranchisement, Strong-Boag maintains that "Blake proved no friend to the supporters of John Stuart Mill." See Strong-Boag, "Citizenship Debates," 78.

78. *Hansard*, vol. 46, April 21, 1898, 4010.

79. Ibid., vol. 18, April 17, 1885, 1169. In 1898, Wilfrid Laurier's government introduced legislation that expressly sought to repeal the *Electoral Franchise Act* of 1885 and to return the federal franchise back to the provinces. Although the Liberal Party argued that it did so for fiscal reasons — because the creation of federal voters' lists had apparently cost the Dominion government an excessive amount of money — the reversion to a provincially controlled federal franchise also coincided with Laurier's long held support of provincial rights. For example, see *Hansard*, vol. 46, March 22, 1898, 2273. Also see Canada, "An Act to repeal the Electoral Franchise Act, and to further amend the Dominion Elections Act," 62 Vic., c. 14.

80. *Hansard*, vol. 18, April 17, 1885, 1169.

81. Ibid., 1170.

82. Ibid., 1171.
83. Goldwin Smith, "The Proposed Constitution for British North America," *Macmillan's Magazine* 11 (March 1865): 413.
84. Ibid.
85. Ibid., "Female Suffrage," *Macmillan's Magazine* 30 (May 1874): 140.
86. Ibid.
87. Ibid. Smith viewed John Stuart Mill as "the real father of the whole [women's suffrage] movement; the arguments of its other champions are mere reproductions of his." See ibid., 148.
88. Ibid., 139; 140.
89. Ibid., 147.
90. Ibid.
91. Ibid., 145.
92. Ibid.
93. Michael Bliss, *Right Honourable Men: The Descent of Canadian Politics from Macdonald to Chrétien*, updated ed. (Toronto: Harper Collins, 2004), 8–11.
94. Ibid., 8.
95. Again see McKay, "The Liberal Order Framework."
96. For example, see ibid., "Canada as a Long Liberal Revolution: On Writing the History of Actually Existing Canadian Liberalisms, 1840s–1940s," in *Liberalism and Hegemony: Debating the Canadian Liberal Revolution*, eds. Jean-François Constant and Michel Ducharme (Toronto: University of Toronto Press, 2009), 397. Within the same book of essays, E.A. Heaman questions such a reading of Macdonald. In her work "Rights Talk and the Liberal Order Framework," Heaman views Macdonald as "a man of deeply conservative leanings" and associates his esteem for property ownership with that of Edmund Burke. See E.A. Heaman, "Rights Talk and the Liberal Order Framework," in ibid., 150–151; 168.
97. This is certainly not to say that no scholarship exists on the conservative tradition in nineteenth-century Canada. Historians such as S.F. Wise have offered lengthy examinations on the subject. Their discussions have tended to end in the year 1850, with the demise of the old Upper Canadian Tory Party. See S.F. Wise, "Upper Canada and the Conservative Tradition," in *God's Peculiar Peoples: Essays on Political Culture in Nineteenth-Century Canada*, eds. A.B. McKillop and Paul Romney (Ottawa: Carleton University Press: 1993), 169–184. More recently, Ian Radforth has appraised the influence of "muscular conservatism" during the Rebellion Losses controversy in Upper Canada in 1849. See Ian Radforth, "Political Demonstrations and Spectacles during the Rebellion Losses Controversy in Upper Canada," *Canadian Historical Review* 92.1 (March 2011): 1–41.
98. *Hansard*, vol. 18, April 21, 1885, 1237.

99. Ibid., 1246.

100. One may also recall Rod Preece's argument that Macdonald believed "it was families, not individuals, who held the franchise.." If this was the case, Macdonald eschewed the liberal notion that the individual formed the basis for society and instead maintained a pre-liberal view of societal construction. Unfortunately, Preece provides no evidence to support his claim aside from the fact that Macdonald only attempted to enfranchise unmarried property-owning women. I have not discovered any further evidence to support such a claim. Considering many of these unmarried women would not have had families, I find the argument that Macdonald desired to empower property owners more convincing. Again see Preece, "Political Wisdom," 475.

101. For example, see the speeches of the Liberal members of Parliament, Malcolm Colin Cameron, James Fleming, Wilfrid Laurier, and John Charlton in: *Hansard*, vol. 18, April 16, 1885, 1140, 1147; April 17, 1885, 1168; May 5, 1885, 1617.

102. Chief Electoral Officer of Canada, 61–64.

103. Ducharme, *Le concept de liberté au Canada*, 6; 25.

104. Ibid., 29–31.

105. Ibid., 8.

106. Janet Ajzenstat, *The Canadian Founding: John Locke and Parliament* (Montreal and Kingston: McGill-Queen's University Press, 2007), 20.

Chapter 2

Macdonald's Relationship with Aboriginal Peoples

Donald B. Smith

John A. Macdonald played a vital role in the formation of Canadian Aboriginal policy both before, and after, Confederation. In 1857, he introduced the *Gradual Civilization Act* in the Province of Canada. Twelve years later he brought forward the first federal *Indian Act*. Under his leadership the Indian policy of the Province of Canada was carried east and west into a full national structure after Confederation. Our first prime minister confronted Louis Riel and the Red River Métis in 1869–70. His administration signed the first three of the numbered treaties in Western Canada from 1871 to 1873. He also served as superintendent general of Indian Affairs for a decade, from 1878 to 1887. The Canadian government's involvement on the Indian residential school system formally began in 1879, during his administration. In 1885 Macdonald again clashed with Louis Riel and the Métis in the Northwest. After noting all of these contributions, surprisingly no one has written a full-length book on our first prime minister's Aboriginal policies.[1] The recent swing away from the writing of Canadian political history by Canadian academics helps to explain this.[2] Let this article serve as a call to action for a full study of our first prime minister' s relationship with Aboriginal Canada.

Upper Canada is the best starting point. In 1820, the Macdonald family, Scottish immigrants from Glasgow, arrived in Kingston, population approximately 4,000. At the time, it was the largest urban centre in Upper Canada.[3] John Alexander, age five, immigrated with his parents and three siblings; Hugh and Helen Macdonald attempted to establish a store in Kingston. After the failure of their first two business ventures the family tried again — this time in the country, at Hay Bay on the Bay of Quinte, about fifty kilometres west of Kingston. In 1824, John, now nine years old, continued with his schooling in Adolphustown. Later his parents sent their son, a gifted student, back to Kingston to attend the Midland District Grammar School, but he returned to the Bay of Quinte area each summer.

The Bay of Quinte had a great influence on young John. Alexander Campbell, his Kingston law partner and political organizer, later recalled that Macdonald spoke "in tone of voice & manner as thoroughly a Bay of Quinte boy as if he has been born there."[4] The Bay of Quinte was most likely the locality where he first met North American Indians, or at least heard "old-timers" talking about them.

The British had been making treaties with the Mississauga, as they termed the Ojibwe on the north shore of Lake Ontario, since the late eighteenth century. John Graves Simcoe, the first Lieutenant Governor of Upper

Library and Archives Canada C-6134.

Macdonald appears before the Six Nations of the Grand Council House at Ohsweken, September 6, 1886. The prime minister bears a flower on his lapel.

Canada, referred to them as "the original proprietors of the Land."[5] The Royal Proclamation of 1763 outlined the procedure to follow when dealing with the First Nations of the Great Lakes. All private transactions involving land were forbidden. Only after public purchase or a treaty with the Crown, could non-Aboriginal settlers occupy First Nations lands. In the 1780s, the Mississauga had completed land agreements with the British. Captain William Crawford, a Loyalist officer who had accompanied the Ojibwe on several raiding parties during the Revolutionary War, negotiated them. The first in 1783, and the second in 1784, led to the acquisition of the huge tract along the northeastern shoreline of Lake Ontario, from Gananoque to the western boundary of the Bay of Quinte.[6] Payment for the first treaty included clothing, guns for those without them, powder, and ammunition, and "enough red cloth as will make about a twelve coats and laced hats."[7] The payment for the second purchase is not recorded.[8] The British regarded these treaties as legal transactions by which they gained title to Mississauga land forever in exchange for specified trade goods, paid for on a once-and-for-all-time basis.

The Ojibwe (or Mississauga) had no legal counsel, and no knowledge of the English language or of English property law. Their concept of land tenure differed from that of the British. They saw the first treaties in the 1780s as affirmations of their alliance with the British. These agreements covered the use of sections of their territory. As Peter Jones, an early Mississauga chief and Methodist minister at the western end of Lake Ontario, confirmed, the Ojibwe at the turn of the century considered themselves free, and independent: "Each tribe or body of Indians has its own range of country, and sometimes each family has its own hunting grounds, marked out by certain natural divisions, such as rivers, lakes, mountains, or ridges; and all the game within these bounds is considered their property as much as the cattle and fowl owned by a farmer on his own land."[9]

For the right to share designated areas of their land the Ojibwe accepted presents, but this did not infer the "sale" or permanent alienation known in English law. An individual family could use a recognized hunting ground, fishing place, or maple sugar bush, but as soon as they stopped frequenting the area ownership reverted to the community. The Ojibwe focused on the use of land.[10] People could possess things, but they were expected to lend and to share as needed or requested. As Roger Spielman has written in his study of Ojibwe discourse: "There seems to be an understanding that relationships with people are far more important than things, and maintaining the harmony of the moment is more important than creating tension by refusing a request or putting more value on things than on people."[11] The Ojibwe accepted British trade goods in return for allowing the newcomers use of portions of their territory.[12]

No deed or indenture nor even a rough map from either of the two treaties exists to describe the tract. Detailed records of the various treaties and surrenders by which the transfer took place are not always available, for the Crown Lands officials had little to do with Indian lands in the beginning. In a landmark essay, "Land Settlement in Upper Canada, 1783–1840," historian Gilbert Patterson noted "that business was carried on by a military 'Indian Department'; scarcely a record or account book was used, the Deputy Paymaster was the only public accountant for monies, and there was not even a permanent clerk for correspondence."[13] The system of record keeping later improved in the 1830s and 1840s, but throughout the period up to 1860 administrative confusion plagued the service.[14]

Shortly after the two "Crawford purchases," British North Americans, who had supported the king in the Revolutionary War, arrived. The Mississauga soon became a small minority. Nearly four thousand Loyalists lived around the Kingston area and the Bay of Quinte in the mid-1780s.[15] Approximately 120 Iroquois who had fought for Britain in the Revolutionary War also settled on the Bay of Quinte.[16] Non-Aboriginals followed, resulting in the British Canadian population rising to about seventeen thousand by 1815.[17]

At the same time as the non-Aboriginal settler population increased, the Mississauga's numbers declined. The North American Indians had no built-up immunity to infectious diseases such as smallpox, diphtheria, or measles, which Europeans had lived with for centuries. British Canadians, in only a generation, had taken over almost all of their land and fisheries. Tensions and frustrations contributed to the widespread abuse of alcohol.[18]

Before the Europeans' arrival, the First Nations had no intoxicating liquor, no previous experience with alcohol. They had no social controls for it, and it wrecked havoc in communities already weakened by great population loss.

By 1820 the Mississauga only numbered about 160 in the Bay of Quinte area and approximately one hundred around Kingston.[19] Non-Aboriginal settlers outnumbered the Mississauga eighty to one. In the mid-1820s, Peter Jones and other Ojibwe Methodists from the Credit River mission just west of Toronto visited the Quinte and Kingston

Mississauga, who recognized points of resemblance between the faiths and similar human values. They began a Methodist mission at Grape Island in the Bay of Quinte. It was only ten acres or so in extent.[20] The non-Aboriginal Methodists chose this site, ten kilometres east of Belleville, as Grape, and neighbouring fifty-acre Sawguin Island, remained free of British Canadian settlement. By 1826 non-Aboriginal settlers had already occupied the large islands from the Bay of Quinte to Kingston. Roughly half a century earlier, the British had promised the Mississauga that they would recognize their possession of the islands in the Bay of Quinte area. But the Mississauga had no written document to prove this. Only in the mid-1850s did government officials locate an important 1797 letter from John Johnson, then the Superintendent General of Indian Affairs. It confirmed that the Mississauga retained almost all their islands.[21]

By the end of 1828, two hundred Mississauga had moved to Grape Island.[22] The Methodists proceeded to build a model Ojibwe mission on a tiny island later evaluated as having a value of forty pounds.[23] Soon Grape Island had a density of approximately twenty people per acre. The Methodist Mississauga first cleared the land, and then built log homes, a chapel, a schoolhouse, and a hospital. Non-Aboriginal and Aboriginal Methodists, such as Peter Jones, taught the skills necessary for lumbering and carpentry. Farming was conducted on neighbouring Sawguin. As Grape Island was not large enough to keep a single cow, they placed their cattle on another island three kilometres or so away. Every day the women travelled by birchbark canoes to milk the cows. The Grape Islanders also had a woodlot on another island three kilometres distant.[24] To supplement their food supply they also hunted and fished. Fortunately Grape Island was a good fishing station in summer. In the fall it was excellent hunting ground for waterfowl, due to the area's wild rice beds.[25]

John A. Macdonald probably heard stories about the Mississauga while living as boy on the Bay of Quinte with his family. The non-Aboriginal settlers overlooked the fact that the British had obtained the Mississauga's land for a pittance, not even paying them for their timber. In any case, even if the payment was low, did not the gift of Christianity constitute ample compensation? Rev. Jonathan Scott described the Grape Island experiment in the *Report of the Wesleyan Methodist Missionary Society in Upper Canada for 1835*. He reported that he had met "some of the white people in the neighbourhood" who compared what they used to think of the Mississauga, and what they saw now. Old non-Aboriginal settlers recalled: "They used to be too filthy to come near — they beat their wives — lay about our streets and our doors drunk with whiskey, and filthy as our hogs."[26] But by the late 1820s, since accepting Christianity, the Mississauga on the Bay of Quinte and around Kingston had become a new people: "We hear them in our woods singing their hymns and praying to God; they are like pious white people now."[27]

In the winter of 1832–1833, Macdonald set up a law office in the town of Napanee. The Mohawks of the Bay of Quinte lived directly west of the town on lands obtained from the British Crown after the American Revolution. The Rev. Saltern Givins, the newly appointed Anglican missionary and unofficial Indian agent for the local Mohawks, regularly visited. The young law student from Kingston sang in his non-Aboriginal church choir in Napanee.[28]

Macdonald had an exceptional memory.[29] Nearly half-a-century after he had first met Saltern Givins, he cited in the House of Commons a story very similar to one the Anglican curate liked to tell. The Reverend Givins' version appeared in a newspaper article he wrote in 1840. He narrated what a North American Indian told a Christian minister:

> On one occasion, expostulating with an aged Indian on the want of industry among his people, he shrewdly remarked. "Why, Minister, you are very unreasonable. When God made the world, He made a great many kinds of animals, but he taught them all different ways of getting a living. He taught the fox to range through the woods and live upon what he could catch. The beaver He taught to live beside the water, He showed him how to dam the river and build a house, and to lie by a stock of provisions for winter. So He also did with different kinds of men. Now you cannot teach the fox to live like the beaver, nor can you make the Indian work and live like the white man. I have a farm, and could live by it; but when the season comes for game or fish, I must have some, and I am tempted to go and look for it, even to the neglect of sowing and gathering my crops."[30]

Apart from the fact that in Macdonald's 1880 version the prime minister has the First Nations person telling him the story, the tale sounds virtually identical to that of the Anglican missionary: "An Indian once said to myself: 'We are the wild animals; you cannot make an ox of a deer.' You cannot make an agriculturalist of the Indian."[31]

Whether or not Macdonald first heard the tale from a First Nations person, or from the Reverend Givins, matters little. It is far more important to learn what he went on to say: "All we can hope for is to wean them, by slow degrees, from their nomadic habits, which have almost become an instinct, and by slow degrees absorb them or settle them on the land. Meantime they must be fairly protected." He believed in the inherent superiority of "British" culture over others. His long-term goal remained the conventional wisdom of the day that the First Nations must be assimilated into the new dominant society. They must leave behind their indigenous social structure, adjust to farming, transform their communal lands into individual family holdings, and eventually abandon the reserve system.

In 1839, Macdonald met a Tyendinaga Mohawk named John Culbertson.[32] He was the son of a Scottish fur trader and the daughter of John Deserontyon, the founder of the Iroquois settlement on the Bay of Quinte. His wife, Sarah Bowen, was non-Aboriginal, the daughter of a Loyalist family. In 1836, the entrepreneurial Culbertson, totally fluent in English, convinced Francis Bond Head, the Lieutenant Governor of Upper Canada, to give him a tract of land, approximately eight hundred acres, out of the Mohawk Territory. Without paying a cent, Culbertson obtained the land. This individual of Mohawk and Scottish ancestry had village lots surveyed for sale around his residence at the east end of the reserve. There he established a village for non-Aboriginal settlers that he named after his grandfather: John Deseronto.[33]

Macdonald met Culbertson when he represented an Iroquois man named Brandt in a murder trial. (The young lawyer already had an intimate connection with death caused by alcohol abuse. As a child of seven, Macdonald had witnessed the murder, or manslaughter, of his younger brother James. The Macdonalds had left the children in the care of a family servant, an old soldier. During their absence the secret drinker struck the boy with great force, either in impatience or anger. The five-year-old fell, fatally injuring himself.)[34]

Culbertson acted as the Mohawk interpreter in the Brandt trial. After his return to Kingston from the Bay of Quinte three years earlier, Macdonald had devoted his practice almost entirely to criminal law. In his cross-examination in the Kingston courtroom, he cleverly extracted from the Crown's principal witness an important admission. The murder of the fellow Mohawk had occurred in a darkened house when everyone was drunk. Under these circumstances it was impossible, Macdonald argued, to be certain who had held the knife. The *Kingston Chronicle* judged Macdonald's defence as "ingenious." Although the jury decided on manslaughter, the judge only imposed a six-month sentence on Brandt.[35]

An entirely different encounter with a North American Indian followed a little over a year later, also in Kingston. On February 1, 1841, Macdonald chaired a Methodist missionary society meeting. Peter Jones from the Credit River mission gave the address. The First Nations speaker had a noticeable presence.

The Upper Canada *Herald* commented on his "easy, simple, natural manner." He "amused the congregation much with an account of the customs and traditions of the Indians in their heathenish state, as well as delighted them in recounting the wonders which had been wrought by the Gospel."[36]

Macdonald had probably first heard of the Methodist Mississauga preacher in the early fall of 1833, after he had returned to Kingston from Napanee, and was preparing to transfer to Hallowell (now part of Picton).[37] Peter Jones became notorious among the settlers after his marriage in New York City to Eliza Field, an Englishwoman. The *Kingston Chronicle*, for example, thundered; "Improper and revolting, we believe that the Creator of the Universe distinguished his creatures by different colours that they might be kept separate from each other."[38] If Macdonald missed the *Chronicle* editorial he might have read the lengthy account in the *Hallowell Free Press,* reprinted from a New York paper. It too spoke out against miscegenation: "The idea is very unpleasant, with us, of such ill-sorted mixtures of colours."[39]

Macdonald was not against intermarriage between the First Nations and non-Aboriginals. By the standards of his day he was a relatively tolerant individual. Still he remained representative of his times. "Deeper in his being," J.K. Johnson has written, "than any conscious rejection of bigotry lay an inborn, unbidden, unquestioning assumption of the inherent superiority of all things British, and the consequent inferiority, in however small degree, of every other living human being."[40]

Macdonald began his political career in 1844, by winning election to the Assembly of the Province of Canada as the member from Kingston. The capital alternated on a regular basis. One could see First Nations people in the two great cities of Canada East. There was the large Iroquois community at Kahnawake near Montreal, as well as the Huron village of Wendake just by Quebec City. Perhaps Macdonald had contact with First Nations people during the sitting of the legislature in Montreal (1844–49) and later in Quebec City (1852–56, 1859–66).

Toronto served as the capital of the Province of Canada from 1849 to 1852, and again from 1856 to 1858. By mid-century Toronto had become the largest city in Canada West with a population of about forty thousand in the mid-1850s, approximately three times as large as Kingston.[41] Toronto had few Aboriginal residents. Only a decade earlier the proximity of the Credit Methodist mission had meant a continuing First Nations presence. Then, in 1847, the Mississauga left.[42] Despite Peter Jones's determined efforts, the Mississauga had failed to secure a title deed, or legal possession of their remaining Credit River lands. Subsequently, they accepted an invitation from the Six Nations or Grand River Iroquois to establish a new community on a corner of their territory.[43] After approximately two hundred Mississauga moved from the Credit River to the settlement they called New Credit, over a hundred kilometres to the west, Aboriginal Canada receded in Toronto's consciousness. Daniel Wilson, who arrived as Professor of history and English literature at University College, University of Toronto, in 1853, later wrote; "In the boyhood of the older generation of Toronto hundreds of Indians, including those of the old Mississaga tribe, were to be seen about the streets." Now, "only at rare intervals" did one see two or three Aboriginal women "in round hats, blue blankets, and Indian leggings."[44]

Only about fifteen thousand First Nations people lived in the Province of Canada in the early 1850s. The non-Aboriginal settlers numbered about two million.[45] Reduced to less than one percent of the total population, the First Nations had become almost invisible to the non-Aboriginal settlers, particularly those living distant from Indian reserves. Many British Canadians expected them to disappear in the near future. As the young Sandford Fleming, later to become known world-wide as the inventor of standard time, wrote in his diary several years earlier: "They are dying away every year and it is supposed their race will soon be extinct."[46] The pressure on their remaining lands was intense. The assessment of Lord Bury, superintendent General of Indian Affairs in 1855, is revealing. He witnessed the British

Canadian settlers' assault on the First Nations' remaining territory, and noted how they, "forcibly squat upon their lands and plunder their timber."[47]

Macdonald, named Attorney General of Canada West in 1854, had little time to make special investigations into First Nations land claims. He had to act quickly just to keep ahead of his numerous duties.[48] When asked in 1857 to provide an opinion on the validity of an 1820 purchase of two thousand acres of land along Dundas Street in the old Credit River Reserve, he did so speedily. The Attorney General of Canada West provided his opinion in early July that it was "an absolute and unconditional Surrender of the land, and that the same belongs to the Crown and the proceeds of sale of such land also belong to the Crown & in no way are held in trust for the Indians."[49] But a key item of information was missing. Hidden in the masses of paper stored in the Indian Department,[50] was a letter from Peter Jones to S.Y. Chesley of the Indian Department, dated November 25, 1854. In the note, Peter Jones recorded Head Chief Joseph Sawyer's recollection of the "surrender" of land along Dundas Street on February 28, 1820. This was five years before the community had converted to Methodism, learned English, and adjusted to farming. Head Chief Sawyer recalled: "All they received at the time was one fat ox some flour and a keg of rum, on which they had a drunken frolic. There are several Indians still living who were present at that council, all of whom can testify that they were entirely ignorant of any sale having been expected at that time."[51]

Macdonald and his fellow legislators believed that the declining First Nation population could be gradually assimilated into the larger society. The reserves were temporary areas set aside to prepare the First Nations for their eventual absorption as Christian farmers into the dominant society. In May 1857, the Attorney General of Upper Canada (Canada West) presented in the Assembly of the Canadas one of the most important bills in the history of Canadian Indian policy, the *Gradual Civilization Act*. Neither he, nor any other cabinet member consulted any chiefs or Indian councils prior to the debate of the proposal.[52]

The bill outlined the procedure by which the First Nations could obtain full legal rights. It stipulated that any Indian adult male judged by a special board of examiners to be educated, free from debt, and of good moral character, could apply. After a successful three-year trial period the applicant could gain ownership of fifty acres of land that subsequently would be removed from the reserve. In short, they would become "enfranchised," that is, made legally equal to their neighbours, with the same rights and privileges. They would cease to be a member of an Indian nation and became full citizens of Canada. Subsequently, the individual cut all his ties with his Indian nation. Moreover, if married, his wife and children would immediately lose their Indian status as well.[53] Macdonald and his fellow legislators hoped a growing number of educated Indians would voluntarily "enfranchise" and, within several generations there would no longer be either Indians or Indian reserves.

In the Assembly of the Canadas the plan encountered little opposition. All but one of the members agreed on its merits. No one pointed out that the bill broke the rules and the spirit of the Royal Proclamation of 1763. The proclamation stated that reserve land was to be exclusively controlled by their governments, and could only be alienated with their own consent.[54] The bill passed without amendment.[55]

Outside of the assembly, First Nations leaders denounced the new legislation,[56] which sought the ending of their land base and increased non-Aboriginal control over their lives. A huge protest meeting was held at Onondaga on the Six Nations territory. Neither Macdonald nor any other Canadian politician paid any attention to their insistence that the government respect their autonomy. The press largely ignored the event. First Nations concerns were not a priority. Ignorance and indifference characterized the dominant society's approach to Aboriginal issues in the Province of Canada.[57]

Little evidence exists that First Nations concerns occupied Macdonald's attention from 1857 to the Confederation debates. The index to the printed volume of Macdonald's letters for the years 1858 to 1861 includes only two references to Indians.[58] Fortunately an 1870 intervention in the House of Commons reveals his outlook on Aboriginal land questions at this time. It shows he sided entirely with the non-Aboriginal settlers. In February 1870, he stated that the Manitoulin Treaty of 1862, "was a good arrangement, and carried out with every fairness to those concerned."[59] He supported the acquisition of the Great Manitoulin Island on the north shore of Lake Huron, even though it had been promised to the First Nations in perpetuity in 1836.[60] For once Macdonald agreed with the newspaper of George Brown, his great political rival. The *Toronto*

Globe had written on July 30, 1863, in reference to the Manitoulin First Nations: "They cannot be permitted to stand in the way of the advance of civilization on this continent."

Very revealing is an 1862 letter, written on North American Indian land rights, by John Sunday Jr., son of the chief of the Grape Island/Alderville Mississauga. It gives an invaluable Bay of Quinte/Rice Lake Mississauga perspective on the losses of Indian land to the European settlers. A quarter of a century earlier, the Mississauga at Grape Island had relocated from the Bay of Quinte to a tract of land south of Rice Lake, about thirty kilometres north of Lake Ontario. In 1862, the young man had just completed the first year of his studies at the Methodists' Victoria College in Cobourg, Canada West.[61] He had a good knowledge of English and of the dominant society. Speaking of the arrival of Europeans, he wrote:

> We gave them land as much as they wanted, and also sold it to them for the merest trifle [...] We have permitted them to clear up our hunting grounds, to build their dwellings and another useful buildings [...] Nor did we say to them when they had become strongly attached to their dwelling places, and also to where they had buried their fathers, "You are mere tenants as well, — we own all the land, which we can recover at any time, and if you do not leave this tract of land, we will recover it by force. You must submit to our laws of the forest as we choose to make them for you."[62]

In the discussions leading up to Confederation, Canadian politicians paid little attention to the needs — or rights — of the Aboriginal peoples. The Charlottetown and Quebec conferences omitted discussion of their role in the new British North American federation. As Richard Gwyn, Macdonald's most recent biographer, summarized: "Whereas the Royal Proclamation of 1763 had declared that Indians 'should not be molested or disturbed' on their historic hunting grounds, no mention of them was made in the *British North America Act*, except to identify Indians as a subject of federal jurisdiction."[63] In total, the *British North America Act* simply states, in section 91 (24), "Indians, and Lands reserved for Indians" are a federal responsibility.[64]

After Confederation, Prime Minister John A. Macdonald's government implemented the policy of assimilation as outlined in the 1857 *Gradual Civilization Act*. The government's *Indian Act* of 1869 simply updated the enfranchisement provisions of 1857. As prime minister from 1867 to 1874, Macdonald expanded the Dominion of Canada tenfold, extending it westward from the Atlantic to the Pacific. Away from Central and Eastern Canada, the Aboriginal Peoples constituted the majority of the population in the 1870s.

Macdonald aimed to build a transcontinental nation, one in which the arable land of the Prairie West would be made available for eastern and central Canadian settlement. Neither he nor his Conservative and Liberal political contemporaries tolerated First Nation and Métis opposition to the settlement of Western Canada. The Red River Métis under Louis Riel had to defend its own territory in 1869–70. In the short term they succeeded, but in the long term they failed. The Métis people could participate in the new Canada that Macdonald attempted to form. They must join Canada as individuals, not as collectivities. The Métis province they aspired to form in 1870 was transformed into a non-Aboriginal one within less than a decade, due to large-scale migration from Ontario.

From 1867 to the year of his death in 1891, Macdonald served as prime minister of Canada, with the exception of the four years from 1874 to 1878. The Liberals under Alexander Mackenzie continued the existing Indian policy. The Conservatives had negotiated the first three of the numbered treaties in the Canadian West and the Liberals concluded the next four. In 1876, Mackenzie brought forward the first consolidated federal *Indian Act*. Both the Conservatives and the Liberals thus worked to abolish the First Nations' self-government, and to work for their eventual enfranchisement.[65]

The Liberals, in one way, went beyond the Conservatives, in that they did consult a major First Nations organization in revising the *Indian Act*, the Grand General Indian Council of Ontario. In the words of David Laird, the superintendent of Indian Affairs, the council requested in 1875 that the "enfranchised" individuals gain the right to hold their lands in fee simple, but to retain the right to sit in council and draw their annuities. He agreed.[66] In February 1876, he also invited three well-educated Ojibwe from Ontario — William Wawanosh of Sarnia; John Tecumseh Henry of the Ojibwe of the Thames; and Reverend Allen Salt, Methodist missionary — to read the draft.[67] The federal government consulted all three men about the proposed bill for five days in Ottawa. In the version of the act they saw, they believed it benefited them as it allowed them to participate fully in the Canadian political state. It did so without requiring them to end their membership in their band. In his diary, Allen Salt reported on the week in Ottawa in mid-February 1876. In one sentence he summarized their reaction: "We liked the Bill and thought that the Indians would like it."[68]

On his return to power in 1878, Macdonald became his own minister of the interior, and with the job came the responsibility for Indian Affairs. He already was prime minister, party leader, minister of the interior, and now he added Indian Affairs, at a time when the Canadian Pacific Railway project demanded a great deal of his time. As minister of the interior he would be responsible for western development. Expansion of Canada — not contemporary Indian issues — would come first. In effect, the prime minister left Lawrence Vankoughnet, his deputy minister in what became the Department of Indian Affairs in 1880, in charge.[69]

Macdonald had to defend his government's Indian policies in the House of Commons. His spontaneous responses in Parliament reveal a great deal about his own personal views of Aboriginal people. Before 1886, neither he nor Vankoughnet had ever been west of southern Ontario, nor had David Macpherson,[70] who replaced an overworked prime minister as minister of the interior from 1883 to 1885.

Macdonald's ignorance of First Nation cultures made his tenure as the head of the Indian Department a difficult assignment. The increasing amount of information arriving in Ottawa added to the workload. Between 1875 and 1880 the number of letters received at the Indian Affairs headquarters more than doubled. In the 1880s it doubled again.[71] The prime minister had to rely ever more on Vankoughnet to make the decisions that counted. Despite the very limited financial resources of the government, Macdonald endorsed the establishment of federally funded Indian residential schools in 1879 to be run by the Christian denominations. He wanted girls, as well as boys, to attend.[72]

Indifference remained the general rule toward Indian Affairs amongst the press. One of the few journalists who did mention the prime minister's views on Aboriginal people made a surprising comment. E.B. Biggar, in his *Anecdotal Life of Sir John Macdonald* (1891), praised him for his knowledge.

Obviously Biggar had little knowledge of Aboriginal Canada as he wrote: "There could be nothing more instructive and entertaining than one of his conversational speeches on Indian affairs, of which department he was head for several years. No question would be asked but he had an answer for it and could give off-hand a history of each appointment, or a clear and instructive statement of every case of difficulty that had come up; while his knowledge of the character of the Indians was marvellous."[73]

Macdonald combined a romantic sentimentalism for First Nations people with a total disregard for their right to keep their ancestral cultures and religions. When he proposed the formation of a Department of Indian Affairs in 1880, he argued that it would advance "the interests of the Indians, civilizing them and putting them in the condition of white men." Then he added an historical reference: "We must remember that they are the original owners of the soil, of which they have been dispossessed by the covetousness or ambition of our ancestors. Perhaps, if Columbus had not discovered this continent — had left them alone — they would have worked out a tolerable civilization of their own. At all events, the Indians have been great sufferers by the discovery of America, and the transfer to it of a large white population."[74]

Yet, in practice, Macdonald showed no such understanding or compassion. Certainly he knew the pain the Plains Indians, in what is now southern Alberta, suffered when the buffalo herds vanished on the Canadian side of the border in 1879. He reported in the Annual Report of the Department of the Interior that year: "The Indians were reduced to such extremities that they eat mice, their dogs, and even their buffalo skins, and they greedily devoured meat raw when given to them."[75] Yet, he felt the little money that government had to spend should go instead for nation- and economy-building projects like canals, railways, and land surveys.[76]

The prime minister's discontent with Aboriginals in western Canada became particularly evident in the mid-1880s, a time when his workload reached new heights. [77] He turned seventy in January 1885. In contrast to his younger days, he had become careless in his administrative practices.[78] After 1883, he developed the habit of putting aside some of his most challenging files to be looked at later. New incoming files soon buried these old ones.[79]

A contemporary First Nation assessment of his performance exists. Robert Steinhauer, a young Cree who attended Victoria College in Cobourg, Ontario, came from White Fish Lake northeast of Edmonton. In early 1886,

Steinhauer made a sharp critique of Macdonald's Aboriginal policy in *Acta Victoriana*, the college magazine. In "The Indian Question," Steinhauer underlined the Western First Nation's disappointments. "Ever since the treaties were signed, there has been much discontent, and complaints made by him [the Indian]. He asks those who have taken the ownership of his country to give him his rights, at least the fulfillment of the promises made to him." They had wanted assistance, but, in the place of competent government intermediaries, they received Indian agents, selected, "because they happen to be friends and right-hand supporters of the Government in power; men whose knowledge of what they were intended to teach was so limited that they were rejected in some places." Ottawa had placed "low and unprincipled characters"[80] in authority over them.

In the mid-1880s, Macdonald's references to Indians in the House of Commons seem very superficial. The prime minister mentioned in April 1884 that "Indians all over the Dominion [were] in all stages of civilization, from near barbarism upwards."[81] At potlatches in British Columbia, the prime minister reported a week later: "They meet and carry on a sort of mystery; they remain for weeks and sometimes months, as long as they can get food, and carry on all kinds of orgies."[82]

The full authority of imperial Canada was soon to be felt on the Saskatchewan Plains. The First Nations and the Métis must not interfere with the building of a united British North America. Worrying indicators surfaced in 1884 that trouble was forthcoming in the Northwest. In June, Louis Riel returned from the United States, to help the Métis in Saskatchewan settle their land claims. Unfortunately, at the same time, the financial problems of the Conservatives' cherished transcontinental project, the Canadian Pacific Railway, increased. Its lack of cash threatened the line's completion. By applying most of his time and energy to the CPR, Macdonald made many mistakes and paid too little attention to his ministerial duties.[83]

A former University of Toronto Classics student, Will Jackson opposed Macdonald and his administration of the Northwest. Then living at Prince Albert, close to the Métis settlements in the South Saskatchewan Valley, Will volunteered his services to help them. The twenty-three-year-old idealist saw justice in their cause and volunteered to become Louis Riel's English-language secretary at Batoche. He assisted Riel in preparing a petition that argued for Aboriginal rights and non-Aboriginal settler self-government. He worked to achieve a new Northwest, creating a relationship of equality between Aboriginal and non-Aboriginal.

When the Canadians took Batoche on May 12, 1885, they seized Jackson, "Riel's Secretary," although he had never borne arms. He had never advocated armed resistance or been present at any battle. While in Riel's camp, the Ontario Methodist had become a Catholic. Only two months before he had accepted Louis Riel as the prophet of a reformed Christian church. The Regina court committed him, in July 1885, to the lunatic asylum at Lower Fort Garry, north of Winnipeg. After several months he walked away from the light security institution. He went to Chicago where he became a spokesperson in the labour movement.[84]

Jackson might well have been delusional and unbalanced during the troubled spring of 1885. The taking up of arms by the Métis against his own people had indeed profoundly disturbed his mental balance. Yet, on the question of the future importance of Louis Riel, Jackson proved the visionary, not Macdonald. In a letter to his lifelong correspondent, Judge James Gowan,[85] the prime minister wrote on December 12, 1885; "The Riel fever will I think die out."[86] Jackson, writing from the lunatic asylum to which he was committed in the late summer of 1885, penned his own assessment. He stated perceptively: "The oppression of the aboriginal has been the crying sin of the white race in America and they have at last found a voice."[87]

During the troubles of 1885, the strain on the prime minister reached a new intensity. On July 6, 1885, he clearly lost control. Baited by the opposition, he declared that the Métis, if given scrip, "will either drink it, waste it, or sell it." Then he referred to the Plains Indian in the Northwest:

> I have not hesitated to tell this House, again and again, that we could not always hope to maintain peace with the Indians; that the savage was still a savage, and that until he ceased to be savage, we were always in danger of a collision, in danger of war, in danger of an outbreak. I am only surprised that we have been able so long to maintain peace — that from 1870 until 1885 not one single blow, not one single murder, not one single loss of life has taken place. Look at the United

States; along the whole frontier of the United States there has been war; millions have been expended there; their best and their bravest have fallen. I personally knew General Custer, and admired the gallant soldier, the American hero, yet he went, and he fell with his band, and not a man was left to tell the tale — they were all swept away.[88]

The prime minister's greatest excess came with the Battleford trials of the Plains Indians accused of participation in the "Rebellion." They were conducted in English, a language none of them understood. None of the accused had legal counsel. The eight men sentenced to death were publicly executed even though Canadian law already banned such spectacles.[89] As Macdonald biographer Richard Gwyn writes, Macdonald must have assented to this plan of public executions. He continues: "By deliberate intent, the eight convicted men were sent to their deaths in front of a huge crowd of their kin brought in from all the neighbouring reserves, including boys from the Battleford Industrial School."[90] A year later Macdonald publicly stretched the truth about Battleford trials. In an Ontario political address, he claimed, according to the *Brantford Daily Courier*, "The government had followed every clemency possible and in not a single instance among half-breeds or Indians had they decreed the sentence of hanging, save where it was actually proven that the offenders had murdered in cold blood."[91]

Macdonald was a rounded character. He represented his age, one of supreme and absolute British self-confidence.[92] His Liberal opponents also had little knowledge of the First Nations and the Métis. In fact, the Liberals had argued to diminish the Conservatives' modest outreach on rations to the Plains Indians in the early 1880s. They argued that the federal government's responsibilities included only the meeting of the narrowly stated terms of the treaties. This led the prime minister to insist continually that his administration was struggling to keep expenditures low. It had, in fact, reduced the Indians to one-half and one-quarter rations.[93] The prime minister told the House of Commons on April 27, 1882, that federal officials "refused food until the Indians are on the verge of starvation."[94]

Macdonald was, in some respects, quite moderate in comparison with one important provincial leader, Oliver Mowat, the Liberal leader and premier in Ontario. "The Christian politician" as he once termed himself, believed that the First Nations had no legal title at all to their lands: "The claim of the Indians is simply moral and no more."[95] The Royal Proclamation of 1763, to which the Macdonald government adhered, and on the basis of which the federal government made Treaties 1 to 3 in the Northwest, was, according to Mowat, "expressly repealed by the Quebec Act of 1774."[96] He believed the federal government had no obligation even to make treaties with the First Nations.

Without question, Macdonald did care about individual Aboriginal people, particularly those anxious to make their way in the dominant society. He went out of his way to help Thomas Green, a bright Iroquois graduate from the Mohawk Institute, the Indian residential school in Brantford, Ontario, and later Brantford High School.[97] He supported Green's successful efforts to complete his B.Sc at McGill University. In 1885–86, he worked in the Northwest as a surveyor. From Regina on March 8, 1886, Green gave the prime minister some very valuable advice. An army was not the way to win over the Plains Indians. Instead Green suggested the following to the prime minister:

> Collect a dozen or so of the principal chiefs of the different tribes of the N.W. Indians, and engage good, honest, and reliable interpreters to accompany them. Give them a trip to Ottawa and allow them an interview. Show them, or at least, allow them to be shown the principal sights & cities of Ontario & Quebec, and above all, have them visit the most prosperous Indian reserves of these provinces. Let them see how their Indian brethren are prospering in those provinces; let them understand that the Indian can subsist like the white man where there is no game; and let them understand that the government do not wish to extermi- nate them, &, &; and I am sure the lessons they would learn, and the pleasing reception you would accord them, would result in a greater & lasting benefit to them & their following and to the peace of the N. West, than the whole army of Canada could achieve.[98]

Macdonald's relationship with the First Nations was more positive in Central Canada than on the Plains. A number of First Nations people in Ontario recognized the prime minister's contribution, particularly after his *Electoral Franchise Act* of 1885.[99] This bill gave the federal vote to all adult male Indians in Eastern Canada who met the necessary property requirements. Macdonald wanted to bring the educated Indians into the system. The formal enfranchisement process outlined in the early Indian Acts had not worked;[100] which led him to introduce the *Electoral Franchise Act* of 1885. It allowed a number of male Status Indians in Eastern and Central Canada to vote without giving up their special rights as Indians, rights gained by treaty or by the *Indian Act*. In short, they gained the franchise without becoming "enfranchised." Peter E. Jones, M.D. (Queen's), the son of the Rev. Peter Jones, and a chief of the Mississaugas of New Credit west of Hamilton, near Hagersville, where the Credit Mississauga had moved in 1847, wrote to congratulate the prime minister. Macdonald read out his letter to the House of Commons: "My Dear Sir John, — I should have written to you some time ago to thank you for making the Indian a 'person' in the Franchise Bill. Other affairs, however, have prevented me from performing my duty … I now thank you on the part of the memory of my father and on the part of myself, as for many years we advocated and urged this step as the one most likely to elevate the aborigines to the position more approaching the independence of the whites."[101]

Support also came from other quarters. From the Georgina Island Ojibwe community on Lake Simcoe in Ontario, Chief Charles Big Canoe and band councillor James Ashquabe wrote to thank the prime minister for his, "earnest efforts to promote the welfare of the Indian people throughout the whole Dominion […] we appreciate your difficulties in dealing with our less civilized brother in the Northwest who has not had the advantages we in Ontario have had [….] we thank you most cordially for the gift of the franchise."[102]

Chief Big Canoe, then in his early sixties, had taught himself both to read and to write English. A farmer, he also kept cattle. At the time of a visit by a reporter from the Toronto *Star Weekly* (who called on him thirty years later), Keche Chemon (Big Canoe) lived in a large frame house, painted white with green trimmings surrounded by a green lawn and flower gardens. Inside his parlour he had an attractive carpet on the floor, good upholstered chairs, and on the central table lay (beside the visitor's book) a book of hymns printed both in English and Ojibwa. On the exterior Charles Big Canoe had adjusted very well to British Canada. But on no account did the respected elder accept Oliver Mowat's definition of Indian land title. When the reporter, in 1915, stated to the chief: "The Government gave this island to the Indians, didn't they?" the chief corrected his visitor: "Oh no! We reserved this island when we sold our other property."[103]

A memorial from Alderville — south of Rice Lake, Ontario, signed by Chief Mitchell Chubb with band councillors Peter Crowe, Joshua Blaker, Allan Salt Jr., E. Comego, and the band secretary George Blaker — also endorsed the extension of the franchise. In the late 1820s and early 1830s, this Mississauga community had lived on Grape Island in the Bay of Quinte area. Blaker's political career began approximately as long ago as the prime minister's. He first served as their band council's secretary in the late 1840s.[104] Later he had been a Methodist mission worker.[105] They wrote:

> Whereas the Right Honourable Sir John A. Macdonald K.C.B. Premier of Canada and Superintendent General of Indian affairs, proposed and obtained the consent of parliament to the enfranchisement of the Indians of the Older Provinces of Canada; and whereas he also eloquently advocated our Rights and protected and defended our character and good name from the insults and slander of our enemies: Therefore be it resolved that we the Chief and council of the Alnwick Band of the Loyal Mississagua tribe in council, assembled, offer on our own behalf, and on behalf of our band our heart felt thanks to him our great Chief, and tell him that we shall always gratefully remember his goodness and Justice and the Honor and dignity he has conferred upon us and that we shall teach our young men to follow in our footsteps in remembering his great character and cherishing the memory of his good words and noble deeds.[106]

On the granting of the franchise to the Eastern Canadian Indians Macdonald wrote Dr. Peter E. Jones on August 31, 1886, that "the statements made by the Grits, who do not wish the Indians to exercise the rights of voting, are altogether false."[107] He continued:

> The object I had in extending the privilege of the franchise to the Indians was to place them on a footing of equality with their white brethren. I considered that it was unjust to the original owners of the soil to be prevented from aiding in the election of men who would represent their interests in Parliament. The Franchise Act has now been in force for a year, and the Indians must see that their treaty rights have not been in the slightest degree affected since it became law. You may answer our Indian friends from me, as Superintendent general of Indian Affairs, that the Franchise Act does not in any way affect or injure the rights secured to them by treaty or by the laws relating to the Red men of the Dominion. They may vote with perfect security [...] I hope to see some day the Indian race represented by one of themselves on the floor of the House of Commons.

Only a week after writing Dr. Jones, Macdonald directly encountered First Nations opposition to his *Franchise Act*. On the afternoon of September 6, 1886, Macdonald visited Ohsweken on the Six Nations Territory near Brantford, Ontario (see image, page 59). He had recently returned from his tour of Western Canada on the newly completed CPR. As shown in a contemporary photo, a huge crowd met him at the Six Nations Council House.[108] According to one press account, a multitude of people, Aboriginal and non-Aboriginal — perhaps as many as eight thousand — had assembled at the village.[109] They awaited his speech at the Six Nations Agricultural Grounds after his visit to the Six Nations Hereditary Council.

The prime minister entered the Six Nations Confederacy Council House[110] around two o'clock. The Council Minutes report: "A large attendance of chiefs & warriors some Whites, and Reporters" were present.[111] Shortly after Macdonald took his seat, Firekeeper Chief John Buck addressed the visitor, "closing with words of greeting and welcome." In his lengthy two-hour speech,[112] translated into Mohawk by

Chief A.G. Smith, the prime minister and superintendent general of Indian affairs did his best to convince the chiefs to endorse the *Franchise Act*. They would not have to sever their ties with their nations. They could keep their laws, language, and own system of governance. As the *Brantford Daily Courier* reported, the prime minister shared with the council a personal message, with a note of levity: "He himself was a Scottish Highlander, and his people still taught the language and wore the dress of their ancestors. He had lately met a deputation of them in Full Highland regalia and a thrill of patriotism had filled his heart as he saw the old costume. It was doubtless the same and always would be the same with the Indians, although he would not advise them to follow the example of his fellows, whose full dress consisted in taking off their trousers. (Laughter.)"[113]

Macdonald's address lasted two hours. He urged them to participate in federal elections. Once he finished, William Smith, the spokesperson for the hereditary chiefs, politely rejected his Franchise Bill of 1885. The council, he explained, had discussed it on several occasions.[114] Why should they participate in Canadian elections? The Grand River Iroquois were a sovereign nation with their own political institutions.[115]

Regardless of their protests, the prime minister continued to regard the traditional Iroquois system of governance as inferior. While his government did not pressure the Grand River Six Nations to adopt the elected system, it did so at Akwesasne, in eastern Ontario, and Kahnawake near Montreal, two other Iroquois communities.[116]

Macdonald worked with two Mohawks who were prepared to adjust to the dominant society, in particular with Oronhytekha, or Peter Martin, the prominent Mohawk doctor who headed the fraternal organization, the Independent Order of Foresters.[117] In 1884, Oronhyatekha spoke and is reported as stating, "Sir John McDonald, as Mr. White had stated, had reason to be a friend to the Indians as he had got the idea of confederation from the confederacy of the Six Nations."[118] Another contact was John Elliott, a young Mohawk leader at Six Nations[119] who sought an elected council on the reserve. Elliott had been a student at the Mohawk Institute when Thomas Green had attended.[120] Those in favour of ending the traditional council's rule had the support of one-fifth of the adult male population of the Six Nations community in 1890.[121]

To understand Macdonald's dealings with Aboriginal people in Canada, one must take into account his vision for the new dominion. He believed in a British Canada, one in which all groups, including the French Canadians,[122] would eventually conform to British values and institutions. He looked forward to the Aboriginal peoples' integration into the new Canada he was trying to build. Optimistically he was convinced that the understaffed and underfunded Department of Indian Affairs, and the equally poorly funded Christian missionaries, could accomplish this goal. In fairness to our first prime minister, it only became known in the mid-twentieth century how slowly cultures change. The expansion of the new discipline of anthropology helped further understanding of how strong and resilient the North American Indian cultures are.

Macdonald knew individuals of Aboriginal background who had become prominent in the dominant society. In French-speaking Canada he had the full support of the powerful Bishop Louis-François Laflèche of Trois-Rivières, whose maternal grandmother was a Métis from the Northwest; and of Father Albert Lacombe, Quebec-born, but active in Roman Catholic mission work in the Northwest. His maternal grandmother also was Métis. Both men made no secret of their Aboriginal background.[123] Other prominent individuals with some North American Indian ancestry included Edward Clouston, the general manager of the Bank of Montreal in 1890, whose mother was an English-speaking mixed-blood.[124] Isabella Sophia Hardisty, the wife of the Bank of Montreal's president, Donald Smith, Lord Strathcona, also had an English-speaking mixed-blood background.[125]

In politics John A. Macdonald knew Isabella Hardisty Smith's brother, Richard Hardisty, the Hudson's Bay Company chief factor at Fort Edmonton. He named him to the Canadian Senate in 1888.[126] The prime minister greatly liked the Conservative premier of Manitoba (1878–1887), John Norquay, an English-speaking Métis from the Red River.[127] One of his Conservative Party contacts in Ontario in 1890 was Solomon White, the mayor of Windsor. The Huron (Wyandot) Indian had given up his Indian status.[128]

In his own cabinet at least two members had linkages to Aboriginal Canada. John Abbott, the government's leader in the Senate and Macdonald's successor as prime minister in 1891, had a tie through his wife, Mary Martha Bethune. The fur trader Angus Bethune (an uncle of Mary Martha Bethune Abbott) had married the English-speaking Métis Louisa MacKenzie.[129]

David Macpherson, minister of the interior, 1883–1885, also had a Native connection through his sister, Frances Pasia. She married the Montreal merchant John Hamilton who had Aboriginal first cousins: the children of his mother's brother, the fur trader Lawrence Herkimer.[130]

Macdonald accepted racial amalgamation. In 1887 his beloved ten-year-old granddaughter came to Ottawa from Winnipeg to attend boarding school. Every weekend Daisy Macdonald stayed with her grandparents at Earnscliffe,[131] their comfortable, agreeable home overlooking the Ottawa River.[132] No doubt, Macdonald heard a great deal about Miss Harmon's School. Daisy's headmistress, Abby Maria Harmon, was the daughter of fur trader Daniel Harmon and his wife, Lizette Laval Harmon, a woman of Cree and French Canadian descent. Former students later recalled Miss Harmon was "proud of her Cree blood and ancestry, and no less proud of her father's reputation as a fur trader and explorer."[133] Canadian historian Stewart Wallace met her about 1900 and later wrote: "I well remember meeting her when I was a child; and she bore unmistakable signs of her Indian ancestry.[134]

Macdonald, born elsewhere, had grown up in Canada. He accepted his new land without condition. His home was here, as he once put it: "All my hopes and my remembrances are Canadian; and not only are my principles and prejudices Canadian, but … my interests are."[135] He wanted the Aboriginal peoples to assimilate into the non-Aboriginal Canadian society and did not understand that they wanted to retain their cultures and identities. His blind spot toward the Aboriginal peoples was one shared by almost all non-Aboriginal Canadians of his generation and can only be understood in the context of his time.

Notes

1. This article is an expansion and reworking of my earlier piece, "John A. Macdonald and Aboriginal Canada," *Historic Kingston*, 50 (2002): 10–29.
2. Ged Martin, *Favourite Son? John A. Macdonald and the Voters of Kingston 1841–1891* (Kingston: Kingston Historical Society, 2010), xiii.
3. Ibid., 3.
4. Alexander Campbell, quoted in Richard Gwyn, *John A.: The Man Who Made Us: The Life and Times of John A. Macdonald, Vol. 1, 1815–1867* (Toronto: Random House Canada, 2007), 43.

5. John Graves Simcoe to Henry Dundas, dated York, Upper Canada, September 20, 1793, E.A. Cruikshank, ed., *The Correspondence of Lieut. Governor John Graves Simcoe, Vol. 2. 1793–1794* (Toronto: Ontario Historical Society, 1924), 61. For full details on the early Mississauga treaties see Donald B. Smith, *Mississauga Portraits: Ojibwe Voices from Nineteenth-Century Canada* (Toronto: University of Toronto Press, 2013), 44–51, 216–220.

6. Donald B. Smith, "The Dispossession of the Mississauga Indians: A Missing Chapter in the Early History of Upper Canada," *Ontario History* 73, 2 (June 1981): 72.

7. Ibid., 74.

8. Extract of a letter from W. Crawford, Esq., to Sir John Johnson, Bart., dated at Cataraqui, August 14, 1784, in Province of Canada. "Report of the Special Commissioners Appointed on the 8th of September, 1856, to Investigate Indian Affairs in Canada," [hereafter Report, 1858.] *Journals of the Legislative Assembly of the Province of Canada*, 1858, vol. 16, appendix 21. This report is not paginated.

9. Peter Jones, *History of the Ojebway Indians* (London: A.W. Bennett, 1861), 71.

10. Anton Treuer, *The Assassination of Hole in the Day* (St. Paul: Borealis Books, 2011), footnote 22, 235.

11. Roger Spielmann, *"You're So Fat!": Exploring Ojibwe Discourse* (Toronto: University of Toronto Press, 1998), 31.

12. Donald B. Smith, *Sacred Feathers: The Reverend Peter Jones (Kahkewaquonaby) and the Mississauga Indians* (Toronto: University of Toronto Press, 1988), 22–31. Very helpful for understanding their viewpoint is George S. Snyderman' s article, "Concepts of Land Ownership among the Iroquois and Their Neighbours," in *Symposium on Local Diversity in Iroquois Culture*, ed. William N. Fenton, Smithsonian Institution Bureau of American Ethnology Bulletin 149 (Washington, DC: United States Government Printing Office, 1951), 15–34, particularly 28.

13. Gilbert C. Paterson, "Land Settlement in Upper Canada, 1783–1840," in *16th Report of the Department of Archives for the Province of Ontario* (Toronto: Clarkson W. James, 1921), 219.

14. Bill Russell, "The White Man's Paper Burden: Aspects of Records Keeping in the Department of Indian Affairs, 1860–1914," *Archivaria* 19 (Winter 1984–85), 55, 57.

15. Brian S. Osborne, "Frontier Settlement in Eastern Ontario in the Nineteenth Century: A Study in Changing Perceptions of Land and Opportunity," in *The Frontier Comparative Studies*, eds. David Harry Miller and Jerome O. Steffen (Norman, OK: University of Oklahoma Press, 1977), 208.

16. Charles Hamori-Torok, "The Iroquois of Akwesasne (St. Regis), Mohawks of the Bay of Quinte (Tyendinata), Onyota' a:ka (the Oneida of the Thames),

and Wahta Mohawk (Gibson), 1750–1945" in *Aboriginal Ontario. Historical Perspectives on the First Nations,* ed. Edward S. Rogers and Donald B. Smith (Toronto: Dundurn Press, 1994), 262.

17. Osborne, "Frontier Settlement," 211.

18. The pattern of the massive social disruption following the intrusion of Western societies in indigenous communities is tightly summarized in Jean-Guy A. Goulet, *Ways of Knowing. Experience, Knowledge, and Power Among the Dene Tha* (Vancouver: University of British Columbia Press, 1998), 110.

19. R.W. Shaw, "The Treaty Made with the Indians at Kingston, May 31, 1819, for the Surrender of Lands," *Ontario Historical Society Papers and Records* 27 (1931): 540–542.

20. For the lease for Grape Island see George F. Playter, *The History of Methodism in Canada: With an Account of the Rise and Progress of the Work of God among the Canadian Indian Tribes* (Toronto: Published for the Author by Anson Green, 1862), 292–293. For a good short summary of the Grape Island experiment see Richard Boehme. *Mission on Grape Island* (Bloomfield, ON: 7th Town Historical Society, 1987).

21. "Mississaguas of Alnwick," in Report, 1858. The letter from Sir Johnson to the Military Secretary, dated Lachine, October 9, 1797, is included in this section of the report. On the basis of this letter the Department of Indian Affairs negotiated a treaty in 1856 for all the islands around the Bay of Quinte.

22. William Case to Robert Alder, dated Alderville, March 16, 1843, Wesleyan Methodist Missionary Society, Box 27, file 185, United Church Archives, Toronto; Jones, *Life,* 261. Entry of October 1, 1829.

23. "Schedule of Islands Claimed by the Band of Alnwick Indians [1861]," RG 10, 731: 165, Library and Archives Canada. [Hereafter cited as LAC.].

24. Francis Hall, "Grape Island Mission, dated New York, October 10, 1828," *Christian Advocate,* October 24, 1828.

25. Ruth Clarke, *Before the Silence. Fifty Years in the History of Alderville First Nation 1825–1875* (Victoria, BC: Fleming Printing, 1999), xii–xiii. This useful study was completed by writer Ruth Clarke at the request of the Chief and Council of the Alderville First Nation.

26. Jonathan Scott quoted in the *Annual Report of the Wesleyan Methodist Church Missionary Society,* 1835, 6.

27. Ibid.

28. Donald Creighton, *John A. Macdonald: The Young Politician* (Toronto: Macmillan, 1952) 27; Many references to the Rev. Saltern Givins and his work in the 1830s among the Mohawks on the Bay of Quinte appear in Deborah Jean Doxtator, "Tyendinaga Land Surrenders: 1820–1840" (MA Research Essay, Carleton University, 1982).

29. P.B. Waite, "Sir John A. Macdonald: The Man,," in *Empire and Nations: Essays in Honour of Frederic H. Soward,* eds. Harvey Leonard Dyck and Hans

Peter Krosby (Toronto: University of Toronto Press, 1969), 40; Gwyn, *John A.*, 105. Donald Creighton, *John A. Macdonald: The Old Chieftain* (Toronto: Macmillan, 1955), 221.

30. The Rev. Saltern Givins, "The Mohawk Indians,," *The Church*, reprinted in the *Kingston Chronicle & Gazette,* December 16, 1840.

31. John A. Macdonald in Canada, House of Commons, *Debates*, May 5, 1880, 1991.

32. Macdonald's reference to the Culbertson family was made in the House of Commons on May 4, 1885. See *Debates*, 1885, 1575. The prime minister mentioned Chief Culbertson and his father without giving their first names. The full names appear in *Canada, Indian Treaties and Surrenders* 2 volumes, (Ottawa: Queen's Printer, 1891). Chief Archibald Culbertson is mentioned in vol. 2, 143; and his father, John Culbertson, in vol. 1, 101, 123, 136. In 1878 the Mohawk chiefs at Tyendinaga prepared an address to John A. Macdonald congratulating him on his recent victory. Chief Archibald Culbertson was one of the six chiefs. Macdonald Papers, MG 26A, volume 304, 138675–76, LAC. Part of the address reads: "We cannot refrain from telling you the peculiar pleasure we experienced on hearing that you had become the *head* of the *Department of the Interior* and consequently *Superintendent General of Indian Affairs* as we have long been aware of the great interest you have always taken and shown for our people in this Dominion."

33. Gerald E. Boyce, *Historic Hastings* (Belleville: Hastings County Council, 1967), 274. I thank Trish Rae for additional background information about John Culbertson.

34. No charge was laid. Gywn, *John A.,* 27–28. Donald Creighton also provides a reference in his *John A. Macdonald: The Young Politician* (Toronto: Macmillan, 1952), 10.

35. Gwyn, *John A.*, 53–54. My thanks to Trish Rae for further details in a notation by Reverend Saltern Givins in the Tyendinaga Parish Church Records: Burials July 11, 1839. I also thank Trish Rae for a copy of the article "Trial of Brandt Brandt, a Mohawk Indian, for Murder," *Chronicle & Gazette and Kingston Commercial Advertiser*, October 2, 1839. A full account appears in William R. Teatero, "'A Dead and Alive Way Never Does': The Pre-Political Professional World of John A. Macdonald" (M.A. thesis, Queen's University, 1978), 200–206.

36. "Missionary Anniversary for Kingston,," *Upper Canada Herald,* February 9, 1841, reprinted in the *Christian Guardian,* February 17, 1841.

37. Creighton, *John A. Macdonald: The Young Politician*, 28–31.

38. *Kingston Chronicle & Gazette,* September 21, 1833.

39. "Romance in Real Life,," *Hallowell Free Press,* September 23, 1833.

40. J.K. Johnson, ed. *Affectionately Yours: The Letters of Sir John A. Macdonald and His Family* (Toronto: Macmillan, 1969), 160.

41. Brian S. Osborne and Donald Swainson, *Kingston: Building on the Past* (Westport, ON: Butternut Press Inc., 1988), 166.

42. The tract of land was formally confirmed as the Mississaugas of the New Credit Reserve in 1903. Margaret Sault, *The History of the Mississaugas of the New Credit First Nation* (Hagersville, ON: Lands, Research and Membership of the New Credit First Nation, n.d.),12.

43. Ibid.

44. Daniel Wilson, "The Present State and Future Prospects of the Indians of British North America," *Proceedings of the Royal Colonial Institute* 5 (1874), 234. My thanks to Bennett McCardle for the reference to this article.

45. Smith, *Sacred Feathers*, 224, 329.

46. Sandford Fleming. Diary entry for June 28, 1845, Sandford Fleming Papers, MG 29 A 8, vol. 80, Diary 1843–45, LAC. I thank Martha Kidd of Peterborough, Ontario, for this reference. Other contemporary forecasts of the extinction of the North American Indian in Upper Canada or Canada West include: John Richardson, "A Trip to Walpole Island and Port Sarnia,," *The Literary Garland* (Montreal), January 1849; reprinted in A.H.U. Colquhoun, ed. *Tecumseh and Richardson* (Toronto: Ontario Book Company, 1924), 70–71; and Samuel Strickland, *Twenty-Seven Years in Canada West* 2 volumes(London: 1853; facsimile edition, Edmonton: Hurtig, 1970), 2: 68.

47. Viscount Bury to Sir Edmund Head, Governor General of Canada, dated Indian Department, Toronto December 5, 1855, Enclosure no. 2, in Correspondence relating to Alterations in the Organization of the Indian Department 1856 (247) vol. 44, in *Irish University Press Series of British Parliamentary Papers, Correspondence and Papers Relating to Canada 1854–58, Colonies Canada 21* (Shannon, Ireland: Irish University Press, 1970): 18.

48. Gywn, *John A.,* 150.

49. John A. Macdonald to R.T. Pennefather, Superintendent General of Indian Affairs, "Copy of Opinion of the Attorney General J.A. Macdonald on Surrenders by Mississaugas of the River Credit," dated July 2, 1857, RG 10, vol. 2242, LAC.

50. Russell, "Paper Burden," 57.

51. Peter Jones to S.Y. Chesley, dated Brantford, November 25, 1854, RG 10, vol. 2225, file 43,957, Pt. 2. LAC.

52. "Civilization of the Indians,," Legislative Assembly, May 15, 1857, *Toronto Globe*, May 16, 1857. See also the account, "House of Assembly: Toronto, 15 May 1857," *The Daily Colonist*, May 16, 1857. Benjamin Robinson is reported in the *Globe*'s summary as stating: "Why should this bill be pressed through, without getting on it the opinion of the Indians themselves or their chiefs. At their Council meetings the Indian chiefs deliberated quite as sensibly as honourable members did in this House, and sometimes even more so,," Robinson had negotiated in 1850 the treaties on the north shores of Lakes Huron, and Superior, still known today as the Robinson Treaties.

53. "An Act to encourage the gradual Civilization of the Indian Tribes in this Province, and to amend the laws respecting Indians." S.C. 1857, c. 26, (20 Vict.) reprinted in Gail Hinge, compiler, *Consolidation of Indian Legislation, Volume 1: United Kingdom and Canada* (Ottawa: Office of Native Claims, Department of Indian and Northern Affairs, n.d.) 114–17.

54. J.S. Milloy, "A Historical Overview of Indian-Government Relations 1755–1940," compiled by J.S. Milloy for Indian and Northern Affairs Canada, December 7, 1992, 41.

55. *Union of the Canadas, Journals of the Legislative Assembly,* 15, 473. Entry for May 22, 1857. In the Assembly, seventy-two members voted in favour, and one (William Lyon Mackenzie) against on May 16, 1857. The *Globe* reported Mackenzie as stating: "Why should we wish to civilize them? What sort of civilization have we here?"

56. John S. Milloy, "The Early Indian Acts: Developmental Strategy and Constitutional Change,," in *As Long as the Sun Shines and Water Flows: A Reader in Canadian Native Studies,* eds. Ian A.L. Getty and Antoine S. Lussier (Vancouver: University of British Columbia Press, 1983), 59; The First Nations almost unanimously rejected "enfranchisement." See Noel Dyck, *What Is the Indian 'Problem': Tutelage and Resistance in Canadian Indian Administration* (St. John's: Institute of Social and Economic Research, Memorial University of Newfoundland, 1991), 51–52.

57. David Thorburn, "Transmits Minutes of a Great Council […] with the Six Nations & a deputation of Chiefs from 15 different Bands from the 20th to 29th Sept. 1858," RG 10, vol. 245A, Docket #11,486–11500, LAC; "Council of Indian Chiefs," *The Grand River Sachem,* October 6, 1858, is one of the few press accounts. My thanks to Anne Unyi, curator of the Heritage and Culture Division, Edinburgh Square Heritage and Cultural Centre, Caledonia, Ontario, for this reference; The *Toronto Globe* only allotted the story less than a hundred words on October 14, 1858. The article stated that the Council was held "last week," but it actually ended two and a half weeks earlier.

58. *John A. Macdonald, The Letters of Sir John A. Macdonald 1858–1861,* ed. by J.K. Johnson and Carole B. Stelmack (Ottawa: Public Archives of Canada, 1969), 593–626.

59. House of Commons, *Debates,* eds. John A. Macdonald in Canada. February 24, 1870, 173.

60. David Shanahan, "The Manitoulin Treaties, 1836 and 1862: The Indian Department and Indian Destiny," *Ontario History* 86, 1 (March 1994), 26–27.

61. 1st and 2nd Terms 1861–62, 2nd Term 1861–62, 1st Term 1862–63, 1st Term 1863–64, 2nd Term 1864–65; Victoria University (Toronto, Ont.) Registrar's Office, Series 2: Student Records, Subseries 2: Arts Records 87.143V 2-2, Registrar of Classes of Arts Students 1855–1878.

62. J. Sunday, Jnr. To the Editor of Petaubun, dated Alnwick, May 28, 1862, in *Petauban*, vol. 2, no. 10 (November 1862).

63. Gwyn, *John A.*, 416.

64. "The British North America Act. VI. Distribution of Legislative Powers," reprinted in *Readings in Canadian History Pre-Confederation*, eds. R. Douglas Francis and Donald B. Smith, first edition (Toronto: Holt, Rinehart and Winston, 1982), 527. Macdonald himself probably inserted this reference to Indians. As J.K. Johnston, a Macdonald biographer writes: "He drafted almost all of what was to be Canada's constitution." Johnson, *Affectionately Yours*, 85.

65. Milloy, "Indian Acts,," 62–63

66. Norman D. Shields, "Anishinabek Political Alliance in the Post-Confederation Period: The Grand General Indian Council of Ontario, 1870–1936" (M.A. thesis, Queen's University, 2001), 58–60.

67. Allen Salt, Diary, 1874–1882. Entry for February 22, 1876, Rev. Allen Salt Papers, 1865–1906, MG 29 H 11, LAC.

68. Ibid., 1874–1882, Entries for February 13 to 22, 1876, Rev. Allen Salt Papers, 1865–1906, MG 29 H 11, LAC.

69. Douglas Leighton, "A Victorian Civil Servant at Work, Lawrence Vankoughnet and the Canadian Indian Department, 1874–1893,," in *As Long As*, eds. Getty and Lussier, 104–119. George F.G. Stanley, *The Birth of Western Canada. A History of the Riel Rebellions* (Toronto: University of Toronto Press, 1960; first published 1936), 216. William Howard Brooks, "Methodism in the Canadian West in the Nineteenth Century" (PhD thesis, University of Manitoba, 1972), 189–191. Waite, "Macdonald," 43.

70. Joyce Katharine Sowby, "Macdonald the Administrator: Department of the Interior and Indian Affairs, 1878–1887,," (M.A. thesis, Queen's University, 1984), 24, 401; Ken Cruikshank, "David Lewis Macpherson." In *Dictionary of Canadian Biography*, vol. 12 (Toronto: University of Toronto Press, 1990), 687.

71. Russell, "Paper Burden," 59, 61.

72. J.R. Miller, *Shingwauk's Vision: A History of Native Residential Schools* (Toronto: University of Toronto Press, 1996), 219.

73. E.B. Biggar, *Anecdotal Life of Sir John Macdonald* (Montreal: John Lovell, 1891), 175

74. John A. Macdonald in Canada, House of Commons, *Debates*, 1880, 1991, May 5, 1880.

75. Canada. *Annual Report of the Department of the Interior*, 1879, 12; cited in Isaac Kholisile Mabindisa, "The Praying Man: The Life and Times of Henry Bird Steinhauer" (PhD thesis, University of Alberta, 1984), 427.

76. Richard Gwyn, *Nation Maker. Sir John A. Macdonald: His Life, Our Times. Volume Two: 1867–1891* (Toronto: Random House Canada, 2011), 34.

77. Waite, "Macdonald,," 46–47; Sowby, "Macdonald the Administrator,," 232; Johnson, *Affectionately Yours*, 159–160.

78. Gwyn, *Nation Maker*, 13.

79. Ibid., 387.

80. R.B. Steinhauer, "The Indian Question,, *"Acta Victoriana* 9,6 (March l886), 5–6.

81. John A. Macdonald, Canada, House of Commons, *Debates*, 1884, 1265, April 1, 1884.

82. Ibid., 1399, April 7, 1884.

83. Gywn, *Nation Maker*, 417.

84. For a review of Will Jackson's life see, Donald B. Smith, *Honoré Jaxon. Prairie Visionary* (Regina: Coteau Books, 2007).

85. Gwyn, *John A.,* 115,

86. John A. Macdonald to Judge James Robert Gowan, private December 12, 1885, Gowan Papers, LAC, quoted in Ged Martin, "Archival Evidence and John A. Macdonald Biography," *Journal of Historical Biography*, 1,1 (Spring 2007), 104.

87. William H. Jackson, Lower Fort Garry, September 19, 1885, to "my dear Family," MG3 C20, Archives of Manitoba.

88. John A. Macdonald in Canada, House of Commons, *Debates*, July 6, 1885, 3119. It would be fascinating to learn when and where John A. Macdonald met George Armstrong Custer.

89. Gwyn, *Nation Maker*, 475.

90. Ibid., 478.

91. "The Great Chief. A Rousing Address on General Topics. The Action of the Government on the Riel Question. A Noble Indication of Administrative Action," *Brantford Daily Courier*, September 8, 1886, 1, col. 3.

92. John Leonard Taylor provides a useful summary in Chapter 14, "Assumptions Underlying Indian Policy," in his *Canadian Indian Policy During the Inter-War Years, 1918–1939* (Ottawa: Department of Indian and Northern Affairs, 1983), 207–11.

93. Noel Dyck, "An Opportunity Lost: The Initiative of the Reserve Agricultural Programme in the Prairie West, in 1885 and After," eds. F. Laurie Barron and James B. Waldram (Regina: Canadian Plains Research Centre, 1986), 127.

94. John A. Macdonald cited in Canada, House of Commons, *Debates,* April 27, 1882, vol. 2, 1186; referenced in Dyck, "An Opportunity Lost," 127.

95. Norah Storey, "Oliver Mowat," *The Oxford Companion to Canadian History and Literature* (Toronto: Oxford University Press, 1967), 174, mentions the premier's description of himself as "The Christian Politician." Oliver Mowat in Regina v St. Catharines Milling and Lumber Company, *The Ontario Reports* 10 (1885) 199.

96. Oliver Mowat in Regina v. St. Catharines Milling, 10 (1885), 201.

97. Elizabeth Graham, compiler, *The Mush Hole: Life at Two Indian Residential Schools* (Waterloo, ON: Heffle Publishing, 1997), 219. "Thomas Daniel Green," *Annual Report 1936, Association of Ontario Land Surveyors*, 124.

98. T.D. Green to The Rt Hon Sir John A. Macdonald, dated Indian Office Regina, March 8, 1886, Macdonald Papers, MG 26A, vol. 424, p. 208289, microfilm C-1775, LAC.

99. A good overview of the act is provided by Malcolm Montgomery in, "The Six Nations Indians and the Macdonald Franchise," *Ontario History*, 57 (1965): 13–25.

100. In 1880, Gavin Fleming, a member of the House of Commons from Brant North (1872–1882), made the following calculation. He first noted that if the low rate of enfranchisement continued (some fifty persons from 1857 to 1880): "it would take 36,000 years to enfranchise the Indian population of Canada." Canada, House of Commons, *Debates*, 1880, 1992, May 5, 1880. I thank Keith Johnson for identifying Gavin Fleming for me.

101. Kahkewaquonaby, M.D., chief to Sir John A. Macdonald, K.C.B., etc., etc., etc., Ottawa, read out in the House of Commons, *Debates*, June 8, 1885. To Dr. Jones's great disappointment Wilfrid Laurier's Liberal administration repealed this legislation in 1898 (Status Indians only obtained the federal franchise in Canada in 1960). Allan Sherwin examines in depth Dr. Jones's connection with Macdonald, in *Bridging Two Peoples: Chief Peter E. Jones, 1843–1909* (Waterloo: Wilfrid Laurier University Press, 2012).

102. Charles Big Canoe, Chief, and James Ashquabe, councillor, to the Right Honourable Sir John Macdonald, Superintendent General of Indian Affairs, not dated, Sir John A. Macdonald Papers, MG 26A, volume 335A, 151507, LAC.

103. La Cerise, "Ojibway Indians of Georgina Island in Lake Simcoe. A Happy and Contented Colony of 130 Members — Old Chief Big Canoe One of Nature's Gentlemen, Who lives in a Well-Furnished Modern House and Idolizes His Grandchildren, Just Like any White Grandfather Would Do," *Toronto Star Weekly*, October 1, 1915, 17. Charles Big Canoe knew his Ojibwa culture intimately. He wrote for example, this preface to Rev. Egerton Ryerson Young's collection of Ojibwa stories, *Algonquin Indian Tales* (New York: The Abingdon Press, 1903), 3: "Dear Friend: Your book of stories gathered from among my tribe has very much pleased me. The reading of them brings up the days of long time ago when I was a boy and heard our old people tell these tales in the wigwams and at the camp fire."

104. George Blaker' s name appears as the secretary in the petition of John Sunday and others to T.G. Anderson, dated Alnwick, March 22, 1849, RG 10, volume 408, p. 61, microfilm reel c-9614, LAC. In an affidavit made on May 15, 1903, in a statement on Mr. Sinclair's Report of the Claims of the Chippewas of Lake Huron and Simcoe, George Blaker gives his age, RG 10, volume 2331, file 67, 071, part one, LAC.

105. See the annual reports of the Missionary Society of the Wesleyan Methodist Church in Canada, 1852/53, xix; 1853/54, xx.

106. Memorial of Mitchell Chubb, Chief; Peter Crowe, councillor; Joshua Blaker, councillor; Allan Salt, councillor; E. Comego, councillor; George Blaker, secretary, John A. Macdonald Papers, MG 26A, volume 335A, 15133, LAC.

107. John A. Macdonald to Dr. Peter E. Jones, August 31, 1886. Ibid., letterbook 24, 8, LAC.

108. Photo number: C/6134, LAC.

109. "The Great Chief. Sir John Macdonald's Visit to the Reserve. 'We'll Vote for the Man Who Gave Us Votes.' An Unparalleled Welcome and Unbounded Enthusiasm. Eight Thousand Indians and Whites Hail The Chieftain. An Objection By The Council Meets With Universal Reprobation by the People," *Brantford Daily Courier*, September 7, 1886, 1, 2, 4.

110. Sheila Staats, "The Six Nations Council House: Historic Building at Ohsweken," *Ontario History* 85, 3 (September 1993), 213–222.

111. The Six Nations in Council September 6, 1886, Minutes. Visit of the Supt. General The Right Honourable Sir John A. Macdonald," RG 10, vol. 886, 233, LAC.

112. "Sir John's Visit," *The Weekly Expositor* (Brantford), September 10, 1886.

113. "The Great Chief. Sir John Macdonald' s Visit to the Reserve, *Brantford Daily Courier*, September 7,1886.

114. "Sir John's Visit," *The Weekly Expositor* (Brantford), September 10, 1886, 4. My thanks to Denise Kirk, local history librarian, Brantford Public Library, for this and other references to Macdonald's visit to the Grand River Six Nations territory on September 6, 1886.

115. Sally M. Weaver, "Six Nations of the Grand River, Ontario," in *Handbook of North American Indians*, vol. 15, *Northeast*, ed. Bruce G. Trigger (Washington: Smithsonian Institution, 1978), 531.

116. David Blanchard, *Seven Generations: A History of the Kanienkehaka* (Kahnawake, QC: Kahnawake Survival School, 1980), 362–67. Thomas Stone, "Legal Mobilization and Legal Penetration: The Department of Indian Affairs and the Canadian Party at St. Regis, 1876–1918," *Ethnohistory* 22, 4 (Autumn 1975): 375–408.

117. There are ten letters from Oronhyatekha to John A. Macdonald in the Macdonald Papers in LAC. So great was the Mohawk doctor' s admiration for the prime minister that he announced, in 1882, that he and his wife had decided to call their newly born son "John Alexander," after Sir John. They planned to do so, "so that in after years we could tell him after whom he was named and to instruct him to emulate his name sake in love and devotion to his country, which go so far to make a true patriot. "Oronkytekha to John A. Macdonald dated January 5, 1882, John A. Macdonald Papers, MG 26a, vol. 390, 185208, LAC. For a sketch of Oronhyatekha's life see: "Oronhyatekha, The Independent Order of Foresters, and the Forester Island Orphanage," *Papers and Records of the Lennox and Addington Historical Society* 17 (1987): 55–75.

118. Dr. Oronhyatekha quoted in "Tyendinaga Reserve. Mohawk Centennial," *Tribune* [Kingston, Ontario?], undated clipping, reporting on one-hundredth anniversary of their landing at Tyendinaga, September 4, 1884, Rev. R.S. Forneri Scrapbook, Diocese of Ontario Archives, Kingston, Ontario. I thank Norman Knowles for this reference.

119. There are a dozen letters from John W.N. Elliott to John A. Macdonald in the Macdonald Papers. On John Elliott, see: "Noted Chief of Six Nations is Buried in East," *Calgary Herald*, May 31, 1921. As a young man Elliott had attended the Mohawk Institute at Brantford, and the Agricultural College at Guelph, Ontario, in the late 1870s. See John W.N. Elliott to John A Macdonald, dated Toronto, November 24, 1886, Macdonald Papers, MG 26A, p. 212175, LAC. He was a grandson of John Smoke Johnson, the speaker of the Six Nations Council for nearly half-a-century, J.W.N. Elliott to John A. Macdonald, dated Ottawa, June 25, 1890, Macdonald Papers, MG 26A, p. 243042, LAC.

120. Capt. J.W.M. Elliott to the Right Honorable Sir John A. Macdonald, dated Six Nations Reserve of the Grand River, October 29, 1886, :Private, John A. Macdonald Papers, vol. 430, 211406, LAC.

121. Weaver, "Six Nations," 532. Weaver wrote of the members of the reform movement of 1890: "Few could claim hereditary chieftainship titles and most felt that education should be a requisite for council office. In 1890 they drafted a petition signed by some twenty percent of the male adults in the community, urging the government to apply the elected system to the reserve, but their activities in subsequent years went unheeded by the federal government.

122. J.K. Johnson, "John A. Macdonald," in *The Pre-Confederation Premiers: Ontario Government Leaders, 1841–1867,* ed. J.M.S., Careless (Toronto: University of Toronto Press, 1980), 226. I thank Keith Johnson for bringing this point to my attention.

123. Nive Voisine, "Louis-Francois Laflèche." In *Dictionary of Canadian Biography,* vol. 12 (Toronto: University of Toronto Press, 1990), 506. Soeur de la Providence, *Le Père Lacombe, "L' homme au bon coeur" d' après ses mémoires et souvenirs* (Montreal: Le Devoir, 1916), 3. For his services in helping to keep the Blackfoot and Peigan Indians out of the Rebellion in 1885, John A. Macdonald moved on June 2, 1886, that the respected Roman Catholic priest be given $1,000. See Canada, House of Commons, *Debates,* June 2, 1886, 1774.

124. Shirlee Anne Smith, Hudson's Bay Company Archives, to Donald B. Smith, December 30, 1988. Carman Miller, "Sir Edward Seaborne Clouston." In *Dictionary of Canadian Biography,* 14: 1911–1920 (Toronto: University of Toronto Press, 1998), 219–222.

125. J.G. MacGregor, *Senator Hardisty's Prairies (1849–1889)* (Saskatoon: Western Producer Prairie Books, 1978), 3–5.

126. Ibid.

127. Gerald Friesen, "John Norquay." In *Dictionary of Canadian Biography* 11 (Toronto: University of Toronto Press, 1982), 642–43. Waite, "Macdonald": 38.

128. "Solomon White," *Commemorative Biographical Record of the Country of Essex, Ontario* (Toronto: J.H. Beers and Co., 1905), 64; Peter E. Paul Dembski, "Solomon White." In *Dictionary of Canadian Biography*, 14: 1911–1920 (Toronto: University of Toronto Press, 1998), 1053–54. "Solomon White dies in Cobalt," *Windsor Evening Record,* November 13, 1911.

129. Carmen Miller, "John Joseph Caldwell Abbott." In *Dictionary of Canadian Biography* 12:1890–1900 (Toronto: University of Toronto Press, 1990), 4. Her father, the Rev. John Bethune (1791–1872), the Anglican Rector and Dean of Montreal was the brother of Angus Bethune (1783–1858), the fur trader. Mary Larratt Smith, *Prologue to Norman. The Canadian Bethunes* (Oakville, ON: Mosaic Press, 1976), 65.

130. Donald B. Smith, "The Herchmers' Secret," *The Beaver,* outfit 310:4 (Spring 1980): 52–58. John Hamilton's half-brothers also had Indian ancestry, through their mother (Robert Hamilton's first wife, Catharine Askin Robertson, after whom the city of St. Catharines is named). One of John Hamilton's half-brothers, George Hamilton, founded what is now the city of Hamilton, which is named after him, John C. Weaver, "George Hamilton." In *Dictionary of Canadian Biography* 7; 1836–1850 (Toronto: University of Toronto Press, 1988), 377–79. Catharine Askin Robertson's First Nation background is discussed by David R. Beasley in *The Canadian Don Quixote. The Life and Works of Major John Richardson, Canada's first novelist* (Erin, ON: The Porcupine's Quill, Inc., 1977), 9–14, see particularly the genealogy provided on page 13.

131. John A. Macdonald to Louisa Macdonald, dated October 14, 1887, and Mary Macdonald to Louisa Macdonald, dated December 10, 1887, in Johnson, ed., *Affectionately Yours*, 172–73.

132. Gwyn, *Nation Maker,* 352.

133. John Spargo, *Two Bennington-Born Explorers and Makers of Modern Canada* (n.p.p.: n.p. 1950), 70.

134. W. Stewart Wallace, "The Wives of the Nor'westers," chapter 7 in his *Pedlars from Quebec and Other Papers on the Nor'Westers* (Toronto: Ryerson, 1954), 68. Wallace would have been intrigued to learn that Sir John's granddaughter attended Miss Harmon's School. Wallace wrote a biography of Sir John, published by Macmillan in Toronto as *Sir John Macdonald* in 1924.

135. John A. Macdonald, quoted in Gwyn, *Nation Maker,* 316.

Chapter 3

Macdonald and the Fenians

David A. Wilson

The Fenians have generally had a rough ride in Canadian historiography. They have been treated with a mixture of contempt and condescension, and dismissed as incurable romantics with a harebrained scheme to liberate Ireland by invading Canada. The views of Donald Creighton were typical: "Nothing could have been more characteristically 'Irish' in the broadest, most farcical meaning of the word than the conception and execution of this great enterprise. With one or two significant exceptions, the leaders of the Fenian movement against British America were a crew of grandiloquent clowns and vainglorious incompetents."[1] C.P. Stacey, in his sketch of the Fenian leader John O'Neill, was equally scathing: "It is hard to believe that O'Neill was a man of much intelligence, for the idea of righting Irish wrongs by attacking Canada, of which he was the most active exponent, was essentially stupid. He was egotistical and credulous. He seems however to have been a brave soldier and a sincere Irish patriot. Unlike many Fenian leaders, he was ready to risk life and liberty for the cause he believed in."[2] More recently, Richard Gwyn struck the same note: "They were talkative, boastful, combative (with each other) and, while brave soldiers individually, hopeless as an organized force."[3] There go the "Irish" (in the broadest and most farcical meaning of the word, of course) — boastful, brave, clownish, credulous, impractical, and incompetent — with their ludicrous walk-on part in Canadian history, providing some comic relief in the grown-up business of nation-building.

Now contrast this with the way that John A. Macdonald viewed the Fenians. Here he is in September 1865, writing to governor general Lord Monck: "I am watching them very closely … and think that the movement must not be despised, either in America or Ireland. I am so strongly of that opinion that I shall spare no expense in watching them on both sides of the line."[4] Two things in particular should be noted about Macdonald's

"GREAT FENIAN SCARE," 9th October, 1869.

comment. The first is its early date. In September 1865, the British government had clamped down on the Fenian leadership in Ireland, but the movement in the United States had not yet turned its attention toward Canada. The second is Macdonald's intention to watch the Fenians on both sides of the border. It was clear to him that the Fenians were both a potential external and internal threat. And watch them he did. Over the next five years, Macdonald's correspondence contained more than 2,400 letters on the Fenians. The vast majority of these letters were not, of course, written by Macdonald himself. But their sheer scale is a good index of his concern. Subsequent historians may have marginalized and mocked the Fenians; Macdonald took them very seriously indeed.

To understand why, we must shed the stereotypical images of Creighton, Stacey, and Gwyn, and think ourselves into the mindset of William Roberts, Tom Sweeny, John O'Neill, and other American Fenians who trained their sights on Canada.[5] The Fenians were far from the first Irish-American nationalists who believed that an invasion of Canada would pave the way for Irish independence. During the War of 1812, an Irish correspondent to the New York *Shamrock* newspaper asserted that "Ireland will be rescued from British bondage on the plains of Canada," and many of his compatriots in New York's Republican Greens militia marched north to avenge the United Irish defeat in the Rising of 1798.[6] In 1848, the Irish Republican Union in New York attempted to coordinate a revolution in Ireland with an expedition against Canada that would wipe out the British Empire in North America.[7] One of its strongest supporters was the young Montreal lawyer Bernard Devlin, who would later emerge as a leading opponent of D'Arcy McGee in Canada.[8] McGee himself, then an Irish revolutionary exile in New York, believed that Canada needed a revolution and that the United States was waiting for the right opportunity to move north.[9] Indeed, the longstanding combination of American annexationism and Irish-American invasion plans goes a long way to explaining why Macdonald and McGee (in his later loyalist years) were so concerned about the Fenians.

It is equally important to understand that the Fenian invasion strategy was not nearly as far-fetched as it retrospectively appeared. In fact, there were good reasons in the winter of 1865–66 for thinking that it might well be successful from an Irish revolutionary point of view. If the famine had produced massive Irish immigration to the United States, the American Civil

War had transformed thousands of those immigrants into soldiers. At the same time, the Civil War had brought Anglo-American relations close to a crisis point. Britain and the United States had nearly gone to war in 1861, and the American government was demanding reparations for the damage caused by Confederate ships that had been fitted out in Britain. Under these circumstances, the Fenian Brotherhood sought ways to turn the American-trained Irish fighting force against the old Imperial enemy.

One possibility was to get thousands of well-armed Irish veterans across the Atlantic to Ireland, where they could form the vanguard of an Irish revolution. But the logistical difficulties were insuperable, and the Royal Navy dominated the Atlantic sea lanes. Besides, in September 1865, the British government cracked down on the Fenian movement in Ireland, arresting its leaders and closing its newspaper. The promise of the Fenian leader James Stephens, that 1865 would be the Year of Revolution in Ireland, was clearly not going to be fulfilled. On the other hand, it would be relatively easy to get Irish-American troops into Canada, where they could strike a blow against the last bastion of the British Empire in North America. Relatively easy: But to what strategic purpose?

Several lines of argument were advanced. Canada could become a base from which to disrupt transatlantic British commerce, or become a bargaining chip in negotiations to secure an independent Ireland. Both these ideas were indeed far-fetched, and deserved all the criticism they got. But there was another, much more plausible scenario. By invading Canada from the United States, defeating the forces of the Crown and establishing a presence on British-American soil, the Fenians could precipitate an Anglo-American war — a prospect that would become more likely if the American government allowed an attack to proceed. In the fall of 1865, Bernard Doran Killian, the treasurer of the Fenian Brotherhood, broached the subject with the American secretary of state William Seward. According to Killian, Seward informed him that if the Fenians were successful, the United States would "acknowledge accomplished facts."[10] Whether or not Seward actually said this — if he did, he certainly did not mean it — the Fenians now believed that they were operating with the unofficial blessing of the American government.

Although the leader of the American Fenians, John O'Mahony, remained skeptical about a Fenian invasion of Canada, he did not rule it out altogether. "The Canadian raid I look upon as a mere diversion, as far as regards our present action," he told the Irish nationalist John Mitchel in November. "Unless it drag[s] the United States into war with England it can only end in defeat to those that engage in it. But it is worth trying in the hope that it may lead to such a war."[11] A Fenian victory in Canada would inspire the revolutionary movement in Ireland at the very moment that British troops were being pulled toward British North America. England's difficulty would be Ireland's opportunity, and Ireland would be freed through Canada.

A few weeks later, the Fenian Brotherhood split on the issue, with O'Mahony preferring to focus on Ireland, and the rival Senate wing under William Roberts drawing up invasion plans for Canada. On St. Patrick's Day 1866, though, the O'Mahony wing decided to steal the initiative from their rivals by organizing an attack on Campobello Island off the Maine-New Brunswick coast, an island that was wrongly believed to be disputed territory between Britain and the United States. The potential for triggering an Anglo-American war appeared obvious. But, contrary to all expectations, the American government intervened against the Fenians. Far from recognizing accomplished facts, the U.S. government prevented them from being accomplished in the first place. The results: total disaster, a price tag of nearly $40,000, and widespread ridicule. This was a failure by any stretch of the imagination.

But the "Eastport fiasco," as it became known, had two unexpected con-sequences. First, it prompted the Senate wing to speed up its plans to invade Canada; unless action was taken quickly, the Fenian Brotherhood would lose credibility, and its members would drift away. The military organizer, General Tom Sweeny, was faced with a tough choice. He could postpone the invasion until he had sufficient men and materiel and risk the disintegration of the movement, or he could launch a premature invasion and go down to defeat. In the event, Sweeny decided to go ahead, on the grounds that a defeat with honour was preferable to doing nothing at all. The Fenians had gone so far that they could not turn back, and a grand revolutionary gesture, even if it was a glorious failure, was better than the ignominy of inaction. Second, the apparent lessons of Eastport lulled the Canadian authorities into a false sense of security. The effectiveness of British North American defence measures, the American intervention against the invaders, and the splits within the Fenian ranks all pointed in the same direction — that no attempt would now be made on Canada.

Partly because of the surprise factor, O'Neill's Fenian army defeated the Queen's Own Rifles at the Battle of Ridgeway before being driven back across the border by superior British forces.[12] Although this was a failure in terms of Fenian objectives, the fact that soldiers fighting under the banner of the Irish Republican Army had entered Canada and beaten the forces of the Crown was a source of pride and inspiration for Irish nationalism. Consider, for example, the response of the constitutional nationalist *Nation* newspaper in Dublin: "There is news this week from America, the first faint mutterings of which have sufficed to flush the cheek and stir the blood of Irishmen from end to end of the land. For today, for the first time in this century, the green flag of Ireland is waving in the sunlight of heaven over serried files of men in arms 'for Ireland;' and whatever other aspect may be worn by the event, howsoever the verdict of colder prudence and clearer judgment may regard it, the popular mind takes in today but this one cardinal fact — that for the first time in well nigh seventy years the red flag of England has gone down before the Irish green."[13] This not only attests to the way in which moral victory could be snatched from the jaws of strategic defeat, but also suggests that the Fenian policy of radicalizing nationalism in Ireland by winning battles in Canada was not entirely off the mark.

But this was only half the story. As Macdonald's comment about watching Fenians "on both sides of the line" indicates, there was also a significant Fenian presence in Canada itself. While the exact figures will never be known, it is clear that sworn members of the Fenian Brotherhood in Canada remained a minority of the Irish-Catholic population. Even in the core centres of Toronto and Montreal, their combined numbers were probably no more than a thousand.[14] In Canada as a whole, it is unlikely that they had more than 3,500 members in an Irish-Catholic ethnic population of over 260,000.

These figures, however, can be quite misleading. Apart from anything else, they ignore the fact that beyond the number of sworn Fenians there were many fellow travellers who sympathized with physical force republicanism, along with others who supported the Fenian objective of a separate Irish republic, but who rejected the means of violence. Many constitutional nationalists had ambivalent feelings about the Fenians, believing that their hearts were in the right place even if their heads were wrong. The Fenians in Montreal reckoned that they could draw on the support of a quarter of the city's Irish-born population, and their success in taking over the St. Patrick's Society shows that they were an important political force in the city.[15] Similarly, the role of the Fenians in organizing St. Patrick's Day parades in places such as Toronto, Ottawa, and Quebec City indicates that they could and did attract wider support.

The Fenians were able to reach a wider Canadian audience through their newspapers. From Toronto, Patrick Boyle's *The Irish Canadian* officially denied any Fenian connections, while disseminating the Fenian message throughout the country. From New York, Patrick Meehan's *The Irish American* circulated in Canada, and from Dublin, Stephens' *The Irish People* reached Canadian readers. When the Dublin police raided the offices of *The Irish People* in September 1865, one of the first things they found was a list of subscribers from Quebec City, and another from Halifax, Nova Scotia.[16]

Although the number of sworn Canadian Fenians was small, they were a pervasive presence throughout Irish-Catholic Canada. Not only in the major cities, but also in small towns from Windsor to Brockville, and in rural townships such as Puslinch and Adjala, there were Fenian circles that were part of the North American network. The fact that the Canadian Fenians operated in the context of a much more powerful American organization gave them an influence out of all proportion to their numbers.[17] A small group of Canadian Fenians — a minority within a minority — was prepared to support an American invasion force by suborning Irish soldiers in the British army, infiltrating the militia, disrupting communications, seizing and destroying military installations, organizing a run on the banks, burning down government buildings, and taking Canadian politicians hostage.[18] From New York, General Sweeny established his own "secret service corps" in Canada; thanks to their activities, when the Fenians crossed into the Niagara Peninsula in June 1866, they knew the terrain better than did the Canadian militia and British troops which were sent to meet them.[19] The imbalance between the numerical and the strategic significance of the Fenians in Canada explains the apparent paradox in Macdonald's attitude toward them. On the one hand, he wrote that the Fenian Brotherhood was "contemptible in point of numbers in Canada," while on the other, he spent considerable time, money and effort tracking their activities and disrupting their organization.[20]

In some respects, Macdonald was confronted with a situation that antici-pated early-twenty-first-century concerns. Within an ethno-religious outgroup, in this case Irish Catholics, there existed a revolutionary minority who intended to subvert the Canadian state and who were working closely and clandestinely with an international revolutionary organization. In response, Macdonald developed a counter-revolutionary strategy in which two components were particularly important: the secret police force that operated against the Fenians in Canada and the United States, and the suspension of habeas corpus in June 1866 along with the renewed suspension of November 1867.

Macdonald had initially established the secret police force in 1864 as a temporary response to an immediate problem — the activities of Southern Confederate agents who were using Canada as a base of operations against the North.[21] He wound the force down after the Civil War, but quickly reac-tivated it when Canadian detectives in the United States picked up stories about Fenian invasion plans. The detectives sent regular reports to the chiefs of the force — Gilbert McMicken in Canada West and William Ermatinger in Canada East — who then evaluated the evidence and sent their summa-ries to Macdonald. This upward flow of information was accompanied by a downward flow of direction from Macdonald, who closely monitored secret police operations and used the force to check other sources of information coming into his office.

Assessing the threat in the winter of 1865–6 proved extraordinarily diffi-cult. The detectives gathered a great deal of information about Fenian circles in the United States and Canada, but got lost in a fog of rumours from rank-and-file Fenians who talked so much that it became impossible to separate fact from fantasy. The main problem, though, was that the secret police were unable to infiltrate the upper echelons of the Fenian Brotherhood. In desper-ation, McMicken suggested to Macdonald that "one of two *Clever Women* whose absolute virtue stands questioned by the censorious might be obtained who by address could get some of the susceptible members of the 'Senate' into their toils and thus as Delilah with Samson possess themselves of their secrets — what think you?" McMicken even suggested a couple of candidates for this patriotic venture.[22] There is, alas, no record of Macdonald's reply.

Precisely because he remained in the dark about the leaders' plans, Macdonald erred on the side of caution. As early as October 1865, we find him giving McMicken advice about how to respond if his men caught

Canadian Fenians drilling; the detectives should order them to disperse, avoid provocation, arrest the leaders afterwards, and capture as many armed men as possible if they resisted. "There is no likelihood of you being called on to act in this way," he added, "but think it as well to give you a general idea of what I think you should do."[23]

Over the winter, as the likelihood of such action became greater, Macdonald increasingly concerned himself with the operational details of the force. Nothing escaped his attention. Among other things, he conferred with McMicken over the number of detectives and their most effective locations, fielded requests for funds and regular payments for the men in the field, made inquiries about the reliability of specific policemen, and passed on information from the British Consulate in New York about Fenian suspects.[24]

By late February 1866, one of McMicken's detectives reported that the Fenian Congress in Pittsburgh was preparing for an invasion around St Patrick's Day.[25] A few days later, another detective who was spying on the Fenians in upstate New York informed Ermatinger that "they all talk about an outbreak on St Patrick's day Week."[26] Meanwhile, the detective stationed in Buffalo learned that large quantities of arms were coming into the city, and similar reports of an imminent invasion were coming in from different sources.[27] There had already been false alarms – the previous year, for example, McMicken had learned that an invasion would take place on November 5 — but this looked like the real thing.[28]

The Adjutant-General of the militia, Patrick MacDougall, had drawn up plans to repulse the invaders after they had advanced into the country. McMicken, in contrast, felt that this was a potentially disastrous strategy: "If they in any body did advance but 50, 40, or 30 miles into the interior from the Frontier," he told Macdonald, "it would raise an excitement in the United States which might be hard to control — My opinion is that every prudent and possible preparation without creating an alarm should be made to prevent their obtaining a moment's foothold on Canadian soil and for this end I am willing to do all and risk all."[29] Macdonald now acted on that advice, calling out the volunteers and concentrating them at the most vulnerable points of the frontier in a show of strength designed to stop the invasion before it started.[30]

He and his cabinet also attempted to prevent any cooperation between the invaders and the Fenian underground in Canada — particularly in

Toronto, where one of McMicken's detectives reported that half the members of the Hibernian Benevolent Society had taken the Fenian oath, and had organized themselves into nine lodges with a total membership of 650.[31] The government feared that the Fenians in the city would use the St Patrick's Day parade to launch an insurrection that would pin down British and Canadian forces during the invasion. To guard against this, D'Arcy McGee applied considerable pressure on the Catholic bishop of Toronto, John Lynch, to withdraw the Church's support for the parade. The bishop duly issued two circulars to that effect.[32] Meanwhile, McMicken travelled to Toronto and arranged a meeting with Michael Murphy, the founder of the Fenian Brotherhood in Canada. After receiving assurances from Murphy that his men would keep the peace, McMicken then set out to persuade the city's mayor, Francis Medcalf, not to call out the volunteers. It took some doing, but McMicken eventually won the argument.[33] In the event, the parade passed off peacefully — partly because the Senate wing had decided they were not ready to launch the invasion, and mainly because Murphy and his men belonged to the rival O'Mahony wing of the Fenians.

As a good O'Mahony Fenian, Murphy left Toronto the following month, to participate in the planned invasion of Campobello Island — only to be intercepted at Cornwall and thrown in jail. In Canada, Macdonald continued to receive reports about Fenian activities on the frontier. "Rumors and reports have been so abundant in regard to the certainty of preparations being made at different points for a concentrated move on Canada," McMicken told Macdonald, "that I have, although somewhat incredulous, been on the watch to obtain something reliable to communicate to you." But there was no hard evidence and it was impossible to see what was going on behind the smoke. Were the Fenians really planning an invasion, or was it all talk to keep up the spirits of the rank-and-file? "It is very difficult at times," McMicken wrote, "to discriminate as to the propriety of doing or not doing in reference to information received."[34]

This state of uncertainty persisted throughout May. "I can gather nothing from any quarter at present of anything being done, indication of a movement of any kind," McMicken wrote Macdonald in the middle of the month, "unless we take the absence of bluster and the unusual quiet everywhere as an indication."[35] In Ogdensburg, a potential launching pad for the invasion, one of McMicken's best detectives had his cover blown and escaped to Prescott, and a potentially valuable source of information was closed off.[36] McMicken became increasingly convinced that there was no reasonable possibility of an invasion, and the British Consul in Buffalo concurred that Fenianism was "virtually dead."[37] Not wanting to be caught napping, Macdonald instructed McMicken to keep Buffalo under constant surveillance, which he did. One of his detectives reported from the city on May 29 that "a great many strange military men" had arrived there over the previous few days, and that each incoming train was bringing more of them. "Something is not right," he concluded.[38]

And indeed, something was not. The "unusual quiet" of the preceding weeks was broken by a rush of reports that hundreds of Fenians were converging on the city. Macdonald telegraphed McMicken, instructing him to send copies of all "direct news" to General George Napier, the commander of British troops in Canada West.[39] McMicken had already telegraphed Napier the previous day, requesting him to send troops to Port Colborne. This was, of course, very much in line with McMicken's views on the importance of pre-emptive action. But, McMicken later told Macdonald, Napier was otherwise engaged with a woman that night and probably put the telegram in his pocket without reading it.[40]

By the time the Fenians slipped across the border in the early morning of June 1, it was too late for pre-emptive action. Having failed to penetrate the top level of the Fenian Brotherhood, McMicken's men reported the Fenian troop buildup only two days before the raid took place, and General Napier had not taken the reports seriously, if indeed he had read them at all. During the invasion itself, one of the detectives infiltrated the Fenian camp, then doubled back to inform the Canadian militia about its size, strength, and location.[41] But his report was already out of date by the time it was made, and seems to have had no bearing on the strategy adopted by Colonel Alfred Booker, who led the Queen's Own Rifles into their defeat at Ridgeway. McMicken was scathing in his comments about Booker's failure: "A greater botch of an easy duty was never made," he told Macdonald. "I feel on this matter very acutely, for had we managed rightly and got hold of these Fenians … in the field, Fenianism would have been wounded mortally — while now they have too good reason to boast and make use of their raid in evidence of their ability to overcome and outwit our forces."[42] McMicken was quite wrong in his dismissive attitude about the Fenians' military ability. In fact, the Queen's Own Rifles were walking straight into a trap, which Booker's military ineptitude ironically enabled them to avoid.[43] But McMicken's assessment of the political impact of Ridgeway was exactly right. It would only be a matter of time before the Fenians would try again.

In the face of this new reality, Macdonald did three things. First, he covered up Booker's incompetence, lest it discredit or undermine his own political position as Minister of Militia — a subject discussed in Peter Vronsky's study of Ridgeway.[44] Second, he suspended habeas corpus — a subject to which we will return. And third, he widened the operations of the secret service. As before, the detectives watched the frontier and kept a close eye on known or suspected Fenians in Canada. But they now paid closer attention to Fenian finances, to assess the organization's state of readiness for the next invasion. Above all, though, they set out to infiltrate the Fenian leadership — something that required creativity, patience, and luck.

One of the key figures here was Detective Charles Clarke, McMicken's top man, who steadily worked his way up the Fenian organization in New York. By the summer of 1867, he pretended to have started up his own Fenian circle in Missouri, and became sufficiently well-acquainted with the American Fenian leader William Roberts to present a pony (courtesy of the Canadian taxpayer) to his son, and attend mass and dinner with his wife.[45] Shortly afterward, he was presented with an Irish Republican Army uniform, and was featured in *The Irish American* as a model Fenian.[46] So far, so good. But everything came crashing down when a woman he had jilted revealed his true identity, and he had to leave New York in a hurry.[47]

Another valuable source of information came via the British Consulate in New York, where Rudolph Fitzpatrick, the Fenian Assistant Secretary at War, had offered his services to the British government, for a suitable price.[48] When, in March 1867, Clarke spent his evenings with Fitzpatrick in New York, neither man knew that the other was a spy. But Fitzpatrick did not remain useful for long. A few months later, he was expelled from the organization for swindling.[49] Charles Carroll Tevis, who had helped plan the Fenian raid, was also on the British payroll from the beginning of 1867. He had "quarreled with the Fenian leaders and is now ready to do them as much harm as possible," wrote the British Minister Frederick Bruce.[50] However, the very fact that he was on the outside limited his value.

The breakthrough came in June 1868, when Macdonald and McMicken received a letter from Thomas Billis Beach, an Englishman who had fought with O'Neill during the Civil War, and who was already supplying information about American Fenianism to the British government. With Macdonald's approval, McMicken met Beach in Detroit, and discussed terms. Beach, or Henri Le Caron as he called himself, would accept a position on O'Neill's staff, and provide detailed information about the invasion plans; in return, the Canadian government would pay him $100 a month.[51] Macdonald agreed, with the provision that the agreement must not be put in writing. "A man who will engage to do what he offers to do, that is, to betray those with whom he acts, is not to be trusted," he reminded McMicken — a point that has frequently been lost on Beach's biographers.[52] It turned out to be an excellent investment. Over the next two years, Beach's information meant that the Canadian government was better informed about the invasion plans than were the Fenian rank-and-file.

Supplementing Beach's information were the reports of William Montgomery, who had joined the secret service in the spring of 1867, and who had been steadily working his way up the Fenian Brotherhood in New York. By April 1870, converging intelligence from Beach and Montgomery pointed to an imminent attack. Meanwhile, detectives stationed in Vermont reported the movement of arms and material toward the border. One report noted that "the superintendance [sic] of this branch of the business seems to have devolved upon Colonel Henry Le Caron." "This Le Caron," the police magistrate Charles Coursol added, "is the same person mentioned in my Report two years ago, and was a very prominent person in the raids at that time."[53] This points to another aspect of Macdonald's strategy. By declining to disclose information about spies and informers to men such as Coursol, who was responsible for countering the Fenian threat in Montreal, Macdonald simultaneously protected his own sources and was able to compare and contrast independent sources of information. Largely as a result of Beach's information, the government knew where and when the invasion would take place, and the names of some of its principal supporters in Canada.[54]

The result was, as McMicken wrote, "the complete discomfiture of the Fenians and their abandonment of the enterprise."[55] Fenian morale was shattered, and the strategy of liberating Ireland by invading Canada was to all intents and purposes abandoned, despite O'Neill's last-gasp freelance effort to foment a Métis rebellion in Manitoba the following year. Despite its initial difficulties and occasional setbacks, the secret police had played a pivotal role in defeating and discrediting the Senate wing of the Fenian Brotherhood. In this sense, Macdonald's counter-intelligence efforts had been a resounding success.

The other main weapon in his anti-Fenian strategy was the suspension of habeas corpus, enacted on June 9, 1866. Clearly, this was a strategy that Macdonald adopted with great reluctance. Despite all the evidence coming in from the secret police during the early months of 1866, the legislation was only enacted after the Fenian raid at Ridgeway. Even then, Macdonald was concerned about the potential for a loyalist backlash that would exacerbate ethno-religious tensions in the country. To prevent this from happening, he authorized a circular to magistrates warning them against "hasty and ill-judged arrests" of suspected Fenians, and ensured that any warrants issued under the Act must first be cleared with the Executive Council.[56] In the event, there was no open season on Fenian suspects in Canada. Macdonald preferred to rely on the surveillance activities of the secret police, and could accurately declare that the suspension had not been "harshly or improperly used."[57]

This policy of restraint was carried through into the first months of the new Dominion, when the earlier suspension had lapsed. In September 1867, McMicken sent Macdonald an urgent letter about two prominent American Fenians who had arrived in Canada to prepare for the next invasion, and called for legislation that authorized the arrest of "suspects" who could not "give a proper account of themselves." Macdonald prudently reminded McMicken that he had no cause to arrest the suspected men: "All that you can do is watch them closely. It won't do to have anything related to *suspects*. Should there be any occasion for it, we can again suspend the Habeas Corpus Act."[58]

Two months later, in November 1867, new intelligence convinced Macdonald that such an occasion had arisen. The British Consul in New York had learned that the Fenians were gearing up for an invasion in the spring of 1868, and McMicken's detectives in the United States were reporting Fenian movements on the frontier.[59] One of them, posing as a U.S. marshall, was shown hundreds of arms around Potsdam, Watertown, and Ogdensburg in upstate New York.[60] Another met a leading Toronto Fenian who talked about caches of rifles and revolvers in Toronto, Montreal, Kingston, and Hamilton, and about the Fenian infiltration of British Army regiments stationed in Canada.[61] Shortly after receiving these reports, Macdonald announced his decision to renew suspension of *Habeas Corpus*.[62]

In making his case, Macdonald reminded Parliament that the Fenian Brotherhood was an international organization, which had engaged in political violence in Britain, and had acquired considerable political influence in the United States. Drawing on his detectives' reports, he said that the Canadian government had "distinct evidence of increasing activity" on the border, and that a second invasion was a very real possibility. Under these circumstances, the government must be given the power to counter potential "foreign aggressors." "The object of the bill," Macdonald continued, "was to prevent parties from making undue raids on our country."[63]

There is no doubt that Macdonald was genuinely concerned about the external Fenian threat. But he also had considerable information from his detectives about the plans of Canadian Fenians to aid and abet a prospective invasion — and he said absolutely nothing about this in public. The silence was probably intended to avoid an anti-Catholic backlash, which would have intensified ethno-religious divisions and produced an atmosphere in which Orangeism and Fenianism would have fed off one another. But it is also likely that Macdonald factored electoral considerations into the equation; he had worked long and hard to cultivate the Irish-Catholic vote and did not want to jeopardize that support with general pronouncements about a Canadian Fenian conspiracy. If this is the case, then the fear of an Irish-Catholic backlash against the Conservatives was also part of the picture.

As it turned out, the suspension of *Habeas Corpus* was used against real or suspected domestic Fenians, after the assassination of McGee in April 1868. Initially, the arrests focused on the friends and acquaintances of the principal suspect, Patrick James Whelan. Increasingly, though, the net was widened to bring in men whom the secret police identified as Fenian leaders in Canada. By the end of May, some twenty-five people had been arrested — a relatively small number, which indicates the highly selective nature of the operation.[64] The targets included prominent Fenians in Montreal, Ottawa, Toronto, and Guelph; Boyle, editor of the *Irish Canadian*, was also imprisoned, which forced the paper to shut down. Those who were arrested on precautionary grounds were generally released fairly quickly, and when Irish-Catholic Conservatives pressed for the release of John Nolan, the secretary of the Hibernian Benevolent Society, Macdonald quickly acquiesced. George Brown, for one, was not impressed. Either the government had released a dangerous man for party political reasons, he wrote, or Nolan should never have been arrested in the first place.[65]

The longer the suspects remained in prison, the greater the risk became of alienating Irish Catholics and creating sympathy for the Fenian prisoners. In early May, Brown — hardly a disinterested observer — commented on a "vague and uneasy feeling in the minds of our Roman Catholic fellow-citizens."[66] By August, the recently released Boyle reopened the *Irish Canadian*, and came out spitting rage against "Orange ascendancy and Tory bigotry and fanaticism."[67] A leading Montreal Fenian who had avoided the roundup looked forward to revenge when the next invasion began. "To be sure," he admitted, "very few have been arrested; but those arrests, being wanton, and the foul and voluminous abuse of our people are regarded as insults, and have created a positive distrust in the Government."[68]

The arrests angered Fenian sympathizers, spread fear among many Irish Catholics, and ran into increasing opposition from Canadian Liberals. But the Catholic Church and conservative Irish Catholics continued to support the government's policy. Macdonald's strategy succeeded in politically isolating the Fenians. Politicians such as Bernard Devlin in Montreal, who had drawn on Fenian support, now pulled back sharply from the movement.[69] The strategy also succeeded in its aim of disrupting the Fenian organization, at least in the short run. By November, James O'Reilly, the Queen's Counsel who oversaw the arrests, was confident enough to declare victory. As the last men were released, he told Macdonald that "Fenianism is dead in the United States, and the prompt action of our Government in making arrests last Spring has effectually stamped it out in this Country. It's now perfectly harmless and no longer to be feared."[70]

This was not in fact the case. The Senate wing Fenians in Canada had another eighteen months of life in them, and it was not the suspension of *Habeas Corpus* but the failure of the 1870 raid that finished them off. Henceforth, Fenians in the country would focus their attention on Ireland rather than Canada.

When that happened, Macdonald shifted his stance with remarkable rapidity. In July 1871, a Conservative supporter and former newspaper editor, Michael Hayes, suggested to Macdonald that he buy the *Irish Canadian* and turn it into "a Catholic constitutional paper, and the organ of the Hierarchy." Macdonald disagreed, on the grounds that Boyle would simply start up another newspaper. No, said Macdonald; it made much more sense to buy Boyle himself, and persuade him to move the *Irish Canadian* by degrees to the Conservative Party. "The paper might be as factious as it pleased about Irish home politics, or even as to New York movements, for all I would care," he wrote. "As long as it pursued that course it would keep up its present subscription list & influence." And it could easily move toward the Conservatives "upon the ground that it sees that justice is at last being done to Irishmen &c &c."[71]

Four years earlier, one of McMicken's detectives had reported that Boyle was selling Fenian bonds in Toronto.[72] Three years earlier, Boyle had been arrested under the *Habeas Corpus Suspension Act* for being part of a movement that had "the purpose of making hostile incursions into Canada," and for being in contact with Fenian emissaries who were planning the next invasion.[73] Now that the Fenians were no longer a domestic threat, none of that mattered — or mattered only insofar as Boyle had the capacity and willingness to bring radical Irish nationalists into the Conservative camp. The strategy worked, at least as far as Boyle was concerned. The Conservatives did indeed wind up financing the *Irish Canadian*, and Boyle did indeed move the paper to the right. Nothing could be a clearer indication of the mixture of pragmatism, prudence, and political calculation with which Macdonald approached Fenianism in Canada. After initial vicissitudes and intermittent setbacks, the secret police had ultimately succeeded in penetrating the upper echelons of the Fenian Brotherhood in New York, and in keeping tabs on Fenians in Canada. The *Habeas Corpus Suspension Act*, along with the assassination of McGee, had prevented the emergence of a Liberal-Fenian alliance, and had temporarily thrown the movement into disarray. Once the movement had been comprehensively defeated in the invasion attempt of 1870, Macdonald moved to co-opt its leaders. He was not called the Machiavelli of Kingston for nothing.

Notes

1. Donald Creighton, *The Road to Confederation: The Emergence of Canada,*

1863–1867 (Toronto: Macmillan, 1996), 304.

2. C.P. Stacey, "John O'Neill." In *Dictionary of Canadian Biography, www. biographi.ca/en/bio/o_neill_john_10E.html*.

3. Richard Gwyn, *John A.: The Man Who Made Us, Vol. 1, 1815–1867* (Toronto: Random House Canada, 2007), 380.

4. Macdonald to Monck, September 18, 1865, vol. 511, 221–22, John A. Macdonald Fonds, MG26-A, Library and Archives Canada [henceforth LAC.]

5. The discussion of the Fenians that follows is drawn from my *Thomas D'Arcy McGee Volume 2: The Extreme Moderate, 1857–1868* (Montreal and Kingston: McGill, Queen's University Press, 2011), 221–24, 247–49, 268–70, 276.

6. *Shamrock*, September 26, 1812; see also September 19, 1812, November 28, 1812, December 19, 1812, and John Caldwell, "Particulars of a North County Irish Family," T3541/5/3, 5, 154, Public Record Office of Northern Ireland.

7. Hereward Senior, *The Fenians and Canada* (Toronto: Macmillan, 1978), 27–31; Brendan Ó Cathaoir, ed., *Young Irelander Abroad: The Diary of Charles Hart* (Cork, Ireland: Cork University Press, 2003), 36.

8. *New York Daily Tribune*, August 25, 1848.

9. *Nation* [New York], March 31, 1849, May 5,1849; Report of informant "EF," June 3, 1848, MS 2038, f. 36; Report of informant "CD," April 15,1848, MS 2040, f. 22, Trinity College Dublin.

10. Quoted in William D'Arcy, *The Fenian Movement in the United States, 1858–1886*, 1947; rpt. (New York, US: Russell and Russell, 1971), 84.

11. O'Mahony to Mitchel, November 10, 1865, quoted in D'Arcy, ibid., 84.

12. The best account of this is Peter Vronsky, *Ridgeway: The American Fenian Invasion and the 1866 Battle That Made Canada* (Toronto: Allen Lane Canada, 2011).

13. *Nation* (Dublin), June 9, 1866.

14. The *Fenian Brotherhood Circular of the Corresponding Society for the Period Commencing 10th Sept. and Ending 28th October 1865* (New York: 1865) shows that $365.10 was raised in Montreal, and $500 in Toronto. Assuming the usual subscription rate of one dollar a month, and allowing for non-payments, the combined figure of one thousand seems like a reasonable estimate.

15. David A. Wilson, "The Fenians in Montreal, 1862–68: Invasion, Intrigue, and Assassination," *Éire-Ireland* 48: 3, 4 (Fall/Winter 2003), 109–33.

16. Fenian Briefs, 1865–69, Carton 5, Envelope 18, Business Papers, "List of the Irish People, up to July 14th," National Archives of Ireland.

17. A point also made by Peter Toner, "'The Green Ghost': Canada's Fenians and the Raids," *Éire-Ireland* 16: 4 (Fall 1981), 46.

18. Wilson, "Fenianism in Montreal," 124–25.

19. Receipt, November 16, 1865, Thomas Sweeney [sic] Papers, New York Public Library; Vronsky, *Ridgeway*, 29, 67.

20. Macdonald to J. Brown, January 2, 1866 [misdated 1865], Macdonald

Fonds, vol. 510, 172, LAC.

21. On the secret police force, see Jeff Keshen, "Cloak and Dagger: Canada West's Secret Police, 1864–1867," *Ontario History* 79: 4 (December 1987), 353–81, and Gregory S. Kealey, "The Empire Strikes Back: The Nineteenth-Century Origins of the Canadian Secret Service," *Journal of the Canadian Historical Association* 10, 3–18, 1999.

22. McMicken to Macdonald, November 3, 1865, Macdonald Fonds, vol. 236, 102943.

23. Macdonald to McMicken, October 12, 1865, ibid., 102889-91.

24. McMicken to Macdonald, September 4, 1865, ibid., 102782-4; McMicken to Macdonald, December 5, 1865, ibid., 103034-7; McMicken to Macdonald, December 8, 1865, ibid., 103046; McMicken to Macdonald, December 15, 1865, ibid., 103066; McMicken to Macdonald, February 1, 1866, Macdonald to Fonds, vol. 237, 103217.

25. McMicken to Macdonald, Windsor, March 5, 1866, Macdonald Fonds, vol. 237, 103296–9.

26. Ermatinger to Macdonald, March 3,1866, ibid., 103278.

27. Tupper to McMcMicken, March 4, 1866, ibid., 103286-7.

28. McMicken to Macdonald, October 2, 1865, Macdonald Fonds, vol. 236, 102868-69.

29. McMicken to Macdonald, November 3,1865, Macdonald Fonds, vol. 236, 102949-51.

30. W.S. Neidhardt, *Fenianism in North America* (University Park: Pennsylvania State University Press, 1975), 37–38.

31. Nolan to McMicken, December 31, 1865, Macdonald Fonds, vol. 236, 103110-13.

32. McGee to Lynch, March 7 and 14, 1866, Bishop Lynch Papers, LAF 0308, 0309, Archdiosesan Roman Catholics Archives of Toronto; "Circular to the Clergy of the Diocese of Toronto," March 9, 1866, Lynch Papers, L AE 0212; Lynch, "To the Reverend Clergy of the City of Toronto," March 15, 1866, newspaper clipping, Lynch Papers, L AE 0615.

33. McMicken to Macdonald, March 18, 1866, Macdonald Fonds, vol. 237, 103398-403.

34. McMicken to Macdonald, May 5, 1866, ibid., 103651-2.

35. McMicken to Macdonald, May 17, 1866, ibid., 103745-7.

36. Clarke to McMicken, May 11,1866, ibid., 103703.

37. McMicken to Macdonald, May 17, 1866, ibid., 103745-7; Hemans to McMicken, May 19, 1866, ibid., 103761-3.

38. McLaughlin to McMicken, May 29, 1866, ibid., 103819-20

39. Macdonald to McMicken, May 31, 1866, ibid., 103854.

40. McMicken to Macdonald, June 10, 1866, ibid., 104063-8; McMicken to

Macdonald, July 11, 1866, Macdonald Fonds, vol. 58, 23259.

41. Clarke to McMicken, June 5, 1866, Macdonald Fonds, vol. 237, 103939-42.

42. McMicken to Macdonald, July 11, 1866, Macdonald Fonds, vol. 58, 23258-9.

43. As explained in Vronsky, *Ridgeway*, 119–63.

44. Ibid., 226, 244, 254.

45. Clarke to McMicken, June 8,1867, Macdonald Fonds, vol. 239, 106025-8; Clarke to McMicken, June 8,1867, ibid., 106021-4; Clarke to McMicken, June 8, 1867, Macdonald Fonds, ibid., 106014-20; Clarke to McMicken, June 10, 1867, ibid., 106032-3.

46. *Irish American*, June 15, 1876.

47. McMicken to Macdonald, September 11, 1867, Macdonald Fonds, vol. 239, 106201-4.

48. Edwards to Stanley, June 13, 1867, Fenian A Files, A279, National Archives of Ireland.

49. Clarke to McMicken, June 8, 1867, Macdonald Fonds, vol. 239, 106014-20.

50. Bruce to Stanley, January 7, 1867, Fenian A Files, A250, National Archives of Ireland.

51. McMicken to Macdonald, June 8,1868, Macdonald Fonds, vol. 241, 107057-9.

52. Macdonald to McMicken, June 15, 1868, Macdonald Fonds, vol. 514/3, 883-4.

53. Coursol to Macdonald, April 1, 1870, Macdonald Fonds, vol. 244a, 109571-8.

54. McMicken to Macdonald, April 26,1870, ibid., 109771-4; McMicken to Bernard, May 23, 1870, Macdonald Fonds, vol. 245, 109883-6.

55. McMicken to Macdonald, July 6, 1870, ibid., 110167-70.

56. Crown Law Department of Upper Canada Circular, RG 13-A2, vol. 15, file 667, LAC; *Canadian Freeman*, September 20, 1866.

57. Canada House of Commons, *Debates*, 1867–68 (Ottawa: Queen's Printer, 1967), November 29, 1867, 158.

58. McMicken to Macdonald, September 25, 1867, Macdonald Fonds, vol. 239, 106226; Macdonald to McMicken, September 28, 1867, Macdonald Fonds, vol. 514, 16.

59. Archibald to Stanley, October 1, 1867, Fenian A Files, A291, National Archives of Ireland; Gilbert McMicken to Macdonald, October 3, 1867, Macdonald Fonds, vol. 239, 106237; McMicken to Macdonald, October 21, 1867, ibid., 106262-3.

60. McMicken to Macdonald, October 29, 1867, ibid., 106269-70; McMicken to Macdonald, October 1867, ibid., 106275; McMicken to Macdonald, November 9, 1867, ibid., ff. 106288-91.

61. Macdonald to McMicken, November 5, 1867, Macdonald Fonds, vol. 239, 106280-82.

62. Canada House of Commons, *Debates*, 1867–68 (Ottawa: Queen's Printer, 1967), November 29, 1867, 158.

63. Ibid.

64. David A. Wilson, "The D'Arcy McGee Affair and the Suspension of Habeas Corpus," in Barry Wright and Susan Binnie, eds., *Canadian State Trials Volume III: Political Trials and Security Measures, 1840–1914* (Toronto: Osgoode Society for Canadian Legal History and University of Toronto Press, 2009), 85–120.

65. *Globe*, July 23, 1868.

66. *Globe*, May 8, 1868.

67. *Irish Canadian*, August 5, 1868.

68. *Irish Canadian*, August 13, 1868.

69. *Montreal Herald*, September 1, 2, 3, 5, 9, 1868.

70. O'Reilly to Macdonald, November 18, 1868, "Papers re. parties charged with Fenianism in Ottawa," RG13A-2, vol. 20, folder 510, LAC.

71. Macdonald to Smith, July 17, 1871, Macdonald Fonds, vol. 519/1, 40-41.

72. Clarke to McMicken, May 10,1867, Macdonald Fonds, vol. 239, 105922-6.

73. Warrants of Commitment, LAC, RG13A-2. vol. 20, file 584, LAC.

Chapter 4

"The Aryan Character of the Future of British North America"[1]: Macdonald, Chinese Exclusion, and the Invention of Canadian White Supremacy

Timothy J. Stanley

In 1885, while debating the *Electoral Franchise Act,* John Alexander Macdonald called upon the Canadian House of Commons to take the right to vote away from people of Chinese origins living in Canada. He justified disenfranchisement on the grounds that the Chinese were not only "aliens" who did not belong in Canada, but that they were also a different species from people of European origins. He warned that, unless those racialized as Chinese were excluded from Canada, "We would have a mongrel race ... [and] the Aryan character of the future of British America should be destroyed ..."[2]

Macdonald's antipathy toward the Chinese is often explained on the grounds that he was expressing the common, if far from universal, prejudices of his age.[3] Particularly in British Columbia, anti-Chinese views were widespread and strongly expressed, and Macdonald was dependent on the support of British Columbia members of Parliament, many of whom had been elected on anti-Chinese platforms.[4]

The idea that Macdonald was merely expressing the prejudices of his age underplays the significance of this particular moment in Canadian history. The 1885 *Electoral Franchise Act* was not only a key act of Canadian state formation in general — defining who made up the federal polity — but it was also a key moment in racist state formation.[5] The act was passed in the era in which a global realignment of nation, "race," and ethnicity was taking place. Macdonald's comments came as racial discourse in the European world was shifting from earlier notions of essentialized differences around culture to ones based on supposed biological concepts. This perspective interpreted differences between human beings as evidence that "races" naturally occur, either as sub-species of *homo sapiens* or as completely separate species within the genus *homo*.[6] Such notions were used to justify European superiority as the European powers were completing their division of the world in the scramble for Africa.[7] At the same time, the local Canadian variation of the British imperial project was nearing completion — in the form of westward expansion and the military occupation of the prairies. Macdonald's comments about the Chinese came as his government was suppressing the North-West Rebellion, even as the Canadian volunteers and British forces were marching on Batoche and "pacifying" the Plains Cree.[8] The Canadian Pacific Railway was also nearing completion and with it the link between Eastern Canada and British Columbia.[9]

It was in this context that Macdonald injected "scientific" racism, i.e., racism based on alleged biological differences, into the Canadian state at the federal level. He was not just expressing popular views, but was rather organizing "race" as a political principle into the world. While racisms are often thought of as individual or even collective prejudices, and/or irrational beliefs, a significant body of literature has established that racisms are exclusions.[10] Racisms are not individualized forms of prejudice or discrimination, but are social systems, what the French philosopher Michel Foucault called a biopolitics of organizing the world and its peoples.[11] In his 1975 lectures at the Collège de France, Foucault argued that racism was not only built into the disciplinary processes and discourses that created the modern state, but that its incorporation into the state was the whole point of the development of these disciplinary processes in the first place.[12] Perhaps less controversially, the American philosopher Judith Lichtenberg argues that, in the United States, those who are privileged by racisms tend to see them as being part of people's beliefs and attitudes. Since they themselves may not share these beliefs or attitudes, they distance themselves from particular racisms. She calls this position "racism in the head." By contrast, she notes that people who are oppressed by racisms, such as African Americans, experience it in everyday life. They tend to see racism as what she calls "racism in the world."[13] Seen in this light, if Macdonald's racism was originally in his head, he organized it into the world through the *Electoral Franchise Act*.

The extensive literature on racisms emphasizes that racial categories are not fixed, but are highly fluid depending on context. Particularly in the case of racialized representations of people of Chinese origins, historians need to be careful of reading their sources as describing an objectively exist-

THE WORKINGMAN'S DELICATE POSITION.

ing external reality, and instead should read them as making knowledge of and fixing dynamic categories.[14] As Peter Ward noted many years ago, anti-Chinese discourse was more a construct of popular Anglo-European imagination than it was descriptive of actual people of Chinese origins.[15] In this respect, Macdonald's comments were not so much about real people of Chinese origins themselves as they were asserting knowledge about what they were alleged to be.

The 1885 *Electoral Franchise Act* created a federal voting system separate from that of the provinces. The legislation gave the vote to those who were British subjects and who met a property qualification, either in the form of direct ownership or rental of property of certain values as identified in the legislation. When introduced into the House of Commons in March 1885, it proposed that the vote would be given to all of those who met the property qualification, including women and First Nations people. However, as it became evident that neither of these measures would have the support of the majority of the House, Macdonald dropped the provisions on women and amended the legislation so that only First Nations men who met the property qualification and who lived east of the Manitoba border would have the vote.[16] Despite having to retreat from some of his earlier commitments, Macdonald would later call the *Electoral Franchise Act* "the greatest triumph of my life."[17] The legislation created a separate federal electoral list that was controlled by electoral officers — all appointed by Macdonald himself. The result was not only an electoral system that he thought would ensure Tory rule indefinitely, he saw it as the culmination of his life-long efforts at achieving power through the judicious application of patronage.[18]

Macdonald initially proposed to disenfranchise the Chinese by amending the clause defining a "person" as "a male person including an Indian" with the addition of the phrase "and excluding a Chinaman." When challenged by the Liberal opposition, he presented arguments in favour of exclusion on cultural grounds. "The Chinese are foreigners," he said. "[W]e know that when the Chinaman comes here he intends to return to his own country; he does not bring his family with him; he is a stranger, a sojourner in a strange land, for his own purposes for a while; he has no common interest with us." For Macdonald, the Chinese worker was like "a threshing machine or any other agricultural implement which we may borrow from the United States on hire and return it to its owner on the south side of the line." He concluded that "the Chinese has no British instincts or British feelings or aspirations and therefore ought not to have a vote."[19]

Arguments calling for anti-Chinese measures on the grounds of their alleged cultural practices were familiar to members of the House of Commons. British Columbia members had been calling for Chinese exclusion since March 1878, when Arthur Bunster, a Liberal MP from British Columbia, introduced a motion barring any man "wearing his hair longer than five and one half inches" from working on the transcontinental railway.[20] As he well knew, the measure applied to workers from China who had to wear their hair in long braided queues as a sign of their subjugation to the ruling Manchus. Bunster called for the measure on the grounds that "Canadians should take measures to protect themselves against the introduction of a population so detestable, and prevent their manhood from degenerating through the use of the opium drug ... and other evils ... which had been introduced by these people, and which gave cause for serious reflection to every father of a family as to the difficulties of guarding against them." According to Bunster, it was the duty of the government to take steps that would "maintain our own race in its vigor and manhood."[21] In 1879, another British Columbia MP, Amor de Cosmos, elaborated at length on Bunster's claims that the Chinese did not come as permanent settlers, but only as temporary residents, that they did not bring their families with them, that they practiced immorality such as smoking opium, staunchly refused the efforts of Christian missionaries, and, perhaps most importantly, that they unfairly competed against racialized white workers.[22] Once railway construction began and there was a significant migration of Cantonese workers to British Columbia, exclusionists repeatedly claimed that the province was being overrun by the Chinese.[23] In 1882, de Cosmos claimed that 24,000 Chinese were expected to arrive in the coming months, which would make for 32,000 Chinese in the province, who would then outnumber "whites."[24] In the 1885 debate, Noah Shakespeare argued that Chinese enfranchisement was dangerous because Chinese merchants controlled the votes of Chinese workers.[25]

Although these comments contrasted "Chinese" to "whites" and were racializing, they did not express difference in the kind of racial terms familiar today. For example, de Cosmos' 1879 diatribe against the Chinese was approximately seven thousand words in length, but all that he said on the subject of "race" was, "There was the difference of race. The Chinese were a race who did not assimilate with the white race."[26] Even here, this comment was descriptive rather than a statement of the innate character of the Chinese. It claimed as a matter of fact, rather than of essence, that the Chinese did not assimilate. This did not mean that these calls for exclusion were not racist, but they were a different kind of racism from the more familiar racisms of the twentieth century built on fixed "socially imagined" differences.[27] In effect, the exclusionists did not argue that the Chinese were inferior to people of European origins, just so different culturally as to be incompatible. This position in the late twentieth century came to be called "the new racism," although as the exclusionists' comments show, it is in fact an old racism.[28] The absence of "race" from calls for Chinese exclusion is not surprising given the fluidity of racial concepts in the English-speaking cultural world before the late nineteenth century.

"Race" is a social and political category, rather than an objective "scientific" one. While to be sure there are populations that have different skin colours and varying genetic distributions, how and whether these translate into popular "race" categories is highly contextual. Despite their apparent permanence, contemporary common sense notions of "race" cannot necessarily be transposed to other contexts.[29] As such, statements alleging "race" difference do not so much describe objectively existing differences as pick out specific differences and fix them as socially and politically important.[30] As with other forms of difference, when it comes to racializing difference, power seeks to fix meanings that are otherwise fluid.[31] During the 1870s and 1880s, what twentieth-century scholars referred to as "race-thinking" was still emerging.[32] In Britain, the United States, and elsewhere in Europe the idea that there was such a thing as what the historian Edward Beasley called "separate, physically distinct and physically inheritable races, with different mental and moral characteristics" was only gradually gaining acceptance as the century progressed.[33] Although, by the mid nineteenth century, western Europeans commonly accepted French naturalist Georges Cuvier's division of human beings into at least three "races": Caucasian, Negroid, and Mongolian. English-speaking people in Canada and the United States also commonly saw people as belonging to different groups such as "whites," "coloured," and "Chinese"; there was little consensus as to what these differences signified. Indeed in mid-nineteenth-century England, "race" referred as much to family or clan-sized groups or even to social types, such as in "the race of London cabdrivers," as it did to anything else.[34] It is in this sense of "race" as "type" that Bunster and de Cosmos were using the term prior to 1885.[35] Thus, there were "Chinamen" just as there were "Englishmen," "Frenchmen," and "Scotchmen." However, by the 1870s in England, attitudes toward "race" understood as skin colour differences were hardening as they had earlier in the United States.[36] In English-Canadian discourse, "race" would continue to be used to refer to ethnic or national groups well into the twentieth century.[37]

Macdonald's amendment introduced Chinese exclusion in similar terms to that which had already been effected in British Columbia, where multiple pieces of legislation discriminated against "Chinamen" and "Indians" without appealing to biology. For example, the 1875 *Qualification and Registration of Voters Act* stated, "No Chinaman or Indian shall have his name placed on the Register of Voters for any Electoral District, or be entitled to vote at any election of a Member to serve in the Legislative Assembly of the Province."[38]

As Macdonald quickly found out, the trouble with cultural arguments about Chinese and Anglo-European difference is that people can and do change their cultural practices. Peter Mitchell, sitting as an independent MP from New Brunswick, an architect of Confederation in his own right, a member of Macdonald's first federal cabinet and, by 1885, one of Macdonald's implacable enemies,[39] countered the latter's views with the argument that even those as culturally different as the Chinese could still become good Canadians: "Every person who comes and lives in this country, and labors and spends his money in the country, even if he is a foreigner — a Chinaman, if you like, the most disliked class of foreigners — if he comes to make Canada his home, we ought to make Canada free enough to include even the Chinaman." He further noted that a number of Chinese in Montreal "are spoken of as a respectable body of men — good, peace-loving citizens" and added, "So long as they comply with the naturalization laws and they become British subjects, and I would give them the vote."[40]

Mitchell's comments led George Eliott Casey, a member of the Liberal opposition to ask whether naturalized "Chinamen" ceased to be "Chinamen" and instead became British subjects.[41] In response, Macdonald changed the amendment to exclude "a person of Mongolian or Chinese race."

Several MPs echoed Mitchell's views. Matthew Hamilton Gault, the Conservative member for Montreal West, suggested that the Chinese "are industrious people" who had "voted in the last election." Louis Henry Davies, one of the members for Prince Edward Island, suggested that a Chinese who had been naturalized had "as good a right [to] be allowed to vote as any other British subject of foreign extraction." Arthur Hill Gillmor, a Liberal member from New Brunswick, told the House, "I do not think that they are a desirable class of persons, but I think that, as British subjects in British colonies, we ought to show them fair play."[42] Gillmor was particularly impassioned in using evidence collected by the Royal Commission on Chinese Immigration to debunk the cultural arguments of the exclusionists. For example, he showed the amount of money that racialized Chinese workers could send out of the country was far outweighed by the amount of money brought into the country by merchants from China.[43]

Faced with such attacks, Macdonald shifted his justification from one involving the supposed cultural practices of those he called Chinese to one fixed by nature, i.e., on the basis of their alleged biology. He told the House that if the Chinese were not excluded, "if they came in great numbers and settled on the Pacific coast they might control the vote of that whole Province, and they would send Chinese representatives to sit here, who would represent Chinese eccentricities, Chinese immorality, Asiatic principles altogether opposite to our wishes; and, in the even balance of parties, they might enforce those Asiatic principles, those immoralities ... the eccentricities which are abhorrent to the Aryan race and Aryan principles, on this House."[44] He further claimed, "The Aryan races will not wholesomely amalgamate with the Africans or the Asiatics." and that "the cross of those races, like the cross of the dog and the fox, is not successful; it cannot be, and never will be." He then warned that "the Aryan character of the future of British North America" was at risk.[45]

At least three issues arise from these comments. First, in claiming that the Chinese and Africans were separate species from Europeans, Macdonald was showing himself to be familiar with nineteenth-century "race" science.[46] This is confirmed by his exchange with David Mills, a member of the Liberal opposition,[47] immediately following his comments. According to Mills, "The hon.

Gentlemen does not seem satisfied with the number and important questions that are involved in the Bill, but he proposes to introduce the very large and complicated question of miscegenation." He noted that Macdonald's comments were "not exactly in accord with Pritchard [*sic*] and Latham, though they may be in accord with the views of Morton, Gliddon and Agassiz."[48] Mills was citing prominent nineteenth-century racial theorists, in effect suggesting that Macdonald was putting forward the most extreme and radical of these views. In the pre-Darwinian European mindset of the early and mid nineteenth centuries, scholars debating the origins of racialized difference effectively fell into two schools of thought. The monogenesis school held that all human beings came out of a common origin, while the polygenesis school argued that different racial groups were the products of separate creations. The former affirmed humanity as a single species, where the latter saw it as a common genus, divided into different species. James Crowley Prichard was one of the most prominent English advocates of monogenesis, while his disciple Robert Latham even questioned the value of "race" as a classification applied to human beings. Samuel G. Morton, George Robbins Glidden, and Louis Agassiz were American scholars and among the most extreme advocates of polygenesis.[49] Macdonald did not deny these associations, although he did deny Mills' suggestion that he intended to disenfranchise African Canadians as well.[50] Macdonald was almost certainly familiar with these theories. Indeed when he changed his amendment to make "race" the basis for exclusion, a member of the House pointed out, "Many maintain that the Indians of British Columbia are of the Mongolian race." Macdonald replied, "That is an ethnological question that I will leave the hon. gentleman to settle with Henry Bancroft."[51] This was almost certainly a reference to Hubert Howe Bancroft, the American historian who had published a five-volume history on "the Native races" two years earlier.[52]

Second, Macdonald is not merely expressing anti-Chinese sentiments, he is also expressing a view of the kind of country Canada should be and of the kind of people Canadians should be. If he was racializing the Chinese, he was also racializing Canadians. His deployment of "Aryan" references arises from familiarity with the theories of Joseph Arthur Comte de Gobineau, which gained popularity in Europe during the early 1880s. Gobineau was a minor French diplomat and literary figure whose 1851, four-volume *Essai sur l'inégalité des races humaines* became increasingly influential in late-nineteenth-century race thinking. "Aryan" originally was a linguistic term referring to the speakers of the primal Indo-European language. Gobineau developed the concept into an explanation for global history. In his view, the Aryans were a racially pure group of the "white race," who had founded all major world civilizations, but who, over time, had became corrupted by lesser races. His views also contributed to changing European attitudes toward the Chinese, who had previously been seen as the most advanced people. In Gobineau's terms, Chinese civilization had become corrupted and corrupting due to its focus entirely on material comfort.[53] Thus, the vision that Macdonald was putting forward is one based on a hierarchy of races in which inferior races corrupted superior ones unless miscegenation was prevented. To found a worthwhile civilization, the Canadian population needed to be racially pure with the most highly developed of Europeans — not contaminated by lesser "races" like the Chinese. In effect, he was suggesting that racialized Chinese were inescapably incompatible with people and things Canadian. While such discourse may not have been entirely new in Canada, Macdonald is the only member of the House of Commons and the Senate during this era to refer to Canada as an "Aryan" country.[54]

The third element in his comments that urges attention is the fact that he clearly pointed out that the problem with the Chinese was not just their biology, or their threat to the national gene pool, but their numbers. The fear he expressed was that they were a sufficient number to control the vote in British Columbia and then impose their corrupting values "on the House." Notwithstanding Macdonald's comments about Chinese workers, since his legislation took for granted that property owners or relatively well-to-do renters would be the voters, Chinese disenfranchisement was not about limiting the number of Chinese workers entering the country. Rather, it was about limiting the power of Chinese merchants who were among the largest property-owners in British Columbia.[55] This concern about Chinese property owners also explains why Macdonald did not extend disenfranchisement to either Africans or First Nations people. As noted, he explicitly denied his intention to disenfranchise the former, even though they too were allegedly a separate species from Europeans.[56] At the same time, except in parts of southern Ontario and Nova Scotia, African populations were not large enough to have a significant effect on the vote.

First Nations, however, were a different story. They had significant numbers and in Western Canada were the majority of the population. Yet, Macdonald was in favour of giving the vote to First Nations and disenfranchising the Chinese. Members of the opposition jumped on this seeming contradiction. Peter Mitchell, for example, noted, "I am in favour of Chinamen being placed on an equal footing with all other persons. Certainly a Chinaman is quite as good as an Indian," to which Macdonald replied, "I cannot agree with my hon. friend at all. Indians are sons of the soil; they are Canadians and British subjects; and therefore, if they have the property qualification, I think they ought to be treated as other British subjects."[57] Macdonald's comments highlight that First Nations were in a different position from Chinese people in relation to Canadian state formation. First Nations were unlikely to disappear, and the whole point of government policy was to coerce them into signing treaties and then assimilate them into the European population. Indeed the purpose of the 1876 *Indian Act* consolidation was to lead First Nations from a state of alleged barbarism to civilization through enfranchisement, the process in which men gave up Indians status and received part of band property as private property.[58] The *Electoral Franchise Act* was at least in part intended to encourage this by not requiring that enfranchised "Indians" give up other benefits associated with band membership.[59] As Macdonald's exchange with Mitchell shows, he originally proposed to extend the vote to all First Nations men who met the property qualification, whether or not they were enfranchised under the *Indian Act*. This drew incredulous responses from members such as David Mills, who accused him of wanting to give the vote to Poundmaker and Big Bear, the leaders of the Plains Cree supposedly in rebellion against the government. Macdonald agreed to this accusation, provided — as always — that they met the property qualification. This led Mills to interject, "So that they can go from a scalping party to the polls," and to try to amend the bill to give the vote only to those who had been enfranchised under the *Indian Act*.[60] As noted earlier, Macdonald eventually compromised by extending the vote to "Indians" east of Manitoba only. In practice, few First Nations people could meet the property qualification, and as such did not constitute a threat to European dominance. Macdonald knew personally some individuals who did meet the property qualification, such as the descendants of the Mohawk Chief

Joseph Brant who lived near his Kingston riding, and he likely was hoping that they would vote for him.[61]

However, the idea that "Indians" could become "Canadians" like their European counterparts while "Chinese" could not illustrates the difference between the existing racism and the new form that Macdonald was introducing in the case of the Chinese. For Macdonald and many of his contemporaries, First Nations were excluded because of their alleged cultural practices; however, as they adopted the dominant Anglo-European culture they could be assimilated into the dominant population. Thus, while colonialism was based on the exclusion of First Nations, Inuit, and Métis people from their traditional territories and ways of being, its cultural racism meant that individuals could, at least in theory, become part of the dominant group if they assimilated to the latter's cultural standards. Macdonald, however, was typecasting people of Chinese origins as being biologically incapable of becoming part of this dominant group. Fixing Chineseness as a racialized category in relation to Canadianness also racialized the latter. Eventually this would undo the culturalist racism toward First Nations in favour of a biological one that treated all First Nations people alike. Starting with the Liberals' 1898 electoral reform that took the vote away from all First Nations people, this continued in the twentieth century in such policies as those governing education that did not differentiate between the different educational needs of communities and individuals.

That Macdonald's disenfranchisement of the Chinese was about the political project of ensuring the dominance of property owners of European origins is supported by the comments of Secretary of State and former Quebec Premier Joseph Adolphe Chapleau. As one of the two commissioners of the 1884–5 Royal Commission on Chinese Immigration, Chapleau was the leading expert in Ottawa on the Chinese. Indeed much of the commission report had been devoted to debunking common anti-Chinese prejudices, finding that the greatest issue for public policy was not the actual difference of the Chinese, but the hostility they excited from racialized white workers.[62] Consequently Macdonald's appeal to biological essentialism appears to have caught Chapleau by surprise. Speaking shortly after Macdonald, Chapleau began his remarks by saying that he was in substantial agreement with Gillmor, who had extensively cited the report. However, he then used his superior knowledge of things Chinese to claim that the Qing consul general in San Francisco had told him that the Chinese did not want the vote and that giving them the vote might complicate the country's international relations.[63] In the end, exclusion was needed, he suggested, "not because they are the dirty, unintelligent, criminal class that they are so often represented to be, I do not believe that; I believe that Chinese immigration is a danger to any new country like our own, not because they are a degraded race, but because their immigration might become dangerously large." The Chinese, he said, were "the superiors, of all other races, in the competition for labor" since they "exercise extreme frugality, and their way of living is one not adapted to our view of civilisation." He further suggested that whatever one's views on the character of the Chinese themselves, there was a strong consensus "that at the present moment, it would be a threat to the particular civilization of America and to our institutions if we allowed that immigration to assume greater proportions at present."[64]

In introducing the *Chinese Immigration Act*, the very next piece of legislation the House debated, Chapleau tied Chinese exclusion to European resettler colonialism:

> It is a natural and well-founded desire of British subjects, of the white population of this Dominion, who come from either Britain or the other European States and settle in this country, that their country should be spoken of abroad as being inhabited by a vigorous, energetic, white race of people; I say it would be much more pleasant to have this said of the Province of British Columbia, than to have that Province even if it grew richer than it is, with two-thirds of its population composed of a race which is not similar to ours, and which cannot assimilate with ours.[65]

He even claimed that John Sebastian Helmcken (one of the major figures of the British Columbia establishment: an old Hudson's Bay Company doctor, speaker of the first colonial assembly of the Colony of Vancouver Island, and a member of the British Columbia delegation that had negotiated the Terms of Union[66]) had told him that the Chinese needed to be kept out of British Columbia, "because we want to be here ourselves, and do not want others to be here. You will not consider it strange if we tell you that as good Englishmen we see no reasons why any men except good Englishmen should live in this country."[67]

The radical nature of Macdonald's Aryan vision and his fixing of "Canadian" and "Chinese" as racial categories sharply contrast with the views of the previous head of government, Alexander Mackenzie. When Bunster first proposed Chinese exclusion in 1878, Alexander Mackenzie mobilized what the political scientist Christopher G. Anderson later would call "liberal internationalism" to reject Bunster's claims about the Chinese.[68] Mackenzie attacked Bunster's resolution as "unprecedented in its character and altogether unprecedented in its spirit, and at variance with those tolerant laws that afforded employment and an asylum to all who came into our country, regardless of color, hair or anything else." He claimed that legislating "against any class of people" entering the country was not seemly for "a British community." Finally, he noted that many Chinese immigrants were from Hong Kong and consequently, "as much British subjects as were the hon. members ... and, as such, were entitled to the rights and privileges of British subjects anywhere over the entire extent of the empire." Mackenzie even disputed Bunster's racializations, saying his characterization applied to only "some of the Chinese people." On the prime minister's urging, the House voted the resolution down.[69]

Mackenzie expressed even stronger views the following year when de Cosmos presented a motion to look into the Chinese presence in British Columbia. Sitting as Leader of the Opposition, Mackenzie asked Macdonald what he thought of the matter. Macdonald replied that he had no objection to forming a select committee as "[i]t was well that the whole subject should be carefully studied before the over-mastering Chinese population came upon us."[70] After several other members of the House from British Columbia expressed anti-Chinese views, Mackenzie stated: "To avow the principle that some classes of the human family were not fit to be residents of this Dominion would be dangerous and contrary to the law of nations and the policy which controlled Canada."[71]

While the 1885 reaction of the House of Commons to Macdonald's appeal to biological essentialism was muted, that of the Senate was much sharper. Even the friends of the premier, senators appointed by Macdonald himself, were vociferous in their opposition to any measure singling out people on the basis of their racial origin. Sir Charles de Boucherville, a Conservative, a former and future premier of Quebec,[72] objected to the clause excluding the Chinese and other Asians on the grounds that it excluded Christians. He tried unsuccessfully to amend the definition clause so that it did not apply to Christians.[73] Another Tory also appointed by Macdonald, Alexander Vidal from Ontario, stated, "I cannot see the propriety of excluding the Mongolians who have shown themselves to be patient, industrious and law-abiding, from privileges which are given to every other member of the human family in this country."[74] Another Macdonald appointee, an independent appointment from British Columbia, further demonstrated senators' uneasiness with exclusion.[75] Donald McInnes apparently either did not understand or did not accept Macdonald's scientific racism. He rather innocently asked Sir Alexander Campbell, minister of justice and government leader in the Senate, about the meaning of the exclusion clause: "Does it apply merely to a Chinaman fresh out of China, or does it apply to a half-breed, quarter breed or octoroon?"[76] When Campbell replied that there were no "half-breed Chinamen" to his knowledge, McInnes claimed that there were and was supported by Josiah Burr Plumb, another Macdonald appointee,[77] who insisted that there were mixed race people in Canada, but that they were children. This led Campbell to state that the exclusion would apply to "any person of Chinese blood." As a result McInnes wondered if the government couldn't further define the class as "[i]t is an undoubted fact that some Chinamen marry white women. They have families, and they bring up their children in a very respectable, intelligent way; and when such children attain the years of manhood, and have the necessary qualification, I think it would be a great hardship to deny them the franchise." He then cited the case of a resident of Peterborough, who was "a most respectable citizen," who had married a white woman, was "well connected," and whose children "were educated in the best schools of the province."[78] Even though McInnes made clear that for him culture trumped biology, and that what Macdonald called "crosses" between East Asians and Europeans were in fact successful, he stated that he would still support the bill.[79] In fact, on the final votes on the amendments, de Boucherville and Vidal voted against the government, while McInnes managed not to be present for the vote.[80]

Senators appointed by Mackenzie made even stronger interventions. In answer to the government's claims that exclusion was necessary to respond to the demands of British Columbia, Senator Robert Poore Haythorne, who helped negotiate Prince Edward Island's entry into Confederation and who was appointed to the Senate as a result,[81] argued that Chinese exclusion would not produce the desired outcomes but would actually damage BC: "refusing the franchise to the respectable Chinaman who fulfills all the duties of a good citizen; who supports his family respectably, educates his children, and pays his taxes, is committing an act which tends rather to injury of British Columbia than its advancement." He suggested that "to get respectable Chinese labor here, you ought to hold out every inducement to them to come; but if you tell the Chinaman that no matter how reputable he may be in British Columbia, he will have no vote at all, it will deter them from coming to the country."[82] Senator Lawrence Geoffrey Power, another Liberal,[83] also denounced the legislation, stating, "We have not heard any good reasons for excluding the Chinese." He commented, "I do not think the Parliament of Canada should make any distinction of race at all; that the Chinese, Negroes, Indians, and Whites should be on the same footing; that no distinction should be made in favor of one or against another race." He further pointed out that it made no sense to give the vote to "Indians" who did not "own property and cannot make a bargain" and to deny it to the Chinese even though they did own property and could make contracts.[84] Power unsuccessfully tried to amend the legislation by striking the exclusion clause completely.[85]

Senators expressed equally strong opposition to the *Chinese Immigration Act* and seemed even more willing to send it back. Although the opponents of the bill were not strong enough to defeat it outright, they almost succeeded in subjecting it to a three-month hoist, a procedural move that would have effectively killed the bill. However, an error on their part (the motion had not been presented in writing) resulted in the legislation coming to a vote.[86] Feeling was so strong against the legislation that the Senate voted down amendments to the *Chinese Immigration Act* in 1886 and 1887. Indeed, in 1887 the speaker had to rule that the Senate could not initiate a bill to abolish it completely, because (by imposing a head tax on Chinese immigration) it was a money matter and money bills could only originate in the Commons.[87]

Racism is commonly understood as a form of individual prejudice and discriminatory actions.[88] In this view of racism, Macdonald's actions in the franchise debate were a toxic mix of prejudice and power. This view of racism is often invoked to justify Macdonald's actions as reflecting the prejudices of his age. If he was racist against the Chinese, so was everyone else. This was in effect what he himself claimed. In 1887, he even admitted that his own views might be prejudiced, "On the whole, it is considered not advantageous to the country that the Chinese should come and settle in Canada, producing a mongrel race, and interfering very much with white labor in Canada. That may be right, or it may be wrong; it may be prejudice or otherwise; but the prejudice is near universal."[89] But as we have seen, far from sharing the prejudices of the age, he was alone in introducing a completely new discourse of scientific racism into the federal Parliament. Indeed, throughout all the debates on the franchise and Chinese immigration, Macdonald was the only member of Parliament to refer to the Aryan nature of Canada or to make claims about the biological incompatibility of East Asians and Anglo-Europeans. As we have also seen, a political project of keeping Chinese property-owners out of Canadian state formation was behind his racist discourse.

Recognizing that Macdonald was not merely expressing prejudicial views, but organizing the exclusion of particular groups into the world focuses attention of the consequences of racism. The exclusion of racialized Chinese people directly voiced and exactly articulated with the colonizing project of settlers from Old Canada and Europe. There was only one problem facing this project. As westward expansion was being completed, as a vast territory was being converted to the potential property of settler men and a new state system was creating its power over this territory, another group of would-be property owners was also entering the territory. In this respect both the *Electoral Franchise Act* and the *Chinese Immigration Act* were pieces of the same whole. The latter was designed to control and severely limit the migration of racialized Chinese workers and their families without killing the China trade that would help pay for the railway. The former ensured that racialized Chinese merchants and entrepreneurs, i.e. racialized Chinese men of property, those who otherwise met the requirements for the franchise and for immigration to Canada, were kept out of the state system and its operations. By positioning Chinese-European difference in biological terms, whether he believed these differences to be true or not, Macdonald knew that he was ensuring that Chinese could never become Canadian, no matter how much they adapted to their new environment.

Seen in this light, the exclusion of the Chinese was a vital element in a larger project of state formation. State formation is not a foregone conclusion, the automatic result of the visions of far-seeing men. It is as much the result of happenstance and of unintended consequence as it is of deliberate, intended outcomes. In successful states, the state system and its operations are legitimized through cultural as well as political projects.[90] Racial state formation is no different. It too is the combination of building state systems and developing broader justificatory projects. In this respect, the *Electoral Franchise Act* made biologically-defined "race" into one of the criteria for deciding who and what was Canadian, and began the re-articulation of other relationships. Although people of Chinese origins had been in the territory that became Canada since before its creation, and were arguably no more and no less "Canadian" than any other migrant communities, from 1885 onward they were to be permanent outsiders to the emergent nation state and their access to its territory severely restricted. Once their alienness was legally fixed, other exclusions, petty and not so petty, would follow while the consequences would be born by generations of people of Chinese origins. Although federal disenfranchisement would be overturned by the Liberals' reinstatement of a provincially based voting system in 1898, racialized Chinese people would not have an unfettered right to vote throughout the country until 1947. Meanwhile, every community of any size in Canada would be divided between those whose family members could emigrate from the old country and those who could not because of their "race."[91] As Macdonald's critics in the Commons and Senate foresaw in 1885, once "race" was introduced as an organizing principle of Canadian law, equally invidious restrictions would follow for other racialized groups.[92]

Like most important acts of state formation, as the 1885 debates show, Chinese exclusion was highly contested. At issue were two competing visions of what Canada should be — a state that was to be the exclusive domain of "the white man," or a colour- and ethnicity-blind state that embodied an ideal of a transcendent multicultural British citizenship and of equality before the law for all of its citizens, including the naturalized foreign-born. Once the monopoly of "the white man" was established, it became the default framework, since all racialized others were either excluded from the territories that became Canada or marginalized in terms of its governing structures, or both. With time, it came to appear natural that Canadians were of course European. What would be forgotten was that white supremacy and its exclusions was a deliberate creation: John A. Macdonald's "greatest triumph."

Note: I would like to thank Frances Boyle, Marie Ainsworth, Ivana Caccia, Amy Chen, Ralph de Smit, and Bryan Smith for commenting on an early draft of this paper.

Notes

1. Canada, House of Commons, *Official Report of the Debates of the House of Commons of the Dominion of Canada* (Ottawa: Maclean, Roger & co, 1885) [henceforth, *Debates*], 18, May 4, 1885, 1589.
2. Ibid., 1589.
3. See, for example, Gwyn, *Nation Maker: Sir John A. Macdonald: His Life, Our Times, Volume Two, 1867–1891* (Toronto: Random House, 2011), 528–533.
4. On anti-Chinese sentiments in British Columbia during this era, see Patricia E. Roy, *A White Man's Province: British Columbia Politicians and Chinese and Japanese Immigrants, 1858–1914* (Vancouver: UBC Press, 1989). While agreeing with Gwyn that Macdonald was a nation builder and practical politician, in discussing his anti-Chinese measures, Roy notes, "In short, John A. Macdonald was a racist …," 63. See also, W. Peter Ward, *White Canada Forever: Popular Attitudes and Public Policy toward Orientals in British Columbia*, third edition (Montreal: McGill-Queen's University Press, 2002).
5. In the best account of the debate over the legislation in the House of Commons, Veronica Strong-Boag calls it, "a key moment in the history of 'rights talk' in Canada" (p. 70). See Veronica Strong-Boag, "The Citizenship Debates: The 1885 *Franchise Act*" in Robert Adamoski, Dorothy E. Chunn, and Robert Menzies, eds., *Contesting Canadian Citizenship: Historical Readings* (Toronto: Broadview Press, 2002), 69–94. On racial state formation, see Michael Omi and Howard Winant, *Racial Formation in the United States: From the 1960s to the 1990s*, Second Edition (New York: Routledge, 1994) and David Theo Goldberg, *The Racial State* (Oxford, UK; Malden, MA:

Blackwell Publishers, 2002). See also, Renisa Mawani, *Colonial Proximities: Crossracial Encounters and Juridical Truths in British Columbia, 1871–1921* (Vancouver: UBC Press, 2009). On state formation more generally, see Bruce Curtis *Building the Educational State: Canada West, 1836–1871* (London, ON.: Althouse Press: Falmer, 1988); Curtis, *True Government by Choice Men? Inspection, Education, and State Formation in Canada West* (Toronto: University of Toronto Press, 1992) and Curtis, *The Politics of Population: State Formation, Statistics, and the Census of Canada, 1840–1875* (Toronto: University of Toronto Press, 2001). See also, Philip Abrams, "Notes on the Difficulty of Studying the State [1977]," *Journal of Historical Sociology* 1,1 (March 1988).

6. For an overview of developments in European discourses of "race," see Edward Beasley, *The Victorian Reinvention of Race: New Racisms and the Problem of Grouping in the Human Sciences* (New York: Routledge, 2010). See also Douglas A. Lorimer, *Colour, Class, and the Victorians: English Attitudes to the Negro in the Mid-Nineteenth Century* (Leicester, UK: Leicester University Press, 1978); Christine Bolt, *Victorian Attitudes to Race* (London: Routledge and Kegan Paul, 1971); Nancy Stepan, *The Idea of Race in Science: Great Britain 1800–1960* (London: Macmillan, 1982); Thomas F. Gossett, *Race: The History of an Idea in America, New Edition* (New York, NY: Oxford University Press, 1997); and Ivan Hannaford, *Race: The History of an Idea in the West* (Washington, DC : Woodrow Wilson Center Press, 1996).

7. See, for example, Robert J. C. Young, *Postcolonialism: An Historical Introduction* (Oxford, UK: Blackwell Publishers, 2001).

8. John L. Tobias, "Canada's Subjugation of the Plains Cree, 1879–1885," *Canadian Historical Review* 64 (1983): 519–48.

9. Strong-Boag, "Citizenship Debates."

10. Here I follow David Theo Goldberg, *The Threat of Race: Reflections on Racial Neoliberalism* (Malden, MA: Blackwell Publishing, 2009).

11. Michel Foucault, *"Society must be defended": Lectures at the Collège de France, 1975–76* (New York: Picador, 2003). On biopolitics, see also, Foucault, *History of Sexuality: Volume 1, Introduction* (New York: Vintage Books, 1990). On racisms as systems, see W.E. Du Bois, *The Souls of Black Folks* (Oxford; New York: Oxford University Press, 2007); Jacques Barzun, *Race: A Study in Modern Superstition* (New York: Harcourt, Brace and Company, 1937); Hannah Arendt, *The Origins of Totalitarianism.* new edition with added prefaces (San Diego, New York and London: Harvest/HBJ, 1979); Franz Fanon, *Black Skin, White Masks* (New York: Grove Press, 1991); Edward W. Said, *Orientalism* (New York: Vintage Books, 1978); Stuart Hall, "Race, Articulation and Societies Structured in Dominance," in UNESCO, *Sociological Theories: Race and Colonialism* (Paris: United Nations Educational, Scientific and Cultural Organization, 1980). See also, Philomena Essed and David Theo Goldberg, eds., *Race Critical Theories: Text and Context* (Oxford: Blackwell Publishers, 2002).

12. Foucault, *"Society must be Defended."* See also, Ann Laura Stoler, *Race and the Education of Desire: Foucault's History of Sexuality and the Colonial Order of Things* (Durham, NC: Duke University Press, 1995).

13. Judith Lichtenberg, "Racism in the Head, Racism in the World," in Naomi Zack, Laura Shrage, Crispin Sartwell, eds,., *Race, Class , Gender and Sexuality: The Big Questions* (Oxford: Blackwell Publishers, 1998), 43–47.

14. Hence I prefer to use the term "racialization" rather than "race." At the same time, I put racializing terms in quotes to question their presumed naturalness. See Timothy J. Stanley, *Contesting White Supremacy: School Segregation, Anti-Racism and the Making of Chinese Canadians* (Vancouver: UBC Press, 2011), esp. 9–10.

15. Ward points out that British Columbians of European origins did not, in fact, know Chinese people well. See "John Chinaman," Ward, *White Canada Forever,* 3–22.

16. Strong-Boag, "Citizenship Debates."

17. Macdonald to Charles Tupper, July 7, 1885, cited in Donald G. Creighton, *John A. Macdonald: The Old Chieftain* [Ebrary Electronic Resource] (Toronto: University of Toronto Press, 1998), 427. Creighton does not discuss the legislation and argues instead that the railway and Confederation were greater achievements. See also, Gordon Stewart, "John A. Macdonald's Greatest Triumph," *Canadian Historical Review* 63 (1982), 3–33.

18. Ibid.

19. *Debates*, 18, May 4, 1885, 1582.

20. Ibid., 4, March 18, 1878, 1207. On Bunster, see "Bunster, Arthur," Parliament of Canada, ParlInfo, Parliamentarian Files [Henceforth, Parliamentarian Files], entry for *www.parl.gc.ca/ParlInfo/Files/Parliamentarian. aspx?Item=8367f9d7-6af3-43a3-aa1d-d11e632b1d95&Language=E.*

21. *Debates*, 4, March 18, 1878, 1208.

22. See also the statement of de Cosmos, *Debates*, April 16, 1879, 1251–1260.

23. I emphasize " Chinese" as during this era the label Chinese was an ascription. People from China did not define themselves as such until the twentieth century. See Stanley, *Contesting White Supremacy*, 173–74.

24. *Debates*, 12, May 12, 1882, 1476–77.

25. *Debates,* 18, May 4, 1885, 1591.

26. *Debates*, April 16, 1879, 1253.

27. Robert Miles, *Racism* (London: Routledge, 1989), 7.

28. Martin Barker, *The New Racism: Conservatives and the Ideology of the Tribe* (London: Junction Books, 1981).

29. For example, in Britain until the 1980s, the category "Black" included people of Chinese origins. Stuart Hall discusses the breaking down of this category in "New Ethnicities," in David Morley and Kuan-Hsing Chen, eds., *Stuart Hall: Critical Dialogues in Cultural Studies* (London: Routledge, 1996), 441–49. For an American

example, see Noel Ignatiev, *How the Irish became White* (New York: Routledge, 1995). See also the interactive website of the American Anthropological Association, "Race: Are We So Different?" *www.understandingrace.org*. It has long been established that genetic differences between populations, however defined, are less than differences within the population. See, for example, Luigi Luca Cavalli-Sforza, "The Genetics of Human Population," *Scientific American*, 231, 3 (September 1974): 81–89.

30. See Stuart Hall and Sut Jhally, *Race: The Floating Signifier* [videorecording] (Northampton, MA: Media Education Foundation, 2002); Robert Miles, *Racism* (London: Routledge, 1989). See also, David Theo Goldberg, *Racist Culture: Philosophy and the Politics of Meaning* (Malden, MA: Blackwell, 1993).

31. Stuart Hall, "The Work of Representation," in Stuart Hall, ed., *Representation: Cultural Representations and Signifying Practices* (London: Sage Publications, 1997), 13–74.

32. Barzun, *Race*; Hannah Arendt, "Race-Thinking Before Racism," *Review of Politics* 6 (1944): 36–73.

33. Beasley, *Reinvention of Race,* 1.

34. Ibid., 2.

35. Beasley provides an excellent review of both English and American discourse. See Beasley, "Introduction: Reinventing Racism," ibid. See also Michael Banton, "Race as Type," *Racial Theories,* Second Edition (Cambridge,UK: Cambridge University Press, 1998), 28–64.

36. In addition to Beasley and Banton, Stephen J. Gould, *The Mismeasure of Man* (New York: Norton, 1981), esp. "Chapter 2, American Polygeny and Craniometry before Darwin: Blacks and Indians as Separate, Inferior Species," provides an overview of some aspects of American discourse, discourse with which Macdonald was evidently familiar.

37. Perhaps the best-known example of such discourse in Canada is the idea of "two founding races." Consider also Andre Siegfried's 1907 work on English-French relations in Canada, *The Race Question in Canada* (Toronto: McClelland & Stewart, 1966).

38. "An Act Respecting the Qualification and Registration of Voters," *Statutes of British Columbia: Up to and Including the Year 1888*, Ch 38, s. 3, 301 (Victoria: Richard Wolfenden, Government Printer, [188?]).

39. See W.A. Spray, "Mitchell, Peter." In *Dictionary of Canadian Biography Online* [henceforth *DCB Online*], www.biographi.ca.

40. *Debates*, 18, May 4, 1885, 1582.

41. Ibid., See "Casey, George Elliott, B.A.," Parliamentarian Files, *www.parl.gc.ca/ParlInfo/Files/Parliamentarian.aspx?Item=22d58154-634c-42ca-b52c-6c59b10242bf&Language=E*.

42. *Debates*, 18, May 4, 1885, 1585. On Gault, see "Gault, Mathew (Matthew) Hamilton," Gladys Barbara Pollack and Gerald J.J. Tulchinsky, *DCB Online*;

on Davies, see J.M. Bumsten, "Davies, Sir Louis Henry," ibid.; and on Gilmor, see Kathryn Wilson, "Gilmor, Arthur Hill," ibid. The debate in the House of Commons is also discussed in Stanley, *Contesting White Supremacy*, 82–85.

43. *Debates*, 18, May 4, 1885, 1585–86.

44. Ibid., 1588.

45. Ibid., 1589.

46. As shocking as this seems, it should be remembered as Beasley, *Reinvention of Race*, 99, reminds us, interbreeding as a criteria for determining different species is not a straightforward question. This was especially the case before Darwin resolved the species question by explaining the gradual evolution of one species into another.

47. Robert C. Vipond, "Mills, David," *DCB Online*.

48. *Debates*, 18, May 4, 1885, 1589.

49. See, Beasley, *Reinvention of Race*. See also, Banton, *Racial Theories* and Gould, *The Mismeasure of Man*.

50. *Debates*, 18, May 4, 1985, 1582. Macdonald apparently consistently rejected attempts at excluding racialized Africans from the same rights as racialized Europeans. See, Gwyn, *Nation Maker*, 529.

51. *Debates*, 18, May 4, 1985, 1582.

52. See Hubert Howe Bancroft, *The Works of Hubert Howe Bancroft [microform]: The Native Races* (San Francisco: AL Bancroft, 1883).

53. Gregory Blue, "Gobineau on China: Race Theory, the 'Yellow Peril,; and the Critique of Modernity," *Journal of World History* 10, 1 (Spring 1999): 93–139. I am indebted to Dr. Blue for bringing this reference to my attention. See also, Beasley, *Reinvention of Race*.

54. Macdonald first expressed his Aryan vision in 1882 when in response to de Cosmo's intervention, he famously stated, "At present it is simply a question of alternatives — either you must have this labor or you cannot have the railway." However, he also explained that he shared "the feeling of the people of the United States, and the Australian colonies, against a Mongolian or Chinese population in our country as permanent settlers." He claimed, "they would not be a wholesome element in this country" since "it is an alien race in every sense, that would not and could not be expected to assimilate with our Arian [sic] population"(*Debates*, May 12, 1882, 1477). As Macdonald's comments show, exclusion was an international movement. Exclusionists in Canada and in other British colonies of settlement closely followed events in the other colonies and were inspired by each other. See Robert A. Huttenback, *Racism and Empire: White Settlers and Colored Immigrants in the British Self-Governing Colonies, 1830–1910* (Ithaca: Cornell University Press, 1976).

55. On Chinese merchants and anti-Chinese racism, see Stanley, *Contesting White Supremacy*. The Royal Commission on Chinese Immigration also had extensively discussed Chinese economic activity in BC.

56. *Debates*, 18, May 4, 1985, 1582.
57. *Debates,* May 4, 1885, 1582.
58. See, for example, the debates over the *Indian Act. Commons Debates: Third Session — Third Parliament,* 1876.
59. Strong-Boag, "Citizenship Debates."
60. See, for example, the exchange between Macdonald and David Mills in the Commons on April 30, 1885, *Debates,* 18, 1484–85.
61. In fact, he overestimated the enthusiasm of First Nations people for the vote. See Strong-Boag, "Citizenship Debates."
62. See Canada, Royal Commission on Chinese Immigration, *Report of the Royal Commission on Chinese Immigration: Report and Evidence* (Ottawa: By order of the Commission, 1885).
63. *Debates*, 18, May 4, 1985, 1590. Although the part of the report authored by Chapleau does record a conversation with the Qinq Consul General, it does not mention any discussion of the franchise. See *Report of the Royal Commission*, 366.
64. *Debates*, 18, May 4, 1985, 1590.
65. *Debates*, 20, 1885, 3010.
66. Daniel P. Marshall, "Helmcken, John Sebastian," *DCB Online.*
67. *Debates*, 20, 1885, 3009. Chapleau also claimed that the presence of racialized Chinese workers excited "race antagonism" on the part of racialized white workers. See ibid, 3006..
68. Christopher G. Anderson, "Restricting Rights, Losing Control: Immigrants, Refugees, Asylum Seekers and the Regulation of Canada's Border, 1867–1988" (unpublished PhD thesis, McGill University, 2006), 213–52; see also Anderson, "The Senate and the Fight against the 1885 Chinese Immigration Act," *Parliamentary Review* 30, 2 (Summer 2007): 21–26.
69. *Debates,* 4, March 18, 1878, 1209.
70. *Debates*, 7, April 16, 1879, 1260.
71. Ibid., 1262.
72. Kenneth Munro, "Boucher De Boucherville, Sir Charles," *DCB Online;* De Boucherville, dropped the "Boucher" in his customary usage.
73. Canada, Senate, *Debate of the Senate of Canada* [Henceforth *Senate Debates*], 1885, Vol. 2, 1276 and 1343.
74. Ibid., 1276.
75. Ben Forster, "McInnes (MacInnes), Donald," *DCB Online.*
76. On Campbell, see Donald Swainson, "Campbell, Sir Alexander," *DCB Online. Senate Debates,* 1885, Vol. 2, 1279.
77. P.N. Waite, "Plumb, Josiah Burr," *DCB Online.*
78. *Senate Debates,* 1885, Vol. 2, 1279.
79. Ibid., 1279.
80. Ibid., 1343.

81. Andrew Robb, "Haythorne, Robert Poore," *DCB Online*. On his appointment, see, "Haythorne, The Hon. Robert Poore," Parliamentarian Files, *www.parl.gc.ca/ParlInfo/Files/Parliamentarian.aspx?Item=d55a8bb9-e5e3-41d3-8e0b-6dfe4127581d&Language=E*.

82. *Senate Debates,* 1885, vol. 2, 1278.

83. "Power, The Hon. Lawrence Geoffrey, P.C., K.C., B.A., LL.B., Parliamentarian Files, *www.parl.gc.ca/ParlInfo/Files/Parliamentarian. aspx?Item=3ea75794-f03a-4c09-b8b3-a2a775257b81&Language=E*.

84. *Senate Debates,* 1885, vol. 2, 1280.

85. Ibid., 1342.

86. See Anderson, "The Senate and the Fight against the 1885 Chinese Immigration Act," 24–5. See also *Senate Debates*, 1885, 2, July 13, 1885, 1291–1301 and July 14, 1885, 1326–29.

87. Anderson, 24. See also, Anderson, "Restricting Rights, Losing Control," 232–43,

88. See, for example, the definition of racism in the glossary provided by the Canadian Race Relations Foundation, *www.crr.ca/*.

89. *Debates*, 23, May 31, 1887, 642.

90. For example, in English state formation, taxation was originally quite literally highway robbery, yet today, people in Canada self assess on income taxes. See, Philip Corrigan and Derek Sayer, *The Great Arch: English State Formation as Cultural Revolution* (Oxford, UK: Blackwell, 1985).

91. See Harry Con, et al., Edited by Edgar Wickberg, *From China to Canada: A History of the Chinese Communities of Canada*, Generations Series (Toronto: McClelland & Stewart, 1982); Peter S. Li, *The Chinese in Canada* (Toronto: Oxford University Press, 1988); Wing Chung Ng, *The Chinese in Vancouver, 1945–80: The Pursuit of Identity and Power* (Vancouver: UBC Press, 1999); Denise Chong, *The Concubine's Children: Portrait of a Family Divided* (Toronto: Viking: Penguin Books Canada, 1994); Shirley Chan, et al. *Finding Memories, Tracing Roots: Chinese Canadian Family Stories* (Vancouver: Chinese Canadian Historical Society of BC, 2006); Lisa R. Mar, *Brokering Belonging: Chinese in Canada's Exclusion Era, 1885–1945* (Oxford: Oxford University Press, 2010); Alison Marshall, *The Way of the Bachelor: Early Chinese Settlement in Manitoba* (Vancouver: UBC Press, 2011).

92. Racisms directed at other groups such as African Canadians, First Nations, and Jews each have their own particularities. See, for example, Barrington Walker, *Race on Trial: Black Defendants in Ontario's Criminal Courts 1858–1958* (Toronto: The Osgoode Society and University of Toronto Press, 2010); Peggy Briston, ed., *We're Rooted Here and They Can't Pull Us Up: Essays in African Canadian Women's History* (Toronto: University of Toronto Press, 1994); Allan T. Davies, *Anti-Semitism in Canada: History and Interpretation* (Waterloo, ON: Wilfrid Laurier University Press, 1992); Constance Backhouse, *Colour-Coded:*

A Legal History of Racism in Canada, 1900–1950 (Toronto: Published for the Osgoode Society for Canadian Legal History by University of Toronto Press, 1999). First Nations and settler relations have not normally been written about in Canada from the perspectives of white supremacy and racism — even though the latter are central to processes of colonization. For an exception, see Daniel N. Paul, *We Were Not the Savages: A Mi'kmaq Perspective on the Collision Between European and Native American Civilizations* (Halifax, NS: Fernwood, 2000). Because of this indelible connection to the territories that became Canada, where they have not faced extermination of the kind Paul describes, First Nations have faced at best marginalization and containment on reserves. See, for examples, James R. Miller, *Skyscrapers Hide the Heavens: A History of Indian-white Relations in Canada* (Toronto: University of Toronto Press, 2000), Edward S. Roger and Donald B. Smith eds., *Aboriginal Ontario: Historical Perspectives on the First Nations, Third Edition* (Toronto: Dundurn Press, 1994); Sarah Carter, *Lost Harvests: Prairie Indian Reserve Farmers and Government Policy* (Montreal: McGill-Queen's University Press, 1993); R. Cole Harris, *The Resettlement of British Columbia: Essays on Colonialism and Geographical Change* (Vancouver: UBC Press, 1997) and *Making Native Space: Colonialism, Resistance, and Reserves in British Columbia* (Vancouver: UBC Press, 2002); Mary-Ellen Kelm, *Colonizing Bodies: Aboriginal Health and Healing in British Columbia, 1900–50* (Vancouver: UBC Press, 1998); and John S. Milloy, *A National Crime: The Canadian Government and the Residential School System, 1879 to 1986* (Winnipeg: University of Manitoba Press, 1999). By contrast, at times, other Asians have faced disenfranchisement, and along with Africans and Jews have faced exclusion from the country. Members of all three groups have faced discrimination in access to public facilities. Michiko Midge Ayukawa, *Hiroshima Immigrants in Canada, 1891–1941* (Vancouver: UBC Press, 2008); Roy Miki, *Redress: Japanese Canadians in Negotiations* (Vancouver: Raincoast Books, 2004); Ann Gomer Sunahara, *The Politics of Racism: The Uprooting of Japanese Canadians during the Second World War* (Toronto: Lorimer, 1981); Hugh J. Johnson, *The Voyage of the Komagata Maru: The Sikh Challenge to Canada's Colour Bar*, Second Edition (Vancouver: University of British Columbia Press, 1989); Robin W. Winks, *The Blacks in Canada: A History*, Second Edition (Montreal: McGill-Queen's University Press, 1997); Harold Troper, "The Creek Negroes of Oklagoma and Canadian Immigration, 1909–11," *Canadian Historical Review*, 53, 3 (1972): 272–88.

Chapter 5

Macdonald and the Concept of Liberty

Michel Ducharme[1]

John A. Macdonald was no philosopher king. He produced no theoretical treatise, rarely discussed political principles or ideas, and almost never used philosophical arguments in his speeches. Until his death, he remained faithful to a commitment he had made in 1844 to his Kingston supporters. As a candidate in the provincial election of that year, he had explained that "in a young country like Canada ... it is of more consequence to endeavor to develop its resources and improve its physical advantages than to waste the time of the Legislature, and the money of the people, in fruitless discussions on abstract and theoretical questions of government."[2] This was to be his lifelong attitude toward politics.

The fact that Macdonald almost never explicitly discussed his values and principles does not mean that he did not have any. This silence does, however, explain why his biographers have seldom addressed the issue. This was certainly the case of Donald Creighton, Macdonald's most capable biographer. In his authoritative two-volume biography, the Toronto historian portrayed Macdonald as a moderate, conservative politician. He structured his biography around Macdonald's political activities and achievements, rather than his ideas and principles.[3] Central to Creighton's argument was the prominent role Macdonald played in the rise and development of the moderate Liberal-Conservative party. His main objective in writing this biography was to demonstrate that even if he had always been a Conservative, Macdonald's brand of conservatism was different from traditional Toryism. According to Creighton, Macdonald had added to his unshakable admiration for the British constitution and Empire "the right note of discreet modernity and forward-looking conservatism."[4] Ironically, even though Creighton celebrated the triumph of Macdonald's moderate "philosophy," he never explicitly defined this philosophy other than in very general terms.

Other historians who have studied John A. Macdonald's life and career generally confirmed Creighton's interpretations. In his short biography, which focused on Macdonald's character and personal skills, Donald Swainson used a sympathetic tone that was reminiscent of Creighton and reached the same conclusion about Macdonald.[5] The same is true of Peter Waite's *Macdonald: His Life and World*. Although the author mainly discussed the social and political context in which Macdonald evolved, he dedicated his first chapter to "the Man and his Ideas." According to him, Macdonald's political program could be summarized very succinctly: "Forget about abstract notions of what government ought to be. Concentrate on the country's development."[6] If Waite did not go so far as to reinterpret Macdonald's career, he did place greater emphasis on Macdonald's nationalism than his predecessors. As for Richard Gwyn, Macdonald's most recent biographer, he downplays the importance of Macdonald's conservatism (whatever this means) and his role in the creation of the Conservative Party in order to emphasize his ability to negotiate compromises, his contribution to the development of Canadian democracy, and his role in the advent of Confederation. In this biography, Macdonald is depicted less as a staunch conservative politician than as a deal-maker, a nation-builder, and a man with a great national vision.[7] The rise of a new Conservative Party in Canada in the decade preceding the publication of this biography may explain this reinterpretation of Macdonald's achievements, Gwyn preferring to see him more as a statesman than as a Conservative politician.

Although each of Macdonald's biographers has chosen to study Canada's first prime minister from a different perspective, each one has also proposed a generally positive interpretation of the man and his career. All have shared a great respect for his achievements, albeit for different reasons. In this context,

Patricia Phenix's iconoclastic study of Macdonald's private life differs from all these previous biographies. Although the book contains very little new information about Macdonald, it reinterprets his life and career in a most unfavourable light. Rather than depicting a great man, politician, or nation-builder, Phenix presents Macdonald as an ambitious, disloyal, and unprincipled politician, as well as a distant husband.[8]

WHITHER ARE WE DRIFTING?

Grip, 16 August, 1873.

Despite their different approaches, all these biographies lack an in-depth discussion of Macdonald's political thought. These historians obviously agreed with T.W.L. MacDermot's view that Macdonald was a man of action, not of reflection; a practical man, "not a man of ideas."[9] Indeed, this interpretation has become conventional wisdom.[10] However, two scholars have dared to challenge such conventional wisdom; Rod Preece investigated the nature of Macdonald's conservatism in what is arguably the best study of Macdonald's political thought to date. Contesting the idea that Macdonald was "devoid of political principles," Preece argued that his political thought was essentially Burkean. The importance Macdonald gave to prescription (or tradition), his openness to piecemeal reform, his devotion to the British form of government (including virtual representation), his loyalty to the British connection, and his attachment to British rights and liberties were all similar to the principles defended by the father of British conservatism. According to Preece, Macdonald's ideals "centred around the idea of moderation, balance, prudence, and order."[11]

The sociologist Stéphane Kelly has also analyzed Macdonald's policies in order to provide fresh insight into his political thought. Kelly's analysis was inspired in part by the work of Peter J. Smith and Gordon T. Stewart, who had, during the 1980s, reassessed the intellectual foundations of the Canadian state. Offering a new reading of the political debates which had occurred in the British North American colonies in the nineteenth century, Smith and Stewart argued that these debates should be interpreted in the context of the opposition between Court and Country ideologies — which had structured eighteenth-century Anglo-American politics — rather than in the traditional framework opposing *liberal* reformers to *conservative* politicians.[12] According to these two political scientists, the Fathers of Confederation shared "a consistent system of values which had its roots in the Court ideology"; they believed in a strong and centralized state focused on executive power and a commercial society sustained by the development of economic infrastructures such as canals and railways. In order to build their desired state and commercial society as well as to promote political and social stability, these politicians used patronage extensively.[13] Kelly, who had previously used this Court versus Country framework to study Lower-Canadian politics between 1837 and 1867,[14] reinterpreted it in the context of *l'américanité* (Americanness) in order to understand better Macdonald's principles. He discussed Macdonald's principles in the context of an opposition between the ideals developed by Alexander Hamilton (Court ideology) and Thomas Jefferson (Country ideology) in the United States at the end of the eighteenth and beginning of the nineteenth century. In this context, Kelly argued that Canada's first prime minister shared Hamiltonian ideals; Macdonald believed in the creation of a centralized, expansionist, interventionist, and "corrupt" state.[15]

Even if these two interpretations are quite distinct — the first being essentially intellectual and quite positive; the second, more political and critical — they are more complementary than antithetical. On the one hand, Macdonald's conservatism is beyond doubt, as demonstrated by Preece. Macdonald believed in the "conservation of the constitution" (with everything that this entailed) and in the necessity of only modifying it carefully, respecting its own logic and development. Comparing the constitution to a tree, he explained that "the treatment bestowed on the tree should vary with its growing wants and development."[16] In this, Macdonald was respecting two basic tenets of conservatism. He was showing respect for the constitution he had received from his ancestors and he was defending its preservation on the basis of its specificity rather than on its conformity to universal principles.[17]

However, as Creighton had argued, Macdonald's brand of conservatism was distinct from old colonial Toryism. As Macdonald put it himself at an electoral rally in 1860: "It is well known, sir, that I have always been a member of what is called the Conservative party. I could have never been called a Tory."[18] This was more than an electoral statement: while Macdonald needed the support of the most radical Tories to remain in power, he sometimes showed his impatience with them and their rigid, outdated principles. He was for instance so annoyed with some of his colleagues and their "stupid attempt to re-animate the dry bones of Pre-Adamite Toryism" in 1860 that he went as far as to say that he "would much prefer cutting the connection" with them rather than "having anything to do with such a reactionary policy."[19] Accordingly, he presented himself as a "progressive Conservative," or "Conservative-Liberal."[20] As far as he was concerned, in 1847 he had joined in the party that was supporting "the Conservative cause, the liberal Conservative cause."[21] Macdonald remained faithful to this appellation all his life, being the leader of the Liberal-Conservative Party until his death in 1891.

Although there might have been some electoral and political considerations in the choice of these labels, it is clear that Macdonald did not see liberalism and conservatism as necessarily being mutually exclusive. If Liberals
and Conservatives made sense of the world they inhabited through distinct
ideologies, they shared many values in the context of the British Empire
and both had sprung from eighteenth-century Whig doctrines. Therefore,
they could sometimes arrive at the same conclusions about politics for different reasons. For Macdonald, this is what had happened in the Province
of Canada in 1854, when the Conservatives and the Hincksite Liberals
realized that they agreed on many issues:

> I have always been a Conservative Liberal, and when I found
> there were very many called Reformers who agreed with me,
> I did not hesitate to enter into an alliance with them.... There
> was really no great question to prevent the Conservative
> party from coalescing with men of constitutional and mod-
> erate views, although they had previously belonged to what
> was called a different party; and from that time until now,
> men brought up in the Conservative school have acted with
> those brought up in the Liberal School — acted as united
> government — acted together, because they think alike.[22]

Later on in life, Macdonald enlisted both Edmund Burke and Robert
Baldwin in the cause of "liberal-conservatism." According to him, Burke
"would have been in this country what we call a Baldwin Reformer, or, in
other words, a Liberal-Conservative."[23]

What set Macdonald apart from old Toryism was, first, his willingness to
build a coalition government with more "liberal" politicians (or Hincksites).
As he explained himself:

> It has been said that neither England nor Canada likes a
> Coalition Government. If coalition between two parties
> means that, for the sake of emolument or position they
> sacrifice principle, then Coalition Governments ought not
> to receive the confidence of the people. But if a Coalition
> Government means, what I contend the coalition of 1854

was, the junction of a number of men who, forgetting old quarrels which have been wiped out, and who, instead of raking up the ashes after the fire of dissension had burned away, and endeavoring to re-kindle it, finally extinguished it, and refused to prolong discord and the ruin caused by it — then I say that coalition is the act of true patriots.[24]

The other major difference between Macdonald and the Tories was his rejection of traditional Tory Anti-Gallic sentiments. This attitude was expressed very clearly to Quebec Lawyer Brown Chamberlin in 1856: "If a Lower Canadian Britisher desires to conquer, he must "stoop to conquer". He must make friends with the French; without sacrificing the status of his race or lineage, he must respect their nationality. Treat them as a nation and they will act as a free people generally do — generously."[25]

While Macdonald's conservatism is beyond doubt, it did not preclude him from sharing a mindset reminiscent of the eighteenth-century Court ideology. In fact, his conservatism fits very well within the eighteenth-century Court tradition since both British and Canadian conservatism and liberalism (as opposed to radicalism) came out of this tradition in the nineteenth century. The same can be said of Alexander Hamilton and the American Federalist Party, whose principles were the basis of the 1787 American Constitution.[26]

There is one concept, however, that was integral to Court ideology and Burkean conservatism in both British and Canadian contexts, but that is almost absent in the historiography of John A. Macdonald: that of liberty. Even if most commentators including Creighton, Gwyn, Preece, and Smith noticed Macdonald's references to this concept in his speeches, electoral addresses, and other interventions, none of them defined what he meant by the word nor how it impacted and shaped his understanding of politics and government. This may be in part because Macdonald himself referred to the concept only when he deemed it necessary during his long career (which admittedly did not happen very often). It could also be because the word's meaning seems so obvious nowadays or even because such a discussion is counter-intuitive considering Macdonald's conservatism. After all, nineteenth-century Canadian conservatives have the reputation of having believed in order, not in liberty. I contend that Macdonald was definitely a great believer in order, but order based on a certain concept of liberty.

Although John A. Macdonald referred to liberty a few times over the course of his long career, he never clearly explained what he meant by the term. Contrary to many of his Tory predecessors, he never felt the urge to discuss this concept thoroughly. His reluctance to discuss abstract concepts, including liberty, may be explained in part by his conservatism. Nineteenth-century conservatives did not like to think at length about abstract concepts and principles. As far as they were concerned, the French Revolution had demonstrated the danger of discussing such principles in public and of reforming institutions according to them. Conservatives participated in theoretical discussions only when they were forced to do so by circumstances. For instance, in Upper and Lower Canada, John Strachan (spiritual leader of the Upper Canadian Tories) discussed the principles informing the British and colonial constitutions only in 1810, when tensions between the United States and Great Britain were building to a crescendo.[27] Jonathan Sewell (Lower Canadian chief justice), John Beverly Robinson (Upper Canadian Attorney General), and Strachan did the same in the context of the 1822 Canadian union project in Britain.[28] Many more conservatives, such as Adam Thom (author of many pamphlets in Lower Canada and editor of the *Montreal Herald*) and Egerton Ryerson (Upper Canadian Methodist leader), got involved in the discussion about liberty in the 1830s when the republican threat became more pressing in both Canadas.[29] Robinson also expanded his discussion in the wake of the Canadian rebellions.[30] In this context, it is possible to say that conservative politicians defended liberty (or their own version of it) only when they felt that it was under threat. That there was no such threat in the colony after the 1837–38 rebellions may well explain why Macdonald remained discrete on this subject. Conversely, this reactive attitude may explain why Macdonald's best interventions about liberty were made in the few years prior to Confederation.

Macdonald may also have been reluctant to discuss the meaning of liberty during most of his political career due to the post-rebellion context. First, the British military victory in 1837 and 1838 confirmed the victory of the modern (liberal) concept of liberty in the colony over the republican one.[31] With few exceptions, there was therefore a broad consensus in the colony about the meaning of liberty after the rebellions, making a theoretical discussion redundant. Liberty meant first and foremost the respect of individual autonomy and rights, not political rights. Second, Lord Durham explained the 1837 Lower Canadian rebellion in racial rather than intellectual terms in his *Report on the Affairs of British North America* (1839); his recommendations, involving precise political measures such as the union of Upper and Lower Canada and responsible government, reframed the debates in the colonies in two ways.[32] Durham's report encouraged French Canadians to develop a strong defence of their nationality and also pushed English Canadian reformers to demand political and institutional reforms without debating the nature of the colonial system. This institutional approach to liberty became dominant in the Province of Canada from the 1840s onward. Macdonald's lack of interest for intellectual debate may reflect this shift toward practical reforms and national concerns rather than intellectual debates about the nature of the colonial political system.

Macdonald's silence might also have been influenced by the international context. He may have preferred not to raise the issue during and after the European Revolutions of 1848–49, in which the idea of liberty had been deployed by many people in ways of which he did not approve. He may also have feared the annexationist movement in the Province of Canada in 1849–50. At the same time, he was also following, knowingly or not, a general trend within the British Empire. Since the 1830s, even Whig and liberal commentators had stopped discussing the intellectual principles that were the basis of the British constitution (including the concept of liberty), choosing instead to focus on its structures and mechanisms (although there were exceptions, such as John Stuart Mill).[33] A comparison between William Blackstone's *Commentaries of the Laws of England* (1765) and Walter Bagehot's *The English Constitution* (1867) is instructive in this regard. While Blackstone began his work with a chapter entitled "Of the Absolute Rights of the Individuals," Bagehot did not consider such a theoretical discussion essential at all.[34] He simply began his work with a chapter about the British Cabinet, which explained the stability of the constitution. As Paul Smith explains, "for someone like Bagehot, the battle for the liberties of the subject was over, because a properly worked system of representative government of its very nature guaranteed them."[35] In many ways, Macdonald's attitude toward liberty was similar to that of Bagehot (even if the former was a conservative and the latter a Whig). For both, liberty was not something to be conquered. It was rather something to take advantage of — and protect if necessary. In this sense, Macdonald's restraint in discussing the concept of liberty is not really surprising. Macdonald nonetheless referred to and defended liberty a few times during his career. But just what did he mean when he spoke or wrote of "liberty"?

• • •

When John A. Macdonald discussed the concept of liberty, he often referred to it as "constitutional liberty." Although he never defined precisely what this meant, he explicitly stated what it did *not* mean: republican or democratic freedom as experienced in the United States. Macdonald made this very clear during the negotiations held in Quebec City in October 1864, regarding the creation of a new British North American federation. For Macdonald, it seemed self-evident that Canada "shall have a strong and lasting government under which we can work out constitutional liberty as opposed to democracy."[36]

In this context, Macdonald's "constitutional liberty" had to refer to the kind of liberty embodied in the British constitution ("our constitution", as he called it).[37] And in fact, it was on these principles that the *British North America Act* of 1867 was established.[38] To understand the founding principles of the British constitution (and therefore Macdonald's thinking), one has to go back to Blackstone's *Commentaries on the Laws of England*, published from 1765 to 1769 (even if Macdonald never seems to have referred to them). As mentioned earlier, Blackstone opened his *Commentaries* by discussing the absolute rights of the British subjects on which the British constitution rested. These "absolute rights" (also referred to as Englishmen's "birth-rights" by Jean-Louis de Lolme in his *Constitution d'Angleterre* published in 1771) were reduced "to three principal or primary articles; the right of personal security, the right of personal liberty, and the right of private property...."[39] This definition of liberty (based primarily on civil liberties, security and property) was characteristic of what I call "modern" liberty. It was very similar to Benjamin Constant's "*liberté des modernes*" (1819), Isaiah Berlin's "negative freedom" (1958) and David Miller's "liberal freedom" (1991).[40]

Macdonald's conception of liberty is also closer to what Hannah Arendt referred to as "rights" and "liberties" and what David Hackett Fischer called "liberty" as opposed to "freedom." If "liberty" and "freedom" are generally considered to be synonymous (as they were during the nineteenth century), it might be useful to make a distinction between them.[41] Arendt and Hackett Fischer argued that these two words (or words families) referred to two very different concepts in the past. Structuring their arguments around the etymology of both words, they gave a political meaning to the word "freedom." For Arendt, freedom referred to the citizen's political participation in republican forms of government; for Hackett Fischer, it referred to the "rights of belonging and full membership in a community of free people."[42] Conversely, liberty and liberties would have referred to individual autonomy, and would therefore have had a "liberal" connotation. Although Hanna Fenichel Pitkin contested the etymological rationale behind this distinction,[43] she acknowledged a difference in the way these two words have been used over the past two hundred years. More relevantly, she also noticed that while Berlin used both word in his discussion of "negative liberty" (which relates to individual autonomy), "he employs the "free" family almost exclusively" when discussing "positive liberty" (or should I say freedom), which relates in part to "democratic self-government."[44] If Macdonald himself used both words (as other promoters of "negative" liberty had done before him), he seems to have used the word "liberty" mainly to refer to individual rights (also called "liberty of the subjects") or colonial autonomy, at least in his published addresses and speeches. According to this interpretation, Macdonald would have believed more in *liberty* than in *freedom*.

This modern concept of liberty appeared in England at the end of the seventeenth century, where it was institutionalized in the wake of the 1688 Glorious Revolution. First discussed by John Locke in his *Second Treatise on Civil Government* (1691), it was developed in the eighteenth century by the first generation of the French *philosophes* (Voltaire, Montesquieu, and Louis de Jaucourt, for instance); British Constitutionalists (Sir William Blackstone and Jean-Louis De Lolme, to name the two most important ones); Scottish thinkers (such as Adam Smith); British Whigs (including Edmund Burke and Charles James Fox); as well as the American Federalists (Alexander Hamilton and John Adams, for example). These thinkers emphasized the civil rights and liberties of subjects and citizens rather than their political rights, even if most of these men were also in favour of representative institutions. This concept was adopted by both British liberals and conservatives in the nineteenth century. Liberals structured their ideologies around it, while conservatives defended it as being part of their inheritance. John A. Macdonald's concept of liberty clearly belonged to this tradition as it referred, first and foremost, to individual rights rather than political rights.

One of the most important such individual rights was equality before the law. Macdonald had proven early in his career that he believed in the rule of law by defending rebels in the wake of the Upper Canadian rebellions.[45] He remained faithful to this principle during his political career. While discussing the creation of what he then called the "Constitutional" League (better known as the British American League) in 1849, in the midst of the annexation crisis, he included "equal rights to all" among his principles.[46] During the debates on the subject of Confederation fifteen years later, he explained to his colleagues that it was:

> [O]f great importance that we should have the same crimi-
> nal law throughout these provinces — that what is a crime
> in one part of British America, should be a crime in every
> part — that there should be the same protection of life and
> property as in another .... under our Constitution we shall
> have one body of criminal law, based on the criminal law of
> England, and operating equally throughout British America,
> so that a British American, belonging to what province he
> may, or going to any other part of the Confederation, knows
> what his rights are in that respect, and what his punishment
> will be if an offender against the criminal laws of the land.[47]

However, his notion of equality did not go beyond this legal equality. He did not see anything wrong with economic and social inequalities, going as far as to defend primogeniture laws in Canada in the 1840s.[48] He even regretted, at the end of his life, the democratic aspect of the social hierarchy in Canada, which encouraged some to promote annexation to the neighbouring Republic:

> The monarchical idea should be fostered in the colonies,
> accompanied by some gradation of classes. At present, with
> some few exceptions, Canadians are all on one democratic
> level, as in the neighbouring Republic, and this fact, among
> others, is appealed to by the annexationists in Canada, as

providing that our national sympathies are with the Americans, or should be so. A great opportunity was lost in 1867 when the Dominion was formed out of several provinces.[49]

This way of conceiving of equality, as merely equality before the law, was a direct by-product of Enlightenment thought and was typical of modern liberty, as opposed to republican liberty.[50] Macdonald also defended other individual rights, such as *Habeas Corpus* (essential for British subjects), "the freedom of speech, and of the press" as well the freedom of religion and the equality between the different Christian denominations in Canada.[51] At the same time, he believed that the government had to guarantee the "protection of life and property."[52] These were the rights Macdonald mainly referred to during his career, even if he did not make too many references to them.

Rather than addressing the issue of liberty through principles, Macdonald addressed it through institutions. This approach was not new in Canada. Robert Baldwin had adopted the same approach in the 1830s and 1840s. The father of responsible government also seldom discussed intellectual principles, focusing his attention on the ways in which colonial institutions worked.[53] In the end, this approach to liberty was closer to Walter Bagehot's view than to Blackstone's. As far as Macdonald himself was concerned, the liberty of the subjects depended on two institutions: Parliament and the Crown.

The British Parliament was central to the British constitution; it was not only the supreme legislative power, but also the sovereign power. This concept of parliamentary sovereignty was defended by the partisans of modern liberty in eighteenth- and nineteenth-century Britain against republican or radical theories.[54] Republicans considered that sovereignty rested with the people (although some British radicals tried to defend the sovereignty of the people within the parliamentary framework)[55] and this legal fiction was the foundation for republican political institutions, which were structured around the legislative power, through which the will of the people could be expressed.[56] British constitutionalists adopted a different take on the issue of sovereignty. First, they did not discuss this issue as much as republicans, focusing mainly on individual civil liberties rather than political rights. (It is worth noting, for example, that John Locke himself never discussed the issue of sovereignty in his *Second Treatise on Civil Government*.[57])

Since partisans of modern liberty considered that liberty existed mainly outside the political realm (albeit not completely), they generally viewed the concept of sovereignty with suspicion. After all, nothing could prevent a sovereign power from threatening individual liberties. To prevent this possibility, British constitutionalists acknowledged the sovereignty of Parliament, an institution characterized by its internal divisions. If the British nation (or people) expressed its will through Parliament, it was not itself sovereign: Parliament was. The nation represented in Parliament was neither the univocal republican fiction, nor the sum of all the individuals, as in modern liberal democracies. It was rather the sum of the diverse interests existing in the realm, organized around the three traditional orders of English society: monarchy (King), aristocracy (Lords), and democracy (Commons). This form of government was known as mixed government. While many Anglo-American thinkers and politicians of all intellectual traditions had promoted the idea of a mixed government in the eighteenth century, only the British Whigs and Tories continued to refer to it during the nineteenth century.[58]

Macdonald's own attitude reflected both Whig and Tory ideas about sovereignty. First, he never referred to popular sovereignty: whenever he mentioned the "people" or the "nation" — he used both words interchangeably — he never conferred upon them any share of sovereignty. In 1865, for instance, he explained that the project for a British North American federation came from a "desire to form one people under one government," really believing "that the union of the colonies was for the advantage of the country, that the joining of these five peoples into one nation, under one sovereign, was for the benefit of all."[59] The nation he referred to was *not* sovereign. This was made very clear by his refusal to submit the project to the colonists through an election or plebiscite. According to him, "it would be obviously absurd to submit the complicated details of such measure to the people ... before asking the Imperial Government to introduce a Bill in the British Parliament."[60] Not only would it be absurd, but an appeal to the people would also be "a fundamental error against constitutional and free institutions."[61] Macdonald based his argument both on a general principle and the British constitution. On the one hand, Macdonald explained that:

[I]n every free country where there is a Constitution at all, the vote must be taken by the constituted authorities, the representatives of the people, and not become a mere form and cover to tyranny, but a measure which accords with the calm and deliberate judgments of the people, as expressed through their representatives.[62]

On the other hand, he thought that there was no disposition in his beloved British constitution to organize such an appeal: "How could … a vote like that … be taken in a country whose Constitution is modelled on the Constitution of England? … There is no means, no system, by which we could make an appeal of that kind, and in order to do it we should have to subvert the principles of the British Constitution." In this context, an appeal to the people "would be a subversion of the first principles of British constitutional government."[63]

John A. Macdonald's stance on this issue also revealed his conception of representation. Macdonald believed that the representatives of the people were no "mere delegates," but were rather elected to make decisions for the people, "to see for them, to think for them, to act for them."[64] This view of representation was very similar to Edmund Burke's in his 1774 address to the electors of Bristol. Burke was then an influential follower of the Marquess of Rockingham, one of the most radical Whig leaders at the time, and not yet the father of British conservatism. In his address, Burke explained that:

[I]t ought to be the happiness and glory of a Representative, to live in the strictest union, the closest correspondence, and the most unreserved communication with his constituents.... But, his unbiased opinion, his mature judgement, his enlightened conscience, he ought not to sacrifice to you; to any man, or any sett [sic] of men living.... Your Representative owes you, not his industry only, but his judgement; and he betrays, instead of serving you, if he sacrifices it to your opinion.... Parliament is not a Congress of Ambassadors from different and hostile interests; ... but Parliament is a deliberative Assembly of one Nation, with one Interest, that of the whole; where, not local Purposes, not local Prejudices ought to guide, but the general Good,

> resulting from the general Reason of the whole. You chuse
> [*sic*] a Member indeed; but when you have chosen him, he is
> not Member of Bristol, but he is a Member of Parliament.[65]

To make his argument more convincing when debating George Brown, the leader of the Clear Grits (or Liberals), Macdonald did not cite Burke, but appealed instead to the authority of a Liberal British MP, Mr. Leatham, "a brother-in-law of Mr. John Bright, and belonging to the advanced Liberal school of English politicians, known as the Manchester school," who had "contended that the responsibility of voting for a measure must rest upon the Legislature alone, and that it could not refer this responsibility to the people."[66] It followed that if the people were not sovereign in theory, they could not be so in practice either. This understanding of the concept of representation was typical of the modern concept of liberty.[67]

But even if Macdonald acknowledged the sovereignty of the British Parliament over British North America, he did not seem to care that much about the concept itself and rarely mentioned it. When he did bring it up, he seemed to have an imprecise understanding of the concept. During the 1865 debates over the Quebec Resolutions, he used the word "sovereignty" to imply many different meanings. He did not contest the sovereignty of the British Parliament during those debates, but he also acknowledged the sovereignty of the Queen (not the Queen-in-Parliament), saying that "in framing our Constitution ... our first act should have been to recognize the sovereignty of Her Majesty."[68] He later added that the Canadian Parliament should be granted "all the powers which are incident to sovereignty" and that the Canadian constitution should confer "on the General Legislature the general mass of sovereign legislation."[69]

Macdonald may have had a *flexible* understanding of what the concept of sovereignty entailed, but he was clear about one thing: even if sovereignty could be shared by the British monarch and the Parliaments of Great Britain and Canada, the provincial legislatures should have no part of it. According to Macdonald, the American Civil War had demonstrated the absurdity of leaving component states their sovereignty. This was, according to him, "the fatal error which they the Americans have committed" in designing their constitution. As far as he was concerned, "the true principle of a confederation lies in giving to the general Government all the principles and powers of sovereignty, and in the provision that the subordinate or individual States should have no powers but those expressly bestowed upon them."[70] Although his definition of "confederation" was inaccurate, Macdonald was consistent since he would have preferred a legislative union to either a confederation or federation.

Such a pragmatic attitude could also have been influenced by the Canadian political context. He may have been hesitant to reopen a debate over sovereignty since the previous attempt to discuss the issue in the 1830s had ended in open rebellions. As for the imprecise ways in which he referred to the concept, perhaps Macdonald did not have any precedent to work with within the British Empire. In any case, his reluctance to discuss sovereignty was typical of the modern concept of liberty.

While Macdonald never seriously discussed the issue of sovereignty, there was no way he could avoid becoming involved in debates about the composition of the British and Canadian Parliaments in 1865. Macdonald was aware of the composition of the British Parliament and the theory of mixed government behind it. He alluded to this very briefly during the debate over Confederation by referring to Henry Hallam's *Constitutional History of England* (1827), which gave a standard account of the evolution of the English constitution toward a mixed or constitutional monarchy.[71] However, he could not go too far in that direction when discussing the nature of the Canadian Parliament, since there was no Canadian aristocracy.[72] He had to justify the bicameral structure of the Canadian Parliament differently.

According to Macdonald, the "nation" (or the "people") represented by the Canadian Parliament was neither a single abstract entity nor the sum of the individuals living on the national territory. Rather, it was a community including "all interests, classes, and communities" living in Canada (this conception of the nation as the sum of interest groups within the country was typical of an eighteenth-century version of modern liberty). In order to respect the British constitution and protect the rights and liberties of these different interest groups, the federal Parliament had to be constituted of two independent Houses: the House of Commons and the Senate. The seats in the lower house were to be divided according to the population, while the seats in the Senate would be distributed equally between the three regions joining the federation. This division was adopted to allow the upper house to represent the "sectional [regional] interests" and defend them "against the combinations of majorities in the Assembly [House of Commons]."[73] This was the Canadian way of following Montesquieu's advice that *"pour qu'on ne puisse abuser du pouvoir, il faut que, par la disposition des choses, le pouvoir arrête le pouvoir."*[74]

By designing the Canadian Parliament in this way, the Fathers of Confederation also guaranteed "the rights of the minority," which were considered "the great test of constitutional freedom." According to Macdonald, only this sort of system, as opposed to a more "democratic" one, could guarantee the rights of minorities: "In all countries the rights of the majority take care of themselves, but it is only in countries like England, enjoying constitutional liberty, and safe from the tyranny of a single despot or of an unbridled democracy, that the rights of minorities are regarded."[75] Although Macdonald boasted about this theoretical achievement in 1865, he did not always uphold this principle after Confederation. For instance, he decided not to intervene in New Brunswick during the early 1870s when Roman Catholics lost their right to be educated according to their faith. At that moment, he preferred to uphold the provincial jurisdiction in the matter: "It is the bounden duty of the Government of the Dominion, in the first place, to support the Constitution. The Constitution would not be worth the paper it is written on, unless the rights of the Provincial Legislatures were supported."[76] Macdonald may have had convictions, but he was also a pragmatic man. In other words, he was a politician.

But it was not only sectional and minority interests that Macdonald intended to protect with this political system. He also (and probably more importantly) wanted to safeguard private property, one of the key individual rights of British subjects. As Adam Smith had said: "civil government, so far as it is instituted for the security of property, is in reality instituted for the defence of the rich against the poor, or of those who have some property against those who have none at all."[77] Macdonald agreed: it was clear for him that in order to guarantee the respect of property in Canada, "classes and property should be represented as well as numbers" in the Canadian Parliament.[78] This desire to protect private property influenced the composition of both Houses of the Canadian Parliament. This was manifested in Macdonald's rejection of the principle of universal suffrage for the House of Commons on the argument that it would be a threat to private property:

Experience had shewn that it left a nation weak and led it toward anarchy and despotism. Unless there was a middle power, unless property was protected and made one of the principles on which representation was based, they might perhaps have a people altogether equal, but they would soon cease to have a people altogether free. ... If the principle of representation by universal suffrage was adopted, the result would be in this country as it has been in other countries, that those who had no property would come to have the governing power, the power of imposing the burdens on those who had property. In all countries where universal suffrage had been introduced, it amounted in the long run to a confiscation of property, and men of property had been obliged as in France, to seek refuge in despotism, to rescue them from the tyrannical power of mere numbers.[79]

Macdonald also favoured the appointment of wealthy senators in order to protect property: "A large qualification should be necessary for membership of the Upper House, in order to represent the principle of property. The rights of the minority must be protected, and the rich are always fewer in number than the poor."[80] Macdonald's proposed arrangement was, in a way, flawlessly logical: a vital principle was protected by an institution based on that same principle.

Although Macdonald accepted the sovereignty of Parliament, he understood that the seat of power in the British system was the Crown (the executive), rather than the legislature. This meant that Parliament was not supposed to govern, but only to keep an eye on the government to make sure it did not abuse its power. It is quite telling in this regard that Macdonald started his defence of the Quebec Resolutions in February 1865 by talking about the executive rather than the legislative power, confirming the primacy of the Crown in the working of the British Constitution: "In the first place ... we have provided that for all time to come, so far as we can legislate for the future, we shall have as the head of the executive power, the Sovereign of Great Britain."[81] The primacy of the executive power over the legislative power was also an important feature of the modern concept of liberty.

There is no doubt Macdonald believed in the "Monarchical principle." But his commitment was to a constitutional monarchy. In theory, the executive and legislative powers were divided in the British constitution. In practice, they had been interrelated since the eighteenth century.[82] In order to avoid conflicts between the Crown and Parliament, the Cabinet was created. According to the Cabinet system (known as Responsible Government in Canada), the monarch governed on the advice of ministers who had the confidence of the House of Commons. By the mid-nineteenth century, the Cabinet system clearly set the British constitution apart from other European and American political regimes. Bagehot even started his analysis of the British constitution by discussing the Cabinet system in 1867.[83] The British Crown was made manifest through two distinct institutions in the second half of the nineteenth century; one formal (the monarch), and one effective (the Cabinet). If Macdonald entered politics too late to participate fully in the debate about Responsible Government in the 1840s, he accepted this system of government very quickly. In this regard, Macdonald's understanding of the functioning of the British executive power was very similar to Bagehot's.[84]

Macdonald actually sought to give Canada a formal head of state in 1865, one that would be neutral and above politics:

> By adhering to the monarchical principle, we avoid one defect inherent in the Constitution of the United States. By the election of the President by a majority and for a short period, he never is the sovereign and chief of the nation. He is never looked up to by the whole people as the head and front of the nation. He is at best but the successful leader of a party. This defect is all the greater on account of the practice of re-election. During his first term of office, he is employed in taking steps to secure his own re-election, and for his party a continuance of power. We avoid this by adhering to the monarchical principle — the Sovereign whom you respect and love. I believe that it is of the utmost importance to have that principle recognized, so that we shall have a Sovereign who is placed above the region of party — to whom all parties look

up — who is not elevated by the action of one party nor depressed by the action of another, who is the common head and sovereign of all.[85]

In the meantime, Macdonald considered that "the Sovereign, or in this country the Representative of the Sovereign, can act only on the advice of his ministers, those ministers being responsible to the people through Parliament." Accordingly, the power of the monarch was limited to the choice of his chief advisor (federal prime minister or provincial premiers): "The absolute, uncontrolled right to choose a premier is, according to Bagehot and other late constitutional writers, the only *personal* prerogative remaining in the Sovereign."[86] Once the prime minister was appointed, the monarch did not have the right to remove him, as long as he had the confidence of the Parliament: "Under the constitution as it now stands, I contend that the Ministry of the day, so long as they have the confidence of Parliament, so long as they are sustained in Parliament, must and will have the right to claim the confidence of the Sovereign or the representative of the Sovereign."[87] The system defended by Macdonald was also characteristic of the institutions developed under the auspices of the modern concept of liberty.

As far as he was concerned, Macdonald considered that this system of government was much better suited for liberty than the American system since, in the United States the situation was quite different:

> The President, during his term of office, is in a great measure a despot, a one-man power, with the command of the naval and military forces — with an immense amount of patronage as head of the Executive, and with the veto power as a branch of the legislature, perfectly uncontrolled by responsible advisers, his cabinet being departmental officers merely, whom he is not obliged by the Constitution to consult with, unless he chooses to do so.[88]

According to Macdonald, these threats to liberty did not exist under the British system.

• • •

John A. Macdonald may have been a man of action, but this does not mean that he was not also a man of reflection. He may have been suspicious of abstract principles, but he was not an unprincipled man. The fact that he may not have been always up to the task in defending some of his principles did not make him a vulgar opportunist; it made him a successful politician and statesman.

One great guiding principle that Macdonald believed in throughout his life was that of liberty. He did not understand this liberty to be an inherent right, but his inheritance as a British subject. His definition of liberty focused on the liberties of the subjects, on civil liberties rather than political liberties and independence. As Macdonald saw it, British rule over Canada had been beneficial: "Under the broad folds of the Union Jack we enjoy the most ample liberty to govern ourselves as we please and at the same time we participate in the advantages which flow from association with the mightiest empire the world has ever seen."[89] Liberty meant autonomy, not sovereignty.

Although his concept of liberty was embodied in a conservative framework, it was very "liberal." Indeed, it was so much so that he did not have problems appealing to Whig thinkers to justify his own beliefs. A study of Macdonald's political thought that takes into consideration both his conservatism and conception of liberty highlights the process by which a *conservative* politician could fully participate in the advent of a *liberal* order.[90] If only for that reason, it is worthwhile to assess and reflect on Macdonald's political thought.

Notes

1. I would like to express my gratitude to Simon Vickers and Michael Lanthier for the assistance they offered in the preparation and writing of this article, and to the Social Sciences and Humanities Research Council of Canada (SSHRC) for its support.

2. John A. Macdonald, "To John Kirby *et al.*," *Kingston Herald*, April 23, 1844, quoted in *The Papers of the Prime Ministers, vol. 1: The Letters of Sir John A. Macdonald 1836–1857*, ed. J.K. Johnson (Ottawa: Public Archives of Canada, 1968), 12.

3. Donald Creighton, *John A. Macdonald: The Young Politician* (Toronto: Macmillan, 1952); idem, *John A. Macdonald: The Old Chieftain* (Toronto: Macmillan, 1955).

4. Creighton, *John A. Macdonald: The Young Politician*, 79.

5. Donald Swainson, *Sir John A. Macdonald: The Man and the Politician* (Don Mills: Oxford University Press, 1971).

6. B. Waite, *Macdonald: His Life and World* (Toronto: McGraw-Hill Ryerson, 1975), 22.

7. Richard Gwyn, *John A.: The Man Who Made Us: The Life and Time of John A. Macdonald* (Toronto: Random House Canada, 2007).

8. Patricia Phenix, *Private Demons: The Tragic Personal Life of John A. Macdonald* (Toronto: McClelland & Stewart, 2006).

9. T.W.L. Macdermot, "The Political Ideas of John A. Macdonald," *Canadian Historical Review* 14 (1933): 264.

10. See also J.K. Johnson, "John A. Macdonald" in *The Pre-Confederation Premiers: Ontario Government Leaders, 1841–1867*, ed. J.M.S. Careless (Toronto: University of Toronto Press, 1980), 223–24. J.K. Johnson and P.B. Waite did not address this issue at all in their biography of Macdonald included in the *Dictionary of Canadian Biography*, accessed May 15, 2012, www.biographi.ca.

11. Rod Preece, "The Political Wisdom of Sir John A. Macdonald," *Canadian Journal of Political Science* 17 (1984): 459–86, 465. Philip Resnick has also argued the influence of Edmund Burke's political ideas on Canada's development in *The Masks of Proteus: Canadian Reflections on the State* (Montreal and Kingston, McGill-Queen's University Press, 1990), 88–106. It is interesting to note that in 1891, Joseph Taché had compared Macdonald to Benjamin Disraeli rather than to Burke. His analysis was however quite superficial: *Lord Beaconsfield and Sir John A. Macdonald: A Political and Personal Parallel*, translated by James Penny (Montreal: 1891).

12. Smith and Stewart were themselves inspired by the work of British and American historians such as J.G.A. Pocock, Bernard Bailyn, and Gordon Wood to name but a few: see J.G.A. Pocock, *Politics, Language and Time: Essays on Political Thought and History* (New York: Atheneum, 1971 [1960)); idem, *The Machiavellian Moment: Florentine Political Thought and the Atlantic Republican Tradition* (Princeton: Princeton University Press, 1975); Bernard Bailyn, *The Ideological Origins of the American Revolution* (Cambridge: Belknap Press of the Harvard University Press, 1967); Gordon S. Wood, *The Creation of the American Republic, 1776–1789* (Chapel Hill: University of North Carolina Press, 1969).

13. Peter J. Smith, "The Ideological Genesis of Canadian Confederation," PhD Dissertation (Political Science), Carleton University, 1983, 375 for the quote; idem, "The Ideological Origins of Canadian Confederation," *Canadian Journal of Political Science* 20 (1987): 3–29; Gordon T. Stewart, *The Origins of Canadian Politics: A Comparative Approach* (Vancouver: UBC Press, 1986). Although Janet Ajzenstat has been influenced by this framework as well, she has come to see the Canadian founding as being liberal: *The Canadian Founding: Locke and Parliament* (Montreal and Kingston: McGill-Queen's University Press, 2007).

14. Stéphane Kelly, *La petite loterie. Comment la Couronne a obtenu la collaboration du Canada français après 1837* (Montreal: Boréal, 1997).

15. Stéphane Kelly, "John A. Macdonald 1815–1891," *Les fins du Canada selon*

Macdonald, Laurier, Mackenzie King et Trudeau (Montreal: Boréal, 2001), 21-65.

16. *The Quebec Constitutional Question: Speech by the Rt Hon. Sir John Macdonald, Delivered April 11th 1878* (Montreal: *Montreal Gazette*, 1878), 2.

17. On conservatism, see Russell Kirk, *The Conservative Mind from Burke to Santayana* (Chicago: Henry Regnery Co., 1953); Roger Scruton, *The Meaning of Conservatism* (Markham, ON: Penguin Books, 1980).

18. *Address of The Hon. John A. Macdonald to the Electors of the City of Kingston, with Extracts from Mr. Macdonald's Speeches Delivered on Different Occasions in the Years 1860 and 1861, &c., &c., &c.* (1861), 9.

19. John A. Macdonald to Charles Lindsey, Quebec, June 19, 1860, reproduced in *The Papers of the Prime Ministers, Vol. 2. The Letters of Sir John A. Macdonald 1858–1861*, eds. J.K. Johnson and Carole B. Stelmack (Ottawa: Public Archives of Canada, 1969), 244.

20. John A. Macdonald to James McGill Strachan, Kingston, February 9, 1854, reproduced in *The Letters of Sir John A. Macdonald 1836–1857* (Ottawa: Public Archives of Canada, 1968), 202; John A. Macdonald at electoral meetings in Brantford and St. Thomas in 1860, reproduced in *Address*, 8, 9.

21. *Address*, 8.

22. *Address*, 9–10.

23. *The Quebec Constitutional Question: Speech by the Rt Hon. Sir John Macdonald, Delivered April 11th 1878* (Montreal: *Montreal Gazette*, 1878), 7. The idea that Burke was a reformer may surprise us today, but so he was considered in his day. He defended the American colonists in the 1770s, lobbied for an inquiry on the Indian administration of Warren Hastings in the 1780s, and favoured both the Roman Catholics' emancipation and the advent of free trade in the 1790s.

24. *Address*, 9.

25. John A. Macdonald to Brown Chamberlin, Toronto, January 21, 1856, in *The Letters of Sir John A. Macdonald 1836–1857*, 339.

26. Arthur Aughley, Greta Jones, and W. Riches, *The Conservative Political Tradition in Britain and the United States* (London: Pinter Publishers, 1992). This book provides an analysis of Alexander Hamilton's philosophy as being conservative.

27. John Strachan, *A Discourse on the Character of King George the Third: Addresses to the Inhabitants of British America* (Montreal: Nahum Mower, 1810).

28. Jonathan Sewell and John Beverley Robinson, *Plan for a Legislative Union of the British Provinces in North America* (London: W. Clowes, 1824); John Beverley Robinson, *A Letter to the Right Hon. Earl Barthurst, K.C. on the Policy of Uniting the British North American Colonies* (London: W. Clowes, 1825); John Strachan, *Observations on a "Bill for Uniting the Legislative Councils and Assemblies of the Provinces of Lower Canada and Upper Canada in One Legislature and to Make Further Provision for the Government of the said Provinces"* (London: W. Clowes, 1825).

29. Adam Thom (Camillus), *Anti-Gallic Letters; Addressed to His Excellency The*

Earl of Gosford, Governor-in-Chief of the Canadas (Montreal: Herald Office, 1836); Egerton Ryerson (A Canadian), *The Affairs of the Canadas in a Series of Letters* (London: J. King College Hill, 1837).

30. John Beverley Robinson, *Address, of the Honorable Chief Justice; on Passing Sentence of Death upon Samuel Lount and Peter Matthews* (Toronto: Guardian Office, 1838); Robinson, *Charge of the Honorable John B. Robinson, Chief Justice of Upper Canada to the Grand Jury at Toronto (Thursday, 8th March 1838) on Opening the Court Appointed by Special Commission to Try Prisoners in Custody on Charges of Treason* (Toronto: R. Stanton, 1838); Robinson, *Canada and the Canada Bill* (London: J. Hatchard and Son, 1840).

31. Michel Ducharme, "La primauté des droits ou La liberté moderne dans les Canadas (1828–1838)," in *Le concept de liberté au Canada à l'époque des Révolutions atlantiques, 1776–1838* (Montreal & Kingston: McGill-Queen's University Press, 2010).

32. Lord Durham, *Report on the Affairs of British North America* (1839), ed. Sir Charles Lucas (Oxford: Clarendon Press, 1912); Sir Francis Bond Head, *A Narrative* (London: John Murray, 1839).

33. On this issue, see Paul Smith, "Editor's Introduction," in *Bagehot: The English Constitution* (Cambridge: Cambridge University Press, 2001), 20. For other commentaries on the British constitution and institutions, see Homersham Cox, *The British Commonwealth; or a Commentary on the Institutions and Principles of the British Government* (London: Longman, Brown, Green, and Longman, 1854); Homersham Cox, *The Institutions of the English Government* (London, UK: H. Sweet, 1863); Henry, Lord Brougham, *The British Constitution: Its History, Structure, and Working* (London and Glasgow: Richard Griffin & Co, 1861); George Cornwall Lewis, *Dialogue on the Best Form of Government* (London: Parker Son and Bourn, 1863); Earl Grey, *Parliamentary Government Considered With Reference to Reform* (London: Richard Bentley, 1864); Edward A. Freeman, *The Growth of the English Constitution* (London: Macmillan & Co., 1872). See also John Stuart Mill, "On Liberty" (1859) and "Considerations on Representative Government" (1861) in *On Liberty and Other Essays* (Oxford: Oxford University Press, 1998).

34. Sir William Blackstone, "Of the absolute Rights of Individuals," in *Commentaries on the Laws of England* (1765; repr., Chicago, IL: Chicago University Press, 1979), 1:1; Walter Bagehot, *The English Constitution* (London: Chapman and Hall, 1867).

35. Smith, "Editor's Introduction," 20.

36. John A. Macdonald, October 11, 1864, as quoted in "Hewitt Bernard's Notes on the Quebec Conference, 11–25 October, 1864," in *Documents on the Confederation of British North America*, ed. G. Browne (Toronto: McClelland & Stewart, 1969), 95.

37. John A. Macdonald, October 11, 1864, as quoted in "Hewitt Bernard's Notes on the Quebec Conference, 11–25 October, 1864," in *Documents on the Confederation*, 98.

38. 30 and 31 Victoria, c. 3.

39. Sir William Blackstone, "Of the Absolute Rights of Individuals," in *Commentaries on the Laws of England* (1765; repr., Chicago: University of Chicago Press, 1979), 1:1, 125; Jean Louis De Lolme, *The Constitution of England: Or an Account of the English Constitution* (1771; repr. London: Henry G. Bohn, 1853), 80–81.

40. Benjamin Constant, "De la liberté des anciens comparée à celle des modernes," in *Écrits politiques*, ed. Marcel Gauchet (Paris: Seuil, 1997), 589–619; David Miller, "Introduction," in *Liberty*, ed. David Miller (Oxford: Oxford University Press, 1991), 2–4; Isaiah Berlin, "Two Concepts of Liberty," in *Four Essays on Liberty* (1958; repr., Oxford: Oxford University Press, 1969), 118–72.

41. For instance, Isaiah Berlin warned his readers in his famous essay entitled "Two Concepts of Liberty" that he would "use both words to mean the same." F.A. Hayek did the same in his *Constitution of Liberty*. As far as he was concerned "there did not seem to exist any accepted distinction in meaning between the words 'freedom' and 'liberty' and we shall use them interchangeably." Most encyclopaedias of political thought still do the same. See: Berlin, "Two Concepts of Liberty," 121; F.A. Hayek, *The Constitution of Liberty* (1960; repr., Chicago: University of Chicago Press, 2011), first footnote of the first chapter; David Miller, ed., *The Blackwell Encyclopaedia of Political Thought* (Oxford: Basil Blackwell, 1987) 163–66, 291; Garrett Ward Sheldon, *Encyclopaedia of Political Thought* (New York: Facts on File, 2001) 113, 187–88; Scott John Hammond, *Political Theory: An Encyclopaedia of Contemporary and Classic Terms* (Wesport, CT: Greenwood Press, 2009), 134, 190.

42. Hannah Arendt, *On Revolution* (New York: Viking Press, 1965); David Hackett Fischer, *Liberty and Freedom: A Visual History of America's Founding Ideas* (Oxford: Oxford University Press, 2005), 10.

43. Hanna Fenichel Pitkin, "Are Freedom and Liberty Twins?" *Political Theory* 16: 4 (1988): 523–35.

44. Pitkin, "Are Freedom and Liberty Twins?" 543, 544.

45. Creighton, *John A. Macdonald: The Young Politician*, ch. 3.

46. John A. Macdonald to David Barker Stevenson, Kingston, July 5, 1849, reproduced in *The Letters of Sir John A. Macdonald 1836–1857*, 155.

47. *Parliamentary Debates on the Subject of the Confederation of the British North American Provinces* [hereafter *Parliamentary Debates*] (Quebec: Hunter, Rose & Co, 1865), 41.

48. Creighton, *John A. Macdonald: The Young Politician*, 107.

49. John A. Macdonald to the 1st Baron Knutsford, Rivière du Loup, July 18, 1889, in *Correspondence of Sir John Macdonald: Selections from the Correspondence of the Right Honourable Sir John Alexander Macdonald, G.C.B. First Prime Minister of the Dominion of Canada*, ed. Sir Joseph Pope (Garden City, NY and Toronto: Doubleday, Page & Company, 1921), 450.

50. On the concept of equality, see André Delaporte, "Idée d'égalité, thème et mythe de l'âge d'or en France au XVIIIᵉ siècle," *History of European Ideas* 14: 1 (1992): 115–36; Harvey Chisick, "The Ambivalence of the Idea of Equality in the French Enlightenment," *History of European Ideas* 13: 3 (1991): 215–23.

51. For the Habeas Corpus, see John A. Macdonald to the Governor General, Quebec, March 6, 1861, in *The Letters of Sir John A. Macdonald 1858–1861*, 306. For the freedom of the press and the freedom of religion, see John A. Macdonald, *Address*, 8, 25.

52. John A. Macdonald to the provincial secretary, December 15, 1858, reproduced in *The Letters of Sir John A. Macdonald 1858–1861*, 112. Macdonald used the same expression in 1865 while defending the Quebec Resolutions: *Parliamentary Debates*, 41.

53. See, for instance, "Baldwin to Glenelg," July 13, 1836, in *Statutes, Treatises and Documents of the Canadian Constitution, 1713–1929*, ed. W.M. Kennedy (London: Oxford University Press, 1930), 335–42; "Baldwin to Durham," August 23, 1838, in *Statues, Treaties and Documents of Canadian Constitution, 1713–1929*, ed. W.M. Kennedy (London: Oxford University Press, 1930), 367–69.

54. Continental liberals were more inclined to appeal to popular sovereignty than their British counterparts. See Nicolas Rousselier, *L'Europe des libéraux* (Complexe, 1991); Philippe Nemo and Jean Petitot, eds., *Histoire du libéralisme en Europe* (Paris: Presses universitaires de France, 2006).

55. James A. Epstein, "The Constitutionalist Idiom," in *Radical Expression: Political Language, Ritual, and Symbol in England, 1790–1850* (Oxford: Oxford University Press, 1994), 3–28.

56. On the sovereignty of the people, see Marcel David, *La souveraineté du peuple* (Paris: Presses universitaires de France, 1996). On the idea of the republican people as a metaphysical reality at the basis of the state's legitimacy, see Michael Dorland and Maurice Charland, *Law, Rhetoric and Irony in the Formation of Canadian Civil Culture* (Toronto: University of Toronto Press, 1996), 146–147. Edmund Morgan has talked about the sovereign people as a fiction: *Inventing the People: The Rise of Popular Sovereignty in England and America* (New York: W.W. Norton & Company, 1988). It might be important to say that the use of the word "people" in English (which is plural) implied a greater respect for diversity than the word "nation" used in France (which is singular).

57. On John Locke and the question of sovereignty, see Jean Terrel, *Les théories du pacte social. Droit naturel, souveraineté et contrat de Bodin à Rousseau* (Paris: Seuil, 2001), 234.

58. For the eighteenth century, see Zera S. Fink, *The Classical Republicans: An Essay in the Recovery of a Pattern of Thought in Seventeenth-Century England* (Evanston, IL: Northwestern University, 1945); Gordon Wood, *The Creation*

of the American Republic, 1776–1789 (1969; repr., Chapel Hill, University of North Carolina Press, 1998), 197–255. Carl J. Richard, *The Founders and the Classics: Greece, Rome, and the American Enlightenment* (Cambridge: Harvard University Press, 1994), chap. 5. For the nineteenth century, see for instance Brougham, *The British Constitution*; Benjamin Disraeli, "Conservative Principles: Speech at Manchester, April 3, 1872" and "Conservative and Liberal Principles: Speech at the Crystal Palace, June 24, 1872," in *Selected Speeches of the late Right Honourable Earl of Beaconsfield*, ed. T.E. Kebbel (London: Longmans, Green, and Co., 1882), vol. 2, 490–502, 523–29.

59. *Parliamentary Debates*, 31.

60. John A. Macdonald to John Beattie, esq., Quebec, February 3, 1865, in *Correspondence of Sir John Macdonald*, 21.

61. *Parliamentary Debates*, 1003.

62. *Parliamentary Debates*, 1004.

63. *Parliamentary Debates*, 1004.

64. *Parliamentary Debates*, 1007.

65. Edmund Burke, "Speech at the Conclusion of the Poll, 3 November 1774," in *The Writings and Speeches of Edmund Burke, Vol. 3: Party, Parliament, and the American War 1774–1780*, ed. Paul Langford (Oxford: Clarendon Press, 1996), 68–69.

66. *Parliamentary Debates*, 1005.

67. On the same issue, see also De Lolme, *Constitution*, 53.

68. *Parliamentary Debates*, 33.

69. *Parliamentary Debates*, 41. He also said at the same occasion that: "The Federal Parliament must have the sovereign power of raising money from such sources and by such means as the representatives of the people will allow." (40).

70. John A. Macdonald, "Discourse in the Legislature (April 19, 1861)," in *Correspondence of Sir John Macdonald*, 11. He also said in 1865 that this was the "weakness of the American system": *Parliamentary Debates*, 41.

71. *Parliamentary Debates*, 34. See Henry Hallam, *The Constitutional History of England from the Accession of Henry VII to the Death of George II* (Paris: L. Baudry, 1827), 3 vols.

72. Macdonald acknowledged that "an hereditary upper house is impracticable in this young country. Here we have none of the elements for the formation of a landlord aristocracy — no men of large territorial positions — no class separated from the mass of the people. An hereditary body is altogether unsuited to our state of society, and would soon dwindle into nothing. The only mode of adapting the English system to the upper house is by conferring the power of appointment on the Crown (as the English peers are appointed), but that the appointments should be for life." *Parliamentary Debates*, 35.

73. *Parliamentary Debates*, 38.

74. Montesquieu, *De l'esprit des lois* (1748) (Paris: Garnier-Flammarion, 1979), vol. 1, 293.

75. *Parliamentary Debates*, 44.

76. John A. Macdonald to the Rev. James Quinn, Ottawa, May 29, 1873, reproduced in *Correspondence*, 213–14.

77. Adam Smith, *An Inquiry into the Nature and Causes of the Wealth of Nations (1776)* (Edinburgh: Adam & Charles Black, 1850), 321.

78. *Parliamentary Debates*, 39.

79. *Address,* 99, 100, 101.

80. John A. Macdonald, October 11, 1864, quoted in "Hewitt Bernard's Notes on the Quebec Conference, 11–25 October, 1864," in *Documents on the Confederation,* 98.

81. *Parliamentary Debates*, 32.

82. See Blackstone, *Commentaries*, 1:2,149–50.

83. Bagehot, *The English Constitution*, chap. 1.

84. *The Quebec Constitutional Question*, 12, 16.

85. *Parliamentary Debates*, 33.

86. John A. Macdonald to Lieutenant Governor of Nova Scotia Rivière-du-Loup, July 20, 1884, reproduced in *Correspondence of Sir John Macdonald*, 316.

87. *The Quebec Constitutional Question*, 5.

88. *Parliamentary Debates,* 33.

89. John A. Macdonald, *Address to the People of Canada* (s.l:s.n, 1891), 7.

90. On the advent of a liberal order in Canada, see Ian McKay, "The Liberal Order Framework: A Prospectus for a Reconnaissance of Canadian History," *Canadian Historical Review* 81 (2000): 617–45. For a discussion about this liberal order, see Jean-François Constant and Michel Ducharme, eds., *Liberalism and Hegemony: Debating the Canadian Liberal Revolution* (Toronto: University of Toronto Press, 2009).

PART 2

Macdonald and the Economy

Chapter 6

First Spikes: Railways in Macdonald's Early Political Career

J.J. BEN FORSTER

In the 1850s, visions of continental empire were emerging in British North America. Businessmen, their political allies, and newspapers of the day projected commercial hegemony, either in terms of establishing hinterland access, or in developing a carrying trade to overseas markets.[1] In the Maritimes, Joseph Howe forcefully articulated notions of evolving a regional, and then a wider continental, hinterland for the Atlantic trade; he and like-minded individuals fostered a groundswell of seaboard railway activism. Commercial interests in the Canadas, among whom Alexander Tilloch Galt played a significant role, had already undertaken serious efforts to gain ocean access by rail in the later 1840s. Many of the potential hinterlands were American as opposed to *British North American*, so the conceptual apparatus was of economic rather than political empire. By the late 1850s, commercial and political railway entrepreneurs had moulded the major railways of Canada West — the Grand Trunk and the Great Western — to gain access to the American Midwest, and railway success or failure pivoted on the fortunes of the American trade.

The colonial dependence on the Imperial connection made financial and approval mechanisms political in character, so railways emerged in part as binding agents for the BNA colonies. The American model of continental imperialism was well understood,[2] and the Canadian/British perspective, as

Doug Owram and A.A. den Otter have shown, was also well developed. The Hudson's Bay Company's hegemony prefigured an imagined western political empire.[3] By the late 1850s, the possibilities of western agrarian expansion for the dynamic Canadas, particularly Canada West, were part of public discourse. George Brown, publisher of the *Globe*, was not shy of touting this

THE GRAND OLD TACTICIAN.

Grip, 25 January, 1890.

consideration. William McDougall, the Clear Grit whom Macdonald later co-opted into the Conservative party and sent west to govern Red River, also articulated these beliefs.[4] In preview and imagination, railways linked the West to inevitable progress, to growth, to imperial expansion.[5]

So in planning, the question was not whether to have railways, but how many, where, at what cost, and at whose expense. In realization, the issue became how to make these immensely capital-intensive enterprises profitable, which often revolved around heavy state-subsidization of the capital costs. In this nexus, we search for John A. Macdonald.

In the search, I propose to link Macdonald's early political correspondence to the under-utilized debates and journals of the Legislative Assembly, and to combine this with life cycle and class/professional contextual perspectives.[6] This perspective owes something to Richard Gwyn's recent effort to shift away from Donald Creighton's view of Macdonald as born, Venus-like, fully formed as a statesman-politician, and to J.K. Johnson's attempt in the 1970s to present Macdonald as a non-politician.[7] However, Johnson's assertion that Macdonald was a businessman in politics, with his politics driven by financial (and sometimes venal) interests,[8] was not balanced, and was met by a deafening historiographical silence.[9] Nor did Brian Young's pungent materialist view of George Cartier, as deeply embedded in the normative class-cultural outlook of entrepreneurial Montreal, stimulate a re-examination of the Kingstonian.[10] Most recently, in Ged Martin's work on Macdonald's evolution away from his Kingston constituency and his particularist interests, we obtain an even stronger sense of how time and place framed the young politician.[11] Cued by these historians — and to some degree by the cheerful cynicism of Oscar Skelton[12] — I intend to show how Macdonald's personal and public interest in railways developed and solidified in the politics of the 1850s. The analysis, in turn, permits some forays into the structure of politics in that era.

We know little of Macdonald's perspectives on railways when they first emerged. His letters from the late 1840s and early 1850s are thin, and those histories that depended heavily on his correspondence, such as Donald Creighton's, reflect this.[13] Creighton's first volume, *The Young Politician*, all 481 pages of it, has only three pages dealing with the Grand Trunk Railway, has one brief mention of the Great Western, has nothing to say about the *Railway Guarantee Act* of 1849 or the *Municipal Loan Fund Act* (both Francis Hincks' work),[14] or about the variety of local railways which might have been of political interest to Macdonald, such as the Brockville and Ottawa, or the Bytown and Prescott, both structured to develop regional hinterlands.[15] Three pages on the Grand Trunk — the longest railway in the world when planned in 1852![16] Was Macdonald really so uninterested in the first phase of railway development when they became for him such a dominant concern in the early 1870s and again in the 1880s? And did he view the early railways simply as a means of weakening his opponents and gaining political advantage, as Creighton implies?

In a word, no. Even in conjectural terms, Macdonald must surely have shared in the near-universal enthusiasm about railways. Once the Grand Trunk passed across Macdonald's doorstep in Kingston and gave him quick access to the Legislative Assembly in Toronto he would have been appreciative; the locomotive works in Kingston undoubtedly brought home to him the local economic and political utility of railway development. Speed of communication was enormously accelerated: by the 1860s, a letter posted in Toronto could reach its recipient in Ottawa the same day, as he understood. And he knew of the visions of empire and imperial connection: there is an 1858 letter to him, kept among all those discarded or lost, urging the construction of a transcontinental railway.[17]

Indeed, Macdonald had a lively record of involvement in the railway excitements of the 1850s. He happily voted, by his own admission, for the *Guarantee Act* of 1849.[18] As a youthful member of the Assembly, he was mentored by Sir Allan MacNab (he of "all my politics are railroads" fame);[19] Macdonald in turn seconded the knight from Hamilton's efforts to get specific individuals on the Railroad and Telegraph Line Committee in 1849.[20] The two men treated each other with courtly warmth and kindness in the Assembly, copiously apologizing for differences of opinion on railway matters.[21] Macdonald, on a notable occasion, also commissioned MacNab to apologize to the House for his absence; MacNab was clearly privy to Macdonald's personal travails.[22] This political friendship, centred so emphatically on railways, has been lost to view by historians. Perhaps this is so because it ended so badly in 1856, when Macdonald helped remove MacNab from his co-premiership of the province and, shortly thereafter, despite protestations that he had no such ambitions, took over MacNab's role.[23] Yet though Macdonald outgrew the relationship with the Hamilton man, it helped frame the younger politician's outlook on railways, on the character of political life, and on business-government relations.

Most strikingly, MacNab repeatedly manoeuvred Macdonald onto the Railroad and Telegraph Line Committee,[24] which reflected well on the younger man's perceived acuity of mind, and his trustworthiness in fostering the great railway enterprises of the decade. The Railroad Committee was the furnace in which railway undertakings were hammered into legislative shape. Macdonald himself gave brief suggestion of the centrality of the committee when urging the first reading of a railway charter bill in 1853. The objections raised to the charter were of no immediate moment he said; the thing would be straightened out by the Railroad Committee.[25] Almost all the log-rolling, the significant compromises, the key decisions about potential routes, took place in the Railroad Committee, by those thought to have the coolest heads, the strongest interests, and the most representative politics from both sides of the House. Getting on the committee was the trick. In this context, it is not surprising that despite the thirty-three pages of references to railways in the Index to the Journals of the House of Assembly from 1852 to 1866, debate in the House on railway matters was relatively limited except for the grand trunk excitements of 1851 and 1852, and later when Grand Trunk indebtedness raised its ugly head.

So much of the real debate took place *in camera* in the committee. Macdonald was on the committee from 1851 through the 1860s, with the exception of one year, during which time his viewpoint on railways must have been shaped in some important regards. He was there in 1852, for example, when the impressive and dynamic British railway promoter and builder William Jackson laid the groundwork for the partnership of Peto, Brassey, Jackson, and Betts (the partnership varied over time, and so did the name) to obtain the construction contract for the Grand Trunk Railway, at goodly rates. He was there, too, when Jackson so readily indicated that the partnership could generate the private financial support necessary for constructing the massive undertaking.[26] Macdonald may well have been caught up in the intense enthusiasms of those moments, as was Francis Hincks, who was enamoured of the possibilities of British private finance.

As it emerged, however, Macdonald's support of railway development was not unequivocal. He had a significant sense of fiscal restraint in the midst of the developing railway barbecue. One does need to keep in mind that the early history of railways in British North America followed on the railway mania in Great Britain in the mid 1840s, and that immense mania was built on the happy belief that railways could be financed entirely in the private sector, and that they would be immediately profitable. George Hudson, the era's British "Railway King," guaranteed high rates of returns on the bonds of his railways, and for a time engaged in Ponzi schemes to seemingly make good his guarantees.[27] But private sector financing dried up in the aftermath of the British railway crash, which helped reveal Hudson's malfeasance. And it was from Britain that the vast bulk of railway construction funding came to British North America and elsewhere.[28] So, while early railway plans in the Canadas emphasized private finance, some reliance on public-sector support became increasingly and obviously necessary in the British North American colonies. The American approach, where a wide variety of public financial support for railways emerged beginning in the 1830s and 1840s, would have been known in the Canadas.[29] The railway crash in Britain, followed by an economic downturn, made private finance difficult to obtain by railway promoters, even in the imperial financial mecca of London.[30] The *Guarantee Act* of 1849 was the consequent modest first step in government support for railways in the Canadas. Macdonald had readily voted for that.

However, he reacted with caution as the first Grand Trunk Railway proposals emerged, involving much greater government aid. When these grandiose plans were presented, purportedly supported by a vast Imperial loan, Macdonald voiced suspicion. Nova Scotian politician Joseph Howe, with New Brunswick premier E.B. Chandler[31] in tow, came to the Canadas in the spring of 1851, asserting that the Imperial government was intending to provide a loan guarantee of £7,000,000 for the construction of an intercolonial grand trunk line.[32] Howe swept almost all before him, but not Macdonald, who wanted the Assembly to delay the consideration of support for the portions of the line that would be outside of Canada West (Upper Canada). He felt that the financial liability of what is now Ontario was in this plan too great, and in the process displayed an economic and political particularism with which George Brown might well have agreed. Indeed, Macdonald voted for the inclusion of a proviso in the bill which would require the supposed Imperial loan to be in place before the line was to be undertaken, though that was defeated.[33] His suspicions were well-grounded: the British government soon indicated that the loan guarantee would not be forthcoming, and the first Grand Trunk proposals receded.

When Francis Hincks returned to the charge in 1852, Macdonald again voiced concern. Macdonald showed an opposition that puzzled both Hincks and Allan MacNab, by first seeking a procedural delay to the Grand Trunk bill because the appropriate documents had not yet been printed in French, and then more directly. As Hincks pointed out, Macdonald could have expressed his opposition in the Railroad Committee. Either Macdonald had developed doubts after the initial enthusiasms of Jackson's Committee presentation had worn off, or Macdonald had kept his counsel for fear that the Railroad Committee would bury his objections and concerns. Macdonald's opposition centred on potential fiscal difficulties,[34] which the opportunistic Hincks could sometimes sweep aside in his eagerness for British financing. Macdonald crossed swords with Hincks repeatedly on these matters, pouring scorn on the apparent pandering to Jackson, the great English lobbyist. Macdonald pointed out that for all the promises, the Peto partnership was not associated with the Grand Trunk Railway (GTR) bill then under consideration, and so the province might be liable for the construction costs.[35] Allan MacNab then rose to express pained surprise and opposition to his young protege's apparent lack of commitment to the centrality of railway enterprise. Macdonald forcefully interrupted, saying that the advantage of railways to the province was of "the greatest" extent, and that his opposition was to the specifics of the current proposal, and not to the general principle, which he fully supported.[36]

Macdonald then seized or created opportunities to make his strong support of railways fully evident. His satisfaction at being able to second Hinck's motion a couple of weeks later to petition the British Crown for guaranteed railway funding support for eastward extensions of the GTR was palpable.[37] Later, while Attorney General for Canada West, he strongly supported an expansion of Hincks' creation of a *Municipal Loan Act* for Canada East, to parallel that already in place for Canada West. These acts, as members of the Assembly were fully aware, were a primary means of extending local financial support to railways through municipal bond issuances that were pooled under provincial fiat.[38] But here too Macdonald expressed fiscal prudence. William Cayley, the Inspector General (finance minister) who brought forward these important amendments to the *Municipal Loan Act*, undertook to mollify opposition by firmly suggesting that the debentures issued by municipalities under the act would be guaranteed by *provincial* credit. Macdonald poured cold water, asserting that such a matter could only be decided by the courts, and refused to give his personal opinion.[39] When an opposition motion was made to modify the act to explicitly provide such a guarantee, Macdonald was key in squelching it.

The boundaries of fiscal restraint were however increasingly violated. In 1855, Macdonald endorsed aid to the Grand Trunk in the way of guaranteeing 6 percent on a GTR bond issue of £900,000. This caused great debate in the Assembly, so much so that in the subsequent election Macdonald undertook to explain his position in a pamphlet to his constituents, arguing that the GTR was in effect getting no more support on a *pro rata* basis than other railways in the province.[40] It was, he wrote, "a rational subscription to an enterprise fostered for the general benefit of the whole country."[41] In 1856, his government sponsored the *Relief Act*, which offered £800,000 for the completion of the Victoria Bridge in Montreal and allowed the GTR to issue £2,000,000 of bonds that took creditor precedence over the 1855 bond issue. He had voted in favour of a massive £3,111,500 loan to that railway, and was co-premier in 1857 (and the *de facto* power in the land), when the Canadas gave up the first rights to the income from the loan, which effectively resulted in giving up claims to the debt itself.[42] It might be thought that Macdonald had by that point deserted his earlier stance of fiscal restraint and control. But his argument in the context of the later 1850s was clear: these vast railway enterprises, particularly the Grand Trunk, could not be allowed to fail. As it was, the credit of the province through private British bond funding, and possibly the province's entire economic well-being, were all dependent on the railways. Despite the very considerable fiscal risk involved, support *had* to be extended. The sheer size of the Grand Trunk, the immensity of *British* private sector involvement in that railway, made the full commitment of the Province to it inevitable. It was too big to fail. That underpinned Macdonald's attitudes, overwhelming fiscal restraint and even prudence. There was, as well, a pragmatic and intellectual shift away from the local and particularistic perspectives that partly fueled his earlier fiscal concerns.

The toils of the railways, most specifically those of the GTR, continued to increase in intensity as the decade moved on. The fiscal difficulties this and other railways faced by the late 1850s lay in their inadequate accommodation of the development of the western American hinterland in the face of steadily escalating competition,[43] not just capital cost over-runs and excessively high operational expenses. By the end of 1857, as the economy suffered a major downturn, the fiscal implications were serious indeed. It needs to be noted that upwards of 70 percent of government revenue at this time was derived from tariffs on imported goods, and in such a downturn, the decline of imports had a major impact on the government's income stream. As the Grand Trunk was by then effectively dependent on government support through bond guarantees as well as direct cash subventions, the dangers railways posed to government finance were considerable. This was understood by Inspector General William Cayley and comprehended in all its implications by the man who took Cayley's place, the formidable Alexander Tilloch Galt. Auditor General John Langton raised the alarm in mid-1858, pointing to an estimated deficit of some £1,000,000. Half of that arose from railway obligations. The other half "had all the appearance of a permanent deficiency upon our present basis ..." Langton wrote to Galt. Indeed, "before we reach the end ..., we must come to direct taxation."[44]

The outlines of this, if not the intricacies, surely was evident to Macdonald, as leader of government. Langton had been given the Auditor Generalship through Macdonald's influence, and as a former member of the House of Assembly and in this office, he had direct access to Macdonald. So through this, and even more emphatically through Galt, Macdonald would have been made aware of the state of affairs. Not surprisingly, both Cayley, and then Galt, increased the tariff, and somehow government finances staggered on without resorting to direct taxation. The evidence suggests that the fiscal boundaries Macdonald had asserted so firmly in the early 1850s when in opposition, and indeed in 1854, when he was in power as Attorney General, had been significantly and knowingly subverted.

Three generations after the railway politics of the 1850s Canadian historians expressed wonderment at the belief those of the earlier era had in the transformative and enriching power of the railways, at the spendthrift ways of governments, at the remarkable blend of idealism, collective greed, and individual venality embodied in the railway project.[45] Those historians had a moral stance increasingly outside the spectrum of behaviours considered commonplace some sixty years earlier, when public economic policy could be shaped to give considerable incidental private gain to the well-informed and well-positioned politician. Moreover, such activities were known, even expected, from members of the political class by their peers. Insider information was to be traded upon, though the trading was to be disguised from the public, as it might raise questions about political altruism. Thus, for example, at the same time as forceful clashes were taking place about extending funding to the Grand Trunk in 1855, a bill that attracted somewhat less attention made its way through the Assembly, fostered by Macdonald, changing the railway's route in Toronto. Questions of route and land were important to making speculative profit, as was suggested in the debate on this matter.[46]

This interweaving of politics and private enterprise, sometimes envisioned as crony capitalism,[47] and at other times as political entrepreneurship[48] was pervasive in the House of Assembly. Francis Hincks, who was co-premier of the province from 1851 to 1854, was hung out to dry and lost control of the Assembly on a railway-associated scandal. He was notoriously discovered to have profited through insider knowledge from railway-linked Toronto municipal bonds to the tune of several years' professional income. Hincks denied that there was any wrongdoing involved and was substantially cleared, but his name by rumour was attached to other dubious railway operations where personal profit was thought to have been obtained.[49] Sir Allan MacNab, the baronet of Hamilton who came next after Hincks as co-premier, infamously said "all my politics are railroads," and acted to profit from railway-associated land holdings. Few others were quite so frank, but railways were a frequent component of the heady mixture of business and politics that prevailed.

It could hardly be expected that Macdonald would be free of such actions when MacNab was a political crony until the mid-1850s and Hincks was a respected opponent with whom Macdonald could co-operate on railway matters. J.K. Johnson has shown how Macdonald operated in conjunction with local Kingston businessmen, and how he pursued personal profit beyond that sphere.[50] This extended beyond local interest and deep into the provincial world of railways. Macdonald acted as solicitor for the railway contractor C.S. Gzowski and Company in 1853 and 1854, for example. The firm had taken on the construction of the western section of the Grand Trunk Railway, and Macdonald not only acted on their behalf, but had personal interest in land that made up potential railway yards or town lots in Sarnia. When a political colleague in London made an inquiry about buying land in the town in anticipation of Gzowski & Co.'s interest in it, Macdonald asserted that "*we must* get the *value* of our land" (italics original). Clearly price had been discussed, and profit had to be kept in mind.[51] During the same time period he slyly boasted to a friend: "Things pecuniary have prospered with me, & without exertion I will be next year a rich man."[52] It needs to be noted that among those interested in this land, other than Gzowski and Macdonald, were A.T. Galt, Luther Holton, and David Macpherson — all railway and political men.[53]

• • •

These manoeuvrings did not end with the hoped-for profit, and from the perspectives of contemporaries, such efforts damaged his reputation.[54] However, the scheming provides a perspective on Macdonald as a figure of his time, influenced by the apparent success of MacNab and his like in working public railway plans to private profit. Not surprisingly, when Macdonald's will was probated in 1891, newspapers could report that "the late statesman held many valuable shares in companies and schemes, to float which he had assisted at various times ... The publication of the fact ... has caused some excitement in the Dominion."[55] While by the 1890s disapprobation might be expressed, such in some part was the way political life proceeded in the Assembly of the Province of Canada.

While Macdonald's railway-oriented work within that narrow and crucial political world remains largely cloaked in mystery, there are occasional glimpses into the story. With him, as with most politicians of the time, there was a blending of public interest with personal, expressed through *sub rosa* conversations and meetings. Endless deal-making, log-rolling, and promises of patronage were essential in a fluid political environment in which flexible alliances and the partial independence of politicians were at the margin more important than declared party allegiances. One might cite the case of Hamilton mercantile powerhouse and politician Isaac Buchanan,[56] who received a full Macdonaldian treatment in relation to Buchanan's Southern Railway project. In 1859 Buchanan desperately wanted the government to provide $40,000 for a minor railway line associated with the Great Southern and in which Buchanan had an interest. Macdonald did not feel this was politically viable. He suggested that Buchanan write to Finance Minister A.T. Galt to see whether some money could be found for this purpose, and then told Galt to let Buchanan down gently in denying the plea.[57]

A year and a half later, Buchanan alarmed Macdonald with talk of leaving the Assembly because of Macdonald's unwillingness to have the province take over municipal debt, which had largely emerged in support of railways. We have seen above how wary Macdonald was of providing open-ended provincial support for municipal indebtedness. Macdonald urged Buchanan not to resign, pointing out that if the Southern Railway "is going to have a chance it must be strong in Parliament & Foley,[58] you, Christie,[59] McBeth[60] [*sic*] & myself will require all our united influences to set it on its legs again."[61] He later urged Buchanan to buy out another investor in the Southern Railway, indicating that the "scheme must fructify 'ere long."[62] Macdonald plotted with Buchanan about advancing the Great Southern Line, in the process revealing an intimate knowledge of the makeup and activities of the Great Southern's

Board of Directors. That he had the same detailed awareness of the Grand Trunk Railway's Board of Directors is hardly surprising given how dependent the GTR was becoming on government largesse by 1856.[63] Macdonald kept close tabs on the goings on in the GTR Canadian Board of Directors through John Ross,[64] a member of the Assembly, a not infrequent cabinet member, a government representative on the board of the Grand Trunk, and its president. Macdonald himself resisted taking a seat on that board himself, for political reasons. That he had influence with that board cannot be doubted.

This brief mention of names establishes a couple of webs — two of many interconnected webs, economic and otherwise — that made Macdonald such a superb politician, and permitted the provincially crucial railway project, to which Macdonald had so substantially tied himself, to advance. In the process, the project showered benefits onto the private sector and onto some of those politicians most closely linked to it, and created moments that bound together or divided essential groups and components of the political process.

What understandings are to be derived from this largely downplayed and even ignored phase of Macdonald's early political career? First, even keeping Johnson's work in mind, one can readily assert that Macdonald was not a financier or promoter, nor did purely fiscal considerations drive his politics.[65] His politics lay in pragmatism and in his ability to persuade and move others. His cabinet-level involvements first emerged because of those abilities and from his formidable legal skills. Railways, in their chartering and in the manoeuvring to put together appropriate parliamentary coalitions to move those charters into place and incidentally to provide benefit to some of those in the coalitions, were to Macdonald a *political* enterprise, not an economic one.

In one way, this paper is a comment on the character of mid-nineteenth-century politics, in which there was a continuum of personal, political, and public interests structured into the very heart of governmental and legislative processes. In the sequence of political leaders — Hincks, MacNab, and Macdonald — the politics of railways was a politics of continuity. Allan MacNab's mentorship of Macdonald could be seen to allow Macdonald to develop his personal interests, his political skills, and his nascent statesmanship. In turn, Macdonald's growing political authority was dependent on parallel and intermingled information flows that he variously disguised, hid, or selectively revealed or acted upon, very occasionally for personal benefit, and more generally to create and maintain the networks of connections through which political decisions were made. The railway project was a crucial component of this process. At the same time one can observe Macdonald's Upper Canadian particularism and Kingston localism evolving into a broader political and state sensitivity.[66]

It can also be suggested that Macdonald's experiences in the politics of the early- and mid-1850s deeply influenced his later approaches toward national railways. One unfortunate lesson was played out in the Pacific Scandal, where for political purposes he willingly accepted generous amounts of monied electoral aid from financier and shipping magnate Hugh Allan, to whom the first transcontinental railway charter did go, after all. That particular bit of crony capitalism — of political entrepreneurship on Allan's part — is little more than an expansive extension of the murky railway politics of the 1850s. Somewhat greater ostensible distance was maintained between the railways and Macdonald thereafter.[67] A second area in which the 1850s had their influence was in the fiscal implications of railways. One might note that Macdonald was not an enthusiast for government ownership; he felt that railways should be private enterprises. He rejected the approach taken by Alexander Mackenzie's government in the mid-1870s. One lesson of the 1850s was, however, that private enterprise was not enough: the private railways of that era required government aid aplenty to remain solvent. As railways were the overarching economic enterprise of the 1850s, they could not be abandoned in their travail, as he clearly articulated. It was not at all surprising that at the time of the election of 1872, he reassured one Hamilton manufacturer that high tariffs were a necessity, given that there would be a need to support railways.[68] The great generosity of the Canadian Pacific Railway charter terms are to be understood in this context. It is to be seen as an effort to get as much of the cost out of the way at the start of the enterprise, and to avoid the political and fiscal ulcer of continued debate and continued subventions. Macdonald perhaps felt he had enough of that in the 1850s and 1860s. It didn't turn out that way, of course.

Yet Macdonald, more than many of his contemporaries, showed fiscal restraint — an unwillingness to overcommit the resources of the state in support of private enterprise, in case it might result in fiscal collapse. The generosity in the CPR charter may be seen, and with much irony, as an attempt to create a context for fiscal restraint in the future. Macdonald's considerable reluctance to provide the company with further financial support during one critical phase in its construction is to be understood from this perspective. Nonetheless, as in the 1850s, once Macdonald was committed, he stayed the course.

And as for empire? The national railway enterprise of the 1870s and 1880s proved its military and imperial utility in the suppression of the rebellions of 1885, in which little pandering to the hinterland, such as took place in the earlier Manitoba troubles, needed to be undertaken. The railway exploitation of the West shifted from the continentalist economic perspective of the 1850s to a national political/economic hegemony with the CPR, attended though that future railway was by vast financial and entrepreneurial risk. There was much profit to be found in due course. But by then Macdonald was no more.

NOTES

1. The shifting trends of railway development in North America is succinctly outlined in G.R. Taylor and I. Neu, *The American Railroad Network, 1861–1890* (Cambridge: Harvard University Press, 1956); A fine biographical expression of continental business ambitions and the role of the carrying trade is to be found in Douglas McCalla, *The Upper Canada Trade, 1834–1872: A Study of the Buchanans' Business* (Toronto: University of Toronto Press, 1979); A classic pre-railway expression is D.G. Creighton, *The Commercial Empire of the St. Lawrence* (Toronto: Ryerson, 1936). However, a more tightly analytical perspective is found in G.N. Tucker, *The Canadian Commercial Revolution 1845–1851* (New Haven, CT: Yale University Press, 1936). The literature is very large, and the references here are merely emblematic. The best source on the idea of railways and commercial empire in British North America is A.A. den Otter, *The Philosophy of Railways: The Transcontinental Railway Idea in British North America* (Toronto: University of Toronto Press, 1997), which is particularly strong in the Maritimes.
2. Alvin C. Gluek Jr., *Minnesota and the Manifest Destiny of the Canadian Northwest* (Toronto: University of Toronto Press, 1965).
3. John S. Galbraith, *The Hudson's Bay Company as an Imperial Factor, 1821–1869* (Berkeley: University of California, 1957).
4. Douglas Owram, *Promise of Eden: The Canadian Expansionist Movement and the Idea of the West, 1856–1900* (Toronto: University of Toronto Press, 1980). Suzanne Zeller, "McDougall, William." In *Dictionary of Canadian Biography*, [hereafter *DCB*] vol. 13. *www.biographi.ca/009004-119.01-e.php?&id_nbr=6901*.
5. On this, one might consult H.V. Nelles, *Philosophy of Railroads and Other Essays*, ed. T.C. Keefer (Toronto: University of Toronto Press, 1972). Nelles has a useful and extensive introduction to the *Philosophy*, which was first published in 1850. A.A. den Otter appropriately co-opted and rephrased Keefer's title, and has an effective chapter discussing railway technology as an imperial ideational factor.

6. Even the debates are not rich on railway matters, except as the Grand Trunk Railway began to devour government finances. See Province of Canada, *General Index to the Journals of the Legislative Assembly of Canada, 1852–1866*.

7. D.G. Creighton, *John A. Macdonald: The Young Politician* (Toronto: Macmillan, 1965).

8. J.K. Johnson, "John A. Macdonald and the Kingston Business Community, 1842–1867," in Gerald Tulchinsky, ed., *To Preserve and Defend: Essays on Kingston in the Nineteenth Century* (Montreal: McGill-Queen's University Press, 1975); and especially Johnson, "John A. Macdonald, the Young Non-Politician," Canadian Historical Society, *Historical Papers*, vol. 6 (1971) 138–153. See also James Keith Johnson, ed., *The Papers of the Prime Ministers, Vol. I: The Letters of Sir John A. Macdonald 1836–1857* (Ottawa: Public Archives of Canada, 1968) and *The Papers of the Prime Ministers, Vol. II: The Letters of Sir John A. Macdonald 1858–1861*, (Ottawa: Public Archives of Canada, 1969). There is considerable suggestive material contained within these texts.

9. Johnson may well have retreated from this perspective, as may be presumed from a reading of his and P.B. Waite's "Macdonald, Sir John Alexander." In *DCB*, vol. 12, 91–612.

10. Brian Young, *George-Étienne Cartier: Montreal Bourgeois* (Montreal: McGill-Queen's University Press, 1981). Also, see Jonathan Swainger's and my more recent work on Edward Blake, which places that man within his legal culture, "Blake, Edward." In *DCB*, vol. 13, 74–85.

11. Gwyn, *John A.: The Man Who Made Us: The Life and Times of John A. Macdonald, vol. 1, 1815–1867* (Toronto: Random House Canada, 2007). See also the earlier J.K. Johnson, ed., *Affectionately Yours: The Letters of Sir John A. Macdonald and His Family* (Toronto: Macmillan, 1969). Ged Martin, *Favourite Son? John A. Macdonald and the Voters of Kingston 1841–1891* (Kingston: Kingston Historical Society, 2010), 35, 37. A sharp contrast is to be obtained between J.K. Johnson, "John A. Macdonald," in *The Pre-Confederation Premiers: Ontario Government Leaders, 1841–1867*, ed. J.M.S. Careless (Toronto: University of Toronto Press, 1980), 197–245, and Ged Martin, "John A. Macdonald: Provincial Premier," *British Journal of Canadian Studies* 20 (2009), 99–122. Johnson pursues Macdonald as a personality profile, with an emphasis on his business dealings, while Martin displays Macdonald as the committed politician within the complex policy and electoral considerations context of the 1850s and early 1860s.

12. Oscar Douglas Skelton, *The Railway Builders: A Chronicle of Overland Highways* (Toronto: Glasgow, Brook & Company, 1916).

13. Moreover, Creighton used the incomplete scrapbook newspaper *Hansard*, as the carefully compiled Assembly debates that Elizabeth Nish (later Gibbs) and others edited were not yet available. Elizabeth Nish (Gibbs), ed., *Debates of the Legislative Assembly of United Canada, 1841–1867* (Quebec: L'Ecole des Hautes Études Commerciales, 1970–1990) [hereafter *Debates*.]

14. For a full treatment of Hincks, see R.S. Longley, *Sir Francis Hincks: A Study of Canadian Politics, Railways, and Finance in the Nineteenth Century* (Toronto: University of Toronto Press, 1943).

15. Creighton, *The Young Politician*, 250–3, and index. See J.M.S. Careless, *The Union of the Canadas 1841–1857: the Growth of Canadian Institutions* (Toronto: McClelland & Stewart, 1967), 139–46, for a succinct treatment.

16. A.W. Currie: *The Grand Trunk Railway of Canada* (Toronto: University of Toronto Press, 1957), 3.

17. Gwyn, *John A.: The Man Who Made Us, Vol. 1, 1815–1867*, 191.

18. *Debates*, August 26, 1851 (Montreal, 1970–1994) 1580–81, 12 Vic. Cap 29, 1849. The provincial government would guarantee up to 6 percent interest on bonds of railways for up to half their cost. The railways had to be over seventy-five miles in length, and one-half completed.

19. Peter Baskerville, "MacNab, Sir Allan Napier." In *DCB*, *www.biographi. ca/009004-119.01-e.php?id_nbr=4565*. MacNab's biographer here identifies him as having "questionable scruples" — MacNab's difficulty in differentiating between personal and public business is evident. He became, in the mid-1840s, the leader of moderate Tories, and between 1854 and 1856 was premier. He was not the best model for the young Macdonald, who rapidly outgrew MacNab politically in the mid-1850s.

20. The formal name of the committee as it then stood was the Standing Committee on Railroad and Telegraph Line Bills. *Debates*, 1849, March 3, 1849, 1297; *Debates*, March 27, 1849, 1570.

21. *Debates*, 1852–53, October 21, 1852, 1166.

22. *Debates*, 1850, 887, June 28, 1850.

23. Macdonald to Henry Smith, November 13, 1856, Johnson, *Letters*, vol. 1, 392–93.

24. This in 1853 became the Railroads, Canals, and Telegraph Lines Committee. *Journals of the Legislative Assembly of the Province of Canada* (May 23, 1851): 18; [hereafter *Journals*]; *Journals* 11(1853), Part 1 (August 23, 1852): 10; ibid., (June 19, 1854): 20 (he was absent by September, likely because he became Attorney General); ibid., (February 21, 1856): 30; ibid., (March 2, 1857): 8; ibid., (March 18, 1858) 148; ibid., (February 17, 1859):71; ibid., (March 7, 1860): 27; ibid., April 5, 1861, 67; ibid., (April 9, 1862): 103.

25. *Debates*, 1852–53 (March 7, 1853): 1886.

26. Oscar Douglas Skelton, *Life and Times of Sir Alexander Tilloch Galt*, ed. G. MacLean (Toronto: McClelland & Stewart, 1966), 32.

27. Hudson's career has generated some biographies, most recently the somewhat adulatory text by Robert Beaumont, *The Railway King: A Biography of George Hudson* (London: Review, 2002).

28. Skelton, *Galt*, 19–22, notes that Alexander Tilloch Galt had great success in 1845 in London selling the stock of the Atlantic St. Lawrence Railroad Company. When he returned the following year to sell the bonds, the market had already become too congested, and he faced great difficulties.

29. George R. Taylor, *The Transportation Revolution 1815–1860* (New York: Harper and Row, 1951) 86–96, and for canals, 48–55.

30. Skelton, *Galt,* 21–24.

31. Michael Swift, "Chandler, Edward Barron." In *DCB*, vol. 10, 157–60.

32. J. Murray Beck, *Joseph Howe, Volume II: The Briton Becomes Canadian 1848–1873* (Montreal: McGill-Queen's, 1983), 32–45. Howe had been in Britain from late 1850 to the spring of 1851, lobbying on railway matters, and had obtained some assurances that a British loan guarantee was forthcoming. The British government, by the end of 1851, denied the support it had previously promised, citing Howe's desire to have the railway run close to the American border (with the possibility of a connection to the United States). Howe had taken care to keep Francis Hincks in the Canadas effectively informed. G.P. deT. Glazebrook, *A History of Transportation in Canada*, vol. 1 (Toronto: McClelland & Stewart, 1964), 150.

33. *Debates*, 1851 (August 12, 1851): 1344; (August 13, 1851): 1378; (August 26, 1851): 1580–81.

34. *Debates* 1852 (October 27, 1852): 1266. Macdonald was possibly partial to a competing bid from A.T. Galt, Luther Holton and David L. Macpherson. See. Skelton, *Galt*, 34–36. Matters become somewhat murky in this context. A different interpretation of his opposition to the Grand Trunk as developed under Hincks and the British connection with William Jackson might be possible. Alexander Tilloch Galt, Luther Holton, and David L. MacPherson (with whom Casimir Gzowski was frequently associated as contractor and more) had struggled mightily to develop a Grand Trunk line, having structured a share subscription for the charter. That the group subscribing had the funds necessary to undertake the railway is unlikely. There remains the possibility that the Galt, Holton, and MacPherson effort (with Gzowski associated, among others) may simply have been a ploy to require the Hincks-Jackson interests to effectively buy them out through contracts and routing decisions. Certainly the Jackson contracting and financial interests won out in 1852–53. Was Macdonald's opposition to the Hincks-Jackson form of the Grand Trunk linked to his involvement in representing Gzowski & Co.? The complex negotiations between the groups are described in part in Currie, *The Grand Trunk*, 11–15.

35. *Debates*, 1852 (October 25, 1852): 1214.

36. *Debates*, 1852 (October 21, 1852): 1166.

37. *Debates*, 1852 (November 8, 1852): 1555; (November 9, 1852): 1555.

38. The pooling agent was the province, so undiscerning investors could incorrectly believe that the bonds were provincially supported. 16 Vic. Cap. 22, 16 Vic. Cap. 123 (1852) , and 18 Vic. Cap. 13 (1854). See Michael Piva, "Continuity and Crisis: Francis Hincks and Canadian Economic Policy," *Canadian Historical Review* 66 (1985) 185–210, which provides a discussion of the acts in context.

39. *Debates*, 1854–55 (December 1, 1854): 1559, 1561.

40. Ibid., 1854–55 (May 1, 1855) 3106–7.

41. Ibid., 1854–55 (May 8, 1855) 3283.

42. A.W. Currie, *The Grand Trunk*, 39–40, 44–45, 312.

43. A.T. Galt to Brassey, Galt Papers, vol. 1, 28–3, Library and Archives Canada. This letter makes it clear that the Grand Trunk and the Canadian canal system were going concerns, and the trade of the American west was necessary. The Baring Papers has two letters confirming Galt's perspective that the increase in traffic was an *immediate* necessity to provide support for the Grand Trunk, and that could only be traffic from the American side of the border. See A.T. Galt to T. Baring, October 13, 1859; November 12, 1859, Baring Papers, LAC. The Toronto and Northern Railway had the same focus.

44. J. Langton to W. Cayley, Department of Finance Records, LAC. This letter probably was circulated, as the one in existence in vol. 3367 is a copy.

45. Skelton, *The Railway Builders*; S.J. McLean, "National Highways Overland," in Adam Shortt and Arthur G. Doughty, eds., *Canada and Its Provinces, Vol. 10: The Dominion Industrial Development II* (Toronto: Publishers' Association, 1913).

46. *Debates*, (May 1, 1855): 3201; (May 10, 1855): 3343.

47. See Andrew Smith, "British Businessmen and Canadian Confederation: Gentlemanly Capitalism at Work," PhD Thesis, University of Western Ontario, 2005, who defines the nexus in Great Britain as "gentlemanly capitalism." See also the resultant book, *British Businessmen and Canadian Confederation : Constitution-Making in an Era of Anglo-Globalization* (Montreal : McGill-Queen's University Press, 2008). There is a vast and growing multi-disciplinary literature on crony capitalism.

48. See Burton W. Folsom, *Entrepreneurs vs the State: A New Look at the Rise of Big Business in America, 1840–1920* (Reston,VA: Young American's Foundation, 1987).

49. William G. Ormsby, "Sir Francis Hincks," in J.M.S. Careless, ed., *The Pre-Confederation Premiers*, 148–96. An extensive discussion of the scandal is Paul Romney, "'The Ten Thousand Pound Job': Political Corruption, Equitable Jurisdiction, and the Public Interest in Upper Canada 1852–6," in D. Flaherty, ed., *Essays in the History of Canadian Law, Vol. II* (Toronto: University of Toronto Press, 1983), 143–99.

50. Johnson, "John A. Macdonald and the Kingston Business Community," and Johnson,"John A. Macdonald, the Young Non-politician." J.K. Johnson and P.B. Waite, "Macdonald, Sir John Alexander," *DCB*, vol. 12, 591–612.

51. Johnson, ed, *Letters*, vol 1, 195 Letter to Crown Land Ordnance Department, June 1853 (copy to C.S. Gzowski & Co.); 204, to Henry C.R. Brecher, March 22, 1854, in ibid.

52. Johnson, vol. 1, Macdonald to John Rose [1853.]

53. Johnson,"John A. Macdonald, the Young Non-politician," 143. It might be noted that several of these men had formerly had an interest in driving a railway through to Sarnia before the town was settled upon as a terminus for the Grand Trunk.

54. Martin, *Favourite Son?* 68.

55. *Barrier Miner* (Broken Hill, Australia, July 18, 1891), 2.

56. Isaac Buchanan, with his brother Peter in Glasgow, was involved in a series of mercantile partnerships that allowed him to become one of the wealthiest men in Canada West by the mid-1850s, and a dominant figure in the political and business life of Hamilton. He entered politics largely because of railways and his interest in the Great Western and then the projected Southern railway. He came into direct conflict with Sir Allan MacNab on railway matters. It is possible that Macdonald's drift away from MacNab was associated with Buchanan's political emergence as an alternative power to MacNab in Hamilton. See Douglas McCalla's *The Upper Canada Trade 1834–1872: A Study of the Buchanans' Business* (Toronto: University of Toronto Press 1979). Also his Buchanan, Isaac, *DCB*, vol. 11, *www.biographi.ca/009004-119.01-e.php?&id_nbr=5402* .

57. Johnson, *Letters*, vol. 2, Macdonald to Galt, October 28, 1859, 183; Macdonald to Buchanan, November 28, 1859, 192.

58. Michael Hamilton Foley was a journalist and a Reform politician who sat for Waterloo North. He held a post in the short-lived Brown-Dorion ministry of 1858. His presence in this potential railway alliance shows how railway politics transcended the amorphous political affiliations of the day. He was also an occasional member of the Railroad Committee. He later was a member of the Macdonald-Cartier ministry in 1864. Bruce W. Hodgins, ""Foley, Michael Hamilton." In *DCB*, vol. 9, *www.biographi.ca/009004-119.01-e.php?&id_nbr=4427.*

59. David Christie, at this time a member of the Legislative Council, was a Reformer and Clear Grit and had sat as a member of the Assembly for West Brant, and so showed how railways were a project that transcended the normal array of political disagreements. J.M.S. Careless, "Christie, David." In *DCB*, vol. 10, *www.biographi.ca/009004-119.01-e.php?&id_nbr=4898.*

60. George Macbeth was a wealthy landowner in southwestern Ontario, and was a conservative sitting member for Elgin West (where much of his property lay) at the time this letter was written. He kept a home in London Ontario. The *DCB* does not note this railway involvement among the many he had. Frederick H. Armstrong, "Macbeth, George." In *DCB* vol. 9, *www.biographi.ca/009004-119.01-e.php?&id_nbr=4557.*

61. Johnson, ed, *Letters*, vol. 2, 337–38, Macdonald to Isaac Buchanan, June 1, 1861.

62. Op. Cit. 401, Macdonald to Buchanan, October 28, 1861. The other investor was James Morton, a strong Macdonald supporter in Kingston, who had been in an ownership position in the Locomotive Works in the city. He was by this point essentially bankrupt, and in a legal dispute with Buchanan, who was himself in severe financial straits. M.L. Magill, "Morton, James," *DCB*, vol. 9. *www.biographi.ca/009004-119.01-e.php?&id_nbr=4615* . It is revealing the Macdonald would even in these circumstances undertake to keep a network of influence and connection on the railway front open and in operation, though it is unlikely that he was fully aware of the extent of Morton's and Buchanan's difficulties.

63. Johnson, ed*., Letters*, vol. 2, Macdonald to Henry Smith, November 13, 1856, 392–93; same to same, December 15, 1856, 404–05.

64. John Ross became an adherent of John A. Macdonald's in 1854, according to his own remembrance, though his biographer viewed him as a leader of moderate Reformers for some time thereafter. He was a member of the Legislative Council. He was crucial in deposing Sir Allan MacNab in 1856, and in moving Macdonald into leadership. He was president of the Grand Trunk Railway. He held cabinet-level positions later, as well as membership in the Board of Railway Commissioners. Macdonald made certain that he was Ross' seat companion on the Grand Trunk when Ross headed home to Belleville and Macdonald to Kingston. The talk naturally lent itself to railways. And see Paul Cornell, "Ross, John." In *DCB*, vol. 10, *www.biographi.ca/009004-119.01-e.php?&id_nbr=5242.*

65. And this is precisely the conclusion one reaches from Johnson and Waite, "Macdonald, Sir John Alexander," *DCB*, vol 12, 591–612.

66. Martin, *Favourite Son?* traces this in a more extended fashion.

67. M. Bliss, *Right Honourable Men: The Descent of Canadian Politics from Macdonald to Mulroney* (Toronto: HarperCollins, 1994), 21–22, outlines how much money Macdonald obtained for political purposes as a consequence of his connection to George Stephen and the CPR. One can see some railway money at work if one consults Ben Forster, Malcolm Davidson, and R. Craig Brown, "The Franchise, Personators, and Dead Men: An Inquiry into the Voters' Lists and the Election of 1891," *Canadian Historical Review* 67 (1986): 17–41.

68. Macdonald to D. McInnes, June 17, 1872, Macdonald Papers, vol. 520, 672–5, LAC.

Chapter 7

Macdonald and Fiscal *Realpolitik*

E.A. HEAMAN

"The strong do what they can, the weak suffer what they must." According to the ancient Greek historian Thucydides, this was the advice that an imperial, aggrandizing Athens gave to the small, defiant island of Melios, which wished to remain neutral in the developing war between Athens and Sparta. When the Melians rejected that piece of Athenian wisdom, retaliation was swift and brutal: Athens destroyed the city state, killing the men and enslaving the women and children. But Thucydides' chilling phrase was actually, according to classicist Mary Beard, something more like "The strong exact (or extort) what they can, the weak comply."[1] Ruthless *realpolitik* is not the usual avenue to understanding Victorian Canada but it can shed light on some tendencies that characterized John A. Macdonald's long period at the helm of the Canadian state.

Macdonald has long been described as governing pragmatically, without much in the way of coherent theorizing or philosophizing behind him.[2] He changed his mind repeatedly on some of the most important policy issues of his day, including tariff policy and the Confederation of British North America, because he relied heavily on political allies of very different outlooks to keep him in power, and had to adapt his views to suit theirs. When the Conservative Party in Canada East or Quebec provided the necessary political alliance, he adopted policies that reflected its interests; when he had to accommodate western grits, he pandered to their priorities. He was professedly and evidentially a Conservative, but conservatives tended to explain and justify themselves rather less than reformers because they did not share the same faith in rational explanation as a mode of managing public opinion. Americanization, for example, was better warded off with blank declarations of loyalty that rallied rather than persuaded: "A British subject I was born and a British subject I will die."[3] Macdonald seems to have shared with French statesman Talleyrand the view that words were given to us to hide our thoughts; moreover, he often urged correspondents to burn letters received from him; and he let others serve as political figureheads.

But, even without a smoking gun, Macdonald's political purposes can be seen in their effects, if we are willing to presume his agency was at work behind the large legislative projects of his many governments. Certainly, Liberals took that view: "We know the great power he possesses with the party opposite; we know that his nod is law."[4] By focusing on one area of policy — fiscal arrangements — over the half-century or so that he dominated Canadian politics, it is possible to identify consistency and coherence. I will focus on three milestones that let me identify the basic problem of Canadian fiscal politics, the means that Macdonald used to address the problem, and the long-term outcome. I will close with some discussion as to how he justified his policies.

SETTING THE SCENE: MACDONALD'S FISCAL PROBLEM

When Macdonald entered politics, the clash over responsible government was at its height. At issue were both political principles and control of the purse strings. The British parliament used its control of tax levies to force the crown into submission. The executive branch of government had no right to initiate money bills and the legislature had ultimate control of government spending. In Canada, no such disciplining of the executive was possible. The executive branch of government could bypass the legislature by drawing monies from Britain and it also fought hard for independent control of monies levied through customs and excise duties in Canada. Responsible government was essentially conceded in the late 1840s when the Earl of Elgin agreed that the legislature could control spending and patronage. Almost immediately, the newly responsible colonies of British North America went on spending sprees that lasted through much of the 1850s.[5] Above all, they

Grip, 1 May, 1886.

DEPENDING ON ONE MAN.

The Party.---O, PRAY DON'T TALK OF GETTING OLD AND GIVING OUT! I CAN'T ABEAR THE IDEA!

invested in railroads. Canadians had watched other countries have railway booms through the 1830s and 1840s while their own quarrels prevented private or public interests from investing in railways. Now that Canadian legislators had control of public spending, they were not content to leave the matter to private enterprise, but instead put substantial sums at the service of railway-building, as much as £3000 of public money per mile of railtrack. In 1849, the Canadian legislature voted almost unanimously to guarantee interest payments for railway debts. It also passed other laws that expanded central and municipal debt-loads for purposes of railway building. The Conservative premier of the mid 1850s, Sir Allan Napier MacNab, famously gave voice to the new politics of Canada: "All my politics are railroads." This was an attitude that Macdonald, his lieutenant and successor as party leader and premier, had taken from the outset of his career. In 1844, when he published his platform in the Kingston *Gazette*, Macdonald declared: "In a young country like Canada, I am of the opinion that it is of more consequence to endeavour to develop its resources and improve its physical advantages, than to waste the time of the legislature and the money of the people in fruitless discussions on abstract and theoretical questions of government."[6] In effect, quarrelling could not resolve Canada's differences but development might. There was a Baconian quality to the suggestion that Canadians might get along better if they had more resources to divide amongst themselves. As Attorney General from 1854 and effective premier from 1857, Macdonald put that philosophy into effect and oversaw much of the early investment in railroads, as initial caution gave way to extravagance.

The result of the spending spree was near-catastrophic debt at all levels of Canadian government. The railways did not generate the expected profits and by the mid-1850s, a number of towns and railway companies were close to, or actually in, default, while the government of the United Canadas was spending nearly half its revenue servicing debts generated by railway projects. Other British North American colonies were in similar straits. The peak of their distress in 1857 coincided with an American fiscal crisis, as the western land and railway bubble there burst and caused a run on eastern banks.[7] The colony was in a full-scale fiscal crisis that had far-reaching effects. One was the introduction of new regulations and bureaucracies to better manage the railways and finances. Another was an increased tariff on imports in 1859, which whetted the appetite of businessmen for protection. Still another was the growing pressure in business circles to amalgamate colonial governments so as to consolidate their debts under an imperial guarantee.

By the early 1860s the worst of the crisis was past — but the Canadian government's interest payments were heavy and the danger of insolvency remained acute. Macdonald was mistaken in thinking that an appeal to loyalty and patriotism would carry his militia bill in the spring of 1862, when American militarization (as a result of the Civil War) threatened Canada. His opponents believed that the "chief danger in Canada just now arises from the embarrassed finances of the Government," as George Brown remarked in the *Globe* (regarding the appointment of a new adjutant general) in January of that year. And so an alliance of reformers brought down Macdonald's government, despite furious accusations of cowardice and disloyalty not only from the Tories but even from British sympathizers.[8] The armies of the United States apparently were nothing compared to the threat that Macdonaldian fiscal irresponsibility seemed to pose to the country. As fighting in the United States intensified, the mood in Canada changed; although the next government did manage to pass a militia bill (and replace the adjutant general), Macdonald had clearly overestimated patriotic fervour. His drinking binge that spring did not help, nor did the fact that most of his initiatives were partisan, or nepotistic (the adjutant in question looked particularly incompetent to the Grits), not to say corrupt. But the bigger lesson was that fiscal weakness undermined even potentially non-partisan initiatives. Macdonald's policy of unity through prosperity would have to be adapted to ensure that the government also prospered. If he were really poor to campaign on a platform of loyalty to the British Crown, Macdonald's political career would be cut short.

A CONSTITUTIONAL FIX FOR THE FISCAL PROBLEM

Macdonald bore that humbling experience of the 1862 election in mind when he and his Minister of Finance, Alexander Tilloch Galt, put together their plans for funding the new Dominion in 1864. They did not have their own way in all matters and much of their work was undone in the courts over subsequent decades, but they were remarkably successful in centralizing fiscal power. The plan for Confederation sent to Britain in 1865 was very obviously designed to strengthen Macdonald's hand fiscally (assuming his election as prime minister). Author Garth Stevenson succinctly summarizes matters: "All of the provinces had depended mainly on customs tariffs and excise taxes for their revenues prior to Confederation, and these sources of revenue were assigned exclusively to the federal government. The provincial power to impose direct taxes was of little immediate value, since such taxes would have been politically unacceptable."[9] Therefore, the provinces would receive subsidies from the general government, primarily a per capita subsidy of eighty cents according to population figures from the last census. But that sum would remain constant, so that the per capita rate would dwindle as the population increased. Nova Scotia and New Brunswick — which, having constituted governments, were in a stronger negotiating position than the future provinces of Ontario and Quebec — demanded better terms and so they were not pegged to the 1861 census: the eighty cents would increase until each population reached 400,000 inhabitants, at which point it would freeze. If federal subsidies did not cover the cost of provincial government, then the provinces must turn to direct taxation.

Fiscal restraint was one way of reining in local governments, in keeping with Macdonald's larger scheme for centralizing as much power as he could.[10] Taxpayers did not feel indirect taxation so intimately and so governments that taxed indirectly could extract more and rationalize less. Direct taxation was a liberal project of governance: it tended to produce small government and vigilant, engaged tax payers who closely scrutinized government spending. English Liberal leader William Gladstone embraced direct taxation and so did George Brown in the *Globe*, which regularly asserted, in the words of a public meeting at Glenmorris, South Dumfries, in 1867, "Protective duties are unjust in principle and mischievous in practice."[11] In British Columbia, John Sebastian Helmecken opposed Confederation and favoured direct taxation. And, as Andrew Smith has observed, opponents of Confederation across British North America recognized that the scheme was likely to lead to inflated federal taxes and it would not only perpetuate, but expand Macdonald's high-spending ways.[12] The larger territory would bring in increased tax revenue and the cost of Canada's debt would go down, thanks to the British government's offer to guarantee the consolidated debt of a confederated British North America. To reformers across British North America, the choice between independence and Confederation seemed, to no small degree, to be a choice between a small, cheap, and virtuous government, closely controlled by self-reliant small producers, and the corruption of a big government that was formally accountable but practically unaccountable to its citizens.

But most Canadians were not orthodox liberal political economists and they abhorred direct taxation. H.V. Nelles observes of late-nineteenth-century Ontario that direct taxation was a "bugbear" and likely to provoke mass revolt.[13] When Macdonald anticipated that Confederation would eventually reduce the provinces to the status of municipal governments, it is not unlikely that he based his predictions on fiscal arrangements. Municipalities taxed directly, but they were perennially short of money. Taxpayers resented paying taxes on their property and they regularly challenged the values that assessors assigned to their properties in any court open to them — sometimes special courts of revision, sometimes the ordinary law courts. They formed ratepayers associations, fomented against municipal political parties, and publicized their complaints in municipal newspapers. Tax hikes tended to lead to immediate electoral reversals. Ratepayer protest was a powerful engine of dissent amongst municipal residents and taxes were never far from the centre of municipal politics. (These were not merely narrow, self-interested debates: the late nineteenth-century municipal public was economically literate and inclined to engage in philosophically and spiritually charged debates about public finances. Macdonald had good reason to seek disengagement from that charged political sphere.)

Income taxes threatened to stir up the same kind of tax-focused politics because they were resented just as directly by the taxpayer. It is not that income tax was inconceivable to legislatures. At the time of Confederation, both Britain and the United States had income taxes, largely necessitated by the expense of wars. Political theorists like John Stuart Mill argued that income tax was, in theory, the most fair of all possible taxes. But he tempered his admiration by conceding that any such tax, to be truly effective, would require an inquisitorial bureaucracy unsuited to a liberal polity. Authorities tolerated high levels of tax evasion so as to stave off more open resistance to the direct taxes.[14] In practice, thus, income taxes tended to be deeply unjust: evaded by professional classes and extracted primarily from wage-earners. British Columbia began to impose income taxes along with property and poll taxes from 1875 and politics in that province became infused with resentment over taxes.[15]

The argument for direct taxation did not enjoy a monopoly on pretensions to virtue. Macdonald could draw upon a century-old philosophy of prosperity to support his fiscal policy. Brown's virtue was severe and political, but Macdonald's was a more easy-going commercial form of virtue that reflected eighteenth-century reasoning about the conditions that permitted the development of liberalism in the first place. According to that reasoning, coercion contrasted with consent and choice as a means of extracting surplus value from ordinary people. Jan de Vries has outlined the changing views of political and economic theorists as they advocated a new consumerist ethos (to replace an older leisure-oriented ethos) that, thanks to scholars like Bernard de Mandeville and David Hume, celebrated the conjunction of British commercial imperialism and liberalism. The argument applied downward to the agricultural labourer as well as upward to the urban bourgeoisie: Hume argued that it was violent and impracticable to force a labourer "to toil in order to raise from the land more than what subsists himself and his family. Furnish him with manufactures and commodities and he will do it himself." By skimming a little bit off the surface of that process of exchange in the form of indirect taxation, the British state was relieved of the kind of direct taxation of peasants that so hindered French tax collection (all too often this practice resulted in such calamities as the seizure of livestock, which was prohibited in England). Thus was the one state unable and the other able to pay for its expensive eighteenth-century wars.[16] By this standard, direct taxation looked French, feudal, and an obstacle to market-oriented activity. Philosophers of direct taxation seemed to have only a negative grasp of prosperity as an effete and corrupting luxury. The conservative tradition that stretched from Hume to Macdonald seemed better at banishing state coercion and creating conditions for a more modern and vigorous form of prosperity.

There could be no objection to vesting the federal government with the power to tax trade and commerce, under the BNA Act, because it controlled the regulation of trade and commerce. Macdonald did not bother to justify that arrangement when he introduced the plan for Confederation; he simply observed "of course, too, it must have the regulation of trade and commerce, of customs and excise. The Federal Parliament must have the sovereign power of raising money from such sources and by such means as the representatives of the people will allow."[17] At the last minute, the British Colonial

Office undermined the federal government's control of trade by vesting residual power over property and civil law with the provinces. The decision to vest the federal government with the power to govern and tax trade has not been seriously analyzed as social and cultural history, but it reflected the cultural and social baggage of the "Fathers" of Confederation. To insist on the priority of trade was to insist on the subordination of other interests. Confederation was designed to persuade Canadians that they should rally around material prosperity. The goal was to develop citizens who would subordinate local identity and culture to trade, or would understand culture primarily in terms of trade.

Broadly speaking, the federal government was designated as the branch of government primarily responsible for governing and administering prosperity throughout the land. The provinces would also pursue prosperity, of course, primarily through the development of resources, but trade was primarily a federal concern and so the federal government would be the one to establish and manage relations between the different economic interests. This claim was key to ensuring that Canada could abandon the old sectarian obstacles to development.[18] The advocates for the new federal arrangement insisted that Confederation would nurture a new "political nationality" based on rational, economic self-interest. Anything that did *not* look like rational, economic self-interest would be devolved to the provinces. But the consequence was a very one-dimensional form of government with scant ability to recognize or respond to the more subtle characteristics of social identity. The outcome was truly terrible for Indigenous peoples, who were its wards. The federal government would spend decades trying to make them conform to an economist's caricature of human motivation, seeing in the expression of other kinds of concerns ample justification for denying them political rights. The sufferings of the First Nations of Canada reflected a refusal on the part of the federal government to recognize poverty as a serious social concern. The fiscal arrangements of Confederation were designed to administer poverty out of political existence, by devolving it to the provinces and by gradually restricting the monies that could be spent upon it. This was not an accidental oversight (as briefs for the Rowell-Sirois commission tended to suggest), but a carefully designed policy that would take an enormous amount of legislative capital to reverse in the twentieth century.

Confederation rested on an optimistic theory that Canadians might have cultural differences but they shared basic economic interests in such things as railways and liberal trade relations. The new political entity that would be Canada would have two legislatures to reflect a view of human behaviour as having two major aspects: a federal parliament to reflect rational economic interest and provincial legislatures to reflect the other kinds of interests such as ethnicity and religion. The two kinds of interests operated at cross purposes: culture, religion, and ethnicity all worked to put Canadians at one another's throats and to prevent them from collaborating on economic progress either individually or collectively. Politicians would be more likely to agree on those shared economic interests in a federal arena stripped of all the non-economic business of government. Thus could George-Etienne Cartier advance a view of Confederation as redirecting the zero-sum political rivalries amongst Canadians into healthy commercial rivalry: "We were of different races, not for the purpose of warring against each other, but in order to compete and emulate for the general welfare." He identified something he called "political nationality," which was oblivious to ethnic origin and religion: "Under the federal system, granting to the control of the General Government, these large questions of general interest in which the differences of race or religion had no place, it could not be pretended that the rights of either race or religion could be invaded at all. We were to have a General Parliament to deal with the matters of defence, tariff, excise, public works, and these matters absorbed all individual interest."[19]

• • •

Cartier had to push the argument for an identity-neutral political identity, one coeval with economic self-interest, to counter the obvious demographic and cultural threat to French Canadians from the numerically superior English Canadians. But Galt, in defending Confederation to his English-speaking constituents in Sherbrooke, had to push the argument still further to counter the obvious demographic and cultural threat to *their* identity. His argument was threefold. First, the interests of English- and French-speaking inhabitants of Canada East were "identical," namely, to ensure that the western trade continued to flow through their province. Second, the numerical superiority of their "race" in the General Parliament secured their interests in that arena:

> The interests of trade and commerce, those in which they
> felt more particularly concerned, which concerned the
> merchants of Montreal and Quebec, would be in the
> hands of a body where they could have no fear that any
> adverse race or creed would affect them. All those sub-
> jects would be taken out of the category of local questions,
> would be taken away from the control of those who might
> be under the influence of sectional feelings animated either
> by race or religion, and would be placed in the hands of a
> body where, if the interests of any class could be expected
> to be secure, surely it would be those of the British popu-
> lation of Lower Canada.[20]

Thus, British identity would be protected in the central government
because that identity amounted to a concern for trade and commerce.
Culture was either non-existent or it would be managed locally. Third,
regarding their local interests, Galt had only a feeble argument that material self-interest would smooth relations there as well. Because each "race"
had its own legislature, each could damage the other and the result would
be mutually assured destruction: "anything which tended to damage that
position would be fatal to the interests both of the one and of the other.
He thought our material interests would have to govern us in this respect."
Any attempt to legislate racial protection — beyond protection for separate
Protestant schools — would inspire resentment and lead to trouble.

Galt had championed the reform since 1858 and had persuaded
Cartier. Macdonald, remarked Galt's biographer, was "the last of the
big men of his province to be brought to see the need of the federation policy" but "the most indispensable in getting it through when at
last converted."[21] Certainly it cohered with Macdonald's policy of unity
through prosperity. The Dominion government would be better equipped
than its predecessor to govern trade and commerce. It would be able
to construct a pan-Canadian political identity rooted in political economy. The constitution rested on an optimistic theory that Canadians
had a double identity — their identity as economic citizens and their
cultural identity — and they were able to distinguish one from the other.
Accordingly, two identities required two distinct political jurisdictions

so as to prevent their future conflation. The invisible hand of the market, once freed of nefarious political influence, offered the best model for reconciling the otherwise irreconcilable differences among Canadians. Ben Forster (Chapter 6) has shown that Macdonald's government, in these crucial years, was basically liberal and laissez-faire in its outlook.[22] Based on that understanding, the key function of the Dominion government would be to keep all the politics out of politics, so to speak, and to facilitate and administer prosperity. In so doing, it would be creating a new and modern kind of virtuous citizen, one who looked to rational marketplace activity to advance his self-interests and who understood that politics should be, at best, a handmaid to that virtue. It is no small irony that Macdonald, Canada's textbook example of a conservative statesman, instigated a new state predicated on an abstract and rational conception of human nature; in other politicians this might be considered the work of a liberal innovator.

The disparate visions of government's role drew upon some version of Adam Smith's liberal political economy, something that helped smooth over differences between the members of the Great Coalition. Smith had argued against a pernicious alliance between large business interests and state powers, and those arguments played very well to the reform model of politics, one that vested ultimate political agency with the self-reliant farmer. Supporters of Confederation could also use that language of small government, direct taxation, and political virtue: they simply applied it to provinces rather than to the general government. Galt remarked, during the Confederation debates, that "it is one of the wisest provisions in the proposed Constitution, and that which affords the surest guarantee that the people will take a healthy interest in their own affairs and see that no extravagance is committed by those placed in power over them, is to be found in the fact that those who are called upon to administer public affairs will feel, when they resort to direct taxation, that a solemn responsibility rests upon them, and that that responsibility will be exacted by the people in the most peremptory manner."[23] The general government, unburdened by any such solemn responsibility, would look rather different. Macdonald's version of political agency led upward to a central government that powerfully represented the best and highest collective interests of the Canadian people. The fact that Macdonald had to defend his decision not to take Confederation to the people enhanced his centralizing teleology. Confederation would, he repeatedly declared, create a "powerful" new country and a "powerful and enduring alliance with England." The only reasons for adopting it were to make Canada both British (Macdonald brandished his favourite rhetorical weapon again) and prosperous: "If the House and country believe this union to be one which will ensure for us British laws, British connection, and British freedom — and increase and develop the social, political and material prosperity of the country, then I implore, this House and the country, to lay aside all prejudices, and accept the scheme which we offer."[24]

Canada would still lack independent treaty-making powers and it would still have to manoeuvre between British and American diplomats from a position of grave weakness, but it would be in a better position to encourage economic development by building up trading relationships and local industries, and sponsoring immigration. There were the military and other responsibilities as well, of course, but Macdonald was no sabre-rattler and the primary responsibility of his federal government would be the governance of trade and commerce, both internally and externally, so far as these things *could* be governed by a still-quasi-colonial government, hemmed in by an imperial power on the one hand and by ambitious provincial governments on the other. But if, politically, Macdonald faced treacherous terrain ahead, fiscal matters were simpler. Macdonald had the power he needed to expand the policies that he had enacted during the union period. Canadian politicians at all levels had overplayed their hand and spent more than they could afford during the Union years, but those policies were not repudiated in the new arrangements.

So what was entailed in the project of nurturing prosperity? Government under such circumstances must be a hybrid of public and private considerations. Such a government must tax to maintain itself and to enact measures of common interest, such as a military force, or a canal. But there was very little conceptual conflation of public and private interests, very little of the quasi-magical transformation of private into public that Jürgen Habermas identified as a constituent of the discursive bourgeois public sphere.[25] Talk was cheap, taxes were not, and Victorian statesmen bore that distinction in mind. Thus, Macdonald was prepared, during the Confederation debates, to insist that the existing government had powers of representation sufficient to impose a major constitutional reform on the people of Canada, but he repudiated any suggestion that the new arrangements involved either the appropriation of property or the granting of money. "Not a farthing of money was being appropriated," exclaimed George-Etienne Cartier, seconding Macdonald's argument.[26] They refused to convene the legislature as a committee of the whole, as a money bill would require, for fear of dragging out the debate.

The appropriation of property in the interests of government was perhaps the most vulnerable part of the mid-Victorian social compact. To maintain maximal legitimacy, a government's reasoning about how it spent its tax monies, especially tax monies raised on trade and commerce, had to fall in line with what seemed reasonably sound business principles. According to liberal economic theories, the policies that most closely approximated market reasoning were the ones most likely to work out well. But equally important, governments must not pass policies inimical to the economic interests of taxpayers; to do so would amount to using their own money against them.[27] Consequently, mid-century political regimes were organized around a profound distinction between the propertied and the unpropertied and they ardently pursued the interests of the propertied. There seemed, to politicians and pundits, something profoundly unjust in the possibility that someone without property could spend his propertied neighbour's tax monies. The interests of the unpropertied citizen must, ultimately, conflict with the interests of the propertied citizen and any profound clash of that sort threatened to debunk the liberal social contract and delegitimize government.

Property was, for Macdonald, far more important as a basis for political rights than race or gender. He considered it one of the great achievements of his political career to stave off democracy and maintain a property franchise. In this respect, Macdonald reflected a trend that historian Sven Beckart identifies in post–Civil War New York: a political alliance of the propertied classes, one that united different kinds of business interests in opposition to democracy.[28] Macdonald devoted most of his political career to advancing the interests of Canadian businessmen, believing that general prosperity must come through their prosperity. Gustavus Myers describes the Macdonaldian brand of politics as "in fact, a business; the Canadian Parliament was crowded with men who were there to initiate, extend, or conserve class or personal interests."[29]

The government of prosperity meant that tax monies should be spent advancing the interests of the propertied. There was absolutely no intention of using taxation as a means of distributing wealth. Local governments would look after social welfare; the federal government did something different with its money. Whereas colonial governments in British North America had had to provide for progress *and* its social costs — in the form of workhouses, asylums, and penitentiaries for example — the new arrangements separated these responsibilities. Thus no concern for poverty or relief entered into the dominion list of responsibilities. There were only two exceptions: marine hospitals, which did not serve a local community in the manner of other hospitals, and penitentiaries, which were put there by the British, as a revision to the draft bill. Galt explained the reasoning behind the draft bill to his constituents at Sherbrooke:

> The management of all the penitentiaries and prisons naturally fell under the scope of the local authorities; also that of hospitals, asylums, charities, and eleemosynary institutions. With regard to these, he would merely say that there might be some which could hardly be considered local in their nature; such, for example, was the Marine Hospital in Quebec City, a seaport where there was an enormous trade, and where thousands of seamen were annually coming in. A hospital where the sick among these sailors were taken in must necessarily be almost national in its character — certainly more national than local; but all would agree that most of the other hospitals and asylums of various kinds should be more properly supported by local than by general resources. Indeed, he hoped the day would come when these institutions would find support from the individual liberality of the people, rather than from the votes of Parliament. Of this they had a magnificent example in Great Britain, where the most useful charities were supported by the free gifts of a liberal people, and he trusted that Canadians would prove themselves in this respect not unworthy scions of the race from which they sprang. (Cheers)[30]

Britain provided the model for Galt's division of responsibilities. At the start of the nineteenth century, Britain, like Canada, was ruled by a corrupt elite. Martin Daunton argues that the British state at the end of the Napoleonic wars was a "tax-eater" state, generally characterized as "Old Corruption," and that it was "undemocratic, bloated, and inefficient," as well as inequitable to classes and interests in its spending. The government spent the first half of the century gaining public trust, by replacing indirect with direct taxation, effectively getting the state out of discreditable negotiations with private interests, and by reining in spending. British governments downloaded much of the responsibility for social welfare to local governments and voluntary societies, where vituperous disputes about social spending were not likely to be translated upward to threaten the central state. One politician observed during the 1850s that "it is evidently wise to put as little on the Government whose overthrow causes a revolution as you can and to have as much as you can on the local bodies, which may be overthrown a dozen times and nobody be the worse."[31]

But if free trade and direct taxation persisted as policy until the end of the century, Avner Offer shows that pressures began to build on the national government to resume some responsibility for social spending from the mid-nineteenth century. Local authorities could not bear the burden; ratepayers in poor areas had to pay much higher rates than those in rich areas. Their representatives argued that the social costs of industrialization and urbanization, which brought enormous wealth to a few, solid prosperity to many, and poverty to many more, had to be understood as national economic burdens. The problems of a poor, working-class borough like Poplar or Bethnal Green could not be considered solely their problems. Local workhouses bore the brunt of the cost, providing cheap accommodation that was supposed to be temporary, but the workhouses were becoming discredited by notorious scandals, as at Andover, in 1845, when the starving inmates fought over the bones they were supposed to be crushing to make fertilizer. Moreover, new institutions for long-term incarceration, above all lunatic asylums and penitentiaries, drew inmates from large territories and frequently exceeded local resources. Offer singles out lunatic asylums as particularly problematic from a fiscal point of view, leading to the reclassification of lunacy as "a national calamity" according to one British parliamentary report of 1871.[32] (Lunatic asylums posed comparable fiscal disputes in British North America. For example, grand juries in Halifax protested against being charged for the growing numbers of pauper lunatics who had only briefly resided in the county: their upkeep cost thousands of dollars and drove up local assessment rates.[33]) Through the 1860s and 1870s, the British Parliament, under pressure from local authorities and from constituency-minded MPs, debated the pros and cons of providing state grants to local poor law authorities, as well as the justice of vesting prosperity in a general government and poverty in a local one. In 1868 the Liberal front bench took up the question: "What would be the view taken in Bethnal Green as to the Thames Embankment? It was not fair, when an improvement was to be made, which might be thought most important by the wealthy, that it should be carried out at the expense of the whole metropolis while at the same time the burdens of the East End were to be borne partially and locally."[34] It was according to this logic that the British government began to tax for purposes of supporting local welfare and that it inserted penitentiaries into the British North America Act as a federal responsibility. It would have done more, but for the protests of Canadian representatives.

Canadians were not well-situated to anticipate these emergent disputes. Instead, they looked backwards at the earlier British experience, believing that progress lay in downsizing and downloading redistributive spending while centralizing spending on public works in the name of a "common good" that was largely defined by the well-being of the business classes. Canada had little of the apparatus of state-administered charity outside of Nova Scotia where the poor laws were in force. Poor people were supposed to turn to local charities (some of which were subsidized with public funds) for help or to go out and build themselves a farm by taking advantage of the Free Land policy. Observers, steeped in British economic theories, had some difficulty in explaining how poverty could exist in British North America at all, given the economic opportunities, including availability of land and absence of taxation. In the Maritime colonies, for example, too many people — including Indigenous peoples, French Canadians, and Highland Scots — apparently preferred leisure and subsistence to the consumption and prosperity that were supposed to enrich both state and society painlessly.[35] Governments in British North America did intervene to nudge people toward market-oriented behaviour, teaching "practical" subjects in public schools and sponsoring agricultural societies and mechanics' institutes, and they sternly penalized such heretical avenues of self-advancement as theft. In doing so, they followed a prescription of increased privatization of poverty. Liberalism and religious doctrine converged in the project to define poverty as a problem of morality and, therefore, of civil society rather than the state. This convergence was especially marked in Quebec where the Catholic Church expanded phenomenally during the middle decades of the century.[36] But it also reflected traditions in other provinces, as in Upper Canada, where "virtually all social services, from poor relief to orphanages, were privately funded and operated," though they received more or less invisible state subsidies.[37]

Canadian politicians had, therefore, both theory and experience behind them when they planned to reduce provincial subsidies over time in the expectation that either direct taxation or, better yet, charity, would suffice to pay for the social costs of economic development. Charitable dependence was unmanly and perhaps provincial dependence on the federal government would ultimately be understood and rejected as unmanly in much the same way. Either way, the federal government would take no interest in such matters. Canadian subsidies to the provinces steadily decreased where populations increased, dipping, by 1881, to 65 cents per capita in Quebec and 60 cents per capita in Ontario where the population had grown more quickly. By the turn of the century, the figures were 54 and 51 cents respectively.[38] Following that same logic, the provinces also tended to pass relief spending on to still lower levels of government. In the Charity Aid Act of 1867-8, for example, the Ontario government provided only for the care of new immigrants; other relief was to be provided by local communities.[39] The binary on spending in nineteenth-century Canada was not so much public versus private as it was between legislatures that spent taxes according to a clientelist model and local (municipal or county) institutions that shared with philanthropy the burden of social solidarity. Federally, the notion of the "public" remained little more than a cover for privileged private interests. Confederation considerably enhanced Macdonald's ability to invoke a lofty national purpose, while permitting him to narrow his government's focus to the interests of the bourgeoisie.

The Grand Finale

It was still just barely possible to believe that poverty might be legislated out of political existence in Canada during the mid 1860s. The social costs of urbanization and industrialization could only be recognized as hard-wired after the fact. In Canada, that process was still just beginning to get seriously underway by 1864. The 1870s is the decade when industrialization leaped ahead and workers' politics entered legislatures and municipal councils. The 1870s was also the decade when Henry George's *Progress and Poverty* conceptually conjoined the two phenomena in his title and put forward an argument for redistributive taxation of land. It spread throughout the United States and Canada as well as Britain (where, indeed, J.S. Mill had made the case for redistributive taxes on land values in 1871). The great depression in the middle of that decade drove most of the Canadian provinces close to bankruptcy. The provinces complained that the reasoning behind the diminishing subsidies failed to reflect the growth of provincial responsibilities. The federal government was largely aloof to such complaints.

Indeed, it was at the end of the 1870s that Macdonald achieved his greatest moment of fiscal realpolitik. Whereas British and American authorities were beginning to entertain redistributive theories of taxation, Macdonald introduced a National Policy of Tariff Protection. Previous tariffs had offered incidental protection to home-grown manufactures but had been designed primarily to raise revenue.[40] The National Policy did an about-face and imposed protective duties on a very wide range of Canadian-made products. It was economic orthodoxy that tariffs were unprogressive: they hindered trade and they were socially unjust, because they hit the poor harder than the well-to-do. Conservative apologists insisted that the necessities of the poor — bread, coal, clothing above all — were spared the steepest increases, but the Liberals at the time (and historians in hindsight) have remained unconvinced. As the Toronto *Globe* noted, in order to cover a $2M shortage in government funds (most of it caused by railway-building initiatives), the Tories imposed $7M in new taxes.[41]

If poverty entered into Tory calculations, it was the poverty of the propertied. There could be no national prosperity without a prosperous business class. Businessmen had suffered during the economic downturn and the National Policy would restore to them their lion's share of the national wealth. Macdonald insisted that Canada could not afford direct taxation: he made the point in the House of Commons as early as 1876 and in 1880 he took the argument into the heart of liberal England when he met a delegation of Manchester businessmen and politicians who urged free trade and direct taxation. In reply, Macdonald gamely took the part of the impoverished high-earners of Canada (income taxes generally had a base exemption of several hundred dollars): "An income-tax would be a failure, because there was nothing to levy it upon; therefore, they were obliged to have recourse to the tariff."[42] Macdonald's critics saw something much more sinister at work: not just a preference for prosperity of the few, but an actual hostility to evidence of prosperity amongst the many. According to the *Globe*'s caricature of Tory reasoning, "The families of the men on fixed incomes are dressed and fed too well for their station in life. It was desirable that they should be taught their places. Were the manufacturers to be pained by the spectacle of the increased comfort of an inferior class, while they were compelled to reduce their own expenditure? Human nature could not be expected to endure such an outrage." The Tories weighed the sensibilities and the prosperity of the few against those of the many and sided with the few: "The mere physical suffering caused to the labouring classes by higher taxation would have been inconsiderable, and their mental distress not worth talking about in comparison with that of the capitalist."[43] Whatever the intention, the outcome was to set back principles of redistribution. Elsewhere, political debates raged about how to spend taxes in the national interest, whether by some form of social redistribution from rich to poor or, at the very least, toward such projects of equalization as state-sponsored education. Those debates scarcely troubled federal politics in Canada. The National Policy refined and rarified his policies of redistributing money upward, from the poor to the rich. Given the refusal to entertain social spending at the federal level, the Dominion government could do nothing else with its enhanced income. Ben Forster describes the coming of the National Policy as "a conjunction of interests."[44] Poverty was not an interest and it was successfully conjured out of federal party politics by one of the greatest statesmen of his age.

Historians have identified little philosophy and much pragmatism in the development of the National Policy, seeing it as an about-face provoked by high American tariffs. But viewing the tariff as revenue rather than as economic policy, the story looks different: a sustained pattern of consolidation of power. I think Macdonald did it because he could do it and because it made him politically impregnable: he never lost another election. The tariff filled government coffers while political donations by businessmen seeking special tariffs filled the coffers of the Conservative party. The Canadian Pacific Railway alone donated more than a million dollars during the last decade or so of Macdonald's tenure. Michael Bliss has observed: "The Conservative Party must have been so flush with CPR and manufacturers' money in the 1880s that general elections were close to meaningless."[45] Again, in the words of Thucydides: "The strong exact what they can and the weak comply."

• • •

The thing still had to be defended to the people, weak though they might be. Doctrinaire Liberals like Sir Richard Cartwright tried but failed to persuade consumers to see themselves as injured taxpayers. In his speeches, Macdonald emphasized job-creation and claimed credit for the fact that the working poor were, at least, *working*.[46] But if he could continue to invoke prosperity, it was no longer the same British formula for prosperity that had underpinned his previous campaigns. British politicians, economists, businessmen, and pundits lined up to denounce the new Canadian protectionism as distinctly un-British and illiberal, lending powerful support to Macdonald's critics at home. Macdonald's reply to such detractors was ostentatiously modern rather than conservative. He and his MPs argued that the new tariff would be legitimate because it would be *scientific*. The rise of science and scientists would transform politics in the twentieth century, but, in the 1870s, it had barely begun to inform statesmen. Macdonald was, once again, doing something innovative when he chose "science" as a line of defence for protectionism. There were grounds for thinking that tariff protection was debunked science. As Andrew Smith shows, D.W. Prowse believed in the mid-1860s that "the fear that Canada might adopt a protectionist tariff policy was groundless … in such a scientific age, a Canadian ministry containing such intelligent men as George Brown and A.T. Galt would no more 'return to the exploded theory of protection' than they would propose to 'defend the Canadian frontier with bows and arrows.'"[47] Free trade as a philosophy enjoyed near hegemonic status during the 1860s in Britain. Adam Smith's theories in favour of freedom of trade as the only sound basis for politics and economics had been updated by classical economists, many of them simultaneously parliamentarians, of whom Mill was only the most prominent and influential, and who oversaw the modernization of that science from relations of force on a (diluted) Newtonian model to inductive Baconian science.[48]

By the end of the 1870s, although marginalism had not yet begun to challenge British or Canadian economic policy, new "historical" schools of thought, emerging in Germany and England in the 1870s, were beginning to undermine the abstract generalizations of classical political economy. When Robert Lowe declared in Parliament in 1870 that "Political

Economy belongs to no nation; it is of no country: it is the science of the rules for the production, the accumulation, the distribution, and the consumption of wealth," he was quickly answered by T.E. Cliffe Leslie, in the *Fortnightly Review*, that "political economy is not a body of natural laws in the true sense, or of universal and immutable truths, but an assemblage of speculations and doctrines which are the result of a particular history."[49] British economists tended to see local British history as somehow universal so the historicism probably did not much alter British economic truths,[50] but historicism could lend greater legitimacy to local experience in Canada. Moreover, Canadians had their own colonial critique of liberal economics in a treatise published in Montreal by John Rae in 1833. Whereas Adam Smith identified individual and national wealth as essentially similar, Rae distinguished them: individuals became rich by seizing a bigger piece of the national economic pie; nations became rich by creating new wealth, primarily through new technologies. The consequences were considerable for state policy: Rae believed that judicious economic legislation — to encourage new technologies for example — could improve a national economy whereas Smith decried any such political meddling. Given their great differences, Rae concluded that Smith's arguments lacked scientific validity. Where "Lord Bacon," the father of modern science, argued for precisely defined concepts and a debunking of common and familiar notions, Smith generalized loosely from common and familiar concepts like capital, wealth, profit, self-interest, and the like, never subjecting them to rigorous analysis. Rae's critique of Smith would, in the long run, go some way toward rehabilitating the notion that a government could intervene in the economy on behalf of the common good, especially when it invoked science, and Macdonald's Tories drew upon it to justify the tariff in 1879.

Macdonald did not take science lightly. He had a long history of support for science. Indeed, during the early 1840s, before he entered politics, reformers and conservatives had been able to make common cause around state sponsorship for science, in the form of a Geological Survey of Canada and funding for agricultural societies that were supposed to encourage a taste for scientific agriculture, while mechanics' institutes encouraged scientific education amongst working men. Macdonald's pre-Confederation governments maintained their funding for these institutions, though he retained only the Geological Survey as a federal agency after Confederation; agricultural societies and mechanics' institutes became provincial responsibilities. Macdonald's government of science was remarkably hands off. Politicians could establish political priorities around the scientific work and decide whether or not to fund it, but they could not evaluate its content and must trust to scientists' judgment of one another's work. In May 1883, for example, Macdonald was forced to defend the work of the Geological Survey of Canada. He invoked the international respect for the chief geologist, Alfred Selwyn, and argued that "it would in some degree interfere with this system, if we were to interpose our own ideas upon scientific matters connected with the survey." It was with "a good deal of diffidence, because I do not profess to be a man much acquainted with the natural sciences," that he proposed expanding the survey to encompass natural history.[51] Similarly, in April 1884, Macdonald voted to supply $5,000 to publish the *Transactions and Proceedings of the Royal Society of Canada* with its valuable scientific papers, "[A]s far as an inexpert like myself can judge."

Macdonald understood political knowledge as distinct from formal knowledge obtained through enquiry. When the governing Liberals moved, in February 1876, for a committee to inquire into "the causes of the present financial depression, with power to send for persons, papers, and records — to report from time to time," Macdonald took this motion as one of non-confidence in the government. Such a committee would be effectively assuming the powers and responsibilities of the government, doing things the government should already have done.[52] In other words, the government's responsibility was to know the condition of the country; if it did not know, then it lacked legitimacy. Because scientific knowledge was so distinct from political knowledge, Macdonald was extremely careful to hire few scientists, lest he lose control of the apparatus of patronage. Keenly aware that few Tory supporters had scientific credentials, Liberals regularly pushed for more scientific appointments: for the civil service in general in 1883; in 1884 for Dominion Librarian (Macdonald quoted arch-liberal Goldwin Smith as an authority to argue that "a man may be a very scientific man or a very literary man, and yet make a bad Librarian")[53]; for cattle inspector; and for military commissions.[54] In 1885, when Liberal MP David Mills demanded that a chief superintendent of mines be a man with "practical scientific knowledge," Macdonald responded that an ability to settle disputes between rowdy miners was more important.[55] In the spring of 1886, Minister of Public Works Hector Langevin practically apologized for including a scientific text in his annual report — the work of a hobbyist in his department — and promised there would be no recurrence.[56]

Only in respect to the tariff, it seemed, could scientific knowledge map on to political reasoning and, in the process, give political decisions some of the special, nonpartisan qualities of scientific knowledge. The tariff was not just a conjuncture of interests; it was also a conjuncture of knowledge. Through the long debates over a protective tariff, Macdonald insisted that a scientific tariff was possible. In 1878 he declared: "We say the present tariff is inartistic, unscientific, deficient in some parts; that it helps to depress and crush our manufacturing interests, to allow an undue and improper interference with our agricultural products in our own markets, and that there ought to be a readjustment in a scientific sense." Others in his government also defended the National Policy as scientific, including Finance Minister Sir Leonard Tilley and Nova Scotian MP, Sir Charles Tupper, who notoriously defended a high tariff on coal, which benefitted Nova Scotia at the expense of central Canada, as "scientific," to the great disgust of Liberals who regularly threw the claim back in his face. Macdonald was more judicious in his argument for the scientific qualities of tariffs: it was grounded in historical particularity rather than abstractions and it served to correct the excessive abstractions of economic theorizing. This was the line he took in debates during the mid-1870s, when he insisted that free trade was mere "superstition" where it refused to consider local circumstances that even Mill (whom Macdonald quoted at some length) considered worthy of consideration.[57] Macdonald lectured the British delegation of 1880 on exactly that point, dismissing the argument by John Slagg, a British MP and vice president of the Manchester Chamber of Commerce, that Mill had "recanted that monstrous doctrine." Other Tory MPs took up the "scientific tariff" argument in the spring of 1879 when the tariff bill came before the House of Commons. John McLennan, a merchant and onetime president of the Montreal Board of Trade, gave it on scientific authority that "[p]olitical economy cannot assume the uniformity of nature in the same way that astronomy does, and hence it has no scientific position from which to slight the doctrines of those who maintain that a new and wholly different *régime* might supersede that which Ricardo and his school have so clearly decided.[58] James Colebrook Patterson, MPP for Essex North, lawyer, and president of the Ontario Conservative Union, quoted another economic authority: "Political economy is not a universal science, of which all the principles are applicable to all men, under all circumstances, and equally good and true for all nations; but every country has a political economy of its own, suitable to its own physical circumstances of position on the globe, climate, soil and products, and to the habits, character, and idiosyncrasy of its inhabitants, formed or modified by such circumstances."[59]

Science from this perspective was neither the Newtonian science of mechanics nor even the Hobbesian science of molecules in motion.[60] Nor was it scientific history: no such beast existed in any serious way in mid-Victorian Canada.[61] Macdonald's scientific political economy was like the natural history and geology that were performed at the Geological Survey of Canada. It was inventory science, a science informed as much by colonial collecting as by the great metropolitan centres, and wherein Canadians excelled.[62] Macdonald could lean on the international prestige of Canadian geologists Sir William Logan and Sir John W. Dawson, both of whom were feted by metropolitan scientists who relied upon local investigations to piece together their theories and maps and inventories. Viewed from that perspective, the inventory of colonial prosperity might similarly be held up as a corrective to overly centralized and formal metropolitan political economy. Of course the science, like the government, would represent and inventory material wealth rather than poverty. That is to say, poverty was no more visible as fact than as interest. The local governments would have to come up with their own sciences for that purpose, their own anatomies of poverty. They did eventually accomplish this feat, but only after the death of Macdonald.

As a young politician, Macdonald watched colonial legislatures struggle and founder from a position of fiscal weakness. As the leading "father" of Confederation, he took that opportunity to strengthen the national government's revenues. He could not extricate that government from fiscal squabbles with the provinces, of course, but he could and did ensure that it would henceforth negotiate from the position of fiscal strength. The new constitution had a broad base for revenue, but a narrow mandate for spending, thereby efficiently and ruthlessly transferring money from the poor to the rich. These were extraordinary innovations. And yet, to no small degree, Macdonald drew on his understanding of the world before Confederation, when voluntarism was in its heyday and geology was the emergent queen of the sciences. It may also be that he was harkening back to the political dreams of the Upper Canadian Toryism from which he sprang, of a prosperous social elite in permanent control of the fiscal and therefore the political apparatus, albeit an apparatus now funded from below rather than above. Amidst all the promises of science and progress, Macdonald effectively laboured to roll back the forces of equality and democratization in Canada, ending the Tocquevillian century. Alexis de Tocqueville had, after all, always argued that equality could be overcome by a "new aristocracy" of manufacturers that would not hesitate to use its expanding ownership of material resources to entrench "permanent inequality of conditions" and control of the political process.[63]

NOTES

1. Mary Beard, "Which Thucydides Can You Trust?" *The New York Review of Books*, September 30, 2010; see also Clifford Orwin, *The Humanity of Thucydides* (Princeton: Princeton University Press, 1994).

2. Rod Preece, "The Political Wisdom of Sir John A. Macdonald," *Canadian Journal of Political Science* 27 (1984).

3. On Macdonald's life and characteristics, Richard Gwyn, *John A.: The Man Who Made Us* (Toronto: Random House, 2007) and *Nation Maker: Sir John A. Macdonald* (Toronto: Random House, 2011).

4. John M. Charlton, *Hansard*, April 27, 1885, 1391. Other Liberal MPs made similar remarks during the same debate — on suffrage (see Colin Grittner in this volume).

5. Michael J. Piva, *The Borrowing Process: Public Finance in the Province of Canada, 1840–1867* (Ottawa: Ottawa University Press, 1992); Andrew Smith, *British Businessmen and Canadian Confederation: Constitution-Making in an Era of Anglo-Globalization* (Montreal: McGill-Queen's University Press, 2008).

6. Donald Creighton, *John A. Macdonald: The Young Politician, The Old Chieftain* (Toronto: University of Toronto Press, 1998), 97.

7. Charles W. Calomiris and Larry Schweikart, "The Panic of 1857: Origins, Transmission, and Containment," *Journal of Economic History* 51, 4 (December 1991): 807–34.

8.   *Toronto Globe* January 24, 1862. Further commentary is in F.H. Underhill, "Canada's Relations with the Empire as Seen by the *Toronto Globe*, 1857–1867," *Canadian Historical Review* 10, 2 (1929): 106–28.

9.   Garth Stevenson, *Unfulfilled Union: Canadian Federalism and National Unity* (Toronto: Gage, 1982.), 33.

10. Robert Vipond, *Liberty and Community: Canadian Federalism and the Failure of the Constitution* (Albany: State University of New York Press, 1991).

11. *Toronto Globe* March 14, 1867.

12. Andrew Smith, "Toryism, Classical Liberalism, and Capitalism: The Politics of Taxation and the Struggle for Canadian Confederation," *Canadian Historical Review* 89, 1 (March 2008): 1–25.

13. H.V. Nelles, *The Politics of Development: Forests, Mines and Hydro-Electric Power in Ontario, 1849–1941* (Toronto: Macmillan of Canada, 1974), 46.

14. Martin Daunton, *Trusting Leviathan: The Politics of Taxation in Britain, 1799–1914* (Cambridge: Cambridge University Press, 2001).

15. Elsbeth Heaman, "'The Whites Are Wild About It': Taxation and Racialization in Mid-Victorian British Columbia," *Journal of Policy History* 25, 3 (2013): 354–84; Elsbeth Heaman, "The Politics of Fairness: Income Tax in Canada Before 1917," in Kim Brooks, ed., *The Quest for Tax Reform Continues: The Royal Commission on Tax Reform Fifty Years Later* (Toronto: Carswell Publishing, 2013), 10–31.

16. Jan de Vries, *The Industrious Revolution: Consumer Behaviour and the Household Economy 1650 to the Present* (Cambridge: Cambridge University Press, 2008); John Brewer, *The Sinews of Power: War, Money and the English State, 1688–1783* (London: Unwin Hyman, 1989); Philip T. Hoffman, *Growth in a Traditional Society: The French Countryside, 1450–1815* (Princeton: Princeton University Press, 1996), 185.

17. *Parliamentary Debates on the Subject of the Confederation of the British North American Provinces,* 3rd session, 8th Provincial Parliament of Canada (Quebec: Hunter, Rose, 1865), 40. The "too" refers to the previous and first item on the list of federal responsibilities: the public debt and property of the Confederation. [Hereafter *Parliamentary Debates.*]

18. See E.A. Heaman, *The Inglorious Arts of Peace: Exhibitions in Canadian Society during the Nineteenth Century* (Toronto: University of Toronto Press, 1999), 179–81.

19. *Parliamentary Debates,* 26, 60. See Arthur Silver, *The French Canadian Idea of Confederation, 1864–1900* (Toronto: University of Toronto Press, 1997).

20. A.T. Galt, *Speech on the Proposed Union of the British North American Provinces, Delivered at Sherbrooke, C.E.* (Montreal: *Gazette*, 1864), 20.

21. Oscar Douglas Skelton, *The Life and Times of Sir Alexander Tilloch Galt* (Toronto: Oxford University Press, 1920) 218–19, 225.

22. Ben Forster, *A Conjunction of Interests: Business, Politics, and Tariffs, 1825–*

1879 (Toronto: University of Toronto, 1986) and "Common Knowledge: Theory, Concept, and the Prosaic in Making the Tariff of 1859," in E.A. Heaman, Alison Li, and Shelley McKellar, eds. *Essays in Honour of Michael Bliss: Figuring the Social* (Toronto: University of Toronto Press, 2008): 119–45. [Hereafter *Conjunction of Interests.*]

23. *Parliamentary Debates*, 68.
24. Ibid., 728, 31.
25. Jürgen Habermas, *The Structural Transformation of the Public Sphere: An Inquiry into a Category of Bourgeois Society*, trans. Thomas Burger (Cambridge: Massachusetts Institute of Technology Press, 1991).
26. *Parliamentary Debates*, 19.
27. Robin L. Einhorn, *Property Rules: Political Economy in Chicago, 1833–1872* (Chicago: University of Chicago Press, 2001).
28. Sven Beckert, *The Monied Metropolis: New York City and the Consolidation of the American Bourgeoisie, 1850–1896* (Cambridge: Cambridge University Press, 2001).
29. Gustavus Myers, *History of Canadian Wealth* (Chicago, 1914); *Toronto Globe*, November 25, 1879.
30. Galt, *Speech on the Proposed Union*, 15.
31. Martin Daunton, "Creating Legitimacy: Administering Taxation in Britain, 1815–1914," in José Luis Cardoso and Pedro Lains, *Paying for the Liberal State: The Rise of Public Finance in 19th-century Europe* (Cambridge: Cambridge University Press, 2010), 29, 45.
32. Avner Offer, *Property and Politics 1870–1914: Landownership, Law, Ideology and Urban Development in England* (Cambridge: Cambridge University Press, 1981), 179, quoting a speech by the Liberal MP for the City of London, George Joachim Goschen, February 21, 1868. [Hereafter *Property and Politics.*] See also Peter J. Gurney, "'Rejoicing in Potatoes': The Politics of Consumption in England During the 'Hungry Forties,'" *Past and Present* 203, 1 (2009): 99–136; Ian Anstruther, *The Scandal of the Andover Workhouse* (London: Geoffrey Bles, 1973).
33. Quarter Sessions of the Peace, Halifax Grand Jury Books, P18, 1852–1862; P1: Quarter sessions of the Peace, 1863–1875, RG 34-312, Provincial Archives of Nova Scotia. See Bruce Curtis, *Ruling by Schooling: Quebec, Conquest to Liberal Governmentality, a Historical Sociology* (Toronto: University of Toronto Press, 2012).
34. Offer, *Property and Politics*, 173.
35. Jeffrey L. McNairn, "The Malthusian Moment: British Travellers and the Vindication of Economic Liberalism in the Maritime Countryside," in Nancy Christie, ed., *Transatlantic Subjects: Ideas, Institutions, and Social Experience in Post-Revolutionary British North America* (Montreal: McGill-

Queen's University Press, 2008): 329–68.

36. Jean-Marie Fecteau, *La Liberté du pauvre:Sur la régulation du crime et de pauvreté au XIXe siècle québécois* (Montreal: VLB, 2004); Roberto Perin, "Elaborating a Public Culture: The Catholic Church in Nineteenth-Century Quebec," in Marguerite Van Die, ed. *Religion and Public Life in Canada: Historical and Comparative Perspectives* (Toronto: University of Toronto Press, 2001), 87–107.

37. Mariana Valverde, "The Mixed Social Economy as a Canadian Tradition," *Studies in Political Economy* 47 (Summer 1995): 39.

38. Jack Jedwab, "The Politics of Finance: A Comparative Analysis of Public Finance in the Provinces of Quebec and Ontario from 1867 to 1896" (PhD Dissertation, Concordia University, 1992), 58.

39. Cheryl DesRoches, "Everyone in their Place: The Formation of Institutional Care for the Elderly in Nineteenth-Century Ontario," *Journal of the Canadian Historical Association* 15 (2004): 57.

40. Ben Forster, *Conjunction of Interests*.

41. See the discussion in Simon J. McLean, "The Tariff History of Canada," *Toronto University Studies in Political Science* 4 (1895): 31. Federal receipts, $14 million in the year after Confederation, rose from $23 million in 1879 to $30 million in 1880. *Historical Statistics of Canada*, Series H1-18, Federal government, budgetary revenue, by major source. *www.statcan.gc.ca/pub/11-516-x/pdf/5500098-eng.pdf.*

42. *Hansard* March 7, 1876, 491 and *Times* (London), August 9, 1880.

43. *Toronto Globe*, November 25, 1879.

44. Forster, *Conjunction of Interests*.

45. Michael Bliss, *Right Honourable Men: The Descent of Canadian Politics from Macdonald to Mulroney* (Toronto: HarperCollins, 1994), 22.

46. E.g. Sir Richard Cartwright, *Reminiscences* (Toronto: W. Briggs, 1912); *Speech of Sir John Macdonald to the Workingmen's Liberal Conservative Association of Ottawa and Le Cercle Lafontaine Delivered in Ottawa on the 8th of October, 1886* (CIHM 32314).

47. Smith, "Toryism, Classical Liberalism, and Capitalism," 9–10.

48. James E. Alvey, "Mechanical Analogies in Adam Smith," *International Journal of Applied Economics and Econometrics* 10, 2 (2002): 165–84, reprinted in K. Puttaswarmaiah, ed. *Growth of Economics in the Twentieth Century: Theories and Practices* (Enfield: Isle Publishing, 2009): 29–38, *http://economics-finance.massey.ac.nz/publications/discuss/dp99-12.pdf.*

49. T.E. Cliffe Leslie, "The Political Economy of Adam Smith," *Fortnightly Review* November 1, 1870; T.E. Cliffe Leslie, *Essays in Political and Moral Philosophy* (London: Longman's, 1879), 148; Roger E. Backhouse, "Economists in Parliament in Britain (1848–1914)," and Massimo M. Augello and Marco E.L. Guidi, "Economists in Parliament in the Liberal Age: A Comparative

Perspective," in Massimo M. Augello and Marco E.L Guidi, eds *Economists in Parliament in the Liberal Age (1848–1920)* (Aldershot: Ashgate, 2005).

50. As A.W. Coats remarked, "In the seventies and eighties historical pronouncements became very fashionable, though it is difficult to judge how far the central body of economic analysis was affected by the change." A.W. Coats, "The Historicist Reaction in English Political Economy 1870–1890," *Economica* ns 21, 82 (May 1954), 150. See also Dimitris Milonakis and Ben Fine, *From Political Economy to Economics: Method, the Social and the Historical in the Evolution of Economic Theory* (London: Routledge, 2009).

51. *Hansard*, May 9, 1883, 1090.

52. *Hansard*, February 16, 1876, 69.

53. Ibid., March 13, 1884, 839; March 20, 1884, 1003.

54. Ibid., March 20, 1884, 1010–12.

55. Ibid., July 12, 1885, 3345.

56. Ibid., April 27, 1886, 883.

57. Ibid., March 7, 1876, 490.

58. Ibid., March 18, 1879, 517–9.

59 Ibid., March 21, 1879, 645; quoting J.E. Cairnes, *The Character and Logical Method of Political Economy* (1861; republished 1875). Patterson's authority, John Elliott Carnes, actually upheld the view that classical political economy was a science, more deductive than inductive and not susceptible to statistical testing; his was a polemical argument directed against the historical school. Nonetheless, for the purposes of Canadian parliamentary debate, his argument supported that of historical and geographical specificity.

60. Steven Shapin and Simon Schaffer, *Leviathan and the Air Pump: Hobbes, Boyle, and the Experimental Life* (Princeton: Princeton University Press, 1985).

61. Donald Wright, *The Professionalization of History in English Canada* (Toronto: University of Toronto Press, 2005); M. Brook Taylor, *Promoters, Patriots, and Partisans: Historiography in Nineteenth-Century English Canada* (Toronto: University of Toronto Press, 1989); Elisabeth Wallace, "Goldwin Smith on History," *Journal of Modern History* 26, 3 (September 1954): 220–32.

62. Suzanne Zeller, *Inventing Canada: Early Victorian Science and the Idea of a Transcontinental Nation* (Toronto: University of Toronto Press, 1987).

63. Terry Lynn Karl, "Economic Inequality and Democratic Instability," *Journal of Democracy* 11, 1 (2000): 149–56.

Chapter 8

The National Policy's Impact on the West: A Reassessment

DAVID W. DELAINEY AND J.C. HERBERT EMERY

At an Ontario political convention in late November 1881, John A. Macdonald spoke about his national vision for Canada. Historian Donald Creighton describes the broader themes of this speech:

> He had made a reality out of a dream and the miraculous success of his policies, seemed to his auditors, to supply an incontrovertible argument against any alternative conception of Canada and its future … it had become, an autonomous nation inside the British imperial system; and if it kept steadfastly to its first and true course, the certainty of transcontinental nationhood lay before it. He contrasted his own national policies with the international trade and railway policies of Mackenzie and Blake. He talked about his schemes for western settlement…. The whole transcontinental, he told the audience — and the whole pavilion yelled applause — would now be finished in five years instead of ten. "I now have some chance," he said proudly, "if I remain as strong, please God, as I now am, of travelling over it in person before I am just quite an angel."[1]

From Confederation until his death in 1891, at age seventy-six, Macdonald was the veritable political and legislative godfather of the Canadian transcontinental nation. His series of nation-building policies — historically referred to in the aggregate as the national policy[2] included, amongst others: the protective tariff, the building of the transcontinental railway, and the Dominion land policies.

Upon the purchase of Rupert's Land in 1870, Macdonald vested absolute control of these vast lands to the Dominion government. This became "…a veritable empire in its own right, with a dominion of public lands five times the area of the original Dominion, under direct federal administration."[3] Macdonald would use the federal power of disallowance to quash provincial legislation, primarily railroad charters, that were not deemed to be in the national interest.[4] He personally administered the cabinet portfolio of the Department of the Interior, through which he directly supervised western affairs, from 1878 through 1888.[5] In this manner, Macdonald pursued this transcontinental vision with a singularity of purpose.

Indeed, Macdonald did live long enough to see the completion of the transcontinental railroad. At age seventy-one on July 24, 1886, Macdonald, with his wife Agnes, reached Port Moody, British Columbia in their Canadian Pacific Railway (CPR) railcar, the *Jamaica*. A reporter later that day noted that "Sir John looks gay as a lark …"[6] Notwithstanding this personal moment of triumph, on his return to Ottawa, foreshadowing the increasing western dissatisfaction with the national policy, Macdonald attended a Winnipeg political convention

> …in the hope of restoring the declining strength of Norquay's government and the waning popularity of Conservative policies at Ottawa. Macdonald defended the "monopoly clause" of the Canadian Pacific charter. It would, he hoped, be given up "speedily". But in the meantime, the national railway must be defended — and if necessary by federal disallowance from the premature encroachments of its American rivals.[7]

For many in the Prairie West, from his contemporaries to the present, Macdonald's national policy was a work of economic imperialism designed to exploit the region for the benefit of eastern interests. Harold Innis, in his ground-breaking work on the CPR, concludes his discussion on the national policy in the following manner: "Western Canada has paid for the development of Canadian nationality, and it would appear that it must continue to pay. The acquisitiveness of eastern Canada shows little sign of abatement."[8] The CPR was the economic life-line for the western community, but, it became the company that westerners loved to hate. Historian T.D. Regher emphasized this

Grip, 11 July, 1880.

STARTLING AFFAIR IN LONDON!

A PROMISING YOUNG WOMAN OFFERED FOR SALE TO THE HIGHEST BIDDER.

point: "No single issue had contributed more to western Canadian discontent within Confederation than the so-called national transportation policies. Since 1883 ... there has been deliberate and admitted freight-rate discrimination against the West."[9] Kenneth Norrie quotes from the July 1973 *Joint Submission of the Western Premiers to the Western Economic Opportunities Conference*:

> ... the patterns of settlement and development has been influenced by economic, financial and tax policies of the federal government, which early assisted the concentration of the nation's business and industrial activity in central Canada. These policies which have led to this concentration of financial and industrial resources and population have worked against the allocation of financial and production resources to bring balance to the economies of all regions of Canada.[10]

Throughout its history, the western regional economy has been poorer and less industrialized than the central Canadian region. Notwithstanding these economic characteristics and despite continuing negative western views on the matter, the argument can be made that Macdonald's national policy was not the cause of these regional economic circumstances. In the absence of the national policy the Western economy would have evolved in essentially the same manner with the same basic characteristics, nature, and structure. In that regard, the national policy was the inappropriate target of western protest. To the contrary, given that the British Northwest was the focus of a new Canadian commercial policy, Macdonald's national policy was a necessary geopolitical response to American nineteenth-century expansionism.

THE NATIONAL POLICY

In 1869, the world's first transcontinental railway, the Union Pacific, was completed in the United States. It ran hundreds of miles south of the forty-ninth parallel; however, Jay Cooke's Northern Pacific, promised to link Lake Superior with Puget Sound, situated an American railroad remarkably close to British territory. By 1871, it had reached the Red River.[11] The revolutionizing nature of railroad technology was not lost on Macdonald; rails were the tools of economic linkage and geopolitical expansion. The latter aspect reflecting American initiatives was particularly troubling to him in 1870: "It is quite evident to me ... that the United States Government are resolved to do all they can, short of war, to get possession of the western territory, and we must take immediate and vigorous steps to counter-act them. One of the first things is to show unmistakably our resolve to build the Pacific railway."[12]

As an added concern, the Dominion desperately needed a new commercial strategy by 1870. Its access to the United Kingdom market had been compromised by the British adoption of free trade at mid-century. The Canadian-American Reciprocity Treaty of 1854 had provided a suitable alternative for some time, but in 1866 the treaty was abrogated and repeated Canadian attempts to restore it had failed. The transcontinental expansion outlined at Confederation thus became the core of a new commercial strategy. It was designed specifically to defend the British Northwest from American encroachment, while emulating the evident economic success of American westward expansion. This plan involved the purchase of Rupert's Land from the Hudson's Bay Company and the construction of a transcontinental railroad. This strategy had the potential to provide an immense new Canadian agricultural frontier for the profitable investment of capital and labour. Macdonald's proposal of a protectionist tariff in 1878 was aimed at attracting foreign capital and promoting Canadian industrialization. Overall, this tariff — coupled with the transcontinental railroad — was designed to ensure that the wealth of the British Northwest would accrue to Canadians.[13]

The articulation of these policies, or the national policy, would create a regionally specialized but nationally diversified economy. Next to the transcontinental railway, the most critical factor determining the overall success of the national policy would be the effectiveness of a land policy designed to promote the rapid settlement of the Northwest. If there were no people, the railroad would fail and the notion of an emerging wheat economy would be nothing but an illusion. It followed that Canadian industrialization would be inhibited. From a geopolitical point of view, these distinct policies, such as the tariff, the railroad, and the rapid settlement of the West, were necessary to affix permanently the British Northwest to the Dominion and keep American designs on the region at bay.

The global depression that started in 1873 triggered a rise in unemployment and led to widespread commercial and industrial failure. The technological advances of the second Industrial Revolution destabilized many of the manufacturing concerns that employed older and less efficient manufacturing processes. Innovations in steel production and steam power led to a decline in trans-ocean and inland transportation rates. Lower transportation prices had the effect of increasing import competition in Canada, leaving domestic producers vulnerable because natural protections were eliminated. Larger and more efficient American producers, protected by the substantial American tariff wall, aggressively pursued the Canadian market to maintain their production levels. In relation to its population, Canadians imported a significantly higher proportion of their finished goods than their southern neighbours. To that point in time, the Canadian tariff had not changed in its basic purpose, that of supplying revenue to the federal government. Despite the incidental protection of this revenue tariff, the Dominion economy remained a small, open economy with a very high reception of imported goods. Crippled by the depression, Canadian industry could not afford to invest in the processes and the equipment necessary to become competitive. The overall effect for Canadian business was a combination of depression, technological change, and competition.[14]

Philosophically, the Maritimes, the agrarian community, and the Laurentian commercial interests were supportive of free trade or its hybrid, reciprocity.[15] The members of the Canadian industrial community, on the other hand, became a powerful advocate for protection. For them, protection was a necessary tool to invigorate the economic climate and enhance the still infant industrialization of the Dominion. For others, "fighting tariffs" were a necessary response to American protectionism. It would force the Americans to open their market and accept a new reciprocity agreement. The "infant industry" argument was an additional reason used to justify protection. Canadian industry needed the time and the stability provided by protection to invest in new technologies and to support development on an operational scale necessary to be competitive. Increasingly, protection became associated with the protection of the "infant nation" and conveniently lent itself to nationalistic impulses.[16]

By the late 1870s, as price deflation affected their commodities, the traditionally free-trade agrarian interests were more willing to support a policy of protection in response to American import pressures.[17] With the gathering momentum, Macdonald adopted protectionism and it proved to be a compelling political strategy.[18] It entrenched the Grits into their traditional and increasingly less popular free trade policy while resonating with nationalistic exponents within the country. Economically, it had the potential to develop employment opportunities, discourage emigration, encourage foreign investment, and promote industrialization. Most importantly, it could end the depression and, perhaps, pressure the Americans to open their market again.[19] With the acceptance of Macdonald's National Policy in 1879, Canadian tariff policy was reoriented, from revenue to one focused on protection.

At the time, the National Policy was not recognized as part and parcel of the transcontinental expansion of the eastern provinces. In 1879, the markets that mattered to Canadian industry were the central and eastern Canadian ones — not the proposed agricultural frontier of the British Northwest.[20] However, as the expansionist strategy progressed after 1880, the tariff, in conjunction with the CPR, became instrumental to Canadian economic control of the new agricultural frontier of the British Northwest.[21] Not surprisingly, the protectionist tariff has come to be associated with the political and economic consolidation of the transcontinental nation which occurred from 1870 to 1930.

The debacle of the Pacific Scandal, which drove Macdonald's Tories out of power in 1873, and the depressionary conditions facing the Grit Prime Minister Alexander Mackenzie, delayed the building of the transcontinental railway. Mackenzie continued the survey work, however, and built a number of key short haul links; but for all intents and purposes, the transcontinental was hamstrung.[22] Following Macdonald's return to power in 1878 and his negotiation of a commercial understanding with a syndicate in 1881, led by Sir George Stephen, the Canadian Pacific Railway Company was contracted by the Canadian Government to build and operate the road.[23]

Under that arrangement, those sections of the transcontinental already built during Mackenzie's government, approximately seven hundred miles of road worth approximately $38 million, were to be assumed by the company. The links, from Lake Superior to Selkirk and from Port Moody to Kamloops, then under construction by the government, would be assumed by the CPR upon their completion. The remainder of the route, from Callander, Ontario, to Kamloops, was to be constructed and completed by the company before 1891. The primary government subsidies to the company included: $25,000,000 and 25,000,000 acres of land. The company's rail monopoly, west of Callander, was to survive for twenty years.[24]

Once the final CPR agreement was reached in 1881, construction on the transcontinental line progressed. The Pembina branch, connecting Winnipeg to the St. Paul, Minneapolis, and Manitoba Railroad at Emerson, had been operational since 1879. This branch line was assumed by the CPR in 1881. It provided the only rail-based export point until the CPR's Winnipeg to Port Arthur branch line was completed in 1883. The main line from Port Arthur to the eastern slope of the Rockies was completed by June 1883. The most difficult rail links in the network, the all-Canadian road over Lake Superior to Winnipeg and westward through the Rockies to Kamloops, were both completed by November 1885. By 1890, the CPR extended eastward to Saint John, New Brunswick, thus linking the Atlantic with the Pacific.[25] The keystone of Macdonald's national policy, the all-important all-Canadian communication link to the West, was complete.

From 1871 to 1930, federal land policy was modified numerous times. It was adapted to the changing requirements associated with the transcontinental railway and the relative success of the policy in attracting sufficient numbers of settlers necessary for the rapid settlement of the region. In 1872 the policy provided for a "free" 160-acre homestead for qualified settlers within the even-numbered sections of agriculturally fit land in the British Northwest. All odd-numbered sections within a band of land on both sides of the proposed transcontinental railway were offered as a material inducement to private interests to build and operate the transcontinental railway. With the passing of the CPR charter on January 1, 1882, the railway belt was extended to twenty-four miles on each side of the proposed road. As of that date, the free homestead was extended to the even-numbered sections within the railway belt. All government controlled odd-numbered sections outside the belt were available for a reserve price of either $2.50 or $2.00 an acre, depending on their proximity to the railway belt.[26]

Under the "indemnity selection" condition within the CPR charter, if any of the odd-numbered sections within the railway belt were deemed to be not "fairly fit for settlement," the CPR had the right to choose an alternative odd-numbered section anywhere within the surveyed prairie lands. A second issue pertained to the railroad lands within Ontario and British Columbia.

A full 49 percent of the total mileage of the transcontinental passed through both Ontario and British Columbia. However, for various reasons, the CPR grant was wholly allocated within the Northwest, even though only 51 percent of the actual road mileage ran through the Prairie West. The net result was that the CPR lands were not limited to the railroad belt — its lands ranged far and wide across the prairies. The selection process also ensured that CPR lands were of high quality.[27] The liberal alienation of western lands to private interests, including through the government agreement with the CPR, ensured that over 54 percent of western lands were offered for sale rather than as free homesteads.[28] This hybrid circumstance of a large block of federally available homesteads and a large block of contiguous railway lands available for sale simultaneously had the effect of creating a powerful alignment of interests between the CPR and the federal government; their shared goal was the rapid settlement of the Northwest.[29]

TRADITIONAL WESTERN VIEWS OF THE NATIONAL POLICY

The railroad did not lead to paradise and the western Canadian farmer battled all nature of plagues to produce his crop. Once it was produced, he was subject to the demands of the railroads, grain handlers, and banks — to say nothing of the vagaries of the Liverpool marketplace. At the same time, he was forced to purchase his farm inputs from eastern Canadian manufacturers at inflated prices due to the protected tariff.[30] The CPR's western rates were materially higher than similar rates charged to eastern shippers and the western economy paid the full freight for product entering and leaving the Northwest on the transcontinental railway.[31] The national policy appeared to "steer" or "direct" Canadian industrialization to central Canada at the expense of western economic diversification.[32] The federal government's land policy was alleged to have distorted the pattern of settlement, either delaying it or placing it in the wrong places.[33] It all amounted, from the western community's perspective, to a form of eastern Canadian economic colonialism of the West. Even with rapid settlement and the wheat boom years after 1896, this siege mentality blossomed into a regional consciousness, a societal grievance which became an ideology and ultimately the source of political movements. As such, the national policy, in many circles within western Canada, continues to be held responsible for the continuing economic inequality between the West and central Canada. Fundamentally, the phenomenon of western alienation is partially a sociological and psychological product of the perceived inequality of Macdonald's national policy.[34]

THE REASSESSMENT

With regard to the tariff, the essence of the western complaint was that it forced the producer to pay higher prices for his input goods; without tariffs, cheaper manufactured goods could be purchased from American suppliers. In that regard, there was little doubt that western incomes were damaged; however, *all* Canadian incomes were damaged by the tariff. As many believed in 1879, this was the price of Canadian nation-building. Described by W.A. Macintosh, in 1939, and most cogently, by Ken Norrie, in the 1970s, the negative economic effect of the tariff to western interests was offset by a commensurate reduction in the "entry cost" paid by the western producer to enter the farming industry. In effect, the "entry cost" was the value of the fixed factor of agrarian production, land, and its value was lower due to the implementation of the tariff.[35] This was an adjustment mechanism not afforded the average Canadian consumer or to established export-oriented concerns outside the western region.

In economic theory, an asset's value is the discounted present value of all the future cash flows that can be earned from that productive factor. This concept is readily applied in nearly every investment transaction within a modern economy. In a similar manner, if the tariff reduced the expected future cash flows expected from the productive use of the western agricultural land, the value of that land would be expected to decrease. More specifically, the land would have to drop in sufficient value such that the potential buyer was indifferent to employing his capital and labour in the Northwest or in a competing agrarian region such as the American Dakotas. As land was the fixed factor, it could not escape the economic effects of the tariff. It is worth remembering that, prior to the investment decision, the producer's capital and labour were perfectly mobile. In such a manner, these mobile factors of production can avoid the cost of the tariff prior to the investment decision. In such a manner, on a return-on-capital basis, the western producer was compensated for the lower future cash flows accruing to a farming operation located within the British Northwest by the fact that the land was made available for a lower cost than similar land available in a lower tariff jurisdiction. As a very small percentage of the Northwest lands were occupied prior to the highest incidence of the tariff in 1888, it follows logic that the tariff did not damage the western community.[36]

When considering the Canadian West and the implications of the tariff, it was a *change* in the tariff that mattered. In 1929, W.L. Mackenzie King, followed by R.B. Bennett from 1930 through 1933, instituted "fighting tariffs" (read "higher" tariffs) as a response to increasing levels of American protectionism. According to Macintosh, this was a particularly damaging policy to the western economy at exactly the wrong time. Conjugated to the difficult climatic and economic forces of the early 1930s, the increase in the tariff exacerbated the farmer's economic situation. Suddenly, the value of his land and his business suffered a capital loss. However, from 1888 until 1929, as there had been a moderate trend toward lower levels of effective tariff protection, this would have provided the western producer with an unexpected capital gain.[37]

In addition to its effect on western incomes, there was an articulated concern that the national policy, as facilitated by the all-Canadian transcontinental and the protectionist tariff, had "directed" or "steered" the coveted industrialization, with its higher incomes and greater employment, to the central Canadian region at the expense, even de-industrialization, of the West.[38] As a compounding irritant, it appeared that the West had paid for that industrialization through the tariff and CPR freight rates — in effect the West had funded a regional subsidy that exported high value manufacturing jobs to the centre.

The apparent reasonableness of such a calculation failed to appreciate a number of economic considerations. The tariff, as a tool of import substitution, almost guaranteed that the industrial supplier would be Canadian — but it did not determine where industry would expand within the country.[39] In theory, with the completion of the transcontinental railroad in 1885, industrialization could have occurred in any geographic location in sufficient proximity to the road. Ultimately where this activity would be located would be determined by the economic principles of competitive advantages, endowments, and the agglomeration effect.[40]

Economic theory suggests that the region that commands the superior portfolio of initial endowments would have the natural and acquired competitive advantage over alternative regions in the struggle for control of the expanded industrial capacity stimulated by the tariff. The region that enjoyed the widest, most diverse, and lowest cost transportation network required to source raw materials and deliver product would enjoy a natural advantage. Industrial regions within close proximity to large concentrated populations enjoyed cost-effective access to large markets and access to a large and skilled labour pool necessary for value added manufacturing. Regions with large concentrated populations enjoyed higher aggregate incomes leading to greater levels of local capital formation and consumer demand. Further, industrial activity accrues to the regions that enjoyed an economic head start. In some instances, those head starts are measured in decades and centuries of prior economic activity. Over those decades, significant infrastructure, capital, organizational capability, entrepreneurial skills, and technological innovations had been accumulated. This translates into more diverse economies, higher capital formation, and superior endowments. Overall, the region with the superior endowment will have a cost of capital advantage, a cost structure advantage, and a market advantage often very difficult to overcome by less developed, newer or poorer regions.

These natural and acquired advantages create a momentum or a gravitational pull; commercial activity begets more commercial activity, thus multiplying the regional competitive advantage over time. This is the effect of agglomeration. Incremental business will locate in areas of successful business for the same reasons that made it a dominant industrial region in the first case, thus multiplying the advantage.

Within this context — endowments, agglomeration, and natural and acquired competitive advantage — there is little doubt that the Canadian industrial heartland enjoyed a competitive advantage over the new, sparsely populated, logistically challenged British Northwest. Additionally, the Central Canadian economy enjoyed a commercial head start of at least a century. It controlled larger aggregate incomes, higher levels of capital formation, more sophisticated industrial and financial organization, larger and more diverse labour pools, greater prior infrastructure development, and a technology advantage. Notwithstanding this point, there was little doubt that the U.S. industrial regions enjoyed a similar advantage over the Central Canadian for the same reasons.

Since at least the late eighteenth century, the Laurentian economy had been in a commercial struggle with the U.S. eastern seaboard for control of the interior trade of the continent. The development of the Erie Canal, in 1825, and the rapid expansion of the U.S. railway networks, in the 1840s–1860s, provided the clear economic advantage to the Americans. The Laurentian response, significant investments in canals in the 1830s–1840s, and the Grand Trunk Railway in the 1850s, was late and failed to turn the tide.[41] This fact, coupled with the United States' superior seaports, significantly larger populations, larger domestic markets, higher incomes, greater capital formations, and superior technologies ensured that industrial activity and trade would be located in Chicago and New York before Toronto or Montreal. To some extent, the 1879 tariff was a response to that competitive advantage.

As an added benefit, the Americans could boast a superior logistical connection to the British Northwest via St. Paul. The Hudson's Bay Company had recognized that fact in the decade leading up to Confederation. With the merger between the HBC and The Northwest Company in 1821, the HBC had abandoned the Laurentian route in favour of Hudson Bay. However, in 1858, with the development of river steam boats and the construction of the extensive U.S. rail network south of the Great Lakes, Governor Simpson directed the fur trade to the Atlantic via the Red River to St. Paul. Simpson had co-opted the "natural" and economically superior north-south trade connection from the British Northwest through Minnesota. This had been the basis of the growing Red River to St. Paul commercial connection since the 1820s.[42]

The American logistical advantage was a function of the difficulty inherent with travel north of the Great Lakes, through the Precambrian Shield.[43] This difficulty was well understood by firms active in the continental trade, such as the Grand Trunk Railway (GTR). As the most strategically aligned and the most established Canadian railroad, Macdonald had approached the GTR to extend its network and build a transcontinental line. The GTR rejected the scheme because it could not conceive of a route that did not borrow the established southern networks through the United States.[44] This demonstrated sound business judgement and a realistic understanding of efficient continental trade. For the management of the CPR, there was no illusion as to the financial advantage in forging a northern route through the Shield. It would never be a profitable route for the CPR; however, it was a necessary condition of acquiring the Dominion contract.[45]

This history and the nature of continental trade were not lost to John A. Macdonald or to the Laurentian commercial interests. If the Dominion was to control the commercial traffic of the Northwest, it had to be channelled through an all-Canadian route. As the American cities were more powerful economic magnets than Canada's industrial centres and controlled the most attractive logistical route to and from the British Northwest, the national policy was designed to purposely exclude the American capture of the trade. In such a manner, the tariff and the CPR were designed to frustrate the economic forces of the "natural connection" through Minnesota.[46] Notwithstanding this premise, Macdonald's economic nationalism had not purposely reserved the resulting industrial activity for central Canada. The economic forces of competitive advantage, agglomeration, and endowments had concentrated the industrial capacity in the most logical place within Canada — the central Canadian industrial heartland.[47]

In the absence of the national policy, the economic linkages to the British Northwest would have been facilitated by the Northern Pacific and the Great Northern Railway.[48] These roads would have funnelled the resultant economic activity through Minneapolis and Chicago. As those areas already enjoyed significant industrial advantages from an endowments viewpoint, the industrialization necessary to service the western Canadian agricultural frontier would have occurred in the upper Midwest United States. In this scenario, Minneapolis and Chicago would have replaced Toronto and Montreal as the key cities in control of the British Northwest hinterland. In such a manner, the Canadian West would not have industrialized to any greater extent than it ultimately did — even if the national policy had not been instituted.[49] As an anecdotal confirmation of this thesis, the economies of North Dakota and Montana are significantly smaller, less industrialized, and poorer than the states of Michigan and Illinois.

Prior to June 1883, the CPR's road consisted of a number of short-haul routes within southern Manitoba — with connections on an easterly route to Lake Superior terminating at Port Arthur and along a southeasterly route to Pembina. Freight rates were set based upon the Grand Trunk's eastern zone winter rates. As the eastern railroads competed with cheaper water transport in the summer but had no such competition in the winter, the GTR's winter rates were the CPR's highest available benchmark. However, as the CPR's financial difficulties escalated, especially during the period from 1883 to 1885 when the difficult Canadian Shield and Rockies links were being constructed, the CPR became concerned about its future. The federal government was forced to step in with loans totalling $22.5 million in 1883 and an additional $5 million in 1884 to prevent the immediate collapse of its railroad constructor. It was within this context that the 1883 rates schedule was issued.[50] From the CPR's perspective the higher rates were required, given the sparse western traffic of the time and the higher operating costs of the region. The 1883 schedule provided for a 50 percent premium over the Grand Trunk winter rates. This rapid increase in rates above eastern ones bred western discontent.[51] However, largely due to the efforts of the Manitoba government, the CPR monopoly was broken in 1888. This had the immediate effect of introducing competition into the national rail industry. In such a manner, the CPR rate for grain shipped from Winnipeg to Thunder Bay was reduced from 36 cents per hundredweight, in 1883, to 10 cents in 1903.[52] This was largely facilitated through the Crow's Nest Agreement of 1897 and the Manitoba Agreement of 1901.[53]

Another annoying characteristic of CPR freight rates for western producers was the fact that western commercial interests were paying the full cost to transport their input goods entering the region and the full cost to transport their produce to market. This apparent double charge can be explained by simple economics. As a global commodity, with no appreciable Canadian domestic demand to consume the western surplus (and, incidentally, an increasingly large American surplus) North American grain prices were equal to the Liverpool price, adjusted for grade, less transport to the farm gate. The Canadian surplus could only be absorbed in Liverpool. To clear substantial volumes, Canadian grain had to meet the global price on a delivered basis. In effect, the producing region absorbed the entire cost of freight and handling. With regard to import goods, prairie demand was inelastic — demand was not overly sensitive to price. This was a function of a large number of small buyers with few local producers of the necessary goods. Thus the eastern wholesaler could charge the full freight to deliver the product. This was an unavoidable characteristic of a primary resource producing hinterland with small populations situated long distances from the centres of industry.[54]

Were the CPR's freight rates an impediment to western development from 1881 to 1900? All other things being equal, lower rates are always preferable to higher rates for a commodity producer; however, westerners could only claim direct and objective harm if the cost of their most logical alternative shipper to the CPR had lower rates for a similar level of service. In the absence of the CPR, the American transcontinental lines would have provided that alternative. As outlined by Ken Norrie and John McDougall, the Canadian Railway Rates Commission conducted a comparison of the relative level of Canadian versus American rail rates in their *Report of the Railway Rates Commission* in 1895. For the eastbound transportation of grain, the commission concluded that the CPR rates were lower than those on the Great Northern and the Northern Pacific for similar distances per hundredweight. On average, the CPR transported Canadian grain on a mileage basis 30 percent farther than did the Great Northern for the same rate or less and 60 percent farther than the Northern Pacific. As an additional test, the commission extrapolated the North Dakota rate schedule upon the western CPR rail network. This analysis suggested that western Canadian rates would be uniformly higher under the Dakota schedule, except at Prince Albert and Edmonton. The Dakota tariff was 2.7 and 5.1 cents per hundredweight lower in those cases respectively. Freight rates in the northwest states were not reduced from their 1893 rates until 1908; thus, the CPR advantage expanded in those critical years of rapid settlement after 1895. This was due to the adoption of the Crow's Nest Rates in the late 1890s and the Manitoba Agreement early in the twentieth century. As a final test, the commission studied the American rates in effect for westbound goods. In those cases, the CPR system resulted in lower import costs for lumber and merchandise. In the case of agricultural implements, the CPR rate was lower than the American on a ton/mile basis; however, the delivered price in the Dakotas was lower because of the lower track mileage from the manufacturing centre in the U.S. Midwest versus the Canadian industrial heartland. In that case, the disadvantage was due to tariff policy, not the CPR rates.[55]

As there are no available rate comparisons for the period prior to 1895, we have relied on a number of observations to support the broader thesis. First, in the absence of the CPR, it would have been unlikely that a Northern Pacific monopoly would have provided the westerner any relief from the "value for service" rate model. Secondly, even when competition was allowed after 1888, the Northern Pacific did not provide any significant or lasting benefit over the CPR rates.[56] Thirdly, as noted by Innis, at least through the early to the late 1880s, the CPR's operating profits were not indicative of a company exploiting its monopoly position in the region.[57] Finally, the "entry cost" argument has additional application in the case of freight rates. If the CPR rates were higher than those rates offered within the Dakotas, the "negative differential" would not have damaged the western producer in any significant manner as it predated any meaningful settlement of the area. The differential would have been perfectly transparent to the producer at the time of his farm investment. This would have reduced the cost of western Canadian agricultural lands; thus, lowering the farmer's initial land investment, or their "entry cost," versus other land investment alternatives (such as in the Dakotas). Consistent with and as discussed in the case of the pre-existing tariff earlier, the net effect was that the producer's return was insulated from the higher Canadian rate through a lower initial investment cost. Any future rate reductions would have provided a capital gain.[58]

According to federal land policy, the primary use for the western lands was to pay for the pacific railway "…by means of the land through which it had to pass."[59] The second requirement was to promote the rapid settlement of the region. Finally, the lands had to be "…administered by the Government of Canada for the purposes of the Dominion."[60] In such a manner and in contravention of the BNA Act and established British precedent, the federal government retained control of the prairie lands. This was "… a veritable empire in its own right, with a domain of public lands five time the area of the original Dominion, under direct federal administration."[61] Macdonald was concerned that local western land administration would delay or otherwise frustrate the national policy. Upon obtaining provincial status, however, all other Canadian provinces retained control of their lands. By 1930, the federal lands were finally vested in the western provinces.[62]

In the twenty-five years after the HBC purchase, western settlement was anaemic. As estimated by Charles Studness, over 250,000 Canadians moved west in the thirty years after 1870. Remarkably, nearly half of them continued onwards to settle south of the border in the U.S. frontier, including the Dakotas, Iowa, Minnesota, and Nebraska.[63] As noted by Norrie: "Homestead entries averaged under 3,000 from 1874 to 1896, and in many years there were nearly as many cancellations as new entries.

In the same period adjacent American lands were filling up, in large part with emigrant Canadians."[64] In the twenty-five years from 1870 to 1895, less than 20 percent of the entire homesteads alienated by 1930 were entered.[65] There were fewer than 75,000 people living in Manitoba and the Northwest Territories in 1871. This had grown to 250,000 people by 1891.[66] Rail access was a constraining factor early in the period; however, the Pembina export point via Minnesota was available as of 1879 and the CPR had completed its line from Port Arthur to the eastern slope of the Rockies by 1883.[67] Conversely, the Dakotas boomed from 1879 to 1886.[68] This trend reversed itself as settlement on Canadian lands proceeded rapidly after 1896. As noted by Norrie: "Homestead entries began to rise in 1897 … They jumped from 1,857 in 1896 to 7,426 in 1900 and 44,479 in 1911. The increase in homesteads was matched by a jump in land sales…. By the end of the decade … the region was rapidly becoming one of the world's leading wheat producers."[69] In the twenty-five years from 1895 to 1920, almost 75 percent of the entire homesteads alienated by 1930 were entered. The ten year period, from 1900 through 1910, experienced most of that growth.[70] By 1911, Manitoba, Saskatchewan, and Alberta had a combined population of 1.3 million.[71]

Critics state that the delay in western settlement, contemporaneous with extensive emigration to the United States, was due to the Dominion's land policy. According to Charles Studness, the Canadian prairies were the superior investment frontier when compared to the Dakotas. The supply of economically superior Manitoba free homestead lands had been constrained by the persuasiveness of the railway grants. Once the finite number of Manitoba homesteads in proximity to key railroads were occupied, the Canadian settler, rather than purchasing a quarter from the CPR, occupied an inferior free quarter in the Dakotas. The extra cost of the purchased quarter was a capital requirement the new settler could not afford and pushed the economic balance in favour of the southern frontier. The Dakotas had more extensive public homesteads available in proximity to key railroads, which absorbed the excess demand from the Northwest.[72] In effect, there were insufficient numbers of free homesteads in proximity to key railroads and the best lands within the British Northwest were controlled by eastern corporate interests, thus delaying settlement. Notwithstanding this thesis, the predominance of historical and economic research supports the premise outlined by Tony

Ward: "While the National Policy was appropriate to induce settlement, it was not sufficient to induce growth, and much of the settlement that did occur before the turn of the twentieth century was premature."[73] In essence, there were a number of exogenous factors that had to be satisfied before any land policy could be effective. The federal land policy did not delay settlement and the hybrid circumstance, stemming from this policy, appeared to be the most efficient and effective solution.

Similarly, Chester Martin argued that the Dominion Lands Policy had been effective. The key to this effectiveness resulted from two characteristics of the land policy. In the first case, the CPR adopted a land sale strategy, for their large holdings, that was very accommodative to quick sale through the employment of attractive commercial terms for potential purchasers. Their primary goal was to materially increase rail revenues, a desired and necessary result of rapid western settlement, which would firmly establish the long-term profitability of their road. This strategy was economically preferable versus maximizing short-term profit from the sale of their lands. From 1893 to 1900, the Hudson's Bay Company sold their lands for an average sales price of $12.10 per acre while the school lands averaged $9.79 in Manitoba, $14.40 in Alberta, and $16.85 in Saskatchewan. The average sales price for the CPR lands was $8.55 an acre.[74] Rapid settlement became "sound railway policy." Second, as dry land farming technology was designed to reduce the probability of total crop failure, given the semi-arid nature of much of the Prairie West, the 160-acre free homestead was too small to profitably apply these techniques. A farm size of 320 acres was of economic size. The hybrid circumstance had ensured that every successful homesteader had a readily available contiguous quarter of 160 acres that he could purchase from the CPR on a timely basis and at a reasonable price.[75] Martin argued that settlement delays were due to exogenous or technological limitations outside of the control of the Dominion and not due to any failure of the policy itself.[76]

Martin concluded that the hybrid system was superior to either extreme. If every section was offered as a free homestead, the best lands would have been filled as 160-acre parcels providing little flexibility for the necessary expansion to 320 acres. Further, the Canadian experience with free homesteads was mixed; from 1870 to 1927, 41 percent of total homestead entries failed to reach patent. In human and material terms, this represented a massive wastage. Despite this wastage, Martin suggests that the homestead system was a necessary requirement to provide early traffic to the railroads and as an important psychological pull to the Canadian West. If a revenue model had been exclusively employed, the likely result would have been slower settlement with significant implications for the profitability and solvency of the CPR. The hybrid system, where in effect half the land was sold and the other half given away, provided the best solution. It created the necessary conditions conducive to rapid settlement and the most efficient alienation of the western lands minimizing the wastage inherent within the homestead model.[77]

Ken Norrie argued that the British Northwest, except for the lands in the immediate area of the Red River, were outside the extensive margin of economic cultivation using established agricultural techniques in effect east of the one hundredth meridian until the late 1890s.[78] Central to this thesis was the idea that Canada could not be viewed in "… isolation but as the northern frontier of the phase of continental agricultural expansion after 1870."[79] This North American phenomenon required the settlement of the sub-humid lands first; then, with those lands filled and with the development, availability, and mass adoption of dry land farming techniques, then the North American semi-arid lands were occupied. Finally, with the critically important development of Marquis Wheat, the extensive margin was expanded into the Canadian northern parkland after 1910. Norrie's examination of the historical facts supported this thesis. The North American sub-humid lands were largely occupied by the mid-1880s. The necessary dry land farming technology was developed by the late 1880s and early 1890s. The short bear market in wheat prices in the early 1890s delayed the process; however, with their recovery after 1895, the conditions were right for the rapid settlement of the Canadian and U.S. semi-arid lands.[80] This explained the apparent paradox of the Dakota land boom and Canadian bust between 1883 and 1890; as the Dakota land boom of the 1880s occurred primarily within the sub-humid lands east of the one-hundredth meridian.[81] With the development of dry land farming techniques and the filling of the North American sub-humid lands by the 1890s, the level of homesteading within the Canadian and the American semi-arid lands progressed rapidly.[82]

CONCLUSION

At its core, the prairie economic complaint was with the inherent nature of the western economy, not with the national policy. An interior continental economy exhibits certain characteristics or endowments which progress toward a certain end independent, and sometimes in spite, of policy. Those characteristics included: small local populations, little transport diversity, long distances from key markets, low capital formation, under-developed infrastructure, and a relatively new economy. They organized themselves around the production of a key export staple reliant on a large and autonomous external demand. Its economy was driven by the extent of the "spreading effects" or the linkages afforded that staple. Alternative occupations of capital and labour in competition to the dominant staple tended to be crowded out. Diverse industrialization was difficult and secondary manufacturing was limited. It faced the high and fixed transportation costs necessary to import goods and necessary to export its product to the world. High and sustained levels of intensive growth are very difficult to maintain in an economy focused on resource extraction and primary industry. These economies tend toward cycles of recurring boom and bust, depending on the commodity and technology cycle.

In addition to geography and endowments, the eastern-based economies enjoyed hundreds of years of previous economic development and significantly larger populations. These large metros, through the process of natural and acquired competitive advantage and the principle of agglomeration, commanded an economic hegemony over the hinterlands. This advantage, once acquired, can be very difficult to overcome. As described by John McCallum's modified staples theory, the Ontario wheat economy of the mid-nineteenth century was able to overcome the Montreal advantage; however, in that case, the conditions accommodative to that result were very specific to the Upper Canadian region and that time.[83] Those conditions were not prevalent within the British Northwest of the later nineteenth century. Ironically, the former "suppressed" agrarian frontier of Canada West became the new metro that "enforced" its hegemony over the new agricultural frontier further to the west.

The economic research argues that the national policy did not damage the western economy nor did it inhibit its industrialization. As outlined by Norrie, it is highly likely that the western economy would have developed exactly as it did in its absence. The policy directed the industrial expansion required to service the British Northwest agricultural frontier to its most logical economic place in Canada. The principles of competitive advantage and agglomeration determined that geographic placement — the pre-existing industrial heartland in central Canada. The policy defeated those same principles and frustrated the more powerful economic connection between the British Northwest and the American Midwest.

As the tariff was implemented before material settlement, it was a cost of production entirely transparent to the farmer before investment. The necessary result was that the fixed factor of production, land, was discounted by an amount sufficient to protect the producer's minimum return. Alternatively, the producer could have employed his labour and capital in the Dakotas. Once the region was settled and the tariff implemented, it was the change in the tariff that was germane to the economic welfare of the established producer. For that very reason, it was economically rational for the agrarian community to support free trade if that political bargain could have been struck. Ultimately, the tariff reduced incomes and constrained production; however, western producers had the ability to reset the basis of their investment decision to account for the costs of the tariff. Arguably, the real "losers" in this case were the original "landowners," including the Hudson's Bay Company, the CPR, and the Government of Canada — each of whom received less for their landholdings than they would have in the absence of the tariff.[84] Nevertheless, only the HBC could claim true damage as the Dominion had the power to change the tariff and the CPR investment decision followed the implementation of the tariff.

A close examination of the western freight rates does not suggest that they were discriminatory relative to U.S. rates for similarly situated producers. In the absence of the CPR, the U.S. railways were the West's only true alternative. If the western economy was able to negotiate a better deal through political action or encouraging the entrance of new rail competitors, this was a rational political response within the national context. However, this does not imply that the CPR rates were discriminatory or damaging to western interests. With regard to federal land policy, the historical and economic literature support the premise that the federal land policy was *appropriate* to induce rapid settlement but not *sufficient* to facilitate this goal until such time as certain exogenous constraints, such as the development of dry land farming techniques and the filling of the North American sub-humid lands, had been satisfied. This finally occurred at the turn of the century.

In 1879, the tariff was not visibly associated with the transcontinental expansion; however, it was an equally important strategy necessary to fuse the British Northwest to the Dominion and to frustrate American designs on the territory. This was not without a cost; the tariff had the effect of reducing the real incomes of all Canadians. Notwithstanding these costs, global protectionism was on the rise in the latter half of the nineteenth century and it was an accepted industrial strategy necessary to generate budgetary revenues and to promote domestic manufacturing. This formula had been fully embraced by the American Republic. Industrialism was consistent with nationhood and, for many in 1879, it was a small price to pay for the survival of a British nation on the northern half of the continent. Given these facts, the 1879 tariff appears a reasonable strategy for Macdonald — to counter the "beggar-thy-neighbour" trade policies of the Americans and, later, to ensure that the trade of the Northwest was captured in Canada. It was unfortunate that the tariff became so clearly a political symbol of Canadian sovereignty, as it diminished the economic flexibility of the Government of Canada to modify materially that strategy for nearly a century.

Macdonald's concern "… that the United States Government are resolved to do all they can, short of war, to get possession of the western territory, and we must take immediate and vigorous steps to counteract them …" was not misplaced.[85] The Canadians needed to project credible political and economic control over the region — through the establishment of a railroad and settlers — before U.S. interests expanded northward. It was unlikely that the British would have defended Canadian economic designs from a concerted American action where a defensible American "interest" such as railways and settlers existed.[86] Given this geopolitical context, the national policy was a wholly reasonable and necessary response. It was designed to emulate the apparent economic success of the American transcontinental nation. At the same time, it was a necessary defensive measure to protect Canadian ambitions in the region. To use Fowke's terms, the national policy was driven by this "national emergency." The necessary result, unlike the American frontier experience, was the peculiar characteristic of Canadian history that led to the federal mega project of western settlement and its development in one concerted burst of national energy. The "all Canadian, all at once, and all the way" transcontinental railway strategy was driven by this emergency as was a land policy accommodative to the rapid settlement of the British Northwest. The measured approach, as outlined by the GTR, may have been a superior commercial strategy, when considering cost and risk, but it was an insufficient geopolitical response to the situation. The unprecedented control and administration of the western lands "for the purposes of the Dominion" was wholly consistent with the necessity for rapid and concerted action.

Western Canadian mythology holds as true that Macdonald's national policy was regressive, capricious, and economically exploitive to Western Canadians. At best, Canadian historiography is neutral to this claim and, alternatively, highly supportive.[87] The economic reality was that prairie life was difficult. The economic statistics confirm these facts. The tariff, the CPR, and federal land policy, amongst other eastern policies, appeared to aggravate the situation. It all amounted, from the western community's perspective, to a form of eastern Canadian economic colonialism of the West. While sympathetic and in full understanding of its origin and nature, this protest, as a struggle against the framework of the national policy, was economically misdirected. In this regard, John A. Macdonald and the national policy are inappropriately held responsible for the apparent deficiencies of the western regional economy. To the contrary, the national policy and Macdonald's bold action were the necessary and timely economic and political acts required to preserve the northern half of the continent for Canada.

NOTES

1. Donald Creighton, *John A. Macdonald: The Young Politician and The Old Chieftain* (Toronto: University of Toronto Press, 1998), 326.
2. As per current historical convention, the capitalized term, the "National Policy," refers to Macdonald's protectionist tariff as that was what it was called in 1878. The un-capitalized term, the "national policy," refers to the whole framework of Canadian nation-building policies instituted by the Canadian government in the late nineteenth century, including the purchase of Rupert's Land, the tariff, the transcontinental railway, immigration, and land policy amongst a number of other federal policies.
3. Chester Martin, *Dominion Lands Policy* (Toronto: McClelland & Stewart Limited, 1973), 9.
4. W.L. Morton, *Manitoba: A History* (Toronto: University of Toronto Press, 1961), 212–16; Creighton, 473–74, 478–79.

5. Creighton, 245–45, 504.
6. Ibid., 461.
7. Ibid., 462.
8. Harold A. Innis, *A History of the Canadian Pacific Railway* (Toronto: University of Toronto Press, 1971), 294.
9. T.D. Regehr, "Western Canada and the Burden of National Transportation Policies," in *The Prairie West: Historical Readings*, ed. R. Douglas Francis and Howard Palmer (Edmonton: Pica Pica Press, 1995), 264–68. [Hereafter "Western Canada."]
10. Ken Norrie, "Some Comments on Prairie Economic Alienation," *Canadian Public Policy* 2:2 (Spring 1976), 213 [Hereafter "Comments."]
11. Vernon C. Fowke, *The National Policy and the Wheat Economy* (Toronto: University of Toronto Press, 1957), 43–57, 69 [Hereafter *National Policy.*]
12. Ibid., 44–45.
13. Ibid., 3–69; Ben Forster, *A Conjunction of Interests: Business, Politics and Tariffs, 1825–1879* (Toronto: University of Toronto Press, 1986), 68–72, 78–85, 130–33.
14. Ibid., 26–28, 33–51, 72–74, 84–85, 88–109.
15. Ibid., 76–77, 124–26.
16. Ibid., 113–26.
17. Ibid., 147–51.
18. Ibid., 171.
19. Ibid., 136–48, 151–78.
20. Ibid., 178–80, 205.
21. Fowke, 56–57, 62–69.
22. G.P. de T. Glazebrook, *A History of Transportation in Canada* (New York: Greenwood Press, 1969), 239–63.
23. Ibid., 263–67.
24. Ibid., 265–67.
25. Ibid., 262–82, 294–301.
26. Martin, *Dominion Lands Policy*, 38—52, 140–42, 143–47.
27. Ibid., 45–52, 73–78.
28. Ibid., 56, 96–99, 227–33; Kenneth Norrie, Douglas Owram & J.C. Herbert Emery, *A History of the Canadian Economy* (Toronto: Thomson Nelson, 2008), 197.
29. Glazebrook, *History of Transportation*, 262–282; Martin, *Dominion Lands Policy*, 10–13, 44, 51–52, 56–57, 82.
30. Gerald Friesen, *The Canadian Prairies: A History* (Toronto: University of Toronto Press, 1987), 188; A.R. M. Lower, *Colony to Nation: A History of Canada* (Toronto: Longmans, Green & Company, 1951), 429.
31. Regehr, "Western Canada," 264–284; Howard Darling, *The Politics of Freight Rates: The Railway Freight Rate Issue in Canada* (Toronto: McClelland & Stewart Limited, 1980), 16–32, 38; Glazebrook, *History of Transportation*, 301–12.

32. Kenneth Norrie, "The National Policy and Prairie Economic Discrimination, 1870–1930" in *Canadian Papers in Rural History, Volume I.* ed. Donald H. Akenson. (Gananoque, ON: Langdale Press, 1978), 22–23 [hereafter "National Policy"].

33. Norrie, "National Policy," 25; Martin, *Dominion Lands Policy*, 11–13; Charles M. Studness, "Economic Opportunity and the Westward Migration of Canadians during the Late Nineteenth Century," *The Canadian Journal of Economics and Political Science* 30, no. 4 (November 1964), 570–84 [Hereafter "Economic Opportunity".]

34. Howard Darling, in his work *The Politics of Freight Rates: The Railway Freight Rate Issue in Canada*, 1–44, and Ken Norrie, in his articles "The National Policy," 13–29, and "Some Comments," 211–24, describe the underlying psychology of the western protest movement. In particular, they outline how the railway freight rate controversies and the national policy contributed to this social and political phenomenon.

35. W.A. Mackinosh, *The Economic Background of Dominion-Provincial Relations* (Toronto: McClelland & Stewart Limited, 1969), 140–146 [hereafter *Economic Background*]; Norrie, "National Policy," 22–25.

36. J.H. Young, *Canadian Commercial Policy* (Ottawa, Queen's Printer, 1957), 33; Norrie et al., *A History of the Canadian Economy*, 193, 200–201.

37. Mackintosh, *Economic Background*, 144–146, 154–170; Norrie, "National Policy," 22–25.

38. Ibid., "National Policy," 22.

39. Ibid., "National Policy," 22–25.

40. Ibid., "Some Comments," 212–24.

41. Fowke, *National Policy*, 6–8, 26.

42. Glazebrook, *History of Transportation*, 216–22, 225–27.

43. Fowke, *National Policy*, 26–27.

44. Glazebrook, 240–41.

45. Ibid., 272–74, 302–06.

46. Fowke, 42–69.

47. Norrie, "National Policy," 22–25.

48. Fowke, *National Policy*, 43–57, 69; Regehr, "Western Canadian," 264–84; Norrie, "National Policy," 16–19.

49. Norrie, "National Policy," 22–24; Mackintosh, *Economic Background*, 150–54.

50. Glazebrook, 262–82.

51. Darling, *Politics of Freight Rates*, 28–29.

52. Conversion from 21.6 cents per bushel in 1883 to 36 cents per hundredweight is based upon a standard weight of 60 lbs per bushel for wheat. See Regehr, 267–74 for rates per bushel in 1883 and cents per hundredweight in 1903.

53. Ibid., 270–71, 273–76; W. Kaye Lamb, *History of the Canadian Pacific Railway*, (New York: Macmillan, 1977), 155–64; Glazebrook, *History of*

Transportation, 306–12; Norrie, "National Policy," 19–22; Norrie, "Some Comments," 219–220; John Lorne McDougall, "The Relative Level of Crow's Nest Grain Rates in 1899 and in 1965." *The Canadian Journal of Economics and Political Science* 32:1 (February 1966), 46–54.

54. Norrie, "Some Comments," 214.
55. Norrie, "National Policy ," 16–22; McDougall, "Relative Level," 46–54.
56. Norrie, "National Policy," 16–22.
57. Innis, *History of the Canadian Pacific*, 244–45.
58. Norrie, "National Policy," 16–22.
59. Martin, *Dominion Lands Policy*, 11.
60. Ibid., 9.
61. Ibid.
62. Norrie, "National Policy," 25; Martin, *Dominion Lands Policy,* 11–13.
63. Studness, "Economic Opportunity," 570.
64. Kenneth Norrie, "The Rate of Settlement of the Canadian Prairies, 1870–1911," *The Journal of Economic History* 35: 2 (June 1975), 410.
65. Norrie et al, *A History of the Canadian Economy*, 201.
66. Ibid., 193.
67. Fowke, *National Policy*, 47–49; Glazebrook, *History of Transportation*, 272–77.
68. Norrie, "Rate of Settlement," 410.
69. Ibid., 410–11.
70. Norrie et al*, A History of the Canadian Economy*, 201.
71. Ibid., 193.
72. Studness,"Economic Opportunity," 570–84.
73. Tony Ward, "Climate Change and the National Policy" *The Canadian Journal of Economics* 29, special issue: part 1 (April 1996), S347.
74. Martin*, Dominion Lands Policy*, 44–52, 73–87, 143–45.
75. Ibid., 73-87, 140–74, 227–46.
76. Ibid., 73–87, 140–74, 227–46.
77. Ibid., 227–46.
78. Norrie, "Rate of Settlement," 410–27.
79. Ibid., 423.
80. Ibid., 423–27.
81. Ibid., 425–26.
82. Ibid., 420–27.
83. See John McCallum, *Unequal Beginnings: Agriculture and Economic Development in Quebec and Ontario until 1870* (Toronto: University of Toronto Press, 1980).
84. Norrie, "The National Policy," 22–25.
85. Fowke, *National Policy*, 44–45.
86. Alvin C. Gluek Jr., *Minnesota and the Manifest Destiny of the Canadian Northwest*, (Toronto: University of Toronto Press, 1965) 28–30, 78–79, 115–

17, 152–54, 157, 159–61, 168–72, 193–94, 204–19, 262–63, 270–71, 278–83, 287–88, 292–93; Kenneth Bourne in his work *Britain and the Balance of Power in North America, 1815–1908* (Berkeley: University of California Press, 1967) provides an excellent synthesis of the British geopolitical challenges, given the rise of American (Northern) power after the Civil War and Prussian after Sadowa in 1866. C.P. Stacey in his work *Canada and the British Army, 1846–1871* (Toronto: University of Toronto Press, 1963) outlines the effects of these changing geopolitical conditions upon the ongoing British challenges of defending the Canadian provinces. These pressures led to the removal of the British garrison from Quebec in 1871 by the Gladstone administration.

87. Innis, *History of the Canadian Pacific Railway*, 294.

Part 3

Macdonald and Government

Chapter 9

Macdonald and the Governors General: The Prime Minister's Use and Abuse of the Crown

Barbara J. Messamore

Few aspects of John A. Macdonald's political career demonstrate his acumen as clearly as his relationship with the Crown. Over the course of a long parliamentary career, Macdonald dealt with some ten different governors general. Other Canadian politicians evinced discomfort with the British aristocrats appointed to preside over them, wavering between prickly churlishness and embarrassing obsequiousness. But Macdonald, while frequently embroiling the governors in controversy, managed to forge bonds of genuine affection and friendship with many of them. A glimpse into these relationships offers a valuable window on the workings of nineteenth-century politics, and also affords insight into Macdonald's character and tactics. It reveals the immense personal charm that was so much a part of the secret to Macdonald's enduring political success. But it also shows Macdonald's willingness to use — even abuse — the Crown as a tool to achieve and hold on to power. At times, the governor general could be an unwitting victim of Macdonald's ambition.

The very process by which Macdonald came to lead the Conservative party in 1856 made use of the Crown. A party revolt that sought to oust the aging Sir Allan MacNab from the leadership placed Governor Sir Edmund Head in an awkward position. MacNab, who for decades had used his political connections in a bid to enrich himself, tried to push his influence too far with a double-dealing arrangement that sought to extort funds from both the Great Western Railway and their rivals, the Grand Trunk — an episode that prefigures some later machinations by Macdonald himself. With his party colleagues turning against him, MacNab, suffering from an attack of gout, was carried into the Assembly, and tried in vain to cling to the leadership.[1] But his cabinet outmanoeuvred him by resigning after surviving a vote on a supply bill. They maintained that a want of confidence had been shown in the administration since there was only a majority among the Canada East members of the Assembly, and not among the members for Canada West.[2] While some pre-Confederation politicians had hoped to introduce systemically the "double majority" principle, this had not been consistent practice, and Head recognized that it was only a pretext. Indeed, he privately railed at "the absurdity in *one* legislature of requiring *two* majorities." The resignation was of a "very mischievous character," he noted. The "*real object* was to "get rid of Sir Allan M'Nab" who "would not relieve them by resigning voluntarily." Faced with the dilemma of a resignation by a government still holding a majority, Head called upon Étienne Paschal Taché and John A. Macdonald to lead his administration.[3]

Unfortunately for Head, the unstable political atmosphere of pre-Confederation Canada soon created another circumstance in which he became an instrument of Macdonald's partisan goals. By late July 1858, Macdonald, along with George-Étienne Cartier, presided over a precarious ministry that had lost a couple of votes over matters that were not considered confidence measures. Hectored by Reform leader George Brown, Macdonald survived a vote on adjournment, but nonetheless tendered his resignation to Head. Just as before, the governor general had to contend with the resignation of a ministry that still possessed a majority. Head confided to the Colonial Office that he had "no alternative" but to accept it and call upon opposition leader George Brown.[4] Macdonald, for his part, was clearly enjoying the spectacle of Brown being put to the test. After asking Head for a delay of a couple of days to garner support, Brown accepted office. "A prudent fish will play around the bait for some time before he takes it," Macdonald scoffed, "but in this instance the fish scarcely waited till the bait was let down. He jumped out of the water to catch it."[5]

Ged Martin has remarked upon Brown's surprising success in drawing support from across partisan lines, including the *rouge* leader Antoine-Aimé Dorion, and a record six Roman Catholics. "Macdonald and his allies faced an urgent need to strangle the new ministry at birth," Martin suggests.[6] Mere hours after the new ministry was sworn in, they went down to defeat in the legislature. Knowing the poisonous atmosphere of the legislature, Head had attempted to guard his own position, letting Brown know in advance that he would not necessarily be prepared to dissolve the legislature should he receive a request from his new ministry.[7] Despite the written caveat, Brown appealed to Head for a dissolution, citing the "unprecedented and unparliamentary" conduct of the assembly. Head refused him. Head confided to a friend that Brown believed "that he could bully me into dissolving and he was mistaken." Head nevertheless recognized that "the exercise of this discretion is a very serious thing."[8]

After unsuccessfully exploring other options, Head called upon George-Étienne Cartier, who in turn reached out to his ally, Macdonald. The return of these two men to office posed a fresh difficulty, however. Macdonald knew the legal requirement, which stipulated that the new ministers vacate their seats and submit to fresh elections, meant that his administration

Grip, 23 August, 1879.

SIR JOHN'S CROWNING VICTORY.

might not have enough manpower to withstand a confidence vote in the meantime. Rather than take the chance, they took recourse in a slick legal loophole. The governor general was obligated to swear the cabinet into new offices, and then back into their original portfolios the following day. The legal provision that had been set up to allow cabinet ministers to change portfolios thus ensured that no one in the Cartier-Macdonald administration need be absent during a critical vote. Head evidently felt that he had no option but to acquiesce in this shady transaction, but his discomfort can be guessed at: he pointedly avoided describing what had occurred in his cryptic correspondence with the Colonial Office.[9] Not even Head's close friend George Cornewall Lewis was privy to the details of how the governor general had been made the unwitting tool of his administration. Head's selective synopsis to Lewis only allowed that he had had three governments within ten days, and that he had been "in hot water."[10] Lewis admitted that he was "unable from the accounts which I have seen to understand the rights of this question," but, having seen the newspapers, shrewdly deduced that it was "a political manoeuvre to keep in office a set of ministers who were afraid to go back to their constituents."[11] Colonial Office officials carefully avoided any comment that might have been construed as interfering in a purely domestic matter,[12] although Colonial Secretary Sir Edward Bulwer-Lytton later confessed his "great doubts" in a private internal minute.[13] The *Times* scolded that the so-called double shuffle contained "much to regret": "We should have been better pleased to have seen the Governor-General refuse to take any part in it." Macdonald and his colleagues were unlikely to enjoy any enduring success, they added.[14] The verdict in a lawsuit brought by Brown and his associates upheld the legality of the manoeuvre, and Head was eager to let his friend Lewis know this. "Whether it was expedient or not is another matter," he added. "I thought & still think that it was not, but this was a point on which I had to take the advice of those who were responsible to the Colonial Parl[iamen]t."[15]

In Canada, the hapless Head became the target of prolonged partisan criticism. Through the *Globe*, George Brown vented his "disgust" for Head's "odious" conduct. While pretending to listen to the advice of his constitutional advisers, the governor general had played "into the hands of their party opponents." Head was accused of abusing his prerogative, and was likened to a "Dictator" who had gone further "than any British king has dared to go since the days of the Stuarts."[16] Letters to the editor clamoured for Head's recall.[17] Thomas D'Arcy McGee charged that the whole scheme had been worked out beforehand: when Macdonald and his ministers resigned they had been in excellent humour, and did not look "like disappointed men." Macdonald rose in angry indignation to deny that either he or the representative of the sovereign were dishonourable conspirators. "Here in my place in Parliament, I say it is *false as hell.*"[18]

Head's actions were not motivated by any partiality to Macdonald, or the result of any conspiracy. His acquiescence in what J.L. Morsion described as "one of John A. Macdonald's tricks"[19] does not demonstrate his personal approval of it, but only that there were not sufficient grounds to refuse the advice of a minister who had the support of a majority.

• • •

While a study of Macdonald's interactions with the governor general offers a glimpse into some of his characteristic machinations in domestic politics, it can also shed light on his strategies in the diplomatic sphere. The negotiations behind the 1871 Treaty of Washington offer an example of the complex interplay between the prime minister and the governor general. Canada, for the first time, had a seat at the table in diplomatic negotiations between Britain and the United States, with John A. Macdonald acting as Canada's representative in these three-way negotiations. His goal was probably impossible: to convince the protectionist Americans to reinstate the free trade deal that they had opted out of in 1866. The offered incentive was access to Canada's inshore fisheries. But because Canada now had a voice in the negotiations, it would be less easy during the election upcoming in 1872 to imply that unsatisfactory terms had been forced on Canada by imperial authorities. Generations of historians have targeted Governor General Lord Lisgar as the scapegoat for Canada's diplomatic disappointment in 1871, for the failure to secure reciprocity. Donald Creighton referred to Lisgar's "astounding" behind-the-scenes proposal that access to the fisheries be sold for a cash payment. J.B. Brebner ventured that Macdonald's work as the sole Canadian delegate to Washington was "fatally handicapped" and "hamstrung" by Lisgar's "underhand" behaviour in sharing his confidential cabinet correspondence with British ministers.[20] But the truth is more complicated, and reflects Macdonald's tortuous strategy to win the best deal he could for Canada while ensuring the blame for any disappointment fell on other shoulders. Lisgar was the instrument through whom Macdonald attempted to exert pressure on Britain, and Macdonald did win some important concessions, despite an embarrassing blunder of his own making.

The option of a cash payment for the fisheries had been a long-standing policy alternative openly discussed by Canadian cabinet ministers, not a last-minute attempt by Lisgar to undercut Canada's position. Amid a very strained era in British-American relations, it was widely understood that free trade was unlikely. Compounding the diplomatic strain that made it unpopular in the United States, hard figures revealed a trade imbalance in Canada's favour under reciprocity. Then, too, American statesmen confidently expected that a denial of free trade would force Canada into a union with the United States, that "glorious consummation" as diplomat Caleb Cushing put it.[21]

Macdonald appears to have recognized this, but saw an opportunity to extract something from Britain in exchange for swallowing this bitter pill. The Americans had also refused to place on the agenda another issue important to Canada: compensation for the recent Fenian raids on British North America by disaffected Irish-Americans. But a changing European landscape made accord with the Americans a high British priority, and Macdonald devised a strategy to exploit this eagerness.

He shared his "private" cabinet correspondence with Lord Lisgar, and asked the governor general in turn to share it with British authorities. This was meant to create the impression that Macdonald was being squeezed by intransigent cabinet colleagues. Macdonald suggested that Canada's parliament, now given the opportunity to ratify the treaty for the first time, would balk if it were not sufficiently generous. Lisgar was caught in an unenviable position in between. He urged Macdonald to adopt a franker strategy: "If you will accept advice from me — not often tendered — you will shew your hand to Lord Kimberley — you will not get less from England by doing so," he insisted. At the same time, he reminded Britain's colonial secretary of Canada's "difficult position" and proposed that Britain assist Canada with aid in the form of a subsidy to enlarge the canals.[22]

Macdonald meanwhile wrote to cabinet colleague Charles Tupper that "we must throw the responsibility on England." Alexander Morris was instructed to manipulate media coverage of the treaty. "Friendly newspapers" should hold back and create the impression that Macdonald approved the treaty, and Macdonald himself would maintain silence. That way, George Brown of the Liberal *Globe* would attack him "for sacrificing the interests of Canada. He will afterwards find out, when it is too late, that he is on the same side as myself, and will not be able to retract." If Brown finds that I am opposed to the treaty, Macdonald explained, "he may take up the loyalty cry ... which might react prejudicially on our party."[23]

Macdonald also stage-managed his public reaction to the final terms. He toyed with the idea of refusing to sign the treaty, and also considered having a statement inserted into it objecting to the terms, something that might also serve to convince the Americans that they had made a good deal.[24] In the end, Macdonald signed his consent to the treaty on May 8, 1871, theatrically remarking to the American representative, "Well, here go the fisheries," and lamenting that Canada gave them away.[25]

The British delegates were not convinced by the performance. Lord de Grey privately remarked on Macdonald's "delight" at the agreement reached.[26] But Macdonald's ability to maintain his aggrieved posture soon suffered a severe blow. Among the "confidential" letters Macdonald asked Lisgar to pass along to Lord Kimberley was one he had written to colleague Francis Hincks. Macdonald wrote that he had "worked out a plan in my head ... Our true policy is to hold out to England that we will not ratify the treaty, and I have strong hopes that in her desire to close every possible cause of dispute with the U[nited] States we can induce her to make us a liberal offer. We should lose all this advantage if we showed any symptoms of yielding."[27] Lisgar passed this along to Kimberley as he had the other letters, but added a puzzled postscript: "'I cannot however think it was written with the intention that it should be placed in my hands."[28]

Kimberley exploded with indignation at Macdonald's "knavery." Prime Minister Gladstone added that he hoped "the 'liberal offer' which Sir J.M. intends to conjure from us will be *nil.*"[29] Kimberley informed Lisgar that he "should be sorry to write what I think of the game he proposes so coolly to play.... He will find out that 'in vain is the net spread in sight of any bird.'"[30] Lisgar noted that Macdonald was "much nettled and disappointed" at a letter sent to him by Lord Granville, but observed that "I am not at all sorry he should be made aware as he now is, that he is not to play fast and loose as he pleases, and deal in matters of weighty concern with the Imperial Gov[ernmen]t as he deals with intriguers in local politics."[31]

Despite the evident carelessness that had tipped his hand, Macdonald succeeded in wringing from Britain a loan guarantee in the amount of £2.5 million. Lisgar urged compensation, and let the British cabinet know that genuine opposition to the treaty could indeed jeopardize its passage. Macdonald had been losing ground in Ontario, Lisgar reported, "and dreads the effect of the general election."[32] When the treaty at last came up for debate in Canada's parliament in May 1872, Macdonald ardently defended it and himself, admitting that he had been likened to Benedict Arnold or Judas Iscariot. "When someone writes my biography — if I am ever thought worthy of having such an interesting document prepared — and when as a matter of history, the questions connected with this treaty are upheld, it will be found that upon this, as well as upon every other point, I did all I could to protect the rights and claims of the Dominion!"[33] Whatever one might think of his tactics, few would dispute that.

Macdonald and Lisgar kept up a correspondence when the governor general returned home at the end of his term. Lisgar shared British political gossip, confessed his longing to get back to the life of a gentleman farmer while in London, and wrote warmly that he had bought "a Turkey carpet for my dining room at B[ailieborou]gh on which I shall hope to see you in some good time occupy a comfortable chair."[34] Macdonald in turn avowed that he found Lisgar's successor lacking in comparison, complaining of Dufferin's "gushing" manner, and that he laid on flattery too thick. Dufferin was "laying himself out to be popular" and proposed to have residences at Halifax, Quebec, and Toronto. "It was amusing to see the dismay with which they saw Ottawa and Rideau Hall," Macdonald noted with a touch of *schadenfreude*. "Lady Dufferin is very charming, with nice, unaffected manners, and much more natural than the *caro sposo*. I think I shall like her much, but in military phrase, I would gladly exchange her for Lady Lisgar, and pay the difference." He also complained of the "hard and unpleasant work" of two months "on the stump" during the "drawn battle" of that year's general election. The unpopular Treaty of Washington had been the major obstacle, he ventured, and "I think H[er] M[ajesty's] Government owe me something for fighting this battle."[35]

Macdonald narrowly survived the 1872 election, only to fall from power in 1873 with the Pacific Scandal revelations. After fighting so hard and failing to win a free trade deal in 1871, it is perhaps ironic that the policy that would sweep the Conservatives back into power in 1878, amid a prolonged economic depression, was the high-tariff National Policy. Macdonald trumpeted the virtues of protectionism, a policy that for years became synonymous with Canadian Conservatism. Yet it is clear that, for Macdonald, the National Policy was Plan B. Refused reciprocity, he had no option, and Macdonald, given lemons, always made lemonade.

• • •

That dramatic fall from power in 1873 only came after a controversial use of the Crown by Macdonald — his use of prorogation in order to stave off parliamentary defeat. Before turning to that episode, however, it might be instructive to consider a controversial prorogation that Macdonald witnessed earlier in his parliamentary career.

In June of 1854, the second session of the fourth parliament of the United Province of Canada had just opened. The planned session was to be a short one: important measures to repeal the seigneurial system and to secularize the clergy reserves, as well as a provision to make the legislative council elective, were vital matters under consideration that would warrant a general election. The Liberal-Reform ministry of Francis Hincks and Augustin Morin did announce that they would pass measures in the current session connected to the recent Reciprocity Treaty and to give effect to the Franchise Bill passed in the last session. But Hincks' and Morin's administration was at risk because of allegations of corruption: Hincks had allegedly profited by manipulation of a municipality of Toronto debenture issue and Grand Trunk Railway stock. Macdonald declared it "immoral that the government should occupy their places, upon the strength of violated pledges, and the grossest corruption, while they enriched themselves by speculations on public property." The ministry was attempting to prevent an inquiry into their own conduct, he charged, adding that he hoped that parliament would not be prorogued until the charges against members of the government were cleared up. He noted that the postmaster general, Malcolm Cameron, had not actually denied the allegations, and insisted that his silence acknowledged guilt. What kept Cameron and Hincks together? They "could not love each other" but must fear each other: "the tie that kept them together was common plunder."[36]

The sitting of Thursday, June 22, 1854, was about to begin, just a few days after the start of the session, and, as the speaker was taking his chair, guns were heard announcing the departure of Lord Elgin from Government House. Sir Allan MacNab rose to ask if the rumours that parliament was to be prorogued were true. Hincks confirmed that they were, and further acknowledged that this was with a view to immediate dissolution, and that the Franchise Bill would not therefore be passed. The House erupted in tumult as the notice to attend the governor general in the legislative council chamber was read and Black Rod hammered on the door.

Elgin became the unwitting target of the disappointed members who were dismayed at the ministry's use of prorogation to thwart them. William Lyon Mackenzie, member for Haldimand, angrily denounced the governor's move to "choke our deliberations." He accused the governor of following "the bad example of former tyrants." Macdonald, for his part, spoke with what a reporter described as "great vehemence," insisting on the right of the House to go on. He was "on his legs, gesticulating violently ... while his face shewed how deeply he was moved.... What he said could not be distinguished, but such words as shameful — disgraceful — unconstitutional — revolutionary,— might now and again be heard." The ministry's action "was done to avoid inquiry into their corrupt practices before the election," Macdonald insisted.[37] The speaker, John Sandfield Macdonald, took the opportunity to rebuke both the ministry and the governor general. He noted that no review of legislation passed would be necessary, since they had not been able to accomplish any "owing to the command which your Excellency has laid upon us."[38] Elgin's annoyance betrayed itself with an involuntary gesture of disdain.[39] Elgin had just written to his wife about his attachment to Canada, but now admitted that the parliamentarians were "trying to diminish my sentimentality for this country by behaving very badly."[40]

This episode — the cynical use of prorogation to dodge defeat — triggered Macdonald's disgust in 1854. Yet it is strikingly parallel to the action he himself took in 1873. And Dufferin as governor general would be accused of letting his preference for Macdonald draw him in to unconstitutional practices.

Despite the early misgivings Macdonald had admitted to Lisgar, his relations with Dufferin were amicable. At the beginning of his Canadian term, Dufferin shared with Kimberley stories of Macdonald's legendary brawls with parliamentary rivals, but insisted that he was "rather a demure personage" who "has now left off anything stronger than tea."[41] Dufferin let Macdonald know he was sorry he could not watch him "handle the ribbons" in parliament; "Everyone seems to agree that your management of the House is as neat a specimen of good coaching as anyone need wish to witness."[42] Correspondence between the two men suggests a genuine affection, and Macdonald succeeded in developing a valuable rapport, as he had with other governors general. Joseph Pope, Macdonald's secretary, later remarked upon the "exquisite admixture of courtesy and deference which characterized his manner towards the Queen's representative, sometimes rather oddly contrasting their respective years." The governors, in turn, demonstrated "consideration and respect … to the veteran statesman who had been chief advisor to them all."[43] Most, in fact, continued to correspond personally with Macdonald after their terms of office had ended.

When the Liberal opposition raised allegations in the spring of 1873 about corrupt practices in the Conservative cabinet's handling of the Pacific Railway contract, a parliamentary committee was assembled to consider evidence. Dufferin prematurely concluded that nothing would come of the Pacific Scandal. He wrote privately to Macdonald, acknowledging the probable "annoyance," but adding that "this business must have afforded you a good deal of amusement … now that the rocket has exploded at the wrong end."[44] To Kimberley, he confessed himself "very glad" that there would be no change in his advisers. "Sir John is by far the ablest public man in Canada. He is very agreeable in his manner, and to me personally most friendly and considerate."[45] Macdonald wrote warmly to congratulate Dufferin on the birth of a "Young Canadian," remarking that the "Backwoods Blackwoods" would soon outnumber the older branch of the family.[46] To the disgust of Liberal leader Alexander Mackenzie, Dufferin asked Macdonald, "the drunken debauchee," to be godfather.[47]

One of the ways in which Macdonald proved to be "friendly and considerate" to Dufferin was in respect to expenses. When Dufferin arrived in Canada, he was evidently unaware of past controversies concerning the expenses of the office. In fact, soon after his arrival he told Lisgar that he had written to Macdonald "to insist on being furnished with a summer residence."[48] Just four years before, Macdonald had fought against an opposition initiative to see the governor's salary reduced from $50,000 to $ 32,000. Macdonald defended the salary on the grounds that several smaller inferior colonies paid their governors more handsomely and that a reduction would lower the status of the office.[49]

Just six months into his term, Dufferin had been dismayed to calculate that he had already spent £5,000 in excess of his £10,000 annual salary, not including the cost of constructing a cottage at Tadoussac, or indeed the thirty-six-ton yacht he purchased around the time of his arrival in Canada. He wrote to Macdonald in urgent terms, appending a list of his future expenditures. These were comparatively restrained, he insisted, comparable to "what in England would be considered a modest establishment for a peer or ordinary country gentleman." The number of servants was not extravagant, nor was the projected £3,000 he planned to spend per year on parties, balls, and entertaining. His only option, "if I am to keep out of gaol" would be to adopt the "economical & stationary tenor" of his predecessors.[50] It was clear that he did not fancy that option: he had written to Kimberley noting that both Lord Lisgar and Lord Monck before him spent every penny of their income in Canada. "Yet they neither of them moved from Ottawa or saw any company. In fact quite between ourselves their mode of living occasioned widely spread dissatisfaction."[51]

It is not clear what immediate relief Macdonald offered, but in early June 1873, as the Pacific Scandal gained traction and Macdonald's ministry seemed increasingly at risk, Dufferin wrote to thank Macdonald for including $5,000 in the supplementary estimates to defray heating and lighting costs, and to remind him that he was still to be credited with an additional £1,000 per year for travel. There was also the matter of an increase in salary to £12,000 per year, "the sum at which according to the calculation I sent you, I considered I might fairly require it to stand," although he admitted that the matter had not been "definitely settled between us." But with an acknowledged $17,000 overdraft at the bank,[52] Dufferin might well have feared the prospect of wringing funds out of the parsimonious Liberals should the Conservatives fall from power. Indeed, later, under Mackenzie's ministry, some awkward scenes over money ensued. Dufferin had been mortified by a visit from a junior representative of the finance minister who sought repayment of an $8,000 advance paid out ten months earlier. "At the least he might have spared me a visit from his Bailiff," he complained to Mackenzie.[53]

Macdonald's open-handedness to the viceroy was not a departure from his usual practice; he had similarly defended Lisgar against attacks over expenditures. Lisgar pointed out to Macdonald that the lack of amenities at Rideau Hall gave rise to the problem, as the house did not have gas or water piped in. Water had to be hauled in barrels, requiring extra staff, and the heating stoves were inefficient and wasteful. The poor design of the roof meant that snow had to be shovelled from it to prevent water from pouring in through the upper storeys. Lisgar's entreaties to Cartier and Hector Langevin seem not to have availed. In fact, Lisgar was evidently irked at Langevin's poor taste in writing to his secretary in such a tone as "he might have addressed ... some subordinate who had been drawing superfluous expenses." Macdonald came to the rescue, however, promising to be an intermediary and shield Lisgar from vexations that the governor general confessed "might well drive a wiser man than me mad."[54] As his term was coming to an end, Lisgar also raised the issue of the governor general's entourage with Macdonald. When he himself was appointed "there may not unnaturally have arisen some disappointment in having no more than a Bar[one]t allotted to you," he admitted modestly. But now that Dufferin was to assume the role, "a man of high rank and the first water of fashion so you should make your arrangements on a scale befitting the value which general opinion in Canada professes to place on monarchical institutions."[55]

In the summer of 1873, Dufferin's early expectation that the Pacific Scandal was groundless was soon undercut by a series of damning revelations. He anxiously confided to Lord Kimberley that it would be "a great misfortune both for myself and for the country if Sir John were to be turned out ... I scarcely see who are the people to replace him."[56] The Liberal *Globe* published leaked letters in which Macdonald asked Sir Hugh Allan for "another ten thousand," and also alleged that other cabinet members had obtained $360,000 from Allan and his associates, who had presumably been given reason to expect that their bid to construct the railway would be successful.[57] Macdonald disappeared to Riviere du Loup on a drinking binge, and, by early August, the *Globe* was even speculating that he had committed suicide, a "dastardly" report, as Dufferin called it.[58] Parliament had been adjourned in May in order to give the committee the opportunity to investigate the Pacific Scandal, with a prorogation planned for August when the task would be complete.[59]

As the August sitting loomed, Dufferin proposed to Macdonald that parliament be merely adjourned in order to give the committee the time needed to make its report. He hastened to add that his wish to see parliament render its verdict was based on his confidence in the result, and that he remained one of Macdonald's "warmest friends and sincerest admirers."[60] Macdonald, though, was concerned that the Liberals would rally together members to defeat him on any vote on adjournment in August. The original plan had been that the sitting on August 13 would be "merely formal," without the need of distant members attending, and with a deputy standing in for Dufferin, who was touring the Maritimes. But with the Liberals strongest in Quebec and Ontario, the opposition would be certain of a majority. [61] Dufferin explained to Kimberley that the new revelations about the scandal made "the aspect of affairs at present … very different" from when the prorogation was first planned.[62]

The parliamentary committee, however, had been unwilling to carry on its work without the use of sworn testimony. An act to enable them to require witnesses to swear oaths had been disallowed by the Judicial Committee of the Privy Council. Dufferin agreed to the appointment of a Royal Commission instead, accepting Macdonald's suggestion to appoint his friend, Justice James Robert Gowan, as one of the three commissioners.

Pledging to offer Macdonald "loyal and generous support to assist you with my best advice," Dufferin returned to Ottawa, arriving on August 13, the very day of the scheduled prorogation.[63] He hoped to act as mediator between the parties, but reconciliation proved impossible. The Liberal *Globe* was demanding that Dufferin refuse to allow his prerogative "to be so grievously abused." A deputation of MPs bearing a ninety-two-signature petition urged him not to prorogue the House until necessary steps had been taken.[64] Some of the signatories were deserters from Macdonald's own standard. The *Globe* reported that the governor general gave "a very long and argumentative reply," setting out his reasons for carrying out the planned prorogation.[65] The governor general and prime minister had already haggled over the length of time that should be permitted until the next session: Dufferin rejected the idea of a prorogation until February 1874, but was willing to move from his first proposal of six weeks to at last allow ten.[66]

The scene in parliament on the afternoon of August 13, 1873, had many echoes of the tumult Macdonald had witnessed in 1854. As the speaker took his chair, Black Rod could already be seen through the glass doors of the chamber, and the Sergeant-at-Arms was bowing at the speaker's table and waiting to announce him. When the doors opened, members of the public rushed in, adding to the chaos. Only about thirty-five Conservatives followed the speaker to the Senate chamber for the prorogation, the opposition assembling at an "indignation meeting" led by Alexander Mackenzie.[67] In the aftermath, the *Globe* warned against transferring the indignation that should be directed toward the ministry to the governor general, but regretted that Dufferin had not shown a mind of his own and had not put "down corruption with a firm hand."[68] Dufferin poured out his frustration with the "disagreeable" business to the Colonial Office. "I had nobody to consult, and the very men who were bound to advise me were those most interested in cajoling me into some false move," he later reflected.[69]

In the interval before the next session, Dufferin badgered Macdonald for details that would exonerate him in the eyes of the imperial government, confidently predicting to Macdonald that there would be "a glorious reaction in your favour," once he was "cleared from these damnable accusations."[70] He repeated this same sentiment in mid-September, alluding to Sir Hugh Allan's "incomprehensible wickedness and folly," and deriding a recent speech by Edward Blake as "a childish performance."[71] To Kimberley, Dufferin mused that if the opposition had been more capable, he might "perhaps have been tempted to have forced the situation a little more." He liked Mackenzie personally, but he was "a poor creature."[72] Macdonald, by contrast, was "very popular, even among his opponents…. Above all things, it is remembered that it is to his skill, talent and statesmanship, that the Dominion owes its existence." The Conservative party contained "most of the Parliamentary talent."[73]

One of Dufferin's great fears was that, when the new session began on October 23, parliamentary discussion might centre on the propriety of his own actions in proroguing parliament and consenting to the commission.[74] He was determined to secure a better source of information about what was going on in the Commons than could be gleaned from his own prime minister or from "untrustworthy" newspaper reports. Incredibly, he proposed that Macdonald arrange "some little closet for me in the House of Commons from whence I could hear what was going on." Macdonald had "half promised" this, he reminded him.[75] Ten days later, Dufferin renewed the request, acknowledging Macdonald's objection to "my appearance in any place where I could be seen or where it would be within the power of anyone to notice me…. The utmost that I asked for was exactly what you describe a 'Dionysius Ear' — a closet no matter how dark or inconvenient."[76]

This episode reveals Macdonald's consummate tact and skill in dealing with a governor with a shaky grasp of constitutional principles. He promised to see "if a plan can be contrived where you can be present without being known" — something he almost certainly had no intention of doing — but expressed doubts if it could be managed, and suggested gently that the governor general "forgo the advantage which a hearing of the debate would certainly be to you." Perhaps understanding Dufferin's need for approval, he painted a scenario in which the opposition, learning of the arrangement, might deride it as unconstitutional, or even make insulting remarks. "The Crown would be brought into contempt." Resisting the temptation to administer a lesson in constitutional history directly, Macdonald did so obliquely, predicting that "The Grand Remonstrance against the Crown's taking cognizance of the proceedings of the House would be quoted *ad nauseam*."[77] Dufferin instead arranged for Lady Dufferin, the staff of Government House, and other visitors to watch parliamentary proceedings from the speaker's gallery and report back to him. Rumours circulated that the governor himself attended in disguise.[78]

With the new session about to begin, Dufferin also worried about what he might have to do if the Conservatives were not defeated, but were sustained by a small majority. To Kimberley, he speculated: "I think it would be perfectly competent for me to say to Sir John, you left off last session with a majority of 35. It is now reduced to a third or a quarter of that amount. You yourself admit … that you spent considerable sums of money at the elections in a way forbidden by the Statutes." Since the "small numerical superiority" is "more or less the result of this illegitimate expenditure … I cannot therefore consider that you any longer possess the confidence of the country."[79] His faith in Macdonald was further shaken when he met with the commissioners the following day, and came face to face with the damning evidence.

An itching need to take action pressing itself upon him, but with no clear sense of what that action should be, Dufferin wrote to Macdonald on October 19. "It is with greater pain than ever I did anything in my life," that he wrote "as a warm and sincere friend desirous of putting you on your guard against eventualities which it is well you should provide against in time. I am the more anxious to do this as the friendly spirit I have evinced towards you during the course of this unfortunate business may have led you to count upon my support beyond the point to which I might find myself able to extend it." He was, however, bound to sacrifice his personal inclinations to his duty to his sovereign, he explained. The usual recourse to the verdict of parliament was perhaps not enough in this case, he added as "this circumstance carries with it the further ill effect of rendering the arbitrament of Parliament itself untrustworthy." Dufferin acknowledged his own distress in warning Macdonald: "Your immediate and personal connection with what has occurred cannot but fatally affect your position as Minister." He assured Macdonald of his conviction that "there is no one in the Country capable of administering its affairs to greater advantage than yourself," and asserted that "your name will be preserved in History as the Founder of the Dominion." He shrank from asking Macdonald to resign — "it's not an announcement but a friendly confidence in respect of a future contingency," — and admitted that no firm conclusions had been "actually formed within my mind, but I feel it is but fair to let you know the tendency of my thoughts at the present moment."[80] The two men met, and while Macdonald, with great dignity, suggested that the letter inclined him to offer his resignation, Dufferin assured him that he had not intended to dismiss him; the prime minister had a right and a duty to meet parliament. If he were sustained by a large majority, the governor general would be satisfied. He might only consider forcing the issue if Macdonald pulled through "with the skin of his teeth."[81]

No sooner had this warning been issued, however, that Dufferin had second thoughts. At the height of his August dilemma over prorogation, Dufferin had cabled the Colonial Office for advice, even as he admitted that he knew "that I am not sent here in order that the Colonial Office may have the trouble and responsibility of governing Canada from Downing Street."[82] Now, he again sent a desperate telegram to Kimberley asking for guidance on the issue of forcing Macdonald's resignation.

A carefully worded dispatch from the Colonial Office passed no judgment on the issue, but Kimberley, in a confidential private letter, expressed his views more freely. It was up to parliament, he told Dufferin, to decide whether there was any substance to the charges. "It is no doubt very tempting to act on one's own opinion," but the governor general should stay within the limits of his constitutional prerogatives. And the imperial government should be especially careful not to interfere.[83] This was not to suggest that Kimberley approved of the Conservatives' conduct. A further letter, two days later, contained his analysis of the scandal in plain terms: "No explanation can explain away the fact that the Gov[ernmen]t received Allan's money to promote the election of themselves and their partisans at the moment when a gigantic contract between the Gov[ernmen]t and Allan was pending. In *this* country such conduct would undoubtedly ruin any government."[84] As much as he sympathized with "the extreme difficulty" of Dufferin's position, and wished to afford him all possible support "both as a Minister and as a friend," Kimberley believed it would be "a grievous mistake" if he attempted to take upon himself "the most important of the functions of the Governor General." He would be attacked for interference, and Dufferin would be seen as a "mere tool of Downing Street."[85]

Kimberley's reminder about the ultimate judgment of parliament forced Dufferin to the uneasy conclusion that he had erred in his warning to Macdonald. According to Charles Tupper, "Sir John was aroused from his bed at two o'clock in the morning and notified that Lord Dufferin had recalled his decision."[86] Dufferin himself offered a very lengthy and detailed explanation to the Colonial Office. He told Kimberley that his narrative would be broken into chapters, and that he should read them in order of date. Dufferin explained that after hearing Kimberley's very precise explanation of his duties, he became convinced that he had overstepped the limits of his role. He called Macdonald back, and revealed that Kimberley had led him to understand that he was "more straitened by the voice of Parliament" than he had at first imagined. The earlier letter of warning should be considered, then, "as in some degree cancelled."[87]

Dufferin seemed torn between wanting to see a decisive parliamentary defeat that would make any action by him unnecessary and an evident admiration for Macdonald's tenacity. Watching the plummeting level of parliamentary support, he observed that in no country in the world did "the rats leave the sinking ship so fast, and if once the tide begins to turn it will drop with a vengeance."[88] Macdonald maintained silence in the House, not speaking to defend himself against any accusations until he was sure no final definitive blow would be delivered. Dufferin told Kimberley that, on November 4, 1873 "all my ladies went as usual to hear the debate, leaving me at home." Earlier in the day, Macdonald had spoken briefly, was obviously tipsy, and "said exactly the wrong thing." Yet three hours later, "pale, haggard, [and] looking as though a feather would knock him down," he electrified the House with his oration.[89] At last, his powers spent, he sank to his seat, his voice gone. To Macdonald himself, Dufferin declared that "[r]ound the breakfast table at Rideau this morning there was a continuous chorus of admiration from all my English friends." Lady Dufferin came home from the debates at three in the morning "brimful of your speech." She "was pleased to keep me awake from 3 to 5, repeating it with appropriate action."[90] Lady Dufferin also wrote to Lady Macdonald, hoping that Macdonald was well after "his great exertions," and assuring her that "we have all been talking with the greatest admiration of his splendid speech."[91] Yet by the following day it was evident that Macdonald's support had melted away. He called upon Dufferin to tender his resignation.

Members of the viceregal household seemed bereft at Macdonald's departure. Lady Dufferin wrote home that "I am trying to become a Grit, but I can't quite manage it."[92] Even Colonel Fletcher, Dufferin's secretary, wrote to Macdonald of his sorrow at "the reverse of fortune," and to express gratitude at the "great privilege" of having worked "in however humble a position, with so great a minister."[93] Dufferin later confessed himself cut "to the heart" that his prime minister's career "should have ended in such humiliation."[94] Perhaps he underestimated the resiliency of a man who would go on to lead the country for more than a dozen further years.

• • •

One of the common features of all the viceregal correspondence is the anxiety caused by Macdonald's occasional "weakness." At times, his lapses into drunkenness were inconvenient, and sometimes a great deal more.[95] In 1862, for example, Lord Monck was eager to see Canada pass a Militia Bill that would create a proper armed force. The matter was of some urgency in the climate of strained Anglo-American relations surrounding the Civil War. But, he confessed to the Duke of Newcastle, "I have never had to deal with men who try one's temper so much as the members of the government here." He complained about sending for "a particular minister to consult him about some matter" but finding "he is not to be found, has left Quebec and it is uncertain when he may return."[96] The subject of the complaint was almost certainly Macdonald, who disappeared on a drinking binge when the Militia Bill was before the House. Monck laid the blame for the defeat of the bill — and the administration — at the feet of Macdonald, who was prevented from attending the debates supposedly by illness, "but really, as everyone knew by drunkenness."[97] In the wake of the ministerial defeat, Monck called upon John Sandfield Macdonald to form an administration, rather than Michael Foley, the nominal head of the opposition.[98] Monck's disinclination to select Foley could be attributable to the fact that he shared Macdonald's weakness. Foley was busy drinking himself to death, something he would accomplish by 1870, and Monck's patience may have been exhausted. Nevertheless, Monck missed the "jobbing and corrupt" previous administration, who at least displayed some ability. The new ministers, while "more anxious to do what is right ... have not amongst their administration ability enough to manage the affairs of a parish!"[99]

Monck's successors would similarly find themselves preoccupied by concerns over Macdonald's health. Lord Lisgar and his wife had frequent occasion to express their anxiety to Macdonald, always in the kindest terms. In the autumn of 1870, Lady Lisgar assured him that "you would be very flattered if you could hear how universal is the joy at your recovery. It is almost worth being ill, to have so much anxiety so universally exhibited." His health was essential not only to those close to him "but for the sake of Canada, who with almost one voice declares you to be necessary to the future of the Dominion."[100] Over the years, many expressed delighted amazement at seeing how often Macdonald was pulled back from the brink. Monck wrote from London to congratulate Macdonald on his appointment to the 1871 Treaty of Washington delegation — an "experiment on your part of diplomacy in leading strings" he called it. "I was additionally glad ... because [this] ... was a proof to me that you had completely recovered from your illness of last year."[101] Dufferin, while admitting in 1873 that the prime minister fell victim to the "old weakness," declared it "marvellous how he can pull himself together when occasion requires it, and with what pluck, good temper, and confidence he meets all these emergencies."[102]

But of course the most challenging problem would fall to Lord Stanley, the governor general who was with Macdonald in May 1891 when it became apparent that the prime minister had suffered a stroke. Perhaps ironically, it was the very strength of Macdonald's leadership, his unquestioned grasp of the helm of the Conservative party, which created the problem. Just two months before, Macdonald had fought to victory in a general election. The previous governor, the Marquis of Lorne, and his wife Princess Louise were among those who telegraphed their congratulations. But the toll on the seventy-six-year-old leader had been harsh, and his secretary, Joseph Pope, remarked on his evident exhaustion and ashen complexion. Scheduled to meet with Stanley on May 12, 1891, Macdonald had to call for Sir John Thompson to come and speak for him, for he found he could not. Stanley confided his alarm to Pope, explaining that he had seen similar symptoms before in one who died of paralysis. Macdonald himself confessed such fears to his secretary, but warned him not to tell Lady Macdonald what had happened. Macdonald made a surprising rally in the days that followed, returning to parliament, hosting two dinner parties, and meeting with Thompson to discuss pending matters with his usual acuity and vigour.[103]

At some point in May — the date on the letter is not clear — Stanley wrote to Macdonald in an apologetic tone, citing the "frank confidence" that had always existed between them. He had come to feel, he said, that "our official & other relations have ripened into something far more than ordinary friendship." Macdonald's health was of "inestimable value" to the country, and equally essential to the party and his friends and family. On that score, he pleaded with Macdonald to make some arrangement to lighten his crushing load. Besides the prime minister's duties, "so harassing & so incessant," Macdonald had assumed the heavy duties of the Railways department, as well as the usual duties in the House of Commons, of which "many ordinary members" complained. "And yet, you concentrate on your own shoulders this triple burden — and refuse to listen to your friends. Would it not be possible to lead the Government from the other House — where the hours are less trying & the atmosphere more serene?" Stanley urged. He begged forgiveness "for the motives' sake if I have written very plainly — for I was brought up as a soldier and not a diplomatist. To stand by & see you overtaxing your strength without saying a word is impossible. You are too brave." He added that he claimed the right "within certain constitutional lines, to help in any difficulties, especially in reference to arrangements to be made — if such there should be — by which jealousy or friction in the Cabinet can be averted or lessened. This is within the legitimate sphere of my duties — if you call upon me to intervene. You *must* know," he added, "how devoted your friends are to you. Therefore pardon this letter from one who does not yield the place to any of them."[104]

Stanley shared his grave concerns with the British cabinet in the weeks that followed. On May 29, Macdonald had suffered another stroke, and could no longer speak; the doctor held out no hope of even a partial recovery. Yet Stanley did not force the issue, advising his ministers to avoid introducing any new legislation "except that previously sanctioned by Sir John." Macdonald could only signify his assent to direct questions. Stanley saw no clear successor in the wings, noting that Macdonald had received little help from his colleagues of late, except Langevin and Thompson, and Langevin's department of public works, and the minister himself, had recently been "gravely compromised" by scandal.[105] Nor was the party able to settle its own leadership; Thompson considered himself unsuitable because he was a Roman Catholic convert, and Macdonald had once told him to rally behind J.J.C. Abbott. On the very morning of his second stroke, however, Macdonald let Thompson know he had changed his mind: Abbott "is too damned selfish."[106]

"I think we can get on for a time," Stanley predicted as Macdonald lay ill, "but I think also that the Government will go to pieces. It was doubtful before — now I think it certain barring accident." At most, he believed they might survive the current session.[107] Macdonald slipped away peacefully on June 6, 1891.

Stanley, to the annoyance of his cabinet, avoided any decision on succession until after Macdonald's funeral. "Everybody [is] angry with the child at Rideau Hall for not doing something," Thompson wrote to his wife.[108] With no clear successor waiting to assume the leadership, the party found it easy to blame the governor general for failing to make a decision. Stanley recognized that no one could rival what he later called the "benevolent despotism" of Macdonald.[109] And indeed in the five years that followed, four leaders came and went, and Stanley's successor, Lord Aberdeen, took a sometimes controversial part in ensuring continuity in the prime ministerial office. Aberdeen became, in John Saywell's words, "the most overworked governor in Canadian history."[110] Macdonald can hardly be criticized for the shortcomings of subsequent Conservative leaders, or for the instability that plagued the party he once led. But it is perhaps fitting that, even in death, Macdonald embroiled the governors in controversy.

• • •

Convention dictates — then as now — that the governors general maintain silence about any role they might play in political affairs, in order to uphold every appearance of neutrality. At various stages of his political career, John A. Macdonald capitalized on this viceregal reticence and involved the unwitting representatives of the Crown in machinations that served his partisan ends. Early in his parliamentary apprenticeship, he had witnessed and condemned such actions by others, but decades of experience offered Macdonald ample opportunity to learn and avail himself of a full range of clever devices to sustain power. The Crown's obligatory silence meant that governors were often forced to stand by and absorb the weight of criticism in public and in the press, unable to refute the inevitable inference that they approved of any ministerial actions. The full story behind such political manoeuvres can only be known well after the fact, through access to private communications. Personal letters between Macdonald and a series of governors general — and letters about Macdonald between governors and successive Secretaries of State for the Colonies — offer a rich source of insight. They provide an unparalleled glimpse into some of Macdonald's more audacious tactics. But they also provide glimpses of Macdonald's remarkable personal charisma. This was the intangible attribute that enabled Macdonald to maintain the admiration, and even friendship, of a series of governors who found themselves at the mercy of his devices.

Notes

1. Peter Baskerville, "Sir Allan Napier MacNab." In *Dictionary of Canadian Biography.*University of Toronto. *www.biographi.ca/009004-119.01-e.php?&id_nbr=4565&interval=20&&PHPSESSID=mdirrero2g1niogl791ild6al1.*
2. David Knight, *Choosing Canada's Capital: Conflict Resolution in a Parliamentary System* (Ottawa: Carleton University Press, 1991), 162–23. For an overview of the ministerial crisis of 1856, see J.M.S. Careless, *The Union of the Canadas: The Growth of Canadian Institutions, 1841–1857*

(Toronto: McClelland & Stewart, 1967), 200–02; Donald Creighton, *John A. Macdonald: The Young Politician* (Toronto: Macmillan, 1952), 235–57; D.G.G. Kerr, *Sir Edmund Head, A Scholarly Governor* (Toronto: University of Toronto Press, 1954), 148–50; James Young, *Public Men and Public Life in Canada.* 2nd ed. (Toronto: William Briggs, 1912), 95–101.

3. Head to George Cornewall Lewis, private, June 9, 1856. Head Papers, MG 194, Library and Archives Canada [hereafter LAC.]

4. Head to Sir E. Bulwer-Lytton, despatch 97, July 31, 1858, Colonial Office Correspondence, CO 42/614, B 229, LAC.

5. Head to E. Bulwer-Lytton, despatch. 102, August 9, 1858, Enclosure, *Toronto Daily Atlas*, August 6, 1858, CO 42/614, B 230, LAC.

6. Ged Martin, "John A. Macdonald: Provincial Premier," *British Journal of Canadian Studies* 20: 1 (2007), 113.

7. Head to Sir E. Bulwer-Lytton, despatch 102, August 9, 1858, Enclosure, Head to George Brown, July 31, 1858, CO 42/614, B 230, LAC. This and other related correspondence is also printed in Joseph Pope, *Memoirs of the Right Honourable Sir John Alexander Macdonald,* 2 vols. (Ottawa: J. Durie & Son, 1894), Appendix 3, and Alpheus Todd, *Parliamentary Government in the British Colonies* (London: Longmans, Green & Co., 1894), 762–69.

8. Head to Lewis, private, August 9, 1858, Head Papers, MG 194, LAC.

9. Head to E. Bulwer-Lytton, despatch 102, August 9, 1858, CO 42/614, B 230, LAC.

10. Head to Lewis, private, August 9, 1858, Head Papers, MG 194, LAC.

11. Lewis to Head, private, September 22, 1858, *Letters of the Right Hon. Sir George Cornewall Lewis, Bart. to Various Friends,* ed. Gilbert Franklin Lewis (London: Longmans, Green & Co., 1870), 348–49.

12. Head to E. Bulwer-Lytton, despatch 102, August 9, 1858, minute by Arthur Blackwood, August 30, 1858; minute by Herman Merivale, August 31, 1858; minute by Carnarvon, 1[?] September 1858, CO 42/614, B 230, LAC. See also E. Bulwer-Lytton to Head, despatch 55, September 10, 1858, CO 42/614, B 229.

13. Minute by E. Bulwer-Lytton on Head to E. Bulwer-Lytton, despatch 108, August 26, 1858, CO 42/614, B 230, LAC.

14. *The Times* [of London], September 15, 1858.

15. Head to Lewis, private, January 2, 1859, Head Papers, MG 194, LAC.

16. *Globe*, August 6, 1858.

17. *Globe*, August 6 and 12, 1858.

18. Head to E. Bulwer-Lytton, despatch 102, August 9, 1858, Enclosure, *Toronto Daily Atlas*, August 6, 1858, CO 42/614, B 230, LAC.

19. J.L. Morison, *British Supremacy and Canadian Self-Government, 1839–1854* (Glasgow: James & MacLehose & Sons, 1919), 324. Constitutional

authority Eugene Forsey correctly defends Head's refusal of Brown's advice. Eugene A. Forsey, *The Royal Power of Dissolution of Parliament in the British Commonwealth* (Toronto: Oxford University Press, 1943), 66–67.

20. J.B. Brebner, *North Atlantic Triangle: The Interplay of Canada, the United States and Great Britain* (New Haven: Yale University, 1945), 197.

21. Caleb Cushing, *The Treaty of Washington* (New York: Harper, 1873), 255.

22. Lisgar to Kimberley, private, July 20, 1871, Kimberley Papers, A 314, LAC. A copy of the letter to Macdonald to which Lisgar refers [dated July 7, 1871] may be found in CO 537/102, B 816, LAC. A lengthy private letter from Macdonald to Lisgar, dated July 21, 1871, explained his fears that the treaty and his government might be defeated and warned that he would "at once abandon any attempt to reconcile my colleagues or the people of Canada to the adoption of the Treaty" if the British government made compensation for the Fenian claims contingent upon acceptance. Macdonald to Lisgar, private, July 21, 1871, Macdonald Papers, C 30, LAC. Macdonald did not leave it exclusively to Lisgar to communicate his concerns; he himself let the British cabinet know that there was considerable resistance to the treaty and resentment of the imperial government. A series of letters Macdonald wrote to Lord de Grey over the summer of 1871 can be found in letterbook, vol. 15, C 29, Macdonald Papers, LAC.

23. Macdonald to Alexander Morris, private and confidential, April 21, 1871, *Correspondence of John A. Macdonald*, ed. Sir Joseph Pope (Toronto: Oxford University Press, 1921), 145.

24. Macdonald to de Grey, private and confidential, April 26, 1871, Macdonald Papers, C 29, LAC.

25. Fish diary, May 8, 1871, Allan Nevins, *Hamilton Fish: The Inner History of the Grant Administration* (New York: Frederick Ungar, 1957), 490.

26. De Grey to Granville, April 21, 1871, in W.L. Morton, *The Critical Years: The Union of British North America, 1857–1873* (Toronto: McClelland & Stewart, 1964), 256.

27. Lisgar to Kimberley May 11, 1871, Enclosure, Macdonald to Francis Hincks, n.d. Kimberley Papers, A 314, LAC.

28. Ibid., Lisgar's postscript.

29. Ibid., Minutes on postscript, Kimberley, May 23, 1871; Gladstone, May 25, 1871.

30. Paraphrasing *Proverbs*, 1:17. Kimberley to Lisgar, private, May 25, 1871, Kimberley Papers, A 314, LAC.

31. Lisgar to Kimberley, private, August 17, 1871, Kimberley Papers, A 314, LAC.

32. Lisgar to Kimberley, private, July 20, 1871, Kimberley Papers, A 314, LAC. A short while later, the Conservatives lost control of the provincial administration of Ontario. A Liberal administration under the premiership of Edward Blake was formed, and it is probable that the failure to secure reciprocity was a factor. Morton, *The Critical Years*, 254, 259–60.

33. John A. Macdonald, speech in House of Commons, May 3, 1872, "The Washington Treaty Debate! In the House of Commons." Supplement to the *Daily Mail*, May 1872, 5. http://ia341329.us.archive.org/3/items/cihm_23749/cihm_23749.pdf.
34. Lisgar to Macdonald, July 27, 1872, Macdonald Papers, C1514, LAC.
35. Macdonald to Lisgar, September 2, 1872, in Pope, *Correspondence of Macdonald*, 177.
36. John A. Macdonald, *Debates of the Legislative Assembly of United Canada, 1841–1867*, vol 12: 1, 1854–1855, Elizabeth Abbott Gibbs, ed. (Montreal: Centre de Recherche en Histoire Économique et Sociale du Quebec, 1982), 70.
37. Ibid., 111.
38. John Sandfield Macdonald, as quoted in John George Bourinot, *Lord Elgin* (Toronto: Morang & Co, 1912), 128–9.
39. Ibid., 129–30. The circumstances surrounding the 1854 prorogation are explored in Careless, *The Union of the Canadas,* 189–191; and Creighton, *John A. Macdonald*, I, 199–203.
40. Elgin to Lady Elgin, June 24, 1854, *Extracts from the Letters of James Earl of Elgin* (Edinburgh: privately printed, 1864), 6. There is little correspondence concerning Elgin's decision to grant the request for dissolution, owing perhaps to the suddenness of his ministry's decision. More significantly, there had been a sudden change of ministry in Britain. Newcastle was no longer secretary of state for the colonies, and his successor, Sir George Grey, had only been in office a few days, and would not have much knowledge of Canadian events.
41. Dufferin to Kimberley, private, July 30, 1872, Dufferin Papers, A 407, LAC.
42. Dufferin to Macdonald, private, March 6, 1873, Dufferin Papers A 414, LAC.
43. Pope, *Memoirs of Macdonald*, 243.
44. Dufferin to Macdonald, private, July 21, 1873, Dufferin Papers, A 415, LAC.
45. Dufferin to Kimberley, private, April 23, 1873, Dufferin Papers, A 415, LAC.
46. Macdonald to Dufferin, private, April 19, 1873, Dufferin Papers, A 410, LAC.
47. Mackenzie to George Brown, July 21, 1873, George Brown Papers, C 1603, LAC.
48. Dufferin to Lisgar, August 13, 1872, copy, Dufferin Papers, A 418, LAC.
49. Pope, *Memoirs of Macdonald*, vol. 2, Macdonald to Charles Tupper, May 25, 1868, 15.
50. Dufferin to Macdonald, December 26, 1872, Dufferin papers, A 414, LAC.
51. Dufferin to Kimberley, February 21, 1873, Dufferin Papers, A 415, LAC.
52. Dufferin to Macdonald, June 3, 1873, Dufferin Papers, A 415, LAC.
53. Dufferin to Mackenzie, February 22, 1876, Dufferin Papers, A 409, LAC.
54. John Young to Sir George Cartier , June 18, 1870; Sir John Young to Macdonald, October 2, 1870, Macdonald Papers, C1514, LAC.
55. "First water" was a nineteenth-century expression now fallen out of use. Lisgar to Macdonald, May 23, 1872, C1514, Macdonald Papers, LAC.

56. Dufferin to Kimberley, private, July 23, 1873, Dufferin Papers, A 407, LAC.

57. See the *Globe*, July 4, 1873, for Sir Hugh Allan's letters to his colleagues discussing arrangements made concerning payments, and the probable grant of the railway charter. Copies of letters and telegrams from Cartier and Macdonald soliciting funds appeared in the *Globe*, July 18, 1873 under the heading "the Evidence Complete" and again in the edition of July 19, 1873.

58. Dufferin to Kimberley, private, August 9, 1873, Dufferin Papers, A 407, LAC.

59. Dufferin to Kimberley, despatch 197, August 15, 1873, William Leggo, *The History of the Administration of the Right Honorable Frederick Temple, Earl of Dufferin* (Montreal: Lovell Publishing, 1878), 140–46.

60. Dufferin to Macdonald, private, July 31, 1873, Dufferin Papers, A 410, LAC.

61. Macdonald to Dufferin, private, July 31, 1873, Dufferin Papers, A 410, LAC.

62. Dufferin to Kimberley, private, August 5, 1873, Dufferin Papers, A 407, LAC.

63. Macdonald to Dufferin, private, July 31, 1873; Dufferin to Macdonald, private, August 6, 1873, and August 9, 1873, Dufferin Papers, A 410, LAC.

64. *Toronto Globe*, July 24, 1873; Dufferin to Kimberley, despatch 197, August 15, 1873, and Enclosure "Memorial" presented August 13, 1873, Leggo, *Administration of Dufferin*, 160–68.

65. *Toronto Globe*, August 14, 1873.

66. Dufferin to Macdonald, private, July 31, 1873, Dufferin Papers, A 410, LAC.

67. For an account of the scene in the Commons see George W. Ross, *Getting into Parliament and After* (Toronto: William Briggs, 1913), 68; Leggo, *Administration of Dufferin*, 136–37; Dufferin to Kimberley, despatch 197, August 15, 1873, Leggo, *Administration of Dufferin*, 166–67; *Globe* August 14, 1873, and Dale Thomson, *Alexander Mackenzie: Clear Grit* (Toronto: Macmillan, 1960), 158–59.

68. *Toronto Globe*, August 14, 1873. This represents a striking contrast to the *Globe*'s position in 1858, when Head refused George Brown's request for a dissolution. At that time the paper rejected any possibility of independent action on the part of the governor, and suggested it was his duty to follow the dictates of his advisers in all circumstances. See *Toronto Globe*, August 6, 1858.

69. Dufferin to Holland, private, October 3, 1873, Dufferin Papers, A 415, LAC.

70. Dufferin to Macdonald, private, August 24, 1873, Dufferin Papers, A 410, LAC.

71. Dufferin to Macdonald September 12, 1873, Dufferin Papers, A415, LAC.

72. Dufferin to Kimberley, private, October 10, 1873, Dufferin Papers, A406, LAC.

73. Dufferin to Kimberley, private, October 11, 1873, Dufferin Papers, A406, LAC.

74. Dufferin to Kimberley, private, October 28, 1873, Dufferin Papers, A406, LAC.

75. Dufferin to Macdonald, private, September 20, 1873, Dufferin Papers, A409, LAC.

76. Dufferin to Macdonald, private, September 30, 1873, Dufferin Papers, A409, LAC.

77. Macdonald to Dufferin, private, September 29, 1873, Pope, *Correspondence of Macdonald*, 226–27.

78. W.T.R. Preston, *My Generation of Politics and Politicians* (Toronto: D.A. Rose Publishing Co., 1927), 84.
79. Dufferin to Kimberley, private, October 13, 1873, Dufferin Papers, A 406, LAC.
80. Dufferin to Macdonald, private, October 19, 1873, Dufferin Papers, A 406, LAC.
81. Dufferin to Kimberley, private, October 26, 1873, Dufferin Papers, A 406, LAC.
82. Dufferin to Kimberley, private, August 5, 1873, Dufferin Papers, A 407, LAC.
83. Kimberley to Dufferin, private, October 6, 1873, Dufferin Papers, A 408, LAC.
84. Kimberley to Dufferin, private, October 8, 1873, Dufferin Papers, A 408, LAC.
85. Kimberley to Dufferin, private, October 29, 1873, Dufferin Papers, A 408, LAC.
86. Charles Tupper, *Recollections of Sixty Years in Canada* (London: Cassell, 1914), 132, 156–57.
87. Dufferin to Kimberley, private, October 26, 1873, Dufferin Papers, A 406, LAC.
88. Ibid.
89. Dufferin to Kimberley, private, November 6, 1873, Dufferin Papers, A 406, LAC.
90. Dufferin to Macdonald, private, November 4, 1873, in Pope, *Correspondence of Macdonald*, 230.
91. Lady Dufferin to Lady Macdonald, November 4, 1873, ibid.
92. Lady Dufferin, "December 15, 1873," *My Canadian Journal, 1872–78* (New York: D. Appleton, 1891), 134.
93. Colonel H.C. Fletcher to Sir John Macdonald, private, November 5, 1873, in Pope, *Correspondence of Macdonald*, 231.
94. Dufferin to Carnarvon, private, March 18, 1874 in C.W. De Kiewiet,. and F.H. Underhill, eds. *Dufferin-Carnarvon Correspondence, 1874–1878* (Toronto: Champlain Society, 1955), 12.
95. See Ged Martin, "John A. Macdonald and the Bottle" *Journal of Canadian Studies* 40 (Fall 2006): 162–85.
96. Monck to Newcastle, private, January 10, 1862, Newcastle Papers, Ne C 11, University of Nottingham, 393.
97. Monck to Newcastle, private, May 23, 1862, Newcastle Papers, Ne C 11, University of Nottingham, 419.
98. For discussion about Monck's use of viceregal discretion in the selection of a ministry, see Joseph Pope, *Memoirs of Macdonald*, I, 242; E.W. Watkin, *Canada and the States: Recollections 1851 to 1886* (London: Ward & Lock, 1887), 95; J.L. Morison, *British Supremacy and Canadian Self-Government*, 324–25; W.P.M. Kennedy, *The Constitution of Canada, An Introduction to Its Development and Law* (London: Oxford University Press, 1922), 270; Donald Creighton, *John A. Macdonald*, I, 334; Bruce W. Hodgins, *John Sandfield Macdonald 1812–1872* (Toronto: University of Toronto Press, 1971), 55; C.P. Stacey, *Canada and the British Army, 1846–1871: A Study in the Practice of Responsible Government* (Toronto: University of Toronto Press, 1963), 142–43; Mackenzie to George Brown, May 31, 1862, as quoted in Dale Thomson, *Alexander Mackenzie*, 68–69.

99. Monck to Ellice, private, October 21, 1862, Ellice Papers, MS 15039 ff, National Library of Scotland, 21–30.

100. Adelaide Young to Macdonald, Tuesday, September (?), 1870, in Pope, *Correspondence of Macdonald,* 136–37.

101. Monck to Macdonald, February 10, 1871, Macdonald Papers, C 1514, LAC.

102. Dufferin to Kimberley, private, August 21, 1873, Dufferin Papers, A 407, LAC.

103. Pope, *Memoirs of Macdonald,* 260.

104. Stanley to Macdonald, May ? 1891, Stanley Papers, A 446, LAC.

105. Stanley to Knutsford, June 4,1891; Stanley to Salisbury, June 4, 1891, Stanley Papers, A 446, LAC.

106. As quoted in John T. Saywell, "The Crown and the Politicians: The Canadian Succession Question 1891–1896," *Canadian Historical Review* 37 (December 1956), 310.

107. Stanley to Knutsford, June 4, 1891, Stanley Papers, A 446, LAC.

108. Saywell, "The Crown and the Politicians," 313.

109. Stanley to Julian Pauncefote, October 11, 1891, Stanley Papers, A 446, LAC.

110. John Saywell, *The Canadian Journal of Lady Aberdeen, 1893–1898* (Toronto: Champlain Society, 1960), xxxii.

Chapter 10

Macdonald, His "Ottawa Men," and the Consolidation of Prime Ministerial Power (1867–1873)

PATRICE DUTIL[1]

The whole of our present system is an experiment.

—Macdonald, 1868[2]

Alexander T. Galt, the minister of finance, wrote to his wife a week before Canada's birth, alarmed at the situation in Ottawa. "I have never before had so much worry [and] anxiety about political arrangements," he confided from the new capital. "Add to all this that Macdonald has been in a constant state of partial intoxication and you may judge whether we have had a pleasant week." Galt feared the worst. "When he [Lord Monck, the governor general] either finds John A. in the state he is in, or hears of it, it is not improbable he may withdraw from him the authority he now holds to form a Ministry, and may render all we have done nugatory."[3] Macdonald seized control of himself, evidently, and the ministry was sworn in as scheduled on July 1, 1867. Galt was reconfirmed as minister of finance. "My public labors have again commenced," he sighed.[4]

Galt — himself a champion of administrative reform — was not the only man to observe that Macdonald was buckling under pressure. Edmund Meredith, a seasoned public servant who had worked closely with Macdonald for over a decade, was undoubtedly aware that Canada's first prime minister was enjoying a bender of historic proportions on the eve of Confederation, but shared none of the fears of the overly sensitive Galt. He knew that Macdonald's herculean work habits would soon kick in again and that concerns for the proper functioning of government would trump whatever political difficulties might arise. There could have been no doubt

THE BEAUTIES OF A ROYAL COMMISSION
"WHEN SHALL WE THREE MEET AGAIN?"

Grip, 23 August 1873.

in Meredith's mind that Macdonald was in command, both of his faculties and of his government.

Macdonald liked to style himself as a man of practical affairs, and he relied extensively on a group of men like Meredith, who have remained very much in the background of our understanding of how he actually managed government. The argument presented in this chapter is that Macdonald's reputation as an indifferent administrator is wrong. In fact, Macdonald proved to be a remarkable government executive. First, he successfully integrated into one prime ministership functions that had belonged to two individuals for the past generation (as premierships had been "shared" since the 1840s). Second, he personally took on a number of portfolios and advanced a vision of government that took advantage of situations as they presented themselves. In so doing, he used his first mandate to establish a prime ministership that centralized power and shaped Canada's machinery of government. Third, Macdonald adeptly executed the most important task of any executive: ensuring that he had the best people working for him. Macdonald did not simply inherit a public service; he actively shaped it and reaped its benefits. He took full advantage of a coterie of senior public servants who were practically as experienced in politics and administration as he was. They were his "Ottawa Men," to use the expression coined by J.L. Granatstein to describe the highly effective cadres who led the bureaucracy from the 1930s to the late 1950s.[5] His ambitious first government, from 1867 to 1872, and the first year of his second mandate until he was defeated in late 1873, cemented the base of a strongly administrative prime ministership that set the path for the future of the post.

Macdonald was devoted to administration and once even voiced a great deal of satisfaction with the way tasks were carried out and jobs were assigned. Still, many people (and the scholars who later echoed their views[6]) were very critical of how he managed the bureaucracy. "It was quite true that the civil service was not worked with that completeness here that it was in England, but there was a very close and satisfactory approximation to it," he told the House of Commons in 1872 that "by degrees it was approaching perfection."[7] The task of administering in the early years of Confederation supposed a great element of trust as communication methods were as rudimentary as the country was large. The system depended on mail — at a time when Ottawa could go for a week without any mail at all, a victim of winter's snow paralysis.[8] To ensure compliance with the wishes of the administrative centre, Macdonald had no choice but to pay personal attention to staffing many positions in the "outside service" even if that sometimes irritated the deputy minister corps. For all the criticism of patronage in early Canada, it is clear that Macdonald engaged in it carefully, mixing both partisan concerns with administrative ability.[9] "I notice what you say about the patronage," Macdonald responded to Joseph Howe's concerns in Nova Scotia in mid-January 1869, "in the present aspect of affairs, where success can only be obtained by a junction of the moderates, both of anti and Union antecedents, it will be advisable to distribute the offices impartially between both sections."[10]

This sort of care was as necessary as it was important for Macdonald in consolidating his "centre" in power, and he was sometimes squarely entrepreneurial in doing so. In 1864 he had created a secret police to keep him personally informed of developments in the United States as the Civil War ended and as Fenian campaigns were whipped up to invade Canada. The threat of the Fenians compelled Macdonald to maintain personal informants south of the border that kept him supplied with news and allowed the Canadian militia to confront, and later defeat, those threats. Macdonald also maintained informants to help him manage the Red River insurrection of 1870.[11] Macdonald's interest in policing continued unabated, and in 1873 he formed the North-West Mounted Police. Those concerns were not the exception; they were key to his careful approach to administration.

MACDONALD AS MANAGER

Macdonald's need for loyalty reflected his philosophy of a management anchored in trust and skill. His approach was instinctive, shaped in equal parts by his own mixed experience in business and in government and in knowing the strengths and weaknesses of both. Almost from the beginning of his legal career, he was exposed to businessmen of all sorts and could not fail to absorb at least some of their outlooks and managerial habits. He had not been in practice five years before being named a director of the Commercial Bank and by the mid-1850s he sat on the boards of a dozen firms in different sectors of the emerging economy of Canada West: brewing, insurance, and public works contracting. Macdonald also became a land speculator, scouting potential tracts that eventually could be used for urban developments or railway passage. In this regard he owned land in Kingston, of course, but also in Toronto and as far southwest as the agricultural heartland of Guelph. He associated himself with some of the leading businessmen of his day, not least with John Rose of Montreal, who would for a time become his minister of finance.[12] Remarkably, Macdonald himself was not able to translate his administrative abilities into wealth. By the late 1860s, Macdonald's debts to the Merchant's Bank, the Bank of Upper Canada, and the Commercial Bank worried him deeply. He had no money, and the only real asset he could monetize to settle an account was the important tract of land he could mortgage in Guelph.[13]

Nevertheless, Macdonald was confident in his personal style of management. "One of the essential ingredients of his leadership style was egoism,"[14] Joseph Pope, his personal secretary from 1882 to 1891, later observed. Macdonald worked hard, with "promptness and sagacity" according to a former career public servant, "that had no precedent."[15] As early as 1855, Macdonald liked to think of himself as contributing to a "working government"[16] and clearly he meant it literally: he threw himself into his work in a similar fashion once Confederation was achieved. Beyond strenuous working habits, Macdonald took the time to consider the consequences of his actions in detail, a managerial habit that served him well. As he observed in a slightly different context, "The great reason why I have always been able to beat Brown is that I have been able to look a little ahead, while he could on no occasion forego the temptation of a temporary triumph."[17]

• • •

Macdonald was fifty-two years old at Confederation, in excellent physical shape, and adjusted his daily schedule to cope with the rigours of administering the new polity. A typical day as prime minister in those years, a twelve- to fourteen-hour affair,[18] was anchored in a rigorous routine. It started with work at home. Macdonald had a pleasant study on the ground floor of his residence and, following a light breakfast, worked much of the morning in the house. Hewitt Bernard, Macdonald's deputy minister of justice (and brother-in-law), lived in the house as well, and could be counted on to help in dealing with that department's heavy affairs. As Attorney General, Macdonald was busy: in any given year, Macdonald had to prepare and oversee the responses to over a thousand requests for legal opinions from other departments, provide countless verbal advice, and had to review the legislation of the provinces, as well as items proposed by members of parliament. Not least, his department had to draft and amend government bills.[19] "Occupied with the thousand and one cares that make up the life of a Prime Minister, it is difficult to understand how Sir John Macdonald found time to fulfill those manifold duties of a departmental character which demanded his attention," wrote Joseph Pope. "Yet, as Minister of Justice, he was ever a busy man, and the state book of the country bears ample witness to his untiring industry as a law-maker and law-reformer."[20] These heavy duties made Macdonald the central pivot for government administration. In his first mandate, his desk was piled high with files on reconciliation with Nova Scotia, acquiring the North West, establishing Manitoba, negotiating the entry into Confederation of British Columbia and Prince Edward Island, treaty negotiations with the United States, implementing a first country-wide census, and starting a massive series of public works. In the first session of the Canadian Parliament, Macdonald himself tabled a bill to allow the construction of the Intercolonial Railway that would link Nova Scotia and New Brunswick to central Canada and proposed resolutions on the desirability of acquiring Rupert's Land and the Northwest Territories (which were passed). Macdonald also devoted months of work in this period to prepare a bill to create a Supreme Court, a project that would be realized later by the Mackenzie government.

When leisurely interludes were possible, Macdonald liked to read newspapers and magazines at home on the sofa in the dressing room on the first floor (Macdonald read a great deal of biography, history, travels — anything but natural science, according to Pope). Anthony Trollope was always a favourite and Macdonald often returned to Philip Stanhope's two-volume *Life of William Pitt*, which had been published in 1861–62. This was no doubt because Stanhope had served in parliament and worked as undersecretary of state for foreign affairs under Robert Peel for a few months in 1835 and as secretary to the Board of Control in 1845 and knew something about both administration *and* politicians.[21] (Some of his hero's administrative habits Macdonald followed diligently. He was fond of quoting Pitt's motto that "The first, second, and third requisites of a Prime Minister are patience." According to Pope, "no statesman ever laid this truth more deeply to heart.")[22]

During the first years of Confederation, the Macdonalds lived in the "Quadrilateral" on Daly Street (at Cumberland Street), a quick walk (even quicker by carriage or sleigh) across the Rideau Canal bridge to the East Block of Parliament where the offices of the prime minister, the ministers, and most of the ministries, as well as the governor general, were installed. The close proximity of the offices was undoubtedly a boon for the bureaucracy and made correspondence unnecessary, much to the frustration of scholars who wish to better understand the machinery of government in this period.

After a quick lunch and a short rest in bed (Canada's first prime minister may have invented the "power nap") Macdonald was in the East Block by the afternoon, meeting with his cabinet — there were no cabinet subcommittees in those days except for the Treasury Board, but they did meet almost daily for much of the year — or working on department files and correspondence. On days of heavy work, such as in the early 1870s, Macdonald's schedule was sometimes so tight that he took no time to eat, prompting Lady Macdonald to insist that lunch be brought to him at his office.[23] After the day's work, if Parliament was not scheduled for an evening sitting, his wife Agnes would collect him. Work often extended into the evening. During the session, Macdonald hosted dinner parties every week for members of Parliament and dignitaries.[24] "He can throw off a weight of business in a wonderfully short time," Agnes observed. "Oftentimes he comes in with a very moody brow, tired and oppressed, his voice weak, his step slow; and ten minutes after he is making clever jokes, and laughing like a school boy, with his hands in his pockets, and his head thrown back." Macdonald scarcely took a day off when in government. By Macdonald standards, the only real rest he enjoyed after Confederation was from 1874 to 1878, while he sat in opposition — and he used that time to rebuild his coalition of supporters, redefine the party program and fight an election to victory. Macdonald worked hard. "He was exacting in his demands," remembered Joseph Pope (who later worked with him). "He required all a man's time. The thought of holidays never entered his mind." Pope felt the demands were justified:

To those who caught his spirit and were willing to be on duty all the year round, no life could be more pleasant than constant association with a statesman who ever conveyed the impression to his secretary that he was a coworker with him in a common cause, who rarely gave a direction unaccompanied by an explanation of the reasons for it, who courted suggestions of all kinds, and even invited criticism of his own work. "I want a memorandum on such a subject," he would say, explaining in a few words what was in his mind. "I wish you would try your hand at it." If the secretary expressed a doubt as to his ability, he would add, "Never mind what mess you make of it, the worst attempt will give me some useful idea. See what you can do."[25]

Macdonald relied heavily on personal secretaries to help him through. The first was Robert A. Harrison, who worked with Macdonald from 1855 to early 1859 (leaving to pursue a career in politics and law that eventually led to the post of chief justice of the Superior Court of Ontario).[26] Harrison was followed by Hewitt Bernard, who then became deputy minister of justice in 1867. In the first Macdonald mandate it was Charles Drinkwater, an employee in the Ministry of Justice, who succeeded Bernard as personal secretary to the prime minister. He worked for Macdonald until the defeat of 1873, and then he joined the Canadian Pacific Railway Company.[27]

If Macdonald was demanding of himself, he also appreciated men who worked hard, were loyal, and who had a certain passion for administrative work. "There was nothing he liked better in a man than the capacity for sticking to his post," wrote Pope.[28] Macdonald gave a sense of what he looked for when he wrote of Sir Edmund Head with admiration that "he is a thorough man of business and attends to the public interests *con amore.*"[29] Agnes Macdonald suspected that "his good heart and amiable temper are the great secrets of his success," a judgment that reflected his approach to management as much as it did to politics.[30]

DEPUTY HEADS

If Macdonald was able to consolidate his personal power as prime minister through his own assertion of personality and by making sure that the people he put in cabinet were loyal to him, he also ensured that the bureaucracy was on his side. In 1855, for instance, he favoured François-Xavier Lemieux in the MacNab cabinet because it was politically expedient, but also because he could be counted on to "not interfere much with his Department." Macdonald often placed more trust in deputy ministers, as he indicated in 1855 regarding a number of ministerial appointments:

> In fact, the office will be altogether managed by [Hamilton] Killaly the departmental head, who is a very competent person, & whose hands will be much strengthened by the change. We have a bran [*sic*] new admin for John Ross [who] has no depart [and] no patronage & Col. [Étienne Paschal] Taché never interferes. [31]

Macdonald had a complex view of the public service. In many ways, he was suspicious of it but he knew that nothing could be accomplished without a loyal and competent public administration. There is evidence that he followed closely what was happening in Great Britain, where in 1854 a report submitted to the government had recommended a more stratified hierarchy for the government's employees, and a system of examinations for its upper ranks. The *Report on the Organization of the Permanent Civil Service*, known mostly by the names of its co-authors, the Northcote-Trevelyan report, also recommended an end to political patronage in securing government employment. Macdonald adapted the thinking to his own view of how public management should be structured. He tabled a civil service bill in 1857 that formally gave the government bureaucracy a pyramidal shape and vertical accountabilities. He established deputy heads for each department, created a classification system for clerks, and introduced the idea of merit by creating a board of examination for aspirants to the public service (the issue of patronage would have to be dealt with differently — if ever, and only if necessary). Macdonald did not adopt all the ideas of the Northcote-Trevelyan Report, however. The report had urged that "Treasury" be given a pride of place, but Macdonald ignored it: he did establish a Treasury Board on the second day of Confederation that would oversee expenditures broadly, but no minister or ministry could dominate the administration except him. He would be *primus* among the *pares*, and the *pares* would be roughly equal in voice, if not in size. An argument was also made for the end of political patronage; Macdonald simply refused. In both cases, there were important managerial concerns. Macdonald could not abide a rival in cabinet, and he needed patronage — particularly outside Ottawa — in order to ensure a loyalty to him and to the government, if he could not win hearts on patriotic grounds.

Ten years later, within months of Confederation, Macdonald tabled a draft *Canada Civil Service Act* to consolidate the Canadian government's bureaucracy from the remnants of the administrations of Canada East, Canada West, New Brunswick, and Nova Scotia that were not retained for provincial purposes. Before the end of the first year of Canada's birth, he issued an order-in-council appointing a "[Royal] Commission to Inquire into the Present State and Probable Requirements of the Civil Service" to make recommendations on how the system could be better integrated and improved. The people charged with the commission were a mix of deputy ministers (Robert Bouchette, William Henry Griffin, John Langton, Étienne Parent, and William Smith) and two individuals who have escaped historical records, Thomas Reynolds and Charles S. Ross. The intention of the commission was to examine the government's functions and operations, now that the government of Canada had made headway in disentangling its operations and transferring functions to the provinces. The report examined both the "departmental staff," as headquartered personnel in Ottawa were referred to, and the "outside service," namely provisionally hired staff in localities spread across the territory, and provided a succinct description of the mandates and issues related to each department. The commission's reports, delivered in 1869, surprised no one in calling for better pay for senior public servants, more consistency in hiring practices, and equitable salaries across the ranks. The second and third reports were devoted to the outside service, and here the commissioners noted that there was a great deal of unevenness in the qualifications of the individuals who were hired and proposed that examinations be held to measure the quality of the various applicants. That the deputies on the commission did not complain much about patronage should not be surprising. It was an integral part of the system and, to a certain degree, they had all profited by it.

Macdonald exerted control of the cabinet through the deputy ministers that reported to him and thus planted the seeds of a system that would allow for a highly centralized executive style. Most of the people he named to these postings in 1867 had long experience with public affairs, but more importantly, Macdonald had had a long experience with them. Indeed, he had had a hand in personally ensuring they had received their positions in the 1850s and 1860s. Most were older than Macdonald, and had deeper experience in bureaucracy and, in many cases, in politics. As Table 1 shows, there was also a remarkable consistency in the ranks of deputy heads, in contrast to ministers. Macdonald shuffled his cabinet regularly, knowing that his men had firm control of the administration.

No one worked more closely with Macdonald than his brother-in-law Hewitt Bernard, who, as deputy minister of justice, headed a staff of seven, including two messengers. Bernard was a busy executive on his own, as Macdonald trusted him to deal with penitentiaries.[32] Spending on the administration of justice in Canada increased from $300,000 per year in 1867 to approximately $1,700,000 in 1873, almost a 600 percent increase over six years.

Macdonald also worked closely with William Henry Lee, the Clerk of the Privy Council. At Confederation, Lee was sixty-eight years old. Born and raised in Trois-Rivières, he had joined the office of the executive council of Upper Canada in 1821 as a clerk and gradually rose through the ranks. In 1853, he was made clerk of the executive council and Macdonald confirmed him as Clerk of the Privy Council at Confederation. Macdonald had worked with Lee for years and had great confidence in him. While there would be six presidents of the Privy Council (Adam Fergusson Blair, Joseph Howe, Edward Kenny, Charles Tupper, John O'Connor, and Hugh McDonald), it was clear that Lee reported to Macdonald. The position was important, even though it was often considered to be little more than note keeping. "There is something in the importance and confidential character of the documents which are prepared by, or pass through the hands of, the Clerks of the Privy Council Office, which may entitle the work to a greater consideration than would attach to similar duties elsewhere," noted the Commission on the Civil Service in 1869.[33] Lee earned $2,600, equal to other deputy heads. Though small, the Privy Council Office (PCO) was already functioning as a central agency. Though it had eleven employees in 1867, no fewer than four of them were messengers, a far greater number than any other department, indicating surely that it was already a coordinating office with a strong gravitational pull. A year later, the number of employees in the PCO had grown to twenty, even though eight were clearly employed for a short time only (presumably as couriers), and stayed in that range until the Macdonald government was defeated.[34]

Macdonald also relied on Edmund Meredith, the Undersecretary of State for the Provinces, who had four clerks reporting to him, as well as a messenger (all the figures on personnel are drawn from the Report of the Commission on the Civil Service). Born in County Tyrone, Northern Ireland, in 1817, a graduate of Trinity College in Dublin (where he won the mathematics medal as well as first prize in Political Economy), and a lawyer, Meredith came to Canada in 1842 to visit his elder brother, and soon decided to stay. He quickly gravitated to Montreal's elite circles, became a mathematics teacher at McGill, posed for Cornelius Krieghoff's "The Shakespeare Club," learned to play hockey (and figured in one of the first descriptions of the game where he was applauded for his speedy skating), and was named principal of McGill University in 1846. He was two years younger than Macdonald, and shared a similar world view.

By the time of Confederation, Meredith had worked with the prime minister for almost twenty years. Meredith was hired as assistant secretary of provincial affairs for Upper Canada in the civil service of the United Province of Canada in 1847. In 1857, Macdonald named him to the Board of Inspectors of Prisons, Asylums, and Public Charities (first as its secretary, and as its chairman from 1864). Both men thought along similar lines regarding penal reform and broad administrative approaches, even though Macdonald favoured more traditional approaches to punishment and was skeptical of rehabilitation promises for hardened criminals. Meredith was a highly competent, at times innovative, administrator and a progressive thinker, but it was soon clear that the business of dealing with the provinces, as undersecretary for the provinces, was being usurped by Macdonald, acting as the government's lawyer. The department was seen to be overstaffed by the Civil Service Commission in its report of 1869.[35] Indeed, it seems the Department of the Secretariat for the Provinces had relatively little to do, allowing Meredith to keep enviable hours during this entire period. Though hardly an enthusiastic public servant by this time, he had Macdonald's confidence. Meredith, a leader in Ottawa society in his own right,[36] resented the control Macdonald wielded and often sought employment elsewhere; first in Toronto, then with the Canadian Pacific Railway, but the prime minister blocked those moves. Macdonald, oblivious to Meredith's public complaints about pay rates, had reason to continue to trust him: Meredith had distinguished himself in the drafting of the Penitentiaries Act of 1868 and had been instrumental in dealing with the first Riel rebellion in 1869. Not surprisingly, Meredith was named deputy head of the Ministry of the Interior in the summer of 1873, when the secretariat for the provinces was abolished. That department would be entrusted with Indian Affairs, Macdonald became its minister, and Meredith's political master.[37]

If Bernard, Lee, and Meredith formed the elements of a key triumvirate in Macdonald's ministerial affairs, he also surrounded cabinet with remarkable talent from elsewhere. His choices from Quebec — undoubtedly guided by George-Étienne Cartier — are a case in point. The senior man was Étienne Parent, the Undersecretary of State for Canada, and an intellectual powerhouse in his own right. His department was responsible for the management of Ordnance Lands as well as Indian Lands, two areas of critical importance and interest to Macdonald. Parent, sixty-five years old at Confederation, was one of the most original and progressive French-Canadian thinkers in the nineteenth century. Born in Beauport, he had studied at the College of Nicolet and the Seminary of Quebec. At the age of twenty he had assumed the editorship of *Le Canadien*, demanding the protection of the rights of francophones and Catholics in light of Britain's plans for political union of the Canadas. The precocious Parent wielded a mighty pen and demonstrated an awesome capacity for work. When *Le Canadien* folded in 1825, Parent turned to the study of law and simultaneously secured a job as translator and law officer of the Legislative Assembly of Lower Canada. He revived *Le Canadien* in 1831, and assumed the position of intellectual leader of the Patriote movement, inspiring the ninety-two resolutions presented to the lower Canadian Assembly in 1834.

Parent was not a firebrand, however, and had no taste for violence. He condemned the call to arms and, by 1837, had completely distanced himself from the movement that he had helped to create. He hoped for good things to come out of Lord Durham's visit to Canada in 1837, but was outraged by the violence of Sir John Colborne's suppression of the riots that took place in early November 1838. Parent continued to fight the idea of union but when that battle was lost, he assumed a prominent part in the struggle for responsible government. He was elected to the Legislative Assembly of United Canada in 1841, and tabled a bill that proposed that French be recognized as an official language. Parent was not a persuasive speaker, however, and found electoral politics unnerving. In late 1842, Louis-Hippolyte Lafontaine asked him to assume the post of clerk for the executive council, and he accepted.[38]

At the age of forty, his career took a completely different turn, but Parent would continue to live two lives. The first dominated with administrative tasks (and travels to Quebec, Montreal, Kingston, and Toronto — capitals changed every three or four years). The second was as an intellectual, delivering penetrating insights on the importance of modern education and commerce in developing French-Canadian society. In 1847, he was appointed assistant secretary of the provinces of Canada (in parallel with Meredith, who was focused on Canada West), and continued to write and lecture on all aspects of social and economic development, making the argument that French Canada had to embrace industry and the ambition of taking its place in the world of the modern economy of banking, technology, and commerce. Its very survival depended on it.[39] He stopped lecturing after 1852, focusing instead on his work as an administrator for the provinces of Canada, and thrived in that environment. At Confederation he was made Undersecretary of State, managing the largest staff at Ottawa's headquarters: twenty-six people, including three messengers (more than the Privy Council!). The department was considerably larger than it should have been by 1869, and was targeted by the Civil Service Commission for cutbacks. At fault was an unnecessarily complicated system for duplicating correspondence and, as noted, an excessive messenger staff.[40]

Though it was never acknowledged openly, it is likely that Parent was probably one of Macdonald's best French-Canadian acquaintances, and that exposure undoubtedly played a role in how the prime minister perceived Quebec. Parent served under Macdonald until his retirement in 1872.

Clearly, George-Étienne Cartier, himself exiled in the aftermath of the 1837 rebellions, had an influence on Macdonald and would have been the one to introduce Parent to him. The second old Patriote reporting to Macdonald was Robert Bouchette, the deputy minister of customs (the official title was Commissioner of Customs and Chairman of the Board of Customs, Excise and Stamps), who was sixty-two years old at Confederation. Bouchette earned a great deal more money ($3,200) compared to deputies who otherwise earned an average of $2,600. He had a staff of twelve, in addition to a messenger and an assistant messenger. Born and raised in Quebec City, his father was Joseph Bouchette, surveyor general of Lower Canada and an enthusiastic Tory. He was trained as a lawyer, but Bouchette enjoyed a wide variety of cultural pursuits, not least his father's vocation as cartographer. Where he parted with his father was on politics and, by the 1830s, Bouchette was drawn to the reformers. In the feverish days of 1837 he founded *Le Libéral/ The Liberal* and was arrested. Released on bail, he fought at Moore's Corner in early December, was caught, imprisoned, then exiled to Bermuda (which was clearly more of a hardship in those years than it is today). He returned to Canada in 1845 and a year later joined the public service. In 1851, he was made collector of customs and nominated to a number of key commissions on a wide variety of subjects. In 1860, for instance, he co-presided a commission on the workings of the Reciprocity Treaty with the United States. The following year, he headed an inquiry into immigration. In 1862, he was asked by Macdonald to carry out a reorganization of the civil service and four years later Bouchette was named the Canadian representative to the Paris Exhibition. Macdonald must have been amused by the presence of an old Patriote in his administration, but Bouchette had proven himself and had earned the prime minister's confidence through the years. Macdonald had to have a special interest in customs because most of the government's budget depended on this department's ability to collect funds.[41]

· · ·

The other two francophones were too young to have participated in the events of 1837, but their dedication to the ideals of the Patriotes, and simultaneously to the Macdonald brand of Toryism, could hardly be doubted. The deputy minister of agriculture was Dr. Joseph-Charles Taché, then forty-six years old. Born in 1820, Taché had studied at the Petit Séminaire de Québec before turning to medicine. Like Bouchette and Parent, Taché had started his career in politics. In 1848, he was acclaimed as member of parliament for Rimouski. He declared himself a partisan of Lafontaine, and remained in parliament until he resigned his seat in 1856. He represented Canada at the Universal Exposition in Paris (1855) and was made a Knight (*Chevalier*) of the Legion of Honour by Napoleon III. Taché then devoted himself to his medical practice and to journalism. By the time of Confederation, he had been a doctor for twenty years. Macdonald knew him well — he was the nephew of Colonel Étienne-Paschal Taché who had been active in so many ministries in the 1850s and 1860s (including premier in 1856–57 and 1864–75).

Taché was appointed deputy of agriculture in August 1864 by the administration headed by his uncle and Macdonald, and by 1867 had a staff of seventeen people in addition to four messengers. Taché was a key eye for Macdonald on European matters. He travelled to France in 1866 and brought to Niagara the first French vines. He was back in France the year of Confederation, represented Canada at the Paris exhibition of that year, and then presented the government's greetings to Pope Pius IX in Rome.[42] The Department of Agriculture was somewhat of a misnomer at Confederation; its staff dealt mostly with patents and statistics, and, not least, health care. The Civil Service Commission of 1869 considered that there was a surplus of staff in the patents division, but that the statistics division needed to be expanded considerably in order to collect and digest the data necessary to the delivery of quality government services, depending on how detailed the government wished the reports.[43] Finally, the issue of maintaining quarantine systems was considered to be of dubious value to the commission, which seemed more at ease in seeing the provinces take care of these functions. The issues were resolved and Taché led the first census of Canada in 1871 with great success.[44]

Toussaint Trudeau, forty-one at Confederation, also represented the new generation. As the Deputy of Public Works (including public buildings), he had thirty-two people working for him, as well as two messengers. Trudeau, though the youngest of deputies, earned considerably more ($3,000 a year) than his more senior peers and his department was booming as a result of Confederation. The relatively small pre-1867 department was now coping with the building of lighthouses, examining harbours and railways in Nova Scotia and New Brunswick, and all the mail that was spawned by the new works. The Civil Service Commission of 1869 recommended more support to the deputy head, particularly in the area of engineering audits. Born in Montreal, Trudeau studied civil engineering in New York City before returning to Montreal around 1853 to take full advantage of the railway boom. He distinguished himself in these affairs, catching the attention of the Cartier-Macdonald government. He was involved in a number of commissions of inquiry and formally joined the Department of Public Works as its secretary in late 1859, and, in 1864, was made deputy commissioner by the Taché-Macdonald administration. He continued as deputy head in this department in 1867 and would be involved in each and every aspect of railway development and other public works. Thoroughly competent, though never overtly partisan, Trudeau was known to be a friend of the government. Macdonald had complete trust in him. Remarkably, he was untouched by the scandals around the Canadian Pacific Railway that brought down the government in 1873.[45]

If affairs ran smoothly in most ministries, Macdonald had more trouble with his Department of Finance where a struggle for domination was fought out between the deputy of finance (or inspector general) and the auditor. William Dickinson was the deputy minister of finance in 1867. As such, he oversaw a staff of fourteen people as well as one messenger — and to the consternation of the Civil Service Commission of 1869, still countersigned every cheque issued by the government![46] It was John Langton, as the Auditor in the finance department, who attracted the most attention (not least because of the impressively long white beard that made him instantly recognizable in the small town of Ottawa in those days). Langton, who commanded the same salary as the inspector general and managed a staff of ten, in addition to retaining one messenger, had distinguished himself by the quality of his ideas in improving the managements of the government's financial accounts in the 1860s. He established the essence of the budgetary system that includes advanced estimates of costs and audited statements that are still used today and disentangled the finances between the provinces and federal government, an area where Macdonald was intimately involved.[47]

Born in England and a graduate of the University of Cambridge, Langton was fifty-nine years old at Confederation. He had arrived in Canada in 1833 and eventually settled in Peterborough, Ontario. He was elected to parliament as a Conservative twice, in 1851 and 1854, where he distinguished himself with his critique of public accounts. Langton was passionate about the development of universities (he oversaw the building of University College in Toronto and eventually served as president of the Literary and Historical Society of Quebec). Macdonald appreciated his talents and in 1855 made sure he was appointed chair of the new Board of Audit — an office Macdonald created in order to ensure that the government kept its accountability tidy.[48] In 1868, he became the leader of the Civil Service Commission, appointed by Macdonald, and secretary of the Treasury Board. When Dickinson retired in 1869, Macdonald named Langton as deputy minister of finance with enough latitude to bring in much-needed reforms in how the Government of Canada maintained its books.[49] In effect, Langton, the old Tory, was the super-bureaucrat of his generation, combining the posts of deputy minister of finance, auditor, and secretary to Treasury Board.

The rest of the deputy minister corps was equally sworn to Macdonald. George Futvoye, the deputy head of the militia, was born in London, England and was sixty years old at Confederation. He had immigrated to Canada on the eve of the rebellions of 1837 and was on hand to work under Lord Durham as inspector of protestant schools in Lower Canada the following year. He then applied his administrative skills as City Clerk in Quebec City. He became a lawyer at the age of forty, but maintained his position in the civil service, rising to the highest position in the Crown Lands Office. His expertise in land issues was unsurpassed and his expertise in administrative issues was prized. At Confederation, Cartier insisted that Futvoye, who had never had any interest or experience in army affairs, be named deputy head of the Department of Militia and Defence. (Cartier's generosity is telling here: the old Patriote entrusted the organization of the militia to a man who had arrived in North America in service to Lord Durham.). Futvoye was hardly an innovator in this area of the public service and in military affairs, but his steady hand in running the department during unpredictable times was invaluable to Macdonald as the government faced armed insurrection in the West. His department's budget literally see-sawed during this administration.[50]

The deputy corps was rounded out by three individuals who were responsible for financial matters, but whose stories remain obscure. T.D. Harington was the deputy receiver general; ten people reported to him, as well as a messenger, but he has left no trace. Likewise with Thomas Worthington, who headed the Department of Internal Revenue and whose staff in Ottawa was no bigger than three people and a messenger. We know a little more about the third, one William Henry Griffin, fifty-five at Confederation, the deputy postmaster general, who had a massive department of forty-three people in Ottawa, in addition to a messenger and three assistant messengers. Born in London, England, he had spent his entire career in the post office when Macdonald named him to the position in 1857, ten years before Confederation. He was also heading a flourishing department as postal operations from New Brunswick and Nova Scotia were integrated. The Civil Service Commission of 1869 recommended adding many more postal inspectors to oversee the number of post offices that had doubled in a short time.[51]

There was no official deputy for the Marine and Fisheries Department in 1867, and, in fact, the employees in that department had no official job description. The department — mostly concerned with navigational issues and the (weak) regulation of the fisheries trade — was undergoing substantial change. The small department now had to cope with the management of harbours and lighthouses as well as the fisheries off Nova Scotia and New Brunswick. It also provided services "to sick and disabled and distressed seamen," but for the time, Lieutenant-Colonel Walker Powell led a team of twenty-eight people and four messengers. The chief concern of this department was the management and supervision of the hundreds of workers dispersed along the coasts. The odd portfolio of Marine and Fisheries seemed to join two departments that had little in common (aside from the obvious link of having to do with water).

Macdonald named Peter Mitchell, the premier of New Brunswick, to be minister of this portfolio after the 1867 election and he, in turn, wished for his friend William Smith to assume the position of deputy head. It was a rare example of Macdonald not having a direct hand in the nomination, but Smith was clearly the Tory friend of a Tory who had demonstrated real prowess in management. Not least, Smith was a Scot, born there in 1821, which tripled his chances of winning Macdonald's favour. After some schooling in Edinburgh, he secured a job in the British customs service in 1840. He was transferred to Saint John in New Brunswick and there assumed progressively more responsible positions. Smith became a member of the Saint John establishment, combining his public service with active involvement in the private sector. By the 1860s he was president of the Saint John Gas Light Company and a director the Scottish Life Association of New Brunswick, among other entreprises.[52] When Macdonald travelled to Washington to participate in the negotiation of the new treaty between the United States and Great Britain, it was Smith he brought along.[53]

Mitchell thought the ministry's structure would be difficult to manage because its branches were "so distinct and so unlike" and hoped to have two deputies report to him. Macdonald turned down that request, looking forward to working with Smith, who seemed a most agreeable candidate for the senior bureaucratic post. Indeed, Smith, the only "non-Canadian" in the deputy ranks, fitted into the upper ranks of the civil service quickly. He was soon occupying seats on the Board of Audit, the Civil Service Examining Board, and the Civil Service Commission. He was also an energetic manager. He personally visited every lighthouse on the lower St. Lawrence by 1873 and oversaw the construction of 111 new lights in the Dominion. His department had eleven inside employees and more than eight hundred outside employees (including fisheries officers) and had direct responsibility for 215 lighthouses and other lights, regulation of harbours and pilotage, marine hospitals, inspection of steamboats, and various other services affiliated with shipping.[54]

In sum, while it is important to consider Macdonald's choices for cabinet,[55] his choices for deputy heads tell a story that illustrates his interest in strong administration. Five of the thirteen deputy heads Macdonald appointed in 1867 had sat in parliament. Seven of them had over twenty years of experience at the executive level and, with the exception of one, had worked with Macdonald before. Macdonald's highly politicized corps of deputy heads included many Scots and all of them (save for one) came from central Canada. Three of the French Canadian deputy heads were given the most important posts: customs, agriculture and public works. Most of them had considerable political experience and included old Patriotes as well as hardened Tories. They worked alongside each other in the East block, building a new country in agreeable compliance with the prime minister. Many of them were distinguished intellectuals and cultivated men whose understanding of public administration equaled their devotion to Macdonald personally. Certainly, they complained that their positions were undermined by Macdonald's practices of patronage, but their words were only paid lip service. Macdonald trusted them, but only to a degree. He still needed to ensure that the entire bureaucracy was professionally compliant to the state, and would continue to pursue that practice.

CONCLUSION

In his famed eulogy of Macdonald, Wilfrid Laurier declared that the late prime minister "was fond of power, and, in my judgment, if I may say so, that may be the turning-point of the judgment of history. He was fond of power, and he never made any secret of it."[56] Macdonald indeed transformed the position of prime minister from being one of accommodation of political realities to an executive position that commanded the obedience of cabinet. He instituted a system that prized industry, coordination, and allegiance to the post of prime minister that has continued to endure.

Macdonald accomplished this centralizing of power by putting himself at the centre. His prime ministership would not be an ornamental one. He could chair cabinet, of course, but kept a hand in each ministry as attorney general and as de facto minister of external affairs. In twenty-first-century parlance, his "environmental scan" was the one that mattered. Because every department had legal issues, he dealt with each ministry. He multiplied veto and decision points through his proxies in the ranks of his thoroughly politicized deputy ministers, and by ensuring a legal review of key departments; through John Langton, he ensured financial controls and reduced discretion in all areas of government activity. Macdonald also centralized his power by installing a powerful cadre of "Ottawa men", a first generation of well-connected, knowledgeable, and innovative individuals who had the capacity to expand the new capital's reach into every corner of the dominion. Through them was Macdonald able to achieve, what to this day remains, the most accomplished four-year mandate in Canada's history. Macdonald's managerial ability was recognized later in his life. J.W. Bengough drew a cartoon of Macdonald in 1887 as "the phrenological chart of the Head of the Country," in which his cranium was divided by description of habits and abilities (what today would be signaled as a remarkable ability to "compartmentalize"). Among them were clues to Macdonald's approach to management generally and to the office of the prime ministership in particular. Bengough noted, "he is not so much a philosopher as he is a practical man" and also observed that Macdonald was "strongly endowed with order which renders him methodical and systematic in whatever he does."

There was real insight in this humorous angle. Macdonald's approach to administration was captured in a few of the vignettes: calculation, combativeness, cautiousness, continuity, firmness, hope, "inhabitiveness" at the office. Above all, however, Macdonald displayed remarkable skill in doing

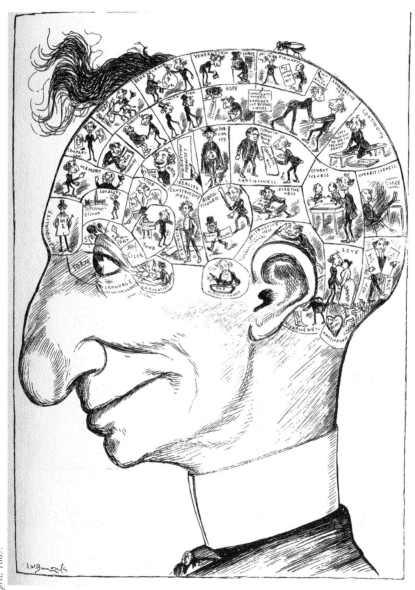

Grip, 9 April, 1887.

Phrenological Chart of the Head of the Country [Sir John A. Macdonald] by William Bengough, 1887.

what the best executives do: select other executives who have similar visions of the world but who also have the skills necessary to get the job done. The deputy heads who worked during the first mandate had all been largely handpicked by Macdonald a decade earlier — many of them had political backgrounds (most had demonstrated themselves as good Tories), were highly educated, and knew their business.

It is not surprising that so much was accomplished during the first six years of Confederation as the government worked to turn the country, in Macdonald's words, "from gristle into bone." Macdonald was as sophisticated in his approach to the bureaucracy as he was to the voting public. Courteous, for sure, but taking no risk in ensuring that the prime minister's will was acted upon by the public service with efficiency and with effectiveness. His approach would continue when he returned to power in 1878. Concerned with administration two years after his re-election, he called for another commission of inquiry into the public service. Not least, and for the rest of his career, Macdonald continued to involve himself in departmental business, first as minister of the interior, from 1878 to 1883 and as superintendent-general of Indian Affairs (from 1878 to 1887). He was president of the Privy Council from 1883 to 1888, and then minister of railways and canals from 1889 until his death in 1891.

Canada was born on the promise of peace, order, and good government. In the eyes of the electors in 1872, Macdonald had delivered some peace, some order, and some good government, but there was grumbling and he had to spend a fatal amount of money to hold on to power. Nevertheless, that first mandate left an important legacy in shaping Canada's governance personally and permanently by institutionalizing an endurably strong prime ministership that commanded a significant managerial role inside the state's machinery. In the critical first five years of Confederation, Macdonald used his position as first minister to augment the role, keeping to himself some of the most critical portfolios to his government's mandate. He added to the government machinery only when necessary, and in this first mandate, mostly to deal with indigenous issues in the newly acquired Western Territories. In effect, he used his administrative role to increase the gravitational pull of the prime minister's office, ensuring that it played a central role in every aspect of decision-making. Macdonald also ensured the centrality of the prime minister as administrative executive by assuring that he could rely on deputy heads who would carry out his will. In this respect, he ensured that his deputy heads were administratively capable and politically astute, and maintained them in their position until they retired; choosing, in contrast, to shift his cabinet members regularly. If, as he wrote, much of the new government was "an experiment," Macdonald did not take many chances.

TABLE 1
DEPUTY MINISTERS AND MINISTERS IN THE MACDONALD GOVERNMENT, 1867–1873

Department	Deputy Minister	Minister
Privy Council	William Henry Lee 1867–73	Edward Kenny, 1869–70 Joseph Howe, 1869 Charles Tupper, 1870–72 John O'Connor, 1872–73 Hugh McDonald, 1873
Justice	Hewitt Bernard, 1867–73	John A. Macdonald, 1867–73
Militia & Defence	George Futvoye, 1867–73	George-Étienne Cartier, 1867–73 Hector-Louis Langevin, 1873 Hugh McDonald, 1873
Secretary of State	Étienne Parent, 1867–73	Hector-Louis Langevin, 1867–69 James Cox Aikins, 1869–73
Marine & Fisheries	William Smith, 1867–73	Peter Mitchell, 1867–73
Secretary for the Provinces	Edmund Allen Meredith, 1867–72	Adams George Archibald, 1867–68 Joseph Howe, 1869–73 Thomas Nicholson Gibbs, 1873
Indian Affairs	William Spragge, 1870–72	Joseph Howe, 1869–73 Hector-Louis Langevin, 1868–69 James Cox Aikins, 1873 Thomas Nicholson Gibbs, 1873 Alexander Campbell, 1873

Receiver General	T. Douglas Harington, 1867–73	Edward Kenny, 1867–69 Jean-Charles Chapais, 1869–73 Theodore Robitaille, 1873
Finance	William Dickinson, 1867–69 John Langton, 1869–73	Alexander Tilloch Galt, 1867 John Rose, 1867–69 Francis Hincks, 1869–73 Samuel Tilley, 1873
Audit	John Langton, 1867–73	
Customs	Robert Shore Miles Bouchette, 1867–73	Samuel Tilley, 1867–73 Charles Tupper, 1873
Inland Revenue	Thomas Worthington, 1867–73	William Pierce Howland, 1867–68 Alexander Morris, 1869–72 Charles Tupper, 1872–73 John O'Connor, 1873 Thomas Nicholson Gibbs, 1873
Public Works	Toussaint Trudeau, 1867–73	William McDougall, 1867–69 Hector-Louis Langevin, 1869–73
Post Office	W.H. Griffin, 1867–73	Alexander Campbell, 1867–73 John O'Connor, 1873
Agriculture and Statistics	J.C. Taché, 1867–73	Jean-Charles Chapais, 1867–69 Christopher Dunkin, 1869–71 John Henry Pope, 1871–73

Source: www.pco-bcp.gc.ca

NOTES

1. I am happy to acknowledge Michael Hudecki, Adam Stecher, and Laura Tonon who each contributed to the preparation of this chapter.
2. Macdonald to Cook, February 3, 1868, Macdonald Papers, vol. 514, LAC, cited in Donald Creighton, *The Old Chieftain* (Toronto: Macmillan Co. of Canada, 1965), 10.
3. A.T. Galt to wife, June 23, 1867, vol. 7, 001174, Galt Papers, LAC.
4. Ibid., A.T. Galt to wife, July 2, 1867, vol. 7, 001181, Galt Papers, LAC.
5. See J.L. Granatstein, *The Ottawa Men: The Civil Service Mandarins, 1935–1957* (Toronto: Oxford University Press, 1982).

6. See Sandra Gwyn, *The Private Capital* (Toronto: McClelland and Steward, 1984), 97. By her account, Meredith had no doubt that Confederation was a *fait accompli*. Sandra Gwyn observed that "it simply never occurred to most politicians, first and foremost among them Macdonald, to be bothered about sound administration or managerial efficiency" (91). Scholars have been equally critical of Macdonald in this regard, particularly his complacency toward abuses in patronage. R. MacGregor Dawson pronounced the post-Confederation years as "an inglorious period" in his *History of the Canadian Civil Service* (London: Oxford University Press, 1929), 24. See also Kenneth Rasmussen, who brings a much more nuanced appreciation of the intellectual underpinnings of "management" of this period in his "Administrative philosophy in Canada: A Study of Federal Public Service Inquiries, 1867–1979" (PhD Dissertation, University of Toronto, 1990).

7. Cited in Dawson, 30.

8. Creighton, 33.

9. On Macdonald's patronage policy, see Gordon Stewart, "Political Patronage under Macdonald and Laurier," *The American Review of Canadian Studies* 10:1 (Spring 1980), and Stewart, *The Origins of Canadian Politics — A Comparative Approach* (Vancouver: UBC Press, 1986); Jonathan Swainger, "Judicial Scandal and the Culture of Patronage in Early Confederation, 1867–78," in Jim Phillips, R. Roy McMurtry, and John Saywell, eds., *Essays in The History of Canadian Law: A Tribute to Peter Oliver* (Osgoode Society for Canadian Legal History and University of Toronto Press, 2008).

10. Macdonald to Howe, January 12, 1869 in Joseph Pope, *Correspondence of Sir John Macdonald* (Garden City, N.Y.: Doubleday, Page, 1921), 84.

11. See Reg Whitaker, Gregory S. Kealey and Andrew Parnaby, *Secret Service: Political Policing in Canada from the Fenians to Fortress America* (Toronto: University of Toronto, 2012), ch. 1.

12. The information in this paragraph is owed to J.K. Johnson, "John A. Macdonald," in *The Pre-Confederation Premiers: Ontario Government Leaders, 1841–1827*, ed. J.M.S. Careless (Toronto: University of Toronto Press and The Ontario Historical Studies, 1980), 200–01, 213.

13. Creighton, 33.

14. Johnson, 209.

15. Henry Morgan, cited in Johnson, 206–07.

16. Ibid., 214. See also J.K. Johnson, ed., *The Letters of Sir John A. Macdonald, 1836–1857* (Ottawa, Public Archives of Canada, 1969). Letter from Macdonald to Henry Smith, September 3, 1855, 301.

17. Ibid., Macdonald to Cameron, January 3, 1872, 161.

18. Joseph Pope, *Memoirs of The Right Honourable Sir John A. Macdonald* (Toronto: Musson Book Company, 1944), 653.

19. "Commission to Inquire into the Present State and Probable Requirements of the Civil Service," *First Report of Canada Commission to Inquire into the Present State and Probable Requirements of the Civil Service* (Ottawa, 1869), 15. The creation of the Department of Justice is well explored in Jonathan Swainger, *The Canadian Department of Justice and the Completion of Confederation, 1867–78* (Vancouver: UBC Press, 2000).

20. Pope, *Memoirs*, 428.

21. Ibid., 642.

22. Ibid., 653.

23. Ibid., 433.

24. Ibid., 643.

25. Ibid., 65.

26. See Peter Oliver, ed., *The Conventional Man: The Diaries of Ontario Chief Justice Robert A. Harrison, 1856–1878* (Toronto: Osgoode Society for Legal History and University of Toronto Press, 2003). Oliver describes the relations between Macdonald and the ambitious Harrison in a short section of a splendid introduction, 12–15; regrettably, there are only a few mentions of Macdonald in the diary.

27. Pope, *Memoirs*, 655

28. Ibid., 55.

29. J.A. Macdonald to Louisa Macdonald, February 21, 1855, in J.K. Johnson, ed., *Affectionately Yours: The Letters of Sir John A. Macdonald and His Family* (Toronto: MacMillan, 1969), 73; Pope, *Memoirs*, 141.

30. Cited in Creighton, 2.

31. Macdonald to Brown Chamberlin, February 2, 1855, in J.K. Johnson, ed., *The Letters of Sir John A. Macdonald, 1836–1857* (Ottawa: Public Archives of Canada, 1968), 235.

32. On Bernard, see P.B. Waite, "Bernard, Hewitt." In *Dictionary of Canadian Biography*, vol. 12, University of Toronto/Université Laval, last accessed April 28, 2014, *www.biographi.ca/en/bio/bernard_hewitt_12E.html*.

33. Civil Service Commission Report, 1869, 13.

34. "Detailed Statement re Staff of the Privy Council Office During Fiscal Years 1867–1891," RG2, vol. 5701, file 2, LAC.

35. Civil Service Commission Report, 1869, 20.

36. See Sandra Gwyn, *The Private Capital*. The first half of the book is focused on Meredith.

37. See letter from J.A. Macdonald to the provincial secretary, July 1855, in Johnson, ed., *Letters of John A. Macdonald, 1836–1857*, 288. Macdonald expresses concern for the low salaries of the judges of the Country Courts in Upper Canada and wants the legislature to enable the government to grant higher salaries "commensurate with the dignity of their position and the responsible nature of their duties."

38. See Jean-Charles Falardeau, "Étienne Parent." In *Dictionary of Canadian Biography*, vol. 10, University of Toronto/Université Laval, 2003–, accessed April 28, 2014, www.biographi.ca/en/bio/parent_etienne_10E.html.

39. The most comprehensive discussion of Parent's ideas is Gérard Bergeron, *Lire Étienne Parent: notre premier intellectuel, 1802–1874* (Québec, Presses de l'Université du Québec, 1993). Claude Couture draws an interesting parallel between Parent and Pierre Elliott Trudeau in his *Paddling with the Current: Pierre Elliott Trudeau, Étienne Parent, Liberalism and Nationalism in Canada* (Edmonton: University of Alberta Press, 1998). Trudeau once said that he was indeed a Tory, "A John A. Macdonald Conservative" — was the thinking of Parent indeed the link between these two prime ministers?

40. Report of the Civil Service Commission, 1869, 17–19.

41. J.A. Macdonald to William Cayley, January 1855, in Johnson, ed., *Letters of John A Macdonald, 1836–1857*, 225. See Yves Tessier, "Bouchette, Robert Shore Milnes." In *Dictionary of Canadian Biography*, vol. 10, University of Toronto/Université Laval, last accessed April 28, 2014, www.biographi.ca/en/bio/bouchette_robert_shore_milnes_10E.html.

42. See Michèle Bernard, *Joseph-Charles Taché: Visionnaire, penseur et homme d'action au cœur du XIXe siècle* (Montreal: XYZ Editeur, 2011).

43. Civil Service Commission, 1869, 36.

44. Taché's work is well described in Bruce Curtis, *The Politics of Population: State Formation, Statistics, and the Census of Canada, 1840–1875* (Toronto: University of Toronto Press, 2002) 238–63. There is no evidence that Taché was "McGee's choice," given the former's long links with the Tories. McGee's famous 1863 *Report on Government Departments* was a Liberal response to years of Tory reform of administrative structures; though Taché certainly would have supported McGee's cry for better statistics, his work was entirely sponsored by the Liberal-Progressive Alliance that governed from May 1864.

45. The source of this material is Glenn T. Wright, "Trudeau, Toussaint." In *Dictionary of Canadian Biography*, vol. 12, University of Toronto/Université Laval, last accessed April 28, 2014, *www.biographi.ca/en/bio/trudeau_toussaint_12E.html*.

46. Civil Service Commission Report, 1869, 32.

47. Civil Service Commission Report, 1869, 26. Langton's contribution to budget-making is briefly discussed in J.E. Hodgetts, *The Canadian Public Service: A Physiology of Government, 1867–1970* (Toronto: University of Toronto Press, 1974), 91, ch..7; see Herbert R. Balls, "John Langton and the Canadian Audit Office," *Canadian Historical Review* 21 (1940), 150–76.

48. See Wendy Cameron, "Langton, John." In *Dictionary of Canadian Biography*, vol. 12, University of Toronto/Université Laval, last accessed April 28, 2014, *www.biographi.ca/en/bio/langton_john_12E.html*.

49. See Balls, "Langton."

50. See René Chartrand, "Futvpye, George." In *Dictionary of Canadian Biography*, vol. 12, University of Toronto/Université Laval, last accessed April 28, 2014, *www.biographi.ca/en/bio/futvoye_george_12E.html.*

51. Civil Service Commission Report, 1869, 33.

52. See Gwynneth C.D. Jones, "Smith, William (1821-97)." In *Dictionary of Canadian Biography*, vol. 12, University of Toronto/Université Laval, last accessed April 28, 2014, *www.biographi.ca/en/bio/smith_william_1821_97_12E.html.*

53. Creighton, *The Old Chieftain*, 82. There clearly was some animosity between Peter Mitchell and Macdonald and the criticisms are laid out in A.L. Burt, "Peter Mitchell on John A. Macdonald" *Canadian Historical Review* 42, September 3, 1961), 209–27.

54. See Burt, ibid.

55. See J.P. Lewis, "The Lion and the Lam Ministry: John A. Macdonald and the Politics of the First Canadian Federal Cabinet" (MA thesis, University of Guelph, 2005).

56. The speech can be found in Pope, *Memoirs*, Appendix XXX, 782.

Chapter 11

Macdonald as Minister of Indian Affairs: The Shaping of Canadian Indian Policy

J.R. MILLER[1]

One would never know from the historiography that John A. Macdonald was Canada's longest-serving minister of Indian Affairs.[2] Neither does existing historical writing inform us that Macdonald played a formative role in the development of post-Confederation Indian policy. The historiography contends that the member of Parliament for Kingston was a shrewd, if perhaps unscrupulous, political tactician; or a visionary nation builder; or even a "non-politician" because he was an active man of business.[3] In fact, the most visible link between Macdonald and Indian matters in the literature is that Donald Creighton subtitled the second volume of his biography of Macdonald *The Old Chieftain*. But Macdonald, in fact, had a lengthy and influential role in dealing with First Nations in Canada. He moved adoption of what was probably the most enduring element of policy a decade before Confederation. And, as prime minister, and as superintendent general of Indian Affairs after 1867, he was instrumental in determining the shape and scope of Western treaties, reserve policy, economic "development" on reserves, and a swath of government program that targeted First Nations' cultural identity, spiritual practices, and traditional governance. For good or ill, Macdonald was an architect of Canadian Indian policy. The foundation that he and his government laid would last largely unaltered until the middle of the twentieth century.

When the young lawyer from Kingston entered the Legislative Assembly in 1844, clear lines of policy concerning Aboriginal lands and culture had been laid down. The key components of that policy were treaty-making and a "civilization" policy. The procedure for making territorial treaties that emerged from the Royal Proclamation of 1763 experienced its development and full effect in Upper Canada. The proclamation, an imperial document designed to regulate and provide institutions of law and government for the North American colonies Britain had acquired from France, provided Crown recognition of a limited Aboriginal territorial right. In the event that any of "the several Nations or Tribes of Indians, with whom we are Connected and who live under our protection" wished to dispose of some of their lands, the proclamation said "they shall be purchased only for Us, in our Name, at some Publick Meeting or Assembly of the said Indians to be held for that Purpose by the Governor...." In other words, according to the proclamation, only the Crown could lawfully take a surrender of territory from First Nations.[4]

It was in the future Upper Canada that the implications of the proclamation's territorial provisions became explicit in treaty-making. Even before the Constitutional Act of 1791 brought Upper and Lower Canada into being, the governor on the spot had begun to negotiate with First Nations in the regions north of Lake Erie and Lake Ontario for access to some of the lands they controlled. The first phase of Upper Canadian treaty-making occurred in 1783–84 with the Mississauga, an Anicinabe people, in preparation for the immigration of thousands of United Empire Loyalists, including some Iroquois, along the Grand River and in the Deseronto area north of Lake Ontario. That stage was followed in the 1790s and first decade of the nineteenth century by more treaties covering other areas along the St. Lawrence and lower Lakes. The initial thirteen treaties recognized access to specific areas for one-time compensation, which was paid in goods. Although there were defects in the negotiation of several of these Upper Canadian treaties, they broadly conformed to the requirements of the Royal Proclamation: negotiations were conducted by a representative of the Crown, and always at a public meeting of the First Nations people affected.

Following the War of 1812, in anticipation of a surge in immigration, the Crown initiated another set of treaty negotiations to deal with lands north of those covered by the earlier agreements. From 1818 on, however, treaties were modified significantly. The one-time payments were now replaced by smaller annual payments or annuities from the Crown to the First Nations signatories. Otherwise, the second phase of the Upper Canadian treaties, down to 1836, duplicated the first. And, again, although there were short-comings in the state's observance of the 1763 rules, the ten treaties made after the War of 1812 generally satisfied the proclamation's requirements. The two sets of Upper Canadian treaties brought all the lands, including especially all the region's arable land, from the lower Lakes to Georgian Bay, and from the Detroit River to the Ottawa, under treaty prior to the formation of the Province of Canada.[5]

The other major result of Upper Canada's growth as an agricultural colony, particularly from the 1820s on, was the emergence of a new attitude on the part of government toward the First Nations. The end of hostilities with the United States, at the close of the War of 1812, ushered in an enduring peace with the new republic that undermined the old foundations of the relation-ship between First Nations and newcomers. Before 1812, their relations had been those of commercial partnership and diplomatic/military alliance. But now, the Treaty of Ghent ended Britain's need for Indian allies, and the rush

FRENCH NONSENSE: OR, "REDUCTIO AD ABSURDUM."

Grip, 5 December, 1885.

of incoming settlement, of which the Macdonald family was a part, finished off the fur trade and its economic partnership between First Nations and Europeans in the region. In the changed environment, the British Indian Department wondered why it was continuing to pay large sums to maintain its relations with First Nations, particularly in the form of annual "presents." And simultaneously, expanding farms undermined the hunting-gathering economy that maintained most First Nations in the region. Another force promoting revision of Indian policy was the emergence in Great Britain of a number of Christian humanitarian organizations, such as the Aborigines Protection Society, that took an interest in the welfare of the indigenous peoples of the British Empire. The result of these forces was the adoption by the Indian Department of a new policy for dealing with indigenous peoples.[6]

After 1830, policy focused not on maintaining Indians as allies or economic partners, but on "introducing amongst them the industrious and peaceful habits of civilized life."[7] Accordingly, a state-sponsored "civilization" policy was developed in the 1830s in Upper Canada, in which Christian churches co-operated with the government and some First Nations leaders to promote sedentary agriculture, Christianity, and basic literacy. The first attempt to implement the policy occurred in the Coldwater-Narrows region between Lake Simcoe and Matchedash Bay, off Lake Huron, where the Indian Department and missionaries worked to settle First Nations in agricultural reserves and provide them with instruction in farming and basic schooling. By 1836, the experiment was a failure, leaving open the question of whether the "civilization" policy should be abandoned or refashioned. An overhaul of Indian policy was one of many areas of government action that fell victim to the confusion and uncertainty that engulfed the two Canadas in 1837–38 and during Lord Durham's mission. The uncertainty still prevailed when the Province of Canada was created.

As Macdonald was winning his first election in 1844, the governor of the colony was working energetically to bring some order out of the chaos into which the "civilization" program had degenerated by the early 1840s. In 1842, Governor General Sir Charles Bagot appointed a commission of inquiry to recommend changes in Indian policy. The gist of the report the Bagot Commission produced in 1844 was a confirmation that the "civilization" policy had failed and a recommendation of new policies that were ominous. The commission proposed that individual land ownership and use, rather than a communal approach, be promoted among the Indians of Upper Canada, and that steps be taken to tighten up expenditures on annual presents. Recommendations to reduce or eliminate the presents, which consumed more than half the amount the imperial government voted annually for Indian affairs in the Canadas,[8] appeared in reports of a series of inquiries between 1828 and 1844. On each occasion, however, Indian opposition and British desire to conciliate indigenous leaders during periods of international tensions with the United States in 1838 and the mid-1840s, prevented the abandonment of present-giving. Thus, the Bagot Commission's recommendation that Indians who became educated should no longer receive presents remained a dead letter.[9] The commission also concluded that Indian education through day schools was a failure and recommended substituting "manual labour schools," a type of boarding school, operated by Christian churches in partnership with the Indian Department.

Implementation of the Bagot Commission proposals was negotiated at a conference in Orillia in 1846, which was attended by First Nations chiefs, missionaries, and Indian Department personnel. An interesting aspect of the First Nations contingent was that it included leaders who were both chiefs of their bands as well as Methodist missionaries. More striking still was the fact that Mississauga Methodists such as Peter Jones (Kahkewaquonaby, or Sacred Feathers) and John Sunday strongly advocated the adoption of manual labour schools. Most significant of all was the fact that the chiefs agreed not only to accept residential schools, but to support their operation with one-quarter of their annuities for twenty-five years. They were opposed, however, to other parts of the department's program. They rejected a proposal to settle in compact settlements, fearing doing so would cause a loss of yet more of their traditional lands to farmer immigrants. Upper Canadian First Nations had earlier articulated their opposition to restrictions on annual presents, rendering that commission recommendation, like compact settlement, a mute letter. What did remain to be implemented, however, were a continuation of the "civilization" program in general and the introduction of the new residential schools in particular.[10]

The short-term fate of the consensus at Orillia on manual labour schools would prove a foreshadowing of the Dominion of Canada's sad experience with residential schooling. Although Mississauga and Iroquois leaders, including especially missionary-chiefs like Peter Jones and John Sunday, had been strongly supportive initially, their enthusiasm soon cooled and turned to indifference or opposition. It is clear that First Nations leaders who agreed to support residential schools expected them to be a path to adjustment to a changing world, not instruments for involuntary cultural change. But the manual labour schools that were created in the 1850s pursuant to the Orillia agreement, quickly turned into oppressive engines of attempted assimilation operated by non-Native missionaries who had little respect for indigenous culture and identity. First Nations responded with passive resistance. In the 1850s they increasingly declined to make their children available to the missionaries who ran the manual labour schools. Another public inquiry lamented in 1856 that "It is with great reluctance that we are forced to the conclusion that this benevolent experiment has been to a great extent a failure."[11]

Sadly, the Province of Canada's experience with treaty-making was not much more successful than with the "civilization" policy. When the province began to function in 1841, its leaders inherited precedents for treaty-making rooted in the Royal Proclamation of 1763. By the 1840s, with almost all the arable land in Upper Canada covered by treaty, non-Natives' ambitions shifted northward to mineral-rich lands along the shores of Lake Superior and Lake Huron. No small part of the reason for this reorientation was awareness that the American government had negotiated a treaty in northern Michigan and American entrepreneurs were extracting riches from the resources there. Unwisely, the Province of Canada issued exploration and mining licences for lands beyond Sault St. Marie to prospectors and miners in the mid-1840s, without any effort to negotiate first with the First Nations whose lands they were. Indigenous reaction took the form of remonstrance, petitions, and, eventually, armed ejection of a mining company from the region. Only then did the Canadian government begin to negotiate a treaty with the First Nations adjacent to Lake Huron and Lake Superior.[12]

The Robinson Huron and Robinson Superior Treaties of 1850 constituted an important evolution of treaty-making practice. It is interesting to note that the Crown's negotiator of these agreements, W.B. Robinson, would become Macdonald's partner only two years later in a spectacularly successful land speculation in farmlands in the south.[13] The 1850 treaties with northern Ojibwa contained the customary provisions for annual compensation to the First Nations for access to their lands, but they also had some significant new features. An important feature of the Robinson Treaties was the escalator clause; it specified that, if resource revenues from the lands in question became sufficient, the Crown would increase the annuities. The creation of reserves was tied directly to a treaty. While there had been reserves in Upper Canada earlier, these had been established apart from treaty-making. Perhaps most significant of all was a novelty in the Robinson Treaties concerning gathering rights. The 1850 agreements explicitly recognized the First Nations' continuing right to hunt and fish on the lands and waters that now were covered by treaty. The First Nations would continue to have "the full and free privilege to hunt over the territory now ceded by them, and to fish in the waters thereof as they have heretofore been in the habit of doing ..."[14]

Reserves and recognition of gathering rights — but not the escalator clause — would become enduring features of treaty-making. Those elements, in addition to the fact that the Robinson Treaties dealt with much larger areas than the earlier Upper Canadian treaties, would form a template for the government in negotiating treaties after 1867. The Robinson Treaties, said federal treaty commissioner Alexander Morris, "were the forerunners of the future treaties, and shaped their course."[15] In the short term, though, the Canadian government learned nothing from its experience between 1846 and 1850 in the north, a prelude to negotiation of the final pre-Confederation treaty. The Manitoulin Island Treaty of 1862 again failed to consult First Nations before authorizing the activities of non-Native interests, in this case fishers, until a confrontation led to negotiations. In treaty-making, as in educational policy, pre-Confederation Canada was a slow learner.

By the time Macdonald was emerging as a potential party leader in the late 1850s, he had begun to play a direct and visible role in Indian policy formation. The Attorney General West rose in the Canadian Assembly in 1857 to introduce a dramatic development in the colony's evolving Indian policy. Macdonald argued that the *Gradual Civilization Act* was a vital step forward in promoting "civilization" of the indigenous people. The bill asserted it was "desirable to encourage the progress of Civilization among the Indian Tribes in this Province, and the gradual removal of all legal distinctions between them and her Majesty's other Canadian Subjects." The measure also averred that it would "facilitate the acquisition of property and of the rights accompanying it." In pursuit of those ends, the statute created the means to usher Indians into full citizenship.[16] The act contained a legal definition of "Indian," and established criteria to determine if a First Nations person was ready to assume "full citizenship." If an adult male could convince a board of examiners that he was educated, debt-free, and of good moral character, he would qualify for a three-year period of probation. If his conduct during this trial were satisfactory, he and his family would be "enfranchised," meaning they lost Indian status and became citizens. The act also said that he was to get twenty hectares of reserve land as a freehold, or land with full title. The Attorney General West apparently saw the act as the embodiment of a carrot-and-stick policy. "The first step that could be taken," he said during debate, "was to let them have a piece of land, and to encourage habits of providence, by letting them know that, if they alienated their lands, they had nothing to fall back upon."[17] The *Gradual Civilization Act* created the institution of "enfranchisement," which hung like a Damoclean sword over status Indians from 1857 until 1985, when the *Indian Act* was amended to remove discrimination against women.

To First Nations, the *Gradual Civilization Act* was linked to other unsettling developments in the late 1850s. The next measure that assailed them concerned the annual presents that had been a bone of contention between First Nations and the Crown since 1816. Little had come of recommendations to reduce the outlay on presents from the 1810s through the 1840s but, in 1851, London decided that the presents were to be reduced gradually each year and eliminated in 1858.[18] This step obliterated the symbolic link between the Crown and First Nations that the latter valued deeply. Worse was to come two years later, when Britain, over the protests of First Nations, transferred jurisdiction over Indian affairs to the colonies. The Province of Canada, with its policies aimed at "civilization," now had full control, subject to no oversight, and with little likelihood of veto by Britain. In 1860, the First Nations of the Province of Canada were abandoned by the United Kingdom and left to the will of the settlers' legislatures.

First Nations chiefs, who assembled at a Great Council with Indian Department officials in Upper Canada in the early autumn of 1858, were threatened by the recent past and looming future. They took the opportunity to object to the *Gradual Civilization Act*, of which one chief said "there is nothing in it to be for their benefit, only to break them to pieces." And they also feared that the *Gradual Civilization Act* and the impending termination of annual presents would lead to abandonment. As they expressed their concern in 1858: "They do not wish to be given over from the Imperial Government to the care of the Provincial one…. If their Great Mother the Queen objects paying the Expenses of Maintaining the [Indian] Department they will consent to do so provided they are not transferred from the Great Mother's care to the Provincial authorities."[19] These complaints and proposals showed that First Nations understood the anti-tribal implications of the *Gradual Civilization Act* and wanted nothing to do with it or the legislators of the settler society that had foisted it on them. Unfortunately for them, Indian Department officials in Canada and policy-makers in London dismissed their fears and their offer. At the Great Council they were told brusquely that "the Civilization Act is no grievance to you," presents were ended, and jurisdiction over Indian policy was transferred to the colonies in 1860.

On July 1, 1867, the new Dominion of Canada inherited and adapted its Indian policy from the former Province of Canada. Under the written portion of the new state's constitution, the *British North America Act* (now *Canada Act*, 1867), jurisdiction over "Indians and lands reserved for the Indians" was assigned to the federal level. Thus, the Parliament of Canada became the creator and implementer of policies to deal with First Nations. In the critical areas of treaty-making, social development, and citizenship the federal government headed by the newly knighted Macdonald followed the plans laid down earlier in central British North America.

Nowhere in the young Dominion was Indian policy a more pressing matter than in the West. The acquisition of Rupert's Land, the Hudson's Bay Company territory, was a term of the Confederation bargain, and successful integration and development of the Northwest was essential if Canada was to thrive. But Macdonald's attitude toward the West was, at best, ambivalent. As he said in 1865, "I would be quite willing, personally, to leave that whole Country a wilderness for the next half century, but I fear if Englishmen do not go there, Yankees will, and with that apprehension I would gladly see a Crown Colony established there." It was fear of American expansionism that governed Macdonald's approach to the West. "If Canada is to remain a Country separate from the United States it is of great importance to her that they (the United States) should not get behind us and intercept the route to the Pacific. But in any other point of view it seems to me that that Country is of no present value to Canada."[20] So, the West had to be acquired quickly — the West which was still overwhelmingly "Indian Country."

• • •

Western treaty-making was an early, clear example of the continuity of Indian policy in the post-Confederation era. For Macdonald's government, deciding how to relate to the Aboriginal peoples of the North-West Territories was a critically important issue. One of the terms of union was a commitment to acquire Rupert's Land from the Hudson's Bay Company [HBC], which Canada did with Britain's assistance in 1869. In fashioning instruments to administer its new lands in the West, Canada initially fumbled badly. It proposed at first to govern the former HBC lands by means of an appointed governor and council, paying no heed to the Métis of Red River and their acquired rights. The resulting Red River Resistance of 1869–70 delayed the transfer of western lands from the HBC to Canada, encouraged American annexationists, and cost the Dominion a considerable amount of money. From this setback, Canada learned that it had to deal more intelligently with the mixed-descent population of Red River, and recognized the necessity to move cautiously in dealing with the First Nations. Friction between official representatives of Canada — first road builders and then an expedition-ary force under Sir Garnet Wolseley — and the indigenous peoples of the region between Kenora and Winnipeg made it clear that negotiations were essential with the original inhabitants to secure Canadian access to lands the Dominion supposedly had purchased from the Hudson's Bay Company.[21] That realization sparked a treaty-making initiative that would enormously expand Canada's influence in the West in the 1870s.

Between 1871 and 1877, Canada concluded treaties with six groupings of First Nations. The numbered treaties — Treaty 1 through Treaty 7 — covered all lands from northwestern Ontario to the foothills of the Rockies, and from the international boundary on the south to a line roughly midway up the present-day Prairie provinces. But it was only the scope of these treaties that was novel. In other respects they faithfully followed what had been laid down in the Upper Canadian treaties, particularly the Robinson Treaties. In return for the lands, Canada, in the name of the Queen, prom-ised initial monetary payments, annuities in perpetuity, reserves separate from areas of non-Native settlement, and several types of assistance with social and economic development. In most areas, agricultural aid was part of the bargain, as well as provision of Euro-Canadian schooling. In all treaty areas, a commitment similar to that in the Robinson Treaties was included to respect continuing hunting and fishing rights. Only in Treaty 6 (1876) were two additional commitments made, promises that responded to the anxiety the Plains Cree of the region were feeling about the decline of the bison. Treaty 6 contained a "famine clause" that promised government aid in the event of a national famine, as well as a "medicine chest clause" that First Nations believed promised medical aid should there be a return of the epidemics that had scoured the plains until 1871. While government quickly came to view the treaties as contracts for the acquisition of Aboriginal land, western First Nations saw them as covenants involving them, the Queen, and the deity. Moreover, they saw the purpose of treaty-making as establishing a kin-like relationship with the Queen's people that would guarantee peaceful relations and mutual support.[22]

Treaty-making was prefatory to post-Confederation policy that aimed, according to the government in 1871, "to lead the Indian people by degrees to mingle with the white race in the ordinary avocations of life."[23] In practice this goal was pursued by means of schooling and enfranchisement according to the untested belief that the former would bring about the latter. There was no empirical evidence for the belief. Under the 1857 *Gradual Civilization Act*, only one First Nations male had applied for enfranchisement. Elias Hill, a graduate of the Mohawk Institute, a residential school in Brantford, Ontario, had applied, been examined, and was pronounced deserving of full citizenship. But then the complications began. Under standard practice, the government would get Hill's band to agree to surrender twenty hectares (fifty acres) of reserve land so that it could be conveyed to Hill as a freehold tenure. Hill's band steadfastly refused to acquiesce, and after many years Hill received only a cash payment in place of the land. Needless to say, such an experience did not encourage other educated First Nations men to apply for enfranchisement. Between 1857 and 1876, Hill's unhappy case was the sole example of enfranchisement under the *Gradual Civilization Act*.

Whatever the concrete results of the 1857 act, the post-Confederation Conservative government showed no inclination to move away from this mechanism for enfranchisement. In fact, the early tinkering with this portion of Indian policy only made matters more complicated. An 1869 statute reiterated the definition of "Indian" that had appeared in the 1857 act, but "stiffened" it by adding what was known in American Indian law as a "blood quantum." Henceforth, "no person of less that one-fourth Indian blood" would be eligible to receive annuities. Effectively, such a person would not be an Indian.[24] More important in the short run was Parliament's passage of a *Gradual Enfranchisement Act* in 1869 that introduced more, and more serious, gender discrimination against women. The 1869 statute stated that henceforth any woman with Indian status who married a man who did not have status, would lose hers. Moreover, all their offspring would be non-status. Although there appeared to be some support for this gender discrimination among Algonkian bands in Ontario, the measure provoked strong opposition from matrilineal Iroquoians, such as the Six Nations.[25] This malignant innovation, which effectively eliminated status for a large number of people, remained part of Canadian law until 1985.

The *Gradual Enfranchisement Act* also ventured into a new area of civil Indian policy. The 1869 measure purported to extend the blessings of British-Canadian governance to bands by providing for the election of chiefs and councils. The act set out a limited area of elective council jurisdiction, and provided that bands could retain their system of "life chiefs" for the time being. But it also empowered the federal minister to remove "life Chiefs ... for dishonesty, intemperance or immorality."[26] The parallels with pre-Confederation legislation about enfranchisement were striking. Concerning governance, too, non-Native legislators were presuming to prescribe what was best. And, as with enfranchisement, provisions about band governance would become more intrusive and onerous over time.

• • •

Thus, before Macdonald lost power in 1873, his government had laid down the foundation of Canadian Indian policy largely by adapting pre-Confederation Province of Canada legislation. It was left to the Reform government of Alexander Mackenzie to codify the various statutes embodying First Nations policy in the *Indian Act* of 1876. What innovation there was to the *Indian Act* was found in form rather than substance. In all essential features the 1876 statute replicated measures that been developed since 1850. Indian status, enfranchisement, regulations concerning reserve lands and band governance, and limited provisions for schooling were the cardinal features of the *Indian Act*. These policies and the well-established tradition of treaty-making with First Nations concerning their lands, which had its origins in the Royal Proclamation, were the main elements of First Nations policy a decade after Confederation.

When Macdonald returned to power in 1878, he chose the portfolio of the Ministry of the Interior. With this department, which had been created only in 1873, came the position of superintendent general of Indian Affairs, or more simply minister of Indian Affairs. As he explained to Edgar Dewdney in 1881, the post was critically important. Although he was old and sometimes ailing, he declared that "I have no intention of giving up my present Department so long as I remain in the Government. Routine matters may be attended to by the permanent Heads, but Indian matters, and the land granting system, form so great a portion of the general policy of the Government that I think it is necessary for the First Minister, whoever he may be, to have that in his own hands."[27] Although he accepted the role at an especially critical time in the development of policy, Macdonald was completely at home in the offices that administered Indian Affairs. Not the least of the reasons for his comfort in Indian Affairs was the fact that his deputy minister was Lawrence Vankoughnet (who had joined the pre-Confederation Indian Department in 1861, became chief clerk in 1873, and then succeeded to the deputy ministry the following year), who was a family friend as well as an experienced administrator. Ties between minister and deputy would be strengthened in 1883, when Macdonald's son Hugh John married Agnes Gertrude Vankoughnet.[28] Vankoughnet presided over a small "inside service" in Ottawa consisting of thirty-eight employees, including part-time clerks. Given the small size of the office and the deputy minister's conscientious — not to say obsessive — habits, Vankoughnet was fully conversant with all aspects of Indian Affairs. If anything, creation of Indian Affairs as a separate department of government in 1880 would have likely made Vankoughnet's sway even greater.[29] Vankoughnet played a vital role in the development and execution of policy until his retirement in 1893.[30]

Edgar Dewdney, whose term as Indian commissioner (1879–88) coincided almost exactly with Macdonald's ministerial role, was another key figure in Indian policy while Macdonald was minister. The English immigrant and sometime member of Parliament for a British Columbia riding by the late 1870s had become a "close friend and confidant" of his leader, and had considerable influence in the shaping of policy in his role as commissioner.[31] Since Dewdney was located in the North-West, it was almost inevitable that friction would develop between him and the centralizing deputy minister Vankoughnet. A clash between the two, following Vankoughnet's 1883 trip to the West, raised the issue of centralized control of policy and personnel versus local direction. Unfortunately, Macdonald never resolved the dispute, and tensions between deputy minister and commissioner continued for some years.[32] Macdonald presided somewhat uneasily over a troika of leadership in Indian matters after 1878.

• • •

Macdonald's choice of portfolio in 1878 reflected and responded to the challenge of developing the recently acquired West. Without a thriving prairie region, could the transcontinental railway that Macdonald thought so important be successful? "Until this great work is completed, our Dominion is little more than a 'geographical expression,'" he observed in 1878. "We have as much interest in B. Columbia as in Australia, and no more. The railway once finished, we become one great united country with a large inter-provincial trade, and a common interest."[33] Absent a prosperous West and a profitable railway through it, Canada was unformed, weak, and vulnerable — especially to American expansionists. It was little wonder, then, that most of the first decade after the Old Chieftain's return to power saw him serving as the political head of Indian Affairs. Without success in dealing with the Indians of the West, settlement would not occur, the railway would not flourish, and the future of a transcontinental Canada would be imperiled. The importance of the West in Indian Affairs during Macdonald's tenure as minister was reflected in the departmental budget. By 1890, Indian Affairs was spending 94 percent of the money Parliament allocated to it in Manitoba, the North-West Territories, and British Columbia.[34]

In shaping First Nations policy in 1878 and beyond, schooling would be a key element. Macdonald thought this was especially necessary in the North-West Territories. "You cannot judge the wild nomad of the North-West by the standard of the Indian of Ontario," he argued. The two groups of First Nations would be treated differently by his government.[35] Canada had inherited commitments to provide educational assistance to western

Indians in the numbered treaties, but even beyond this immediate pressure there was a well-established tradition of supporting several of the Christian churches' day and boarding schools in the eastern provinces. Macdonald, like Canadians in general, approached the task of fashioning a schooling policy with a complicated set of suppositions. Their perception was based on an assumption of cultural superiority and a belief in the potential of indigenous peoples to adapt to Euro-Canadian ways. In other words, their approach was culturally, rather than racially, inspired. If that were not the case — if the differences between First Nations and settlers were the product of "race" — as that loaded term was understood in the nineteenth century — there would be no point in providing them with missionaries, schools, and agricultural instruction. Like most Canadians, Macdonald believed there was significant potential in doing so. As he said once in Parliament, "The general rule is you cannot make the Indian a white man.... You cannot make an agriculturist of the Indian. All we can hope for is to wean them, by slow degrees, from their nomadic habits, which have almost become an instinct, and by slow degrees absorb them or settle them on the land. Meantime they must be fairly protected."[36] This approach dominated Macdonald's Indian policy.

Although six of the seven numbered treaties promised the First Nations a "school on reserve" (the seventh promised only the provision of teachers), the new policy put residential schools front and centre. In 1879 Macdonald appointed Nicholas Flood Davin, Tory newspaperman, future Regina editor, and member of Parliament, as a one-man commission to recommend a Native schooling policy. He concluded what the federal government was already being told by church leaders: day schools were not effective and should be avoided in favour of custodial schools. Davin's rationale for the residential schooling policy rested in large part on an American model, the Carlisle School in Pennsylvania, whose proprietor was known for his policy of "aggressive civilization." Davin recommended that "industrial schools" should be adopted in the North-West Territories for both First Nations and Métis, and that they should be operated by the Christian churches. Given the complexity of the issue and other pressing matters such as chartering the new transcontinental railway, it was several years before a new Macdonald government launched the policy with the creation of one Anglican and two Roman Catholic schools in what are now Alberta and Saskatchewan.[37]

The new policy incorporated most, but not all, of Davin's recommendations. Although Davin had recommended that industrial schooling be provided for both First Nations and Métis children, the new schools officially were only for First Nations. In practice, that policy meant that the Department of Indian Affairs, established in 1880, would pay to support only the children of status Indian parents. In fact, the denominational body that ran the school picked up the cost of the schooling and subsistence of the small minority of students who were Métis. The theory underlying the new institutions was that industrial schools would be larger, better-supported financially by government, and more ambitious in their academic and vocational pedagogical objectives than the smaller and less academically inclined boarding schools that existed in a few locations in both western and eastern Canada. As time went on and disillusionment with the brave new experiment settled in with both government and some missionary bodies, the real differences between industrial and boarding schools would steadily diminish until, in 1923, Ottawa abolished the distinction and thereafter classified all such institutions as residential schools. Although the early decades of the industrial schools policy proved disappointing, the number of such institutions nevertheless spread through most of the Prairie West and into British Columbia in the 1880s and 1890s. The custodial schooling policy, established under Macdonald's leadership in Indian Affairs, would prove enduring, if toxic. These schools lasted until the late twentieth century.

Although Macdonald's views about schooling on the whole were conventional, in one respect he held unusual opinions. Like most middle-class Victorian Canadians, Macdonald saw education as a social elixir, providing a form of upward mobility for the population at large, and a means of acculturation for Aboriginal peoples in particular. Where the Tory leader parted company with some of his peers, though, was in his attitude toward educating girls. In common with many of the missionaries operating the new schools, he believed that it was critically important to school the nurturing female. The "children of the household are generally as much if not more influenced by the Mother's example and by the advice and instruction given them by her as they are by the example set them by the father." If male First Nations graduates of the industrial schools married untutored women, "the result will probably be that either they will themselves relapse in to savagery, or the progeny from these marriages following the example and teaching of the mother will not improbably adopt the life and habits of the pure Indian." Therefore, Macdonald argued to his colleagues in 1884, it was "of the greatest importance with a view to the future progress of the Indian race in the arts of civilization and in intelligence that every effort should be made to educate and train the young Indian females as well as the male members of the different Bands of Indians scattered through the Territories."[38] And a couple of years after the industrial schools were started, they were opened to girls as well as boys.

• • •

Since the assumption behind residential schooling was that education would serve an acculturating function that would lead First Nations to become more like Euro-Canadians, it is not surprising that policies dealing with governance were also prominent during Macdonald's tenure as minister. First Nations communities would evolve, with tutoring of their young in residential schools, to the point that they would be heading for full citizenship. At that point, according to official expectations, they would avail themselves of the voluntary program of enfranchisement to give up their Indian status and become full citizens. That being the case, how they would operate politically as citizens-in-training was an important consideration. The young Dominion had already laid the groundwork in governance in the 1869 *Gradual Enfranchisement Act.* That measure, which had effect only in the central provinces, provided that the government could "order that the chiefs of any tribe, band or body of Indians shall be elected." It did, however, agree that "life chiefs" would not ordinarily be disturbed in office. But any chief, life or hereditary, could be removed if dishonest, intemperate, or immoral.[39] These provisions were incorporated into the 1876 *Indian Act,* although the government took advantage of the codification of legislation to lengthen the list of deficiencies for which life chiefs could be deposed to embrace "dishonesty, intemperance, immorality, or incompetency."[40]

During Macdonald's tenure as head of Indian Affairs, the experimentation in governance continued. An 1880 amendment enabled DIA officials to impose Euro-Canadian electoral practices on a band — whether it wanted them or not.[41] A major step came with the 1884 *Indian Advancement Act,* a measure intended mainly for the First Nations of central and eastern Canada, who were viewed as being more acculturated and likely to work more effectively with elective institutions. The measure provided that bands designated by the government would elect their chiefs and councils in annual elections, and would also enjoy slightly broader jurisdiction than was provided for band governments by the *Indian Act*. Simultaneously, the 1884 statute kept band governments under close supervision by providing that the agent would preside over the deliberations.[42] The *Indian Advancement Act* was consistent with the generally accepted view that First Nations were capable of making "progress" toward full citizenship, if properly tutored.

The same thinking permeated Macdonald's inclusion of limited voting rights for some Indians in his monumental 1885 *Franchise Act*. The prime minister considered this statute an extremely important measure; he described it as "the greatest triumph of my life" to political confidant Sir Charles Tupper.[43] It would serve as the capstone on the edifice of nationalizing the former colonies into one political community by making uniform federal provisions for voting. It would also ensure that a vigilant leader, such as he, could use appointment of the officials responsible for revising voting lists as another powerful tool for holding supporters to his party.[44] What startled many observers at the time, however, was that the bill granted the vote in federal elections to adult Indian males who met the property qualification. In the face of protests, Macdonald compromised by restricting the provision to Indians east of Manitoba. As Donald Smith has noted, the 1885 *Franchise Act* allowed eastern First Nations to obtain the vote in federal elections without giving up their Indian status.[45] Considering the context in which the bill was debated and adopted, this inclusion of some Aboriginal people was remarkable. Much of the debate coincided with the Northwest Rebellion, and opposition Liberals did their utmost to exploit the superheated emotions that existed at the time over the insurrection. They accused the Macdonald government, for example, of making it possible for bloodthirsty Indians to go "from a scalping party to the polls."[46]

All the same, the willingness of the Conservative government to include eastern Indians in the bill's provisions was noteworthy. So, too, was the language Macdonald used in defending the First Nations clause of the *Franchise Act* against Liberal criticism. There was nothing equivocal or half-hearted about Macdonald's case for a limited First Nations franchise. "So I say that the Indians living in the older Provinces who have gone to school — and they all go to school — who are educated, who associate with white men, who are acquainted with all the principles of civilization, who carry out all the practices of civilization, who have accumulated round themselves property, who have good houses, and well furnished houses, who educate their children, who contribute to the public treasury in the same way as the whites do, should possess the franchise."[47] In other words, First Nations policies, such as schooling, were intended to promote acculturation, and those who became acculturated through education and other means should be given some of the rights of citizens. The criteria of satisfactory cultural adjustment were clear: education, Euro-Canadian lifestyle, ownership of private property, and a stake in the political community. While such views might seem narrow and old-fashioned in the twenty-first century, in 1885 they were more progressive than those of many in the Canadian mainstream. There was little doubt about that fact, given the vituperative Liberal speeches on the *Franchise Act*.

Macdonald's relatively enlightened attitude on Indian voting and female schooling was not matched by his response to First Nations' restiveness in the West. In fact, even prior to the *Franchise Act*, Dominion policy toward North-West First Nations leaders had begun to turn in a harsher direction.

There had always been a tough foundation beneath the individual policies: First Nations would move toward Euro-Canadian ways and put behind them their distinctive identity, culture, and practices. Indian Commissioner Hayter Reed expressed this view late in Macdonald's tenure as superintendent general: "The policy of destroying the tribal or communist system is assailed in every possible way, and every effort made to implant a spirit of individual responsibility instead."[48] Macdonald was only a little less blunt during his final year as minister: "The great aim of our legislation has been to do away with the tribal system and assimilate the Indian in all respects with the inhabitants of the Dominion, as speedily as they are fit for the change."[49] The problem was that by the late years of Macdonald's superintendency, it was becoming clear that there was resistance or indifference to the supposed benefits of the government's policies among many in Indian Country. Voluntary enfranchisement did not occur in significant numbers, and many band councils continued to prefer their hereditary or "life chiefs" to the elected variety that the Department of Indian Affairs favoured.

Because of disappointment at the results of its policies, the government turned increasingly to coercion in the mid- and late-1880s. By 1883, the federal government had begun to flex its muscles with First Nations. In the West, even though the post-treaty transition to reserve life and farming was going poorly, thanks in large part to the government's wretched delivery of things that had been promised to the First Nations in treaties, retrenchment set in. In 1879, the collapse of the bison economy left Plains First Nations especially vulnerable to government pressure. Macdonald was apprised of the looming crisis as early as 1878, and by 1879 was sufficiently convinced by the warnings to signal it would be necessary to provide help:

> The rapid disappearance of the buffalo, which is the staple article of food of the Indians and half-breeds of the North-West Territories, induces the belief that these people must in a few years be fed at the expense of the country, unless they in the meantime acquire some other means of subsistence than the buffalo hunt now affords. In order to enable them to become self-supporting as soon as possible, facilities must be provided by which they may acquire some practical knowledge of agriculture and of the care of stock. They will probably require some small supply of provisions each year while they are engaged in tilling and sowing their lands.

At the same time, he indicated that aid would not be liberal: "Such assistance, however, should only be extended to those Indians who prove to be in earnest in endeavouring to become self-subsisting."[50] Government would decide if bands were "in earnest" in farming.

Macdonald dealt with the growing problem in the West with a mixture of assistance and menace. Arrangements were made for Indian agents to dispense food as necessary and, in 1880, he told Parliament, "It is better to feed them than to fight them, and I know no other way of doing this" than by "induc[ing] the Indians to cultivate the soil."[51] On the other hand, food was also used as a weapon. Leaders of First Nations who had refused to conclude treaties, such as Big Bear (Mistahimusqua), were effectively starved into signing, as Big Bear did in 1882. And in spite of the hardship that existed by

1883 — Lawrence Vankoughnet toured the West that year and returned to write what Macdonald described privately as "an uncomfortable report" on conditions[52] — parts of the DIA budget were trimmed (although the overall allocation increased because of the investment in new industrial schools). Indian Affairs exploited food as a weapon, instituting a policy of "no work, no rations" on the western reserves. These measures were inspired largely by the advice of Indian Commissioner Edgar Dewdney, who viewed an emerging First Nations diplomatic offensive with alarm. As the commissioner observed the efforts of chiefs such as Big Bear and Piapot to unite chiefs of the scattered bands into a force that would press the government for improvement of the treaties, he concluded that the government must stop the movement and subdue the leaders.[53] The ranks of mounted police in the North-West Territories were increased in 1884, and the *Indian Act* was amended in coercive and interfering ways. Limitations were placed on ammunition that could be supplied to Plains First Nations; Pacific coastal peoples found the potlatch, their socially important winter ceremony, prohibited.[54]

When the Northwest Rebellion broke out in the spring of 1885, Dewdney — with Macdonald's acquiescence — moved to exploit the insurrection in order to crush the Plains Cree's diplomatic offensive. During the troubled days of that spring, Dewdney created an extra-legal pass system with a proclamation that all First Nations in the North-West must remain on their reserves or be treated as rebels. After the rebellion had been quashed, the proclamation evolved into a policy that required Plains Indians to obtain a pass signed by their Indian agent or be found illegally off their reserves. Macdonald was aware that various proposals to restrict First Nations mobility had been considered since 1882, though it was also clear that such interference with movement was a violation of treaty promises. Such qualms disappeared in the spring of 1885. A pass system that had no basis in either legislation or executive order was implemented notwithstanding treaty commitments.[55] After the Métis insurrection, the federal government fabricated reasons to attack the leadership of the Plains Cree. Although they, and other prairie First Nations, had not supported the rebellion, Ottawa used the courts and administrative measures to hobble them. Even before the rebellion, Macdonald had offered "to write Stipendiary Magistrates as to long terms of punishment at certain seasons" to counter "those Indians who incite others to disorder."[56] Afterward, important leaders such as Big Bear and Poundmaker, neither of whom had been guilty of rebellious behaviour, were tried, convicted, and incarcerated.[57] Other bands were declared "disloyal" and subjected to a series of measures such as loss of horses and weapons, abolition of their governing institutions, and even non-recognition of the bands themselves.[58] Macdonald summarized his policy bluntly: "The execution of Riel and of the Indians will, I hope, have a good effect on the Métis and convince the Indians that the white man governs."[59]

These actions were taken *even though* Macdonald knew that the role of First Nations in what was a Métis insurrection, inspired and led by Louis Riel, was minimal, uncoordinated, and often undertaken by some members of bands against the wishes of civil chiefs such as Big Bear. The criminal courts were used aggressively: more First Nations men were tried than Métis, innocent chiefs were imprisoned, and a public mass hanging of Indian murderers at Battleford was designed to intimidate the First Nations. Some twenty-seven bands were declared "disloyal" and subjected to a range of sanctions. And all of this was done, as the prime minister explained to the governor general, for reasons of state policy rather than justice. "We have certainly made it [the rebellion] assume large proportions in the public eye," Macdonald wrote to Lansdowne. "This has been done however for our own purposes, and I think wisely done."[60]

Given the impact of the Northwest Rebellion, it is not surprising that the last years of Macdonald's leadership of Indian Affairs were marked by harsh new policies, especially toward western First Nations. In addition to maintaining such draconian measures as the ban on the potlatch on the North-West coast and the extra-legal pass system on the Prairies, the Department of Indian Affairs began to push some ideologically driven policies in the area of economic development on western First Nations. There already were systems of surveillance and control on the economic behaviour on these reserves, of course. For example, the permit system, a provision in the *Indian Act*, required a reserve farmer to get signed authorization from the Indian agent to transport reserve produce to town for sale. Officially, the motive for this measure was paternalistic — to protect reserve farmers from being taken advantage of by unscrupulous non-Native merchants, including alcohol peddlers. Unofficially, the permit system also provided another check on reserve residents' mobility. In the latter years of the 1880s, the permit system would be joined by two other notorious, and notoriously damaging, policies.

• • •

Individual ownership of parcels of reserve land has long been — and is still — an obsession of Canadian governments and some of the social engineers that advise them. Since the 1830s in Upper Canada, bureaucrats had been encouraging adoption of ownership in fee simple by occupiers of tracts on reserves in the belief that private ownership would create an incentive to improve the lands and use them efficiently, thereby enhancing productivity of reserves and the material well-being of reserve residents. In other words, governments believed that by owning land as Euro-Canadians did, First Nations would assimilate economically and throw off their dependence on the state for assistance. The problem was that individual ownership in fee simple ran up against the communitarian mores of First Nations, who preferred communal approaches to individualist ones. Individual land ownership was perceived as just another example of the non-Native majority's desire "to break us to pieces," as a Mohawk chief had complained of the 1857 *Gradual Civilization Act*. Therefore, most First Nations ignored or resisted the efforts to get them to shift toward individual ownership. On some reserves individual use within a framework of group ownership of reserve lands developed. The introduction of location tickets in the 1869 *Gradual Enfranchisement Act*, which identified rights of usage for particular tracts with specific residents, went largely unremarked.[61] Some groups chose to adopt location tickets, others did not, and reserve life went on as it had.

In the more coercive post-rebellion era, such a laissez faire approach to the promotion of possessive individualism would no longer do. Fortunately for Canada's Department of Indian Affairs, a solution was in sight. In 1887, the U.S. Congress adopted what was known as the Dawes Plan, a program to impose private property ownership on Native Americans that was inspired by the same ideological assumptions as prevailed in non-Aboriginal Canada. The following year, the Dominion introduced what it called "severalty" into the *Indian Act*.[62] Like the American system, severalty provided for subdivision of reserve land into individual tracts. Unlike the American approach, the Canadian scheme was voluntary: severalty required the concurrence of the band council because Canada had a well-established convention, grounded in the Royal Proclamation and embodied in the *Indian Act* since its inception, that not even the state could take Aboriginal-controlled land without the agreement of its owners. The consequences of the different approaches of the countries were striking. In the U.S., the Dawes Plan worked enormous harm on western Native American groups, with millions of acres wrested from tribal control and often sold to non-Natives. In Canada, where few communities participated, reserves remained intact for another decade. When the assault on western reserves occurred between 1896 and 1913, it was by means of coerced and fraudulently obtained "surrenders" that paid lip service to the *Indian Act*, rather than severalty.

The final major policy of the Macdonald era was contemplated but not adopted until after Macdonald handed over the reins of Indian Affairs in 1887. Between 1889 and 1897, the department aggressively pursued a policy known as "peasant farming" on western reserves.[63] Officially, the rationale for this lunacy was "science," or what passed for it in the late nineteenth century. The prevailing view was that Aboriginal peoples went through a three-stage evolution — from savagery to barbarism to civilization. Specific forms of economic organization were associated with each stage, and it was believed by people such as Hayter Reed, the man who succeeded Dewdney as Indian commissioner, that First Nations had to go through each stage in order to succeed. Thus, First Nations recently settled on reserves should not try to leap to large-scale commercial farming with the mechanized equipment that their non-Native neighbours were beginning to adopt. Nor should they farm collectively like a minority of their neighbours, who increasingly turned to co-operatives for production, marketing, and consumption. No, if First Nations were to succeed they had to farm for a time like European peasants — on small tracts of land, raising limited volumes of grains and root crops with hand implements only. This approach was demanding — not to mention difficult to defend when everyone else was moving as rapidly as they could to mechanized production. Undoubtedly the "peasant farming" policy asked a lot of reserve producers, but "science" demanded it. The fact that the use of hand tools would limit production, thereby reducing complaints from pioneer farmers who objected to "subsidized competition" from reserve farmers, was incidental. Science was all.

Adopted two years before Macdonald's death, "peasant farming" would persist as department policy until 1897, provoking frustration, resistance, and hardship all the while. Although western First Nations objected to it and some Indian agents pointed out it was counterproductive, Hayter Reed, first as Indian commissioner and then as deputy minister from 1893–97, insisted on its retention. While there was not a lot of good news for First Nations in the election of the Laurier government and the appointment of Clifford Sifton as minister of Indian Affairs in 1896, Sifton's sacking of Reed in 1897 and the quick abandonment of "peasant farming" were undoubtedly two positive details. It was during the Laurier prime ministry, however, that the greatest and most damaging assault on western reserves occurred. As well, in 1898, at the behest of the Laurier cabinet, the limited provision for First Nations voting in federal elections east of Manitoba was repealed.[64] It is possible that for some First Nations with long memories, the Macdonald years, when the Old Chieftain was superintendent general of Indian Affairs from 1878 until 1887, might have seemed to be "the good old days" of government policy. As two scholars who examined Canadian Indian policy carefully noted, "Without his guidance, one is tempted to think that there might have been much more interference and experimentation with the Indian way of life and a much greater impetus toward integration than was the case."[65]

Though little-known, Macdonald's role in the development and implementation of Indian policy was extremely significant. He was the longest-serving minister of Indian Affairs in Canadian history, with involvement in Indian policy for over forty years. His first exposure to matters of land ownership, economic development, education, and governance occurred during the Union period, when the foundations of much of later policy were laid. In the 1850s, in particular, he would have become familiar with the treaty-making tradition based on the Royal Proclamation that had been taking shape since the 1780s. As Attorney General West, Macdonald moved the introduction and acted as government spokesman for the critically important *Gradual Civilization Act* of 1857. This measure created enfranchisement — jettisoning Indian status and adopting full British-Canadian citizenship — that would play a lengthy, damaging role.

• • •

In addition to the creation of post-Confederation Indian policy, Macdonald's career in Indian Affairs epitomizes a critically important feature of that policy's history. The persistence of John A. Macdonald in government symbolizes the continuity in Indian policy, the reality that post-Confederation Dominion policy was in large part a continuation of pre-Confederation Province of Canada policy. While there were departures after 1867, such as voting rights in the *Enfranchisement Act,* the wrong-headed governance provisions of the *Gradual Enfranchisement Act* (1869) and the permit system, other key provisions were carryovers. The examples of continuity included residential schooling, a fixation on individual land ownership on reserves, the partnership of church and state for delivery of social programs to Indians, as well as treaty-making and enfranchisement. As both an agent and symbol of the continuity in policy, Macdonald, superintendent general of Indian Affairs from 1878 until 1887, has much to teach us about Native-newcomer relations, as he does in most areas of Canada's public life.

Notes

1. The research on which this chapter is based was supported by several grants from the Social Sciences and Humanities Research Council of Canada and the Canada Research Chairs program. The section of this paper that deals with the 1868–76 period has benefited from my reading of a chapter on Indian policy in an unpublished manuscript by Ted Binnema. I am grateful to SSHRC, the CRC program, research assistant Carling Beninger, and Dr. Binnema for their assistance, as well as to Bill Waiser for reading and suggesting improvements to an earlier version.

2. Macdonald's nine and one-third years as superintendent general of Indian Affairs between 1878 and 1887 eclipsed the runner up, Liberal Charles Stewart, who in the 1920s served a total of eight and one-quarter years in the post. Government of Canada, Privy Council Office, *Guide to Canadian Ministries since Confederation,* Accessed May 6, 2010, *www.pco-bcp..gc.ca/mgm/1st.asp?lang=eng&=1.* Apparently Macdonald's successors have not been keen to highlight his role in Indian Affairs. The Old Chieftain is the only former minister of Indian Affairs whose portrait did not hang in the ministers' gallery of Indian Affairs in Gatineau, Quebec, in the mid-1990s. See Blair Stonechild and Bill Waiser, *Loyal Till Death: Indians and the North-West Rebellion* (Calgary: Fifth House Publishers, 1997), 241.

3. Joseph Schull, *Laurier: The First Canadian* (Toronto: Macmillan, 1965); D.G. Creighton, *Sir John A.Macdonald: The Young Politician* and *Sir John A. Macdonald: The Old Chieftain* (Toronto: Macmillan, 1952, 1955); J.K. Johnson, "John A. Macdonald: the Young Non-Politician," Canadian Historical Association, *Historical Papers* 6: 1 (1971), 138–53.

4. Royal Proclamation of 1763, in *British Royal Proclamation Relating to America, 1603–1763,* Clarence S. Brigham, ed., vol. 12 of *Transactions and Collections of the American Antiquarian Society* (Worcester, MA: American Antiquarian Society, 1911), 215–18.

5. For an account of the Upper Canadian treaties see J.R. Miller, *Compact, Contract, Covenant: Aboriginal Treaty-Making in Canada* (Toronto: University of Toronto Press, 2008), chapters three and four.

6. For the origins, contents, and evolution of the new civil policy, see John S. Milloy, "The Era of Civilization: British Indian Policy for the Indians of Canada" (D. Phil dissertation, University of Oxford, 1978).

7. Sir G. Murray to Sir J. Kempt, January 25, 1830, *British Parliamentary Papers*, (Irish University Press Series), "Correspondence and Other Papers Relating to Aboriginal Tribes in British Possessions," 1834, no. 617, 88.

8. J. Douglas Leighton, "The Development of Federal Indian Policy in Canada, 1840–1890," (PhD Dissertation, University of Western Ontario, 1975), 99, 110.

9. John Leslie, *Commissions of Inquiry into Indian Affairs in the Canadas, 1828–1858* (Ottawa: Indian and Northern Affairs Canada, 1985), 131–2, 17–18, 19–20, 40–1, 52–3, 84, 90–2, 104.

10. *Minutes of the General Council of Indian Chiefs and Principal Men*, Held at Orillia, Lake Simcoe Narrows, on the Proposed Removal of the Smaller Communities and the Establishment of Manual Labour Schools (Montreal: *Canada Gazette* Office, 1946), Baldwin Room, Toronto Reference Library, passim. Dr. John Leslie's conclusion about the outcome of the Bagot Commission is that its report only "set the civilization programme on a new and more optimistic course." *Commissions of Inquiry into Indian Affairs in the Canadas*, 106.

11. "Report of the Special Commissioners Appointed on the 8th of September, 1856, to Investigate Indian Affairs in Canada," *Journals of the Legislative Assembly of the Province of Canada*, 1858, vol. 16, appendix 21, unpaginated. On this pre-Confederation experiment in residential schooling — including attitudes of First Nations leaders, Orillia Conference, and 1850s implementation — see J.R. Miller, *Shingwauk's Vision: A History of Native Residential Schools* (Toronto: University of Toronto Press 1996), 77–85.

12. For the prelude and negotiation of the Robinson Treaties of 1850, see Miller, *Compact, Contract, Covenant*, 109–18.

13. Johnson, "Macdonald: The Young Non-Politician," 142.

14. The Robinson Superior Treaty, in Alexander Morris, *The Treaties of Canada with the Indians of Manitoba and the North-West Territories* (Saskatoon: Fifth House, 1991; originally Toronto: Belfords, Clarke and Co., 1888), 303. The gathering rights clause of the Robinson Huron Treaty had identical wording, ibid., 306.

15. Ibid., 16. Morris was the principal Crown negotiator of Treaties 3, 4, 5, 6, 1873–76.

16. *Statutes of Canada* (20 Vic, cap. 26), June 10, 1857, preamble. To follow Macdonald's involvement and contribution, see Province of Canada, *Journals of the Legislative Assembly*, vol. 15, Session 1857, liii, 48–49, 427, 455, 473–74, 589, 721.

17. Account of the May 15, 1857 Legislative Assembly session, in the *Toronto Globe*, May 16, 1857, 2.

18. Leslie, *Commissions of Inquiry into Indian Affairs*, 131–32.
19. Minutes of the Great Council, September 20–29, 1858, Records of the Department of Indian Affairs, RG 10, vol. 245, part 1, 145566, Library and Archives of Canada [Hereafter LAC.]
20. Macdonald to Edward Watkin, March 27, 1865, Sir John A. Macdonald Fonds, 511, 9–11 (reel C-24), LAC.
21. Miller, *Compact, Contract, Covenant*, 141, 145–46.
22. Ibid., chapter six.
23. William Spragge, Deputy Superintendent, Indian Affairs, Report of the Indian Branch of the Department of the Secretary of State for the Provinces, Annual Report for the year ended 1870, 4; Canada, *Sessional Papers (No. 23)*, 1871.
24. *Statutes of Canada* (32–33 Vic, cap. 6) 1869, clause 4.
25. Ted Binnema, "'Framed to Meet the Views of the Indians': The Development of the *Indian Act*, 1868–1876," (unpublished paper). Dr. Binnema relies on evidence from correspondence between the Indian Affairs branch and First Nations leaders, as well as minutes and resolutions of the Grand General Council of Ontario.
26. *Statutes of Canada* (32–33 Vic., cap. 6), 1869, especially articles 10 and 11.
27. Macdonald to Dewdney, May 10, 1881, Edgar Dewdney Fonds, Series 8 Macdonald correspondence 1878–1888, M-320, 389 (accessed March 14, 2012), Glenbow Archives.
28. "Macdonald, Sir Hugh John." In *Dictionary of Canadian Biography* online. University of Toronto Press, 2014. Accessed October 6, 2013, *www.biographi.ca/EN/index.html.*
29. Leighton, "The Development of Federal Indian Policy in Canada," 341–42 and 403.
30. Douglas Leighton, "A Victorian Civil Servant at Work: Lawrence Vankoughnet and the Canadian Indian Department, 1874–1893," Ian A.L. Getty and Antoine Lussier, eds., *As Long As the Sun Shines and Waters Flow: A Reader in Canadian Native Studies* (Vancouver: University of British Columbia Press, 1983), 104–19. John Leslie and Ron Maguire, *The Historical Development of the Indian Act,* 2nd ed. (Ottawa: Indian and Northern Affairs Canada, 1979), 73, say that the deputy's influence "climaxed" under Vankoughnet. "By the early 1880s, all major decisions were being made by this office."
31. Brian Titley, "Edgar Dewdney, 1879–1888," in his *The Indian Commissioners: Agents of the State and Indian Policy in Canada's prairie West, 1873–1932* (Edmonton: University of Alberta Press, 2009), 66.
32. Joyce Katharine Sowby, "Macdonald the Administrator: Department of the Interior and Indian Affairs, 1878–1888" (MA thesis, Queen's University, 1984), 124–29 and 136. Titley, "Dewdney," 73, takes a different view, holding that Macdonald sided with Dewdney.
33. Macdonald to Sir Stafford Northcote, May 1, 1878, in Joseph Pope, ed., *Correspondence of Sir John Macdonald,* (Toronto: Oxford, [1921]), 240–41.

34. Leighton, "Victorian Civil Servant," 111.

35. Canada, House of Commons, *Debates,* 1881, 1427, March 17, 1881 [discussing permit system.]

36. Ibid., 1880, 1991, May 5, 1880.

37. Miller, *Shingwauk's Vision,* chapter four.

38. Department of Indian Affairs, Annual Report 1884, *Canada Sessional Papers (No. 3) 1885,* 11; RG 10, Black Series, vol. 3675, file 11, 422–2, 17458, (draft) Memo to the Privy Council, December 30, 1884. As Richard Gwyn points out in relation to the initial draft of the 1885 *Franchise Act,* Macdonald's views on the status of women were enlightened for his times. *Nation Maker: Sir John A. Macdonald: His Life, Our Times. Volume Two: 1867–1891* (Toronto: Random House Canada, 2011), 519–22.

39. *Statutes of Canada* 1869 (32–33 Vic., cap. 42), article 10.

40. Ibid., 1876 (39 Vic., cap. 34), article 62.

41. Ibid., 1880 (43 Vic., cap. 28), article 72.

42. Ibid., 1884 (47 Vic., cap. 28).

43. Macdonald to Tupper, July 27, 1885, Macdonald Fonds, vol. 526, Letter book no. 23 (reel C-34), LAC.

44. Elections Canada Online, "A History of the Vote in Canada," Accessed October 1, 2010, *www.elections.ca/content.aspx?section=res&dir+his&document =c.* Gordon Stewart, "John A. Macdonald's Greatest Triumph," *Canadian Historical Review* 63, 1 (March 1982), 3–33.

45. Donald B. Smith, "John A. Macdonald and Aboriginal Canada," *Historic Kingston* 50 (2002), 17. Early drafts of the enfranchisement bill contained limited female enfranchisement, but the provision was dropped.

46. House of Commons, *Debates* 1885, 1850, May 4, 1885. See also Gwyn, *Nation Maker,* 419–20.

47. House of Commons, *Debates,* 1575, May 4, 1885. Macdonald went on to say, ibid., 1576, that the same could not be said of First Nations in the North-West.

48. Hayter Reed to superintendent general, October 31, 1889, Canada, *Sessional Papers (No. 12) 1890,* 165.

49. Return to an Order of the House of Commons, May 2, 1887, *Sessional Papers (No. 20b) 1887,* 37; quoted in Malcolm Montgomery, "The Six Nations Indians and the Macdonald Franchise," *Ontario History* 57, 1 (March 1965), 13.

50. Canada. *Sessional Papers (No. 7) 1878, Department of the Interior,* Macdonald's Report of the Deputy Superintendent General of Indian Affairs, April 10, 1879, 10–11.

51. House of Commons, *Debates,* 1941, May 3, 1880.

52. Macdonald to Dewdney, November19, 1883, Dewdney Fonds, 473, Glenbow Archives.

53. Stonechild and Waiser, *Loyal Till Death*, 62–64.

54. *Statutes of Canada* 1884 (47 Vic., cap. 27), especially sections 2 and 3.

55. Sowby, ""Macdonald the Administrator," 182–86.

56. Dewdney Fonds, Series 8 online, M-320, 546, Macdonald to Dewdney, February 23, 1885.

57. John L. Tobias, "Canada's Subjugation of the Plains Cree, 1879–1885," J.R. Miller, ed., *Sweet Promises: A Reader on Indian-White Relations in Canada*, (Toronto: University of Toronto Press, 1991), 220–32; Bill Waiser, "The White Man Governs: The 1885 Indian Trials," Barry Wright and Susan Binnie, eds., *Canadian State Trials. Volume III: Political Trials and Security Measures, 1840–1914* (Toronto: University of Toronto Press for the Osgoode Society for Canadian Legal History, 2009), 451–80.

58. Stonechild and Waiser, *Loyal Till Death*, 195–57, 214–32.

59. Dewdney Fonds, Series 8 online, M-320, 587, Macdonald to Dewdney, November 20, 1885, Glenbow Archives.

60. Macdonald Papers, vol. 23, 271–72, Macdonald to Lord Lansdowne, September 5, 1885; in Stonechild and Waiser, *Loyal Till Death*, 221. Concerning the government's manipulation of the Rebellion to defeat the Cree diplomatic offensive, see ibid., 145, 158–59, 169, 192–93, 195, 196, 198, 214–27, and 231.

61. E. Brian Titley, *A Narrow Vision: Duncan Campbell Scott and the Administration of Indian Affairs in Canada* (Vancouver, University of British Columbia Press, 1986), 9.

62. The most complete account is Sarah Carter, *Lost Harvests: Prairie Indian Reserve Farmers and Government Policy* (Montreal and Kingston: McGill-Queen's University Press, 1990), chapter six.

63. Ibid.

64. Montgomery, "The Six Nations Indians and the Macdonald Franchise," 16–24.

65. John Leslie and Ron Maguire, The *Historical Development of the Indian Act* 2nd ed. (Ottawa: Indian and Northern Affairs Canada, 1979), 51. Leslie and Maguire's judgment is based on their view that at a time "when a primarily agricultural society believed strongly in the perfectability [*sic*] of man, the Indian Affairs Department was guided by the essentially sceptical and conservative Sir John A. Macdonald." See also ibid., 73 and 86. The judgments of Sowby ("Macdonald the Administrator") and Gwyn (*Nation Maker)* are not dissimilar. Both conclude Macdonald was more tolerant and progressive about Indian matters than most of his contemporaries.

Chapter 12

Macdonald's Appetite for Canadian Expansion: Main Course or Leftovers?

BILL WAISER

Over half a century ago, John Bovey, who served for years as head of the British Columbia Archives, chastised Prime Minister Sir John A. Macdonald for his "temporizing policy" in the northern regions of the young dominion. That policy, according to Bovey, consisted of "doing nothing until more facts become known while doing nothing to ascertain more facts." The Macdonald government did not know "what to do about the remoter [*sic*] parts of the North-West Territories and in their ignorance and indecision … preferred to do nothing."[1] This interpretation influenced two generations of northern historians. Indeed, the standard story is that Macdonald did not really want any additional territory beyond the boundaries of the new Canada in 1867, and only moved to acquire the territory when the American shadow loomed over the region. And even after Canada acquired the territory, he did little, if anything, to expand the Canadian state into the region. It would appear, then, that Macdonald's sobriquet, "Old Tomorrow," was deserved in this case and that he was less of a nation builder then he is usually portrayed. "The practical watchword of [his] administration was economy," charged Bovey, a policy that "long survived the interment of Macdonald's bones."[2]

This assessment is too harsh. The story of the Canadian expansion beyond the boundaries of the original Canada is more nuanced, more complicated. Yes, Macdonald acted in response to the perceived American threat, but he was motivated by a vision of Canada that was not only transcontinental, but also reached to the North Pole. Yes, the Macdonald government can be criticized for doing little to secure the northern reaches of Canada, but so too did the British government — before it transferred the Arctic Archipelago to Canada — and so, too, did the American government after it purchased Alaska. It could even be argued that the failure of the United States to challenge Canadian control of the southern North-West Territories in the 1870s and 1880s — because it was believed in American circles that the Confederation experiment was doomed to fail and the Dominion would soon fall apart — justified Macdonald's inaction after his government accepted the gift of the Arctic islands. Despite Macdonald's policy, he continued to look for ways to exploit Canada's frontier regions. The Conservative leader had been a keen supporter of the Geological Survey of Canada, even before Confederation, and looked at the territory in terms of its potential. This so-called "doctrine of usefulness" is often associated with the Conservative National Policy. But as historian Craig Brown has argued,[3] it also found expression in the creation of Canada's first national park at Banff in 1885, and was more than a matter of simple resource exploitation. Quite simply, Macdonald believed that Canada's territorial inheritance would not only enable the young dominion to survive on the same continent with an aggressive United States but would also be the means to greatness.

• • •

One of Macdonald's most-quoted statements about Canadian acquisition of the North-West region was made in a letter to Sir Edward Watkin in March 1865. Watkin, as president of the Grand Trunk Railway, wanted to extend the rail line from the Atlantic to the Pacific and hence pushed for some form of British North American confederation. Macdonald was not as initially enthusiastic about the idea of a transcontinental nation. "I would be quite willing, personally," he observed on the eve of a trip to London to discuss the confederation agreement, "to leave that whole country a wilderness for the next half-century, but I fear if Englishmen do not go there, Yankees will."[4] These words nicely captured Macdonald's quandary

— how he was essentially bound by political necessity, and not personal enthusiasm, to Canadian acquisition of the North-West. He and his largely Montreal-based supporters subscribed to the old commercial empire of the St. Lawrence, while the drive to settle the British North-West was a Reform plan, spearheaded by George Brown, to satisfy Toronto's economic ambitions.[5] But if the Great Coalition of 1864 was to bring about constitutional renewal in place of deadlock, then territorial expansion into the western prairies had to be a planned feature of the Confederation deal (section 146 of the *BNA Act*). Even then, Macdonald was reluctant to assume control of such a large parcel of land. As Richard Gywn has observed in the first volume of his Macdonald biography, the Conservative leader was preoccupied, if not overwhelmed, with the problems of the United Province of Canada, and his interest in territorial expansion "varied from negligible to non-existent." His response, in Gywn's words, was "cautious to a degree."[6]

This caution was readily apparent in Macdonald's letter to Watkin. Despite his worry that the United States might one day intercept the route to the Pacific and thereby foil the entry of British Columbia into the Canadian union, Macdonald confessed to Watkin: "My own opinions are unchanged ... it seems to me that that country is of no present value to Canada. We have

Grip, 20 November, 1886.

"Another Fervent Appeal to the Breeches Pockets!"

unoccupied land enough to absorb the immigration for many years, and the opening up of the Saskatchewan would do to Canada what the prairie lands of Illinois are doing now — drain away our youth and strength."[7] Ontario expansionists, on the other hand, looked at the situation through a different lens. Believing that Canada faced a future of stagnation and uncertainty unless it was able to break out from the constraints of the Canadian Shield, expansionists like Brown had successfully transformed the image of the western interior by the late 1850s. Once dismissed in Canadian minds as a frozen wilderness, it was now regarded as a potential agricultural hinterland that would provide the means to empire and make possible sea-to-sea nationhood.[8] It was also an essential part of Canada's national inheritance — rightfully hers — because of the historic ties between the region and the old Montreal fur trade that ended with the amalgamation of the Northwest and Hudson's Bay companies in 1821. In fact, the prospect of an agricultural Eden in the West had such powerful appeal that the southern limit of the so-called fertile belt, once confined to the Saskatchewan country, was extended to the forty-ninth parallel.[9] But two obstacles stood in the way of this vision. One was physical — building a reliable, all-Canadian transportation link north of Lake Superior between Central Canada and the North-West. The other was constitutional — annexing the West would necessarily mean a new political arrangement that would undermine the current equal balance between Canada West and East representation in the united parliament. Confederation consequently had to be achieved first, with adequate protections for the province of Quebec, before expansion westward could become a reality. Even then, expansionists were interested only in the fertile southern plains and generally ignored the vast and remote territory to the north. During the lengthy confederation debates, northern Canada was, surprisingly, briefly mentioned only twice in the speeches. There appears to have been some doubt about the wisdom of assuming responsibility for a country that would have increased by seven times the original Canada of 1867 (from 600,000 square kilometres to almost 4,800,000 square kilometres). It was the kind of empire that should have belonged to other, older nations — not a young dominion that would not have control over its external affairs.

What changed Macdonald's reluctance, and that of others, was the apparent threat of American encirclement. On March 30, 1867, one day after Queen Victoria signed the *BNA Act*, the United States and Russia signed an agreement for the purchase of Russian Alaska. This deal is often held up as the American response to Canadian confederation. After all, why did American secretary of state William Seward hurry through the negotiations in secrecy? But as historian Shelagh Grant has maintained in her new book on Arctic sovereignty, the timing was "a fortuitous coincidence."[10] Seward was more worried about internal American opposition to the purchase and wanted to announce the treaty as a fait accompli. Interestingly, one of Seward's most convincing arguments in favour of the deal was that it would effectively eliminate another foreign power from the North American continent and thereby remove a potential roadblock to American manifest destiny. The *New York Herald* agreed, reporting that the "deal would sandwich British Columbia between American territory and make inevitable its annexation."[11]

Even before Confederation became a reality, the United States seemed to have been manoeuvring to outflank the new dominion and threaten its future takeover of the North-West. Chief Justice Draper of Upper Canada had raised this prospect in 1857, when the future of the region was being debated in Canadian political circles. "If something is not done," he warned about American intentions, "that territory will in some way or another cease to be British Territory."[12] The American purchase of Alaska seemed to confirm Draper's prediction and was clearly upsetting for both Great Britain and Canada. Sir Frederick Bruce, the British ambassador in Washington, bluntly noted that "a step had been taken toward the absorption of the entire continent"[13]— probably echoing a similar statement by American Senator Charles Sumner that the Alaska purchase was "a visible first step' in the occupation of the whole North American continent."[14] Quebec East politician Alexander Galt was equally vehement about the implications of this new development. Just three weeks before Alaska formally came into being on June 20, 1867, he warned: "If the United States desire to outflank us on the West, we must lay our hand on British Columbia and the Pacific Ocean. The country cannot be surrounded by the United States — we are gone if we allow it.... We must have our back to the north."[15] In other words, since the United States was transcontinental, then Canada had to be transcontinental and expand, sooner rather than later, to the Pacific Ocean.[16]

Just how realistic this American threat was is debatable. Certainly, it became a constant refrain in Macdonald's verbal political arsenal. "The

Hudson's Bay question must soon be settled," he said during the negotiations to secure the North-West, "the rapid march of events and the
increase of population on this continent, will compel England and
Canada to come to some arrangement respecting that immense country."[17]
Macdonald also thundered during the 1869–70 Red River Resistance: "the
United States government are resolved to do all they can, short of war, to
get possession of the western territory and we must take immediate and
vigorous steps to counteract them."[18] But even though Secretary of State
Seward had continental ambitions that included the possible purchase
of Greenland, he believed that his dream could be achieved without the
resort to arms, that the territory stretching to the North Pole would fall
into the American lap.[19] This view was shared by many American officials
at the time, and was perhaps best elucidated by a July 1867 *New York
Times* editorial marking the creation of Canada: "When the experiment
of the 'dominion' shall have failed, as fail it must, a process of peaceful
absorption will give Canada her proper place in the Great North American
republic."[20] In retrospect, then, the threat alone was what really mattered.
As one scholar observed, "the confederation movement badly needed some
unifying sentiment," and the threat of American aggression underlying
the Alaskan purchase was "shrewdly used ... as a political lever to harmo-
nize the various prejudices and local interests which stood in the way of
a Canadian union."[21] The anxiety over what the United States might do
consequently helped bring the colonies together and led to the eventual
Canadian takeover of the North-West.[22]

When Canada finally secured control of the vast territory west of
Ontario in July 1870, the Macdonald government decided that agricultural colonization would best be focused on the southern prairies and
introduced a number of policies designed to facilitate that process (treaties, survey system, mounted police force, and transcontinental railway).
Indeed, successive Canadian governments up until the First World War
devoted considerable attention to the settlement of Manitoba and the
southern North-West Territories (later Saskatchewan and Alberta). The
remainder, a vast wilderness area stretching northwest and northeast to
the shores of the Arctic Ocean, Hudson Bay, and Labrador, was temporarily left in limbo by the Canadian state. This federal neglect was justified,
according to archivist Bovey, because it was cheap: "This obsession with

saving money, or more correctly not spending it, was to be a persistent theme in northern history once the region became part of confederation."[23] But the Macdonald government already had a formidable challenge in settling the western interior as long as the American settlement frontier remained open and the northern reaches of the territories were sparsely populated by Aboriginal peoples, relatively remote, and of questionable value. In fact, what often gets overlooked or ignored is that the United States did not do anything to challenge Canadian sovereignty directly in the region — despite Macdonald's dire warnings to the contrary. President U.S. Grant and Secretary of State Hamilton Fish genuinely believed that the Red River troubles were the beginning of the end of the dominion experiment, "that Confederation was disintegrating and that the soon-to-be-separate Provinces would almost immediately petition for annexation to the Republic."[24] Besides, the Americans were equally guilty of ignoring their new northern possession. Alaska had no government nor federal funding for seventeen years.[25] Although Macdonald regularly trotted out the American threat to Canada, he could confidently leave the northern territories alone for the time being. It was not a matter of being indifferent to the region, as some scholars have claimed; it was more a matter of concentrating on what was possible given the nation-building tasks at hand. What is often forgotten or overlooked is that during the last four decades of the nineteenth century, the dominion lost an estimated two-thirds of a million people, mostly to the United States. It was not until 1901 that more people came to Canada than left.[26]

The Canadian government next had the opportunity to extend the country's boundaries to include the Arctic islands when British officials unexpectedly raised the matter in 1874. Lord Carnarvon, the secretary of state for the colonies, had become worried about the status of the islands in response to a request for a mining licence on Baffin Island and quietly recommended that they be transferred to Canadian control. But the matter was complicated by the fact that neither the British nor Canadian governments knew exactly the boundaries of the territory in question. Officials in the Alexander Mackenzie government were also somewhat surprised because they had innocently assumed that the islands had been part of the Hudson's Bay Company territory that had been acquired in 1870. They were also uncertain if transfer was possible under section 146 of the *British North America Act* and wanted any transfer to be handled by an imperial act of Parliament.[27] Carnarvon, on the other hand, was worried about American designs on the region and, in the interests of urgency, suggested that an imperial order "would be quieter, faster, and more certain of passage."[28]

Because of the number of questions that hung over the transfer, it was not until May 1878 that the Mackenzie government finally introduced resolutions in Parliament (a Joint Address to the Queen from the Senate and House of Commons) calling on the British government to extend the northern boundaries of Canada to include the Arctic Archipelago.[29] The immediate response from an independent member was that Canada had enough territory to manage. But before David Mills, the minister sponsoring the resolutions, could reply, Macdonald, now sitting in the Commons as Leader of the Opposition, rose to the backbencher's challenge. He warned that the country faced the real prospect of encirclement if Canada did not assume responsibility for the islands: "[W]hen England had abandoned that country, and Canada was so faint hearted as not to take possession of it, the Americans would be only too glad of the opportunity, and would hoist the American flag and take possession of that territory." He continued: "An American was said to have boasted on the natural limits of the United States, that it was bound by Cape Horn and the Aurora Borealis; we must cut them out of that, we must extend our territory to that bright luminary." This sentiment, buttressed by Macdonald's assurance that the territory would not "cost Canada any more than it had cost England, until settlements were made there," appealed to the other members of Parliament, and the resolutions were unanimously approved.[30]

Macdonald's argument for acquiring the Arctic Archipelago clearly had its foundation in the late 1860s, when the American purchase of Russian America appeared to challenge Canadian acquisition plans in the North-West. Like then, the 1878 decision was a strategic one, meant to prevent the United States from moving into the North American attic and undermining the future vitality and well-being of Canada. It was also cheap — it would not cost anything to assume the British claim, according to the former prime minister, and the islands could probably be left untouched for years, if not decades, pending some kind of development.[31] But what was also striking about Macdonald's remarks regarding the need to assume control of the Arctic islands was the expression of a kind of Canadian manifest destiny. A decade and a half into the life of the Dominion, gone was the reluctance and hesitation that had characterized Macdonald's earlier, pre-Confederation position on territorial enlargement. He could now speak of Canada becoming master of all the northern half of the continent. It was a vision that stirred the imagination of other parliamentarians at the time, including those from Quebec. During the same debate, Hector Langevin, a prominent Conservative, argued that annexation of the archipelago was a natural or logical extension of Confederation. "The future greatness of this Dominion and its position on the continent," he told the House, "requires that from the boundary of the United States to the North Pole should be Canadian territory."[32]

The Arctic islands were officially transferred to Canadian control by order-in-council on July 31, 1880. By coincidence, Macdonald, having returned to power as prime minister, was in London at the time that the document was being drawn up and was consulted about a possible transfer date, effective September 1, 1880.[33] Much has since been made of the fact that the British government completed the transaction by order-in-council instead of passing an act that clearly defined the new northern boundaries of Canada. One scholar found the process nothing short of ridiculous: "The Imperial Government did not know what they were transferring, and on the other hand the Canadian government had no idea what they were receiving."[34] It would appear, though, that Macdonald was acutely attuned to the sensitivity of the matter, and that is why he dropped the original Canadian demand that the transfer be completed by an Imperial act of Parliament. During the 1878 Commons debate on the resolutions, he counselled "the less publicity ... the better," since the Americans were not above challenging the British claim.[35] It has also recently come to light that the British government knew exactly the limitations of its title, and that sober fact, and not any uncertainty, accounted for the British desire for speed and urgency. In fact, the documentation on the transfer was retained by the Colonial Office until 1921 in what appears to have been a deliberate attempt to keep the Canadian government in the dark about the shakiness of the British claim to the entire archipelago.[36] So, it is not fair to criticize Macdonald for accepting a territorial gift whose boundaries were so imprecise, especially when the transfer was being done at the initiative of the British government.

The transfer of the Arctic islands was supposed to settle the matter of Canada's northern boundaries. But when the federal minister of justice sought information about the new Arctic territory from the Hudson's Bay Company in 1882, the company sheepishly confessed that it knew very little about the region.[37] Faced with this lack of information, and already burdened with the task of settling and developing the Canadian prairies, the Macdonald government formally chose not to "legislat[e] for the good government of that country until some influx of population or other circumstance shall occur to make such provision more imperative than it would at present seem to be."[38] Northern historians have rightly claimed that this federal indifference would serve to weaken Canada's claim to the North, especially during the twentieth century.[39] The Macdonald's government northern policy, however, was "predicated on resource potential and costs [and] such costs could be justified only if there were valuable minerals or other resources worth protecting."[40] That is why Macdonald insisted that officers of the Geological Survey conduct field work in the more remote regions of the Dominion in the search for valuable minerals or other resource opportunities.

Macdonald's support of the Geological Survey of Canada actually predated Confederation. Faced with the disagreeable prospect of shutting down the survey because of the lack of funds, director Sir William Logan had turned to Macdonald in the spring of 1856 and secured his help, as attorney general for Canada West, in shepherding a new survey bill, with a larger appropriation, through the Legislative Assembly. "The time had arrived," Macdonald spoke of the practical benefits of the agency in defence of the increased grant, "when the survey should be carried out on a much larger and efficient scale. It was of great importance that the present generation should have the advantage of knowing the resources of this country — that those benefits should not be solely derivable by their children."[41] Eight years later, as the co-leader of a shaky coalition with Étienne-Paschal Taché, Macdonald performed the same duty on behalf of the survey, but this time made the agency not only permanent, but attached to a government department.[42]

The Geological Survey of Canada would become a key component of Macdonald's national development policies. Just how important, and in what capacity, was underscored by geologist Dr. George Mercer Dawson before a meeting of the Ottawa Field-Naturalists' Club when he called for fieldwork on practical grounds. "Explorations ... are absolutely essential to civilized society," he argued. Failure to examine "this great aggregate of territory" would stand "as a reproach to our want of enterprise and a justifiable curiosity."[43] This emphasis on positive, constructive information was a hallmark of government-supported exploratory work during the late nineteenth century. When Canada expanded westward and northward in 1870, and again in 1880, the new territory, with its diverse natural life, could have served as an important testing ground, a vast natural-history laboratory, for the celebrated British naturalist Charles Darwin's "theory of natural selection." But Darwin and his ideas were largely ignored in Canada.[44] Instead, government-sponsored scientific exploration was essentially Baconian in nature and concentrated on careful, methodical observation, listing, and description of resources in an attempt to discover their possible uses. Victorian Canadians put great faith in the problem-solving capabilities of science; scientific knowledge was equated with industry, progress, and manpower.[45]

This "inventory" science, with its emphasis on statistical information was precisely the kind of work that Canadian politicians could understand and therefore appreciate. The national development policies of the Macdonald governments (1867–73 and 1878–91) were based on the widely held assumption that Canada's resource wealth was unlimited and that if these resources were made "useful," then the country's great future was assured.[46] In fact, the Macdonald government expected the survey to provide simple, practical information that could be immediately used by private interests to unlock the resource wealth of the young dominion. The Conservatives did not believe in science for its own sake, but rather in the use of science to further economic growth and promote national strength and prestige — what one intellectual historian has described as "an entrepreneurial scientific ideology."[47] Since the federal treasury provided the funds for the survey, the Macdonald government insisted that it had every right to demand certain returns from the investment and expected positive constructive information.[48]

Macdonald's idea of the purpose of science, and the particular role of the survey, were perhaps best illustrated in February 1877, when the Mackenzie government introduced a new bill that, among other changes, formally broadened the mandate of the agency to include other areas of inquiry, such as natural history. The opposition leader reminded the House that "the survey was instituted, as its name indicated, for the purpose of making a geological survey of the whole country" and that the study of the country's flora and fauna should be "merely subsidiary and incidental," especially when there were not enough funds for this kind of work.[49] Macdonald did, however, implement one of the outstanding provisions of the 1877 *Survey Act* when he returned to office and transferred the survey offices from Montreal to Ottawa in the spring of 1881. This relocation, which brought the survey directly under federal control, was part of a general plan in the early 1880s to make the department an increasingly development-oriented agency that would help unlock Canada's seemingly unlimited resource wealth. To this end, the Macdonald government increased the annual appropriation by 20 percent in April 1882. The following year, it transferred the salaries of the survey's permanent officers to the civil service list, thereby making more of the annual budget available for field operations.[50] This improved financial situation enabled survey men to probe the more remote regions of the Dominion. During the 1880s, for example, Dawson toiled up the Yukon River, while Robert Bell roamed the Hudson Bay Lowlands and A.P. Low penetrated the interior of northern Labrador. The survey also embarked on a systematic aerial mapping program to produce a geological map of Canada (and its potential mineral deposits) on a scale of one inch to approximately 6.4 kilometres.

Macdonald's dismissal of natural history work as "secondary" to the real aims of the survey changed somewhat after he and his wife travelled to British Columbia on a Canadian Pacific Railway passenger train in the summer of 1886. (On that same trip, Lady Agnes Macdonald rode on the cowcatcher at the front of the CPR engine on a leg of the route from Lake Louise to Vancouver.) The journey west was Macdonald's first opportunity to see the natural wonders of the newly created reserve at Banff, and as he later told the House of his experience, "It is a place of ideal beauty."[51] The setting aside of Banff as a reserve in 1885, and then as Canada's first national park with the Rocky Mountains Park Act two years later, was a physical expression of the Macdonald government's "doctrine of usefulness."[52] The prime minister, according to historian Craig Brown, wanted to set aside the hot springs in the area as a commercial asset for the government and looked to developing the park into a world-class tourist attraction. "I do not suppose in any portion of the world there can be found a spot … which combines so many attractions and which promises … large pecuniary advantage to the Dominion," Macdonald lectured the House during the Commons debate over the creation of the park. "It has all the qualifications necessary to make it a great place of resort," he continued "and if carefully managed, it will more than many times recuperate or recoup the Government for any present expenditure."[53] What the prime minister had in mind to bring the area "into usefulness" was the building of a spa and bathhouses, a hotel, and a subdivision where people could lease property and erect villa-like structures (with suggested twenty-one-year leases).[54] He even allowed that "there may be places where the property may be used for industrial purposes without interfering with the beauty of the park as a whole."[55] Much like a promoter peddling some restorative elixir, Macdonald wanted to sell the scenery at Banff, including the flora and fauna, year after year.

That the creation of Banff was in keeping with the overall philosophy of Macdonald's National Policy has recently been questioned by environmental historian Alan MacEachern in *Natural Selections*, his study of national parks in the Maritimes. MacEachern contends that members of both sides of the House during consideration of the Banff bill viewed resource extraction as incompatible with national park status and leaned toward preservation.[56] But in reading the lengthy Commons debate, it is readily apparent from the discussion between parliamentarians on both sides of the House, including Macdonald, that they believed that wilderness alone did not make for a national park. The reserve had to be developed and managed — in other words, the landscape had to be made over into a park, needed improvements, before it could attract tourists. "The point is worth noting," observed Craig Brown, that "the reservation in its 'wilderness' state was *not* a park as that term was understood in the 1880s."[57] Or, as Macdonald himself put it so succinctly during the debate, "There is only one way of *making* that portion of the country what it *ought* to be." [emphasis added][58] And tourism and recreation were understood to be synonymous with national park status. In looking back at the acquisition of northern lands, first in 1870 and then 1880, it could be argued that the Macdonald government had acquired the vast territory for essentially negative reasons — to keep it out of American hands. Ottawa was genuinely worried that the United States would take advantage of any absence of an Anglo-Canadian presence in the region and looked to prevent such a calamity. But the territorial inheritance also gave rise to the widespread notion in the late nineteenth century that Canada was blessed with millions of acres that, in the words of a Conservative senator from Manitoba, had been "prepared by the hands of God for civilized man."[59] Any development, including government expenditure, in more remote territory, though, would largely have to wait until the southern prairies had been settled. As Senator L.G. Power declared on March 27, 1888, in response to the suggestion from one of his colleagues that Canada's great northland be colonized, "It will keep.... We have plenty of time before us." And he could have added thousands of homesteads waiting for prospective settlers in the southern North-West Territories. This "wait-and-see" attitude was certainly cheap, but it was also prudent under the circumstances — until time and resources were found that would reward immediate attention. The ensuing exploitation, as exemplified in the establishment of Banff National Park in 1887, would be shaped and informed by the idea of usefulness. That was Macdonald's consistent credo since Confederation and the one that makes best sense of his government's policies and actions in the ensuing decades. After all, leftovers are usually best the next day.

NOTES

1. J.A. Bovey, "The Attitudes and Policies of the Federal Government toward Canada's Northern Territories, 1870–1930" (MA thesis, University of British Columbia, 1957), 41.
2. Ibid., 27–28.
3. R.C. Brown, "The Doctrine of Usefulness: Natural Resource and National Park Policy in Canada, 1887–1914," in J.G. Nelson, ed., *Canadian Parks in Perspective* (Montreal: Harvest House, 1970), 55.
4. J.A. Macdonald to E. Watkin, March 27, 1865, quoted in J. Pope, *Memoirs of the Right Honourable Sir John Alexander Macdonald* (Ottawa: J. Durie, 1894), 398. [Hereafter *Memoirs*.]
5. See D.G. Creighton, *John A. Macdonald: The Young Politician* (Toronto: Macmillan, 1952).
6. R. Gwyn, *John A.: The Man Who Made Us* (Toronto: Random House, 2007), 215, 223.
7. Quoted in Pope, *Memoirs*, 398.
8. D. Owram, *Promise of Eden: The Canadian Expansionist Movement and the Idea of the West* (Toronto: University of Toronto Press, 1980), 59–78.
9. E.H. Oliver, ed., *The Canadian North-West, Vol. 2* (Ottawa: Government Printing Bureau, 1915), 958 [deed of surrender.]
10. S. Grant, *Polar Imperative: A History of Arctic Sovereignty in North America* (Vancouver: Douglas and McIntyre, 2010), 128. [Hereafter *Polar Imperative*.]
11. Ibid., 127.
12. Quoted in Bovey, "The Attitudes and Policies," 13.

13. Ibid., 128.
14. Quoted in A.W. Shiels, *The Purchase of Alaska* (Fairbanks: University of Alaska Press, 1967), 47.
15. Quoted in P.B. Waite, *The Life and Times of Confederation, 1864–1867: Politics, Newspapers, and the Union of British North America* (Toronto: University of Toronto Press, 1962), 306.
16. W.L. Morton makes this observation in *The Critical Years: The Union of British North America, 1857–1873* (Toronto: McClelland & Stewart, 1964).
17. J.A. Macdonald to Bischoff, October 17, 186, quoted in Pope, *Memoirs*, 398.
18. J.A. Macdonald to C.J. Bridges, January 28, 1870, quoted in J. Pope, ed., *Correspondence of John A. Macdonald* (Toronto: Doubleday, 1921), 124–24.
19. Grant, *Polar Imperative*, 118, 132.
20. Quoted in Gwyn, *John A*, 431.
21. D. Balasubramanian, "Wisconsin's Foreign Trade in the Civil War Era," *The Wisconsin Magazine of History* 46: 4 (1963), 262.
22. Grant suggests that "'Fear' was the common factor in both purchases." Just as fear prompted the United States to buy Russian America to keep it from falling into British hands, so, too, did fear prompt Canada to secure the Northwest. Grant, *Polar Imperative*, 137.
23. Bovey, "Attitudes and Policies," 55.
24. J.G. Snell, "American Neutrality and the Red River Resistance, 1869–1870," *Prairie Forum* 4: 2 (1979), 193.
25. Grant, *Polar Imperative*, 129.
26. W.P. Ward, "Population Growth in Western Canada, 1901–71," in John E. Foster, ed., *The Developing West* (Edmonton: University of Alberta Press, 1983), 158.
27. Ibid., 157–62; G.W. Smith, "The Transfer of Arctic Territories from Great Britain to Canada in 1880, and Some Related Matters, as Seen in Official Correspondence," *Arctic* 14: 1 (1961), 59.
28. Smith, "Transfer of Arctic Territories," 65.
29. The resolutions dealing with "The Northerly Boundaries of Canada" can be found in Canada, House of Commons, *Debates*, May 3, 1878, 2386.
30. Ibid., 2390.
31. Bovey, "Attitudes and Policies," 54–55.
32. *Debates*, May 3, 1878, 2391.
33. Grant, *Polar Imperative*, 166.
34. M.R. Howden, "Memo re the Arctic Islands," unpublished article, 1921, cited in Smith, "Transfer of Arctic Territories," 69.
35. *Debates*, May 3, 1878, 2390.
36. Grant, *Polar Imperative*, 167.
37. Ibid., 174.
38. This wording comes directly from Privy Council, No. 1839, September 23,

1882. A copy of the order-in-council was forwarded to the British Colonial Office. See Smith, "Transfer of Arctic Territories," 68.

39. See, for example, W.R. Morrison, "Eagle over the Arctic: Americanizing the Canadian North," *Canadian Review of American Studies* 18: 1 (1987), 63–76 and M. Zaslow, *The Opening of the Canadian North* (Toronto: McClelland & Stewart, 1971).

40. Grant, *Polar Imperative*, 176.

41. *Debates of the Legislative Assembly of United Canada*, 13, 4, 22 April 1856, 1716.

42. M. Zaslow, *Reading the Rocks: The Story of the Geological Survey of Canada, 1842-1972* (Toronto: Macmillan a, 1975), 91.

43 G.M. Dawson, "On Some of the Larger Unexplored Regions of Canada," *Ottawa Naturalist* 4 (1890–91), 31, 39.

44. See A.B. McKillop, *A Disciplined Intelligence: Critical Inquiry and Canadian Thought in the Victorian Era* (Montreal: McGill-Queen's University Press, 1979).

45. C. Berger, *Science, God, and Nature in Victorian Canada* (Toronto: University of Toronto Press, 1983), 6–16.

46. Brown, "The Doctrine of Usefulness," 55. See also W.A. Waiser, "The Government Explorer in Canada, 1870–1914," in J.L. Allen, ed., *North American Exploration, vol. 3 A Continent Comprehended* (Lincoln, 1997), 412–60.

47. T.H. Levere, "What Is Canadian about Science in Canadian History?" in R.A. Jarrell and N.R. Ball, eds., *Science, Technology, and Canadian History* (Waterloo: Wilfrid Laurier University Press, 1980), 20.

48. V. De Vecchi, "Science and Government in the Nineteenth Century," 'PhD dissertation', University of Toronto, 1978, 8–10, 164–65, 222–23.

49. *Debates*, February 27, 1877, 314.

50. W.A. Waiser, *The Field Naturalist: John Macoun, the Geological Survey, and Natural Science* (Toronto: University of Toronto Press, 1989), 67.

51. *Debates*, May 3, 1887, 233.

52. Brown, "The Doctrine of Usefulness," 52.

53. *Debates*, May 3, 1887, 233.

54. This policy would lead to cottages with multi-year leases in several of western Canada's national parks, in particular Prince Albert and Riding Mountain. See B. Waiser, "'A Case of Special Privilege and Fancied Right': The Shack Tent Controversy in Prince Albert National Park," in C. Campbell, ed., *A Century of Parks Canada, 1911–2011* (Calgary: University of Calgary Press, 2011).

55. *Debates*, May 3, 1887, 246.

56. Alan MacEachern, *Natural Selections: National Parks in Atlantic Canada* (Montreal: McGill-Queen's University Press, 2001), 18.

57. Brown, "The Doctrine of Usefulness," 50.

58. *Debates*, May 3, 1887, 233.

59. Quoted in B. Waiser, *The New Northwest: The Photographs of the Frank Crean Expeditions, 1908–1909* (Saskatoon: Fifth House, 1993), 4.

PART 4

Remembering Macdonald

Chapter 13

Politics, Posturing, and Process in Shaping Macdonald's Public Memory (1891–1911)

Yves Y. Pelletier

Within four years of his death on June 6, 1891, five monuments in honour of John A. Macdonald had been erected. Was this unprecedented display of respect reflective of a consensus? French sociologist Maurice Halbwachs argued that collective memories of leaders, events, and places are constantly being rearranged. "We reconstruct (the past) through an effort of reasoning, what happens is that we distort the past, because we wish to introduce greater coherence," he wrote. "It is then reason or intelligence that chooses among the store of recollections, eliminates some of them, and arranges the others according to an order conforming [to] our ideas of the moment."[1] Halbwachs asserted that the collective memory of social groups was determined by a contest between rival reconstructions of the past, each one of which seeks to achieve dominance by adapting historical facts to circumstances at any given point in time. The final acceptance of those representations by the population serves to form national memories. The Italian political theorist Antonio Gramsci had gone further and argued that the economic hegemony of one class over another was more often achieved by means of political and ideological domination, expressed through consent to the adoption of public symbols (and not necessarily by coercion).[2] Ian McKay has noted that any hegemony is "never a once-and-for-all achievement of some unverifiable majority consensus."[3] Thus the representations of a certain historical figure must be measured over time to determine if a consensus prevails. British social anthropologist Mary Douglas argued that the official memory shaped by institutions — governments, private sector, civil society, for example — work for their own benefit, even if that means hiding their influence to gain legitimacy.[4] The art of shaping public memory can also be the product of the state, or of certain groups using the power of the state to justify the very political act of commemoration.

This chapter explores the efforts of Canada's political leaders to promote and challenge the memory of Macdonald in the two decades following his death.[5] Until the First World War, senior members of the Liberal-Conservative Party as well as the Liberal Party tried to shape, through their words and their actions, the legacy of Canada's first prime minister. For the Liberal-Conservative Party, the intense commemoration of Macdonald was concentrated in their years in office before losing the 1896 election. They focused largely on the unveiling of Macdonald statues in five communities: Hamilton (November 1, 1893), Toronto (October 13, 1894), Montreal (June 6, 1895), Ottawa (July 1, 1895), and Kingston (October 23, 1895). The presence of Macdonald's political successors and allies at these events raised the profile of these local commemorative efforts to a national level. They also provided a forum to praise Macdonald's accomplishments and celebrate not only *his* memory, but his successors'.

The Liberal Party also took advantage of opportunities to frame the political legacy of Macdonald. During the years in opposition (1891–1896) and in government (1896–1911), they made several attempts: Laurier's eulogy in the House of Commons two days after his death; the 1892 debate in the House of Commons regarding the erection of a Macdonald memorial on Parliament Hill; the highly partisan 1893 Liberal Party policy convention which united roughly 2,500 party delegates from across the country; the various representations of Macdonald made during the 1905 parliamentary debate regarding the creation of new provinces out of portions of the North-West Territories; and finally the public debate prior to the 1911 federal general election regarding reciprocity with the United States.

• • •

The art of commemoration is often more about the intent of the speaker than the object of the commemoration and this was evident during the unveiling of the statues. Sir John Thompson's ascent into the position of prime minister of Canada following Macdonald's death came with complications, as his Catholic faith was a source of concern to Protestant conservatives. In response, he attempted to "reassure Protestant public opinion, especially in Ontario, by including a recognized Protestant advocate in his government"[6] and appointed N. Clarke Wallace, the grand knight of the Orange Order and

Grip, 13 June, 1891.

"Now let his errors be buried and forgotten!"

MP for York-West, to cabinet.[7] Wallace was added to the speakers' list for the Hamilton unveiling, alongside Thompson, who delivered the keynote address.

Thompson's speeches contained a striking message, namely that Canada was a very difficult country to govern. In reflecting on history, Thompson mentioned that, in the past, half the population had taken arms against the other in order to deal with what he called the "burning questions." Many of these questions resulted from the "rivalries of race," and, according to Thompson (who was facing a schools question in Manitoba that pitted French against English), Macdonald had succeeded in resolving many of these tensions. The prime minister also suggested that, by looking at Macdonald's statue, Canadians would be inspired to do more for the interests of Canada as a whole. With such reasoning, Thompson attempted to reach out to and build support among Protestant Ontarians for his own leadership.

Thompson's sudden death in December 1894, while visiting Queen Victoria at Windsor Castle, left the Liberal-Conservative Party in considerable disarray. Governor General Lord Aberdeen called upon Sir Mackenzie Bowell, a cabinet minister and close friend of Macdonald, to form the next government. Bowell, it turns out, also was a frequent speaker at ceremonies unveiling Macdonald memorials. Bowell liked to emphasize Macdonald's efforts in seeking to "establish upon a solid foundation British power on the greater half of the North American continent."[8] He also liked to hail Macdonald's close collaborations with others, his acknowledgement of the value of diverging opinion, and his role as a conciliator of races.[9]

As prime minister, Bowell emphasized his political links with Macdonald and his legacy, arguing that he had assisted Sir John in taking decisions and determining directions. Like Thompson, he highlighted Macdonald's ability to unite French and English Canadians and two main religious faiths. In addition, Bowell implored the younger generation in the audience to follow in Sir John's footsteps so that they would contribute to Canada's greatness: "[Macdonald's] life-work was a more enduring monument than bronze or marble ... and history [will] show that he was the brightest star that ever shone in the visible constellation of this country, which he loved so much."[10] Thus this new prime minister tried to increase the party's popularity by encouraging Canada's youth to follow Macdonald's Liberal-Conservative path. He also portrayed himself as a natural successor to Macdonald, who supported and shaped his predecessor's policies and who would follow the same course of action as prime minister.

The enthusiasm for Macdonald displayed before the new monuments was not universally shared. When Wilfrid Laurier spoke of Macdonald in the House of Commons two days after the prime minister's death, he gave the impression that death had diminished the hostility between both men. In 1893, Sir Oliver Mowat, the Ontario premier, described Laurier's eulogy to Macdonald as "an appreciative speech which, for its spirit and eloquence, was commended alike by friends and opponents."[11] In reality, Laurier was not all that generous as his eulogy was very critical of Macdonald as a partisan politician. The Liberal Party's quest to form government instead emphasized Macdonald's failings and the Liberal-Conservative Party weaknesses as a whole. As such, the Liberal Party drew mostly negative representations of Sir John A. Macdonald during their years in opposition and, not surprisingly, tarred the Liberal-Conservative Party with the same brush. Even in government, between 1896 and 1911, the Liberals seldom invoked the public memory of Macdonald. When Laurier or other members of the Liberal Party did bring out Macdonald, they did so to advance party objectives. Laurier framed his creation of the provinces of Alberta and Saskatchewan as a measured and incremental approach in contrast to Macdonald's rushed and heavy-handed action in the case of the province of Manitoba. The Liberal Party also attempted to alter the perception of Macdonald's ultimate support for reciprocity to broaden public and political support for this economic policy. In each instance, a common goal existed: to gain a political advantage for the Liberal Party through its efforts of shaping Macdonald's public memory.

Laurier's willingness to commemorate Macdonald as a nation builder, all the same, cannot be ignored. His 1891 eulogy lauded his skill in transforming Canada from "two small provinces, having nothing in common but a common allegiance, united by a bond of paper, and united by nothing else — to the present state of development which Canada has reached."[12] Laurier recognized a "uniter." In light of such achievements, Laurier expounded on this theme by noting that he was:

> [O]nly too glad … to remember only the great services he has performed for our country — to remember that his actions always displayed great originality of views, unbounded fertility of resources, and, above all, a far-reaching vision

beyond the events of the day, and still higher, permeating the whole, a broad patriotism — a devotion to Canada's welfare, Canada's advancement, and Canada's glory.[13]

This representation of Macdonald, which did echo the views expressed by the leaders of the Liberal-Conservative Party, might suggest that a collective memory of Macdonald acceptable to both national parties had already been achieved. However, positive representations of Macdonald as a nation builder by members of the Liberal Party were limited to that single event. On subsequent occasions, Laurier and the Liberal Party did not acknowledge Macdonald as a nation builder and diminished his role in Confederation and in the building of the Canadian Pacific Railway. Outside of the House of Commons, and especially in front of partisan audiences, the Liberal Party offered strong criticism of Macdonald's nation building policies, notably his economic policies. In 1893, the Liberal Party described the National Policy as:

[F]ounded upon an unsound principle, and used, as it has been by the Government, as a corruptive agency wherewith to keep themselves in office, has developed monopolies, trusts and combinations; it has decreased the value of farm and other landed property; it has oppressed the masses to the enrichment of a few; it has checked immigration; it has caused great loss of population; it has impeded commerce; it has discriminated against Great Britain.[14]

Not mincing his words, Laurier argued that Macdonald's National Policy hindered the development of Canada. A brighter future would be achieved under a Liberal government.

During Laurier's tenure as prime minister, the Liberal Party was mostly silent on Macdonald. In itself, this strategy aimed to reduce the public awareness of Macdonald and his public memory. That being said, on a few occasions, members of the Liberal Party still had a few opportunities to influence the public memory of Macdonald as a nation builder. As prime minister, Laurier controlled Canada's economic policies, most of which were not dissimilar to the original National Policy. Laurier often alluded to the difficult birth of Manitoba as a Canadian province to show how awkward

Macdonald was as a nation builder. "Laurier wanted to enhance the reputation he enjoyed as the builder of modern Canada," acknowledged his biographer Réal Bélanger.[15] As such, he proceeded with a promise he had made: the transformation of parts of the North-West Territories into one or more autonomous provinces. Laurier argued that one of the key reasons driving his decision to create new provinces stemmed from the fact that the territories had met a certain level of maturity in regards to the influx of population and the establishment of administrative centres. Laurier heralded this slow transformative process from territory to province as a means of avoiding future conflict. He highlighted his approach in contrast to the conflict that erupted over the establishment of Manitoba. In this regard, he stated:

> If we go back to the history of those days, perhaps the opinion will not be unwarranted that it would have been a wiser course, if instead of bringing Manitoba at once into the confederation full fledged and fully equipped as a province, that maturity had been reached by gradual stages extended over a few years. If that course would have been taken, perhaps some mistakes would have been avoided from the effects of which we have not yet completely recovered.[16]

Among those unidentified "mistakes" were the Red River Rebellion, the North-West Rebellions, the hanging of Louis Riel, and the creation of denominational schools similar to the ones in Quebec, which led to the Manitoba Schools Question. Each of these events had an impact on the development of the province, with many of the linguistic and religious struggles extending beyond the borders to become national debates. Laurier does not actually name Macdonald directly in his speech, although it can be inferred from the quotation. As such, in a single sentence, Laurier labelled Macdonald's government as incompetent as its actions sparked complex political challenges in Manitoba and beyond. In the end, Laurier's criticism of Macdonald's handling of the creation of Manitoba aimed to demonstrate his own superior leadership style and his superior ability in nation building.

• • •

While the Liberal Party was painting a portrait of Macdonald, so too were the Liberal-Conservatives. The theme of Macdonald's leading role in the adoption of the *British North America Act* was central in the unveiling of the five Macdonald statues, with almost only Conservative speakers. On those occasions, his former colleagues did not portray Macdonald as merely one among many Fathers of Confederation. Thompson declared during the Hamilton unveiling ceremony that: "Of no man of any period can it be more truly said that he was the father and the founder of his country."[17] Indeed, Macdonald's liberal and conservative allies in achieving this Confederation objective — Sir George-Étienne Cartier (Quebec), George Brown (Ontario), Sir Charles Tupper (Nova Scotia), and Sir Samuel Leonard Tilley (New Brunswick) among others — were forgotten during the four unveiling ceremonies in Ontario. As a result, Macdonald became *the* Father of Confederation.

Even during the unveiling of the Macdonald memorial in Montreal, the Francophone speakers raised Macdonald above other political figures, including those from Quebec. Sir Joseph-Adolphe Chapleau, who served as Macdonald's secretary of state for ten years prior to becoming lieutenant-governor of Quebec, clearly placed Macdonald's role in bringing about Confederation above everyone else, a fact strengthened by his use of the phrase "father of our country" to describe Macdonald. Sir Adolphe-Philippe Caron, minister of militia and defence and one of the few Quebec Liberal-Conservatives to support Macdonald after the Riel hanging, also labelled Macdonald as *"le père de notre pays, le fondateur de notre pays."*[18] Labelling Macdonald as the father and founder of the nation was indeed an important step in positioning Macdonald as *the* Father of Canada within Quebec. He noted: *"Comme il serait heureux, car il réaliserait, comme nous le réalisons tous, qu'il a vécu pour son pays et que son pays a grandement apprécié son travail et qu'il honore glorieusement son défunt."* (Translation: "How happy Macdonald would be, because he would realize, just like we realize it, that he lived for his country and his country greatly appreciated his work and honour him in death.")[19] As such, French and English Canadian Liberal-Conservative speakers elevated Macdonald above other national political figures, including Sir George-Étienne Cartier. The Liberals, in contrast, observed silence on this issue. Macdonald, for them, was indeed *a* Father of Confederation and criticizing that fact was futile.

The representations of Macdonald as a nation builder were very common during this period.[20] The members of his party enumerated many examples to make their case: the adoption of the *British North America Act*, the creation of new provinces, the development of canals, the support for protectionist tariffs through the National Policy, the purchase of the Hudson Bay Company's territory, the construction of the Canadian Pacific Railway, and the alliance with Quebec through Sir George-Étienne Cartier and Thomas D'Arcy McGee.[21]

Finance minister and New Brunswick member of Parliament Sir George Eulas Foster spoke admiringly of "the finesse, the spirit with which [Macdonald] met strife of creed, strife of race, strife of sectionalism," each of which he attempted to settle through "prudent compromise."[22] Sir Mackenzie Bowell, a longtime ally of Macdonald (who appointed him to the Senate) as well as a future prime minister, focused on Macdonald as a conciliator between Canada's French- and English-Canadian groups, for "[i]n Sir John Macdonald's mind bigotry and intolerance had 'no' place."[23] As such, he highlighted Macdonald's ability to unite French and English Canadians and two main religious faiths. Respect for citizens of a different creed was one of the most important ways, Thompson suggested, by which Canadians could put Canada above personal interests. Such sentiments were important, as his government would likely be divided again in regards to the Manitoba School Question.

French Canadians also heard about Macdonald as a unifier of Canada's official languages communities, in their own language. Former House of Commons speaker and then leader of Quebec's Liberal-Conservatives Joseph-Aldéric Ouimet argued that it was Montreal's duty to honour Macdonald's memory in perpetuity, as previous speakers did not exaggerate his political acumen. He was successful in his enterprise of bringing together the various provinces of British North America, and forging a single community of interest despite the various populations that make up our country[24] Ouimet's remarks clearly ignored the religious and linguistic struggles that had erupted in Canada since Confederation. As such, Ouimet aimed to promote the idea that only a single community of national interest could ensure the further political and economic progress of Canada. Liberal-Conservatives used the image of Macdonald as the main conciliator between Canada's two founding language groups to encourage French and English Canadians to work together and thus achieve a brighter, more prosperous future for Canada.

Laurier's attitude toward Macdonald was also revealed during the debate in the House of Commons regarding the erection of a Macdonald memorial in Ottawa. In April 1892, not ten months after Macdonald's death, the government was asked of its intention regarding the erection of a statue in Macdonald's memory on the grounds of the House of Commons. The response from Prime Minister Thompson was affirmative: as "soon as a vote in Parliament is obtained" to secure the required $10,000 fund.[25] The government's memorial in Ottawa would be funded by taxpayers, as opposed to private fundraising for the other monuments.

The budget debate provided a forum for the Liberal Party to react not only to the allocation of public funds to commemorate a former prime minister, but also to question whether he was worthy of the honour. Laurier expressed concerns that public funds were being used for partisan purposes. He argued that monuments in honour of public men "would be better left to private initiatives instead of to pay for it out of the public treasury."[26] He clearly preferred Macdonald to be remembered as a former leader of a political party, and not a national figure. Moreover, Laurier did not wish to remove Macdonald as a target for continuing partisan attacks that could benefit his party in the forthcoming federal general election. The only other Liberal MP who spoke on this motion was James McMullen, a veteran MP for Wellington-North (Ontario).[27] As a longtime political opponent of Macdonald, McMullen was opposed to state funding for a Macdonald memorial. "I do not think it is right," he said,

> [t]hat the whole country should be asked to pay for a monument to the deceased leader of half of the people of this Dominion, and I am sure that the other half are of the opinion that it was to their misfortune that he should have governed the country so long.... I do not think it is right that you should, by numerical force, compel the Reformers of this country, who are not disposed to recognize the long reign of Sir John A. Macdonald as having been a blessing to this country, to contribute their money to the erection of his monument.[28]

Macdonald's death clearly had not mellowed McMullen's opposition, suggesting that not all Canadians were ready to accept Macdonald as a symbol of Canada and as an historical figure worthy of national commemoration.

Laurier and McMullen's criticisms of this budget motion did not go unanswered. George Foster noted: "I should hope there is no Conservative from one end of this country to the other, who should be ungenerous enough to say of him after his death what the hon. gentleman has said of Sir John Macdonald."[29] Foster argued that, in death, past animosity should be forgotten. He felt a need to defend the memory of his former leader and to build bipartisan support for this motion, but to no effect. In subsequent events, members of the Liberal Party never invoked Macdonald as a symbol of Canada.

Remarkably, Macdonald's real or imagined human failings were downplayed by adversaries in the two decades after his death. His well-known penchant for drink was never referenced by either party spokesmen. Rather, the Liberal Party left it to its press to formulate negative attacks relating to Macdonald's human shortcomings, with the harshest criticism coming from the *Hamilton Evening Times,* the *Montreal Herald,* and *La Patrie.* In an editorial following Sir Mackenzie Bowell's encouragement to Canada's youth that they should emulate the former prime minister, the *Hamilton Evening Times* fired a salvo:

> How many men, Conservatives and Liberals, who knew Sir John Macdonald for thirty or forty years, and were familiar with his private life and his public actions, would wish their sons to take him as a model? His career was successful: he died in office; he got what his ambition craved.... But one John A. Macdonald in a century is as many as any country can stand. Canada will do much better in the twentieth century without double shuffles, Pacific scandals, protective tariffs, gerrymandering, milked contractors, and fraudulent franchise act. The death of one man does not make wrong right, nor black white. [30]

The Liberal *Montreal Herald* aimed its criticism at the five Macdonald memorial organizing committees and the Liberal-Conservative speakers as by "their political complexion, and their partisan enthusiasm, we shall be reluctantly forced to the conclusion that there is much vanity and vexation of spirit in the make-up of Tory hero worship — after the hero is dead."[31] The erection of Macdonald statues led the *Hamilton Herald* to comment wryly that, with the rapidly growing number of statues in Macdonald's honour, "[t]here will soon be enough of them to give a dinner party."[32]

Montreal's Liberal-leaning *La Patrie* often ignored the unveiling of these five Macdonald statues, or only very briefly referenced them.[33] Unable to resist the taunt of the Montreal unveiling ceremony, *La Patrie* published an anonymous letter to the editor by a "brave Canayen" (these were often written by the editors). Poking fun at some of the details of "Johnny's" statue, the letter launched another barrage against the old chieftain, accusing him of strengthening Ottawa at heavy cost to the provinces:

> *On a couronné l'œuvre d'une statue de l'abondance ou de la richesse–reposant sur des lions–soit la richesse et la force; c'est très bien, grâce à sir John qui les auraient introduites dans le pays. Mais, il y a un mais ... que viennent faire autours ces six ou sept enfants, maigres et décharnés, soulevant les armes des provinces canadiennes pour cacher leurs squelettes? Ne disent-ils pas bien haut que la richesse que sir John a apportée au pays il l'a gardée pour lui seul sans en faire profiter les enfants du pays qui ont des corps de crève faim!*[34] (Translation: Macdonald's statue reflects the strength and the wealth that he brought to Canada, but Macdonald is surrounded by six or seven emaciated children who hold provincial shields to hide their skeletons. Does this not say clearly that the wealth Sir John brought to this country, he kept it for himself without regards to the children of this country with their malnourished bodies?)

The letter also implied that the distribution of wealth which had come from Canada's continuous economic and infrastructural development was not shared equally among all social classes. In effect, Macdonald had enriched himself through his political actions, leaving the lower socio-economic classes, especially French Canadians, in poverty. A few days later, *La Patrie* figuratively defaced the Macdonald memorial in Montreal. Reviewing the Macdonald statue recently finished in the national capital by sculptor Philippe Hébert, the editors noted that the base of the Ottawa construction at least did not resemble a *vespasienne* (a French public urinal) as was the case for the Montreal monument in Dominion Square.[35]

• • •

Macdonald, as a loyal British subject who contributed to the British Empire, was a constant theme during the unveiling ceremonies. In Hamilton, Thompson claimed he had just uncovered "the image of one of the most illustrious men of our generation," a man of equal worth to Wellington and Nelson.[36] He declared that Macdonald was as faithful a servant of the Crown as had ever lived within the realm of England, a fact that even Queen Victoria was said to have acknowledged. Finally, he also claimed that this new memorial represented "a new milestone reached in the history of the British Empire."[37] Other speakers echoed the same theme. Sir Mackenzie Bowell described Macdonald's overall political objectives as being to "establish upon a solid foundation British power on the greater half of the North American continent."[38] As such, he stressed the importance of the British connection for Canada's prosperity. Finally, Sir George Foster noted that one of main lessons future generations of Canadians could learn from Macdonald was a love of imperialism, including pride in being a British subject.

Many of the speakers used Macdonald to highlight their perception of Canada's pre-eminence within the British Empire as a result of Macdonald's efforts. For example, Foster used his speech to define Canada as the "premier colony of that great Empire at whose undying altar fires [Macdonald] prayed and watched for more than half a century."[39] For his part Sir Charles Tupper, cabinet minister, noted that Macdonald's political career was known throughout the British Empire. He asserted: "from almost every quarter of the globe [people] were … familiar with his career."[40] As such, many speakers used this theme to paint Macdonald as the man who fashioned Canada as the greatest British colony.

Despite frequent representation of Macdonald as a British subject by Liberal-Conservatives, Laurier attempted to alter this image on several occasions. He focused on representations of Macdonald as anti-British for not supporting the policy of free trade that Britain was promoting during the same period. The representation of Macdonald as a free trader was indeed founded on historical records as Macdonald pursued reciprocity with the

United States throughout much of the 1870s. The Liberal Party was thus historically accurate in depicting Macdonald as someone who sought reciprocity with Canada's southern neighbour.

During the federal general election of 1891, Laurier characterized Macdonald as anti-British, as Macdonald's protectionist economic policies differed from Britain's free trade policies. Macdonald then fired back at Laurier, depicting the Liberal Party's policy of reciprocity with the United States as the promise of economic union and, eventually, annexation. As such, Macdonald played on the sentiments of Canadians of British ancestry by suggesting that he, the "Old Leader," would pursue the "Old Policy" of protectionism as a means of ensuring strong relations with the "Old Flag." The message seems to have resonated with many Canadians, as Macdonald was re-elected in the 1891 general election with a majority government.

• • •

After the March 1891 federal general election, Laurier continued to suggest that Macdonald actively discriminated against the United Kingdom. The Liberal Party's criticism of Macdonald as anti-British became even more constant and fierce following Macdonald's death in June 1891. For example, during the 1893 Liberal Party policy convention, Laurier restated that the United Kingdom's economic policies were anchored in the principle of freer trade, the very same policy he wished to introduce in Canada. "The fact that England is free trade and the Canadian Conservatives are protectionists shows that there is … a diversity of interests between England and Canada," argued Laurier.[41] The difference in economic policy between the United Kingdom and Canada under Macdonald's leadership led Laurier to conclude yet again that Macdonald "discriminated against Great Britain."[42]

That position would echo almost twenty years later, when the Laurier government announced a tentative reciprocity agreement between Canada and the United States. Confident that Canadians were secure enough in their national identity to move forward with an economic arrangement with the United States that would be beneficial to the Canadian economy without setting off fears of cultural or political annexation, Laurier had signed a reciprocity agreement in January 1911. As the policy debate shifted from the narrow economic merits of the reciprocity agreement to Canada's national existence, references to Macdonald were sprinkled in the speeches delivered by Liberal MPs during the electoral campaign of that year. The effort aimed to represent Macdonald yet again as a supporter of reciprocity with the United States. Agriculture Minister Sydney Fisher, for instance, argued that what Macdonald had really sought, and failed to secure, was reciprocity with the United States:

> At the same time when Sir Charles Tupper … and Sir John Macdonald [were] waving that [British] flag, both of them were trying to get from the United States just exactly the arrangement that we have got to-day. They were trying to get it by going on their knees to Washington, while we have Washington coming to us.[43]

Beyond disparaging Macdonald's diplomatic skills, Fisher sought to demonstrate that Macdonald had shared the same policy objective as the Liberals and that his successors were merely hypocritical.

For its part, the Liberal-Conservative Party protested this use of Macdonald's memory, and instead emphasized that it was continuing "the old leader's" policy. The party leader, Robert Borden, offered his own political jousting by concluding he had not heard a convincing argument for the government's position on the reciprocity agreement. Borden responded with open disdain to Laurier's use of "old" speeches to attempt to demonstrate Macdonald's support of reciprocity:

> A very considerable part of the time of my right hon. friend yesterday was devoted to resuscitating very old speeches of himself and others of twenty years ago. Has the right hon. gentleman been asleep? Must we in future dub him Sir Wilfrid Rip Van Winkle? … [T]his is not 1879.[44]

The reference to American author Washington Irving's famous fictional character implied that Laurier had been asleep for the past twenty years, and had lost touch with modern economic needs. Borden rarely invoked Macdonald by name, as he knew Macdonald had at different times promoted freer trade with the United States. However, he did cite Canadian

Pacific Railway magnate Sir William Van Horne, who had stated that the proposed agreement would see "the magnificent work of a generation traded away for a vague idea or a childish sentiment."[45] The work of that generation would indeed be the work of Macdonald's generation. Van Horne, it is worth noting, was biased in his assessment of reciprocity, fearing that reciprocity would endanger the very industries that had assured his material success: The National Policy increased east-west trade and thus the use of the Canadian Pacific Railway. Seeing his profits threatened by reciprocity pushed him to campaign aggressively "to bust the damn thing."[46]

The criticisms made by Conservative MPs did not alter the Liberal Party's position of using Macdonald's public memory to help support its position during the 1911 federal general election campaign. Finance Minister and former Nova Scotia premier William S. Fielding used some examples in his own campaign literature. He wrote an essay to defend his party's position on reciprocity, noting that: "The Conservative policy of higher tariffs was only accepted by its own friends because it was declared by Sir John Macdonald himself and by other statesmen of his party to be the best possible road towards obtaining reciprocity with the United States."[47] He then addressed "The Annexation Bogey" charged about his party:

> Sir John Macdonald ... and other public men of the Conservative Party were not deemed disloyal when they laboured without success to obtain a reciprocal trade agreement with the U.S. It will be difficult to persuade anyone that the Canadian Ministers of to-day are disloyal when they have carried on reciprocity negotiations which have been crowned with the success that was denied to their predecessors.[48]

If the Liberal Party could convince Canadians that their actions were in the best economic interest of Canada and would not alter Canada's loyalty to the British Empire, they realized that they might find electoral success in the plan.

The 1911 election ended the Liberal Party's fifteen-year reign. The precise issues that motivated Canadians to vote for one party or another are difficult to determine. Some Canadians may have voted specifically on the merits of reciprocity. Others may have voted for a new government and a younger political leader. Then there was the issue of support to the British government's arms-building efforts. Despite the electoral outcome, the Liberal Party found merit in trying to reshape the public memory of Macdonald into that of a free trader. The dominant representation of Macdonald at the time was as a "National Policy" protectionist. As such, the representations of Macdonald as a protectionist advanced by Liberal-Conservatives, and those of a free trader advanced by the Liberal Party, were impossible to reconcile. The representation of Macdonald as a supporter of reciprocity would have been strengthened, had the Liberal Party won the 1911 federal election. The Liberal Party's electoral defeat allowed the Liberal-Conservatives to continue defining Macdonald as a supporter of protectionism.[49]

The Liberal-Conservative Party embarked on efforts to build a national myth around Macdonald immediately following his death. His former party colleagues portrayed Macdonald as the man who shaped Canada's destiny almost exclusively by himself. The myth-making around the now historical Macdonald was meant to inspire Canadians and to instil continued support for their party's objectives in subsequent elections. This messaging contrasted with the Liberal Party's approach to foster a negative image of Macdonald's political legacy, an election-focused counteroffensive to paint Macdonald as a partisan politician with malignant motives and ineffective and self-serving policies. As such, the Liberal Party's attacks extended beyond Macdonald in an effort to portray the Liberal-Conservative Party with the same brush. Overall, their criticism of Macdonald and his party was a direct attempt to sell voters on the idea of a better and more prosperous future under a Liberal government. During Laurier's years in government, the Liberal Party was mostly silent on Macdonald and his legacy, reintroducing his memory to undermine Borden's party.

As a result of political representations of Macdonald and media depictions, two very partisan versions of Macdonald emerged from this political battleground. The first, introduced by the Liberal-Conservative Party, was a leader who Canadians should emulate because of his ability to reconcile races and religion, develop Canada on British principles, and transform Canada into the most important colony within the British Empire. The other, introduced by the Liberal Party, was a leader who used the machinery of government to keep his party in office, who brought Canada down a dangerous economic path, and who introduced policies that delayed Canada's development. The public memory of Macdonald emerging from both national parties aimed to advance their respective party's political objectives. In the absence of a hegemonic discourse acceptable to both national political parties, two irreconcilable Macdonalds emerged. In the end, party loyalty likely played a key role in determining which version of Macdonald one chose to remember during this period. Macdonald was clearly not a "hegemonic figure" in the first two decades after his death, but the five statues erected (and now refurbished) still stand proudly. In the last fifty years, three more have been created (Regina, Victoria, B.C., and a second one in Ottawa, located in the Macdonald-Cartier Airport). Macdonald may have won the battle for a certain dominance of the public landscape, but his public memory remains contested, even today.

NOTES

1. Lewis A. Coser, ed., *Maurice Halbwachs: On Collective Memory* (Chicago: The University of Chicago Press, 1992), 183.
2. Roger Simon, *Gramsci's Political Thought: An Introduction* (London: Lawrence and Wishart, 1991[1982]), 18.
3. Ian McKay, "The Liberal Order Framework: A Perspective for a Reconnaissance of Canadian History," *Canadian Historical Review* 81, 3 (September 2000), 638.
4. Mary Douglas, *How Institutions Think* (Syracuse, NY: Syracuse University Press, 1986).
5. Yves Y. Pelletier, "The Old Chieftain's New Image: Shaping the Public Memory of Sir John A. Macdonald in Ontario and Quebec, 1891–1967" (PhD Thesis, Queen's University, 2010).
6. Brian P. Clarke, "Nathanial Clarke Wallace." In *Dictionary of Canadian Biography* online, assessed on February 10, 2014, *www.biographi.ca/en/bio/wallace_nathaniel_clarke_13E.html.*
7. P.B. Waite, "Sir John Sparrow David Thompson." In *Dictionary of Canadian Biography* online, accessed on February 10, 2014, *www.biographi.ca/en/bio/thompson_john_sparrow_david_12E.html.*
8. "The Unveiling," *Globe*, October 15, 1894: 5.
9. Ibid.
10. "Monument Unveiled," *Montreal Gazette*, June 7, 1895: 2.
11. Macdonald Memorial Committee, *The Proceedings at the Unveiling*, 27–28.

12. Canada, *Debates from the House of Commons* (Ottawa: Brown Chamberlain, 1891), June 8, 1891, 885.

13. Ibid., 885.

14. *Official Report of the Liberal Convention: Held in Response to the Call of Hon. Wilfrid Laurier, Ottawa, Tuesday, June 20th, and Wednesday, June 21st, 1893* (Toronto, 1893), 71.

15. Réal Bélanger "Sir Wilfrid Laurier." In *Dictionary of Canadian Biography* online, accessed on February 10, 2014, www.biographi.ca/en/bio/laurier_wilfrid_14E.html.

16. Canada, *Debates from the House of Commons* (Ottawa: S. E. Dawson, 1905), February 21, 1905, 1423.

17. Macdonald Memorial Committee, *The Proceedings at the Unveiling of the Statue of the Late Sir John Alexander Macdonald in Hamilton on the First Day of November 1893* (Hamilton, Macdonald Memorial Committee, 1893), 12–13.

18. "Le Monument Macdonald," *La Presse*, June 7, 1895: 1.

19. Ibid.

20. Macdonald Memorial Committee, *The Proceedings at the Unveiling*, 22.

21. "To the Memory of Sir Macdonald." *Globe*, October 24, 1895: 2.

22. "Monument Unveiled," *Montreal Gazette*, June 7, 1895: 5.

23. "To the Memory of Sir Macdonald." *Globe*, October 24, 1895: 2.

24. "Le Monument Macdonald." *La Presse*, June 6, 1895: 6.

25. Canada, *Statues of Parliament Hill: An Illustrated History* (Ottawa: National Capital Commission, 1986), 8–15; Canada, *Debates from the House of Commons* (Ottawa: Brown Chamberlain, 1891), May 23, 1873: 205.

26. Canada, *Debates from the House of Commons* (Ottawa: S.E. Dawson, 1892), June 30, 1892: 4458.

27. Library of Parliament, History of Members of Parliament, available online and accessed on June 4, 2013, at *www.parl.gc.ca/parlinfo/Lists/Members.aspx?Parliament =1924d334-6bd0-4cb3-8793-cee640025ff6*, search by name "James McMullen."

28. Canada, *Debates from the House of Commons* (Ottawa: S.E. Dawson, 1892), June 30, 1892, 4458. Sir John Thompson first noted that the government wished to introduce a vote on this matter on April 4, 1892. See: Ibid., April 4, 1892, 918.

29. Canada, *Debates from the House of Commons* (Ottawa: S.E. Dawson, 1892), June 30, 1892, 4458.

30. "Montreal's Memorial," *Hamilton Evening Times*, June 7, 1895, 4. See also, "Correspondence: Sir John Macdonald," *Montreal Herald,* June 13, 1895, 4.

31. "The Maisonneuve Monument," *Montreal Herald*, June 10, 1895, 4.

32. Untitled, *Hamilton Herald*, October 24, 1895, 2.

33. "Inauguration de la statue," *La Patrie*, October 15, 1894, 4.

34. "Le Monument Macdonald," *La Patrie*, June 7, 1895, 4.

35. "L'honorable M. Laurier et le monument Macdonald," ibid., June 11, 1895: 1.

36. Macdonald Memorial Committee, *The Proceedings at the Unveiling*, 12. The unveiling of a bust of Sir John A. Macdonald inside St. Paul's Cathedral in London in November 1892, only steps away from the tomb of these two decorated British war generals, facilitated the imagery. See "The Memorial Bust of Sir John Macdonald," *Globe*, November 29, 1892: 4.

37. Macdonald Memorial Committee, *The Proceedings at the Unveiling*, 12.

38. "The Unveiling," *Globe*, October 15, 1894: 5.

39. "Monument Unveiled," *Montreal Gazette*, June 7, 1895: 5.

40. "The Unveiling," *Globe*, October 15, 1894: 5.

41. *Official Report of the Liberal Convention: Held in Response to the Call of Hon. Wilfrid Laurier, Ottawa, Tuesday, June 20th, and Wednesday, June 21st, 1893* (Toronto, 1893), 34.

42. Ibid., 71.

43. Canada, *Debates from the House of Commons* (Ottawa: C.H. Parmelee, 1911), February 28, 1911, 4416. See Anne Drummond, "Sydney Arthur Fisher." In *Dictionary of Canadian Biography* online, accessed February 10, 2014, *www.biographi.ca/en/bio/fisher_sydney_arthur_15E.html*.

44. Canada, *Debates from the House of Commons* (Ottawa: C.H. Parmelee, 1911), March 8, 1911, 4832.

45. Ibid., March 8, 1911, 4831.

46. T. Regher, "Sir William Cornelius Van Horne." In *Dictionary of Canadian Biography* online, accessed February 10, 2014, *www.biographi.ca/en/bio/van_horne_william_cornelius_14E.html*.

47. W.S. Fielding, *The Maritime Provinces and the Reciprocity Agreement* (Halifax: Chronicle Print. Co., 1911), 9.

48. Ibid., 13.

49. The 1911 election is dissected in Patrice Dutil and David MacKenzie, *Canada, 1911: The Decisive Election that Shaped the Country* (Toronto: Dundurn Press, 2011).

Chapter 14

A Legacy Lost: Macdonald in the Memory of His Successors

PATRICE DUTIL AND SEAN CONWAY[1]

As it was, I missed Sir John Macdonald and laid
myself and the Party open to what might
have appeared to be indifference to his memory.

—W.L. Mackenzie King
(Diary, February 1, 1937)

On the occasion of the one-hundredth anniversary of John A. Macdonald's death on June 6, 1991, an important gathering took place at the Cataraqui Cemetery in Kingston and Prime Minister Brian Mulroney delivered the keynote address. He talked about the "difficult moments" his government had endured in its seven years but found comfort, he said, from his caucus and from the people in the land. In this sense, he implied, he was much like Canada's first prime minister. It was a remarkably rare occasion, for Canadian prime ministers generally share an ahistorical predisposition and have seldom invoked Canada's first prime minister in their speeches. Macdonald's views on trade, industry, relations between the English and the French, national unity, religion, indigenous people, and even politics have largely been ignored. Canada has traversed crises of all sorts of magnitude without its leadership ever invoking the memory of the man who had, more than any other, guided the formation of the country. Macdonald has not been the only Canadian prime minister to be so ignored, but the political culture north of the forty-ninth parallel has had no patience for historical reminders. There has been no equivalent talk of the high ideals and accomplishments of Washington, Jefferson, Jackson, Lincoln, Theodore Roosevelt, Franklin D. Roosevelt, Truman, Kennedy, or Reagan. When Canadian prime ministers have brought up Macdonald, remarkably, it was in moments of political trouble when there was a need to show how challenging the job could be. Macdonald was employed to justify their own political lives and deeds, especially in times of deep personal political crisis. Otherwise, his legacy was lost in the rhetoric of his successors.

It was not always so. At his death, there was a sense that Macdonald had left a legacy of lessons in politics and statecraft for people who would succeed him as prime minister. On Monday, June 8, 1891, two days after Macdonald died, Wilfrid Laurier rose as leader of the Opposition to pay homage to his fallen adversary.[2] Laurier was eloquent as few could be about the late prime minister's historical importance, but was particularly sharp-eyed in his assessment of the man's career. Macdonald, he stated, had no equal in the "supreme art of governing men." He admired Macdonald's ability,

> stating that his ability to congregate together elements the most heterogeneous and blend them into one compact party, and to the end of his life keep them steadily under his hand, is perhaps altogether unprecedented. The fact that during all those years he retained unimpaired not only the confidence, but the devotion — the ardent devotion — and affection of his party, is evidence that beside those higher qualities of statesmanship to which we were the daily witnesses, he was also endowed with those inner, subtle, indefinable graces of soul which win and keep the hearts of men.[3]

Laurier considered that "the life of a statesman is always an arduous one, and very often it is an ungrateful one" but predicted that Macdonald's name would be well remembered. There was a lesson here that Laurier was delivering to his own party. Made leader of the Liberal party in 1887, he had performed poorly in the 1891 election and many considered that his best days as leader were now behind him.[4]

Prime Minister John Thompson, the fourth man to hold the office, gave a long oration in Hamilton, Ontario, when a statue of Macdonald was unveiled on November 1, 1893. Thompson spoke of Macdonald lovingly: as patriot, nation builder, parliamentarian, statesman, imperialist, and gentleman but did not fail to hint at his own challenges in governing. "The history of Sir John Macdonald is the history of a long and successful struggle with the greatest difficulties which government in the colonies has presented during the past fifty years," he said. "Of these difficulties the statesmen of older countries have but a faint idea. In Canada they seem to have been greater than anywhere else."[5] A year later, Thompson again gave a keynote address at the unveiling of the Macdonald statue in front of the Legislative Building at Queen's Park in Toronto that stood in some contrast with the Hamilton speech. Noting the nation-building skills of his old boss, his loyalty to Britain, and his love of Canada, Thompson made no point of signalling governing difficulties, a sign of his own growing political fortunes (and personal unawareness of his failing health).[6] Mackenzie Bowell, however, who was now only thirty-six days from assuming the post of prime minister himself, spoke after Thompson. He wistfully noted that Macdonald was "a master in the science of civil governing":

Grip, 13 August, 1887.

It has often been said that he was not only ambitious for power, but that he dominated over those who were associated with him by an iron will. This is an error. While he delighted in the thought of ruling and guiding the destinies of his country, no man ever more freely courted the frank opinions of his colleagues, no man ever listened with greater attention to such opinions, and no man more readily yielded to the judgment of others. I speak of him as one who was his colleague for thirteen years, and therefore know whereof I speak.[7]

It would take another twenty years before Laurier would use the Macdonald name again, and one of the rare occasions where a prime minister called Macdonald to justify a policy. Laurier was defending his position on Reciprocity with the United States in the 1911 election, a time when his administration was most fragile. Pointing to Macdonald's many attempts to open free trade with the Americans through the 1860s and 1870s, he proclaimed that he had been able to deliver on what Canada's first prime minister had always wanted. Launching his campaign in Simcoe, Ontario, on August 15, Laurier rallied the crowd with words that would soon be repeated many times: that Sir John A. Macdonald had been "the Moses of Reciprocity who failed to reach the Promised Land; he would be the Joshua who would lead the people of Canada to the goal."[8]

Mackenzie King, Laurier's successor as Liberal leader, often reported in his diary that he had conjured up an image of Macdonald in a dream or in noting coincidences.[9] Canada's first prime minister was present in the private thoughts of Mackenzie King for a number of reasons. First, there was a small personal connection. Like Macdonald, King was rooted in the powerful Scottish-Canadian community of the nineteenth century. George Baxter, one of Macdonald's teachers at the Kingston Grammar School, was a brother-in-law of King's notorious grandfather, William Lyon Mackenzie, the leader of the Upper Canadian Rebellion of 1837.

There was also a tie to the Kingston area in that the beleaguered and impoverished Mackenzie family settled there in 1850, after a decade of very difficult post-rebellion exile in the United States. The Mackenzie Kingston relatives played a critical role in stabilizing the family at that time and Mackenzie King's mother always remembered the Kingston interlude as an important time in her young life. Decades later, her famous son often recalled the Kingston relatives and the Kingston connection with considerable fondness.

Young Mackenzie King actually saw John A. Macdonald in 1882, while the latter campaigned in the general election of that year in King's hometown of Berlin (Kitchener), Ontario. King at one point wrote: "What I remember from that occasion was not any political argument, but rather, that Sir John was presented with some flowers by a pretty young lady whom he then embraced."[10] It seems clear that Macdonald made a very positive first impression on the then eight-year-old boy. All his life, King remembered precisely where he was and what he was doing when he heard the news that the great man had died in 1891 (King was sixteen at the time).

Macdonald's son, Hugh John, was a friend of King's father, and eventually became a good friend to Mackenzie King after he became prime minister. In his diary, Mackenzie King made many positive references to Macdonald's son following their meeting on November 2, 1920 (King thought Hugh had "his father's nose and charm of manner").[11] As Liberal leader and prime minister, King visited Hugh John in Winnipeg on a number of occasions during that decade, until Macdonald's death in 1929. King was asked to be an honourary pallbearer. Unable to attend the funeral, King sent a wreath inscribed with "In remembrance of a lifelong friend of my father and myself." King noted in his diary that Hugh John's passing reminded him of "the connectedness of things."[12]

It is obvious from the King diary that he thought of Macdonald on occasion, though not always in positive terms. Like most Liberals raised in the mid-to-latter part of the nineteenth century, King had both a grudging admiration and a partisan dislike for Sir John. As with his fellow Liberals — Wilfrid Laurier, Oliver Mowat, and Richard Cartwright — Mackenzie King, however, could not help but admire the political mastery of the man. The fact was that Macdonald, the Conservative politician, had beaten the Liberals throughout most of his career. He also outsmarted them with such parliamentary *legerdemain* as the Double Shuffle of 1858. In 1882, with his famous gerrymander, Macdonald had "hived the Grits" into what seemed like permanent opposition. He had only lost one election to the Liberals in his entire career (in 1874).

King, a devout and abstemious Presbyterian, often expressed a great deal of private concern about Macdonald's attraction to alcohol. Shortly after he became minister of labour under Wilfrid Laurier in 1909, an aide to the governor general advised him that if he wanted to be truly successful in Canadian politics, he should be much more careful with liquor than Macdonald had been. It seemed to have been an easy lesson to learn for King, who otherwise lived out a record-setting tenure as prime minister while scarcely mentioning Macdonald's name publicly.[13]

King gave a speech at Queen's University convocation in October 1919, a few months after he had been elected leader of the Liberal Party, and quoted Wilfrid Laurier extensively, but uttered not once the name of the local hero.[14] Indeed, the fiercely partisan King probably did more than any other prime minister to make sure Canada forgot its first prime minister — even though on a few occasions King visited Kingston with the specific intention of privately visiting the gravesite.

The first visit occurred on October 20, 1925, when King was in the final days of contesting his first general election as prime minister and took a considerable amount of time away from his campaigning to visit Sir John's grave. He met his favourite fortune teller, Mrs. Bleaney, at the Belvedere Hotel for what the King diary tells us was "a remarkable interview." Also present on this occasion was a Mrs. Fenwick, a distant relative of Macdonald. Mrs. Bleaney told King that he possessed a very good soul; that he could have been a great clergyman, or physician because, unlike his enemies, who were inspired by jealousy and selfishness, he was high-minded and concerned only with the public good. Bleaney inaccurately predicted that he would marry a rich widow and she apparently gave King false comfort about his immediate political prospects.

When this remarkable interview at the Belvedere was concluded, the prime minister, Bleaney, and Fenwick visited Cataraqui Cemetery, where King was very impressed with the elegant simplicity of Macdonald's grave. He thought the phrase "at rest" on the tombstone was particularly appropriate for someone whose life had been so full of political battle. King noted that "[m]y grave will be like that." He did, however, think that the words "Prime Minister of Canada" should have been added to the headstone.[15] When the graveyard visit concluded, King resumed his campaign with a large Liberal rally at the Grand Theatre in downtown Kingston. A few days later, the King Liberals suffered a significant political setback, coming second to a Conservative Party led by Arthur Meighen and King was personally defeated in his riding of York North.

King returned to Kingston in August 1927, as part of the Diamond Jubilee of Confederation, and participated in a wreath-laying ceremony at the Macdonald statue in City Park, where he was joined by British prime minister Stanley Baldwin and the Prince of Wales. "It was done in a great hurry. — I was a little surprised Baldwin did not proceed less in haste & display more reverence in the act. It was a sort of business affair." Still, King revealed in his diary that it was "a real pleasure" that he, a Liberal prime minister, was able to celebrate "one of the fathers of Confederation & a former PM of Canada — an honoured leader of another party."[16] The British link was symbolic and ironic as Baldwin later oversaw the passage of the *Statutes of Westminster* that officially recognized Canada's independence in crafting its own foreign policy.

Macdonald was not a priority on this sixtieth anniversary of Confederation. King delivered seven speeches during that summer of 1927 to mark the event and never mentioned Macdonald by name or by title, happier to refer a few times to the role of the "fathers of confederation" particularly at the Quebec Conference of 1865. King, however, was willing to focus an entire speech on Laurier (who had opposed Confederation in 1867, but whose statue on Parliament Hill was unveiled in July 1927).[17] These speeches were augmented by twenty other addresses and published as *The Message of the Carillon and other Addresses*. The (unindexed) collection revealed how irrelevant Macdonald was in King's view of the world: "The Canada of 1867 was ... vastly different from the Canada of 1927, the Canada of today."[18] The section "Canada and the Empire" — a subject of considerable interest to Macdonald — included eight speeches, and one of them, entitled "Citizenship," devoted three pages to Abraham Lincoln and included one line to Macdonald (the only one in the entire 274 pages), which came as a passing reference to self-improvement.[19]

King felt a need to visit Macdonald's grave on the eve of the 1935 federal election. As the Leader of the Opposition, he had travelled to Kingston in early August to prepare his troops for the upcoming battle to unseat the Conservative government of R.B. Bennett. On this occasion, he was accompanied by his local candidate and very good friend, the distinguished

Queen's professor Norman McLeod Rogers. According to the King diary, "on a lovely summer morning" the Liberal leader returned to the Macdonald grave with Rogers in tow. While at the cemetery, King decided that he had to visit the old Baxter homestead, the same farmhouse that had provided refuge to the Mackenzie family many years earlier. The only problem was that by 1935, the Baxter homestead was occupied by very prominent Conservatives and not surprisingly, candidate Rogers was very uneasy about making such a trek. The leader prevailed and the visit occurred.[20] King won a return to power, and on New Year's Eve of 1938, he acquired a bust of John A. and welcomed it to Laurier House.[21]

Macdonald was a silent presence in the "King Years," but the Liberal PM was not entirely cold to his predecessor. He invoked him in his speech following the plebiscite relieving the government of its 1939 conscription pledge.[22] On June 7, 1941, to mark the occasion of the fiftieth anniversary of Macdonald's death, King returned to Cataraqui Cemetery in the company of two other Macdonalds: Angus Macdonald, the minister of naval affairs and the MP for Kingston and Malcolm MacDonald, the British High Commissioner to Canada. Hugh Gainsford, the twenty-two-year-old great-grandson of Macdonald, was also present.

Among the many dignitaries sharing the platform with King that day was his archrival, former Prime Minister Arthur Meighen, who noted the extraordinary wartime context and said in opening his speech that the event was taking place "under the shadow of the blackest clouds that overcast this world; we meet amid the fires, the thunders of war, distant perhaps in space but not in meaning, threatening all we possess and all we are." Meighen made the argument that if Macdonald had been alive, he would have supported the war effort and worked to reconcile the various parts of the country in order to guarantee a strong effort for Britain. "With him Canada was first not in any narrow sense of singleness or priority but only of, or subordinate to a selfish Canadian purpose, the oneness of our interest, the oneness of our security, and the oneness of our destiny with the British Empire," said Meighen. "From the first message to his people, delivered in this City of Kingston in 1844 to his last great appeal in the year of his death, he never ceased to affirm his conviction that our prosperity rested on the permanence of our place in that empire and that our freedom as a nation depended on its unity and its strength. In this he was powerfully supported by his colleagues from French Canada, who believed in him and shared his faith. They knew well what we all know in our country and what the crashing events of this hour are driving home to every quarter of this continent — that the cornerstone of liberty must not be broken if liberty must not be broken if liberty is to survive; and that cornerstone is Britain."[23]

Meighen emphasized the hard work that went into Macdonald's career. "Do not make the mistake too often made of thinking that these talents stood alone," he reminded the audience:

> [O]r that they were the basic and enduring talents which accounted for his usefulness to Canada. The truth is he was the most practical of men, a toiler, a builder devoted indefatigably to getting things done. No one can read his history, his letters, and especially his speeches in parliament, without realizing the comprehensive grasp of facts, the order with which, under his hand, those facts fell into position, and consequently the firmness of conviction with which he could drive home his conclusions. Contrary to the general belief, he could reason just as well as he could appeal. His mind was quick, clear and vigorous, his nature earnest and tenacious; without these solid qualities he never would have reached the place he occupies in history as a parliamentary leader.[24]

For Meighen, this was a lesson for wartime Canada to be learned from Macdonald. "For the heavier tasks of today there is more to be learned from him than from any other," he said. "If we govern ourselves, each one of us, by the principles which governed him; if we work as he worked; dare as he dared; and follow the star that lighted his life, we will serve our country as we ought to serve it and, with God's help, we will save it."[25]

According to his diary, King thought that Meighen's speech was "very good but with blemishes; poorly delivered."[26] King could have been critical of his own performance, as his five-minute speech was hardly eloquent: "Patriotism was the central purpose of Sir John Macdonald's life. Throughout, his dearest wish was to see this country a strong united nation under the British crown. Sir John not only lived to see his dream realized and his prayer answered, but both, in memorable part effected by his own exertions."[27] King's speech was belaboured, focused heavily on Macdonald's personal qualities as a self-made man, and inevitably tied Macdonald to Canada's mission in helping Britain fight the war.[28] For the prime minister, this visit was full of personal nostalgia. As he reviewed the troops at Kingston that day, King wondered to himself what his father's father, who had been stationed at the Kingston Garrison in 1837, would have thought about the fact that one hundred years later, his grandson — and the grandson of the rebel of '37 — had become prime minister. Canada needed the qualities Macdonald had displayed as it marked the second year of its participation in the war against the Nazis. King, eager to avoid the kind of divisive policies that had fractured the country during the First World War, hoped that something of Macdonald's gifts could be extended to him.[29]

Surely, King reflected in his diary, his life story suggested much about the romance and possibility of the Canada that Macdonald had helped create. King took a different comfort from his Tory ghost as war clouds grew even darker. On Wednesday, December 3, 1941, King recorded in his diary that he had had a vision of "someone telling me that Sir John A. Macdonald had been in Ottawa with a view to seeing me and to let me know of his help and goodwill. The countenance of the person who gave me the message was still glowing with a sort of radiant light. Seemed to be greatly pleased."[30] On Sunday, December 14, 1941, a week after the attack on Pearl Harbor, King noted that he had had "a clear vision of Sir John Macdonald's coming again to talk with me. He seemed quite concerned about developments. I also got some impressions about the way conscription was being forced but, on the whole something seemed to work out satisfactorily. This latter part of the vision may only have been what my mind had been working over."[31]

He turned to Macdonald during his severest political crisis of the war, when his popular minister of national (air) defence Charles Gavan "Chubby" Power resigned after the government passed an Order in Council to send conscripts overseas. King used a quote from Macdonald in his speech to the House of Commons. He noted in his diary that the passage "helped to focus not only the attention of the House but the attention of the country on how tremendously critical the situation is. It helped to force it right to the fore." It was a "miracle," a "strange and remarkable circumstance.... This all makes me believe more than ever in the way in which certain forces are working together in the Beyond to help."[32]

As the war in Europe neared its end in February 1945, King again visited Earnscliffe and pondered the bust of Macdonald that stood in its lobby. He returned home to Laurier House and turned to his books. He looked up Pope's biography of Macdonald and happened on a passage where Macdonald revealed to Sir Charles Tupper that "the government was getting too old." King noted that "it seems significant that I should have picked on these particular books…. Each spoke in their way of trials of public men and the uncertainties of leadership."[33]

A final event that connected Mackenzie King to Macdonald occurred in Ottawa on December 9, 1946. The Rideau Club had decided to hold a special dinner in conjunction with the unveiling of a portrait of the first premier. The club had asked Mackenzie King, one of its longest-serving members, to deliver the keynote address. King was positively delighted with this opportunity ("I will paint [with] him words"), and he thanked the establishment crowd at the Rideau Club for offering such an honour to "a Liberal of rebel stock." In his remarks, King told his audience that he remembered vividly how he felt upon hearing the news of Sir John's death, that something vital, something mystical, had departed the land. He praised Macdonald for his warm humanity, his love and skill in the practice of politics, his prophetic vision of Confederation, and his appreciation of the English-French relationship that was so central to Canada. King observed that among Macdonald's many personal strengths were those of "patience and forgiveness." No great leader, said King that evening, could go far in politics if he did not possess much patience and forgiveness.[34]

On April 4, 1947, King again had a vision early in the morning. He saw himself talking with Macdonald. "He was seated at a desk which seemed to be rather high up and in a prominent position. He was most friendly and was writing some statement that was ever pleasing to me. What the nature was I cannot at the moment say. It seemed to me that Sir John possesses great strength and to be in the plenitude of power. That was the thought that his figure brought to me…. It seemed to me that Sir John symbolized my present position as PM of Canada."[35]

Mackenzie King was similar to Macdonald in many ways. Like Macdonald, he spent most of his adult life in politics. To use Macdonald's phrase, both men understood politics as "the long game" (and, unsurprisingly, King was proud to surpass Macdonald's tenure on June 7, 1946).[36] Both were conciliators and bridge-builders; risk-takers and survivors. Both had a keen eye for able people and an ability to manage such talent. Both King and Macdonald were popular with women. Both had an intuitive, nuanced understanding of Canada and Canadians. Both believed and acted on the fundamental principle that the French-English partnership was essential to Confederation. And finally, while King might complain about Macdonald's political victories over the Liberal Party, he admired to no end his "political astuteness."[37] King himself, now at the end of his own political life, could generally match the great Macdonald when it came to political calculation and manoeuvre.

But there were real differences in personality and style that distinguished these two men. Mackenzie King was abstemious, a bit priggish and parson-like. No one would ever have used such words in their description of Macdonald: there was something roguish, something mischievous about the man. There was no evidence that King's colleagues felt the same personal attachment to him that Conservatives felt for Macdonald, although he took pride late in January 1940, as Canada launched its war efforts against the Nazis, that "Sir Wilfrid and Sir John Macdonald or any leader in Canada never had a parliamentary following more completely one hundred percent behind him than I had this morning within the period of some twenty hours even if I must have occasioned disappointment in the breast of every single member."[38]

The men who succeeded King as leaders of the Liberal Party would seldom wax eloquent about Macdonald. Among the Liberals, there is no record of Louis St-Laurent mentioning the legacy of Canada's first prime minister. Largely because he was prime minister during the centennial of Confederation, Lester Pearson did, however, on many occasions, hail Macdonald. "What a great man he was," Pearson said of Macdonald before an audience on January 11, 1967: "Human, wise, flexible, tolerant, but determined ... and among the men who made Canada he must take pride of place."[39] Pearson highlighted Macdonald's ability to work with Cartier and Brown, and spoke admiringly of how they "met the challenges of their times and were equal to its problems and its opportunities.... They were proud of their work; they had faith and confidence in what they had done; not for them was pessimism or self-doubt ... 1867 was a glorious combining of man's vision and energy and practical common sense in overcoming difficulties and obstacles to reach a great objective."[40]

Remembering his thinking while writing his memoirs a few years later, Pearson took aim at his critics and relied on Macdonald's example to justify his actions. Pearson was at the helm as Canada witnessed a new awakening in Quebec and had responded by creating a Royal Commission on Biculturalism and Bilingualism and bringing fresh talent from Quebec directly into cabinet. "I have often been attacked as a believer in two nations," he wrote:

> Our critics were trying to crucify Canada on a cross of words. It is a dreadful experience to see disputes develop over semantic differences (this time over the word "nation"), especially when there are those who for reasons of their own are eager to distort these semantic difference into differences of substance. This misrepresentation is so easy, and has been tried so often, that one is almost afraid to use the word "nation" at all. The French in Canada are a nation in the sense that they are a separate people. As Sir John A. Macdonald said of them: "Treat them as a nation and they will act as a free people do — generously; call them a faction and they become factious."[41]

Pierre Trudeau, like St-Laurent, scarcely had a thought for Macdonald — except for one occasion when joking with a reporter, where he admitted that he was something of a Conservative, but only in the "John A. Macdonald Tradition." John Turner, more of a student of history, reflected on how the leadership of his own party had ignored Macdonald's lessons. In a speech he gave in Orillia on January 11, 2001, he lamented the fact that Macdonald's stature in Canada was nothing compared to Washington in the United States or Cromwell, Pitt, and Disraeli in the United Kingdom.[42] Turner, whose political and prime ministerial career was relatively short, could only admire John A. Macdonald's longevity. "Our wonder grows when we reflect that that career was continued through 47 years of parliamentary life. He was the leader of his party for 36 years; he was a minister of the Crown for 35 years; he was premier of this Dominion for over 20 years. The public life of the average American statesman is very short: Lincoln was before the public but nine years, Cleveland, 15 years; Sir John A. Macdonald, 47 years." Turner dwelled on the political realities of the 1860s that were overcome to realize Canada and the key policies Macdonald pursued as prime minister. "In the final analysis, he not only did more than anyone else to bring Canada into being, but he also ensured her survival through the early, difficult years. In doing so he earned, or should have earned, the title 'Father of Our Nation.'"

Turner continued, perhaps a little wistfully, in his search for the qualities that could summon such support. "I still think he was our greatest prime minister," he said. He talked about Macdonald's humanity, his ability to remember names, his sense of humour, his thoughtfulness in going out of his way to extend small gestures of support and friendship. "He was great as a political leader, he was known as the Old Chieftain. He was born a leader; he had the peculiar quality which we call magnetism, which I suppose is another word for love. Magnetism is that quality which compels a man to walk ten blocks out of his way in order to meet you, instead of walking ten blocks out of his way in order to avoid you. Magnetism was the quality which Sir John held."[43]

Sean O'Sullivan, a member of the Progressive Conservative caucus, observed that Turner consciously emulated his political hero by treating his peers with particular respect and generosity. Pierre Berton told the story of David Thompson, the Liberal MP for Haldimand, who was returning to the House of Commons after an extended illness. His party leader, Edward Blake, gave him a curt nod, whereas Macdonald rushed over, slapped him on the shoulder, and exclaimed "I hope you'll soon be yourself again and live many a day to vote against me — as you've always done."[44] Thompson couldn't help but wish that Macdonald was leader of his party. Turner, O'Sullivan wrote, knew this anecdote and liked to relate it. He was conscious of his own interpersonal skills and not oblivious to their political value. "If I were to make any boast," Turner once declared proudly, "I know more people in Canada than any other single Canadian. Count on it. I can walk down any main street of any town in this country and within five minutes somebody there I will know by their first name."[45]

• • •

Conservative prime ministers proved more willing to refer to Macdonald, but hardly abused the privilege. Robert Borden was in the House of Commons visitors' gallery when Laurier pronounced his famous eulogy of Macdonald, and recalled it as "eloquent and impressive," but never made a habit of associating himself with the first prime minister.[46] This changed slowly over time. During the debates on the creation of the Canadian navy in 1909, Borden positioned himself against Laurier's vision that Canada would eventually sever its relations with the British Empire. Instead, he argued that "we should follow the idea of Sir John A. Macdonald who foresaw and predicted a cordial and healthy alliance with the mother country."[47] Campaigning in the 1911 election, he occasionally wrapped himself in Macdonald's legacy to oppose Laurier's proposals for Reciprocity, but hardly belaboured the point. To Laurier's claim that he was following Macdonald's example in seeking better trading terms with the United States, Borden reminded his audiences that, in 1891, Sir John had called Reciprocity with the U.S. "veiled treason." Reciprocity might have been attractive at one point in Canadian history, but in the prosperous Canada of 1911 it was no longer necessary and even dangerous.[48] Borden only referenced Macdonald nine times in his otherwise comprehensive memoirs, and never in his collected correspondence and speeches, *Letters to Limbo* (eventually published in 1971).[49] He mentioned Macdonald's advice "that one should never select a colleague by the standard of one's personal likes or dislikes," particularly in selecting cabinet members however. Borden, unlike Macdonald, was often very unpopular among parts of his cabinet and caucus.[50]

The record is just as thin in terms of R.B. Bennett's use for John A. Macdonald. Bennett, who had maritime roots but who made his fortunes, both financial and political, in Western Canada, was a good Tory — but not a particularly history-minded one. As a student at Dalhousie, Bennett had heard Macdonald speak and told a friend that the experience inspired him to think that he too could become prime minister one day,[51] and had a certain Leonard Tilley, a member of the House of Commons for New Brunswick, nominate him for the leadership of the Conservative party at the 1927 convention. Tilley was an old friend whose grandfather had long been associated with Macdonald.[52] Following his defeat in 1935, Bennett moved to Britain and was shortly thereafter named to the House of Lords. At one point, he rose to defend the independence of Canada in negotiating treaties and pointed to the reality that such ability was not incongruous with an active participation in the British Empire. "It is always in my mind that the late Sir John Macdonald, than whom no greater Britisher ever lived, said at the time that the Treaty of Washington was negotiated, that he almost felt impelled to give up his position because he was being urged so constantly to make sacrifices on the part of Canada in the interests of the relations between the United States and this island. But he remained, and, as your Lordships know, the Treaty of Washington was approved by the Canadian Parliament, but not by the American Senate."[53]

John Diefenbaker, who assumed the helm of the Progressive Conservative Party in 1952, made the most use of Macdonald in his later years in power, both to justify himself in his appeal to his caucus and to the voters. In a speech he gave at a dinner in Kingston in 1965 to commemorate Macdonald's one hundred-and-fiftieth birthday he, much like Mackenzie King, tied his family background to Macdonald's. He recalled that the latter's parents had left Sutherlandshire, while his own great grandparents lived only twelve miles away at Kildonan and would have left the area at roughly the same time. Diefenbaker likened himself to Macdonald as "one who descended from the same group."[54] Diefenbaker, who had lost ministers over his foreign policy and suspected many in his party to be disloyal, remembered that Macdonald had "stood against Tories in his day."[55] When Diefenbaker eventually lost the support of his caucus in 1967, he used Macdonald to teach the Tories a lesson. In his book *Those Things We Treasure*, he wrote the following:

> [T]o those who have given me their loyalty and support, there are no words to express my feelings. We weren't always right. One time an Ontario leader came to Macdonald and said "You know, Sir John, I'm always with you when you are right." Sir John told him where he might go. "What I need is people who are with me when we're wrong," said Sir John. In democracy, you can't always be right. But you can be honest. I am asked — and I am speaking to young Canada now — are there any rewards in public life? There are — not monetary but there is a tremendous satisfaction in being able to say "I tried, I stood." A leader has to take responsibility. He has to have courage.[56]

Diefenbaker's memoirs are filled with lessons from Macdonald and points to experiences he felt he shared with the first prime minister. He wrote about how Macdonald was legendary in his handling of hecklers, beggars for Senate appointments, demands for plum jobs.[57] He even reflected on the fact that he used to point his finger at members of the opposition who accused him of wrongdoing.[58]

In terms of policy, Diefenbaker likened his vision for northern development as comparable to Macdonald's national policy, chiding the Liberals for their apparent belief that "what was good for General Motors was not only good for the United States but good for Canada."[59] Where the Liberals, he noted, pursued economic continentalism, the Progressive Conservative party in 1957 "offered a policy of positive government" rooted in the Macdonald tradition:

> We saw the historical origins of our policy in the first Conservative ministry in Confederation. Macdonald had known instinctively that the goals of an economically independent and viable Canada could not be realized except by positive, even heroic, government action to ensure the establishment and development of east-west lines of communication and trade. His railway, immigration, settlement, and tariff policies were all testimony to this. Macdonald's National Policy had been fully enunciated in 1878. It was now 1957 and the Liberals continued to demonstrate that they had not learned the fundamental truths concerning Canada's very existence as a nation. We were offering a new national policy of regional and northern development. Our objective was to continue Macdonald's historic task of nation-building within the context of modern requirements and circumstances. We wanted to get government back to the people, to involve them more intimately in the shaping of their own destinies, to release their energies, their enthusiasms, and their imagination. We wanted to make ours an Elizabethan Age worthy of its predecessor, an age of adventure and high endeavour. Government, in our view, was as much a matter of inspiration as it was of administration.[60]

In a speech he gave in early January 1967, Diefenbaker reflected on his views of the United States and again invoked Macdonald. Macdonald, he said, "was convinced that the continental imperialism of the United States was and always had been a serious threat to Canada. For him, therefore, the maintenance of good relationships with the United Kingdom was a basic political necessity. It was to be continued indefinitely; at the same time it must chance to suit the new circumstances until the old imperial connection had become virtually an alliance of political equals. He anticipated the present concept of the Commonwealth."[61]

Diefenbaker also admired Macdonald's ability to govern men: "He had a marvellous knowledge, a rare insight into men and their motives, an inflexible will admirably united to a remarkable power of adaptability to the circumstances," Diefenbaker noted. "He possessed a gift of leadership which had been compared to the feat of the juggler in keeping half a dozen balls in the air at once, an extraordinary ability for holding together diverse elements of interest. Above all he possessed the uncommon ability of evolving success out of defeat and his greatest disaster was soon followed by his greatest success."[62]

Diefenbaker even tied his pro-British views to those of Macdonald. He had this to say about Macdonald's policies on Canada / U.S. relations:

> He believed in an independent Canada associated in partnership with the United Kingdom and other countries in the Empire beyond the seas. He was the first among statesmen of the British Empire to give utterance to the concept of the Commonwealth of British Nations. He vigorously asserted that Canada should have the right to act as an independent national along with Australia, New Zealand, and other nations yet to be formed — that Canada and these national should be co-equals with the Mother country bound together by a common allegiance to the Crown. It was Macdonald who, in the face of strong opposition at home and abroad, inaugurated the system of High Commissioners to the United Kingdom. The Statute of Westminster which was passed 40 years after his death embodies many of the ideas for which he stood in his day.

He foresaw that Canada and other nations within the British family, though free to do otherwise, would make common cause with Great Britain voluntarily against her enemies.[63]

Chiding Lester Pearson's claims of working toward national unity, Diefenbaker rose in the House on Macdonald's birthday on January 11, 1967, to set the record straight and to point out how national unity was achieved. "Macdonald lived in the era of great uniters of nations; the era of Lincoln, Cavour, Bismarck. These three in their respective countries brought about unity by bloodshed or force," he said. In contrast, Macdonald "was able, with the assistance of Cartier, Brown, Tupper, with the eloquence of D'Arcy McGee and all the galaxy of other greats of that era, to bring about Canadian confederation, not through the means of the three leaders I have mentioned but by consultation, co-operation, compassion and common sense."[64]

The next Progressive-Conservative prime minister to invoke Macdonald was Brian Mulroney and, in 1991, on the hundredth anniversary of Macdonald's death, he had reason to summon Macdonald's ghost. The defeat of his attempt to amend the constitution (the Meech Lake Accord) had failed only a year before, and a special commission, the Citizen's Forum on National Unity, led by Keith Spicer, was just about ready to release its report. It observed that "there was a fury across the land." The war in Iraq had just ended, but Canadian servicemen remained on the Arab peninsula. To cap it off, the economy was in a severe recession, the worst since the Great Depression, and Mulroney's popularity had sunk to near-record lows. "Some days, I think I know in some small degree what Sir John A. felt," said Mulroney: "Being Prime Minister of Canada is not a picnic, even in the best of times."

Brian Mulroney, the prime minister who had reversed the trade policy that had been the cornerstone of Macdonald's economic plan, spoke fervently about Macdonald, particularly as his government suffered through the difficult years of the early 1990s. His speech on the hundredth anniversary of Macdonald's death reminded his listeners more about current realities than of those of Macdonald's time. He quoted Macdonald: "We are a great country, and shall become one of the greatest in the universe if we preserve it. We shall sink into adversity and insignificance if we suffer it to be broken," and then continued himself:

These words are a bequest to the nation. But what we make
of them is entirely up to us. We can, in his words, "sink
into insignificance", or we can work for a better Canada.
We have it within our power to renew Canada and build a
stronger country for a new century. Canada today stands
at the forefront of the world's industrialized countries, the
second most desirable country among 160 surveyed in
which to live, according to a recent UN report. Millions
of people around the world would love nothing more than
to share our citizenship, in a strong and humane nation.[65]

Like many who had preceded him, Mulroney sought, a century later,
the image of Macdonald as unifier, a man who could depend on his caucus
for steadfast support and a country that would follow his vision. Brian
Mulroney liked to invoke Macdonald:

My dream ... has always been that one day we would live
up to our potential as a country. We never have quite lived
up to our potential as a country. That was Sir Wilfrid
Laurier's dream. It was also Sir John A.'s dream. And they
still remain our greatest prime ministers. We've got such
a great heritage and a great opportunity with our limitless
land, our water, our resources, and our northern frontier.
There's space to be alone when we want to; our two languages, our many cultures, our spirit of freedom and our
tolerance, our respect for the law, our faith still in parliamentary democracy. I think we all in this room want this
nation to endure because millions of Canadians, I know,
share my dream for our country — for a Canada that is
strong and sovereign and united.[66]

Facing a party convention in early August 1991, Mulroney reminded
his audience of Macdonald's defeats and resurgence and argued that his
decisiveness on issues of foreign policy and economics was likely to be a
source of strength in the upcoming election, as it had been for Macdonald.
"I am not here as prime minister to speak for any special interest, I am here

taking strong decisions in difficult time for a united Canada. I am before you, tonight — bloodied and sometimes bowed — but completely determined to fight another winning battle for a better Canada."[67]

Mulroney also spoke at length about the state of discussions on the future of Canada since the failure of the Meech Lake Accord in late June 1990, likening his situation to that of Macdonald in 1860, when the PM faced separatism in Nova Scotia, parts of New Brunswick, and refusal from Prince Edward Island and Newfoundland.

> Throughout, Macdonald maintained the cohesion and unity of purpose of the Conservative Party, which he saw first and foremost as the instrument of unity and prosperity for the fledgling Canada. Before building a united Canada, John A. built a united party. He realized that compromise and the merger of some of the numerous political groupings were essential. He was able to bring together a group of people who, up to that time, had spent much of their energies opposing one another. Though an enthusiastic practitioner of partisan politics — and a very good one at that — he was generous and open in his vision of Canada. He named Joseph Howe, the leader of the Nova Scotia block of separatists, to the Cabinet. He was understanding and loyal toward the French majority in Quebec. He was willing to listen and to accommodate. He was sustained by his party, which remained united and confident, even when he doubted himself. Some days, I think I know in some small degree what Sir John A. felt.

Mulroney insisted that national unity was the top priority and went on to give a short lesson on the merits of federalism, the need "to accommodate Quebec," and the need to compromise. No constitution should be expected to be "perfect," he said, and pointed to the weaknesses of Macdonald's policies in a way that had not been done since Wilfrid Laurier in 1891: "Because he was a man of large frailties and greater dreams, Macdonald knew that an insistence on perfection could become the enemy of the good," he wrote.

> [Macdonald] sought to guard against that impulse by
> reassuring Canadians that honourable compromise was a
> sign of confidence, wisdom and maturity in nation-build-
> ing, the opposite of rigidity, weakness and fear. He also
> sought to defend the national interest against demands
> of the special interests. For all his impressive qualities,
> Macdonald himself was not a perfect leader: he misjudged
> the fears and aspirations of the Métis and Native People,
> for example; his handling of the second Riel Rebellion
> alienated both aboriginal peoples and the province of
> Quebec during his own lifetime, and are today still a blot
> on our history[68]

Given his historical importance as a statesman, policy-maker, and politician, Macdonald has cast a surprisingly short shadow in the memory of
Canada's politicians. Since his death in 1891, there have been few references
to him and his accomplishments, and his memory has been evoked on
occasions limited to birth and death days. Almost unfailingly, his name
was mentioned to appeal to better days of national unity (as in the case of
Mackenzie King and Arthur Meighen, Lester Pearson, Brian Mulroney) and
party unity (almost in all cases, but most notably with John Diefenbaker,
who also used Macdonald to legitimize his emphasis on Commonwealth
issues). With the exception of Laurier and Borden (for opposite reasons),
Macdonald's economic policy disappeared from the record as Canada inex-
orably integrated into the continental sphere. As King reproached himself
in the 1930s, the reality is that the prime ministers of Canada have been
indifferent to his memory. No prime minister evoked Macdonald's name
in justifying the building of infrastructure, in approaching federalism, in
developing the state or in improving democracy, and Macdonald is largely
absent from their memoirs. Instead, it was mostly a folksier Macdonald that
was brought to mind, the comical Macdonald, the friendly Macdonald who
overcame endless difficulties to see better days and who somehow could
convey the difficult nature of the prime minister's job in Canada. At least
that was the hope of those whose lips uttered the name.

NOTES

1. The authors would like to thank Arthur Milnes for his generous help in locating some of the source material used in this article, as well as the research assistance of Ms. Laura Tonon.
2. *House of Commons Debates*, Monday, June 8, 1891, 884–87.
3. The speech is reproduced in Joseph Pope, *Memoirs of the Right Honourable Sir John Alexander Macdonald, G.C.B., First Prime Minister of the Dominion of Canada* (Toronto: Oxford University Press, 1930), Appendix XXX.
4. See Christopher Pennington, *The Destiny of Canada: Macdonald, Laurier and the Election of 1891* (Toronto: Penguin, 2011).
5. In Joseph Pope, *Memoirs of the Right Honourable Sir John Alexander Macdonald*, Appendix XXXI, 785.
6. See *Globe*, October 15, 1894. Thompson died a month later, on December 12, 1894.
7. Ibid.
8. See Patrice Dutil and David MacKenzie, *Canada 1911: The Divisive Election that Shaped the Country* (Toronto: Dundurn Press, 2011), ch. 7.
9. Mackenzie King Diary online, January 14, 1941, *www.collectionscanada. gc.ca/databases/king/index-e.htlml*.
10. R. MacGregor Dawson, *William Lyon Mackenzie King: A Political Biography, Vol. 1 1874–1923* (Toronto: University of Toronto Press, 1958), 13.
11. See King Diary, November 2, 1920.
12. King Diary, March 30, 1929.
13. See the diary entry for November 26, 1909, where he recounts that Sir John Hanbury-Williams (the governor general's secretary and military secretary) told him about "the care I should take in public life in the matter of wines etc. at any times. He felt I had a great career, he knew I would never want for financial help if it were needed, that I should be the premier of this country, but to look at Sir John Macdonald & see how his career had been marred by this one failing …" King learned early in his prime ministership with great satisfaction that Macdonald had a habit of asking each new minister for a letter of resignation. See diary entry for December 24, 1921. King decried alcohol's role in politics generally. In his diary entry for December 17, 1937, he lamented yet another attack by Mitch Hepburn. "It is all a shameful business, and would indicate his mind is becoming unhinged. Duplessis has talked like a man who had been drinking. I understand he & Hepburn were drinking most of the time they were together. The wine of power has gone to their heads.… It is a shameful exhibition of the management of public affairs."
14. See "The University and Public Life" in W.L. Mackenzie King, *The Message of the Carillon and other Addresses* (Toronto: Macmillan Company, 1927), 225–32.
15. King Diary, October 20, 1925.

16. King Diary, August 5, 1927.

17. King was positively obsessed with writing the speech on Laurier and his diary for all of July 1927 is replete with frustrations.

18. Ibid., 20.

19. Ibid., 143.

20. King Diary, August 8, 1937.

21. Ibid., December 31, 1937.

22. See Allan Levine, *King* (Vancouver: Douglas & McIntyre, 2011), 356.

23. A. Meighen, *Unrevised and Unrepented II: Debating Speeches and Others* (Kingston: School of Policy Studies, Queen's University. 2011) 237–40.

24. Ibid.

25. Ibid.

26. King Diary, June 7, 1941

27. See the *Ottawa Citizen*, June 9, 1941.

28. *Commemoration Service: Fiftieth Anniversary of the Death of Sir John A. Macdonald, June 6, 1891* (Kingston, n.d.) 9–12.

29. King Diary, June 7, 1941.

30. Ibid., December 3, 1941.

31. Ibid., December 14, 1941.

32. Ibid, November 27, 1944: 2.

33. Ibid., February 24, 1945.

34. Ibid., December 9, 1946.

35. Ibid., April 4, 1947.

36. See Levine, 381. Interestingly, King kept track early of his tenure, noting on the eve of his fifth anniversary in office, on March 25, 1927, that Macdonald stood "1st" and that he was now fourth, having passed Alexander Mackenzie. See Mackenzie King Diary online, 126, entry for March 26, 1927 (4812). Upon hearing of Robert Borden's death, he noted in his diary on June 10, 1937, that his tenure only ranked behind Laurier and Macdonald. By the summer of 1943, a weary King grew convinced that he would never surpass Sir John's record. See the entry for July 31, 1943, 726. King recorded a vision in his diary entry on August 3, 1941, in which he saw Macdonald hovering around a number 7. He wondered if the 7 "meant that many more years of active service, or a mystical sign indicating God's purpose in relation to my work at present, or from now on…. It was a good sign, of that only I am sure. It seemed to me that Sir John's presence signified length of office, — or length of service (on the 7th of this month, I will have been 22 years leader of my Party). The 7 may have meant in relation to Sir John that I will have squared my accounts, so to speak, in that time. It seems to me I would have about that many more years to run equal Sir John's term of office as P.M. — This thought is significant & confirmative." King retired on November 15, 1948, seven years and four months later.

37. King relates in his diary his personal debate in describing Macdonald's political prowess as "charlantry" or as "astuteness." See King Diary, December 8, 1946.

38. Ibid., 90, entry for January 26, 1940. He repeated the same claim two days later, see 242.

39. http://archives.cbc.ca/politics/prime_ministers/clips/9693/.

40. Ibid.

41. L.B. Pearson, *Mike: The Memoirs of the Rt. Hon. Lester B. Pearson, Volume 3* (Toronto: University of Toronto Press, 1972), 237.

42. "Speech to the Orillia Museum of Art and History's Annual Sir John A. Macdonald Birthday Celebration, 11 January 2001 — Orillia, Ontario," in John Turner, *Politics of Purpose: 40th Anniversary Edition* (Kingston: School of Policy Studies, Queen's University), 173–79, 180.

43. Ibid., Turner declared Macdonald "our greatest prime minister" in the summer of 2012. See *Hill Times*, July 2, 2012.

44. Pierre Berton, *The National Dream* (Toronto: McClelland & Stewart, 1970), 98.

45. Roy MacGregor, "My Time is Now!" *Toronto Star*, June 17, 1984. We are in debt to Professor Paul Litt for this anecdote.

46. *Robert Laird Borden: His Memoirs, Vol. 1, 1854–1915* (Toronto: McClelland & Stewart, 1969), 12.

47. Ibid., 120; the same lesson is drawn on 175.

48. See Patrice Dutil and David Mackenzie, *Canada, 1911* (Toronto: Dundurn Press, 2011), ch. 7.

49. Toronto: University of Toronto Press, 1971.

50. *Robert Laird Borden: His Memoirs, Vol 1, 1854–1915* (Toronto: McClelland & Stewart, 1969), 107.

51. John Boyko, *Bennett: The Rebel who Challenged and Changed a Nation* (Toronto: Key Porter, 2010), 38–39.

52. Ibid., 154.

53. R.B. Bennett, *The Authentic Voice of Canada: R.B. Bennett's Speeches in the House of Lords 1941–1947* (Kingston: School of Policy Studies, Queen's University, 2009) 31.

54. John Diefenbaker Centre, John Diefenbaker Papers, "An address by the Right Honourable John G. Diefenbaker to a dinner commemorating the 150th Anniversary of the Birth of Sir John A. Macdonald, Kingston, Ontario, 11 January 1965," 2. We are grateful to Arthur Milnes for drawing this document to our attention.

55. Ibid., 3.

56. J.G. Diefenbaker, *Those Things We Treasure* (Toronto: Macmillan, 1972), 151.

57. J.G. Diefenbaker, *One Canada: Memoirs of the Right Honourable John G. Diefenbaker, Vol. 1* (Toronto: Macmillan, 1975), 159, 236.

58. Ibid., 241.

59. Diefenbaker, *One Canada, Vol. 2*, 11.

60. Ibid., 15.

61. John Diefenbaker Centre, Diefenbaker Papers, Speech, January 11, 1967.

62. Ibid.

63. Ibid., January 10, 1867.

64. It is interesting to note that Donald Creighton told Michael Bliss that he felt that Diefenbaker had only "crudely pretended to be a Sir John A. buff." See Michael Bliss, *Writing History: A Professor's Life* (Toronto: Dundurn Press, 2011), 114.

65. "Notes for an address by Prime Minister Brian Mulroney, 100th anniversary of Sir John A. Macdonald's Death. Kingston, Ontario, June 6, 1991." It is interesting to note that the one book published on Macdonald during the Mulroney years noted that "it is obvious that Brian Mulroney is not a Tory of Sir John's stamp." See Cynthia Smith and Jack McLeod, *Sir John A.: An Anecdotal Life of John A. Macdonald* (Toronto: Oxford University Press, 1989), 7.

66. Brian Mulroney, "Canada: A Vanishing Identity," Speech at St. Francis Xavier University, April 3, 2002, Antigonish, Nova Scotia.

67. Brian Mulroney, *Memoirs: 1939–1993* (Toronto: McClelland & Stewart, 2007) 869–70.

68. Ibid. In an address to the Public Policy Forum's dinner in honour of former prime ministers in Toronto on May 3, 2012, Brian Mulroney, the only speaker to give a historical cast to his speech, spoke at length about Macdonald.

Chapter 15

Understanding Macdonald: Reviewing a Biographical Project

GED MARTIN

One of the fixed principles of a traditional training in humanities essay writing was avoidance of first-person pronouns. I disclaim that tradition in this chapter, not for egotistical reasons, but to take stock of my own biographical project on John A. Macdonald by seeking to integrate attempts to answer three related questions. A biographical project and a biography are different things. Biography tells a story in a narrative form.[1] It seeks to explain the personality whose career is being chronicled, but its linear form imposes limitations in tackling thematic issues that may surface at long intervals throughout a life. A biographical project can pursue themes that may span many decades, bringing together shards of evidence to suggest new perspectives. Its drawback is that it tends to assume that readers already know the "story," perhaps forcing some of them to consult the *Dictionary of Canadian Biography* for the "facts." Thus biography provides a narrative account to a large audience at the risk of discounting underlying elements which surface only rarely, whereas a biographical project can perhaps offer a deeper understanding of the subject, but in a form only accessible to a smaller, mainly academic, readership.

One example of these contrasting approaches is the question of the possible impact upon John A. Macdonald of the 1837 rebellions. Narrative reconstruction is not straightforward, not least because Macdonald himself kept very quiet about the fact that he had fought against William Lyon Mackenzie's rebels at Montgomery's Tavern: "I suppose I fought as bravely as my confreres," he commented in 1883.[2] There is evidence to suggest that he was critical of government arrogance at the time, and may have concluded that Canadian society and government were fragile structures that could not, and should not, be forced to handle provocation and confrontation. This hypothesis depends on analysis of the scattered references that he made to the rebellions, in 1860, 1884, and 1887, each of which has to be set into its own context of time. Yet there are revolutionary implications in a biographical interpretation of John A. Macdonald, which assumes that 1837 was not a passing adventure — but rather a shockingly formative episode in his life. We are accustomed to thinking of him as an amoral deal-maker who manipulated material incentives that set aside issues of principle to construct unlikely coalitions. If, instead, we interpret him as somebody who knew from first-hand experience that the rigid pursuit of theoretical principle could lead to deaths on the battlefield, then his accommodating and apparently opportunistic handling of issues such as the secularisation of the clergy reserves and the coming of Confederation may appear in a new and positive light.

My survey concentrates on three areas in which I have published interim conclusions. Two of these are methodological, fundamental but easily overlooked — the question of sources for Macdonald biography, and the nature of the biographies themselves. The third, the issues surrounding his alcohol problem, illustrates some of the themes arising out of biography.

The John A. Macdonald Papers, in Library and Archives Canada, represent a very extensive collection of political papers.[3] I am one of a declining band of historians who has actually handled Macdonald documents: for many years now, access has been solely through microfilm, and sets of these are widely distributed across Canada. Unfortunately, microfilming was carried out as far back as 1950, and some pages are hard to decipher. However, more recently, Library and Archives Canada has begun a program to make the Macdonald Papers available online. Democratic access is welcome, but it raises issues about the nature of the collection. Far too rarely do scholars attempt to interrogate the provenance of a collection of private papers.

Close to the end of his life, Donald Creighton condemned "arid scholars," whose "long years grubbing in archives" had "led them to place an exaggerated valuation on the evidence of unpublished documents — which

Grip, 13 June, 1891.

"The Empty Saddle."

they themselves have toiled so hard to get."[4] The irony is that Creighton based his own two-volume biography of Canada's first prime minister on the Macdonald Papers, whose "richness" conferred "independent authority" upon his research.[5] Creighton's magic touch fostered the easy misunderstanding that because the Macdonald Papers are evidently extensive, they must also be comprehensive.[6] It is worth noting that there are lacunae in the collection. For instance, it contains remarkably little material on Macdonald's family life. This is all the more regrettable, since what does survive can only whet our appetites.[7] John A. Macdonald was a married man for thirty-eight of his seventy-six years. In both of his marriages, politics often took him away from home, but not a single scrap of matrimonial correspondence survives to or from either Isabella or Agnes.

The biographical implications of this massive gap may be illustrated by comparison with what we know of Macdonald's sworn foe, George Brown. Maurice Careless's biography of Brown has unfairly suffered in the light of what he himself called "Professor Creighton's monumental biography." In fact, it is a splendidly readable and richly documented study, with its second volume particularly benefiting from extensive quotation from Brown's letters to his wife, Anne Nelson.[8] Unfortunately, in a bizarre way, this rich source becomes biographically counter-productive. George Brown was a bully and a bigot. The venomous invective of his newspaper, the Toronto *Globe*, injected elements of intolerance and sectarianism into public life, which made him an unusually divisive figure. Yet, although unrestrained in his condemnations of opponents, he regarded the slightest criticism of his own behaviour or motivation as an offence akin to blasphemy, which merited unforgiving abuse of the perpetrator. Only by evaluating the toxicity of Brown's role in Canadian public life can we comprehend just how remarkable was the coalition of 1864, in which he temporarily joined with John A. Macdonald, a particular target of his animosity. To fail to grasp George Brown's negative and deeply unpleasant qualities is to downgrade mid-Victorian Canadian politics into a phantasmagorical sepia-tinted Doonesbury cartoon, in which even the most outrageous personalities do not really "count."

Brown's biographer, Maurice Careless, was a kind and generous person. No doubt it was too much to expect him to live with his subject for so much of his career and not make allowances for Brown's innate nastiness.[9] His discovery of the matrimonial correspondence made possible "the re-assessment of the man and his many-sided activities in a way previously impossible."[10] The interpretational problem is that even the greatest of monsters may appear benign in his own domestic life, and Brown found great joy as a husband and a father. By contrast, the absence of any matrimonial correspondence from the Macdonald Papers robs us of the opportunity to pose the same kind of questions about the role of his two wives in his political life. In the early years of his second marriage, he excluded Agnes from political discussions, disapprovingly ignoring her altogether when she lobbied him on a patronage matter.[11] However, this may have changed as the years passed. "Sir John ... it is whispered, is in the habit of consulting her when he is about to take some important political step," claimed an admittedly uncritical biographer in 1883.[12] Perhaps that was the impression that Agnes wanted to circulate in Ottawa, but she did take the unprecedented step of writing to the governor general, reportedly on the night of her husband's death, urging him to appoint Tupper as Macdonald's successor.[13] In the absence of any correspondence (and the couple often travelled separately, so letters were certainly written), we shall never know how far their matrimonial alliance evolved into a political partnership.

We do not have Macdonald's matrimonial correspondence for the simple reason that somebody destroyed it — either Macdonald himself, or Agnes or possibly his secretary and authorised biographer, Joseph Pope. Indeed, Pope recorded, in February 1917, that he had burnt some politically embarrassing letters — surprising few, he insisted, and many of them to the discredit of others — yet historians do not seem to have picked up on this intriguing admission.[14] By definition, we do not know what has been lost, but it is possible to hazard some guesses. In 1875, Macdonald fell out with his son. Virtually all that survives from this episode is a dignified letter from Hugh John withdrawing from the law firm of Macdonald and Patton ("it will be much pleasanter for you not to have me in the office"). The row centred on the young man's decision to get married. Perhaps Macdonald thought he was too young (at twenty-five, Hugh was three years younger than his father at the time of his own first marriage), but the absence of any further documentation prompts the speculation that Macdonald objected to Hugh John's decision to marry a Catholic — a common prejudice in an era when mixed marriages could raise conflict over the education of children.[15] Was correspondence destroyed (perhaps even by Macdonald himself) because it showed him in an unfavourable light?[16]

Indeed, we may go further and speculate on Macdonald's reasons for preserving a private archive at all. Richard Cartwright's theory, that the collection was a vast dirt file, is primarily evidence for the venom of the feud between the two men. Macdonald could hardly have revealed that supporters had, in effect, taken bribes without confessing himself to be the source of corruption, while the revelation of the sins of any one of his followers would have shaken the trust of them all. In any case, Cartwright's belief that Macdonald "could generally lay his hand on any document he wanted, even after a long lapse of years" does not seem to have been true of the "appalling mass" of paper that had been generated by the final decade of his career.[17] Lawyers had the habit of filing documents, but Macdonald was not consistent in his observance of the practice. He had to admit that he had destroyed an incriminating letter from Sir Hugh Allan, outlining the terms on which he would finance the 1872 Conservative election campaign. However, the opposition years 1873–78 are exceptionally thinly documented, although we might have expected that this was precisely the period when Macdonald needed to keep track of promises made and deals struck. Although he gave the advice "never write a letter if you can help it, and never destroy one,"[18] he was hardly faithful to either principle himself.

Of course, not only did Macdonald write many letters, but one of the delights of his archive is that copies of dozens of them are preserved in letter books. These too mainly cover the years when he was in government, and they cannot always be taken at face value. Unfortunately, merely because Macdonald himself insisted that he wrote to a correspondent "with perfect candour," we are not justified in endorsing Joseph Pope's confidence that he was "evidently expressing his inmost sentiments."[19] Macdonald targeted the presentation of his comments at his correspondents, and we need to search out the context in which key missives were penned. One important example of this is his letter to Malcolm Cameron in December 1864, in which Macdonald predicted that they would live to "see both the Local Parliaments & Governments absorbed in the General power." Dropped into the standard form of linear biographical narrative, those words have the capacity to sizzle: here, surely, is the smoking gun which proves the conspiracy theory that Macdonald was an unscrupulous centraliser. Fortunately, the only major biographer who has used the quotation, Richard Gwyn, has the sophistication to put it in context as Macdonald "spin." Cameron was one of the few Upper Canada Conservatives to oppose Confederation, mainly because he objected to the American-style federal features in the Quebec scheme that would guarantee provincial autonomy. Cameron refused to be seduced by such vague predictions and, a few weeks later, he and Macdonald clashed in an assembly debate, with Macdonald genially demolishing Cameron's belief that a legislative union could have been achieved in the face of overwhelming French and Maritime resistance.[20] Cameron was that rare political phenomenon, a gentleman, and Macdonald could rest safe in the confidence that he would not flourish an embarrassing private letter.

The same principle applies not merely to individual letters, but to Macdonald's dealings with specific correspondents. Comparison of three archives of his political allies illustrates how Macdonald operated at different levels of openness. Creighton used the papers of Alexander Campbell, if perhaps sparingly, but he did not have access to those of J.R. Gowan and T.C. Patteson, which have become available to historians in more recent times. Campbell was Macdonald's long-time political associate who served in his cabinets for two decades. Even if Macdonald never treated him as an equal, Campbell was a cabinet colleague for seventeen years, and his concerns required some measure of serious response.[21] With the hero-worshipping Gowan, Macdonald's correspondence operated on a principle of manipulative inclusivity: he valued Gowan's friendship, no doubt, and made him bask in the epistolary warmth of his goodwill. But his letters contained political messages that were certainly intended for circulation among Gowan's Barrie neighbours.[22] With Patteson, a young Englishman hired to launch the *Toronto Mail*, the element of "spin" was even more blatant, with Macdonald often feeding a definite line of argument for editorial reproduction.[23]

Two examples should demonstrate that Macdonald's letters should not be uncritically accepted as evidence of his thinking, although they can indeed be interpreted as indications of how he wished other people to view events. In the aftermath of his humiliating defeat over the 1862 Militia Bill, he wrote to Gowan:

> I think you will agree that I chose a soft bed to fall on. My U[pper] C[anada] friends stood to me as one man and I fell in a blaze of loyalty. We are now in a position to put the present people out whenever we like — but I am opposed to taking that course just now, but our impatient spirits may *force* a vote on.

Signing himself "In great haste" and adding the flattering postscript that the letter was written "in the midst of a great hubbub in the House," Macdonald was making Gowan feel a valued confidant, a man whose sound judgement was recognised in those opening words: "I think you will agree ...". Perhaps the judge was sufficiently flattered to forget that just six weeks earlier, his insightful friend had reported that the parliamentary opposition were "broken up — weak & disjointed — so now I have them on the hop."[24]

In March 1875, Macdonald wrote in similar tones to Patteson — and this, it should be remembered, was just a year after Mackenzie's Liberals had routed him at the polls and a time when Macdonald's own leadership of his party was insecure. His French allies, he reported, were "in very good heart just now," and expected to "sweep" Quebec at the forthcoming provincial elections. Thus far, Macdonald was on sure ground, for the Bleus did indeed coast to victory. From then on, the letter retreats ever deeper into fantasy. "That once done Quebec is safe & the moderate Rouges in the Commons, seeing the Handwriting on the wall will join us." Ontario would also fall into place. "With the Ont[ario] and Quebec Gov[ernment]s in our favour we can force next session McK[enzie] to resign and Lord D[ufferin] will grant us a dissolution."[25] He did not explain just how this fairy tale was to come about. "Moderate" was an uncharacteristic adjective for Macdonald to apply to any sub-species of Rouges: French-speaking Reformers were the one major political category whom he never ensnared in his welcoming net. Since Ontario had re-elected the Mowat Liberals with a handy majority just two months earlier, a change of provincial regime seemed unlikely. Macdonald, of all people, knew that the point of Confederation had been to separate central and provincial politics into distinct spheres: the day might come when Ontario and Quebec would form a common front against Ottawa (as it did against Macdonald himself in 1887) but no mechanism existed by which mutinous provinces could oust a Dominion ministry. As for the flamboyant Dufferin, it was surely patently clear that nobody could predict what he would do in a political upheaval. In short, to accept these statements made to Gowan and Patteson at their face value would be to do great damage to the conventional view of Macdonald's political sagacity. It is unlikely that he would ever have ventured such implausible predictions to the sceptical Campbell. The biographical problem is that to assemble a fast-moving narrative that combines morsels from the Gowan and Patteson

Papers with more solid missives to Campbell is like adding up a column of figures in both American and Zimbabwean dollars.[26]

• • •

Consideration of the Macdonald biography follows naturally from analysis of sources.[27] The swing away from the writing of political history in Canadian academe over the past half century is paralleled by the relative lack of scholarly biographies of public figures, although the countervailing compensation is that most of those that do exist are highly competent and informative. Nonetheless, it is striking that such works are usually regarded as windows rather than oil paintings: once a biography has been published, it is common parlance among historians that its subject has been "done." This is in sharp contrast with Britain, where many major figures receive multiple coverage: Churchill, for instance, generates an unstoppable literature. Nor is this simply a result of a smaller population. In Ireland, where the university sector is far smaller and much less well resourced than in Canada, biographies of iconic figures such as Collins, de Valera, and Parnell continue to appear at steady intervals. It is worth reflecting that we owe some of the most challenging life story material in Canadian history to the fact that a handful of personalities have been the subject of more than one study: thus Mackenzie King's involvement with spiritualism and Pierre Trudeau's early flirtation with separatism were elements that would not have emerged had coverage of their lives been restricted to a single (even if multi-volume) biography.

Macdonald is unusual in having been the subject of four two-volume biographies, by Macpherson (1891), Pope (1894), Creighton (1952–55), and Gwyn (2007, 2011), as well as many other single-volume works and interpretative essays.[28] Surprisingly, coverage within the four double-deckers is uneven. Although Macpherson was John A.'s nephew, his massive compilation is of little value. Pope was reluctant to provide "a connected narrative" beyond 1873: as a civil servant, he had to consider the possibility that he would find himself working for a Liberal government, as he did two years after he had published.[29]

Perhaps the most curious, and remarkably little noted selectivity in emphasis came from Creighton's acknowledgement of his motive for writing about Macdonald at all. In 1969, he acknowledged that the "protagonist" in his impressive 1937 study, *The Commercial Empire of the St. Lawrence, 1760–1849,* had been the great river itself. Unfortunately, its imperial potential had been destroyed by Britain's move to free trade, a betrayal that provoked some previously loyal Canadians to consider joining the United States. To carry the story beyond 1849, Creighton required an alternative central figure, and he "stumbled upon" the career of Macdonald as "the only satisfactory method of writing the second phase" of the Laurentian story. Hence, Macdonald appears in the pages of Creighton not just as a man, but also as the vehicle for the creation of a Canadian destiny — a view that has been enthusiastically and explicitly taken forward by Gwyn. This aura of nation building has given Creighton's work a grandeur that transcends a mere life story, but it comes at a price. Just as the St. Lawrence River has no headwaters but flows out of Lake Ontario at Kingston, so the young Macdonald emerged fully formed in the same city, a weapon providentially forged for a career of nation building. As a result, Creighton is not much concerned about the shaping of Macdonald prior to 1849, the year that the young politician began to make his impact upon the scene. Magnificent though it is in conception, *The Young Politician* fails to engage with one of the most basic tasks of biography, tracing the adult back to the youth. Indeed, well qualified though he was to write about Canada's past, Creighton was perhaps singularly ill-suited to comprehend another human being. There is no Law of Biography that states that only nice people should engage in the exercise, but there can be little doubt that Creighton was a cold and confrontational personality, both as a colleague and also as a father.[30] Yet there was also a deep vein of creativity in this complex scholar, which is bizarrely reflected in overtones of Wagner's *Ring Cycle* in his life of Macdonald, with hints of the Rhine, the sacred Ring, and the hero who must overturn the Götterdammerung of 1849. For Creighton, *The Commercial Empire of the St. Lawrence* and his two Macdonald volumes constituted "a trilogy on one theme."[31]

These two-volume biographies radiate the impression that Macdonald was a larger-than-life figure, far more important than any of his contemporaries. The medium is the message, but it is possible to suspect that the message may sometimes be overstated. Three of the four works (Macpherson, the slightest of them, is the exception) divide their two volumes at 1867, with Creighton asserting that Macdonald's career "naturally" divides in the year of Confederation.[32] The 1867 young politician/old chieftain divide may be convenient but it is analytically simplistic: in reality, Macdonald's career passed through a series of shorter phases. Arguably, the real caesura in his political life came not in 1867, but three years earlier, when he came close to abandoning politics in order to rescue his personal finances — just weeks before the Confederation issue burst into life. He had spent "twenty long years," he told an audience in Halifax later that year, "dragging myself through the dreary waste of Colonial politics," with the clear implication that he had reached the end of that particular road.[33] If anything, 1867 fell within a transitional phase of regional and special interest deal-making from which arguably he did not finally escape until he recovered power in 1878.

By forcing the sub-periods of Macdonald's career into the pre- and post-Confederation straitjacket, it is easy to assume — indeed that array of double volumes tells us we *must* assume — that John A. Macdonald was the dominant political figure throughout. Gwyn is relentless in his assumption that every pre-Confederation ministry in which his hero served was "Macdonald's government," with premiers such as MacNab and Taché dismissed as facades.[34] Macdonald was certainly seen as a key member of successive ministerial teams, but this does not mean that he dominated them. Biographers have passed lightly over his nine-month premiership of the Province of Canada in 1857–58.[35] It was hardly Macdonald's fault that his brief spell at the head of government was frustrating and fruitless: the coalition lost its Upper Canada majority in the December–January general elections, not least because it had successfully discharged the reform program it had set itself back in 1854. Macdonald himself was exhausted by three years in office, accompanied by financial and health problems (both largely self-inflicted), all of which left him ill-equipped to deal with the death of his first wife. It is a measure of the overall failure of the Macdonald biographies to integrate his public and private life that it may surprise many readers to discover that his first wife died in the midst of a hard-fought election campaign. Unfortunately, one of the few authors to have noted the connection was entirely incorrect to state that "Isabella's death boosted John A.'s flagging political fortunes."[36] In fact, he faced an unusually prolonged session of parliamentary trench warfare with which he could barely cope. Far from dominating and manipulating the political scene in the last years of the province of Canada, Macdonald's star was in the descendant. In July 1859, he even contemplated resignation upon discovering that a major policy commitment had been made without consulting him.[37]

We should be equally wary about accepting the myth that Macdonald emerged from the telephone box of Confederation garbed in the super-hero costume of the Old Chieftain. Macdonald, now Sir John, was chosen as the Dominion's first prime minister because of his skills in managing people and balancing factions. The limitations of his authority were dramatically demonstrated when Kingston's Commercial Bank ran into trouble in the fall of 1867. A modern-day prime minister of Canada would no doubt find a way to save a financial institution that was crucial to the economy of his own riding. Macdonald was presiding over an untried combination of associates, including Maritimers who needed to protect themselves against the down-home allegation that the new structure was being run according to Central Canadian interests. The cabinet declined to shore up the Commercial Bank (which, in turn, had kept Macdonald's own unstable finances afloat for several years past) — but it was the prime minister's name that appeared at the foot of the telegram that consigned Kingston's bank to oblivion.[38] The first prime minister's position was not secure: George-Étienne Cartier resented his relegation to the role of Quebec lieutenant and, in 1868, he seemed ready to respond to feelers from George Brown for a renewal of their alliance of 1864.[39] Symbolically, Macdonald's fall from office, in November 1873, was partly triggered by his inability to incorporate a newly arrived faction into his struggling parliamentary coalition. In the normal run of events, the six MPs from Prince Edward Island, who arrived mid-crisis to take their seats as the representatives of Canada's newly acquired sixth province, would have been the kind of loose fish who would add to Macdonald's narrow working majority. Arriving in Ottawa at the height of the Pacific Scandal, they sniffed the wind and four of them switched to the opposition. Old Chieftainship could not survive rookie opportunism.[40] It was not until his return to power in 1878 that Macdonald came to dominate parliament and cabinet, but even so his ascendancy in Ottawa contrasted with wider limitations on his authority.[41] His writ never ran in Quebec, where his lieutenants quarrelled fiercely for local control, while each of his election campaigns represented a desperate attempt to overcome his innate minority status in Ontario. The recent labelling by four political scientists of the contests of 1878 to 1891 the "Macdonald dynasty" is an unusually fatuous attempt to impose social-sciences pattern-making on objective reality.[42]

The consistent portrayal of Macdonald as a dominant figure throughout his career has required the downgrading of both allies and rivals to walk-on status. Campbell, his longest-serving associate, has certainly suffered in the comparison: detested by Pope (for reasons that remain obscure) and patronised by Creighton (for reasons that are all-too transparent). In reality, Campbell was a more sympathetic and maybe even more noteworthy figure than he has been portrayed. Disguised from us have been the facts, obvious to contemporaries but carefully masked by Victorian propriety, that he was physically handicapped throughout his adult life and, certainly in his later years, subject to violent epileptic seizures: a compassionate modern Canada, a country that cares about disability, might find something of contemporary moment to celebrate behind this conventional facade of this papier-maché Father of Confederation.[43]

George-Étienne Cartier is another character who is too often viewed as "exactly what Macdonald needed as French lieutenant," an approach that downplays the fact that it was Cartier who led the ministry from 1858 to 1862, and Cartier who provided the numbers to strike the deal with George Brown in June 1864.[44] The bizarre episode that ushered in Cartier's four-year period of office is an example of the way the Macdonald myth has distorted an admittedly speculative set of events. George Brown had formed a government on August 2, 1858, but had been forced to resign two days later after being defeated in the Assembly and refused an election by the governor general. Members of the outgoing Macdonald cabinet now regrouped, with some reinforcements, under Cartier's leadership. Had they reappointed themselves to the offices they had held prior to August 2, they would have been obliged to fight by-elections to defend their status as incoming ministers. Happily, somebody recalled a useful provision in the *Independence of Parliament Act* of 1857, which abolished the requirement to fight by-elections if ministers moved from one portfolio to another within thirty days — a sensible device to facilitate internal cabinet reshuffles. Since it was less than thirty days since they had left office, Cartier's team decided to swear themselves to new posts, before switching back the following day to their previous jobs: hence the derisive tag, "double shuffle."[45] Whose idea was the double shuffle? It was "more than probably Macdonald, the old master of manoeuvre" who recalled the convenient loophole, said Creighton.[46] Other biographers have been more definite.[47]

It is certainly plausible to assume that a former law officer would have been the source of the wheeze, but why not Cartier — Attorney General East in 1857, and the incoming premier who was responsible for the government's strategy and who defended the shuffle in parliament? The "evidence" for Macdonald as the progenitor of the double shuffle relies essentially upon

back-projecting the assumption that he dominated pre-Confederation politics and therefore was the source of all its ideas. As it happens, murky though
the affair must remain, there is some counter-evidence that biographers have
ignored. The political chronicler J.C. Dent reported: "An attempt has been
made to excuse Mr. Macdonald's participation therein upon the ground that
he all along disapproved of it; that he opposed it at the Council Board, and
only consented to it at last ... because he was wearied by ... the importunity ...
proceeding from his colleagues." This is not special pleading — Dent himself
was unimpressed by the evidence that he recorded — and, of course, the story
could represent a subsequent attempt at damage limitation, an unscrupulous
attempt by Macdonald to distance himself from a controversial stroke.[48]
Macdonald, exhausted from his premiership and racked by personal worries,
was probably telling the truth when he claimed that he had been "unwilling to have anything to do with the new arrangement" but had acceded to
Cartier's insistence on his continued participation.[49] This certainly reflects
an alternative view to the general assumption that he was pulling the strings.
Essentially, in Macdonald biography, you pays your money and you picks
the Macdonald of your choice. For what it is worth, I do not believe that the
double shuffle has the "feel" of a Macdonald political ploy. His correspondence as Attorney General West shows a respect for the spirit of the law and,
always proud of his ability "to look a little ahead,"[50] Macdonald might well
have foreseen that a dubious ploy could leave him open to prosecution — as
happened, in a case launched by the Grits later that year.[51]

The role of biography, as a filter determining our perceptions, may also be
illustrated by the example of another contemporary of John A., his namesake,
John Sandfield Macdonald.[52] Macdonald, one of the few Canadian politicians to be enduringly recalled by a nickname, "Sandfield" served (uniquely)
in every parliament of the province of Canada, from 1841 to 1866, before
becoming the first premier of Ontario (1867–1871). He created perhaps the
first great moment in the history of Canadian bilingualism, exercising the
age-old privilege of the Speaker to reprimand Lord Elgin — the monarch's
representative, in this case — at the end of the 1854 session, and immediately repeating his rebuke in flawless French. He is also responsible for one
of the great one-liners in Canadian politics, his defiant question to a deputation importunately seeking local favours: "What the hell has Strathroy ever
done for me?" Like Campbell, he battled years of ill health to take part in

public life: there is surely something attractive about a man who disclosed his suspicion that he had "a touch of the horse distemper" just weeks before his doctors told him he was suffering from a fatal heart condition.[53]

With the hindsight of knowing that Confederation was just around the corner, historians have usually dismissed Sandfield's two-year stint as premier of the Province of Canada, which began in 1862, as the nadir of the Canadian Union, and the indisputable proof that the old system had reached terminal rock bottom.[54] This tends to obscure the extent to which he was a key, maybe even a pivotal, political figure in the decade before 1864 — in other words, at that time, equal in stature to his Kingston namesake. When Macdonald's ministry emerged from the 1857–58 elections severely weakened by loss of seats in Upper Canada, it was to Sandfield that he turned in the hope of shoring up his position. He was prepared to pay a high price: not just a cabinet seat for Sandfield himself, but also the nomination to two further places — in effect, the majority share of the Upper Canada section of the ministry.[55] Sandfield's refusal condemned Macdonald's administration to a brief and weak existence. Sandfield's resignation from the premiership in March 1864 may look like a belated recognition even on his part that the old factional game was played out, but at the time he "very freely boasted in the bar-rooms" that his decision to step down while he retained a formal, if narrow, majority was a tactical move to ensure his early recall, after which he could insist on a general election.[56] Indeed, the minority cabinet that Macdonald joined seemed set fair to prove Sandfield's point when it, too, collapsed three months later. One element in the formation of the remarkable coming together of sworn foes in the Great Coalition of June 1864 that has never been stressed was their common determination to keep Sandfield out in the cold.

• • •

How does the filter of biography affect the way we view the two Macdonalds? The standard account by Bruce W. Hodgins appeared in a series called Canadian Biographical Studies, a spin-off from the *Dictionary of Canadian Biography*, which aimed to rescue "men [this was 1971, when gender-specific vocabulary was not questioned] who seemed often to be merely secondary figures."[57] Thus, by definition, to be included in the Canadian Biographical Series was to be of lesser importance. The format further underlined this by a restriction on word-length. Hodgins rose to the challenge of chronicling Sandfield Macdonald in 40,000 words. By contrast, Creighton's two-volume biography of the other Macdonald ran to about ten times that length.

Unfortunately, the implied message — that John A. Macdonald was invariably ten times more important than his namesake — makes it impossible to interpret a key episode in the careers of both of them. Sandfield's claim to feature in the collective Canadian memory rests in part on the fact that he was Ontario's first premier — appointed to the role as part of an alliance with none other than the newly minted Sir John A. Macdonald. It seems a perverse start to Old Chieftainship to designate as premier of the Dominion's largest province a rival who had been one of the dissident rump of four Upper Canada critics to have opposed Confederation to the very last. Biographers have used various strategies to deal with the mystery. Creighton's was particularly effective: he ignored it. Readers of *The Old Chieftain* may become aware by literary osmosis that Sandfield had netted a key job, but insofar as there had been a rapprochement, it was implied that the prodigal anti-Confederate had bowed to the demands of destiny of his *own* overdue volition: in the aftermath of the first Dominion elections, we learn that Sandfield had "campaigned for the unionists."[58] Another biographer conjures the issue away with an aside identifying the new premier as "once John A.'s foe but now his ally" — the historian's equivalent of "In a bound, Jack was free."[59] The only strategy for confronting the episode that is congruent with the John A. Superman theory is to portray it, in the manner of Gwyn, as "one of the most adroit political seductions that Macdonald ever consummated," turning "Little John" into Ontario's "first Conservative premier": I have never encountered the nickname and I do not care to imagine what Sandfield would have thought of the partisan label.[60] The reality was captured by Pope, who wrote that Macdonald "came to the conclusion that John Sandfield Macdonald was just the man to undertake the task" of founding Ontario, and the reason for this decision was explained by Macdonald himself, in a letter to a supporter. Without Sandfield, he admitted, "the whole province would have been governed by a Grit Government."[61] It is only by starting from a position of appreciating that John A. Macdonald did *not* command the entire political landscape of Canada that we can assess the problems he encountered — and, indeed, his ingenuity in overcoming them.

• • •

One experience shared by Cartier and Sandfield Macdonald was that their political careers ran into the ground as their health collapsed. Understandably, biography portrays decline and death as the sad tailpiece that curtails a career, whether or not it had risen to the heights of achievement. A life cycle may resemble a theatrical drama, but that does not mean that the acts are *the same length in every story*. Cartier and Sandfield Macdonald both appear in their Act Five as old men, broken and on the point of exiting the stage. It comes as something of a surprise to calculate that Cartier was fifty-eight when he died, Sandfield fifty-nine.[62] By contrast, John A. Macdonald turned fifty-nine in January 1874, a low point in his career at which he had been ousted from office in the Pacific Scandal and was by no means secure in the leadership of a party about to be hammered at the polls. Had he died at that point, his biographers would have been fewer and, of necessity, less exultant. Their predominant theme would probably have been one of tragedy, that the man who had done so much to create Confederation was destroyed by it: perhaps, in Creightonian hyperbole, the Canadian Icarus who soared too close to the sun of nationhood.[63] It may seem thunderingly obvious to point out that dead politicians do not contribute to the body politic (except, occasionally, as symbols, like Louis Riel). Nonetheless, the fact that Macdonald lived to be *seventy-six* needs to be emphasised as a key element in the mythic status that ultimately gathered around him. Of course, it is possible to spend seventy-six years on this planet and to achieve either very little or, worse still, something that the world could well do without.[64] On the minus side, Macdonald's longevity probably compounded the difficulty of identifying a successor. "You'll never die, John A.!" was an inspirational slogan but it was not an efficient strategy for transferring power to a new generation.[65]

The focus upon Macdonald the nation builder has left correspondingly less biographical space for his family relationships, notably those with women. Indeed, in a witty essay, Barbara Roberts argued that Creighton not only had difficulty in portraying Macdonald's spouses, Isabella Clark and Agnes Bernard, as individuals in their own rights but tended to imply that it was his marriages that accounted for Macdonald's notorious problem with alcohol.[66] However, as with so many men, there was a prior female influence in his life, that of Helen Shaw Macdonald, his mother, "a remarkable woman" in Pope's tribute, who — in the words of her son — "kept the family together" through the first difficult years in Canada.[67] To appreciate her influence, we need to counteract one of the implicit elements of biography, the onward-and-upward spirit that goes hand-in-hand with its linear narrative form. Macdonald's arrival in Canada, at the age of five in 1820, is implicitly seen as the necessary first step to his rise to the leadership of his adopted country. But this obscures the extent to which emigration to Canada, especially for a family from Scotland's commercial class, represented a massive humiliation.[68] Helen's husband was no more successful in Canada than he had been at home, and she channelled her hopes into John Alexander, the only one of her three sons to survive childhood, backing his political career right down to her death.[69]

Although Helen Macdonald's influence over her son was considerable,[70] it would be implausible to suggest that she "programmed" the young John A. to marry his cousin, and her niece, Isabella Clark. But mothers were capable of having a say in their children's choices of partner, no doubt reminding them of the importance of marrying within their class and religious denomination.[71] Did his mother's double relationship to Isabella, as both aunt and mother-in-law, crowd in upon the bride, and could this explain the mysterious illness from which she suffered throughout her years with Macdonald? Attempting to answer this question raises a fundamental issue in biographical method. Calling upon a combination of limited computer skills and the jack-of-all-trades confidence of a longtime historian, I have concluded that Isabella suffered from trigeminal neuralgia, a stabbing and agonising pain in a facial nerve, known at the time as *tic douloureux*, for which no effective treatment was then available (it is treatable today with medication or surgery). However, in a study of Isabella's medical history, James McSherry dismisses trigeminal neuralgia and argues instead that, far from suffering from "an authentic organ disease," her condition was psychosomatic. He does not quite go so far as to term her a silly woman, but there is an arch lack of sympathy in his conclusion that "by some curious perversity, exacerbations always developed when John was busy on political or legal affairs." I prefer my own assessment, but this is a perennial failing of mine. The analytical problem is that James McSherry wrote as a qualified medical practitioner, whereas my doctorate is in British empire history. I believe that he misread the family correspondence to interpret facial pain as more generalized headaches. As a historian, I am presumably entitled to hold forth on the interpretation of sources, but am I justified in setting aside the professional competence of the Director of the Student Health Service at Queen's University?[72]

Perhaps the diagnosis matters less than the impact upon the Macdonalds' lives. Trigeminal neuralgia is extremely painful but, even allowing for Isabella's apparent reliance upon opium, did it necessarily cause her to take to her bed and remain there?[73] Was she, as McSherry concludes, "hysterical" and "manipulative"?[74] Did she use her affliction to create space for herself? For an apparently immobile invalid, she certainly showed dogged determination in 1845 to travel to Georgia, where it seems she had previously lived. Remarkably, she remained away from Kingston, and apart from her husband, for almost three years — except for his brief visits, during one of which she became pregnant.[75] If she was trying to create space for herself, we have to ask: space against whom? Her larger-than-life mother-in-law perhaps; or did she seek isolation from Macdonald himself? McSherry sympathises: "One can only wonder at John A. Macdonald's patience and kindness, for life with Isabella must have been a sore trial."[76] But this is to assume that the benign hero was in control of the situation. Those who were close to him were less confident of his ability to transcend what one friend called "this bitterness in your cup of life."[77] Biographers have not picked up on the allusion by his sister Margaret to "poor John however willing nearly as useless as a child" in his handling of Isabella's illness.[78] We seem to be back here to the ironic title employed by Barbara Roberts: was it his wife's condition that drove Macdonald to drink?

Macdonald's alcohol problem was high on the list of subjects that I sought to confront, and that I regarded as a test case to establish the value of an analytical biographical project over the traditional form of life story. Through its linear form, biography has the capacity to provide faithful narrative accounts of Macdonald's lapses into inebriation, but it is not ideally structured to group the episodes in order to assess and explain them. That capacity may not always be fully exploited, for — as with any form of historical writing — there is scope for selection and differential emphasis in telling the story. It is difficult to recapture now just how straitlaced of a society was English Canada (and Quebec was hardly swinging) for much of the twentieth century. One intending biographer, G.R. Parkin, even consulted the governor general "as to the advisability of mentioning the intemperance question." Lord Minto was no intellectual but he did command vast reserves of common sense: passing over the issue would be "to omit what is really well known to anyone acquainted with Canadian history — besides he completely triumphed on this weakness."[79] A product of Ontario Methodism and writing in joyless Toronto, Creighton was impressively open about Macdonald's "weakness", perhaps more so in his second volume after the first had clinched his status as the Old Man's chronicler. Nonetheless, as an outsider looking at Canada, it seemed to me that there had been an absence of engagement with the issue that complicated the way Canadians thought about themselves and their country. It was almost as if there were two Macdonalds, the visionary statesman who had created Canada and the genial drunk who ran the country through the hazy spectrum of a gin bottle. Indeed, as the statesman faded in the popular memory, so the caricature loomed larger. Putting the two together touched a nerve of national insecurity: if Macdonald was the architect of Canada and Macdonald was prone to alcohol abuse, what sort of country was the product?

Hubris is an ever-present threat to confident scholarship, but I venture to claim that my article in the *Journal of Canadian Studies* for 2006 deals comprehensively with the question.[80] Other episodes of drunkenness will no doubt surface,[81] but the main outlines seem clear. First, Macdonald had an intermittent alcohol problem from 1856 until about 1876. Second, he was a binge drinker ("sprees" was the favourite term at the time) who "broke out" occasionally, and not somebody who was either permanently intoxicated or necessarily dependent upon large intakes of booze to get through his daily round. Nonetheless, and third, there were occasions when his weakness had political repercussions.[82] Fourth, Lord Minto made a good, but generally overlooked point: Macdonald had eventually overcome his problem.

The first major point to note is that dating Macdonald's alcohol problem to the twenty years from 1856 to 1876 utterly undermines the standard division of his career at 1867. Indeed, the chronology renders all the more remarkable his achievements in designing and mentoring Confederation. The periodisation is also intriguing because it coincides with the decline of his electoral support in Kingston. As premier of the province, he carried the city by a massive 1,189 votes to nine in 1857; he lost the riding in 1878. There were other factors in play. These were the two decades in which Kingston had to face the bleak reality that it had lost the race to become Canada's capital and Ontario's largest city. In office almost continuously from 1854, Macdonald made the transition — in S.J.R. Noel's categorisation — from being a "patron" of local interests to the next level, becoming the "broker" who handed out the pork to the regional barons. Not surprisingly, Kingston could not understand why John A. Macdonald's increasing elevation at provincial and later Dominion level in fact limited his scope to bank-roll his own constituents.[83] "Some of the electors were displeased at my neglect," he admitted after the "stern contest" of 1872.[84] Their member's alcohol problem probably symbolised his incapacity, especially when he punched his opponent at an election meeting that year.[85]

Why did he drink? The timing of the episodes provides some clues. One basic cause was overwork: the drinking decades were also the core years in which he held government office. The foundations of the later Canadian civil service were set during this period, but at the time a great deal of administrative work fell upon ministers in person. Since the major decisions by any department often involved either legal or legislative implications, a great deal of business crossed the Attorney General's desk, usually requiring longhand correspondence. In addition, Macdonald passed through phases of severe financial worry. As he admitted in 1855, he had "speculated too heavily in real estate," putting down deposits to buy properties in the hope of selling them on for a quick profit. When the boom slowed down, he was at his "wits' ends" to pay the instalments on the purchase price.[86] He stayed afloat financially thanks to a huge overdraft from Kingston's Commercial Bank (of which he was a director) but when that enterprise failed, his debts passed to a Montreal institution that politely foreclosed on him in 1869 for all he possessed, and he took to the bottle again.[87] Domestic pressures constituted a third trigger: he started to drink heavily after a crisis in Isabella's health early in 1856, and the tragic realisation that his daughter by Agnes would have a lifelong disability was probably a factor in his collapse in 1869. Macdonald's associates seem to have accepted his binge drinking as an outlet for the pressures in his life. "It seems he breaks out in this fashion once or twice in the year," a British statesman noted with some amusement in 1870, adding that "the habit is so well understood that no especial notice is taken of it."[88]

Unfortunately, it was not the case that Macdonald confined his overindulgence to recreational end-of-session sprees. He was incapacitated by alcohol during the debates on militia reform in 1862, and so contributed to the fall of the Cartier ministry. He was allegedly drunk during the Fenian raid of 1866, an inconvenience since he was minister of militia at the time. There was a further bout, which delayed the introduction of the bill to create the province of Manitoba in 1870.[89] Nor were his shortcomings disguised from the public.

Macdonald himself apparently authorized announcements in 1858 and 1862 that he was joining the temperance movement. The *Toronto Globe* lambasted his drunkenness in 1866 and 1870.[90] Arguably, Macdonald only survived the latter campaign of well-documented denunciation because he collapsed and nearly died from a legitimate ailment, gallstones.[91] Canadian public life has not lacked colourful drunks, but nobody else made it to national leadership clutching a bottle. The historian's old friend, paradox, comes to our rescue here. As British Colonial Secretary Lord Carnarvon put it in 1866, "in spite of his notorious vice," Macdonald was "the ablest politician in Upper Canada."[92] Macdonald's modern-day admirers may perhaps prefer to pass over his alcohol problem. In reality, it is only by focusing upon his weakness that we can fully appreciate the sheer ability that made him an indispensable politician, *despite* a problem that curtailed and destroyed many other political careers, then and since. Macdonald himself claimed that his supporters "would rather have John A. drunk than George Brown sober."[93] The verdict should be broadened: many Canadians preferred a John A. who was occasionally drunk to the leadership of any of the dozen or so potential alternatives.

Integral to the story of Macdonald and the bottle — but usually omitted from the popular caricature — is the key fact that he overcame his weakness in the mid-1870s: the governor general, Lord Dufferin, for instance, believed in 1877 that the problem was solved. Macdonald's own explanation, to Dufferin, was that "his constitution has quite changed of late": indeed, by 1881, his digestive system was in such poor repair that his Ottawa physician suspected cancer and sent him to England for treatment.[94] However, a truly incapable drunk might perhaps not have been deterred by the failure of his own metabolism, and we should seek for other explanations. There is probably much in Biggar's opinion that "Sir John's very weakness was a secret of his popularity with a certain class of men,"[95] but by the 1870s the increasing politicisation of alcohol issues was reducing its value. Ontario legislated to lock up inebriates in 1873; Nova Scotia followed in 1875. An aggressive national temperance movement, the Dominion Alliance, was launched in 1875, and a new form of platform agitation, involving heart-rending confessions by reformed drunks, arrived in Canada in 1877.[96] The passage by the Mackenzie Liberals of the 1878 *Scott Act*, which provided for local plebiscites to close the bars on a county or municipality basis, was further evidence of the strength of the political temperance movement, but it also pointed to the potential for mobilising the drink trade as a revenge-seeking electoral base. However, it behoved a political leader seeking to mop up the backlash and project a sober persona. Hence, and probably uniquely, Macdonald threatened legal action to quash claims that he had been drunk during an all-night debate that year. (He had indeed fallen asleep, which is hardly surprising.)[97] Perhaps contemporaries were being formally polite in attributing Macdonald's longevity to wifely "influence, watchful care and rare judgment": Agnes had not vanquished his weakness in the first decade of their marriage.[98] My own hypothesis, a pretentious word for guesswork, is that Agnes at thirty had failed to control his drinking as a trophy wife (a role for which she was always too strong-minded anyway), but Agnes at forty slipped naturally into a maternal role — replacing the most dominant woman in her husband's life, his mother Helen. A lifelong if perhaps not particularly fervent Presbyterian, Macdonald quietly converted to the Church of England, his wife's denomination, in 1875. This little-noticed event may represent a shift within their relationship, and probably reflects some kind of personal crisis. Unfortunately, the absence of any matrimonial correspondence makes it pointless to speculate further.[99]

Was Macdonald an alcoholic (a term, incidentally, that seems to have been coined in 1891, the year of his death)? I confess that I did not go deeply into this question, for which shortcoming I plead two main reasons.[100] The first is a variant of the issue already encountered in relation to Isabella Macdonald's mystery illness: how useful is it for somebody who lacks medical qualifications to attempt such a diagnosis, and a retrospective one at that? The further complication here is that healthcare professionals themselves hold different views about the classification of alcohol abuse, with some arguing that the concept of "illness" encourages heavy drinkers to avoid confronting their own problems.[101] The second hazard is semantic. The disease theory groups together different forms of alcohol abuse, one of which is "bout drinking," long periods of controlled consumption punctuated by occasional indulgence in helpless binges — John A. Macdonald's notorious "sprees."[102] In that precise sense, and that alone, it might be possible to label the John A. Macdonald of 1856–76 as an alcoholic. Unfortunately, in popular usage, the term predominantly conveys the notion of somebody who is permanently incapacitated, generally raucous, and incoherent. There seemed to be no point in engaging in a detailed historical reconstruction of Macdonald's drink problem and then rounding it off with a one-word classification that would only reinforce the censorious misunderstanding that my research was intended to dispel. And we should not overlook that vital element in the story, that Macdonald overcame his problem throughout the last decade and a half of his life. If there is any point in a distinction between a recovering alcoholic and a reformed drunk, then he most certainly belongs to the second category, somebody who in later years could consume alcohol in moderation without losing control. His characterization by one historian as a "chronic alcoholic" is certainly an exaggeration: chronic alcoholism is a condition that causes irreversible physical and mental damage, and the term can hardly apply to a man who successfully fought a midwinter election campaign at the age of seventy-six (even if the effort did, in effect, kill him). John A. Macdonald did not survive to become Canada's oldest prime minister because he was "preserved in giggle-juice" but because he succeeded in overcoming his problem with the bottle.[103]

The essays in this volume are intended to remind Canadians that January 2015 will mark the bicentennial of John A. Macdonald's birth. It is perhaps inconvenient that this landmark will be straddled by the 150th anniversary of the movement for Confederation, from the Charlottetown and Quebec conferences of 1864 to the passage of the *British North America* [now *Constitution*] *Act* and the proclamation of the Dominion in 1867. The people of Canada will decide how they wish to commemorate these events, but there does seem to be a danger that we shall see a revival of that insidious schizoid duality of caricature that portrays two John A. Macdonalds: one statesmanlike, the wise progenitor of the nation and the other folkloric, amoral, and alcohol-sodden. It will be important to soar above these two stereotypes, and elide the public and the private facets of Canada's first prime minister into one rounded personality. Perhaps our basic problem in recapturing the real Macdonald is that we seem to know so much about him, through rich archival sources and creatively crafted biographies. We need to remember that much that we think we know comes to us through the self-projection of his own correspondence and the imaginative reconstruction of admiring biographers. Finding out about Macdonald is invariably great fun. Understanding him is a far greater challenge.

NOTES

1. I have attempted to do this in Ged Martin, *John A. Macdonald: Canada's First Prime Minister* (Toronto: Dundurn Press, 2013)..

2. *Debates of the House of Commons*, 23 [*recte* vol. 13], May 10, 1887, 367–68. Macdonald's biographers have yet to catch up with his participation in the Yonge Street fight. Even Macdonald's admiring friend J.R. Gowan only discovered that they had been comrades-in-arms on the fiftieth anniversary of the clash, in 1887. J.K. Johnson, "Sir James Gowan, Sir John A. Macdonald and the Rebellion of 1837," *Ontario History* 60 (1968), 61–64.

3. The following paragraphs draw upon Ged Martin, "Archival Evidence and John A. Macdonald Biography," *Journal of Historical Biography*, I (2007), 79–115 (available via *www.ufv.ca/jhb*). I also draw upon Ged Martin, *Favourite Son?: John A. Macdonald and the Voters of Kingston 1841–1891* (Kingston: Kingston Historical Society, 2010).

4. Donald Creighton, *The Passionate Observer: Selected Writings* (Toronto: McClelland & Stewart, 1980), 75.

5. Donald Creighton, *John A. Macdonald: The Young Politician* (Toronto: Macmillan, 1952), 7.

6. R. MacGregor Dawson, *William Lyon Mackenzie King: A Political Biography, Vol. I* (Toronto: University of Toronto Press, 1958), vii.

7. J.K. Johnson, ed., *Affectionately Yours: The Letters of Sir John A. Macdonald and His Family* (Toronto: Macmillan, 1969). As Johnson remarks, there are "many long and puzzling chronological gaps" in the surviving correspondence. Many of the 205 letters were received by relatives and were probably added to the collection after Macdonald's death. Fortunately, we know something of the home life of his second marriage: Louise Reynolds, *Agnes: The Biography of Lady Macdonald* (Ottawa: Carleton University Press, 1990). Unfortunately, its most promising source, Agnes Macdonald's own diary (Library and Archives Canada [LAC], MC26A, vol. 559A) was written only intermittently, and in the early years of their marriage. Its stilted quality suggests that it was similar to the diary kept by Cecily in Oscar Wilde's *The Importance of Being Earnest*: "simply a very young girl's record of her own thoughts and impressions and consequently meant for publication." See especially the entry for November 17, 1867: "Of course one keeps a Diary with a vague consciousness that at some time or other, some person or other, will read some part or other." It ends with a direct question to the reader: "Do you think it was very wicked of me to rest my head on his shoulder tonight while he read me Locksley Hall?" My answer would be that as they had been married for nine months and Tennyson's poetry was eminently respectable, no impropriety was involved.

8. J.M.S. Careless, *Brown of the Globe: vol. ii, The Statesman of Confederation, 1860–1880* (Toronto: Macmillan,1963), esp. viii, 374–75.

9. As he did in J.M.S. Careless, *Brown of the Globe: Vol. I, The Voice of Upper Canada, 1818–1859* (Toronto: Macmillan, 1959), 44–45.

10. Careless, *Brown of the Globe: Vol. I, The Voice of Upper Canada, 1818–1859*, viii. In fact, extensive extracts from family correspondence had been published as an appendix in Alexander Mackenzie, *The Life and Speeches of Hon. George Brown* (Toronto, 1882), 217–40.

11. Agnes Macdonald diary, entries for July 5, 1867, March 26, 1868, vol. 559A, MC26A, LAC; P.B. Waite, "John A. Macdonald: The Man," in H.L Dyck and H. Krosby, eds., *Empire and Nations: Essays in Honour of Frederic H. Soward* (Toronto, 1969), 36–53, esp. 44.

12. J.E. Collins, *Life and Times of the Right Honourable Sir John A. Macdonald ... Premier of the Dominion of Canada* (Toronto: Rose Publishing, 1883), 507.

13. Maurice Pope, ed., *Public Servant: The Memoirs of Sir Joseph Pope* (Toronto: Oxford University Press, 1960), 79, states that Agnes wrote to Lord Stanley on the night of Macdonald's death. Since he died at 10:15 p.m., this would suggest that she wrote immediately. Louise Reynolds quotes Pope's summary of the letter unwittingly giving the impression of the original text. See *Agnes: The Biography of Lady Macdonald*, 138. I am grateful to Dr. Barbara J. Messamore for help on this point.

14. Pope, ed., *Public Servant*, 265.

15. Johnson, ed., *Affectionately Yours*, 117; Donald Creighton, *John A. Macdonald: The Old Chieftain* (Toronto: Macmillan, 1955), 201. An alternative explanation for the absence of correspondence could be that both Hugh John and Macdonald himself were living in Toronto at the time, so their disagreement might have been a face to face one.

16. For much of his political career, Macdonald's relationship with his riding was conducted on an absentee basis, yet there seems to be surprisingly little meat in the surviving correspondence about Kingston affairs.

17. Richard Cartwright, *Reminiscences* (Toronto: W. Briggs, 1912), 48. The phrase "appalling mass of correspondence" was used by Maurice Pope, and almost certainly reflects his father's assessment. Pope, ed., *Public Servant*, 263.

18. J. Pope, ed., *Correspondence of Sir John Macdonald* (Garden City, NY: Doubleday, 1921), xxiii.

19. J. Pope, *Memoirs of the Right Honourable Sir John Alexander Macdonald GCB, First Prime Minister of the Dominion of Canada*, 2 vols., (Ottawa: J. Durie, 1894), i, 102, 104.

20. Richard Gwyn, *John A.: The Man Who Made Us: The Life and Times of John A. Macdonald, Vol. 1, 1815–1867* (Toronto: Random House, 2007), 329–30; "Archival Issues," 89–96.

21. A calendar of the collection, which quotes extensively from the Macdonald letters, is available online. Campbell Papers, F23-1. Archives of Ontario [hereafter AO].

22. "Archival Issues," 97–106. The Gowan Papers, MG 27, I E17, LAC.

23. T.C. Patteson Papers, F1191, AO.

24. Macdonald to Gowan, private, June 3, April 21, 1864, Gowan Papers, LAC.

25. Macdonald to Patteson, private, March 15, 1875, Patteson Papers, AO.

26. One other Macdonald source deserves to be rehabilitated. Creighton firmly omitted from his bibliography, E.B. Biggar, *Anecdotal Life of Sir John Macdonald* (Montreal: J. Lovell and Sons, 1891). Many of Biggar's stories can be independently verified (for instance from the *Parliamentary Debates*). The Macdonald family travelled to Canada with his orphaned cousin, Maria Clark (Macpherson) who later also became his sister-in-law. Although ten years older, she was still alive and alert in Kingston when Macdonald died in 1891, and was obviously the source of many tales of his early life. Ibid., 14n.

27. Ged Martin, "Macdonald and His Biographers," *British Journal of Canadian Studies* 14 (1999), 300–19.

28. J. Pennington Macpherson, *Life of the Right Hon. Sir John A. Macdonald* 2 vols., (Saint John: Earle Publishing House, 1891); Joseph Pope, *Memoirs of the Right Honourable Sir John Alexander Macdonald First Prime Minister of the Dominion of Canada*; Donald Creighton, *John A. Macdonald: The Young Politician* and *John A. Macdonald: The Old Chieftain*; Richard Gwyn, *John A.: The Man Who Made Us: The Life and Times of John A. Macdonald, vol. 1, 1815–1867* and *Nation Maker: Sir John A. Macdonald, His Life, Our Times, vol. 2, 1867–1891*. For reviews of other works on Macdonald, see Donald Swainson, *Sir John A. Macdonald: The Man and the Politician* (Kingston: Quarry Press, 1989 ed.), 161–66 and Ged Martin, *Favourite Son*, xi–xiv. A biographical sketch of Macdonald appeared in a London (England) newspaper as early as 1859; the first full-length biography in 1883: *Canadian News* (London), January 5, 1859: 10–11; J.E. Collins, *Life and Times of the Right Hon. Sir John A. Macdonald.* "Anybody can write anybody else's life," Macdonald commented, "you cannot stop them." Pope, *Memoirs* I, 183 n.

29. Pope, ed., *Public Servant*, 84.

30. Gwyn, *John A.: The Man Who Made Us*, 441.

31. D. Creighton, *Towards the Discovery of Canada: Selected Essays* (Toronto: Macmillan, 1972), 160 (written in 1969). This point is well made by Carl Berger, *The Writing of Canadian History: Aspects of English-Canadian Historical Writing since 1900* 2nd ed., (Toronto: Oxford University Press, 1986), 223–25, but does not seem to have had an impact on Macdonald biography. For Creighton's love of opera, P.B. Waite, "Introduction" to the 1998 single-volume reissue of the Macdonald biography by the University of Toronto Press, xxii, and Creighton, *Towards the Discovery of Canada*, 20. I have learned much from Dr Donald Wright who is engaged in an intellectual biography of Creighton. Wright notes the influence of Wagner on Creighton's writing in *Dictionary of Canadian Biography*, xx (*www.biographi.ca/en/bio/creighton_donald_grant_20E.html*, consulted 20 August 2013).

32. Creighton, *The Young Politician*, xii.

33. E. Whelan, ed., *The Union of the British Provinces* (Gardenville, QC: 1927), 45.

34. Gwyn, *John A.: The Man Who Made Us* , 169, 287. Biographers tend to boost their subjects, but there seems to be more than just Tammy Wynette Syndrome about Donald R. Beer's conclusion that "there is no direct evidence of John A. Macdonald's special contribution" to the formation of the coalition of 1854. Beer's account of the MacNab ministry shows Macdonald as an emerging force, but also portrays him as caught up in factional manoeuvres by others against MacNab and obliged to defend his position against rivalry with L.T. Drummond. Donald R. Beer, *Sir Allan Napier MacNab* (Hamilton: Dictionary of Hamilton Biography, 1984), 324–74, esp. 334.

35. Ged Martin, "John A. Macdonald: Provincial Premier," *British Journal of Canadian Studies* 20 (2007), 99–120.

36. Patricia Phenix, *Private Demons: The Tragic Personal Life of John A. Macdonald* (Toronto: McClelland & Stewart, 2006), 131.

37. Pope, *Memoirs*, i, 217. The resignation letter (to Cartier, July 11, 1859) appears to be a draft and may not have been submitted. J.K. Johnson and C.B. Stelmack, eds, *The Papers of the Prime Ministers, Vol. II: The Letters of Sir John A. Macdonald 1858–1861* (Ottawa: Public Archives of Canada, 1969), 161.

38. Max Magill, "The Failure of the Commercial Bank" in G. Tulchinksy, ed., *To Preserve and Defend: Essays on Kingston in the Nineteenth Century* (Montreal: McGill-Queen's University Press, 1976), 169–81; Ged Martin, *Favourite Son?*, 89–90.

39. J.M.S. Careless, *Brown of the Globe, vol. ii: The Statesman of Confederation, 1860–1880* (Toronto, 1963), 62–67.

40. Not specified in *Old Chieftain* but see Andrew Robb, "David Laird." In *Dictionary of Canadian Biography*, xiv, 579, accessed April 30, 2014, *www.biographi.ca/en/bio/laird_david_14E.html*.

41. For Macdonald and his post-1878 cabinet, Ged Martin, *John A. Macdonald*, 156–59.

42. L. Leduc, J.H. Pammett, J.I. McKenzie, and A. Turcotte, *Dynasties and Interludes: Past and Present in Canadian Electoral Politics* (Toronto: Dundurn Press, 2010), 61–75.

43. Ged Martin, "Alexander Campbell: The Travails of a Father of Confederation," *Ontario History*, CV (2013), 1–18. Campbell's symbolic utility is probably reduced by the fact that his marriage broke up, and he twice committed his estranged wife to asylums.

44. Gwyn, *John A.: The Man Who Made Us*, 178.

45. Ged Martin, *Britain and the Origins of Canadian Confederation 1837–1867* (Vancouver: University of British Columbia Press, 1995), 15–16; "John A. Macdonald: Provincial Premier," 113–16.

46. Creighton, *The Young Politician*, 268.

47. "Macdonald found in the statutes a provision..."; "Macdonald immediately realized the implications of the situation. He arranged...."; "Macdonald ... had already found his loophole. He had all his old ministers re-sworn....." W.S. Wallace, Macdonald (Toronto, 1924), 43; Swainson, *Sir John A. Macdonald: The Man and the Politician*, 50; Gwyn, *John A.: The Man Who Made Us*, 176. By contrast, a modern biographer of Cartier assumes that the incoming premier was responsible for the dodge. A. Sweeny, *George-Étienne Cartier: A Biography* (Toronto: McClelland & Stewart, 1976), ch. 2.

48. J.C. Dent, *The Last Forty Years: Canada Since the Union of 1841*, 2 vols (Toronto: G. Virtue, 1881), ii, 387. Dent censured Macdonald for giving way to something he claimed to know was wrong. He showed his disapproval by beefing up Luke 13:47. "Who so knoweth his lord's will and doeth it not shall be beaten with many stripes."

49. J.K. Johnson and C.B. Stelmack, eds, *The Papers of the Prime Ministers, vol. ii: The Letters of Sir John A. Macdonald 1858–1861* (November 15, 1858), 100.

50. Creighton, *Old Chieftain*, 126.

51. The case against Macdonald and his associates failed, but the prosecution was launched in the name of a bankrupt, leaving the defendants with no chance of recovering costs.

52. Bruce W. Hodgins, *John Sandfield Macdonald, 1812–1872* (Toronto: University of Toronto Press, 1971).

53. Ibid., 28 (Speaker), 106 (Strathroy), 118 (horse distemper).

54. I challenged this compulsive denigration of Sandfield Macdonald in *Britain and the Origins of Canadian Confederation, 1837–67* (Vancouver, 1995), 42–44. It is worth noting that, for all his failings, Sandfield carried militia reform in 1863; Hodgins, *John Sandfield Macdonald*, 87–88. Historians who have condemned Sandfield for seeking to avoid divisive issues during his two years in office have generally been respectful of the same skills when displayed by Mackenzie King for almost three decades.

55. Ibid., 36–37.

56. *Montreal Gazette*, March 25, 1864.

57. Foreword by Alan Wilson in Hodgins, *John Sandfield Macdonald*, v. I am grateful to Dr. Hodgins for his comments.

58. Creighton, *Old Chieftain*, 4.

59. Swainson, *Sir John A. Macdonald: The Man and the Politician*, 83.

60. Gwyn, *John A.: The Man Who Made Us*, 427–28.

61. Pope, Memoirs, II, 20; Hodgins, *John Sandfield Macdonald*, 92.

62. Étienne Taché and Joseph Howe also both come across as extremely venerable in the final phase: both died at sixty-nine.

63. Biographers would no doubt have echoed Lord Dufferin's regret, in March 1874, "that a career so creditable to himself, and so serviceable to his Country, as that of Macdonald's should have ended in such

humiliation." C.W. de Kiewiet and F.H. Underhill, eds., *Dufferin-Carnarvon Correspondence 1874–1878* (Toronto: The Champlain Society, 1955), 12.

64. Robert Mugabe of Zimbabwe, heading toward ninety at the time of writing, is a case in point.

65. J.R. Colombo, *Colombo's Canadian Quotations* (Edmonton: Hurting Publishers, 1974), 379, attributes the phrase to a friendly heckler who was reported in the *Toronto Mail* of December 18, 1884. I discuss the impossibility of Macdonald's retirement from office in Ged Martin, *John A. Macdonald*, 155–59, 172–84.

66. Barbara Roberts, "'They Drove Him to Drink': Donald Creighton's Macdonald and His Wives," *Canada: A Historical Magazine* 3 (1975), 51–64.

67. Pope, *Memoirs*, I, 12.

68. Noting the poverty of new arrivals from Britain and Ireland as they came up the St. Lawrence in 1817, an observer recorded that "they frequently lament having quitted their own country." The Macdonalds followed the same route three years later. F.M. Carroll, *A Good and Wise Measure: The Search for the Canadian-American Boundary, 1783–1842* (Toronto: University of Toronto Press, 2001), 101.

69. Ged Martin, *Favourite Son?*, 30, 45; Creighton, *The Young Politician*, 314.

70. In his will, written in 1890, twenty-eight years after his mother's death, Macdonald specified that he was to be buried "near the grave of my mother, as I promised her that I should be there buried." Biggar, *Anecdotal Life*, 319.

71. After an exhausting labour to give birth to her first child, in New York in 1847, Isabella unhesitatingly and dutifully asked John A. to write to her mother-in-law in Kingston to name the child. Johnson, ed., *Affectionately Yours*, 52.

72. James McSherry, "The Invisible Lady: Sir John A. Macdonald's First Wife," *Canadian Bulletin of Medical History* 1 (1984), 91–97, reprised in J. McSherry, "The Illness of the First Mrs John A. Macdonald," *Historic Kingston* 34 (1986). The family letters, including two which mention the "tic," are in Johnson, ed., *Affectionately Yours*, 31–72.

73. Another sufferer, the Marquess of Anglesey, who had lost a leg at the battle of Waterloo, served in the British Cabinet, attending meetings with a bandage around his face to cope with the pain. Marquess of Anglesey, *One Leg: The Life and Letters of Henry William Paget First Marquess of Anglesey 1768–1854* (London: Leo Cooper, 1961), 177. But for cases that ended active careers, see the *Dictionary of Canadian Biography*, xv (Lecoq, Charles) and *Oxford Dictionary of National Biography*, Pemberton, Christopher, *www.oxforddnb.com/view/article/21820*, accessed March 14, 2012.

74. McSherry, "Invisible Lady," 96.

75. Johnson, ed., *Affectionately Yours*, 35–43; Creighton, *The Young Politician*, 111–14, 130. Biographers have not noticed that Macdonald was forced to leave his wife in the Deep South and return to Canada in the middle of the Oregon crisis, which threatened to boil over into an Anglo-American war.

76. McSherry, "Invisible Lady," 97.

77. LAC, Macdonald Papers, vol. 336, F.M. Hill to Macdonald, August 14, 1845.

78. Margaret Macdonald to Margaret Greene [1845], in Johnson, ed., *Affectionately Yours*, 34.

79. Minto to Parkin, January 23, 1902, in Stevens and J.T. Saywell, eds., *Lord Minto's Canadian Papers: A Selection of the Public and Private Papers of the Fourth Earl of Minto* 2 vols., (Toronto, 1983), 2, 115.

80. Ged Martin, "John A. Macdonald and the Bottle," *Journal of Canadian Studies* 40 (2006), 162–85. Much of the information in the following paragraphs is referenced in that article.

81. Richard Gwyn has found a hangover as early as 1839 (Gwyn, *John A. The Man Who Made Us*, 264). David Banoub reports an episode in the Cartier Fonds in Montreal's McCord Museum, which he dates to 1860–64.

82. I stand by my interpretation that Macdonald was primarily a binge drinker, but there were also phases (such as the 1872 election campaign) when his alcohol intake over an extended period was enough to impair his judgement: Ged Martin, "Macdonald and the Bottle," 174.

83. S.J.R. Noel, *Patrons, Clients and Brokers: Ontario Society and Politics, 1791–1896* (Toronto: University of Toronto Press, 1990), esp. 185; Ged Martin, *Favourite Son?*, passim.

84. J. Pope, ed., *Correspondence of Sir John Macdonald*, 175 (letter to Lord Lisgar, private, September 2, 1872).

85. Ged Martin, *Favourite Son?*, 94.

86. Ibid., 171.

87. Creighton, *The Old Chieftain*, 38–42.

88. J. Vincent, ed., *A Selection from the Diaries of Edward Henry Stanley, 15th Earl of Derby (1826–1893) between September 1869 and March 1878* (London, 1994), 58–59.

89. Creighton, *Young Politician*, 332, 448–49; *Old Chieftain*, 67. Creighton was careful not to commit himself to acceptance of the second and third episodes.

90. *Globe*, August 20, 24, September 5, 1866; April 27, 29, 30, May 5, 1870.

91. Creighton, *The Old Chieftain*, 70–71. The *Montreal Gazette* magisterially reprimanded the *Globe* for conducting a vendetta, November 4, 1870. Medical bulletins during Macdonald's 1870 illness made little allusion to diagnosis, but Pope's explanation ("biliary calculus") seems plausible. Problems with Macdonald's gallbladder would explain earlier bouts of illness, notably in 1864 when he collapsed at a banquet in Ottawa, and so tend to discount the interpretation that his drink problem affected his health. However, the life-threatening nature of his collapse in 1870 might suggest the possibility of severe acute pancreatitis, a condition frequently caused by a combination of gallstones and alcohol abuse. However, speculation is

probably fruitless: Macdonald's medical advisers had no access to imaging technology or blood tests; modern-day scholars have perhaps too much access to the Internet. Pope, *Memoirs*, i, 76, and see Biggar, *Anecdotal Life*, 106, for an intriguing undated episode in Toronto in the late 1850s.

92. Carnarvon to Derby, October 11–12, 1866, fos 105–12, PRO 30/6/138, Carnarvon Papers, UK National Archives.

93. Biggar, *Anecdotal Life*, 194.

94. De Kiewiet and Underhill, eds., *Dufferin-Carnarvon Correspondence, 1874–1878*, 351; Creighton, *The Old Chieftain*, 311–14.

95. Biggar, *Anecdotal Life*, 194.

96. C. Heron, *Booze: A Distilled History* (Toronto: Between the Lines, 2003), 142, 160–61; J.L. Sturgis, "Beer Under Pressure: The Origins of Prohibition in Canada," *Bulletin of Canadian Studies* VIII (1984), 83–100; A.J. Birrell, "D.I.K. Rine and the Gospel Temperance Movement in Canada" *Canadian Historical Review* 58 (1977), 23–42.

97. P.B. Waite, "Sir Oliver Mowat's Canada: Reflections on an Un-Victorian Society," in D. Swainson, ed., *Sir Oliver Mowat's Ontario* (Toronto: Macmillan, 1972), 21–22.

98. Biggar, *Anecdotal Life*, 326, quoting 1891 commemorative sermon by Dr James Wild of Toronto, 326, and cf. 192; Ged Martin, "Macdonald and the Bottle," 174–79.

99. Reynolds, *Agnes*, 80–81. It would be cynical to suggest that Macdonald foresaw the 1876 reunion of most of Canada's quarrelsome Presbyterian factions, which would have rendered him liable to the congregational censure by those groups who formed the core of the Liberal Party.

100. I consulted N. Kessel and H. Walton, *Alcoholism* (2nd ed., Harmondsworth UK: Penguin, 1999).

101. On this, see Heron, *Booze*, 10.

102. Kessel and Walton, *Alcoholism*, 90–91.

103. A.A. Travill, "Sir John A. Macdonald and His Doctors," *Historic Kingston* 29 (1981), 85. Travill's study focuses on Macdonald's Kingston physicians, so we still lack an analysis of the medical treatment he received after he effectively shifted to living in Ottawa in the mid-1860s. The reference to "giggle-juice" comes from Allan Fotheringham, *Look Ma ... No Hands: An Affectionate Look at Our Wonderful Tories* (Toronto: Key Porter, 1984), 20.

Rediscovering Macdonald

RICHARD GWYN

A considerable man.

—Benjamin Disraeli, 1879

For me, it is beyond doubt that Macdonald was the most important of all our prime ministers and a strong case can be made that had there been no Macdonald, there would be no Canada today. Confederation itself, pretty obviously, was his conception. Others played critical roles, above all George Brown and George-Étienne Cartier. But Macdonald alone, devious, guileful, alluring, inexhaustibly resilient, was irreplaceable. His post-Confederation achievements were just as transformational: Macdonald more than tripled the size of the country he inherited, giving it coherence by stretching it out from sea to sea and by bounding it by salt water on three of its sides. He stitched together this utterly improbable country — "an eel skin of a settled country," in the phrase of American journalist Horace Greeley — by building a trans continental line to the Pacific and, in defiance of the horrendous additional cost, by insisting that this line run entirely within Canada rather than avoid the "empty" Precambrian Shield above Lake Superior by using already existing American railways. He began the transformation of an ill-assorted collection of British colonies into a national community with his

National Policy of high tariffs that caused Canadians to start to know each other because they now bought and sold amongst each other. He created the North-West Mounted Police (NWMP) that both ensured that Canada's west would develop decisively differently from the United State's topographically and demographically identical west and that itself was the first-ever distinctively Canadian institution.

The context in which he did all of this, and a good deal more, was as important. The new nation was not merely divided and fractious and absurdly elongated, but was inherently fragile. Its alluring and powerful neighbour was far wealthier and more developed. It was demographically very similar: dominated by an Anglo-Saxon majority, though there was a critical difference in the presence of French Canadians here and African Americans there. Canada's national distinctiveness, such as it was, was either negative, with most Canadians identifying themselves principally as not being American, or was derivative because it was borrowed from its far-away Mother Country. Canadians were reminded of the fragility of their new nation right after Confederation, when the first-ever federal and provincial elections were held. In Nova Scotia, by far the more substantial of the two new Maritime provinces, the result was that of the fifty-five elected members of all kinds, all but three were committed to taking the province out of the Confederation. This was the political equivalent of a newly built ship discovering a huge hole in its hull the instant it entered the water. The widespread view was that so illogical a state could not last, and most of few observers in Britain and the United States who knew anything about Canada expected that the new entity would come to terms with economic and geographic realities and join dynamic, booming, post-Civil War America.

For any leader to accomplish his country's survival against such odds indeed did require "a considerable man," as Disraeli recorded in his diary after he met Macdonald in his country house north of London, on September 1, 1879. The pair had talked through dinner and on into the early hours of the following day, their topics ranging from the affairs of the British Empire to "the poets and philosophers of Greece and Rome."

This recognition that Macdonald possessed uncommon qualities has generally been denied him. Not by the public of his day, who accorded him six victories in seven elections. Nor by public opinion today, it being largely favourable and forgiving of Macdonald, with the important exception of many of Canada's indigenous peoples. Today, a plastic figurine of him, the only one for a prime minister except Laurier, sells quite well. He is on a mug available at most souvenir shops. In CBC-TV's "Greatest Canadian" competition he came in eighth (albeit behind a hockey commentator, Don Cherry). Quite a few of his quips still arouse smiles, such as his response to a suffragette who demanded to know why he but not she had the vote:

OUR SWEE. LITTLE CHERUB;

OR, SIR JOHN LOOKING DOWN FROM A HIGHER AND BETTER SPHERE.

Grip, 16 October, 1891.

"Madame, I cannot conceive." Tales of his drunkenness continue to be treasured, although relatively few know he quit as early as the mid-1870s. Only he and Pierre Trudeau have gained anything like a lasting hold on Canadians' imagination.

The view of experts has been quite different. Many historians have been content to mark him down as a charming, clever, cynical, crafty, leader and have given him cameo appearances in some of their studies, but not much more. No grand ideas, no originality, no "vision thing"; instead, his was merely an obsessive determination to gain power and to hang onto it for as long as possible, by any means.

There have been exceptions of course and above all others, by a wide margin, is Donald Creighton's magisterial and magnificently researched two volumes of the 1950s, *The Young Politician* and *The Old Chieftain*. Creighton, though, had to revive Macdonald from virtual oblivion. The extent to which Macdonald was forgotten until Creighton is shown by the fact that one of his greatest accomplishments, the creation of the NWMP, is never mentioned in Creighton's pages. Macdonald's role as architect of this extraordinary, nation building institution was finally recognized in 1972, by Royal Canadian Mounted Police historian Stanley Horrall in his article, "Sir John A. Macdonald and the Mounted Police Force for the Northwest Territories" in the *Canadian Historical Review*. The NWMP is an obvious case example, not only as already remarked because it was the first distinctively Canadian institution (and the only such for many decades) but because Macdonald's original plan was that it should be formed of "a co-mingling of the races," or staffed by Métis and Indians was well as by Euro-Canadians, French as well as English. Or his observation to his friend Judge James Gowan that while he and the Conservative Party benefitted greatly from the overwhelming support he could count on in Quebec, "from a patriotic rather than a party view, is it not to be regretted that the French should not be more equally divided between the two existing parties," going on to warn that "their unanimity had to be paid for."

Peter Waite's *Macdonald: His Life and World* (1975) is a beautifully written and fairly balanced chronicle of his career. Waite took Macdonald's full measure in a way seldom matched: "His greatest gifts to Canada were his intelligence and his tolerance.... His intelligence was large and refreshing, and he had an extraordinarily well-stocked mind." That revisionist view gained little traction. Four years later, *The Journal of Canadian Studies* devoted an entire 1979 issue to the one-hundredth anniversary of the National Policy. The topic was thoroughly described and extensively argued. Missing, though, was any reference to the most interesting aspect of what Macdonald had set out to do — one indeed requiring an intelligence that was "large and refreshing." Macdonald was doing the same thing for exactly the same reason and at exactly the same time as German Chancellor Otto von Bismarck, namely building a tariff wall so that behind it he could build a national community. Indeed, Macdonald had so mastered the subject that he was able during the Commons debate to discomfort his opponents — all true believers in free trade as good Liberals — by pointing out that their great hero John Stuart Mill had in fact decreed that high tariffs could be a valid nation-building tool.

This book of essays on new interpretations on Macdonald is long over-due. Here are two of my most compelling examples of why he needs to be rediscovered: two policies that Macdonald either implemented or attempted to enact in the mid-1880s and both exceptionally imaginative and generous to an astounding degree. Both policies were "Canadian firsts." Macdonald wanted native people to gain the franchise, an act at that time of immense symbolic importance, without losing any of their rights under either the *Indian Act* or under any of their treaties. The second, which attempted to extend the vote to women, was an international "first" (or close to the first: women gained the vote in eighteenth-century revolutionary France, but only briefly; the Isle of Man, if indeed a country as it claimed, gave women the vote in 1881).

Macdonald's policy pre-dated the granting of the vote to women in Canada in 1918 by a third of a century. He wanted to amend the act so that the "Persons" clause would read "Persons means men … or women who are widows or unmarried." He anticipated the famous "Persons" judicial decision of 1929 by almost half a century. By the manner of his extension of the vote to Indians — a model of integration as opposed to the discredited alternatives of either assimilation or apartheid — Macdonald was even further ahead, almost by a century. His initiative affecting indigenous people did not out-live him, though: in 1898 it was cancelled by the newly-elected Wilfrid Laurier. Thereafter, native people continued to be denied the vote, all the way to 1960 when John Diefenbaker restored Macdonald's initiative.

This story needs to be broadly appreciated. The evidence for his actions has all along been hiding in plain sight, in the pages of *Hansard*. Yet few historians have judged it worthwhile to explore Macdonald's attempt to extend the vote so broadly. Olive Dickason's *Canada's First Nations* (1992) devoted some attention to it. More specialized audiences can find part of the story in a 1980 article in the *Saskatchewan Law Review* by Richard Bartlett, while brief references to it are made in J.E. Chamberlain's book, *The Harrowing of Eden,* and in Donald B. Smith's article "Aboriginal Rights in 1885" in R.C. Macleod's book, *Swords and Ploughshares.* Smith's own chapter in this book describes how Macdonald was well acquainted with many indigenous Canadians and how this might have affected his approach. As for Macdonald's attempt to extend the vote to women, commentary on it is all but nonexistent but for a singularly ill-informed passage in the chief electoral officer's pamphlet, *A History of the Vote in Canada* (available online). The single extended view of Macdonald's project has been provided by Colin Grittner, who wrote his M.A. thesis at Carleton University in 2009 on this topic and who has a chapter of his own in this volume.

• • •

Now, to the actual cases; women, first.

No evidence exists to explain why and how Macdonald came up with the idea of extending the vote to women in 1885. At this time, the subject itself was only a distant aspiration even in the minds and hearts of the most ardent of advocates such as Susan B. Anthony in the U.S., Emily Pankhurst in Britain, and, in Canada, of Emily Stowe. It is true that the British House of Commons had debated women's suffrage many times since the 1860s and the Swedish parliament considered the idea in 1884, but Macdonald himself never mentioned the subject in any earlier letter, nor made any previous public comment about it. What made Macdonald special in all this was that he was the prime pinister, not an ordinary parliamentarian. This puts his act in an altogether different category.

Instead, he suddenly just did it, or tried to. Early in 1885, just before Louis Riel began his rebellion, Macdonald introduced into the Commons a Franchise Bill to reform radically the existing system, principally by transferring responsibility for the administration of federal elections to Ottawa from the provincial governments where it resided (as with the states of the United States today) largely by an oversight in the last-minute hurry to complete the *British North America Act*. This was the bill's overt purpose. Its covert purpose was to transfer to Ottawa control over all the patronage involved, above all that of appointing the influential returning officers in each constituency. The opposition immediately identified the threat and resisted ferociously. The debate on the legislation degenerated into a filibuster that continued for months.

A great deal has been written about what became the *Franchise Act*, the most extensive commentary being that of the American historian Gordon Stewart in the 1983 *Canadian Historical Review* under the title, "Macdonald's 'Greatest Triumph,'" a phrase taken from Macdonald's own, later, triumphalist claim. Stewart, though, limited his commentary to Macdonald's ruthless quest to expand his patronage opportunities, and as well to recounting the convoluted tactics he employed to make changes in to the legislation's property-ownership requirements that would limit the size of the electorate in fulfillment of his deep skepticism about democracy. Macdonald spoke on the matter on April 27, 1885. He preceded his speech by noting that the definition of "Persons" in the legislation would now be broadened to include some women. He then explained why he was doing it.

He began, "Mr. Chairman [the House was in Committee], with respect to female suffrage, I can only say that, personally, I am strongly convinced, and every year for many years I have been more strongly convinced, of the justice of giving women otherwise qualified [owning sufficient property, as was the standard requirement] the suffrage." He continued, " I am strongly of that opinion, and have been for a good many years, and I had hoped that Canada would have the honour of first placing women in the position she is certain, eventually, after centuries of oppression, to obtain … of completely establishing her equality as a human being and as a member of society with man." He concluded, "It is merely a matter of time."

Into that short passage, Macdonald compressed everything worth saying: that the deed was "only a matter of time"; that he hoped Canada would have "the honour" of being the first to do this, and, most remarkably, that a woman after the "centuries of oppression" would eventually achieve not merely the vote but "completely establish her equality as a human being and as a member of society with man." The extraordinary expansiveness of

444 · Macdonald at 200

Macdonald's view about the potential role of women in public life suggests he may well have read John Stuart Mill's *Subjection of Women* and have accepted Mill's thesis.

Macdonald, who seldom relied on rhetoric to sway audiences, ended his run of it at this point. Not long after making these arguments, he gave up and withdrew the legislation's section concerning votes for women. (All his Quebec MPs were adamantly opposed, and by one contemporary calculation only four Conservatives were ready to vote for the measure.)

It might thus seem that nothing had happened, which might explain the neglect of historians. Rather, two accomplishments of potentially profound consequence had taken place. Macdonald had become the first national leader in the world to advocate votes for women. And Canada's parliament had become the first at a national level to discuss specific legislation to achieve this goal.

The standard defence of this negligence is that Macdonald could not have meant a word of what he said. This is the presumption that frames the brief commentary in the present-day chief electoral officer's current pamphlet (in its second edition, of 2007). There, his initiative is dismissed, as "a sacrificial lamb" that he never intended should "survive the final reading of the bill" while earning some advantage along the way. Sacrificial offerings can only fulfill their purpose if the chosen lamb is seen to be valuable. In those days, votes for women had a minus political value. Even if all of the small number of women who would qualify initially marked their ballots for Macdonald out of gratitude, incomparably more men would have cast against him the votes they had long possessed. Woman's suffrage was then not a serious subject for more than a small minority of women and, as doesn't need to be said, for almost no men. That was a time when it was assumed near-universally that women were put on earth to be "The Angel of the House." During the debate in the Commons, one Liberal member argued that extending the vote to them would "make women coarser" while another pointed out that "the majority of Canadian women are more proud to be known as good mothers than as voters." Moreover, a great many women thought the same way, not least among them the strong-willed Lady Macdonald: her opinion being that women, "do more harm than good, as women generally do, when they point their dainty fingers into the political pie." The cynical, corrupt, politician thus knew perfectly well that his suffrage policy would cost him a great many votes.

That Macdonald sought initially to extend the vote to so few women — only those either unmarried or widows — strikes a false note to contemporary ears, but in fact his tactic demonstrated how serious he was. In the debate, Macdonald quoted his own maxim, "never refuse a step in advance," or take whatever you can get whenever it is available. He said that he himself saw no reason why wives should not also have the vote, but that he recognized that many feared the result would be to divide husbands and wives. Nor was this limitation original to Macdonald: it had been resorted to the year before in Ontario when the vote in municipal elections was extended to women. (Since municipalities had no constitutional existence and national parties were not involved, this initiative set no precedent at the national or provincial level.)

Not that politics was ever absent from Macdonald's calculations. As his secretary, Joseph Pope, wrote in his *Memoir*, Macdonald believed that, "women, as a whole, were conservative." What really mattered were Macdonald's personal relations with women. As *Globe* editor John Willison put it in his *Reminiscences* "there was among women a passionate devotion to Sir John Macdonald such as no other leader in Canada has ever inspired." Since Willison was for a long time the confidant of the irresistibly charming Wilfrid Laurier, this was the highest possible praise. Clearly at ease in the company of women, Macdonald's own attitude toward them was neither patronizing nor predatory. The best illustration resides in another of his initiatives, one similarly little known. This derived from the interest Macdonald took in the ability of the newly established Salvation Army to attract to its meetings life's losers — the unemployed, the homeless, the paupers, the ex-convicts, the ex, or continuing, drunkards.

In his pragmatic way, Macdonald set off to find out personally how the Salvation Army accomplished this attraction, his interest having been prompted by the way the growing new class of urban workers suffered so much more severely during recessions than did rural dwellers who could get by — just — on their small farms. So, he went to a Salvation Army meeting in Kingston, where an army unit was located. He came into the hall, sat in the middle of the audience and remained to the meeting's end: behaviour impossible to imagine in any other prime minister. Just by being there he signalled that he accepted women taking part in public life, this because the army's founder, General Booth, insisted that women should hold senior positions in the institution. The commander of the Kingston unit was a Captain Abigail Thompson. She ran the meeting while giving orders to men, a practice that, because done in public, scandalized respectable opinion of the day. Not Macdonald. He returned the next evening, and the evening after that (later, General Booth, the Salvation Army's creator, at one time dined with Macdonald in Ottawa). This does not prove that Macdonald meant what he said about votes for women. It does confirm he was quite untroubled by women holding public offices, and so unlikely to worry greatly about women holding the vote.

Other evidence augments the likelihood Macdonald meant what he said. Although he failed in 1885, he did not give up. In 1890 he circulated a memorandum among his ministers seeking answers to such questions as how many provinces allowed female suffrage in municipal elections, how many actually voted, and whether they could be members of school boards. He had to have been gathering material for a speech that was never given, as Macdonald passed away in June 1891.

• • •

Now to one of the least-known of Macdonald's dealings with native people: acts as generous and as enlightened as this initiative of his are difficult to come by amongst all of those exercising political power over Aboriginals, not only in his own day, but in our own as well.

The chronicle of Macdonald's offer to Indians of enfranchisement, without any loss of their distinctive rights, is comparatively straight-forward. He proposed it and implemented it despite ferocious opposition criticism; among these being that he was "sending a scalping party to the polls," and that, "Indian suffrage is an encroachment on the privileges of free men, and of white men." The most vivid expression of the prevailing opinion of the time was the parliamentary debate of 1898, when his initiative was repealed by the Laurier government: one Liberal member then told the house, "It is a derogation to the dignity of the people and an insult to free white people in the country to place them on a level with pagan and barbarian Indians."[1]

In his dealings with First Nations' people, Macdonald made serious mistakes, most especially during the early 1880s when the Department of Indian Affairs (of which he was the longest-serving minister ever) responded ineptly and tardily to the pitiable, near-starving, conditions of many Plains Indians as a result of the sudden disappearance of the buffalo. He made other mistakes after the Saskatchewan Rebellion of 1885, when he was angered by the "disloyalty" of those few non-Métis native people who took up arms and murdered a number of settlers. Macdonald approved, at the very least failed to resist, a series of repressive measures by his officials such as the classification of many bands as "disloyal" and thus ineligible to receive food rations. He stood by as an illegal pass system that severely restricted the ability of Indians to leave their reserves was implemented. For these actions and inactions, Macdonald has deservedly been severely criticized by historians.

That is only half the story. Among all the national leaders who succeeded Macdonald to this day, it is impossible to identify any who better understood Indigenous peoples, or who was innately more sympathetic to them.[2] In his own day, there was without question nobody near equal to him among leading politicians. Macdonald's program of providing food aid to native people so they could become farmers as a substitute for the buffalo, was repeatedly criticized severely by Liberal Leader Edward Blake and his Indian Affairs critic, David Mills. Both argued that such an intervention in the free market would make native people "permanent indigents." Mills once summoned up Charles Darwin to justify his argument, pointing out that "the doctrine of the survival of the fittest is a necessary law of human existence" and that by providing food to Indians unwilling to become farmers, "we frustrate the operations of that law."

Contrast that attitude with the argument Macdonald advanced to justify his proposal that the definition of "Persons" in the *Indian Act* of 1876 be changed to "'Person' means male person, including an Indian" instead of "an individual other than an Indian". In his speech of May 4, 1885, Macdonald went back into history to describe what had happened to the runaway slaves who had come to Canada by way of the Underground Railway. He said: "They were uneducated, having no tradition of freedom, having none of the independence of free men, but at the end of three years they took the oath of allegiance and became voters, and they are voters." He then contrasted the treatment of newly-arrived slaves with the condition of the country's own aboriginals: "Here are Indians, aboriginal Indians, formerly the lords of the soil, formerly owning the whole of this country. Here they are, in their own land, prevented from either sitting in the House, or voting for men to come here and represent their interests. There are one hundred and twenty thousand of these people, who are virtually and actually disenfranchised, and justly complain that they have no representation…. They are British subjects now; they desire to remain so, and as British subjects they have the same rights as the white man."[3]

This was not Macdonald's finest performance in defence of his determination to enable native people to gain the vote without losing any of their special rights. That actually had happened a few days earlier when, on April 30, he was confronted by perhaps the most difficult circumstances any national leader could have to face, namely that events had put him into the position of asking for special treatment for aboriginals at the very moment when some of them had taken the lives of some of his own people. Three weeks earlier, the so-called Frog Lake Massacre had occurred when members of Cree chief Big Bear's tribe killed all but one of the unarmed adult white males in this tiny hamlet, including two priests. At the same time, the band led by Poundmaker had surrounded civilians as well as some policemen in a makeshift fort at Battleford, and while none had been attacked, a great deal of property had been burnt and houses ransacked, with women and children reduced to a state of terror. In response, Macdonald yielded not an inch. He did this in an exchange with Mills who wanted to know whether he really intended to offer the franchise to persons such as these. Mills began by asking whether Macdonald's scheme included "Indians residing on reserve." As recorded in *Hansard*:

> SIR JOHN A. MACDONALD: "Yes, if they have the necessary property qualification;"
>
> MR. MILLS: "An Indian who cannot make a contract for himself, who can neither buy nor sell anything with the consent of the Superintendent General — an Indian who is not enfranchised?"
>
> SIR JOHN A MACDONALD: "Whether he is enfranchised or not."
>
> MR. MILLS: "This would include Indians in Manitoba and British Columbia?"
>
> SIR JOHN A MACDONALD: "Yes;"
>
> MR. MILLS: "Poundmaker and Big Bear?"
>
> SIR JOHN A MACDONALD: "Yes"
>
> MR. MILLS: "So that they can go from a scalping party to the polls."[4]

This exchange corrects an error made by some who have written that Macdonald's scheme was limited only to the peaceable native people of the east, an assumption that caused them to describe his offer as of limited application. Rather, he continued to fight for all First Nations people to be treated as equal, no matter the behaviour of some of them, only yielding when he could no longer defend the politically indefensible. Moreover, both Macdonald's original offer of the vote to all First Nations people as well as the version he eventually enacted — limiting its application to native people in eastern Canada — actually made native people more than equal in the sense that those who gained the vote would retain important privileges withheld from all other Canadians, such as exemption from taxes. That he could achieve so much under such difficult circumstances prompted Olive Dickason to write that "it speaks volumes for Macdonald's political expertise that he was able to get the bill passed." By the time his measure was reinstated, by John Diefenbaker in 1960, far too much mistrust and pain and neglect had accumulated for any alteration in the voting rules to make any difference in relations between Indians and other Canadians.

To have extended the vote to Native people in so enlightened a manner and to have attempted so far ahead of his time to do the same for women, as well as, of course, to have completed the transcontinental railway and his other achievements such as the North-West Mounted Police, Macdonald had to have been not merely a clever politician but, "a considerable man."

Beyond much question, in my view, if it were not for Macdonald there would be no Canadians. He did not "make" Canada; rather, he made certain that no one and no event or force would unmake the odd, near-impossible country he had created. In having for too long abandoned the telling of the full Macdonald, historians have not told Canadians their full history. It is my hope that this book will go far not only in educating readers on rich new interpretations of Macdonald, but that it will inspire many others to pursue this work and make Macdonald relevant to their own times.

Notes

1. The comment is cited in Olive Dickason, *Canada's First Nations: A History of Founding Peoples from Earliest Times* (Toronto: McClelland & Stewart, 1992), 289.
2. A handy measure of Macdonald's uncommon interest in Native people is that he was minister of Indian Affairs for ten years, the longest tenure in the portfolio ever.
3. *Hansard* for May 4, 1885, 1575.
4. Ibid., April 30, 1885, 1484.

Contributors

Sean Conway's life as an historian (MA, Queen's) was interrupted when he was elected to the Ontario legislature at the age of twenty-four in 1975. He served in the Ontario legislature until 2002 and was a cabinet minister in the Ontario government from 1985 to 1990. He is currently a fellow at the Centre for Urban Energy at Ryerson University, a public policy adviser at Gowlings, and chairs the board of directors of the Ontario Centres of Excellence Project.

David W. Delainey is president of a financial firm in Calgary. He earned a Bachelor of Commerce (Finance and Economics) from the University of Saskatchewan (1990) and is now a part-time student in the Department of History at the University of Calgary.

Michel Ducharme is associate professor of History at the University of British Columbia. His books include the award-winning *Le concept de liberté au Canada à l'époque des Révolutions atlantiques (1776–1838)* (McGill-Queen's University Press, 2010) and the edited collection (with Jean-François Constant) *Liberalism and Hegemony: Debating the Canadian Liberal Revolution* (University of Toronto Press, 2009).

Patrice Dutil is professor of politics and public administration at Ryerson University. His publications include *Canada 1911: The Decisive Election that Shaped the Country* (with David Mackenzie) (Dundurn, 2011) and *Devil's Advocate: Godfroy Langlois and the Politics of Liberal Progressivism in Laurier's Quebec* (RDP, 1994). He is the editor of *"The Guardian": Perspectives on the Ministry of Finance of Ontario* (University of Toronto Press, 2011) and *Searching for Leadership: Secretaries to Cabinet in Canada* (University of Toronto Press, 2009). He is the president of the Champlain Society and the founder of *The Literary Review of Canada.*

J.C. Herbert Emery is the Svare Professor in Health Economics, with a joint appointment between the Departments of Economics and Community Health Sciences at the University of Calgary. He has published many articles on aspects of Canadian political history and is the editor of *Canadian Public Policy.*

J.J. Ben Forster is professor of history at Western University. He is the author of *A Conjunction of Interests: Business, Politics, and Tariffs 1825–1879* (University of Toronto, 1986).

Colin Grittner is completing his PhD in history at McGill University.

Richard Gwyn is a columnist for the *Toronto Star* and a broadcaster. He is the author of many books including *The Northern Magus: Pierre Trudeau and Canadians* (McClelland and Stewart, 1981); *Nationalism without Walls: The Unbearable Lightness of Being Canadian* (McClelland & Stewart, 1995); *John A.: The Man Who Made Us: The Life and Times of John A. Macdonald, Volume One, 1815–1867* (Random House, 2007); and *Nation Maker, Sir John A. Macdonald: His Life, Our Times, Volume Two, 1867–1891* (Random House, 2011).

Ged Martin is currently a fellow of the Royal Historical Society and an emeritus professor of the University of Edinburgh. His many books include *Britain and the Origins of Canadian Confederation* (UBC Press, 1995), *Favourite Son? John A. Macdonald and the Voters of Kingston, 1841–1891* (Kingston Historical Society, 2010), and *John A. Macdonald: Canada's First Prime Minister* (Dundurn, 2013).

Roger Hall recently retired after teaching history at Western University for over forty years. He is the general editor of the Champlain Society publications. His publications include (with Gordon Dodds and Stanley Triggs), *The World of William Notman: The Nineteenth Century Through a Master Lens* (McClelland & Stewart, 1993); *A Century to Celebrate: The Ontario Legislative Building, 1893–1993* (Dundurn Press, 1993), and edited, with S.W. Shelton, *The Rising Country: The Hale Amherst Correspondence, 1799–1825* (Champlain Society, 2002).

E.A. Heaman is associate professor of History at McGill University. She is the author of *The Inglorious Arts of Peace: Exhibitions in Canadian Society during the 19th Century* (Toronto, 1999) and *St. Mary's: The History of a London Teaching Hospital* (McGill-Queen's University Press, 2003).

Barbara Messamore is professor of history at the University of the Fraser Valley. She is the editor of the *Journal of Historical Biography* and the author of *Canada's Governors General, 1847–1878: Biography and Constitutional Evolution* (University of Toronto Press, 2006) and the editor of *Canadian Migration Patterns from Britain and North America* (University of Ottawa Press, 2004).

J.R. Miller is professor of History at the University of Saskatchewan. His books include *Bounty and Benevolence: A History of Saskatchewan Treaties* (with Arthur J. Ray and Frank Tough) (McGill-Queens University Press, 2000), *Big Bear (Mustahimusqua)* (ECW Press, 1996); *Skyscrapers Hide the Heavens: A History of Indian-White Relations in Canada* (University of Toronto Press, 1989); *Shingwauk's Vision: A History of Native Residential Schools* (University of Toronto Press, 1998).

Yves Y. Pelletier is currently the president of Education Connections. He completed his doctorate at Queen's University and worked for many years in the government of Canada before becoming assistant deputy minister in the Ministry of Post-Secondary Education in the Government of New Brunswick.

Donald B. Smith is professor emeritus of history at the University of Calgary. His works include *Honoré Jaxon: Prairie Visionary* (Coteau Books, 2007), *Long Lance: The Glorious Imposter* (Red Deer Press, 1999*), From the*

Land of Shadows: The Making of Grey Owl (Western Producer Prairie Books, 1990), and *Sacred Feathers: The Reverend Peter Jones (Kahkewaquonaby) and the Mississauga Indians* (University of Nebraska Press, 1987).

Timothy J. Stanley is associate professor of history and education at the University of Ottawa. He has published in numerous scholarly journals.

Bill Waiser is professor of history at the University of Saskatchewan, and is author (with Stuart Houston) of *Tommy's Team: The People Behind the Douglas Years* (Fifth House, 2010), *Tommy Douglas* (Fitzhenry &Whiteside, 2006), *Saskatchewan: A New History* (Fifth House Publishers, 2005), *All Hell Can't Stop Us: The On-To-Ottawa Trek and Regina Riot* (Fifth House Publishers, 2003), *Prisoners: The Untold Story of Western Canada's National Parks* (Fifth House Publishers, 1995), and many other books.

David A. Wilson is professor of history and Celtic studies at the University of Toronto. He is the editor of *Irish Nationalism in Canada* (McGill-Queens University Press, 2009) and the author of *Paine and Cobbett: The Transatlantic Connection* (McGill-Queen's University Press, 1988), *Ireland, A Bicycle and a Tin Whistle* (McGill-Queen's University Press, 1995), *Thomas D'Arcy McGee, Volume 1: Passion, Reason, and Politics, 1825–1857* (McGill-Queen's University Press, 2009), and *Thomas D'Arcy McGee, Volume 2: The Extreme Moderate, 1857–1868* (McGill-Queen's University Press, 2011). He is the general editor of the Dictionary of Canadian Biography.

Acknowledgements

A book like this inevitably relies on good-humoured collaboration and we have been well served in this regard as editors. Our first thanks go to the contributors to this collection, for their thoughtful work and for respecting deadlines (well, mostly). We are very proud of this group: the oldest just turned eighty, one is in his twenties. They come from every part of Canada, and two of them were born in Britain, like our subject. Our second debt goes to Kirk Howard, the president of Dundurn, who enthusiastically leaped on this project, but the whole team at Dundurn receives our applause with a particular standing ovation for Laura Harris, our patient and careful editor.

Along the way we have been helped by good friends who deserve our heartfelt gratitude. Dr. Andrew Smith, now teaching in the United Kingdom, was a wise counsel when this project was still at its conception stage. Sandra Martin lent her keen eye to demystify the confusions and her sharp pen to clarify passages. Professor Jean-Paul Boudreau, the Dean of Arts at Ryerson University, was generous in his support at critical points in this venture, not least in funding the indexing of this volume. Ms. Julia Macan, then of the Department of Politics and Public Administration, was central to the success of the symposium that was held at Ryerson University in December 2010 that brought together almost thirty researchers.

Not least is our debt of gratitude to the Social Sciences and Humanities Council of Canada, which funded much of the symposium. Its contribution made possible this meeting of minds and the book that has emerged from it.

Index

Abbott, John J.C., 81, 274

Abbott, Mary Martha Bethune, 81

Aberdeen, Lord, 274–275, 362

aboriginal issues. *see* First Nations

Act respecting elections of members of the House of Commons, 35, 313

Act to define the Elective Franchise, 34

Acta Victoriana, 73

Adam, Graeme Mercer, 16

Agassiz, Louis, 123

Akwesasne, 80

Alaska, 342, 345, 347, 348

Alberta, 72, 240, 241, 325, 346, 363

Alderville, 78

Algonkian nation, 322

Allan, Sir Hugh, 10, 185, 265, 267, 270

Alnwick Band of Mississauga, 78

American Civil War, 96–97, 101, 156, 197, 272

American Federalist Party, 147, 151

Anderson, Christopher G., 128

Anecdotal Life of Sir John Macdonald (Biggar), 16, 71–72

Arctic archipelago, 342, 346, 347–350

Arendt, Hannah, 150–151

   Chinese cultural practices viewed as incompatible, 115, 119, 120–122, 124, 126–127, 131–132

   Chinese Immigration Act, 127, 130, 131

   Macdonald's Aryan vision, 123–124, 128, 131, 133

   Macdonald's remarks on people of Chinese origin, 115, 118–119, 122, 123, 128, 131

   naturalization of Chinese residents, 121–122

   racial state formation, 115–116, 125, 131, 132–133

   racial theory, and "scientific" racism, 116–117, 120–121, 122–124, 126–127, 128–129, 131–132

supporters of Chinese enfranchise-
ment, 128, 129–130
Ashquabe, James, 77
Athens, 193

Bacchi, Carol, 31, 32
Bagehot, Walter, 149, 153, 160, 161
Bagot Commission, 314–315
Baldwin, Robert, 146, 153
Baldwin, Stanley, 385
Banff, 352–353, 354
Baskerville, Peter, 37
Batoche, 73–74, 116
Battle of Ridgeway, 99, 104–105
Battleford trials, 75, 332, 448
Bay of Quinte, 59, 60, 61–62, 63, 64
Beach, Thomas Billis (aka Henri Le
Caron), 106
Beard, Mary, 193
Beasley, Edward, 120
Beckart, Sven, 206
Bengough, J. W., *15*, 20, *29*, *117*, *143*,
173, *195*, *255*, *283*, 302–*303*, *313*,
343, *361*, *407*, *439*
Bennett, R.B., 233, 385, 393–394
Berlin, Isaiah, 150, 151
Bernard, Hewitt, 14, 286, 289, 292, *305*
Berton, Pierre, 19, 392
Bethune, Angus, 81
Big Canoe, Chief Charles (Keche
Chemon), 77–78
Biggar, Emerson Bristol, 16, 71–72, 426
Blackstone, William, 149, 150, 151, 153
Blake, Edward, 42–43, 48, 267, 392, 447
Blaker, George, 78
Blaker, Joshua, 78
Bleaney, Mrs., 384
Bliss, Michael, 45, 212
Board of Audit, 299, 301
Board of Inspectors of Prisons,
Asylums, and Public Charities, 293

Bonaparte, Napoleon, 13
Booker, Alfred, 104–105
Borden, Robert, 373–374, 393, 400
Bouchette, Robert, 291, 295–296, *306*
Bovey, John, 341, 346–347
Bowell, Sir Mackenzie, 362, 367, 369,
371, 381–382
Bowen, Sarah, 64
Boyle, Patrick, 100, 108, 109, 110
Brandt trial, 64–65
Brantford Daily Courier, 75, 80
British American League, 152
British Columbia, 73, 115, 116, 119,
121, 123, 124, 127–128, 129, 130,
198, 199, 230–231, 287, 324, 326,
343, 345, 352, 448
British Columbia Archives, 341
British Consulate, New York, 105
British North America Act, 43–44, 69,
150, 200, 207–209, 239, 319, 343,
344, 347, 366, 367, 428, 443
British North American federation, 154
British Parliament, 153–156, 157, 194,
207–209
Brown, Craig, 352, 353
Brown, George, 16, 68, 109, 156, 174,
178, 197, 198, 200, 213, 254–255,
256, 259, 343, 344, 366, 397,
408–409, 417, 426
Bruce, Sir Frederick, 105, 345
Buchanan, Isaac, 183–184
Buck, Chief John, 79–80
Bulwer-Lytton, Sir Edward, 256
Bunster, Arthur, 119, 121, 128
Burke, Edmund, 38–39, 41–42, 46,
48, 146, 151, 155–156
Burkean conservatism, 39–40, 41, 144,
147
Bury, Lord, 66–67

Cameron, Malcolm, 261–262, 410–411

Campbell, Sir Alexander, 59, 129, *305, 306*, 411, 412, 416–417

Campobello Island, 98, 103

Canada Act, 319

Canada Civil Service Act, 291

Canada's First Nations (Dickason), 442

Canadian Biographical Studies, 419–420

Canadian Historical Review, 440, 443

Canadian Illustrated News, 95

Canadian Pacific Railway (CPR), 21, 71, 73, 79, 116, 119, 186, 212, 224, 225, 229–230, 236–239, 240, 241, 242, 244, 289, 298, 352, 364, 367, 374

Canadian Parliament, 157–158, 194–195, 200, 201, 319.

Canadian Railway Rates Commission, 238

Canadian-American Reciprocity Treaty of 1854, 227

Careless, Maurice, 408–409

Carleton University, 18, 442

Carnarvon, Lord, 347, 348, 426

Caron, Sir Adolphe-Philippe, 366

Cartier, George-Étienne, 175, 202, 203, 206, 254, 255–256, 265, 294, 295, 299, 305, 366, 367, 390, 397, 416, 417, 418, 421, 425

Cartwright, Sir Richard, 213, 383, 410

Cataraqui Cemetery, Kingston, 379, 384, 386

Catholicism, 103, 109, 158, 209, 361, 409

Cayley, William, 180, 181

Census of 1861, in Ontario and Quebec, 198

Census of 1871, first Canadian, 287, 297

Chamberlin, Brown, 147

Chandler, E. B., 178

Chapleau, Sir Joseph Adolphe, 126–127, 366

Charity Aid Act of 1867–8, 210

Chief Big Bear, 125, 330, 331, 332, 448

Chief Poundmaker, 125, 332, 448

Chinese Immigration Act, 127, 130, 131

Chubb, Chief Mitchell, 78

Citizen's Forum on National Unity, 397

Clark, Isabella. *see* Macdonald, Isabella (née Clark)

Clarke, Charles, 105

Cleverdon, Catherine, 32

Clouston, Edward, 81

Coalition governments, 146–147, 184, 204, 343, 408, 415, 419

Collins, Joseph Edmund, 16, 23–24

Colonial Office, 200–201, 254, 256, 267, 269–270, 349

Comego, E., 78

Commentaries of the Laws of England (Blackstone), 149, 150

Commercial Bank, Kingston, 285, 286, 416, 425

The Commercial Empire of the St. Lawrence, 1760-1849 (Creighton), 17, 413–414

Committee of the Whole, 31, 37

Confederation, 152, 157–158, 197–199, 200–202, 204–206, 210, 319, 344, 364, 385, 397, 410–411, 424, 428.

conscription, 386, 388

conservatism, 19th century, 38–39, 45–46, 147–148, 151–152

Considerations on Representative Government (Mill), 40–42

Constitutional Act (1791), 33, 34, 46–47, 312

Constitutional History of England (Hallam), 157

constitutional liberty, 150

constitutionalism, 47–49, 145, 149, 150, 153–154, 155

Conway, Sean, 22, 379–404, 451
Coursol, Charles, 106
CPR charter, 185, 230
Crawford, William, 60
Credit River mission, 61, 65, 66, 67
Cree nation, 82, 116, 125, 321, 331, 448
Creighton, Donald, 17–18, 21, 94, 145, 175–176, 223, 257, 311, 406, 408, 411, 413–414, 417, 420, 421, 424, 440
Crowe, Peter, 78
Crow's Nest Agreement of 1897, 237, 238
Culbertson, John, 64–65
Cuvier, Georges, 120

Dalhousie University, 17, 393
Daunton, Martin, 207–208
Davies, Louis Henry, 122
Davin, Nicholas Flood, 325–326
Dawes Plan, 333–334
Dawson, George Mercer, 350–351, 352
de Boucherville, Sir Charles, 129
de Cosmos, Amor, 119, 120, 121, 128
De Lolme, Jean-Louis, 150, 151
de Vries, Jan, 200
Delainey, David W., 21, 223–250, 451
Dent, J.C., 418
Department of Agriculture, 297
Department of Finance, 298
Department of Indian Affairs, 62, 66–67, 70, 71, 72, 79, 81, 294, 304, 305, 311–340
Department of Internal Revenue, 299
Department of Militia and Defence, 299, 305
Department of Public Works, 297, 298
Department of the Interior, 72, 224, 323–324

Deputy Ministers and Ministers in the Macdonald Government, 1867-1873, *305–306*
Deseronto, 64, 312
Devlin, Bernard, 96, 109
Dewdney, Edgar, 323–324, 331, 334
Diamond Jubilee of Confederation, 385
Dickason, Olive, 442, 449
Dickinson, William, 298, *306*
Dictionary of Canadian Biography, 405, 419
Diefenbaker, John, 394–397, 400, 441, 449
direct taxation, 180, 198–199, 200, 208, 211–212
Disraeli, Benjamin, 391, 437, 438
Dominion Alliance (temperance movement), 426–427
Douglas, Mary, 360
Drinkwater, Charles, 289
Ducharme, Michel, 21, 49, 141–169, 452
Dufferin, Lady, 260, 268, 271
Dufferin, Lord, 260, 262–271, 272–273, 412, 426
Durham, Lord, 148–149, 294, 299, 314
Dutil, Patrice, 13–24, 22, 282–310, 379–404, 452

the "Eastport fiasco," 98, 103
Election Act, 33–34
Electoral Franchise Act
    biologically-defined "race," 132
    books written about, 442
    definition of "person," 30, 33, 35, 118, 441, 443, 447
    disenfranchisement of Chinese residents, 115–119, 121–130, 131–133

and First Nations, 77, 78–80, 118,
124–125, 328–329, 336, 441,
446–449

the Franchise bill, 28–29, 33, 38,
77, 80, 261, 262, 442–444

Macdonald's comments on,
328–329

and women's enfranchisement,
27–30, 32, 36, 37–38, 39,
42–43, 46, 48, 49, 118, 441,
442–446

Elgin, Lord, 194–195, 262, 418

Elliott, John, 80

Emery, J.C. Herbert, 21, 223–250, 451

The English Constitution (Bagehot), 149

Erie Canal, 235

Ermatinger, William, 101, 102

European Revolutions of 1848-49, 149

Fathers of Confederation, 144, 158,
201, 366, 417

Field, Eliza, 65

Fielding, William S., 374

First Nations. *see also specific nations*
Bagot Commission, and residential
schools, 314–316

the Battleford Trials, 75, 332, 448

the Brandt trial, 64–65

"civilization" policies, failure of,
314–315

communal land ownership versus
individual, 333

Credit River mission, 61, 65, 66, 67

Crown ties, 312–313, 316–317,
318, 319, 321

Elias Hill (sole case of enfranchisement), 321

expected assimilation into Euro-
dominant society, 21, 64, 67,
70, 72, 80, 81, 82, 125–126,
326, 327–328, 329, 333

famine, and food rationing,
330–331, 446

Grape Island, 62–63, 69, 78

legislation
band governance, and the
Indian Advancement Act
(1884), 322, 327–328

the *Electoral Franchise Act*, 77,
78–80, 118, 124–125, 328–
329, 336, 441, 446–449

the *Gradual Civilization Act*
of 1869, 58, 67–68, 70,
317–319, 321–322, 327,
333, 335, 336

Indian Act of 1876, 58, 70–71,
77, 125, 318, 322–323, 327,
328, 331–334, 441, 447

"peasant farming" policy,
334–335

the Royal Proclamation of 1763,
59–60, 68, 69, 76, 312, 313,
316, 333, 335

schooling policy, 324–327, 329

Macdonald's dealings with, 20–21,
22, 23, 71–73, 74–75, 76–80,
446–449

Macdonald's remarks on Indian
affairs, 63, 64, 72, 74–75,
79, 125, 318, 323, 324, 325,
326–327, 328–329, 330, 332,
447–448

treaties
with the British, and property
issues, 59– 62, 66–67,
68–69, 73–74, 76, 333

harshness, post Rebellion,
331–332

reserves, and gathering rights,
317, 320–321

the Robinson Treaties of 1850,
316–317, 320, 321

Upper Canadian territorial treaties, 312–313, 317, 320
Western treaty-making, 318, 319–321, 324–327, 330
Fish, Hamilton, 347
Fisher, Sydney, 373
Fitzpatrick, Rudolph, 105
Fleming, Sandford, 66
Foley, Michael, 272
Forster, J.J. Ben, 21, 172–192, 204, 212, 452
Fortnightly Review, 214
Foster, Sir George Eulas, 367, 369, 371
Foucault, Michel, 116
Franchise Act (and Franchise Bill). *see Electoral Franchise Act*
French Canadians, 149, 202, 294–295, 362, 366, 367, 370, 391, 399, 412, 418, 438, 440
French Revolution, 13, 148
Frog Lake Massacre, 448
Futvoye, George, 299, 305

Galt, Sir Alexander Tilloch, 173, 181, 182, 183, 197, 202–203, 204, 207, 213, 282–283, *306*, 345
Garner, John, 33
Gault, Matthew Hamilton, 122
Geological Survey of Canada, 214, 215, 217, 342, 350–352
George, Henry, 210–211
Georgina Island Ojibwe, 77
Gillmor, Arthur Hill, 122, 126
Givins, Rev. Saltern, 63, 64
Gladstone, William, 198, 259
Glidden, George Robbins, 123
the *Globe*. *see Toronto Globe*
Glorious Revolution (1688), 151
Gobineau, Joseph Arthur Comte de, 123–124
Governors General, 253–281

Gowan, James Robert, 74, 266, 411–413, 440
Gradual Civilization Act of 1869, 58, 67–68, 70, 317–319, 321–322, 327, 333, 335, 336
Gramsci, Antonio, 359
Grand Central Indian Council of Ontario, 70
Grand River Iroquois, 66, 80, 312
Grand Trunk Railway (GTR), 173, 175, 176, 177, 178, 179, 180, 181, 184, 235, 236–237, 254, 261, 342
Grant, Ulysses S., 347
Grape Island, 62–63, 69, 78
Great Council, Upper Canada, 318, 319
Great Northern Railway, 236, 238
Great Southern Line, 182, 183
Great Western Railway, 173, 176, 254
Green, Thomas, 76, 80
Griffin, William Henry, 291, 299–300, *306*
Grip, 15, 20, *29, 117, 143, 174, 195, 225, 255, 283, 303, 313, 343, 361, 407, 439*
Grittner, Colin, 20, 27–57, 452
Gwyn, Richard, 19, 23, 27–28, 69, 75, 94, 142, 175, 343, 410, 413, 414, 415, 420, 437–450, 452
Gwyn, Sandra, 19
Gzowski & Co., 182–183

Habeas Corpus Suspension (Act), 101, 105, 107–109, 110
Hackett Fischer, David, 150–151
Halbwachs, Maurice, 359
Hall, Roger, 13–24, 451–452
Hallam, Henry, 157
Hallowell Free Press, 65
Hamilton, Alexander, 145, 147, 151
Hamilton, John, 82

Hamilton Evening Times, 369
Hamilton Herald, 370
Hansard, 442, 448
Hardisty, Richard, 81
Harington, T.D., 299, *306*
Harmon, Abby Maria, 82
Harmon, Daniel, 82
Harmon, Lizette Laval, 82
Harrison, Robert A., 289
Hayes, Michael, 109–110
Haythorne, Robert Poore, 130
Head, Sir Edmund, 254, 255–257, 289
Heaman, Elsbeth A., 21, 49, 193–222, 453
Helmcken, John Sebastian, 125, 196
Henry, John Tecumseh, 68–71
Herkimer, Lawrence, 80
Hibernian Benevolent Society, 101, 107
Hill, Elias, 319
Hincks, Francis, 175, 176, 178, 184, 257, 259–262, *304*
Hincksites, 144
Hodgins, Bruce W., 419–420
Howe, Joseph, 173, 178, 285, 292, 305, 399
Hudson, George, 177
Hudson's Bay Company, 81, 174, 227, 235, 239, 241, 244, 319, 320, 344, 347, 350, 367
Hume, David, 200
Huron nation, 66

income tax, 199, 211–212
Independence of Parliament Act, 417
Independent Order of Foresters, 80
Indian Act of 1876, 58, 70–71, 77, 125, 318, 322–323, 327, 328, 331–334, 441, 447
Indian Advancement Act (1884), 322, 327–328

Indian Department/Indian Affairs. *see* Department of Indian Affairs
"The Indian Question" (Steinhauer), 73
Innis, Harold, 238–239
Isabella Clark's medical condition, 421, 423, 425, 427
"inventory" science, 217, 351
The Irish American, 100, 105
The Irish Canadian, 100, 108, 109–110
The Irish People, 100
Irish Republican Army, 99
Irish Republican Union, 96
Irish/Fenian issues. 21, 94, 95, 96, 97–102, 103–105, 106, 107, 108, 109, 110, 111, 112, 113, 114, 258, 277, 285, 307, 425
Iroquois nation, 61, 64, 66

Jackson, Will, 73–74
Jackson, William, 177, 179
John A. Macdonald Papers, 406, 408, 409
Johnson, J. K., 18, 65, 175, 182
Johnson, John, 62
Jones, Peter (Kahkewaquonaby, or Sacred Feathers), 60, 61, 65, 66, 67, 77, 79, 315
Journal of Canadian Studies, 424, 441
Journals of the House of Assembly, 176

Kahnawake (near Montreal), 66, 80
Kelly, Stéphane, 144
Kenny, Edward, 292, 305, *306*
Killian, Bernard Doran, 97
Kimberley, Lord, 258, 259, 263, 264, 265, 266, 267, 268, 269–270, 271
King, Mackenzie, 382–386, 387–390, 400, 413
King, W.L. Mackenzie, 233, 379
Kingston, Upper Canada, 14, 58–59, 61, 382–383, 424, 425

Kingston Chronicle, 65
Kingston *Gazette*, 196

La Patrie, 369, 370–371
Lacombe, Father Albert, 81
Laflèche, Bishop Louis-François, 81
Lafontaine, Louis-Hippolyte, 295, 296
Laird, David, 69
Lake Erie, 312
Lake Ontario, 59, 60, 312
Lamoureux, Diane, 31
Land Settlement in Upper Canada,
    1783-1840" (Patterson), 61
Langevin, Sir Hector-Louis, 215–216,
    265, 274, 305, *306*, 349
Langton, John, 181, 291, 298, 302, *306*
Latham, Robert, 123
Laurier, Sir Wilfrid, 17, 43, 45, 48,
    302, 335, 360, 363–365, 366, 368,
    369, 372, 375, 380, 382, 383, 384,
    385, 393, 398, 399, 400, 441, 445
Le Canadien, 294
Le Caron, Henri (alias of Thomas
    Billis Beach), 105
Le Liberal/The Liberal, 296
Lee, William Henry, 292, 305
    Borden, 393
    Laurier's homage to Macdonald,
        380, 382
    Mackenzie King's connection to
        Macdonald, 382–386, 387–390
    Meighen's praise for Macdonald,
        386–387
    Mulroney's invocations of
        Macdonald, 379, 397–400
    Pearson's admiration for
        Macdonald, 390–391
    R.B. Bennett, 393–394
    Thompson and Bowell, 381–382
    Turner's remarks on Macdonald,
        391–392

Leslie, T.E. Cliffe, 214
Letters to Limbo (Borden), 393
Lewis, George Cornewalle, 256
"The Liberal Order Framework in
    Canada" (McKay), 40
Liberal-Conservative Party, 145, 360,
    362, 363, 364, 366, 367, 369, 371,
    373, 375
Liberalism, 19th century, 40, 43,
    151–152
Liberal-Reform ministry, 261
Library and Archives Canada, 406
Lichtenberg, Judith, 116–117
Life of William Pitt (Stanhope), 287–288
Lisgar, Lady, 272
Lisgar, Lord, 257–260, 263–264, 265
Locke, John, 151, 153
Logan, Sir William, 217, 350
Lowe, Robert, 213–214
Lower Canada, 148, 149, 294
Lynch, John, 103

MacDermot, T.W.L., 144
Macdonald, Daisy, 82
Macdonald, Helen (née Shaw), 13,
    58–59, 421–422
Macdonald, Hugh, 13–14, 58–59
Macdonald, Sir Hugh John, 14, 323,
    383, 409
Macdonald, Isabella (née Clark), 14,
    415, 421–423, 425, 427
Macdonald, James, 64
Macdonald, John A.
    personal life
        alcohol problem, 197, 265, 271–
            273, 282–283, 369, 384,
            406, 421, 423–428, 440
        family and early life, 13–14,
            58–59, 422
        ill health and death, 273–274,
            359

wives. *see* Macdonald, Isabella;
  Macdonald, Lady Agnes
photos and illustrations, *6, 7, 15,*
  29, 117, 143, 146–147, *174,*
  195, 225, 255, 283, 302–*303,*
  343, 361, 381, 407, 415, *439*
political life
  as Attorney General of Canada
    West, 34, 67, 179, 180, 196,
    287, 317, 318, 350, 418
  early career, 63, 64–66,
    285–286
  liberal conservatism, 144–146,
    162, 204
  as Minister of Indian Affairs,
    311–340
  as Minister of Militia, 425
  as Minister of the Interior, 71,
    224, 294, 304, 323–324
  the Pacific Scandal, 184, 229,
    261, 263, 264, 265–271,
    298, 416, 421
  the Parliamentary "double
    shuffle," 253, 254, 255–257,
    383, 417–418
  policy for penitentiaries, 206,
    291, 292, 294
  as Superintendent General of
    Indian Affairs, 58, 78, 79–80
political style
  anti-democratic tendencies, 38,
    45, 150, 152, 158, 206, 443
  character strengths and flaws, 14,
    16, 143, 369, 389–390, 392
  conservative ideologies, 38–39,
    45, 47, 142, 144, 145–146,
    147–148, 194
  pro-British tendencies, 45,
    64, 65, 67, 81, 144, 205,
    371, 372, 386–387, 394,
    396–397

statesmanship and political skill,
  22, 23, 141–142, 144–145,
  162, 183–184, 193–194,
  267, 268, 284, 286, 289,
  380, 389–390, 392, 396,
  424, 449
remarks made by
  on the 1837 Rebellion,
    405–406
  on the 1871 Washington Treaty,
    259, 260, 300
  on Arctic islands, Canadian
    claim to, 348, 349
  on Banff, and the Rocky
    Mountains Park, 352–353
  on being a Conservative Liberal,
    145, 146
  on a British North American
    federation, 154
  on Brown, 286
  on Confederation, 205
  on constitutional liberty, 158
  on constitutionalism, 155
  on corruption of Hincks and
    Morin, 261, 262
  on criminal law, and legal
    equality, 152
  on development of Canadian
    resources, 196
  on Dufferin's wish to view par-
    liamentary proceedings, 268
  on election of neutral head of
    state, 160–161
  on the Geological Survey of
    Canada, 215, 350
  on his drinking, 426
  on Lady Dufferin, 260
  on letter-writing, 410, 412
  on managing government, 284,
    285
  on the Militia Bill, 411

on ministerial appointments, 290
on the office of the US presidency, 161
on parliamentary representation, 156, 158, 159
on private property, 158–159
on Provincial Legislatures, 158
on Sandfield Macdonald, 420
on the scientific tariff, 216
on social classes, and annexation issues, 152–153
on sovereignty, 156–157, 159, 160–161
on the West, 245, 319, 324, 342, 343–344, 345–346
Macdonald, John Sandfield, 262, 272, 418–419, 420, 421
Macdonald, Lady Agnes (née Bernard), 14, 19, 224, 271, 273, 288, 289, 352, 408, 409, 421, 425, 427, 444
Macdonald, Mary, 14
MacDougall, Patrick, 102
MacEachern, Alan, 353
Mackenzie, Alexander, 70, 128, 185, 229, 263, 264–265, 267, 287, 322, 412
Mackenzie, George, 14
MacKenzie, Louisa, 81
Mackenzie, William Lyon, 262, 382–383, 406
Macmillan's Magazine, 43, 44
MacNab, Sir Allan, 34, 176, 179, 182, 183, 184, 196, 253–254
Macpherson, David, 71, 82, 182
Macpherson, J. Pennington, 16, 413, 414
Manitoba, 236, 237, 238, 240, 241, 287, 324, 346, 362, 363, 364–365, 425, 448
Manitoba Agreement of 1901, 236, 237
Manitoba Schools Question, 362, 365, 367

Manitoulin First Nations, 68–69
Manitoulin Island Treaty of 1862, 68, 317
Marine and Fisheries Department, 300–301, 305
Martin, Chester, 241–242
Martin, Ged, 22–23, 175, 255, 405–436, 453
Martin, Peter (Oronhyatekha), 80
McDonald, Hugh, 292, 305
McDougall, John, 238
McGee, Thomas D'Arcy, 96, 103, 108, 110, 257, 367, 397
McInnes, Donald, 129
McKay, Ian, 40, 45, 359–360
McLennan, John, 216–217
McMicken, Gilbert, 101–102, 103–105, 106, 107
McMullen, James, 368
McSherry, James, 422–423
Medcalf, Francis, 103
Meech Lake Accord, 397, 399
Meehan, Patrick, 100
Meighen, Arthur, 385, 386, 400
Meredith, Edmund Allen, 282–284, 293–294, 295, 305
The Message of the Carillon and other Addresses (King), 385
Messamore, Barbara, 22, 253–281, 453
Methodist missions, 61–63, 65, 78, 315
the Métis, 16, 58, 70, 73–74, 81, 107, 320, 325, 326, 331, 332, 400
Michaud, Jacinthe, 31
Militia Bill, 271–272, 411
Mill, John Stuart, 40–42, 43, 44, 48, 149, 199, 211, 213, 216, 441, 444
Miller, J. R., 22, 311–340, 453
Mills, David, 122–123, 125, 215–216, 348, 447, 448
Ministry of Justice, 292, 305
Ministry of the Interior, 71, 72, 224, 294, 304, 323–324

Mississauga nation, 59–61, 65, 66, 69, 77, 78, 312, 315
Mitchel, John, 98
Mitchell, Peter, 121–122, 125, 300, 301, 305
Mohawk Institute, 76, 80, 321
Mohawk nation, 63, 64–65, 80
Monck, Lord, 264, 271–272, 282
Montgomery, William, 106
Montreal Herald, 148, 369
Moore, Christopher, 19
Morin, Augustin, 261
Morris, Alexander, 259, *306*, 317
Morton, Samuel G., 123
Mowat, Sir Oliver, 75–76, 78, 363, 383
Mulroney, Brian, 379, 397–400
Municipal Loan Fund Act, 176, 179, 180
Murphy, Michael, 103
Myers, Gustavus, 206

Napier, George, 104
Nation newspaper (Dublin), 99
National Policy of Tariff Protection, 21, 211, 212–213, 216, 261, 342, 353, 364, 367, 374, 375, 438, 441
Natural Selections (MacEachern), 353
Nelles, H. V., 199
New Brunswick, 28, 158, 198, 230, 287, 291, 297, 300, 399
New Credit, 66, 77
New York *Herald*, 345
New York *Shamrock*, 96
New York Times, 346
Newfoundland, 399
Nolan, John, 108–109
Norquay, John, 81
Norrie, Kenneth, 226, 232, 238–240, 242, 243
Northcote-Trevelyan Report (*Report on the Organization of the Permanent Civil Service*), 290–291

Northern Pacific Railway, 236, 238
The Northwest Company, 235, 344
North-West Mounted Police (NWMP), 285, 331, 346, 438, 440, 449
North-West Rebellion, 116, 331, 332, 365
North-West Territories, 239, 286, 319, 323, 324, 329, 330, 340, 341, 345, 353, 359, 364, 439
Nova Scotia, 47, 124, 198, 209, 216, 285, 287, 291, 297, 300, 399, 426, 438

Offer, Avner, 208
Ojibwe nation. *see* Mississauga nation
The Old Chieftain (Creighton), 17, 311, 420
O'Mahony, John, 97–98
O'Neill, John, 94, 96, 99, 106–107
Ontario, 70, 71, 76, 77, 124, 177, 198, 199, 210, 230–231, 243, 260, 266, 320, 322, 324, 344, 361, 412, 416, 420, 426, 445
Ontario Conservative Union, 217
O'Reilly, James, 109
Orillia, 315, 316
Oronhyatekha (Peter Martin), 80
O'Sullivan, Sean, 392
Ouimet, Joseph-Aldéric, 367

Parent, Étienne, 291, 294–295, 305
Parkin, George Robert, 17, 423–424
Pasia, Frances, 82
patronage system, 118, 122, 144, 161, 182, 195, 215, 285, 290, 291, 292, 443
Patterson, Gilbert, 61
Patterson, James Colbert, 217
Patteson, T.C., 411, 412–413
Pearson, Lester, 390–391, 397, 400
Pelletier, Yves Y., 22, 359–378, 453

Penitentiaries Act of 1868, 294
Phenix, Patricia, 19, 143
Pitkin, Hanna Fenichel, 151
Plains Indians, 72, 75, 76, 116, 125,
  321, 330, 331, 446–447
Plumb, Josiah Burr, 129
Pope, John Henry, *306*
Pope, Sir Joseph, 17, 36, 38, 263, 273,
  286, 287, 288–289, 409, 413, 417,
  420, 421–422, 445
Powell, Walker, 300
Power, Charles Gavan "Chubby," 388
Preece, Rod, 36, 38, 39, 144, 145
Prichard, James Crowley, 123
Prince Edward Island, 28, 130, 287,
  399, 416
Privy Council Office (PCO), 292–293,
  304, *305*
Protestantism, 361–362
Province of Canada, 58, 65–66, 68, 146,
  149, 182, 261, 293, 313, 314, 316, 318,
  319, 322, 335, 343, 415, 418, 419
Prowse, D. W., 213
Public Archives of Canada, 18

*Qualification and Registration of Voters
  Act* (1875), 121
Quebec, 28, 43, 46, 69, 76, 193–194,
  198, 209, 210, 266, 294, 295, 344,
  365, 366, 367, 385, 391, 399–400,
  412, 416, 440
Quebec Act of 1774, 76
Quebec Resolutions, 156, 159
Queen's Own Rifles, 99, 104–105
Queen's University, 18, 384, 423

Rae, John, 214
Railroad and Telegraph Line
  Committee, 176, 177, 178, 179
Railway Guarantee Act (1849), 176, 178
Reciprocity Treaty, 261, 296

Red River Métis, and rebellion, 58, 70,
  81, 285, 320, 346, 347, 365
Reed, Hayter, 329, 334, 335
Reform Party, 33, 254–255, 322, 343,
  368. *see also* Brown, George
Regher, T. D., 225–226
Relief Act, 180
Report of the Railway Rates Commission,
  238
Report on the Affairs of British North
  America (Durham, 1839), 149
Republican Greens militia, 96
Republicanism, 153
Revolutionary War, 60, 61
Reynolds, Louise, 19
Rice Lake Mississauga, 69
the Rideau Club, 389
Rideau Hall, 260, 265
Riel, Louis, 58, 70, 73, 74, 294, 332,
  365, 366, 400
Ring Cycle (Wagner), 414
Roberts, Barbara, 421, 423
Roberts, William, 96, 98, 105
Robinson, Sir John Beverly, 148
Robinson Treaties, 316–317, 320, 321
Rocky Mountains Park Act (1887), 352
Rogers, Norman McLeod, 386
Rose, John, 286, *306*
Ross, Charles S., 291
Ross, John, 184, 290
Royal Commission on Biculturalism
  and Bilingualism, 391
Royal Commission on Chinese
  Immigration, 122, 126
Royal Commission (on the Pacific
  Scandal), 266
Royal Commission to Inquire into
  the Present State and Probable
  Requirements of the Civil Service,
  291–292, 293, 295, 297, 299,
  300, 301

Royal Proclamation of 1763, 59–60, 68, 69, 76, 312, 313, 316, 333, 335

Rupert's Land, 224, 227, 287, 319, 320

Russia, 344–345

Ryerson University, 20

Salt, Allan Salt Jr., 78

Salt, Rev. Allen, 70–71

Salvation Army, 445–446

Saskatchewan, 73, 240, 241, 325, 344, 346, 363

Saskatchewan Rebellion of 1885, 447

Sawguin Island, 62

Sawyer, Joseph, 67

Scott, Rev. Jonathan, 62–63

Scott Act (1877), 426

Second Treatise on Civil Government (Locke), 151, 153

Seward, William, 97, 345, 346

Shakespeare, Noah, 119

Shaw, Helen. see Macdonald, Helen

Sifton, Sir Clifford, 335

Simcoe, John Graves, 59

Six Nations Confederacy Council, 79–80

Six Nations Iroquois, 66

Six Nations territory, 68, 79–80

Smith, Adam, 151, 158, 204, 213, 214

Smith, Andrew, 198, 213

Smith, Donald B., 20–21, 58–93, 328, 442, 453

Smith, Donald, Lord Strathcona, 81

Smith, Goldwin, 43–45, 48, 215

Smith, Isabella Hardisty, 81

Smith, Paul, 149

Smith, Peter J., 144

Smith, William, 80, 291, 300, 301, 305

Southern Railway, 183, 184

Spielman, Roger, 60–61

Stacey, C. P., 94

Stanhope, Philip, 287–88

Stanley, Lord, 273–74

Stanley, Timothy, 20, 115–40, 454

Statutes of Westminster, 385, 396

Steinhauer, Robert, 72–73

Stephens, James, 97

Stevenson, Garth, 198

Stewart, Gordon T., 144, 443

Strachan, John, 148

Studness, Charles, 239, 240

Subjection of Women (Mill), 444

suffrage, 20, 23, 27, 28, 30–32, 34–37, 38, 39, 41,42,44, 46–49, 51, 54, 56, 158–59, 218, 439, 442, 443, 446 Sunday, John, 315

Sunday, John Jr., 69

Survey Act (1877), 351

Swainson, Donald, 18, 142

Sweeny, Tom, 96, 98, 100

Taché, Sir Étienne Paschal, 254, 290, 297, 350

Taché, Joseph-Charles, 296–297, 306

Taschereau, Thomas Linière, 45–46

Tevis, Charles Carroll, 105

Thompson, David, 392

Thompson, Sir John, 273, 274, 366, 367, 368, 371, 381

Those Things We Treasure (Diefenbaker), 394

Thucydides, 212

Tilley, Sir Samuel Leonard, 216, 306, 366, 393

Tocqueville, Alexis de, 218

Toronto Globe, 16, 68–69, 174, 197, 198, 211, 212, 256–257, 259, 265, 266, 267, 408, 426, 445

Toronto Star Weekly, 77

Toryism, 145, 146, 147, 211, 212, 218, 296

Treaty of Ghent, 13, 313

Treaty of Washington (1871), 257–260, 261, 272, 394

Trudeau, Pierre, 391, 413
Trudeau, Toussaint, 297–298, *306*
Tupper, Sir Charles, 216, 259, 270, 292, 305, *306*, 328, 366, 371, 373, 389, 397, 409
Turner, John, 391–392
Tyendinaga Mohawk, 64

United States
    the 1871 Washington Treaty, 257–260, 261, 272, 300, 394
    Alaska purchase, 345, 347, 348
    Canadian-American Reciprocity Treaty of 1854, 227
    Dawes Plan adopted by Congress, 333–334
    emigration to the US (Dakotas), 347
    expansionism, 319, 324, 341, 342, 343, 344–346, 347, 348, 353, 396
    reciprocity agreement, 372–373, 374, 382, 393
University of Toronto, 66
Upper Canada Rebellion of 1837, 148–149, 295, 296, 314, 382, 405–406

Van Horne, Sir William, 374
Vankoughnet, Lawrence, 71, 323, 324, 331
Victoria, Queen of England, 344, 362, 371

Victoria College, 72–73
Vidal, Alexander, 129
Vronsky, Peter, 105

Waiser, Bill, 22, 341–356, 454
Waite, Peter B., 18, 142, 440
Wallace, N. Clarke, 361–362
Wallace, Stewart, 82
War of 1812, 96, 312, 313
Ward, Norman, 31
Ward, Peter, 118
Ward, Tony, 240–241
Waters, John Francis, 16
Watkin, Sir Edward, 342, 343
Wawanosh, William, 70–71
Wendake (near Quebec City), 66
Western Canada. 58, 70, 72, 79, 232, 247, 355, 356, 393, 454
Whelan, Patrick James, 108
White, Solomon, 81
Willison, John, 445
Wilson, Sir Daniel, 66
Wilson, David A., 21, 94–114, 454
Women's Property Laws, 37, 38, 47
World War II, 386, 387, 388–389, 390
Worthington, Thomas, 299, *306*

Young, Brian, 175
The Young Politician (Creighton), 17, 175, 414, 440

Of Related Interest

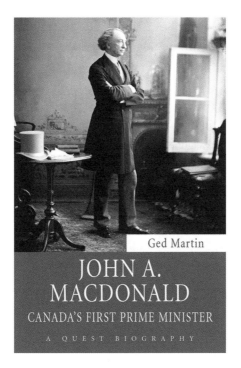

John A. Macdonald: Canada's First Prime Minister
by Ged Martin

Shocked by Canada's 1837 rebellions, John A. Macdonald sought to build alliances and avoid future conflicts. Thanks to financial worries and an alcohol problem, he almost quit politics in 1864. The challenge of building Confederation harnessed his skills, and in 1867 he became the country's first prime minster.

As "Sir John A.," he drove the Dominion's westward expansion, rapidly incorporating the Prairies and British Columbia before a railway contract scandal unseated him in 1873. He conquered his drinking problem and rebuilt the Conservative Party to regain power in 1878. The centrepiece of his protectionist National Policy was the transcontinental railway, but a western uprising in 1885 was followed by the controversial execution of rebel leader Louis Riel.

Although dominant nationally, Macdonald often cut ethical corners to resist the formidable challenge of the Ontario Liberals in his own province. John A. MacDonald created Canada, but this popular hero had many flaws.

Available at your favourite bookseller

 DUNDURN

Visit us at
Dundurn.com
@dundurnpress
Facebook.com/dundurnpress
Pinterest.com/dundurnpress